THE GRAND DESIGNER

Rosemary Hannah gained exceptional first-hand knowledge of Mount Stuart when she lived on the island of Bute. In 2000 she was awarded a PhD degree from the University of Durham for a thesis on the third Marquess. She has published in academic journals, including *Architectural History*, on the interface of art, architecture and patron in the Victorian period. She is currently Church History Co-ordinator for the Theological Institute of the Scottish Episcopal Church.

THE
GRAND
DESIGNER

THIRD MARQUESS OF BUTE

Rosemary Hannah

BIRLINN

To my mother, Joy Armstrong

This edition first published in Great Britain in 2013 by
Birlinn Ltd
West Newington House
10 Newington Road
Edinburgh
EH9 1QS

www.birlinn.co.uk

ISBN: 978 1 78027 134 7

The publishers gratefully acknowledge the support of the Carnegie Trust and the
Marc Fitch Fund

MARC FITCH FUND

towards the publication of this book

British Library Cataloguing-in-Publication Data
A catalogue record for this book is available on request from the British Library

Typeset by Carnegie Book Production, Lancaster
Printed and bound in Britain by T.J. International Ltd, Padstow

MIX
Paper from
responsible sources
FSC® C013056

Contents

List of illustrations

Fourth plate section (colour)

House of Falkland (Fife) was a home which Bute left largely unchanged except for new decoration. Falkland Palace (Fife), Greyfriars Convent (Elgin), where the architect was John Kinross, and Castell Coch (a rural retreat north of Cardiff, designed by William Burges and completed by William Frame after Burges's death) are all buildings which Bute commissioned for restoration but in which he never lived.

Preface and Acknowledgements

'Bute does it for the fun of the thing, I'm sure'[1]

When the eighteen-year-old fabulously wealthy 3rd Marquess of Bute met the most outrageous of Gothic designers, William Burges, it was the start of a lifetime's collaboration with artists and architects which would pour Bute's original mind into fabulous buildings in an astonishing variety of styles, from the intricate Gothic of Cardiff Castle through the Arabian nights ostentation of Mount Stuart to the sumptuous Renaissance Falkland Palace. Bute was far more than a patron for his amazing buildings; he was also very much a collaborator in their art and architecture. That would have been enough achievement for a lifetime for most people, and more than enough to justify describing Bute as 'the grand designer'. For Bute it was only part of his life's work. His 'designs' for education were just as grand. He sought to re-shape the education for the priesthood in Scotland, and to create a centre for liturgical excellence in Oban, in both cases with indifferent success. His fight to save St Andrews University, and to make it into a modern university fit for the age and for the future, succeeded – yet another of his grand designs. Sadly, he was dying as he fought to save the University. Because those who bitterly opposed him controlled the Dundee newspapers, their hostile story has become the version commonly accepted. New research for this book gives a more balanced account.

In one sense, however, Bute was anything but grand. He had little sense of personal self-importance. His wealth was as much a burden as a delight, and he valued his title chiefly as a tool to be used consciously to win allies for his causes. Most of his closest friends were from the middle classes. Bute was, in every way, an astonishing man. Lord Rosebery, as a former Prime Minister, commented smugly that he had known every interesting person of his generation; he considered Bute the most remarkable of them all. Above all, Bute had a lively sense of the absurd and a cutting wit. This was one of the things which attracted him to Burges's Gothic architecture, which is suffused with playfulness, something I missed when I first encountered the Victorian Gothic as a teenager.

Bute is especially beloved in Cardiff. True, it was his father, the 2nd Marquess, who created a busy port and a prosperous town out of something not much more than a fishing village, but it was the 3rd Marquess who saw the Victorian heyday of the town, who endowed numberless charities, and converted a modest castle into a towering Gothic extravaganza.

As a teenager, I thought Cardiff Castle a fraud. Instead of a building with Georgian elegance, or Victorian red-brick modernity, the patron and his architect had perpetrated a hideous and unoriginal fraud. I grew up. I came, gradually, to understand that Victorian Gothic was in fact one of the most original of all styles, a style that took the knowledge and wisdom of the past, and then had a great deal of light-hearted fun with it.

In middle age, I found myself living next to another of Lord Bute's amazing houses, Mount Stuart. At that time it was still a private dwelling-house, and was as closed and as mysterious as the man for whom it had been built. The best source for Bute's life was the biography by his friend, the Benedictine-baronet-Abbot Sir David Hunter Blair, a man whose social skills were greater than his originality, and who was bemused that anybody, however bored, could offer small talk along the lines of: 'Isn't it perfectly monstrous . . . that St Magnus hasn't got an octave?'[2]

Hunter Blair was so torn between his amusement at Bute's social inexpertise, his anger over past trouble between him and Bute, his respect for Bute's learning, and his awe of Bute's wealth and social position, that it is a very patchy portrait that emerges. One thing was clear: Hunter Blair thought that if Bute had received a more normal upbringing, he would have been a better man. Was that right? Did Bute's childhood cripple him, and if so, was his mother to blame? Moreover, Hunter Blair raised as many questions as he answered. Why did a man so in love with the mediaeval put central heating in his houses? Why had Bute's marriage been rumoured to be unhappy,[3] and was it really so? Why was there such a long gap between the first child born to him and the second? What was the truth behind Bute's behaviour to Marie Fox?[4] There were questions, but no answers.

One of the challenges of writing this biography has been the sheer weight of previously unpublished material. It was impossible at the beginning to anticipate the shape it would take, and researching it was not unlike unravelling the plot of a real-life soap opera. The breadth and depth of Bute's interests constantly threatened to overwhelm the story of the man himself. Bute is a difficult, unexpected figure, one of the last of the truly great Victorians to lack a modern biography. I trust these pages will go some way to explain the link between the man, his buildings, and his other projects, including his rescue of St Andrews University.

Stylistically, I have tried very hard to preserve the flavour of the original writing: where I found words underlined, I left them underlined instead of shifting them to italics, not least because the latter leaves one with a dilemma with doubly-underlined words. Where I found italics, I preserved them. I have also retained some idiosyncratic spellings and abbreviations including Bute's habitual initial shortening of 'ex' to X or x, thus writing words such as 'xcellent' for 'excellent'. The preferred spelling of the title is Marquess, but I have used Marquis in quotations where that spelling is used. The family name pre-1900 is usually Crichton Stuart, although the modern form is Crichton-Stuart (with hyphen); the *British Museum General Catalogue of Printed Books* prints this as Crighton Stuart (with a g and omitting the hyphen), and the *Dictionary of National Biography*, while spelling the name correctly, enters Bute's biography under 'Stuart'. The correct Christian name of the 3rd Marchioness is Gwendolen, not Gwendoline, although the more common spelling is often found in documents relating to her. The modern spelling of the family home on the Isle of Bute is Mount Stuart; the older spelling, all one word, is used where it occurs in quotations.

Apart from a continuing fascination with Bute himself, one thing has emerged from those five years: the kindness I have met with from almost all those whom I have bothered in the pursuit of my goal.

I am fairly certain that my admission to the archives at Mount Stuart arose from a misunderstanding, which, having once been made, was honoured by John Bute. He once asked me why I wanted to write about his great-great-grandfather. I answered as best I could, but I hope that as he reads these pages he gets a better answer, and one that in part repays his great kindness in giving me early access to his archives. I would also like to thank the Mount Stuart Trust for generously offering the free use in this book of all photographs in their gift.

Of all those to whom I have been a nuisance, Andrew McLean, archivist at Mount Stuart, must have suffered most, though he has never suggested it by word or look. Not only has he been superbly professional at his job, but he has also been a companion on the way, always ready to laugh, to commiserate, and above all to enthuse over the latest discovery. His has been the ready, sympathetic, listening ear into which I have been able to pour enthusiasm and never have it dampened. Latterly his deputy Lynsey Nairn shared her office with me, bore with my sighs, fielded my queries and listened endlessly. Thanks also to both of them for taking additional photographs for the book, and work on the preparation of images for it.

I had no right at all to call upon the generosity of Diane Walker, but she has kindly and unstintingly supplied help in all kinds, from a whistle-stop tour of Cardiff to a wealth of information on the death and burial of various members of the Bute family. The impeccable generosity and unfailing kindness of Matthew Williams, Keeper of Collections at Cardiff Castle, have extended far beyond anything that I will ever be able to acknowledge. Whenever the magnitude of the task before me dampened my spirits, he made me laugh. Many additional thanks for his work photographing details for reproduction here.

Ninian Crichton-Stuart, Hereditary Keeper of Falkland Palace, opened his personal family archives to me, and entertained me quite literally royally. The privilege of staying in the Palace is something I will never forget. They also kindly allowed me to view and reproduce their family images for this book. Pam McIlroy generously shared her intimate knowledge of the Falkland properties with me, and passed on to me the word-of-mouth history of the Marquess. I would also like to thank the National Trust for Scotland for allowing me and Kimberly Bohen free rein to photograph Falkland Palace, and especially the staff there, who most kindly facilitated our visit.

I would like to thank the Catholic Diocese of Aberdeen, who readily gave permission for Greyfriars to be photographed, and opened the building (now sadly unoccupied) so that Jeff Lowndes could record some of its beauties. I owe an especial thanks to Jeff and Kimberly who so freely gave of their time and talents; without that, this book would be much the poorer.

Libraries opened their doors, and their staff worked hard to help me. I would like to thank the staff of: Rothesay Public Library, Durham University Library, Glasgow University Library, the British Library, the Scottish National Library, and the Mitchell Library, Glasgow.

A great deal of my work has been done in archives far from home, and I would especially like to thank those who helped me struggle to decipher doubtful Victorian handwriting and impossible signatures. My thanks and acknowledgements go to: the Principal and Chapter of Pusey House, Oxford; the Earl of Harrowby for entry to the Sandon Hall Papers, Staffordshire; the archives of the Scottish National

Library and the British Library; the National Archives of Scotland; the Ayrshire Archives; the National Museum of Wales; Cardiff Central Library; Paisley Burgh Library; the Scottish Catholic Archive and the Sneyd family.

I would like to thank the priests at Cumnock and Galston for their kindness in allowing me to see their churches, and the minister at Cumnock Parish Church for his help with this project. I would also like to thank Ian Maclagan LLB, FSA Scot., for his advice on Victorian Scots law, and David Hamilton, head of the Renal Unit at Glasgow Western Infirmary and medical historian, for his invaluable help on the causes and symptoms of Bright's disease. To him is due the graphic description of the suffering of the Hastings family. The causes of Bute's death were unravelled by Dr Julia Lowe, MB, ChB, FRCP (UK) M.Med Sci (Clin Epi), who is Associate Professor of Medicine at the University of Toronto, and to her insight and acuity we owe an understanding of how and why Bute died so tragically young.

My former husband, Angus, helped me with the correction of the early drafts of this book, translated letters from French and Italian for it, and was supportive throughout. Sheila Wright undertook a huge amount of work to get the later chapters to a readable condition.

Everybody who has seen this book has been delighted with its high production values. My publishers, Birlinn, have realised the work of many years by turning my words into a beautiful publication in a way few authors today can hope for. They have been unfailingly helpful and encouraging. Singling people out from a team is an enterprise fraught with danger, but especial thanks are due to Hugh Andrew who heads the firm, and to my managing editor, Mairi Sutherland, who has the patience of a saint, and the tact of an angel. I would also like to thank my agent, Duncan McAra, for steering a new author safely through the publishing of her first book, and for his constant faith in my work.

My last, and my greatest, acknowledgement goes to Dr Sheridan Gilley. It is no conventional thanks that I owe him. Not only has he readily offered me any help from the vast body of knowledge lodged sometimes on his bookshelves but more often in his head, but his steady faith in this work, his constant encouragement, his careful nurturing have given me a faith in it, and in myself, that I might otherwise not have found. If this account of Bute's life makes interesting reading (as I hope it does), then that is due to his encouragement to tell it as a story. He was the audience for which I originally wrote this, his the reaction I imagined, as I tried to allow Bute to come out of the shadows and tell of the laughter, the pain and the triumph of his life.

Stuart family tree

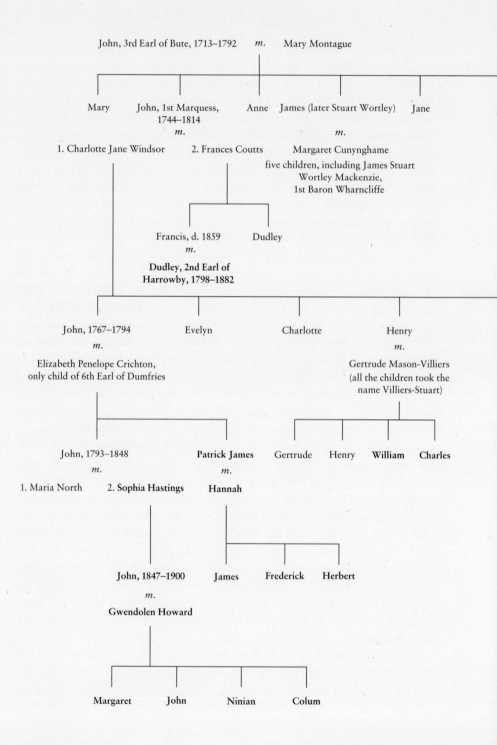

John, 3rd Earl of Bute, 1713–1792   *m.*   Mary Montague

Mary   John, 1st Marquess, 1744–1814   Anne   James (later Stuart Wortley)   Jane

m.

m.

1. Charlotte Jane Windsor   2. Frances Coutts   Margaret Cunynghame

five children, including James Stuart
Wortley Mackenzie,
1st Baron Wharncliffe

Francis, d. 1859   Dudley

m.

**Dudley, 2nd Earl of
Harrowby, 1798–1882**

John, 1767–1794   Evelyn   Charlotte   Henry

m.

m.

Elizabeth Penelope Crichton,
only child of 6th Earl of Dumfries

Gertrude Mason-Villiers
(all the children took the
name Villiers-Stuart)

John, 1793–1848   **Patrick James**   Gertrude   Henry   **William**   Charles

m.

m.

1. Maria North   2. **Sophia Hastings**   Hannah

John, 1847–1900   James   Frederick   Herbert

m.

Gwendolen Howard

Margaret   John   Ninian   Colum

Only significant marriages are recorded.
Names in bold indicate characters significant in the book.

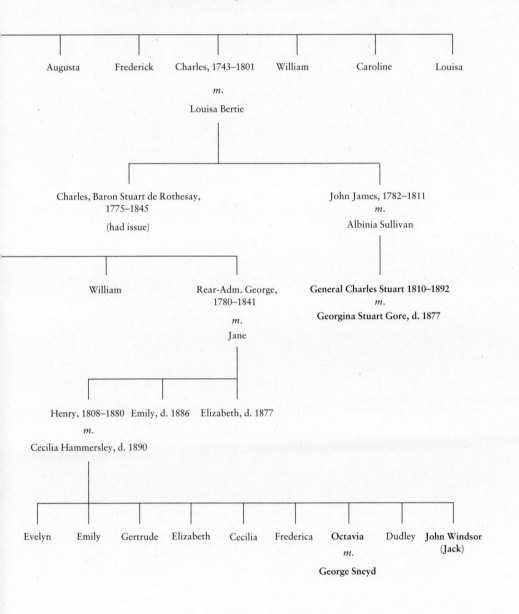

Hastings family tree

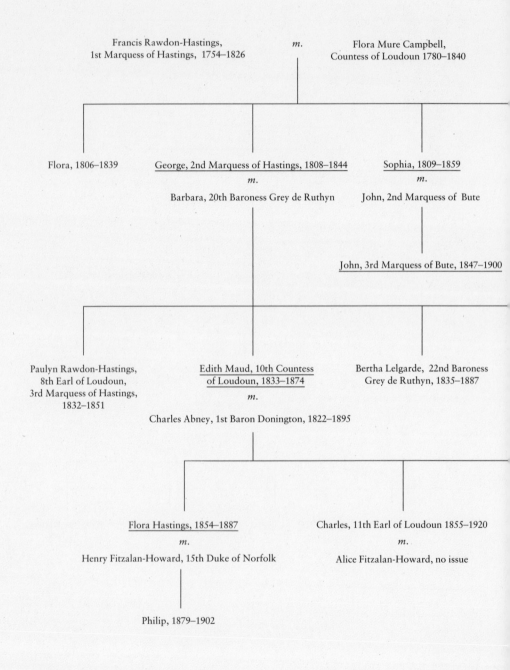

Francis Rawdon-Hastings, 1st Marquess of Hastings, 1754–1826 _m._ Flora Mure Campbell, Countess of Loudoun 1780–1840

Flora, 1806–1839

George, 2nd Marquess of Hastings, 1808–1844
_m._
Barbara, 20th Baroness Grey de Ruthyn

Sophia, 1809–1859
_m._
John, 2nd Marquess of Bute

John, 3rd Marquess of Bute, 1847–1900

Paulyn Rawdon-Hastings, 8th Earl of Loudoun, 3rd Marquess of Hastings, 1832–1851

Edith Maud, 10th Countess of Loudoun, 1833–1874
_m._
Charles Abney, 1st Baron Donington, 1822–1895

Bertha Lelgarde, 22nd Baroness Grey de Ruthyn, 1835–1887

Flora Hastings, 1854–1887
_m._
Henry Fitzalan-Howard, 15th Duke of Norfolk

Charles, 11th Earl of Loudoun 1855–1920
_m._
Alice Fitzalan-Howard, no issue

Philip, 1879–1902

Only those marriages which are significant to the biography of Bute are shown.
Persons whose names are underlined died of Bright's disease.

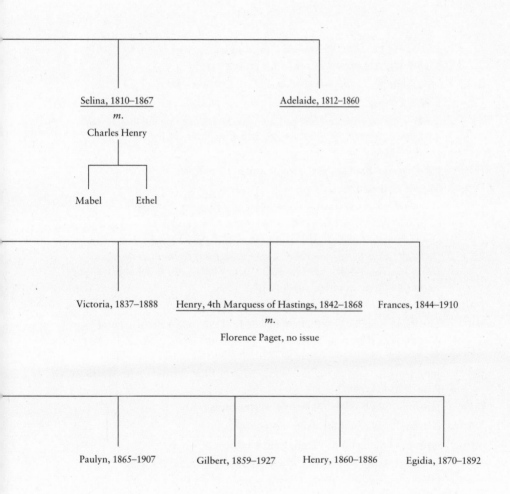

Selina, 1810–1867
m.
Charles Henry

Adelaide, 1812–1860

Mabel   Ethel

Victoria, 1837–1888   Henry, 4th Marquess of Hastings, 1842–1868   Frances, 1844–1910
m.
Florence Paget, no issue

Paulyn, 1865–1907   Gilbert, 1859–1927   Henry, 1860–1886   Egidia, 1870–1892

Abbreviations

AC   J. A. Venn, LittD, FSA, *Alumni Cantabrigienses,* Part II vol. VI (Cambridge University Press: Kraus reprint, 1978).

AO J. Foster, *Alumni Oxoniensis* (Parker & Co.: Oxford, 1888).

BL   British Library.

BP   *Burke's Peerage* (Peter Townend, ed., *Burke's Genealogical and Heraldic History of the Peerage, Baronetage and Knightage,* 103rd edition, London, 1965).

BU   Papers in the Bute archive, Mount Stuart House, Isle of Bute.

CCL   Cardiff Central Library

CDS   *The Catholic Directory for the Clergy and Laity of Scotland* (J. Chisholm: Aberdeen, 1888).

CP   George Edward Cokayne, *The Complete Peerage of England, Scotland, Ireland, Great Britain and the United Kingdom, Extant, Extinct or Dormant,* vols I–XIII, ed. The Hon. Vicary Gibbs, H. A. Doubleday (St Catherine Press: London, 1910–1940).

DNB   *Dictionary of National Biography.*

HB   The Right Rev. Sir David Hunter Blair Bt, OSB., *John Patrick Third Marquess of Bute K.T. (1847–1900), A Memoir* (John Murray: London, 1921).

JD   John Davies, *Cardiff and the Marquesses of Bute* (University of Wales Press: Cardiff, 1981).

JSPR   *Journal of the Society for Psychical Research.*

NAS   National Archive of Scotland, Edinburgh.

NLS   National Library of Scotland, Edinburgh.

SP   Sir James Balfour Paul, ed., *The Scots Peerage* (David Douglas: Edinburgh, 1908).

SR   *The Scottish Review.*

WB   William Burges papers in the Bute archive.

1   Infancy

'All that should make a Parent's heart thankful'

When the 3rd Marquess of Bute lay dying, his daughter heard a carriage rattle up to the door. The door was answered. Nothing was there.[1] She knew at once that she had heard the ghostly death carriage of the Hastings. By tradition, spirits announced the forthcoming death of the head of the House of Hastings with a carriage heard but invisible. It seems almost fair that John Patrick Crichton Stuart should have been accorded this privilege.

He was not, of course, by any reckoning, the head of the Hastings family; that was his still-living cousin the Earl of Loudoun, Charles Abney-Hastings.[2] Bute was only a Hastings through his mother. With his interest in the supernatural he would have appreciated it, however, in a way Charley would not have. Perhaps the ghosts made allowance for that, or for the fact Bute was dying of Bright's disease, or, as it is now known, kidney failure, which had killed his mother and was an 'almost hereditary' disease in the Hastings family.

Bute was the late-born son of a second marriage. His father, John, 2nd Marquess of Bute,[3] had made a happy first marriage to Maria North,[4] but she was an invalid, and their marriage remained childless. The 2nd Marquess meanwhile devoted his amazing energy to the development of the run-down estates in Wales which he had inherited from his paternal grandmother.[5] The city of Cardiff was largely of his making, springing up around the docks he built, which gave an easy outlet for the coal that South Wales began to produce, a good deal of it mined on the land he leased for development. He personally superintended all the details, as well as the broad sweep of his estates. He was laying the foundations of enormous wealth; just how much wealth the next generation was to find out.

In retrospect, it is easy to see that the 2nd Marquess managed his business enterprise wisely. At the time it seemed less certain. He sold the family estate at Luton (bought by his great-grandfather the much-vilified Prime Minister Earl of Bute) and borrowed heavily to finance the expansion of Cardiff. When he remarked that he was willing to think well of the prospects of his income 'in the distance'[6] he was tacitly recognising just how heavy his borrowing had been, and how the tide of finance might yet turn against him.

The 2nd Marquess's first wife Maria died in 1841, and in 1845 he married again. He was fifty-two and his sight was seriously impaired. His bride was thirty-five years old. She was Lady Sophia Hastings,[7] the daughter of Flora, Countess of Loudoun in her own right,[8] and of the 1st Marquess of Hastings.[9] It looked as if the 2nd Marquess was securing a companion for his old age not a potential mother for a putative heir.

This must have been reassuring to his younger brother, Lord James.[10] Their parents having died young, both John and James Crichton Stuart had been brought up by their mother's father, the old Earl of Dumfries, and John had inherited that title and the estate in Ayrshire on the death of the Earl in 1803.[11] He inherited the Bute lands and title from his father's father in 1814.

His brother James had gradually come to expect that these titles and estates, and the wealth his brother was beginning to create in Cardiff, would come to him. He too had married, and he had a family. His expectations were hardly shaken when the 2nd Marquess remarried.

Yet, however little Lord James anticipated it, shortly after her wedding Sophia became pregnant. Her child was stillborn in the seventh month.[12] To add to the pain, it was a boy. Lord James must now have been confident that either he or his eldest son James Frederick would inherit everything. After all, Sophia did not come from a very healthy family.

Lady Flora,[13] Sophia's eldest sister, had taken up one of the few careers open to respectable aristocratic spinsters: a Lady-in-Waiting to the Princess Victoria, mother of the Queen. Her tragic story is well known. She had been alone with Victoria's *bête noire*, Sir John Conroy.[14] Her belly began to swell, and she was sick. Ugly rumours flew around. The young Queen believed them. It was not pregnancy, however, but cancer which was the cause, and Flora, who had been publicly humiliated by the rumours, was only able to establish her innocence by an exhaustive intimate examination. Victoria tried to make amends, but it was too little and too late. Lady Flora died aged thirty-three.

Sophia nursed Flora through her painful illness, afterwards publishing her sister's poems.[15] Within six months, her mother, too, was dead; and her brother, George, 2nd Marquess of Hastings, died four years later.[16]

The whole family blamed the Curse of the Hastings, invoked by the marriage of George to Barbara Grey de Ruthyn.[17] Legend had it that back in the middle ages there was a dispute over who should inherit the Hastings coat-of-arms: an heir descended through a daughter, who was also a member of the Grey de Ruthyn family, or a male Hastings. So bitter was the dispute that the Hastings claimant cursed any member of his family who married a Grey de Ruthyn.[18]

In 1847, two years after her marriage to the 2nd Marquess, it became plain that Sophia was again pregnant, and on 12 September she gave birth to a son 'at half past five o'clock in the afternoon'.[19] So it was that John Patrick Crichton Stuart became heir to the earldom of Dumfries, the marquisate of Bute and the curse of the Hastings. His parents, however, were both too overjoyed to let a mediaeval curse enter their minds.

Lord Bute wrote to a friend: 'I now give you my news, and I know you will be rejoiced to hear that Lady Bute by the blessing of God gave me a little boy yesterday afternoon.'[20] He wrote again, confirming that they were both doing well, not this time by the careful hand of an amanuensis, but in his own difficult scrawl.[21] Since by this time he rarely wrote in his own hand, it is a measure of his joy, and perhaps his disbelief, that he, who was fifty-four, and his thirty-eight year old wife, had a son and heir. That she was scarcely less happy is confirmed by her answer to felicitations; she found her little boy was 'indeed all that should make a Parent's heart thankful'.[22]

Now, for the first time in his life, Lord James was no longer heir presumptive to the Bute estates. His life had not been fulfilling. He had made a career in politics, and had come almost at once into conflict with his brother John: he was elected member for Cardiff in 1818 and again in 1826; he was a popular MP and supported reform whilst his brother opposed it. Lord James would not change his opinions to suit his brother, so, at the next election, John put in a candidate against him. Lord Bute's candidate won, and Lord James was out of Parliament until his election for Ayrshire (his home county) in 1835.[23] In private, relations between the two men steadily worsened.[24] To his sister-in-law's disgust, Lord James regarded the child as only a temporary disruption to his prospects; he did not expect the late-born child of two ageing parents to survive.[25]

Lord Bute naturally wanted to take his son to Cardiff, the town he had created, and arrived early in March 1848. Already worrying over business matters, he received a letter from his brother which deeply distressed him.[26] On 18 March, he and his wife entertained friends to dinner. The party broke up at ten o'clock and Bute retired to his room. Getting no reply when she called to him, his wife walked into his bedroom to find him lying dead in bed.[27] She had hysterics, a fact ever after held against her as proof of an unsound mind.

Considering his reputation for punctilious business management, the mess in which the 2nd Marquess left his personal affairs after his death is odd. Perhaps, like other great men, he did not believe he would die; probably he intended to make detailed provision for his son (then just six months old), his wife and brother during his stay in Cardiff.[28] In the wake of his unexpected death, however, a horrible legal tangle ensued. Bute had made a will in July 1847, when it was apparent that his wife was likely to carry her second child safely to term. Despite naming separate trustees for the English estates (O. Tyndall Bruce, J. M. McNabb and Lord James) and the Welsh (Bruce and McNabb only), it made no mention of the Scottish estates, which were later found to be intestate. Nor did the will make any provision for James, the failed politician in his fifties, with a family to support, who had spent all his life in his brother's shadow, subsidised by him, distrusted by him, and in expectation of great wealth and a title upon his death. Now, seeing his prospect of inheriting a great estate go down before the interests of a baby still not in short frocks, Lord James was furious and desperate. He was convinced that his brother must have made provision for him somewhere, and went through every drawer to find some paper which would give him a secure claim on the estate. When he planned to go to Scotland, Sophia commented: 'if he is to ransack the Bureaux I do not know what will be the consequence ... I know there are many relics of those who have been loved and cared for.'[29]

Once the first shock passed, Sophia behaved with great determination and self-reliance. She chose as confidant her late husband's agent, an executor under his will, O. Tyndall Bruce.[30] She first wrote to him a month after her husband's death, because she had nobody else to turn to for help and advice.[31] After that she wrote at least weekly, and in times of stress daily. Her letters became informal and personal as the correspondence continued. Normally neat, her handwriting disintegrated into a scrawl under pressure, though her style remained forceful and coherent. Of stress, she had plenty. Her son had not been left any proper provision for his minority, and Lord James, concerned with resolving his own difficulties, did nothing to make his sister-in-law secure, or the young Marquess comfortable.

Sophia was not in an enviable position. She was the widow of the creator of one of Europe's busiest ports, and the mother of a son who must be reared as heir both to an ancient line and a modern fortune. Given this, her jointure of £3,500[32] was not large. A house, and a separate allowance for her son, would have brought it into line with the arrangements made for other widows.[33] Without these, it was inadequate. Bruce's advice to her was to argue for a more handsome settlement for herself, to be secure even if her son were to die, rather than to seek a proper allowance for her son.[34]

Lord James had the poor taste (given his position) to harp on the same theme.[35] Naturally, Sophia rebelled. She had buried a beloved sister, her Marquess brother, both parents, her first child and her husband. She was not going to build her future on the surmise of the death of her healthy child. She fought determinedly for a suitable settlement for her son, perfectly reasonably, since he was already the inheritor of his father's wealth, and the 3rd Marquess of Bute. As 'it has pleased God that Lord Bute has a child of his own I feel I am bound to expect for that child what I should have no right to for myself', wrote Lady Bute, continuing a little desperately, '& tho' he may not live I do not think his death should be assumed as probable, for any of the arrangements. The better taste would be for everything to go on as far as possible as it did in Lord Bute's lifetime.'[36]

With the Scottish estates intestate, Lord James, as the new Marquess's nearest male relative, became 'Tutor-at-Law', that is to say, responsible for managing and administering those estates.[37] He refused Lady Bute the use of either of the two houses he now controlled as her own home. One of these was Mount Stuart, the Georgian house on the Isle of Bute. Set in pleasant woodland, facing to the east, with its lands rolling down to the sea, it was where the widowed Marchioness had borne both her sons, and buried the first. The second, Dumfries House, an Adam gem, was not in Dumfriesshire but in Ayrshire, near Cumnock. Lord James was financially mean too. Bitterly considering his suggestion of £1,400 p.a. for the young Lord Bute, Sophia commented 'I consider his offer as miserable'.[38] With her usual directness, Sophia encapsulated the position thus: 'I do not see why the child should be pinched when, if he live by God's mercy, he is likely to be very rich at the end of such a minority. Nor, if it be God's will that he die, is there any reason that he and I should be pinched that Lord James and his family may have the more to squander hereafter.'[39]

What most enraged her contemporaries was that she did not have any inhibitions about dealing with areas of life generally left to men. One of these was the law, of which she had a much better grasp than many of the men around her. During her bitter struggles over a place of residence, she pointed this out to Lord Harrowby,[40] himself a lawyer, and a cousin by marriage. 'My family', she commented smugly, 'are a legal family in Scotland, and I know from my own knowledge [Lord

James] has already incurred deep responsibility in his breach of the law.'[41]

Lady Bute's attitude to Lord James was undoubtedly coloured by the letter her husband had received about ten days before his death. It has been suggested that it was uncommon for Victorian widows to experience anger and a desire to blame someone for their husband's death, which is now an accepted part of the grieving process for many people,[42] but Sophia blamed Lord James wholeheartedly: 'the immediate cause of [Lord Bute's] death was a letter written by his brother Lord James Stuart'.[43] She was convinced, too, that he was mad; this had been her husband's judgement, after that same letter.[44] She did make an attempt to be fair to Lord James: 'I believe he means to be kind but his letter is written in his most disagreeable style of inflated pompous condescension and self importance.'[45] She added a little pitifully that it was not at all the style she was accustomed to. Presumably, the admirable 2nd Marquess did not talk down to his wife.

Lady Bute was not alone in her poor opinion of Lord James. McNabb was the other executor of her husband's will. His natural caution as a lawyer did not hide his opinion of Lord James. He told his fellow executor that if Lord James took any active role in the management of the English Estates, they should ask him for a formal guarantee that any claims against him would not have to be paid by them. McNabb assumed that maladministration would be inevitable. Lord James also succeeded in forcing the South Wales trustees' hands and making them agree, very much against their first intention, that he could continue to live in Cardiff Castle,[46] thus occupying all three of the Bute houses, and leaving nowhere for the infant 3rd Marquess and his mother.

Much that Sophia wrote has the ring of determined level-headedness about it. She planned to take over administration for the annuities of 'poor relations, old servants or old servants' children'.[47] She was 'inclined to think it would be more wholesome for my own mind to be obliged to think of some sort of business and not to be too much at ease'.[48] She was quite at home, if sometimes exasperated, negotiating for her own jointure and the allowance for her son. Her arguments never relied on emotion but on well-argued logic.

She told her confidants, too, about her 'Child', as she usually referred to him, responding that he was well; no ailments, real or imaginary, were mentioned. Obviously devoted to him, she retained her sense of humour:

He continues, thank God, to thrive so well that I can scarcely hold him for his weight – He is quite well & did I tell you? he has said

'Mamma'. He is growing so interesting to me that I am fearful of tiring my friends with details of him.

The nearest she came to any sign of neurosis was in an early letter to Bruce. Just a month after her husband's death, Lady Bute explained that she was giving Lord James a sword of her husband's as a remembrance of him:

> I had a superstition not to give <u>him</u> anything with a coronet and cipher – and yet I knew not what to chuse & could not pass him by without the offer of a remembrance – and Baby could not value the sword <u>at present</u>. Thank you – He is quite well and very hearty.[49]

The only way Lord James could legitimately hold such a coronet was, of course, by the death of the baby.

Lord James was miserably spiteful. He forbade Sophia to give orders to any of the servants in any Bute house she visited.[50] He only ever referred to his nephew as 'Lady Bute's son' or 'her son'. He refused for years to surrender to her the family plate left for her use in her lifetime.[51] He made snide remarks about her in nearly all of his letters, occasionally implying that she was verging on madness: 'I fear Lady Bute is in a very nervous state.'[52]

Lady Bute fought back with vigour. She finally persuaded the south Wales trustees to get Lord James to leave Cardiff Castle in the summer of 1849,[53] complaining bitterly that 'Lord and Lady James left the house in a disgraceful state of filth and ruin'.[54] She rented Dallars House, a small country house in Ayrshire, near to both Dumfries House and her old home at Loudoun, which gave her a Scottish base. She also leased Largo House near St Andrews for the summer months, where her son was 'enchanted' by bathing in the sea.[55] Lord James's own friends lost all patience with him, and repeated attempts were made to allow Lady Bute one of the Scottish homes as her own.[56] She, or rather her son (for he, not his uncle, was the owner of all these properties), was finally allowed to live in Mount Stuart from about 1853.

Sophia was helped by being part of a close family of her own. George and Flora were dead, but her sisters Selina[57] (by now married to a Mr Henry) and Adelaide[58] were intimates, especially Adelaide, who was unmarried. It seemed as though the Hastings family could not escape tragedy. In 1851, the young 3rd Marquess of Hastings,[59] a Rifle Brigade officer not yet twenty years old, died after falling into Birkenhead Dock.[60] Lady Bute and her sister were 'overwhelmed by the calamity'. The new Marquess of Hastings was his young brother Harry,[61] still only nine years old. His eldest sister Edith[62] was eighteen and virtually took the place of their mother, who had remarried.[63]

Very conscious that she was already being criticised by her brother-in-law, Lady Bute was scrupulous to avoid scandal, remarking 'one cannot be too prudent in my position as to character'.[64] A widow still of marriageable age, she largely avoided the company of men. She compensated by a wide circle of women friends, all approximately in their middle years, mainly unmarried, and all able and intelligent. Lady Elizabeth Moore,[65] a distant cousin, some six years older than Lady Bute, was a particular friend. Lady Elizabeth was strong-minded, witty and interested in almost everything. But Sophia's son was her greatest companion, and her greatest delight. From the very beginning she took pleasure in teaching him herself. The first letter of Bute's that is still preserved was written when he was four years old. Lady Bute included an account of its composition and despatch: 'They are his own words & I held his hand as he is particularly fond of writing letters, which he folds, puts the seal on the wax & the stamps on himself & then gives with sedateness to the servant "for the post".'[66]

Bute's letter was short and to the point: 'I am very happy & Mama is pleased with me.' A year later he was writing rather more: 'I was in my nursery picking some wheatheads out of the corn I had picked in my walk in the morning & putting it into a bowl . . . Afterwards I meant to get a pestle and mortar . . . and make a little bit of bread.'[67] Letters give a vivid picture of his life. One sent to Bute from the well-known authoress Agnes Strickland[68] enclosed pictures of 'horses, dogs, foxes, hares and a cat-a-mountains' cut out by 'my sister Elizabeth'. She continued, 'Ask Mrs Lamb, your kind nurse, to read you the description of them all from some pretty book of natural history,' and advised him to learn to read 'at once, and beg your dear Mamma to allow you to devote half an hour twice a day to learning to read'.[69] Did 'Mamma' in fact put the letter-writer up to this request? It does read a little like a sugar-coated pill. Certainly, as he learnt to read, either Bute or his mother requested printed letters so that he could read them himself.

Some correspondents were bent upon improving the young Bute. He was sent two bottles of water, one from the Dead Sea 'which will remind you of the fearful judgements of God upon sin & wickedness of those who obey not his will'.[70] In contrast there was a bottle of water from the Jordan, where the obedient Jesus was baptised. Others had the measure of a small boy a little more realistically. One correspondent did not have 'time to write you a printed letter, but . . . I daresay you won't mind having this read to you'.[71] Also highly improving were the letters from 'Godmother Aunt North'.[72]

Susan, Lady North was the last surviving North child. Maria, Lady Bute, had been her elder half-sister. She was genuinely devoted to Bute, as though he were her nephew and not her half-brother-in-law's son by another wife. She had very little idea how to interest a child, but was a faithful correspondent. 'I am very sure that you do wish me many happy returns of my Birthday but perhaps you do not think that not a little part of my happiness depends on your being a good boy.'[73] There is no evidence that Bute gave Aunt North cause for concern. Other correspondents were more light-hearted. There is a charming letter with an indecipherable signature where selected words have been omitted, and little printed pictures have been cut out and glued in. Just in case the code was not broken, a separate envelope gave the solution. Thus the sheep turns out to be a wether, for weather.[74]

Another correspondent, Sir Francis Hastings Gilbert,[75] later appointed guardian to Lord Bute, wrote that he looked forward to meeting Bute in St Andrews, to 'renew our games of cricket, though I believe golf is the great game there, of which however I never yet could understand the science, so you will have to teach me'.[76] At St Andrews there was sea bathing,[77] shell collecting, visits to Principal and Mrs Lee, and to see the mechanical toys of Sir Hugh Playfair. Bute remembered also the spectacular three-tailed Donati's Comet of 1858.[78]

Letters also show us something of the young Bute's early instinct for giving. Hunter Blair, with his determined insistence that no good thing ever came from Lady Bute, attributed Bute's generosity to the example which he received later in his life from the Galloway family,[79] but Bute showed an early delight in giving. Already in March 1853, his dutiful Aunt North remarked, 'I am sure the servants must have been pleased with all the nice things you gave them on your Mamma's birthday.'[80] Bute sent Henry Hunter Blair (uncle of Bute's biographer), who was going to Australia, 'the stuff for a coat' and a book. The book seemed a 'good one', a phrase capable of two interpretations, and Henry added 'I have no doubt I shall profit very much by the reading of it'.[81] There were gifts to young friends as might be expected. But others were definitely not in this category. Mrs Tyndall Bruce got a surprise: when Bute had promised her a travelling suit, she had thought the boy was joking. Then one morning her servants brought in a brown paper parcel, which, unwrapped, showed foxes' heads. She had been given furs. Her astonishment and delight were real.[82] Unlike most children, little Lord Bute could afford serious presents. Equally evidently, he must have had adult help to choose well for his mother's friends.

Another correspondent, a regular member of Lady Bute's close circle of woman friends, was Miss Eleanora Boyle,[83] or Nora as she was usually known. The large Boyle family were the children of the late Lord Justice Boyle of Scotland.[84] John Boyle[85] was one of the trustees of the Welsh estates, and his sisters were both 'intimate friends'[86] of the Marchioness. An early letter from Nora was full of fun, and suggests a thoroughly normal little boy: 'Dear old man, Lady Mary[87] & I miss somebody screaming on the stairs very much, and we have no one to hug us except each other, and she hugs Pincher, but you know I never do that.'[88] 'Dear man' or 'dear old man' were the usual affectionate terms for Bute in the Boyle family.[89] Nora's dislike of Pincher, Lady Bute's dog, was another standing joke. Her elder sister, Hamilla Augusta,[90] usually known as Augusta, was also a close friend.

Nora avoids calling the little boy 'Bute', which he was to almost all his regular correspondents. Most people did not have enough rank, or enough of a blood tie, to address the child by his Christian name. Some years later, his guardian referred to him as a 'young potentate'.[91] Though all young boys with a claim to be 'gentlemen' might hide their Christian names from each other, they were usually well-provided with brothers, sisters and cousins who would use the familiar first name. Few indeed were the children so exclusively called by their title.

A shared interest of the Bute circle was natural history. Adelaide encouraged him to keep a fresh-water aquarium. 'Cousin Edith' (Sophia's brother's daughter, Harry's sister) was much concerned with stuffing a lobster at Bute's direction.[92] All these letters are pleasantly informal in character, as though one relaxed adult were writing to another. Bute was perfectly at ease with the companionship of adults. There is a painting of him and his mother made when he was nine years old, and formally dressed in Highland costume. He lolls back on his mother untidily, one foot crossed behind the other. At their feet the family pets appear: the small terrier Mungo and a hedgehog. Mother and child seem completely at ease with each other, although Bute eyes the outside world with a hint of reserve.

In 1854 there was a serious rift between Adelaide and Sophia, the more painful as family and friends were dragged in to side with one or the other. It was sparked by Sophia's dislike of Lady Adelaide's marriage to Sir William Keith Murray of Ochtertyre, and made Sophia miserable.[93] She subsequently caught scarlet fever, which friends with the usual shaky Victorian sense of the causes of infection put down to her unhappiness, and no sooner was she well than Bute caught German measles, followed by measles. Perhaps it was to aid their convalescence that in August 1855, just before his eighth birthday, they embarked on a trip to Belgium and Germany.[94]

From the moonlight drive to the ferry at Folkestone, it was an enchanted journey for the young Bute, so much so that themes from it were to haunt his adulthood. His diary was dictated, largely to his mother (to judge by the handwriting), so he was not deterred from making long entries. Yet he had a remarkably free hand in what he said. Despite her celebrated dislike of Roman Catholicism, she had no qualms about visiting Catholic churches. On one occasion, staying too long to enjoy a church, they found themselves in the service. Lord Bute saw his first Catholic Mass:

> we had not been there long, when the bells began to ring and soon after the organ began and a man took a long taper and lit more of the candles, and the people began to come in a considerable number. A priest in his robes walked down the aisle and went into a confessional whispering-box. Then a lady in black went into it, but while I was staring at the marble monuments I was told to look at the high altar and I saw ... a priest in white robes with a golden kind of hood ascending ... the organ played very loud and made a disagreeable mixture of sounds ... then came various kneelings and prayings ... then the voices grew louder and the censer was flung in the air, and the bell was rung furiously.[95]

This account was a mixture of the standard evangelical phrases of dismissal ('kneelings and prayings'), of childish curiosity (the lady and the confessional box), of genuine observation (the 'white robes with the golden kind of hood'), genuine dislike (of the 'disagreeable sounds' of the organ) and of something like real appreciation (of the censer flung in the air and the furious bell). Later, at Munich, Bute was to record another beautiful church: 'It is a Protestant church now I am glad to say.'[96] He approved of the sixty-four splendid marble columns.

Bute gave three pages of description to his first Catholic service, whereas the zoological gardens, despite his fondness for them, got only half a page. Later, however, his first theatrical performance, the play *Aladdin*, earned five rapturous pages. After this, until his mother's death, miniature theatres were to be a regular entertainment, giving the lie to suggestions that Sophia's religion was joylessly narrow, since the really strict disapproved of the theatre at this date, although the moral content of a puppet theatre was a good deal more easily policed than the public stage.

Every day was a round of new pleasures – provided, like the little Bute, you were able to find your pleasures in churches, museums, battlefields and castles. Many eight-year-olds would have found it tedious. After his usual quiet life, the marble pillars, inlaid floors, painted ceilings, pictures and ancient silver came to Bute with great freshness. He had one great advantage over most little boys. The adults who surrounded him made it their business to interest him in everything he saw. Gradually, the *dramatis personae* of the trip emerge. Apart from 'Mamma' there were 'Mrs Lamb, Dr Hood and Nora'. Dr Hood,[97] by this time seventy-four years of age, was an Englishman who had spent most of his life in Scotland. He was the redoubtable first Rector of St Paul's Episcopal Church, Rothesay, newly built to serve the Episcopalian congregation on the island. Both his age and the fact he was a clergyman rendered him an unexceptionable companion for Lady Bute, and gave Bute some contact with an adult male who was not a servant. Nora was sometimes a companion for Bute, and sometimes for his mother. Mrs Lamb was Bute's much-loved nurse.

There is a good deal of horror in the diaries. Cruelty 'haunted' the adult Bute, to use his own word. It is hard to know if the young Bute was getting a satisfying shudder or real aversion from what he saw. Perhaps he himself did not know. One museum had a drum 'covered with human skin'.[98] Dr Hood escorted him to various torture chambers, although most were bare: 'nothing to be seen except for the beams on which the wheel was said to be suspended'.[99] At Brunswick in 'a church' he saw numerous coffins: 'one of them contained Queen Caroline of England. There were many cushions attached to the coffins with metal bases, containing I was told the heart of those within. One of these hearts was taken out and shown to me. It was that of Duke Leopold.'[100]

Chance acquaintances also interested him, from the man who spoke such perfect English that Bute found it hard to believe he was indeed German, to the green tree frog

we caught ... that afternoon. We put him on a tree and he climbed beautifully. Every little projection he seized with his little paws, just as a boy would with his hands and we saw his pulses beating in his back. He was very neatly made, but we let him go away.[101]

Some pleasures were typical of those enjoyed by most children: 'I dined up at an actual dinner party at Mr Forbes! ... I am sorry now that I did not take more sugar plums than one, for Mama says it is the custom to carry away some.'[102] The party turned and headed for home, taking a boat down the Rhine, and telling legends of the river as they sailed. At Cologne, Bute summed up the mood of the trip: 'Dr Hood finished the drawing of me which he had begun at Baden & Nora played on a very fine piano-forte. Mama had a cup of coffee & I had my tea & we were all very happy.'[103]

There were still delights in store. Bute saw the tomb of Charlemagne at Aix-la-Chapelle with its 'immense slab of stone with CAROLOMAGNO simply placed on it' and 'three rows of arches one above the other with marble pillars'.[104] They said goodbye to Dr Hood, and had a photograph taken for him 'with my head in a vice'.[105] There was a visit to a toyshop to buy presents for Bute and for his friends and relatives. There, 'the people were very cross' and 'we were glad to get out of that scolding house'.[106] Bute was used to content and cheerful people.

At the end of the first trip the party visited Cousin Edith who had married Charles Clifton in 1853; Bute met their two children, Charles[107] and Flora.[108] Edith's unreasonable husband made their marriage miserable. In the many surviving documents referring to him, not one voice is raised in his praise. The usual verdict on Edith's marriage was voiced by Lady Selina: 'Poor soul, she has had much to bear.'[109]

This was the first of three such trips, but the only one for which there is a complete record. There is a fragmentary journal for the second, scribed by Nora Boyle. In 1857, a correspondent was hoping that Bute's third trip to Brussels afforded 'as much pleasure as the first did'.[110]

Bute was of an age when most aristocratic boys were at school, and his male relatives, by this time, were putting pressure on his mother to at least get him a tutor,[111] but for a long while she prevaricated. Even when the tutor arrived (at the end of 1858), Bute had frequent and lengthy holidays, and days spent 'running about'.[112] In itself, this was an education. Lady Bute entertained a good deal, and her young son was often 'kept running about, charging ladies' plates at luncheon'.[113] He grew up assuming that it was normal for women to be interested in the serious subjects that men were. Lady Bute also continued to have her own ideas about his education. Sophia had edited her father's journals and her sister's poems; now she assisted her eleven-year-old son to start a small newspaper. The *Mount Stuart Weekly Journal* was begun at the end of 1858 to 'convey to our absent friends some knowledge of how we are occupied', in which it succeeds now as then. Bute was the editor, and he copied the whole out in his own hand, and as a good editor should, he solicited contributions from all the talented associates he could find. Occasionally, however, he was forced to note that 'No contributions have been sent in, not withstanding the repeated prayers for them.'[114]

There was a serial, a pastiche of melodramatic Victorian historical novels, contributed anonymously (in fact written by Lady Bute), which followed the breathless adventures of the loyal Marie, lady-in-waiting to Empress Maud (of Stephen-and-Maud fame). The subject was, of course, chosen because of the connections of Cardiff Castle with the story of the Empress. Her beleaguered position must have appealed to Lady Bute, and each short episode is full of strong women characters. The Misses Boyle acted as sub-editors, something the publication needed; Bute had a somewhat shaky grasp of spelling. On the other hand, he could hit the exact stylistic note for every feature of the paper. A dead bullfinch got the full treatment for his obituary: 'every effort was made to restore the vital spark but in vain . . . he was a Bird much admired, loved and respected'. In true Victorian style, there followed details of the funeral. Wrapped 'in silk he was deposited in [a wooden box] & the whole sewn up in calico, the seams of which were covered in wax. He was placed beside the body of his talented friend "Paris" in the vault of particular pets.'[115] The whole is surrounded by a carefully ruled and inked black border.

Shortly after this, Lady Bute and her son travelled to the other family home in Scotland, Dumfries House, and the publication was renamed *The Pilgrim's Weekly Gazette and Mount Stuart Weekly Journal*. From this issue comes a piece of editorial comment that sets the tone for the fervent Scottish nationalism of the circle.

That eminent man, Mr A. J. Boyle,[116] we rejoice to say, has returned to his native country. In these days of centralisation, Scotland cannot allow all her sons to be absorbed by the sister country. If 'Scottish rights' are not to be for ever abandoned, if her identity as a nation is not to be wholly lost sight of, let her rouse herself to cherish those who can best uphold her.[117]

In Victorian Scotland, Christmas was not celebrated, but gifts were given at the New Year; and amongst other presents in 1859, Lady Bute had given her son a 'Lilliputian Theatre'. Celebrations included performances of *The Miller and his Men,* reviewed in the journal:

the whole play was gone through very successfully, including a tremendous explosion in the last scene, the appearance of which was artfully managed by a device of Lord Bute's; while the sound was produced by the bursting of a large biscuit bag, procured for the purpose.[118]

Regular book reviews appeared, one being of Catherine Sinclair's *Beatrice, or The Unknown Relatives,*[119] which contained 'a discovery of Popish wickedness, with a harrowing interist' [sic].[120] It had been published in 1852, in the wake of the Protestant 'No Popery' furore over the restoration of the English Catholic hierarchy, and had outsold *Uncle Tom's Cabin*. If Lady Bute had been concerned that Bute was not quite hostile enough to Roman Catholicism, this book would have possibly been a suitable corrective – although a sceptical reader might have found it far-fetched enough to promote more hilarity than disgust.

In this edition, the paper acquired a proper printed mast-head with an engraving of Mount Stuart House. In the same issue, Bute tells of his first visit to the criminal courts in Edinburgh. As well as his own version of the cases, Bute glued in reports from the newspapers. The paper soon carried another trial, this time of Donald Chance Infatuation, commonly known as Downy. Not this time in the High Court, but 'in the renovated hut, we mean fort, we say renovated because it was fitted out expressly for the occasion, having a glass window, table covered with green baze [*sic*], desk and 3 stools'.[121] There was a little difficulty in persuading the accused into this court, and he did not, because he could not, reply to the charge in his own voice. He was a dog. A visiting minister from Bute was the judge and Bute was counsel for the prosecution. The indictment is carefully laid out. Not only the language but the exact form and shape of legal documents is reproduced.[122]

The main surviving evidence for the prosecution is a statement from John P. C. Stuart, as on this occasion he correctly styled himself:

> Master Carter, Master Jessop, and myself were playing at 'Tom Tinkers ground' in the Flat Holms on the 5th inst. Master Carter had walked quietly away in the direction of the cowshed and Master Jessop and I were following at some distance, when, without the least provocation, the prisoner and his father rushed upon and barked at him (Master Carter) – this is the whole thing.[123]

The incident is explained in the only other surviving statement, that by Jane Chapman. She had deposed that 'he never hurts fowls ... [but] barks at and assaults everybody who is not well clothed'.[124] Master Jessop was the butler's son and he would have been respectably dressed. It was Master Carter who was attacked by the dog because he was roughly dressed.

This incident shows that Bute was allowed to play with children from other backgrounds. He could cajole adults into his pastimes, in this instance to act as judge in the little court. He enjoyed taking on very different roles and playing them out, just as he liked mastering the pastiche of various literary styles. It shows his ability to get to the essence of something as complicated as a legal trial, and in a short time. Every element of this little case is punctiliously correct. And there is another aspect: Bute would not allow his friends, however roughly dressed, to be attacked by the estate dogs.

Bute recorded the end of his winter holidays in this last winter edition of his paper.[125] It was about this time that he himself printed a bill (advertising a lecture) at Duncan Ballantyne's printers: he had the opportunity to appreciate all the aspects of producing and printing. Bute's breadth of general knowledge was very remarkable, even from this early date. He had the time and means to follow up anything that interested him, and his interests were many and varied. If his formal education was lacking, he had learned how to investigate anything which interested him. He was very fond of his mother's friends and his older relatives, and indeed his younger distant cousins, Flora and Charley (the children of his Cousin Edith). It was not enough. In the 19 February issue of his little paper he complained of 'the very monotonous life enjoyed (?) by the Editor'.

The next issue of the paper did not appear until July when, apologising for 'our long silence' the Editor explained that they had been in Edinburgh, Ayrshire, and Peebles before travelling to Cardiff, where 'the pleasure and excitement of arriving ... has been sadly marred by the illness of the Marchioness of Bute'. This is the first mention of Sophia's illness, though in June it had prompted her to make a new will, arranging the guardianship of her son. Lord James Stuart's death from heart disease in September 1859 came too late to change her plans. She liked his eldest son, James Frederick,[126] a judgement which events were to prove sound. Following the conflict with her sister Adelaide, and in the light of her cousin Edith's unhappy marriage, she turned to new guardians. She probably hoped for most from Sir Francis Gilbert, but lacking one overwhelmingly obvious choice, had the good sense to appoint three, which would ensure that a majority opinion would always carry the day. The others were her redoubtable spinster cousin Lady Elizabeth Moore, and Charles Stuart,[127] already trustee of the south Wales estates. Bruce had died in 1855, and McNabb had retired. Their places had been taken by Stuart and John Boyle,[128] another of the numerous Boyle siblings.

Charles Stuart, a colonel who had served as military secretary to Lord Canning, the first Viceroy of India,[129] was descended from the 3rd Earl of Bute's third son Charles. Stuart had been warned of the seriousness of the Marchioness's condition by John Boyle, and came to Cardiff to resume his duties as trustee. A very conventional man, he was less occupied by the estate than by the way Bute was being brought up, which horrified him. Bute, now twelve, was still not at school, and was being taught (when he was taught) by an inadequate tutor,[130] whom the boy despised ('understandably', recorded the fair-minded Stuart). His religious education was still wholly in the hands of his mother. Boyle thought that Bute would soon rebel against his mother's rule, perhaps not reckoning how deep Bute's love of her was, or how strong his impulse to please her. Yet there is no doubt that Bute was yearning for a wider life and for adventures.

In every issue, now, there was reference to her Ladyship's health, the only record we have, apart from Stuart's comment that she looked 'thin and ill'.[131] She tried drives out, a short break down the coast from Cardiff, and once it was possible to record that 'Her Ladyship has had no attack of breathlessness the last three days.'[132] The very last issue of the journal in late November commented that she was 'at present still suffering from astha [sic] & cough'.[133] The newspaper did not record the cause, probably because nobody thought Bute should know that his mother was suffering from Bright's disease, the Victorian name for all forms of kidney failure, one of the effects of which is that the body cannot rid itself of water. It was this which would have caused Sophia's breathlessness.[134]

The little 'Mount Stuart Gazette' suggests Bute's life was kept as normal as possible. There were dancing lessons, and a trip to see the last portions of the East Bute dock and its canal opened to the public. This was illustrated by a pen drawing by Bute,[135] whose illustrations increasingly enlivened the paper. He had a strong, concise style of drawing, able and lively. News of the family pets continued to be a mainstay, with a new hedgehog causing much anxiety: 'He resorted into the chimney in his apartment and remained there for more than two days . . . many means had been resorted to in order to hint to him that his presence was strongly desired either above or below.'[136]

By December, the Marchioness had reached Edinburgh. Bute wrote to his 'own dearest cousin Charley' that Mama had a 'brutal cold'. The last entry, on 22 December, still cheerful and unconcerned, recorded: 'Mr Bruce and I threw a little loose snow at each other in the Meadows.'[137] There is something a little pathetic in the picture of a boy so bereft of companionship of his own age that he has to turn to an adult to play in the snow with him.

The letter to Charley was never finished or signed. Lady Bute's health worsened, and it could no longer be hidden that she was seriously ill. The monotony and the happiness of Bute's life were alike at an end for many years.

2   Custody

'A susceptible and excitable young person'

Lady Bute was dying, and her family and friends began to gather round her in the Edinburgh hotel. Seeking the 'good death', so important to the Victorians,[1] Adelaide came, and the sisters were reconciled.[2] Their niece Edith joined them, and Mr and Mrs John Boyle and John's sister Augusta. One of the Church of Scotland's most senior ministers, Dr Norman Macleod,[3] who had buried Sophia's sister, Flora, and mother, came to her bedside to console her.[4] Ironically, he was later to comfort the widowed Queen, whom the family still blamed for Flora's suffering.

Charles Stuart, Bute's guardian, was telegraphed to come and hear Lady Bute's last concerns about her son, and support young Bute; but it was Christmas, and he stayed in Hampshire with his wife. On 27 December Lady Bute was 'insensible after two terrible fits'.[5] She rallied and regained consciousness, but died at four o'clock on the afternoon of 28 December 1859. Bute, occasionally overcome by storms of grief, took his place as head of the family, and began making the appropriate arrangements. Within two hours of her death he had given instructions for a cast to be taken of her face 'with view to a future bust',[6] ordered a 'leaden coffin',[7] arranged the inscriptions to go on it, requested a post-mortem examination and made arrangements for 'Locke & other servants about his mother to be cared for'.[8]

Stuart was telegraphed again and urgently pressed to travel to Scotland.[9] He chose not to leave until the following evening by the overnight train. The first person he met at the hotel was Lady Edith, whom he disliked. This made him a good deal gloomier than Sophia's death. What really confused him was Bute's emotional state.

His grief was violent & returns in fits and starts, he is often quite cheerful and laughing ... I went up with [Miss Boyle] to see poor

Lady Bute's body. The face was placid and serene in expression. The boy followed us in & kissed her face, then uncovered her hand & kissed it & left the room in quiet tears.

Stuart dismissed the weight of arrangements Bute had taken on as 'The boy busies himself much about the vault & coffin.' The post-mortem confirmed that she had died of Bright's disease.

Stuart then left to bring in the New Year with friends at Ford in the Borders,[10] unaware that leaving the mourners in order to join a cheerful celebration would cause offence. The disruption of the New Year holiday meant that the body could not be moved until 2 January. Early on that day, Lady Elizabeth Moore arrived. She had intended to spend the winter on the Mediterranean, but telegraphed with the news of Lady Bute's death, she started for home, not breaking her journey of three days and two nights, and arrived in time to accompany the coffin to Bute.[11] Stuart, however, remained in the Borders, still celebrating the New Year.

The funeral party left Edinburgh early, and travelled by rail to Glasgow and then by the *Dolphin* steamer, privately chartered, to Rothesay. The journey took all day.[12] Bute bitterly recalled how Stuart: 'left [my mother's] body ... to be attended on that long and troublesome journey, in the depth of winter, only by women, servants, and myself, a child of twelve'. Bute dated his disgust at Stuart from this incident, feeling the 'gross disrespect'[13] to Sophia implied in it.

The Scotsman gave the funeral party as 'the Marquis of Bute, Colonel Charles Stuart and Mr A. T. Boyle, Dr Matthews Duncan, her Ladyship's physician and Mr A. Bruce, S.S.C.'. These were the persons the Bute household expected, but others as well as Stuart may have avoided the terrible journey. Stuart's personal journal, an invaluable insight into his day-to-day thoughts and actions, shows he was not there. Whether or not Bute was really alone except for servants and women, there is no doubt that his guardian was comfortably with friends, while Bute made the most traumatic journey of his life.

Bute arranged for his mother's body to rest in the ground-floor sitting room, with candles around, a nice compromise between his own love of ceremony and her dislike of ostentation. Charles Stuart finally arrived on 4 January with Bute's cousin, James Frederick Crichton Stuart, and stayed to attend the funeral. The next morning at 'About 11½ the company began to arrive, Bute came downstairs & received all kindly and composedly – though he looked pale and nervous ... then Dr Norman MacLeod ... prayed most beautifully. Bute fidgeted to the window afterwards to see the hearse & the coffin put into it.'[14] It was beyond Stuart to see how far Bute felt himself responsible for the ceremony, or how much comfort he derived from such things.

Under lowering skies, the procession moved the five miles by the shore road to Rothesay. As well as the extended Stuart clan, island notables and clergy of all denominations came to pay their last respects, as did the Bute tenant farmers. In all there were 250 in the cortège, and almost every vehicle on the island was pressed into use. The day was cold and overcast, but no rain fell. 'In the same carriage as chief mourners with the Marquis were his cousins, Col. Stuart and Mr Villiers Stuart.'[15] Charles Stuart was amazed at Bute. 'The boy seemed happy to be with young men and really was as outwardly cheerful as if he were going to a wedding, though he may have been feeling much inwardly. I felt grieved that the crowds of people who stared into the carriage should see him grinning.'[16] The possibility that Bute felt triumphant in the face of his mother's well-made death, and his own successful arrangements for her appropriate ceremony of exit from this world did not occur to him. Stuart's religion, sincere as it was, did not allow exultation in faith following a death.

The coffin was carried to the mausoleum in the grounds of the parish church (known as the High Kirk), with family members bearing the pall above it. Charles Stuart was not accustomed to the stark simplicity of a Presbyterian funeral – nor much impressed by it. 'The coffin was simply laid down without a word by the bearers. The ladies with Lamb and Locke were ranged along the wall of the Mausoleum.[17] Bute peered about him till all was settled, then knelt & I hope prayed beside the coffin & again returned and kissed it.' Stuart could not imagine the disposition that needs to put its innermost emotions into a fitting outward form. Just as he had earlier misunderstood Bute's feelings of exultation and thought them mere happiness, he now doubted the sincerity of his grief. Yet the feeling, the prayers, were not less real for being acted out. Onlookers other than Stuart were more impressed. *The Buteman* described the scene.

Within the vault were several ladies in company with the deceased's sister, Lady Adelaide, witnessing the last duty being silently performed. The coffin, which was covered with rich black velvet, and plainly mounted, bore a brass plate simply recording her Ladyship's name, date of birth and decease ... [when] the funeral party in numbers entered the vault the touching spectacle was witnessed of a motherless and fatherless boy with his right hand upon his mother's coffin kneeling to bid a last adieu.

The ceremonial over, Bute suffered a reaction as the gravity of his loss hit him. 'He went home with Lady E. Moore, Miss Boyle & Lamb, quite overcome', recorded the bemused Stuart.

After luncheon, Stuart at last had his interview with Lady Elizabeth: 'She does to be sure "multiply words" but I think that we understand one another.'[18] The next day, Lady Elizabeth found an opportunity to try and impress her view of Bute on Stuart: 'she opened & gave us her opinion of Bute's talents, peculiarities, precocity & determination at most tedious length. But I think there was much truth in what she said.'[19] She later confided that at this time she found that whilst 'he was not to my view agreeable, I fancied him a stern, high-minded strictly "honourable man" incapable of any meanness trickery or falsehood'.[20] At that moment they were fairly well in accord. Ominously, however, Stuart added that he feared Lady Elizabeth would humour Bute too much, 'for he must learn to obey & not merely to reason'.[21]

The usual practice in Scotland was to have the eulogy the following Sunday. Accordingly, Rev. John Robertson, minister of Scoulag, the little church by the shore in the Mount Stuart policies, which served the locals and the servants of the big house, preached a fine, direct sermon. A 'dark dispensation' had deprived the mourners of one firm yet gentle, loving and wise: 'May he who met the two disciples on their sad way to Emmaeus ... join Himself to us ... to give us ... consolation and peace.'[22] Stuart was again bemused: 'The extraordinary boy remained to all appearance totally unmoved, only decently attentive.' He might not have been any happier with a wild outpouring of grief, which would probably have been the result if Bute had not to some degree distanced himself from the occasion and assumed a formal mask. Sitting in his father's pew, leaving his mother's seat empty, he was firmly embarking on a more adult life.

That afternoon, Stuart interviewed Bute about his future. He began with the essential aristocratic sport of horse-riding, suspecting (unfairly) that Lady Bute had not tried to interest her son in it. A good seat and, above all, courage on a horse were inextricably bound up with the image of a gentleman. Stuart was not delighted that 'evidently he has no taste for [riding]. He asked if he might learn to fence to which I at once assented. He asked if he might learn navigation (which he wishes to know because there are technical phrases, he told me, in Peter Simple,[23] which he does not understand!).'[24]

Stuart left Bute on 11 January. Of the three nominees in Lady Bute's will, Sir Francis Hastings Gilbert was consul at Scutari, so was not available to be guardian to Bute. This left Lady Elizabeth and Charles Stuart. The two guardians were appointed by the Scottish Court of

Session on 18 January. Stuart and Elizabeth Moore began a fraught correspondence.[25] Just a month after Lady Bute's death, Stuart wrote to Lady Elizabeth with plans for taking the boy, his tutor Mr Stacey and his servant Meikle into his own house.[26] A regular theme of Stuart's was the need to remove Bute from the care of his nurse, Mrs Lamb.

Stacey was a new addition to the household, picked by Lady Bute as she became ill. The son and brother of Cardiff clergymen, Francis Edmond Stacey was the nephew of E. P. Richards, 'the co-architect with the second marquess of the fortunes of the Bute estate'.[27] He was also a Fellow of King's College, Cambridge, and probably some fifteen years older than Bute. A former cricket 'blue', he seemed just the man to encourage Bute to develop an interest in sporting pastimes.[28] Meikle, formerly butler at Dumfries House, was Bute's private servant, and a replacement for Lamb. Stuart did not propose any regular contact with Lady Elizabeth. In effect, Bute was to lose not only his mother but every trace of his life with her: his nurse, his home, his adult friends.

Lady Elizabeth replied, urging caution. She began in a conciliatory way: 'with regard to the subjects you have named respecting a boy's Education "Public & Private schools" tutors etc. I feel that this is so entirely your concern that I hardly venture to hazard an opinion upon topics I have never been accustomed to think of.' Lady Elizabeth was showing traditional female deference to the male areas of responsibility, but she was only backing off to make her claims elsewhere.

> From my intimate knowledge of his (Bute's) singular character ... I do not think it is for his advantage (or yours) to remove him hastily from my care ... gradually accustom him to the necessity of a change ... If conversed with rationally, he is far too wise not to see and understand the real state of the case. I have talked to him of school, of young & pleasant companions. I have told him he must work hard at Latin and other languages and that he cannot pass the whole of his childhood at Mount Stuart.

Lady Elizabeth had undertaken two battles, the first to persuade Bute to leave her and the second to persuade Bute to like Charles Stuart, who was doing nothing to make her task easier. Lady Elizabeth urged Stuart to come back to Mount Stuart and to win Bute's confidence: 'it will not be accomplished in five minutes for he has a great deal of Scotch caution (and reserve when he pleases) and childlike as he naturally is in some ways he is as old and shrewd and long headed as a grown up man in other ways'.[29]

Instead of co-operating, Stuart went on the offensive. He said that the role of guardian was so onerous that no one 'who has bread to eat would undertake the task except from a feeling of duty and humanity . . . but if I am to hold it my judgement must be altogether unfettered'.[30] Lady Bute had left a careful balance of power which with Sir Francis out of the running was already disrupted. Now, by insisting he virtually hold the guardianship alone, Stuart was making a nonsense of Lady Bute's will, as Mr Bruce[31] gently pointed out when he told Lady Elizabeth that he regretted what she told him about Stuart's approach and spoke of 'Lady Bute's wisdom in selecting . . . another in whom she placed equally great . . . confidence'. Stuart was determined that Bute should see himself as one boy amongst many, but Bute, freed from his mother's stifling care, was taking on himself an essentially grown-up role. He made no fuss about parting from his nurse, and sleeping in his own room. He was compensating for his terrible loss with growing power and responsibility. Yet Stuart wished Bute to lay these consolations aside.

Stuart believed Bute had 'ideas of importance' and wished to educate him 'morally'.[32] He harked obsessively on this theme. When Lady Elizabeth suggested it would help Bute to acclimatise to the society of children to invite to Mount Stuart some distant relatives whom Bute knew, Stuart replied, 'I think that it is the society of thoroughly independent boys who do not know him as a young potentate that Bute requires.'[33] Stuart did not want Bute acclimatised, he wanted him shocked. When Bute himself invited Stuart to Mount Stuart, the latter wrote to Lady Elizabeth of 'a little misapprehension in Bute's mind when he asks us to visit him . . . & it is perhaps a pity that he should not know that whilst under-age his guardians occupy exactly the position towards him . . . (of) his poor mother . . . I should not notice it at all if I did not think it was so essential that he should not become or continue self important.'[34] In short, he objected strongly to the fact that Bute behaved more like an adult than a boy. He wanted to change him, and change him radically. Bute had come of age in taking responsibility for his mother's last journey and burial. He was far less prepared to be a boy after this than he had been before it.

Bute, desperate to escape Stuart's care, wrote to Mrs Stuart at the end of January, asking her to intercede with her husband to allow him to enrol as a midshipman in the Navy. Stuart's reply is balanced and reasoned – and utterly ungenerous. He explains that his guardians would bear a heavy responsibility in sanctioning such a hazardous course, and that Bute, who had been tenderly cared for by his nurse, was quite unprepared for the tough life of a 'middy'. So far, so good, but then Stuart goes on the attack, assuming that Bute feels he would 'pass five or six years of [his] life more pleasantly and idly . . . than . . . at school and college'. The possibility that Bute, fired by Captain Marryat's tales of a boy living a man's life at the age of fourteen, would rather have relied on his wits and abilities than go into the care of one who was determined to belittle and reduce him never occurred to Stuart. Nor does he seem to understand the terror felt by one wholly accustomed to the adult world upon being faced with a mass of other boys at school. Stuart put salt into this wound, speaking of 'the daily rubs you must meet with [at school] & the knocking about of boys older and bigger than yourself'.[35] He refers again to the need for Bute to be free of the care of a nurse: 'neither I nor any boy that I knew was ever touched by a female servant after eleven years of age.' This was, of course, the convention,[36] but the ceaseless references to the subject suggest there was more emotion than rationality behind his mentions of the 'uneducated servant's influence'[37] and the need for Bute to avoid the scorn of his fellows.

It was perhaps not just a desire to free himself from Stuart that motivated Bute. Writing in 1866, Lady Elizabeth recalled writing to Stuart when 'Lady Adelaide Murray with the "Viper" were scolding and ill treating the lonely Orphan child left in my charge, so that I became miserable & would gladly have placed you anywhere to be quit of them.'[38] The 'Viper' was Miss Augusta Boyle. Stuart had taken the unwise step of employing Lady Adelaide and Miss Boyle to provide an unbiased account, as he thought, of what was toward at Mount Stuart. Both ladies were engaged in a desperate power struggle with Lady Elizabeth, who, as guardian, unsurprisingly felt it was her role to direct Bute and the household. Thus the information Stuart got was far from impartial. Worse, his spying system was soon discovered and so he became associated with the worst behaviour of one faction. As he liked Augusta and disliked Lady Elizabeth, he was very late in coming to see that she had right on her side.[39] Bute was caught up in battles between adults who had very different ideas of the way he should behave, and 'susceptible and . . . excitable'[40] as he was, it is not surprising that he should have longed for escape to a world that seemed at once simpler and more challenging.

Stuart's next letter damned him in Bute's eyes. Stuart had been speaking to Sir John Stuart the Vice-Chancellor about the forthcoming petition to the Court of Chancery which would see the two guardians officially appointed over the young Marquess. Stuart laid out a sensible plan, that Bute should travel to Geneva or 'some other Protestant place' for the summer, to learn French from native speakers and classical languages from his tutor. Bute would then go to a private school for 'eight or nine months' and then in midsummer 1861 to Eton or Harrow. So far, so good.

Then Stuart broached the question of money for himself to support the Marquess:

> I should suppose that about £5000 per annum will be allowed. It is right I should tell you that the Court have in other cases ruled that maintenance is in some degree to be looked upon as the salary of an office . . . some pecuniary advantage (I might say compensation) in the way of saving a portion of the guardian's private income may be fairly made by the person who has custody of the 'infant' . . . The Custody does involve in many respects a scale of living & establishment more expensive than I have been accustomed to, and at the end of nine years to reduce again materially may not be altogether pleasant.[41]

It does not require a particular prejudice against Stuart to see a man determined to feather his own nest a little, whilst carrying out duties for which he had no taste. One prejudiced against Stuart would see a man undertaking the charge of a small boy solely for financial gain. Bute was prejudiced against Stuart, and he read the letters. 'I can trust no one', he cried.[42] Lady Elizabeth replied promptly that she 'did not understand . . . regarding Bute's future "maintenance"' but she would be glad for Stuart to have the money for his own sake. She herself did not want to claim anything unless she had actually parted with money on Bute's behalf.

The guardian of Bute's person did not control his wealth, which came mainly from the south Wales estates. These were run, as they had been since his father's death, by two trustees: at this time Charles Stuart and John Boyle. The wealth from Wales was gradually accumulating, as was wealth from the Scottish estates, administered by the Tutor-at-Law, who was now James Frederick Crichton Stuart. The income from the English and Welsh estates was estimated at 'upwards of £76,000 p.a. and the income from the Scotch estates as about £17,000 p.a.'.[43] Yet the trustees, whilst they were responsible for Bute's wealth, were not in a position to benefit from it to any extent. They were essentially salaried servants. A guardian could benefit from their position in the way a trustee could not.

Stuart had carefully considered this. In his meeting with Sir John Stuart he

> went the length of asking how far it might be right for a guardian to put by his own income & live on his ward. He replied that it

would not be right in a guardian to live entirely upon his ward, but that it had been ruled that the office was in the nature of a salaried appointment – that I might keep up an increased establishment & probably save out of my private income. In short, the court gives what it thinks necessary having regard to the minor's income & the guardian only has to keep his ward properly provided for.[44]

Stuart, with the highest legal opinion behind him, felt quite comfortable at the prospect of gaining from his guardianship. The Court of Chancery felt that some remuneration for the job was reasonable. Stuart might save, not the money he got for Bute, but (a nice distinction) his own money. The only concern was to see that neither Bute's loss nor Stuart's gain was out of proportion. Clothes, food, carriages, riding-horses, the whole style of the home must reflect the nobility and wealth of the young charge. The necessary funds drawn to keep Lord Bute in a suitable style could easily be made enough to allow other, less wealthy persons, to live more comfortably than they had dreamed possible, entirely at his expense, whilst saving their own money. Since this was sanctioned by the Court of Chancery, Stuart considered it wholly moral and honourable. But Bute adhered absolutely to Lady Bute's strict values: he would have been sincerely shocked at any suggestion of profiting from any labour of love. This was more than abstract ethics. Bute's feelings were deeply hurt at seeing himself as a desirable commodity, valued not for himself, but for the money he brought, and also as a burden so great that it could only be sweetened by a whole new standard of living.

Yet Bute was not solidly hostile to Stuart when at last he arrived back at Mount Stuart at the end of February: 'Agreeably surprised by Bute's rushing down to welcome us full of excitement about the volunteer uniform . . . a lucky thought of mine.' His manner to Stuart was 'frank and affectionate'.[45] If Stuart had only been able to compromise in his way of managing Bute, he would have had a much easier time; but he saw no option other than insistence on blind obedience, and he ignored all of Bute's best intentions. 'I see clearly . . . that everyone & everything gives way to him, & he naturally expects this to be the case,' said Stuart. 'The inevitable struggle depresses me, because I cannot (not naturally liking young people) depend on my temper in carrying it through.'[46] All his life Bute had conformed, and been a good and dutiful son. For the first time, there was an authority-figure he could hate, and hate him he did.

Failing all else, the carrot of another trip to the Continent might, like the volunteer uniform, have helped to win Bute round, but on this visit Stuart found out some surprising facts about Bute that made him cancel the projected trip abroad. Lady Bute, despite being a staunch Protestant 'of an uncompromising kind' and responsible for Bute's religious education, had not been able to put a stop to Bute's attraction to Roman Catholicism. Walking in the grounds of Mount Stuart, Stuart fell in with Lady Elizabeth, and for once heard her out, because he could not escape. He learned that Bute had: 'Great interest in R.C. doctrines and ceremonies, a tendency to voluntary humiliation & fasting, & strong aesthetic tastes especially for churches and pictures. Added to this a great love of theological argument & reasoning, & at present mighty little [balance?].' Plainly all sorts of temptation in this direction might lurk on the Continent, so poor Bute was to take his undiluted classical education at home.

There were other troubles to face. Bute wanted to live in one of his own homes, and sneered at Stuart's house. 'He told Miss Boyle that Stacey will have no shooting at Hubborne, so one sees which way the cat jumps & that Stacey is not likely to be long in <u>my</u> service.' In fact, no servant was ever long in Stuart's service. His diary reveals a succession of them arriving, seemingly good and industrious, only to be dismissed as they proved unsatisfactory. Poor Stuart acknowledged his failings. 'How I wish I had more energy & temper in my dealings with my own servants. I do dislike speaking & when I do speak express myself so angrily & in this fear I ever deteriorate.'[47]

Bute's relationship with his servants was a relaxed and carefree one. Stuart was right that the young potentate had no doubt that he would be obeyed, but equally he was quite at home with those from social strata other than his own. 'Found Bute skylarking with Stacey & some of the servants – he says for himself – for the last time.'[48] This simplicity of manner with servants made Stuart uneasy, as did Bute's obedience to his nurse. Stuart, who so desperately wanted Bute to learn to obey and not reason, saw sinister overtones when Bute obeyed Lamb.[49] Stuart's attitude to Bute's nurse, Mrs Lamb, is particularly difficult for modern minds. He was undoubtedly right in thinking that other boys of Bute's age would have mocked him for still being in her care, and he could not see how a servant could ever be a mother-substitute. Mrs Lamb was uneducated: a letter she wrote to Bute when he was about to leave Harrow, finally seeking another post nearly five years after she had ceased to care for him, is semi-literate and full of spelling mistakes. But it is warm and well-balanced – she promised that at any time she would come to visit him, or he could come to her – and there is no hint of the 'toadying' of which Stuart made such an issue. 'I was very unhappy to give myself away from my dear Lord Bute but you sea [*sic*] you are to be the same after as now my dear.'[50]

Stuart only recognised book-learning and the traditional values of males of his own class. He did not recognise the wisdom of women like Mrs Lamb. But Bute's attitude to servants was based on the fact that nobody, least of all Bute, doubted that he was a gentleman. In contrast, when Stuart offered assistance to a lady and gentleman on a train, it was not very graciously received. Stuart's insecurity surfaced at once: 'I always fancy that I look like a gentleman, when dressed as one, but I wonder if I really do?' Shy as he was, Bute was at ease with his own role and his fellow men. He would have been puzzled by Stuart's reaction to a visit to the National Gallery in London, which 'has a dingy appearance. The company today contributed. What can the shop keepers & artisans really think of the grotesque saints and martyrs of the tre- & quattro cento masters?'[51] The twelve-year-old Bute was better placed to appreciate both the art and the artisans.

Bute's weakness was that he had not yet learned to question the rightness of his own judgements; his view of his universe was wholly self-centred. He made no effort to give Stuart the benefit of the doubt. In time, Bute forgave Stuart, but never doubted that he had been wronged. Stuart failed to understand Bute's emotional swings, yet he was not the monster Bute made him. In February *The Gazette* had brought Stuart the news he had long hoped for: 'I am a pucka [*sic*] Major General. I have now the title I must die under. I . . . can never profit by the death of a fellow creature in the way of advancement!'[52] For a regular soldier at this period advancement usually came when a vacancy was created by death, usually death in action, and it troubled Stuart that he had benefited by this.

Stuart returned home to Hampshire, and Lady Elizabeth, Stacey and Bute travelled south by stages to join him. In Edinburgh Bute had a bout of influenza. He was still unwell in London. Lady Elizabeth saw that from his 'agitation & alarm . . . he could neither take food or sleep soundly'.[53] She tried hard to persuade Stuart to visit him, hoping that the bogeyman would seem less horrible in the flesh than in the imagination. She cannot have been helped by a letter Bute received from Stuart's wife, which was supposed to welcome him into her care. It began well enough with regrets for his poor health and her own warm feelings towards him. She knew that he had 'gone through a great trial in parting from so many whom you love . . . and coming to comparative strangers. But it is <u>God</u> who has sent you this trial' and if this was not enough, she then reminded him of her sufferings, for she had a 'little stranger boy coming to live with

me, of whose ways and temper and habits I know nothing'.[54] Mrs
Stuart's words suggested strongly she thought it a good thing Bute
had lost his mother (not surprising, as Stuart undoubtedly thought
this) and that she was just as much to be pitied as Bute. He was an
unwelcome intruder in her home.

As Bute wrote: 'I prayed, I entreated, I agonised, I abused the
general; I adjured [Lady Elizabeth] not to give me up to him. She was
shaken but not convinced . . . [In London] my prayers and adjurations
were trebled.'[55] Added to this was his determination to avoid a private
school.

It is possible to feel heartily sorry for both parties in this conflict.
Stuart did not want the charge that was thrust on him, but he was
prepared to carry it out to the best of his ability. He was not the
best man to have the care of any boy,[56] and he was incapable of
understanding that it was intolerably painful and unhealthy for Bute
to surrender all his links with the past. His idea that no one of Bute's
age should be allowed any voice in his treatment was too fixed to allow
any negotiation, even when it was clear to everybody else in the case
that Bute, accustomed to being consulted on every point, could not
return to the ranks of properly subservient boyhood.

Lady Elizabeth was undoubtedly highly intelligent, and well-read.
She was always quick to catch an inference, or make a connection, as
when Stuart was first accused of taking the post of guardian to feather
his own nest. It would be impossible to accuse her of obsequiousness;
she always had a sharp word for any action of which she disapproved,
and like Lady Bute was one of those women with the unwelcome gift
of saying aloud what others thought in private. More than anything
else she lacked the knack of living on an even emotional keel. She
was cordially disliked by Lady Selina,[57] who believed that she was
deeply hostile to her, and also spiteful. Bute, however, was to love
her all her long life. With her growing mistrust of Stuart on one side,
and pressured by Bute on the other, Lady Elizabeth did not have it
in her to bow to the inevitable. Stuart had the entire English male
establishment behind him. Every man in the Court of Chancery would
have felt that the best course for Bute was to follow the inevitable
path for upper-class boys: private school followed by public school.
In those circumstances the most practical option for Bute, and Lady
Elizabeth's best chance of influencing events, was to persuade the boy
to overcome his dislike of Stuart as far as possible. She chose instead
to make a fight of it.

By 3 April 1860, Stuart's not-very-extensive patience was at an end.
He was tired of excuses for the delays in handing Bute over. Unfairly,

he blamed Lady Elizabeth for Bute's fear of him. He decided that their 'ideas of the proper manner of bringing Bute up differ so widely' that he was going to ask the Court of Chancery to decide that he should have exclusive charge of Bute. To make certain that she understood this was not simply a dispute about schools, but was about the way Bute should be handled, he added that Lady Elizabeth seemed to feel 'that Bute himself ought to be consulted, <u>a point on which I regret to feel compelled to differ with you entirely</u>'. On 11 April there were meetings between the Vice-Chancellor Sir John Stuart and Lady Elizabeth and her counsel, which did not go well for Lady Elizabeth.[58] Stuart refused to meet Lady Elizabeth, although he was beginning to wonder if Bute's dislike of him was being prompted by Stacey.

A court hearing was set for 17 April. The preceding night, Lady Elizabeth and Bute, with Stacey, fled by train to Scotland. Undoubtedly their destination was chosen by Bute, who was bolting for the place he felt safe. Ironically, if they had gone to Lady Elizabeth's native Ireland (as Stuart at first thought they had) they would have been secure from all further proceedings. Stuart reacted by withdrawing every penny from the joint account set up for the guardians, and leaving Bute dependent on Lady Elizabeth's private money for everything, even his pocket money (which was two shillings and six pence a week). Lady Elizabeth and her legal advisor (George Maclachlan, an Edinburgh-based lawyer) believed that Bute was a 'domiciled Scotchman' and was out of the jurisdiction of the English courts when their decision was taken, and that they had no further hold on him. Bute and Lady Elizabeth lived quietly at The Granton Hotel in Edinburgh, while Bute continued his studies with Stacey.

In May, Stuart suggested that a new guardian should be appointed, who would have care of Bute, arrange his education and receive the maintenance for him. Whilst a suitable person was located, Bute should be placed either with Lady Adelaide, or Charles or Mrs Stuart, or Mr Stuart Wortley, or Mr John Boyle, and live at Dumfries House, thus preserving his Scotch domicile.[59] Lady Elizabeth wondered if this was the first step towards a compromise. Maclachlan thought it was 'a scheme to effect the total separation of the Marquis from your Ladyship'.

Stuart and his wife came to Scotland, to try and persuade Bute to surrender himself to them. The General did not feel he was getting the support he deserved from James Frederick Crichton Stuart, Bute's Tutor-at-Law. Jas. Fred., as Stuart called him, was counselling compromise, and was dismissed as 'a dish of skimmed milk'.[60] Mr Bruce, with whom Lady Elizabeth and Bute had taken refuge at

Falkland, succeeded in giving both parties the feeling that he was on their side. It was through Bruce that Stuart eventually heard that Bute disliked Lady Adelaide more than anyone else, and that Bute was beginning to think 'petticoat government' unmanly.[61]

The fact that the Stuarts were Low Church did nothing to help. The Low Church dislike of 'balls and theatres' (the young Bute loved dancing) was a further difficulty. Now anonymous letters started arriving at Lady Adelaide's, and Stuart anxiously mulled over their contents: Lady Elizabeth was working Bute up against his relations until he was frightened. Stuart suspected the writer was Miss Tyndall[62] – O. Tyndall Bruce's niece, and cousin to the Mr Bruce who had inherited Falkland. She, as later events were to prove, had her own game to play.[63] Factions were developing. Meikle, Bute's servant, was supporting Stacey, and was against Lady Elizabeth. Stuart could not see the danger to Bute of living in this web of deceit and faction.

A revealing little episode took place. Mrs Stuart wrote to Bute reminding him 'of our plan for visiting the Antiquarian Museum – which you know so well'.[64] She hoped he and his tutor would come on the arranged day. Bute, always shy in person and much bolder on paper, felt a refusal was easier when not face-to-face. 'I was not aware that the latter was a definite arrangement . . . I have got an arrangement that will prevent my complying,' he wrote.[65] When crossed, Mrs Stuart attacked with martyred innocence. Instead of calmly pursuing the plan, which might well have won Bute over, she at once went on the offensive: 'I am very much grieved & surprised at the note you have written . . . It was not like the son of parents such as you had. When you are older, I am sure you will feel this.' As if this was not enough to set Bute's teeth on edge by deliberately loading him with guilt, she added a postscript. 'There was not, perhaps, any "definite arrangements" (those are very long words!)'[66] By Bute's standards, they were perfectly ordinary words; from the age of eight he had been mastering the correct terms for everything that interested him. Too late the Stuarts came to accept that it was Bute's own letter.[67] Stuart's temper was not improved: '[Bruce's] account of him [Bute] is rather discouraging – he so evidently wants the sound thrashing that may be too long delayed to do good.'[68]

While the two parties were so far apart, it was impossible to imagine any satisfactory compromise. One guardian had to be outright victor. Stuart went back to the Court of Chancery. The legal advisors for Lady Elizabeth did their best. Mr Maclachlan dashed down to London in response to a telegram reading 'Come up immediately'.[69] As telegrams buzzed back and forth with increasing urgency, his partner stayed in

Edinburgh to advise Lady Elizabeth. Chancery did not accept Bute was outwith its jurisdiction, and in July Lady Elizabeth was removed from the office of guardian, and ordered to deliver up Bute into Stuart's custody. As Lady Elizabeth complained: 'an amiable, intelligent & noble-minded youth . . . has met with no more consideration than an American slave'.[70]

This is not surprising, as English establishment attitudes, severely alienated from Scotland a hundred years before during the Jacobite rebellions, and only slowly thawing under the waves of the picturesque mediaevalism let loose by Sir Walter Scott and the fashionable 'Balmorality' promoted by Victoria, still had little sympathy for the independent rights of the Scottish people, or understanding of the profoundly different culture which they cherished. One difference was this very attitude to youths. The age at which a young person was deemed to be able to make sensible decisions on their own behalf was (and is) much lower north of the Border.[71] Most importantly, the Scots legal system (based on different principles from the English) gave particular rights to a parentless minor from the age of fourteen, when they could appoint their own 'curators', endorsed by the Court of Session, the highest civil court in Scotland. From among them, the minor was entitled to choose one to care for and supervise him. If Bute could keep out of the jurisdiction of the English courts until he was fourteen, he could pick his own Guardian. As he was now rising thirteen, his date of freedom was not far away.

Lady Elizabeth and her advisors believed that in Scotland she was not under the jurisdiction of the English Court. She had absolutely no intention of complying with the order to surrender Bute. The simplest way to avoid complying with any court order is to avoid being served in person with the papers of the court, and Lady Elizabeth began dodging writs. Bute and Lady Elizabeth were, of course, accompanied by servants, one of whom was Jack Wilson, afterwards gamekeeper at Mount Stuart. It was they, and especially Wilson, who bore the brunt of this constant vigilance. On one occasion he knocked a writ-server down the hotel stairs, and he slept outside Bute's door at night, lest anyone crept up on him.[72] For a sensitive boy like Bute, these conditions of virtual siege were very disturbing.

Repeated and devious attempts to serve the papers of the English Court having been evaded, General Stuart petitioned the Scottish Court of Session to enforce the order of the Court of Chancery. This was what Lady Elizabeth had been waiting for, and she at once accepted the papers served by the Court of Session. She wished to present her case under Scottish law. The petition was finally heard on 18 July 1860. It springs to life under General Stuart's pen. Mr Dundas presented the case for Colonel Stuart, 'not fluently',[73] describing the Marquess as a 'susceptible and excitable young person' and arguing that Lady Bute (who had herself been appointed a guardian under English law) had intended an English guardianship and English education for her son. Lady Elizabeth Moore 'has not the shadow of a legal title or right, either natural or derived, for retaining custody of the child'.[74] She had acquired her guardianship from her appointment by the Court of Chancery, which had now withdrawn it. Lord Bute drew the bulk of his wealth from English estates (Wales is part of the English legal system) and held a British title. He was not Scottish.

Mr Gordon, 'a younger man of reddish hue',[75] represented Lady Elizabeth, who was 'the grandniece of the first Marquis of Hastings . . . maternal grandfather of the present Marquis of Bute'.[76] The relationship prompted the Lord Justice Clerk, presiding, to remark to laughter: 'She is at all events a Scotch cousin.'[77] Gordon pointed out that when Lady Elizabeth became aware of the need to preserve Bute's 'Scottish rights', she had 'restored him to Scotland'. Gordon described as 'a little strong' Stuart's withdrawal of all the funds deposited at the Union Bank 'subjected to the drafts of both guardians' and his paying these into his own account. Gordon drew attention to the impeccable Scottish antecedents of both of Bute's parents, and to his Scottish titles, including the Earldom of Bute (which he held as well as the later British Marquisate). Lord Bute had been born in Scotland of two Scotch parents. He added that 'when the order of 7th February appointing Lady Elizabeth Moore and General Stuart as guardians was pronounced the Marquis was in Scotland, he was not within the jurisdiction of the Court of Chancery'.[78] Before Gordon had finished, it became pretty clear by the remarks and questions of the court that there would be little chance of Bute's removal to England with Stuart being granted, but it seemed still likely that Bute might be placed in Stuart's hands to be kept in Scotland.

'Old Mr Patton' was James Frederick's counsel and he 'expressed J.F.'s anxious desire the infant should be consigned to [Stuart]'.[79] Poor James Frederick, who had throughout done his best to keep the peace, and to be fair both to Stuart and to Bute, found himself in trouble. He not only inherited the duty of managing the Scottish properties, but was (by definition, since the post of Tutor-at-Law fell to this person) the nearest male relation on the male side. There would be a presumption, in normal circumstances, that he would be the guardian of the Marquess, and, as the Lord Justice Clerk pointed out, he had duties under Scotch law which he had not fulfilled. The Lord Justice

Clerk (unfairly) felt that the Tutor-at-Law had taken little interest in the case. He was even less impressed that the latter appeared to be considering sending Bute out of Scotland without consulting the court. If he did do that 'he would be immediately removed from his office – that has been done over and over again'.[80]

In view of the allegation that Stuart wanted the custody of Bute only for the money, it was unfortunate he appeared so anxious to gain custody of him even if it meant remaining in Scotland. When Stuart overheard the opposing counsel say as much during the recess, he was anxious to refute the charge. '"The only thing I care for", I said, "is that he should be taken from Lady Elizabeth. I should rather he should be consigned to some other person but to me – but I am prepared to take him and stay with him."' But when Bell tried to put matters right in this way, he unfortunately lost his temper, and in an enlightening outburst let his client's true estimate of Lady Elizabeth appear, saying that remaining with Lady Elizabeth would damage Bute's character and morals. The Scottish Court took no charitable view of a respectable aristocratic Scottish spinster in middle age being described as immoral, and Mr Bell offered an immediate apology. Too late, for he had sunk the last of Stuart's case. In summing up

the Solicitor General came to my willingness expressed, now suddenly, to take charge of Bute in Scotland & bind myself by recognisances not to take him back into the jurisdiction of the Court from which alone I derive authority & contrasted it with Bell's assertion that I was not anxious for the charge, he had me on the hip completely, and elicited laughter even from the grave judges. And yet, if truth were known, how perfectly true Bell's statement was, for if I do deserve credit for disinterested desire to do my duty, it is in this.[81]

Stuart believed absolutely in the purity of his own motives. The court decided that further investigation into the views of the Tutor-at-Law, and possible future care of the Marquess, should be made. Rejecting Charles Stuart's suggestion that he care for Bute in Scotland, they fully accepted that Bute was a Scotsman with all the rights that entailed. They ordered that he should remain in the care of Lady Elizabeth until the Court met again to consider his future.

Bute and Lady Elizabeth had won the first round. They went with Mr Stacey, and a number of servants including Meikle, to Dumfries House.

'An engine ... kept at high pressure'

Life for Bute soon fell into a more relaxed pattern. He was supposed to be working hard to reach the standard of formal education demanded by public school. A few of his exercises still remain, probably from this period. In Latin he was working on Caesar's *De Bello Gallico*, a straightforward original text. The mathematical problems he resolved were quite simple ones: if soldiers take seventy-five steps, each of a yard, in a minute, how far would they travel in two and a half hours? He was also working on exercises designed to improve his English style.[1] In fact, Bute did very little work at Dumfries House. Tired out and in a place he loved, he spent much of his time reading novels and writing nonsense verses.[2] Alas, not one of these has survived. Lady Elizabeth invited distant child relatives to stay, and did not interfere with Bute, believing the good reports from Mr Stacey.

Stacey 'went out fishing & shooting & diverted himself'. Lady Elizabeth settled to herself 'that he was a vain trifling young man, spoiled by the easy life at Dumfries House ... by not having a head over him'. A bill shows he also diverted himself by buying a good deal of new saddlery at Lord Bute's expense. Bute was in good health and obedient. It was only when the visitors left Dumfries House that Lady Elizabeth began to be 'astonished & dissatisfied'.[3]

All the principals in this case were now clearly aware of being on show. Their letters to one another, both foes and allies, could be produced, neatly copied, in court. Inevitably, there came to be two versions of events – allies sent one another frank letters, and also guarded ones, the latter being retained as copy letters. Foes, of course, were sent only carefully considered official letters, and most of Lady Elizabeth's were written following advice from Maclachlan.[4] She composed a careful account of Stacey's misdemeanours for the court,[5] but she wildly poured out the whole matter to her brother. She remarked that Bute should do more work. 'The lessons were carried on in such earnest that B was <u>always</u> engaged ... but one thing did strike me – that the more he was left alone in the society of his wise tutor the more silly his conversation became!' From being mature, gentlemanly and charming, Bute 'was changed!! <u>Anything so insolent so abusive so insulting you never heard</u> ... It only convinced me some frightful devilry had been going on. His intellect is so weakened, that it was as if I had been talking to someone half drunk.'[6]

Lady Elizabeth was always suspicious that any event might turn out to be the iceberg-tip of a conspiracy: this time she faced a real one. Later Bute wrote an account of what Stacey had said, which included a remark about Bute that Lady Elizabeth hotly denied making: 'The mother insulted me and I suppose the son is following in her footsteps.'[7] Stacey had plainly engineered circumstances in which Lady Elizabeth could be blamed that Bute had been given an excessively heavy workload. Having caused much upset to Bute, Stacey then committed what, to Victorians, was a cardinal sin. He encouraged Bute to write and receive 'clandestine correspondence'.[8] Behind Lady Elizabeth's back, Bute wrote letters to his solicitor George Maclachlan complaining about her, letters that were designed to get him transferred from her charge to Stacey's.

Stacey had brandy smuggled into Dumfries House, and from references to Meikle's being a drunkard,[9] and drunkenness in the stable department, it seems the men-servants were easily bribed to side with Stacey.[10] Bute was told that Lady Elizabeth had approved the brandy. If Stacey had introduced Bute, too, to brandy, it would make perfect sense of her allegations that he planned to '<u>weaken [Bute's] mind</u> – to destroy his principles – to introduce him to vice gradually in order to have complete power over the unfortunate Child'.[11] Bute himself, when he came to this area of Stacey's wrongdoing, said only that 'Mr Robertson will tell you about the Brandy'.[12] It is not surprising Bute's behaviour was changing. He was now thirteen, and he had rarely enjoyed those long periods with peers away from all supervision, which allowed most boys to develop views and patterns of behaviour which adults might not consider desirable. Constrained to be a dear obedient boy in the company of older women, no wonder he was able to be somebody different with a sportsman in his twenties.

Lady Elizabeth laid out clearly and simply the course of action which should be taken: 'The Blackguard Tutor must be got rid of <u>quietly</u>.'[13] She would join James Frederick in recommending Bute's going to the Scots Episcopal boarding school, Glenalmond, and Bute would no longer need a tutor. Stacey's job would come to a natural end. Perhaps Bute disliked the idea of Glenalmond, because she panicked. She fled from Dumfries House towards the end of October, abandoning the household of servants but taking Bute with her. It was a bad mistake, and one for which she and Bute were to pay dearly.

Both parties turned at once to George Maclachlan. Stacey saw him on 24 October; Lady Elizabeth, who had gone to the George Hotel in Glasgow, then summoned Maclachlan to her side. Next day Mr Stacey arrived at the George in a very excited state, which seems to have convinced everybody he was not fit to have charge of Bute. 'His language & deportment were maniacal. He forced himself into Lady Elizabeth's private room & behaved with the greatest rudeness & violence & in the course of an excited conversation with Mr Maclachlan he said that he could stab Lord Bute to the heart.'[14] Maclachlan admitted that it might just have been Lady Elizabeth whom Stacey wished to stab. Stacey intended to marry a 'young lady' – none other than Miss Tyndall[15] – which, as all Fellows had to be unmarried, would require him to surrender his Fellowship and the income that went with it. The plan was a comic opera plot to enable them to marry and live comfortably. Little wonder the letters Stuart had received in July were biased propaganda, as Miss Tyndall stood to gain as much as her fiancé by getting Bute out of Lady Elizabeth's hands. The other conspirator was Meikle. As long as they stuck together, these three had a strong case to make, especially given Stacey's uncle's previous confidential relationship to the Bute Estate. With the fabric of the little conspiracy apparent, all hope of winning Bute's trust was gone. Stacey saw his prospects of future happiness crumbling.

Any normal person would have recognised that they had played their hand and lost. But for weeks after this incident, Stacey made various furtive efforts to get back into contact with Bute, and was once stopped by Sheriff's officers, behaving oddly outside Edinburgh.[16] Bute had it underlined once again that people were attracted to his money, and not himself. Bute also lost Lady Elizabeth. She could only escape the allegation that she had allowed Bute to fall into real moral danger by claiming that she had imagined a conspiracy where there was none. Neither allowed her to keep Bute in her care. Mr Maclachlan, upon whom Lady Elizabeth had leaned throughout, explained: 'If you had remained at Dumfries House & everything had gone on quietly & smoothly the Court would have been very disinclined to have interfered & yr. Ladyship would have had the charge of the Marquis of Bute until he was fourteen ... the probability is now that the Court will take the matter into their own hands.'[17] The fact that this is in the 'official' bundle of copy letters shows that things had gone so badly wrong that an admission of defeat was the only course of action. Her dignified official comment that she was not struggling to keep Bute in her possession[18] was disingenuous.

James Frederick had stopped trying to compromise with Stuart. He suggested that Bute should be sent to 'a Scotch Nobleman who is highly respected ... I can confidently assure you that you will be treated as one of his own children.'[19] By the time the Court of Session resumed consideration of the case on 20 November, the Tutor-at-Law and Lady Elizabeth had agreed that Bute was to be placed under the charge of the Earl of Galloway.[20] Maclachlan told Bute he rejoiced 'to think that you will now enjoy a life of tranquillity undisturbed by vexations'.[21] As one who knew him well, and had earned his unqualified trust, Maclachlan understood just how distressed Bute had been by the whole train of events after his mother's death. The ideal compromise had been reached. Bute escaped from the hands of the dreaded Stuart, and received a kindly but conventional upbringing whilst staying in Scotland. Above all, the constant sense of embattlement, the stress and the uncertainty had been resolved. As a Scottish orphan, he knew that, at the age of fourteen, his fate would be largely in his own hands, in any case.

Meanwhile Stuart had been considering his position. He was besieged with advice that he should abandon his determination to take Bute into his personal care. At the time of his last diary entry, at the end of August, he had decided that he would not do this unless Bute himself 'should earnestly ask me'.[22] A family council was, however, to be held. Sadly, the notebook was full, and although Stuart doubtless continued his journal, the volume does not survive.

The Scottish court was about to consider the claim of General Stuart and settle it, almost certainly against him, when the House of Lords, on 13 December, issued an injunction prohibiting all further consideration of the case.[23] Probably Stuart had used his influence behind the scenes to ensure the battle would be decided in the English courts. Perhaps the family encouraged him to continue his struggle, or perhaps he was driven by some other deep-seated motive, barely understood.

Overnight, all tranquillity vanished. Whilst Bute was to stay in the hands of Lord Galloway, and so have something like a normal life for the time being, all the legal battles, upheaval, mud-slinging and jockeying for position were to start up again.

In the meantime, the Galloways were the perfect family for Bute. Randolph and Harriet Stewart[24] had been married for twenty-seven years. They had twelve living children. Deeply religious, Lady Galloway liked young people and had the gift for taking them seriously without forgetting their youth, so was able to treat Bute with sympathy and good sense. Best of all, Bute was at once plunged into a group with children both younger and older than he was. He was rapidly at ease with the Galloway children. One of the Galloways said Bute was greatly attached to their brother Walter,[25] whose bright, cheery nature appealed to him. 'I remember our old housekeeper, after some great escapade, saying, "Yes, and the young marquis was as bad as any of you!"' Obsessed with death, he would collect the bleached skulls from the seashore and 'conduct some kind of ceremonies over these remains after dark, inviting us children to take part, sometimes dressed in white sheets'.[26] Stories of his drawing the other children into his games of ritual burial show how easy he found it to mesmerise others into sharing his rich inner life, an ability which later allowed him to collaborate with artists and craftsmen in the creation of his fantastic buildings.

Bute took Mr Maclachlan's advice and wrote to James Frederick and Colonel Stuart: 'Lord and Lady G. did indeed receive me as a child of their own, which I felt deeply . . .' He probably sent the same letter, or a version of it, to Lady Elizabeth, who replied with her usual candour: 'I like to think of your being surrounded with kind friends and in the midst of a cheerful party of young companions, for it is not improving to live alone or entirely with grown up people which has been too much your case all your life. Of the disadvantages of this, I became fully aware latterly.'[27] She reassured him on the well-being of Mungo, Bute's own beloved little terrier,[28] whom she now had in her keeping. Whether because of the hostility of the Galloway family to her, or because Bute was too busy with his studies and his games with the Galloway children, Bute lost contact with Lady Elizabeth, who quickly took offence.[29] From then on, her hostility to the Galloways was implacable, and she feared they would starve him, imprison him and shorten or end his life, as well as convert him to Catholicism. This was unfair. Lady Galloway was a High Church Anglican, and as opposed to Roman Catholicism as Lady Elizabeth herself.

Bute's preoccupation with death was then intensified with the loss of yet another family member, also to the dreaded Bright's disease, when Lady Adelaide died in December 1860. Despite his unwillingness to be handed over to Lady Adelaide, Bute very much thought of himself as a Hastings, as well as a Crichton Stuart. He went to the funeral, his liking for formal terms producing a tragi-comic effect in his description of it. 'Sir William met us in the hall and took us to the drawing room – he seemed very much dejected . . . We committed the Body to that grave from which it will rise at the last day, in the form of the Church of Scotland without any other form besides the two ordinary reverences to the dormant member of Christ.'[30]

More revealing is the account that Bute wrote of a time he was allowed to stay in the family chapel and witness a service of Holy Communion. He was with Janie,[31] three years his junior. The silence was unbroken, except for the wind and the footfalls of the small congregation moving to the sides of those 'they loved in this world' and Bute was so moved he trembled all the time. Unable to see, he imagined each action of the celebrant, and the solemnity of the gathered family carried him 'nearer heaven step by step'. He was happy, yet wept, when the bread was at last placed on Lord Galloway's hand.[32]

The language of the passage was very mature, but the naked intensity of religious feeling more remarkable. Bute emphasised the drawing together of the human family, joined in love and in physical proximity. Their solidarity emphasised the loneliness of the thirteen-year-old who had no earthly family at all, and at this point the account moved directly into a description of Bute's excitement and trembling. Given the intensity of his emotions, the fact that he was on the threshold of adolescence, and his longing for emotional closeness, perhaps it is not surprising that he fell in love with one of the girls,[33] much to the embarrassment of the adults.

Meanwhile, Bute's life continued on a more ordinary plane. Although the Boyle family had sided with Charles Stuart throughout the great contest of 1860, they now wrote to Bute regularly, enclosing snippets about the Isle of Bute, remembering earlier happy days. His aunt, Lady Selina, also sent him news of his cousins, Lady Edith, and her brother, Harry, the Marquess of Hastings. Being much older than Harry, Edith felt responsible for him. Edith was suffering from Bright's disease, made no better by her constant anxieties over her brother. Harry had been expelled from Oxford, for gambling Lady Selina thought.[34]

Bute was doing a good deal of riding, which the Boyles were confident he would be enjoying.[35] His mother had tried to introduce him to the sport with a donkey and a quiet pony, and visits to an Edinburgh riding academy, and to some degree he had mastered this essential upper-class pursuit. However, the trenchant Lady Elizabeth was right in her summing up of Bute's attitude. 'There are few animals he cares for so little as for horses – an elephant would amuse him infinitely more – or almost any other beast you could name.'[36]

The Galloways and Lady Elizabeth were still deeply hostile to each other, and their indignation reached fever-pitch, with the unfortunate Bute caught in the cross-fire. She was unjustifiably convinced that the

Galloways meant harm to Bute, or to make him a prize in marriage. In fact they were highly embarrassed by his love for their daughter.[37]

As the date for the House of Lords hearing, 17 May 1861, came closer, Bute became once again very nervous. The Lords had no sympathy for a middle-aged woman who was not supported in her views by a man. The Lord Chancellor, John Campbell, Baron Campbell, was Scottish, and had received a Scottish education, but he showed no appreciation of the Scottish point of view. The legal establishment, which was in theory British, was in practice wholly English. Worse, the facts of the case were not even fairly presented. The Lord Chancellor at once dismissed all suggestion that Bute had any right to a view on his future care: 'If a child is to be a fit judge of such matters why should he have a Guardian at all?' He accepted that Bute had 'been brought up without any sort of control, and had received no education whatever'.

The Lord Chancellor went on to accuse Lady Elizabeth, who was a keen advocate of Bute's going to public school, of forming 'the resolution of keeping the poor, ill-used boy entirely to herself and the nurse'. He said that no human being could doubt it would be in the interests of 'the infant' to be removed from Scotland, and given into the care of an English guardian and sent to an English public school.[38] *The Scotsman* pungently commented that, on that reckoning, all Scottish orphans ought to be educated in England: 'the Lords says that . . . it is for his benefit to be educated in England, and that he must be educated there, whether he will or not, until he reach the age of 21'.[39] Scotland has always prided itself on its schools and its universities, of which it has four of mediaeval foundation.

The judgement meant that Bute was wholly in the power of Charles Stuart, and lost the right to decide his own fate once he was fourteen. He realised by now that going to school was inevitable, and went philosophically to May Place, a preparatory school in Malvern run by Mr and Mrs Essex, and favoured by the Galloway family. He settled in fairly happily. In June he wrote to Lady Selina with no greater unhappiness than a sense of imprisonment, and a longing for release. If she or his cousins came to visit there was an inn, 'with a nice garden full of old fashioned tulips'. He had 'blundered in & out of about half-a-dozen' friendships, and formed two lasting ones, with 'C. Romilly and W. Sinclair (the nephew of the authoress)'. Bute was no fan of Holman Hunt: 'Mr Essex has just got [an engraving] of "Behold I stand at the door and knock". I have seen the original. I dare say my taste is ibominable [*sic*] but I cannot say that I admire it so exceedingly as other boys do. Can't you come and see me, it would be so nice?'[40] Mr Essex summed up the situation: '[Bute] is certainly happier at school than I hoped or expected, and if this shows a considerable power of adapting himself to circumstances it is a good augury for the future.'[41] Bute was on excellent terms with his school-fellows, though he preferred 'romps' to organised games. Essex found Bute's opinions puzzling, combining an admiration for the Covenanters, and yet a liking for 'the Romish priesthood and ceremonies'.[42] Essex's summing up of Bute's religious position was shrewd and well-informed. He must have been a good listener.

It was originally intended that Bute would spend the summer with the Galloway family. Typically, however, Charles Stuart had offended Lord Galloway[43] and the Villiers Stuarts.[44] Bute therefore was to spend his whole holiday with Charles Stuart on the Continent. Mr Essex told Lord Galloway that he thought Bute wanted to see Switzerland and Italy and had 'sufficiently conquered his repugnance to General Stuart not to look upon <u>his</u> presence as a serious drawback to his enjoyment'.[45] James Frederick was less sanguine. Whilst admitting that Stuart was 'much liked' by those who knew him well, James Frederick thought him 'not a man who would take any trouble for popularity and I believe it to be especially up-hill work for him to ingratiate himself with a boy'. He hoped Bute's quick perception of character would come to his aid, and he deeply regretted Stuart's quarrelling with the Villiers Stuarts.[46]

It was Paris which made the most lasting impression on Bute. He fell in love with the Sainte Chapelle: 'I do not think I ever saw anything so beautiful, with possibly the exception of Cologne Cathedral.' Bute kept a travel diary, in exactly the style of Stuart's diary, down to the formatting of the page headings. Later, the Stuarts looked forward to reading Bute's travel diaries, which he plainly intended to be public documents. This one has the literary and guarded air of confidences designed to be read by others. Bute was in some ways very mature, and in his ability to use written English exceptionally so. In his relationship with Stuart he was almost powerless. He must have had to be very careful with a man who was both short-tempered and a believer in a 'sound thrashing'. One power Bute did have was the power of his pen. By wishing to see what Bute wrote, the Stuarts handed him a weapon against themselves, a weapon he used with adolescent zeal. He set out to use ambiguity to stir the Stuarts and underline their inability to control him in the way they wished, whilst still being able to claim a technical innocence.

This was never more so than when Bute wrote, as he often did, of seeing the Host in Catholic churches: 'Walked back [from the English church] . . . & went into the Madeleine on the way. Mass was still going on so we stood near the door with a lot of other people who had come in to worship the Host for a few minutes.'[47] It is left provocatively unclear whether or not Bute also worshipped the real presence of Christ in the Host – challenged by Stuart, it would be easy to return to the ranks of a Protestant sightseer. Yet the natural reading of the passage, and especially the capitalisation of the word 'Host', suggests Bute was one of those so worshipping. The technique seems to have been successful, for Bute recorded the presence and position of the Host in all the Catholic churches he entered. Stuart must have been dismayed; all the English and classical education of May Place had not dented Bute's love of Gothic beauty, continental churches and, worst of all, Catholic practice.

At Wildbad, Stuart and Bute met up with Mrs Stuart, who was taking a cure. She told him later that she had 'dreaded' his coming and pitied him for having to come: 'But I saw your poor, young, sad face in that room at Wildbad ... my childless heart reached out towards you with a warmth that surprised myself!'[48] Bute certainly had a better relationship with Mrs Stuart than with her husband. Although they disagreed about the death of Lady Flora so strongly that Bute wrote to his Aunt Selina, begging her to support his claim that 'my aunt [Flora] was stript by 3 men by Her Majesty's order', Bute was careful to add that there was no other topic on which they disagreed so strongly.[49]

The party journeyed through Switzerland, where in a Catholic canton Bute found the road 'disfigured with bleached and broken crucifixes, carved in the worst possible manner'.[50] They crossed into Italy, where he enjoyed swimming in the lakes. He had indeed learnt to fence, and walking had always given him pleasure; these and swimming were the only forms of exercise he enjoyed.[51] Then Bute had a serious illness, which the English doctor later diagnosed as smallpox. Before this Bute was rising at the early hours that Stuart approved. After his illness, he went back to spending half the morning in bed. The party returned late to England, and Bute was not yet well enough for school. Before he returned, he sorted out the personal effects left by his mother and Lady Adelaide.

That September Bute was fourteen, and he duly chose the curators for his Scottish properties. They were Col. William Stuart (Charles's cousin), Charles Stuart, Sir Francis Hastings Gilbert, Sir James Fergusson, David Muire MP and A. T. Boyle. But what should have been a day of freedom, when he placed himself in the care of a guardian of his choice, was reduced to a business arrangement. Despite this, it was an occasion for further conflict. Charles Stuart told Anderson (lawyer for the Scotch Tutor): 'I have an insuperable delicacy in suggesting myself & the boy does not seem to think of me'.[52] This delicacy, in fact, proved not insuperable. Lord Galloway, neither an intemperate man, nor a radical, and certainly not a partisan of Lady Elizabeth, was disgusted.

> I did and do complain of the impropriety and the imprudence of Genl. C. S. having forced himself into the office of curator, and of his indelicate mode of so doing – however he may attempt to shelter himself under the chancellery wing. This act ... was not in accordance with Lady Bute's wishes, of which I have the best evidence: and was so distasteful to Bute that he disclaimed it in his own act, though he signed the deed, which I ... accepted.

Galloway felt that if he had made the full circumstances known to the Court of Session, it would not have allowed Stuart to be appointed. Stuart had been 'indiscreet' and perhaps worse, and the whole thing had a bad effect on Bute's mind, whilst adding to the expense of the estate and decreasing the efficiency of its management.

> Finally Genl. Stuart was [trustee?] of the boy's property in England and Guardian of his person. Wherefore force himself (in a most objectionable manner) into the office of curator in Scotland which has no reference to the person, but to the property?[53]

The large family, upon whom Bute had no call but that of unforced affection, continued to welcome him, despite the fact that Galloway felt 'painfully the awkwardness of his position'[54] since Bute was still in love with his daughter.[55] Lady Galloway was the person closest to Bute at this time. He consulted her about his prayers. She replied warmly and humbly: 'I am very anxious you should use a book fr. yr. Prayers, I am sure you will find it a help in keeping up your attention ... though alas! With all, how sadly remiss we are and how fearful the wanderings of one's thoughts – at least I know it is so with me.'[56] Whenever others needed some insight into Bute it was to Lady Galloway that they turned. Although his attraction to the Catholic Church horrified her, and she feared that it would pass to her own children, yet she was always ready to welcome Bute.

At the start of the spring term in 1862, when Bute was fourteen, he started at Harrow. For much of his time, he was in the House of the renowned scholar B. F. Westcott,[57] whose most enduring memorial is the Greek New Testament he edited with Hort. Westcott was a gentle man, more inclined to forgive than to punish, with a warm interest in nature and art to set beside his formidable learning. Academically, Bute made progress. His 'scholarship' (that is to say, his grasp of classical grammar and the formal aspects of language) remained his weakest area. His writing in his own language remained outstanding, and great things began to be expected of him.[58] He certainly learnt how to pick up a new language fast, and how to work hard. In 1860, he had had no French, yet one of the books he left behind at Harrow in 1864 was Hugo's *Les Misérables*, which implies a competent knowledge of the language. A quiet, withdrawn figure, Bute only revealed his warm, impulsive side to a few real friends. One of these was the serious-minded George Sneyd, another, the much more light-hearted Adam Hay Gordon, a fellow Scot, known as 'Addle'. Somewhere between the two he found the necessary outlet for his mercurial spirits, his deep seriousness, and his love of fun and joking.

Another kindly adult was interesting himself in Bute's affairs. Bute spent the generous public school holidays of the winter 1862–3 at Sandon Hall in Staffordshire, the neo-Jacobean home of Lord Harrowby, who was the son-in-law of the 1st Marquess of Bute.[59] In the following November, Lord Harrowby became his joint guardian.

In the spring of 1863 Bute had a very bad attack of whooping cough. It was as he was recovering from this illness that he wrote what was to be the prize-winning poem at Harrow that year. It cost a long day 'of headache and backache and . . . many sheets of Hieroglyphics'.[60] An atmospheric piece on the set subject of Edward, the Black Prince, it alternates between mediaevalism and splendidly ringing descriptions of nature. The Headmaster, congratulating him, was unsure if he would be well enough to return to collect his prize in July.[61] In the same year, Bute also won a prize for translating a set piece of English verse into Latin verse.

That summer he stayed with the Galloways who saw the stress he was under. Bute still thought the decision of the House of Lords which handed him into the care of Stuart a 'grievous wrong' and that Stuart had been 'dishonourable' to accept it when he knew how Bute felt about him. His social interactions with the Stuarts had been 'unfortunate' and Bute had become more hostile to them:

> the detriment to his character is very apparent of living in a state of forced submission, and concealment of his real feelings. It was not only to us that he spoke upon the subject, but he sought a private interview with a neighbour, a Scotch lawyer . . . and spoke in the strongest terms of the cruelty and unhappiness of his position.[62]

It was only seeing his bottled-up feelings at last given an outlet that could give one any idea of how deep they were, said Lord Galloway.

In the Galloway home he was welcomed and valued, in an atmosphere where he felt confident enough to be himself. Yet his happiness there showed him plainly how miserable he was with the Stuarts.

It was usual for boys to be confirmed whilst at school; this would have meant Bute's giving his allegiance to the Church of England. He could not do this, and told Westcott that he feared the Reformation had been 'a great mistake'. This caused some real difficulties at Harrow, and perhaps the depth of his feeling surprised his schoolmasters and the Stuarts, though not Lady Galloway, Bute's confidante.[63] Joining the Church of England would both take Bute away from the Presbyterian Church of Scotland of his childhood, and also from the Catholic Church. Pressuring Bute made him fasten all his attention on controversies among the denominations, and drew him into more theological reflection.

There were many reasons why Bute found the Church of England unattractive, and they included its being the Church to which the Stuarts belonged. Bute also disapproved strongly of the fact that it had been started, not from principle, but to give Henry VIII a divorce. He thought it unblushingly Erastian:[64] used to prop up the state, rather than to worship God. Another consideration weighed even more heavily. It was not just that the Crowned Head of England was earthly head of the Church of England. It was that Queen Victoria was that head. Bute was half Hastings. He said repeatedly that he regarded his Hastings cousins as sisters, though he said as little as possible about his wild cousin, the Marquess. In that family the cruelty to Lady Flora was still a living issue. When Bute was fourteen he had seen Lady Flora's death as murder: 'Mrs Stuart . . . talks about the giddiness of youth, and bad advice, and forgiveness. And, as I tell her, if the woman was not the queen one wouldn't hear anything but lamentations over such early blackness and cruelty of heart.'[65] The issue perfectly concentrated his mind on the evils of the link between English Church and State.

His Hastings relations were much in his mind in the summer of 1864, for his cousin the Marquess, Harry, caused a major scandal, and did his best to involve as many as possible of his family. Harry can easily appear simply as a spoilt and precocious troublemaker, but since his teens, he had known that he was dying. The symptoms of Bright's disease had appeared when he was fourteen,[66] and although it would not necessarily kill him quickly, kill him it undoubtedly would. No wonder he lived his life with reckless speed.

When Harry left Oxford, his main interest became horse-racing. He ran his own horses and betted heavily on them, allegedly with the intention of breaking 'the ring'. He was bored by staid society, and plunged into the seamy side of London. Nevertheless he also mixed with the social circle into which he had been born, and he met a young girl so petite and beautiful that she had earned the title of 'the pocket Venus',[67] Lady Florence Paget, daughter of the Marquess of Anglesey. Her own reputation was also far from impeccable; however, with her beauty and her birth she had attracted suitors, and was engaged to marry Henry Chaplin, another sporting young man, and a friend of the Prince of Wales. Chaplin's relations were outraged,[68] but powerless. Their wedding was fixed for early August 1864.

On 16 July she went alone to the 'fashionable store of Messrs Marshall and Snelgrove in Oxford Street',[69] where she was met, probably by Freddy Granville or his newly-wedded wife. The Granvilles had just made a runaway match themselves. She went from there to St George's Church, Hanover Square. Harry had asked his sister to pick him up in her brougham at a quarter to eleven that morning; she was late. They went to a shop together, then back into the carriage. He asked her to take him to St George's. It was only as they drove up to the church that he told her that he was going there to marry Lady Florence. Harry did not wish to give his sister a chance to think through his course of action, or how she was damning herself by becoming involved in it. He calculated that the more his family shared in the wedding, the harder it would be for them to condemn him, and that if Lady Edith had no time to think, she would react with sisterly love and help him, as she did. She was, however, very taken aback to find that the bride did not have a single relative to support her. The bride was already waiting at the church. Lady Florence had 'provided a marriage-bonnet for which a footman went as soon as she entered the vestry'. The Granvilles were also there, and Lord Marsham had just arrived, 'summoned by Hastings "upon business of the greatest importance" and was almost at the altar before he knew what the business was'. He was not happy, and refused to give the bride away, so this task was performed by Granville, the only other man there, except the clergyman. 'Edith was in mourning, which distressed her very much, as a bad omen.'[70]

In the Victorian era, marquesses and their daughters attracted the attention which today is reserved for media celebrities – and Hastings, with his exploits in the gin palaces of London, and his public and expensive forays on the Turf, had made himself a huge following of those who idolised him. An equally interested body enjoyed deploring him. The romance of the clandestine marriage further increased the scandal.

In a great scandal, there is something pleasant in being one of the few to know the details beyond all speculation. Bute had an account from his cousin Lady Edith. He was very attached to her, and remained a close friend of her eldest son, Charley. He discussed the matter with Lady Selina, who was Harry's aunt as well as his own. He was convinced that only Florence and Harry, and a few of his friends knew anything beforehand of the wedding, and that the others had just been involved at the last possible moment. But the wedding itself was not a matter of last-minute impulse. A special train had been ordered, triumphal arches had been prepared to greet the happy couple, and two cooks had been labouring for a week to prepare a banquet.

Bute also had the pleasure of having been consulted on the action taken next. He thought that 'the peculiar circumstances aside', the marriage was not a bad one. Bute never espoused double standards for men and women.[71] It was widely believed that Lady Florence had borne at least one, and maybe two, children, but 'Hastings is probably tolerably foul himself, and they certainly are very much attached to each other.' He thought the family should make the best of a bad job, and hoped that the marriage would cause both principals to settle down, and Harry to curb his excessive expenditure. He had promised to sell his racehorses. Lady Selina had passed some other information to the sixteen-year-old Bute. 'As to Lord Hastings, I had certainly heard it whispered that he was physically incapable of doing his duty to his wife. I never knew it for certain before.'[72]

By the autumn of 1864, Bute was seventeen, and the question of his entering university was being considered. The original idea had been that he would go to Trinity College, Cambridge, but Westcott thought that 'Bute would not distinguish himself at Cambridge and would not get his first class'. He considered Bute capable of this at Oxford and that working for it would keep him from endlessly considering which church to join. At Oxford he would be 'sure of his first; because it is not a wide and accurate knowledge of language that is required; but the careful getting up of certain definite books in history: metaphysics and classics: and this he would do well'.[73]

Benjamin Jowett, the Master of Balliol, had contributed to a then infamous book of essays which reflected the new approach to Biblical texts, treating them as historical documents.[74] Conservative Victorians had a stultifyingly reverential attitude to the Bible, and those who cared for Bute worried Jowett might turn Bute into a liberal, a fate only just less terrible than his becoming a Roman Catholic. But after earnest discussion, they finally decided Balliol would be a safe option. The problem was to secure a place there for Bute. What happened next is obscure, but it proved impossible for Bute to go to Balliol, unless he got a scholarship. Westcott reported Bute's reaction.

> When I told Ld Bute the substance of Dr Scott's note he was evidently very disappointed. After a few minutes reflection he proposed to offer himself for the scholarship examination . . . the proposal at first surprised me, for he knows that the examination turns in a good measure upon scholarship which is his weakest point. I can only say that this resolution would involve the necessity for hard work, and hard work in subjects for which he has no inclination.[75]

His Harrow masters thought he stood little chance of success.

Bute spent Christmas at Sandon Hall, wretchedly unhappy. He was beginning, as he himself put it, to be 'very ill nervously'.[76] He found Sandon uncomfortable, and he complained bitterly.[77] Returning to school, he undertook a great deal of uncongenial work. He burst out to Westcott that he did not know how he would get through the term. Westcott reassured him that if he was doing his duty, God would help him through. He asked why, given he felt as he did, Bute was still at Harrow. Bute replied that he was staying only because it was so distasteful to himself to stay. Westcott was sensible enough to reply that Bute could not expect any 'blessing or satisfaction from such self-inflicted misery'. Bute replied that as he did not know what course of action God wanted from him 'he thought it best to take the one least pleasing to himself'. Westcott was 'not only satisfied but thoroughly pleased' with this answer, which nicely indulged just the right level of Victorian spiritual masochism, and told him:

> I felt that if he ought to leave us, God would make it plain before many weeks were over, but I have really no anxiety about his health . . . I think we may all be very grateful for the way in which the question has been discussed:– after the boy's first outburst of passion, nothing could have been better than his behaviour throughout.[78]

Bute had learnt to assume the appearance of calm expected of a boy of his age and class, but he remained the same passionate person beneath the surface.

In the midst of all this, somebody persuaded the Archbishop of Canterbury to write to Bute urging him that the Church of England was the true Catholic Church.[79] Only Lady Galloway had ever pointed out that both denominations worshipped the same God. Nobody thought to tell Bute that he would get into one or another Oxbridge college and it did not matter much which one. Cocooned in a world of privilege, they failed to assess the triviality of the choices before Bute and pressured him into believing that the choices he made were of life-changing importance; he accepted their judgement and made himself ill over it. When his indirect appeal to Westcott failed, and he was not released by kindly adults from a burden beyond his strength to bear, he found the only honourable escape that he could – illness. He collapsed.

As a boy terrified of being handed over to Charles Stuart, Bute had suffered from sleeplessness and an almost total lack of appetite. These were early forewarnings of the anxiety and depression which dogged him throughout life, although this adolescent episode was the most serious, and as he grew older he learned to a large degree how to manage his condition. This was the more remarkable, as the Victorians had no diagnosis of the disease of depression, and no treatments for it. Photographs of him taken at this time show him almost painfully thin. As he recovered, he wrote, as will be seen, of fatigue, the desire to die, the inability to undertake his usual activities, and of being 'unstrung' by what sounds like acute anxiety.[80] Lady Edith was sure that Bute's problems were caused by overwork. 'You must be aware that even an engine can only be kept at high pressure for a certain time & up to a certain point', and Bute's head was not iron and steel.[81]

Bute blamed Harrow for his illness and shrank from the idea of studying. But he had begun to be ill during the holiday at Sandon, and Charles Stuart did not believe 'that the usual amount of study exacted from a young man can be unwholesome for him'.[82] In a backhanded way, Stuart was probably right. It was the pressure of his relationship with the Stuarts which had pushed Bute towards illness, though the addition of an excessive work load finally tipped the balance. For years Bute had been under great stress, first watching his mother die, then fighting the attempts to take him into Stuart's custody. He had acclimatised to family life with the Galloways, and then spent two terms at a private school, before starting another new school, Harrow. He had had to adjust to life with the Stuarts, and whether he had found it more exhausting to fight Stuart or to maintain cordial relations with his wife, only Bute knew. He was assailed by doubts about his religion, which caused great distress both to those he cared for and those he wished to annoy. He was subjected to further pressure to persuade him to change his beliefs. He topped all this by determining to follow a path of study for which everyone agreed he was ill-equipped, which made no use of his talents, and demanded ones he did not have, and from which he was unlikely to achieve the end he sought. That he then collapsed is not surprising.

The project of travelling, instead of a final term at Harrow, had been suggested by Westcott. One cure for illness popular with the better-off was to seek a more favourable climate, preferably abroad. Bute, with a tutor, doctor and carefully selected friends (selected by Stuart that is, and not himself) set off for the Mediterranean and the Holy Land.

4   Travel

'Very much wrought up and excited'[1]

Bute had been too ill to make a swift recovery, but, slowly, he began
to be active again. He did not understand the possible phases of his
illness, so he did not realise how hopeful a sign this was. His day at
the Pyramids made Georgina Stuart 'gasp. What a full day it was for
body and mind!'[2] Bute sent his friend Sneyd an account of the day,
too. 'At midnight started for the pyramids of Gheezeh, from there to
Sakkara, thence to Memphis and home about five last night.'[3] Did he
recognise that it was also a sign of his recovery that he was 'able to
resume [his] habits of devotion'? Lady Galloway was his confidante,
because as she remarked, 'perhaps there is no one to whom you could
[open your heart] but myself'. Even with her he was reserved, not able
to say what he felt 'upon another subject' because he knew she was
'a better Christian' than he was. 'Oh Bute, you are sadly mistaken',[4]
exclaimed Lady Galloway.

From Egypt, Bute went on to Palestine. Georgina Stuart put what
Bute must have felt into words: 'the holy awe of knowing that there
our Saviour trod!'[5] It was a deeply significant time for Bute, and he
turned to his close friend Sneyd. 'You will see ... that I have lived to
see Jerusalem, and one of the objects of my life is accomplished and
over. When I thank God for this it is because His will has been done,
for I wish I was in my grave before this. If this journey was intended
to give me any taste for life it has hitherto failed utterly – what am I
to say or do?'[6]

Alone in a foreign land, and with companions he had not chosen,
his sense of isolation was overwhelming. Finally he let his misery out
to Sneyd, painfully conscious at the same time that his friend might
be distressed or disgusted by the very confidences that brought him
relief.

I do not know whether you care to read this. I must write to you. I only tell you I am not writing words to be read or repeated at [Harrow]. These things are very sad and ghastly for me, though you may [or] may not, and perhaps cannot sympathise, with the ailing of a brain which has been overtasked. I am totally, utterly alone here, except that I sometimes exchange thoughts with a friar of the Franciscan convent here, whom I have become accidentally acquainted with.

Bute followed this agony with a calm, elegant account of his journey, including a 'horrid French steamer'. More of his real feeling appears when he describes the Holy Places he visited, including 'the beautiful brilliant garden of Gethsemane – In the morning I went to Bethany. In the evening I went again to Sepulchre. On Friday we all had crosses tattooed on our arms.'[7] A Franciscan friar, Aloysius Stafford,[8] walked with him to Bethlehem, Bute pouring confidences into his ear.[9]

It is traditional Catholic practice for the believer to be encouraged to offer their pain to Christ, to make it a type of concrete prayer, so that by suffering in and through him, that pain may be transformed. Did Stafford try to set Bute's feelings in the context of Jesus's suffering? 'I spent the afternoon with F. Aloysius who took me in the evening to Gethsemane and opened for me the Cave of the Agony.' In the garden of Gethsemane Jesus faced his coming suffering on the cross. He asked his disciples to stay awake, but they all slept, leaving him utterly alone and in a mental agony so great that he sweated drops of blood. The resonances of this much greater suffering with Bute's life are plain to see. It is easy to make light of the pain of this rich young man, who appears to have had everything in the world to make him happy, but mental illness is as real and as terrible as physical sickness. If Bute had found a context and an outlet for his pain in Catholicism, then his attraction to Rome was not, as others believed, simply sensual worship and mediaeval ceremonial, but the endless wellspring of the healing of heart, mind and soul.

He ended his letter to Sneyd with a bitter attack on Harrow, and a plea to keep the most revealing parts of his account private. It was very much part of the public school ethos that boys should treasure their memories of the school. Bute wrote that 'Harrow itself I could and would curse every day of my life; if there is a thing I hate and loathe it is her.' Bute was unsure if and when he would recover: 'It is hardly ten days since the memory of Harrow gave me fits of nervous pain which unstrung me for a minute or two at a time.'[10]

Bute sent Mrs Stuart letters, as well as keeping a journal for her to read on his return: 'On the night of May 24–25 I assisted at the celebration of the Ascension on the very spot where it happened, the most curious and interesting Christian Festival I have ever seen.'[11] He did not specify which denomination was celebrating the festival, and Mrs Stuart could believe, if she wished, that it had been a High Anglican celebration. It was almost certainly Roman Catholic. He received a certificate from the Franciscans of Mount Sion, certifying he had visited the Holy Places and describing him as '*devotus Peregrinus*', a devout pilgrim. He was touched to think himself linked with pilgrims through the ages. Also, through the Hastings line, he believed he was descended from a schismatic Pope (known only through legend) known as 'the Pilgrim of Treves'.[12] It was safe for him to tell Mrs Stuart, with conscious artistry, of Samaria and the 'augustly miserable shrines where Christians worshipped in a poverty worthy of God'. Later he went to see 'what is called a *ziki*, performed by Darveeshes [Dervishes] in a Mosque. This was the only Muslim function I have seen. It was very solemn & impressive.'[13] Intensity from the participants was what impressed him most in a religious ceremony.

Bute returned to England, and in the autumn of 1865 went to Christ Church, Oxford, to enjoy greater autonomy than he had known before. He occupied the beautiful rooms later made famous through the photographs of his successor in them, Charles Dodgson, better known by his *nom-de-plume* of Lewis Carroll. Bute did not fit, by temperament or tastes, into the hard-drinking, riding and gambling set of young nobles. Nevertheless, he made friends among more serious young men, of whom the closest was probably Lord Dalmeny, later Lord Rosebery.[14] Dalmeny was enormously clever and very witty, with an acid, biting tongue, and, like Bute, a man with few intimates.[15] Bute was shy with strangers and preferred the company of his few close friends, among whom he could be his unguarded self. He continued walking, fencing, and swimming. He covered a certain amount of the prescribed curriculum. His tutors urged him to work hard and hurry through what was tedious to him in hope of finding work more to his taste, but he did not. He was bored with the classics, and also worried that much study would plunge him back into serious illness.

He was particularly ill-served by the narrow academic disciplines of his day. Today he could have won academic distinction studying comparative religion. As it was, his absorption in the Hindu scriptures was thought to be merely a distraction from real work. He loved the account of the death of Krishna:

'Then the illustrious Krishna, having united himself with his own pure, spiritual, inexhaustible, inconceivable, unborn, undecaying, imperishable and universal spirit, which is one with Vasundera, abandoned his mortal body and the condition of the threefold qualities.' To my mind this description of the great Saviour becoming one with universal spirit approaches the sublime.[16]

But he gave most of his energy to considering the merits of the Christian denominations. At Oxford, he had another option presented to him: Anglo-Catholicism. The Anglo-Catholics were members of the Church of England, and among their most prominent representatives at Oxford were Professor Edward Bouverie Pusey[17] and Henry Parry Liddon.[18] Pusey was by this time leading a largely reclusive life. When his friend Newman had become a Catholic, he had stayed behind in the Church of England, viewed by many with a suspicion amounting almost to disgust. Pusey's protégé at Oxford was Liddon, a little man blessed with an ascetic face. Photographs show finely chiselled features, with a determined chin, a marked nose, and lovely, animated eyes. Here, perhaps, lay something of the secret of his charm and ability to attract others. Unlike Pusey, who had had a romantic and tragically short marriage, Liddon was celibate, and outside his family, his most intense relationships were with other men.

The Anglo-Catholic approach to personal and spiritual discipline was austere, but its adherents indulged themselves in the forms and colours of the worship of the Middle Ages and contemporary Romanism. They re-introduced the traditional vestments and altar furnishings, which changed colour according to the time of year, measuring out the fasts and feasts of the Church: 'spiritual haberdashery' one irate bishop called it. They generated anger by their re-introduction of the priest hearing the individual confessions of his parishioners.

The basic tenet of Anglo-Catholicism was that the Church of England was still a part of the Catholic Church and they did not see themselves as Protestants at all. In Anglo-Catholic theory, there were three main branches of the Catholic Church: the Roman Catholic Church, the Catholic Church in England (which was the Church of England) and the Orthodox, or Eastern Church. This last branch had been separate from the eleventh century, following controversy over the authority of Rome and whether the Holy Spirit proceeded from God the Father alone, or from the Father and the Son. What mattered to Anglo-Catholics was that the Orthodox Church reached in an unbroken line to the very earliest days, and did not acknowledge a special authority of the Pope. Liddon himself wrote that 'if the East did not run out like a jetty, breaking up the advancing wave of the Roman argument, our position, I admit, would be a much less defensible one'.[19] What the Anglo-Catholics did not want was to acknowledge the supremacy of Rome, or the additions Rome had made to what a Christian was supposed to believe.

What they did want was all the beauty of the ritual of the High Mass. The Anglo-Catholic church of St Barnabas in Oxford was one of the very highest. Rev. Francis Kilvert was taken to worship there on a trip back to his old University, and his reaction was typical of those who were critical of the ritualists:

> As we came out of Church Mayhew said to me, '*Well*, did you ever see such a function as that?' No, I never did and I don't care if I never do again. This was the grand function of the Ascension at St Barnabas, Oxford. The poor humble Roman Church hard by is quite plain, simple and Low Church in its ritual compared with St Barnabas in its festal dress on high days and holidays.[20]

Bute did not warm to ornate High Church worship. He was already very familiar with the Roman Mass, and perhaps the High Church tendency to overdo ritual struck him as play-acting by amateurs.

Bute's anxious guardians had already approached those at the college who might, they hoped, be able to help keep him from Rome. H. L. Mansel[21] was their chief point of contact. He emerges from his encounters with Bute as a remarkable man with a profound understanding of the workings of the human mind. Hearing that Bute had been impressed by Dr Pusey's writings, Mansel managed to engineer a meeting between them. Whereas Bute's guardians had thought to keep him away from really High Church men, Mansel felt that Bute might well find a compromise there that would keep him from Rome. He also had the sense to see that only those as serious, as sensitive and as concerned with truth as Bute himself could win his trust. Mansel was soon able to assure Lord Harrowby that Bute 'is losing somewhat of the brooding turn of his mind and is entering more with relief here than he did at Harrow'. He was, however, still dwelling on his grievances, and especially upon the old wrong which he felt had been done him by Stuart.

That Christmas he spent at Dumfries House, probably with the Stuarts. It was 'comfortable if not merry or ideal'.[22] He also felt himself short of money, which, given his riches, seemed to him to be 'absurd'. His allowance was £2,000, which seems a generous sum for an undergraduate at the time.[23] Hunter Blair claims that his 'lavish alsmgiving' had made him hard-up. Bute was approached all the time by persons seeking help, both individuals who had hit hard times, and more formal charities. Acutely aware of his privileged position, he found it difficult to turn any away.

After Christmas he returned to Oxford, and to his religious controversies. Liddon was at this time the mentor of a number of young men at Balliol College, to which Bute had tried so hard to gain entry and had failed. Amongst their number was Gerard Manley Hopkins. With Hopkins at Balliol and Bute at Christ Church, there is no record that the two young men ever met.

In May 1866, Liddon

> walked out with Lord Bute. He talked incessantly about liturgies – he believes that he has specimens of every ancient one in Xtendom. He described his visit to Armenia.[24] I twice got near to the question of first confession but could not succeed in bringing it on.[25]

The fascinating, direct and emotional Bute encountered in his writing vanished when Bute was ill at ease. He said little or nothing, or else spoke incessantly on a single subject which he found both safe and appealing. Augustus Hare was later to complain that he wound himself into his theme like a serpent and 'almost loses himself, and certainly quite lost me, in sentences about "the Unity of the Kosmos"'.[26] It did little to gain him new friends, and from the tone of this passage it would seem that Liddon did not warm at all to him. Yet the technique successfully avoided subjects he did not want raised. If the Church of England was part of the Catholic and Apostolic Church, then Liddon had the authority to hear confessions and to pronounce absolution. If authority lay only in the Roman Catholic Church, he did not. Bute was dodging the question. That very evening, Liddon heard Hopkins's confession. It is only looking back that we realise that certain days epitomise the full flavour of a period of history.

That summer Bute again set off for Constantinople and the Middle East. He was away for four months, sparing himself and the Stuarts a difficult summer. He went with Rev. George Williams,[27] an unnamed doctor, his cousin James Frederick, and his friend Harman Grisewood,[28] three years his senior, who later converted to Roman Catholicism.[29] Bute wrote to Sneyd, who was relieved that Bute seemed to be finding them pleasant company. Bute made an 'intimate'[30] of George Williams, whose book *The Holy City* had been his guide on his first visit to Jerusalem. Williams should have been the perfect companion on such a trip, for he was an Anglo-Catholic with a deep interest in the Orthodox Church, and was later president of the Eastern Church Association, which was devoted to increasing understanding between the Anglican and Orthodox Churches. The first hint of tensions to follow came in Sicily, where Bute reported he had been told that 'the English church here is most painful. Indeed I have hardly heard of anything so truly awful as something I was told by an eye witness today. Mr W. said "but that was not much"!' [31] Bute was very bitter against the Church of England, and he expressed this in a slighting, jeering way of speaking of it. [32]

Sicily was perhaps more of an experience than a pleasure. The party ascended Etna at night on mules with 'saddles more uncomfortable than words could describe. Their pace was about 2½ miles per hour, which it was too easy to reduce but impossible to accelerate.' [33] After midnight, they

> emerged upon the summit between the peaks, and at the same time the full moon, silver, intense, rose from behind the lower with a vivid light and shed a flood of radiance over the tremendous scene of desolation. As far as the eye could reach there was nothing visible but cinder and sky, the last starless, the former a plain of black dust in which we sank some 18 inches at every step.

Descending, they rested at a local inn. 'G[risewood] was in his bed less than half an hour, in which time he killed 4 b–s, 3 fleas, 2 gnats, & a mosquito, after which he got up and lay on the floor, having two hours of repose altogether in the night. I saw nothing but felt – '.[34] Two days later, Bute was 'so ill as to be nearly always insensible',[35] and the others, believing the bed bugs had made him ill, did their best to protect him as he recovered.

> My bed was carefully divested of all clothes and the boards examined. Then it was carefully drawn out into the middle of the room, isolated as far as possible from everything else and the feet covered with insect powder, after which we spread on it the rugs and a carriage cushion and I lay down in my dressing gown. By these means I managed to pass a most hopelessly uncomfortable but safe night upon my three planks.[36]

The party sailed from Sicily to Chios, a Greek island off the coast of Asia Minor just south of Lesbos, where Bute was not impressed by his first experience of the Greek Orthodox Church. In each Roman Catholic Church, a consecrated wafer of bread, the Host, is kept in a tabernacle. There was a tabernacle in the Orthodox churches, too, but

Bute was dismayed that nobody visited the churches to worship Christ in the sacrament. Bute also misunderstood the place of the icons in the Orthodox Church, speaking of: 'Pictures ... exposed to receive an exaggerated homage, unknown and undreamt of in the West'.[37] At this stage he failed to realise that an icon is more than a picture to Orthodox worshippers; it becomes a window through which to experience the reality behind it.[38]

Part of Williams's purpose in the trip was to visit the Metropolitan of Chios, in order to discuss the possible reunion of the Orthodox and Anglican Churches. The Metropolitan arrived to visit

> bringing six or eight clergy with him. These all sat in the hall while his Grace was entertained in the drawing room ... He rose for me. I knelt down and kissed his hands then took a chair. Mr W talked with him about reunion, over which he is rather zealous.

Bute shrewdly remarked that 'It seemed to me rather as if they just wanted to show the riches of the church to us & Mr Williams in particular, and to make an exhibition of friendliness, not to say triumphant condescension. They can afford to be generous.'[39] Talks did not go well. Bute reported gleefully that he heard the Patriarch of Constantinople had censured the discussions.[40]

As Bute was punctiliously correct towards Orthodoxy, and plainly considered it better than Anglicanism, yet markedly inferior to Roman Catholicism, he irritated Williams. With Bute condescendingly siding with those interests in Orthodoxy opposed to the recognition of the Anglican Church, and with his own negotiations going badly, no wonder Williams became irritatated. Yet, whatever reservations Bute had about Orthodox worship, he enjoyed to the full the experience of Greek hospitality. The Metropolitan entertained the visiting party to dinner, which

> was laid in the great corridor, out of which all the rooms seem to open, and which serves as a hall. The table was dressed with flowers. The windows being open at both ends there was a through draught. We sat down.

It was a fast day, and the dinner was various fish dishes splendidly cooked, enjoyed by everyone except Bute, who detested fish.

> Then we went back to the divan and commenced a grand smoke, which lasted several hours. It was carried on with chilbooks filled

with the strongest and most delicate drugged Turkish tobacco, fresh pipes being brought in continuously as soon as the old ones were 1/3 smoked. At intervals we did cigarettes.[41]

He concludes the account tongue firmly in cheek: 'About 8.30 we had final Benediction, with more solemnity than usual.'

After Chios, the party sailed to Constantinople. Bute records the approach to the city.

I lay down to sleep in my clothes wrapped up in a plaid, on top of one of the paddle boxes. About 3 am we approached Constantinople and I sat up. It was intensely still, the light intense, but grey, the water as smooth as oil, the only sound the thud of the paddle wheels. Ahead was a great veil of silver mist shrouding all the waters and far away rose over this two vast domes with minarets clustering round them, all grey and shadowy, like the domes in a mysterious picture I once saw, with no apparent foundation on earth. They got afterwards clearer and clearer, and the last brighter and brighter orange and the people on board woke up and there was a smell of coffee and hot oil and what not.[42]

Bute was amazed at the contrast between the beauty of the ancient buildings, and the condition of the 'anything but throughfares'[43] which were 'paved with a weak imitation of shingle ... which would have been disgraceful to the Borough of Rothesay in a back street'.[44]

He felt that viewed from outside for the first time, S. Sophia, 'the largest Byzantine building and one of the finest churches in the world', was an 'unimpressive bulk' of whitewashed walls and low grey domes', but he was deeply moved inside, where they 'looked into the vast space of the interior between columns of priceless marbles, the plunder of the greatest heathen shrines'.[45]

More than anything, though, he was deeply stirred by the 'Dariveeshes' or Dervishes, dancing devotees of Islam.

The Dariveeshes began to follow one another round the ring ... the first Dariveesh ... began to turn himself slowly round and round, moving slowly towards the centre of the room, the next did the same but moved round him ... till the whole space was filled with revolving figures, all moving round in a great circle except the one in the middle. As each one started the wind slightly inflated his skirt but they were so heavy that nothing could be seen above the ankles, and when fully blown out they remained like a carving without a fold altering. The faces of the Dariveeshes were fixed and their eyes shut, their heads thrown back or hanging to one side . . . The peculiar revolving motion is in imitation of the cherubim who revolve before the throne of God . . .

Bute remembered that some Christians, like the Copts, walk round and round their altars, and that there was 'solemn dancing' before the altar at Seville but concluded

> it cannot be much more solemn than the Muslim one, as far as its actions go. I left the Mosque very much wrought up and excited. There are who are not impressed by this. There are also who always laugh at a service in a language they do not know, and who see nothing awful in the holy Mass.[46]

Perhaps this refers to Williams. He must have been aggravated by Bute's contrasting reaction to the Patriarch of Constantinople whose profile was 'much the same as that of a wedge or a sheep, to which animal indeed he has a striking resemblance'.[47]

Bute's preference for the orderly yet ecstatic Islamic Dervishes over the muddle of Orthodox worship was temperamental. What Bute looked for in an act of worship, more than anything else, was a mixture of intensity and good orchestration. He wanted to feel that everyone was sharing in the same experience, with a nice combination of passion and decorum. People who love the Orthodox rite welcome the freedom to find their own way to worship during it. Unity there is, but it is the liturgy that gives it. Bute did try Orthodox services. One Sunday, with Williams away, he rose early (with some difficulty) and went to 'the Greek Cathedral of Pera', but he found the service 'was perhaps the most disagreeable function I have ever assisted at. The church was crammed with people, in a state of restlessness and irreverence', and 'the singing being really inexpressibly painful'.

> A man lighted the glass chandeliers, of which there are literally as many as the church will hold . . . The countless lamps were of course burning long before. I think I never saw so many lights – and all in the bright daylight of an Eastern morning. The heat, dirt, smell and streams and cascades of melted wax may be imagined . . . In my opinion the function was almost as much spoiled as slurring, drawling, irreverence, bad music and bad taste could spoil it. Everybody began to go out at the canon, so that the words of consecration were hardly audible for the noise.[48]

Bute was no less hostile to the Anglican church. He did attend the 'small function' in the Embassy chapel which marked St James's Day 'celebrated in the ordinary manner, using the English rite. There were four persons present.'[49] Bute does not comment on the nominally Anglican Embassy staff who could not be bothered to worship on special feast days. Bute avoided stating the obvious.

The party travelled into the Levant, where they met the Maronite[50] Bishop Bistani who invited them to stay in his palace. Bute accepted the invitation as soon as was polite. He liked the bishop,

> a remarkably handsome and reverend looking person, about 50, with a long silvery beard. He wore a cassock of reddish purple silk, under a coat of blue black cloth, and a large turban of black silk. His ring was a fine amethyst. His manner was perfect. The Chaplain – his name was Father John, Yohanna – was a dear old man with a long white beard, dressed in blue-black cassock, coat, and turban, like the other priests. He spoke French well.[51]

Having been present at the Bishop's Mass in his private chapel Bute wrote that 'so august and moving a ceremony I never saw'.[52] Williams simply did not understand any of this. He continued to hold his own 'little Sunday service', which Bute attended 'only twice during the four months'. But of course not only was Bute still collecting liturgies; he was always one of those who travelled to experience as fully as possible the areas to which he went. His reaction was doubtless partly conditioned by the fact that the Maronites were in communion with the Church of Rome, but it was not simply that. He worshipped with the locals when possible, just as he liked to stay with them, rather than in the tents in which the rest of the party stayed. Bute was, in the end, more swayed by his reaction to the persons he met, than by the ideas they espoused. Williams did not understand this either.

Nor did Williams know, of course, that something significant had occurred for Bute at the end of the Mass in the Bishop's chapel: 'While the Bishop was at his prayers after b d q m s B M V'. Whatever happened was intensely private, and shielded with the cryptic letters. The final capitals must refer to Blessed Mary the Virgin, whose initials Bute usually gives in that order.

Bute had hesitated to inconvenience the Bishop by accepting a bed for the night, until it became clear that he already had a visitor, a cousin who was a teacher. Bute and Mr Bistani shared a room. 'My bed was intensely luxurious with all kinds of quilts and mattresses and featherbeds, some silk, and all the linen of the most delicate kind. It was put on boards on trestles. I slept well.' In hot climates Bute slept naked, and he was much amused by Mr Bistani who 'took off nothing except his outer clothes, not even his stockings'.[53] Perhaps what struck Bute most in the palace, however, were the courtyards and rooms open to the air either above or through arches. The mixture of room and open air fascinated him. The 'most perfect apartment' was the one

> where his Lordship receives. The far end was open in one great arch . . . commanding a view of the most wonderful beauty, whether one looked down upon the valley when it basked in sunlight, or up into the sky, covered with stars. A stone divan spread all round these sides of the room. The centre of the floor was a tank about 7 inches deep, of a vescia piscis shape[54] with a small jet in the middle. The room was built in the purest and chastest oriental taste of white stone, relieved with dark red in the arches, and the shafts of the windows, and the floor of simply tessellated marbles. The roof was of plain, open timber.

The next day, Fr Yohanna spent some time with him in this room, before taking him 'into the higher court of the palace', an upper floor room

> which is laid out as a garden, apparently for use as well as ornament, for the domestic cabbage is not excluded, and into a charming room off it where we sat and smoked in the window.[55]

The peace, beauty, cleanliness and devotion of the Bishop's palace must have showed to the greater advantage, because tempers were becoming frayed. Williams was making long excursions into the countryside to visit things which interested him, leaving the others to wait his convenience, and meals were often long delayed by his non-appearance. James Frederick, a former military man, was not amused by this behaviour. Things came to a head after a long day which ended with them stumbling around in the dark when confused directions led to the whole party missing their tents and having to backtrack for some miles. Bute went to bed at once and 'fell into a sort of stupor or dead sleep . . . the others', he added, 'had a most terrific row of which I was happily unconscious.'[56]

Williams was plainly still angry long after he returned to Britain. Bute does not record in his diary the times that he had attacked the Stuarts for 'pocketing' his maintenance, but Williams had listened and been horrified. Bute had also revealed his attachment to the Roman

Catholic Church, especially his devotion to the Virgin Mary.[57] Why this last upset Williams is a little hard to understand. In the view of Low Church Anglicans it was idolatry, elevating a human, Mary, and directing to her the reverence due to God alone. But George Williams was not Low Church. He was an Anglo-Catholic especially sympathetic to the Eastern Orthodox, where Mary was of enormous importance. Hymns praising her were sung, and she was the focus of faith and devotion, and asked for her prayers. Williams should have been quite at home with Bute's attitude.

Bute was sincerely religious. He was also in some ways a very worldly young man. One of the few who seem to have been aware of this was Sneyd, to whom Bute opened himself up in a letter from Constantinople. Sneyd replied that he was delighted

> to find that you are beginning to have a sort of idea that the gratification of the passions is not the only end worth living for & I hope & pray that the fear which is now backed by the sort of sullen assurance & intention which does not let the better nature interfere may by God's Grace be so gradually weakened & destroyed that it may at last be merged into a firm determination to the contrary & a deliberate resolve to abstain for believe me, my dear Bute, that with such a resolve & faith in God's help, we can contain & repress our passions.[58]

Despite the clumsy Latinate sentence structure, the main meaning is clear. While the rest of the world tended to see Bute as spiritual, Sneyd saw him as a victim of his passions. There seems to be something more serious than the usual Victorian anathema against masturbation. Indeed, Stuart had been worried by Bute's 'extreme purity' because 'it is probable that at his time of life health may be impaired by resistance to temptation'.[59] Whilst it is hard to imagine that Bute ever thought sensual delight the *only* end worth living for, Sneyd, knowing Bute as well as any, was aware of how the sensual appealed to him.

Williams had been puzzled that Bute 'told both the Greek Orthodox Bishop of Chios and the Patriarch of Constantinople that he was a Presbyterian'.[60] But this was not, as Williams thought, part of Bute's 'duplicity'. It was a simple statement of fact. With the Orthodox Church out of the running, Bute had narrowed himself down to two possible Churches, the Presbyterian Church of his childhood, with its comparative social respectability and its freedom from queen and state, or the Catholic Church.

Bute was nineteen in the September of 1866. In November Stuart went to see Williams, who was not well. Williams repeated to Stuart all that Bute had told him during the long summer abroad, doubtless with an added edge of personal animosity created by the tensions of the ill-assorted travelling party. Stuart understandably exploded. Bute had left Stuart's letters unanswered, and he now finally understood this was because of Bute's hostility to him. He had also finally understood that Bute was accusing him of appropriating maintenance that the courts allowed from Bute's estate. Hotly protesting that Lord Harrowby and 'other honourable men' knew 'how small a part of it is in any degree beneficial to me & how justly that is my due' he maintained his behaviour had been strictly honest. He was furious, and while he would not resign as guardian, he refused to offer Bute a home, or to handle the maintenance money. He added that he hoped Bute would find friends 'able and willing to make Cardiff & Mount Stuart agreeable for you as we have hitherto endeavoured to do'. He ended that Bute owed Mrs Stuart 'more than the gratitude and affection of a life could repay'.[61]

Bute answered Stuart promptly, fully and provocatively. All the old hurts and battles were fresh to him.

> Surely you must distinctly remember that, six years ago, talk was made of your turning some of the maintenance to your own benefit, founded on a letter wh. you wrote to Lady Elizabeth Moore ... You cannot doubt that at that time the question was at least an open one in the mind of myself personally, & it is impossible that you can ever have supposed that from that hour to this I have for a single instant altered any of the opinions I had then ... time has only confirmed my beliefs. You conquered me, but my thoughts have always been the same.

'You conquered me'; to Bute the conflict was personal and bitter. Any difficulties he had made for Stuart, all bad behaviour, Bute could justify to himself. It was as though he was a country under enemy occupation, where insurgency became a merit. He explained that he had spoken of these things only to those 'whom I foolishly imagined to be too much gentlemen to retail to you for my injury'. He seemed unaware that it was Stuart who had been injured by being defamed in the eyes of the world. Bute added that

> You say 'a part' of the maintenance wh. you consider only too 'justly your due' 'is in any degree beneficial to you.' I own the utmost I ever hinted exceeded this by but little & I confess that till I had read this I

had always mentally admitted the possibility of your explaining your letter to Lady E. M. in a sense different to that usually assigned to it . . . I shall be very glad to make my 'home' altogether with Lord Harrowby.

One can only hope that the old scores Bute sought to pay off by these words were real ones. He added a postscript which caused yet more trouble: 'to Mrs Stuart I should be very happy to write. I shall probably hear some news which may interest her at the dance at Blenheim in a few days.'[62] Six years had not weakened Mrs Stuart's ability to feel injured, and she replied with truly histrionic flair.

By General Stuart's desire I opened your letter, before sending it on to him at Cardiff. The whole tone of it – & the PS about myself caused me such exquisite pain (for your sake alone) that it brought on a severe spasm of my heart. Pray don't write to me – I should not read the letter . . . you will see how little Ball gossip could accord with my present feelings . . . Nor should I be justified in risking another attack for the sake of those who do value my life.[63]

Bute, who it is to be hoped did appreciate the times when Mrs Stuart had been a peacemaker between him and Stuart, had meant no ill by the 'ball gossip' remark. Georgina Stuart's letters were full of harmless gossip. It is easy to condemn her as a silly woman, but she did care for Bute, and she was really ill after reading his letter.[64] She could never express any anger or sense of loss on her own behalf; she had instead to feel sorrow or pain on behalf of her attacker. It does not mean her emotions were not deep.

Bute told Lord Harrowby of what had happened in a letter cocky with self-righteousness:

You must first please remember the position Genl. Stuart and myself have always been in, of master and slave, jailer and prisoner, wild beast and hunter. I have noticed since I came up to ch. ch. the Stuarts both had intensified the dislike with which they always regarded me and increased its vulgar results in the way of insults, annoyance and abuse.

Bute tells that when he had gone to Scotland to visit a close friend (both Dalmeny and Addle were Scottish) Mrs Stuart had accused him of going to debauch himself 'in the vilest manner' and in the following storm, he had got from General Stuart 'the lowest blackguarding' he had ever had. Bute then tells just how he had spoken of the spending of his maintenance monies

> But it is for talking about this . . . or rather, shrugging my shoulders and wondering where on earth the maintenance all went to, that the present thunderbolt is declared to fall. He refers me to you to know how the maintenance has been spent, and also how little he takes, saying you know all about it. Please be so good as just to throw a little light on these points if it doesn't bore you, as it would be a great favour to me.[65]

Bute instructed Lord Harrowby that he would, in future, give Bute a home.

Harrowby replied with enviable calm.

> I have been shocked but not surprised, that matters have at last come to that pass . . . You very early adopted a notion, that Gen. Stuart was only activated by an interested motive to carry out your mother's wishes . . . and you absurdly exaggerated the pecuniary advantages which he would derive from it . . . He may not have pleased you . . . he may possibly have been abrupt and peremptory on some of the many trying occasions of intercourse with one who had set himself against him. But that was no reason why you should impute low notions to a man of honour . . . You will hardly [think?] something like a surplus of 1000£ a year is an exceptional consideration for the trouble & anxiety & sacrifice of prospects & home comforts wh. a man in Gnl. Stuart's position had to make in your case. A mother would have been allowed the same advantage for the same charge.[66]

All this gives a very good picture of the hell that Bute and Stuart had succeeded in creating for each other between 1861 and 1866. Harrowby is undoubtedly right in his picture of an adolescent deliberately being difficult, and anyone with experience of this sort of situation will sympathise with Stuart. Yet he was a man established in his role in the world, with a successful career and a wife he adored, and in the relationship with Bute he held (literally as well as metaphorically) the whip hand. Bute was a child, desolate and powerless. Harrowby then refused to offer Bute a home. He remembered the Christmas when Bute had been so miserable at Sandon. Very probably he also disliked Bute's cavalier assumption that Harrowby would welcome him without his needing to ask politely and formally.

Mansel passed on to Bute a detailed account of how Stuart had spent the maintenance money. That document no longer survives, but Stuart gave Harrowby a somewhat rougher account of it. About £2,000 went on supporting the poor on the estates and old family retainers. Keeping Mount Stuart, Cardiff Castle and Dallars House in reasonable condition accounted for £1,300. Then Bute's education, and Stuart's travel to Bute's homes, and his entertaining others there on Bute's behalf, and Bute's travels cost about £3,000. Stuart reckoned he had about £1,000 for his own use out of the estate. Had he not had been Bute's guardian he 'might, (or might not) have sought and obtained professional employment' but because he was, he could not do so, and so his 'claim to a regiment has thereby been materially weakened'.[67]

Bute's reaction to all this was chastened.

> I have just heard Genl. Stuart's statement from Mr Mansel. I have nothing which I need here to say except that what I have meant is what it declares, and that I certainly did not know that such was lawful, as I am now informed that it is ... I am sorry, indeed, very sorry, that I left a bad impression on you the winter that I was at Sandon. I pray you to remember that at the time I was very ill nervously ... in extenuation of any ill breeding I may have shown toward you, or any other; you all treated me far better than I could ever have deserved, and truly nothing could be further from my wishes than to repay your kindness with ingratitude and rudeness. It seems you are being shown some private letters which I wrote at the time, complaining of my extreme lowness. I think if you saw everything I wrote then the impression you receive might be different.[68]

In time, Bute forgave Stuart. It is nowhere on record he ever came to feel he did not have much to forgive.[69]

Whatever his feelings, he still had a champion in the redoubtable Lady Elizabeth. She pointed out that Stuart had in fact taken somewhat more: 'the maintenance is called "£7000" omitting the additional £500 (when he became sole guardian) – in six years a trifling item of £3000.' Sir James Fergusson of Kilkerran[70] became Bute's new guardian.

Bute came to feel that the conflicting personalities of Lady Elizabeth and Charles Stuart in part created the whole sad business. They both died in September 1892. Bute reflected then that, even in the world after death, he could not imagine peace between them.[71]

5 Oxford

'A feminine tone about his ... mind'

Bute was not the only undergraduate at Oxford considering his religious position in the autumn of 1866. In October Liddon heard that 'Addis of Balliol, Garrett of Balliol and Wood of Trinity have just joined the ch. of Rome and that Hopkins of Balliol is on the point of following.' He later added ruefully 'The Balliol secession had been entirely put down to my account. I "looked like" a RC and that sort of thing which does not matter, and will all be the same 100 years hence.'[1]

What had happened elsewhere at Oxford was a reproach to Bute. He walked with Addle Gordon to Wantage, and to the 'ancient Catholic chapel of East Hendred' where the Host had been kept and Mass celebrated without a break, even in the most difficult times for Catholics. Bute 'knelt so long in prayer before the altar that he had twice to be reminded by his companion of the long walk home they had in prospect'.[2] The round trip is some twenty-seven miles.

If Bute thought that his new guardianship would make those around him more sympathetic to his Catholic leanings he was mistaken. By November, Mansel was concerned enough about Bute's growing attraction to Rome to approach Lord Harrowby. He explained that the 'Eastern journey this summer' had set Bute against the Orthodox Church, which had increased his attraction to the Roman one. He offered a perceptive diagnosis of the situation. It was not an intellectual attraction, against which there were plenty of good arguments, and, in the University, plenty able to put them forward, but 'much more a matter of feeling and taste'. Mansel put this down to his liking for rituals and 'a feminine tone about his own mind' due to his having been reared by his mother which made him 'cling to the idea of a female protector' the Virgin.[3]

The idea that Catholicism, with its devotion to the Virgin and female saints was feminine and intuitive while Protestantism was masculine and rational, was a standard aspect of Victorian 'No Popery' polemic,[4] which Bute would have denied. Yet in many areas of life beside religion, Bute's judgements sprang from his intuition and sympathy. He enjoyed female company of all ages, not just the young and attractive, and lacked any interest in the traditional male pursuits of hunting, fishing and shooting.[5] Combine this with his passion for art, architecture and beautiful places, and the profile of Bute's interests was more typical of a woman of his period than of a man. Mansel's own rational approach failed and he commented in exasperation: 'He catches any sneer or taunt against both the body of the English Church or the Scots Episcopacy. An epigram which falls in with his prejudices has more weight than an argument, and an epigram and verses are not things to refute.'[6]

Bute spent Christmas at Dumfries House with Sir James Fergusson. He revealed to Sir James's wife, Lady Edith (another of the outspoken women he loved so well) that he intended to become a Catholic in the spring. But it was not until just before Easter that he announced that he intended to take the definitive step of formally joining the Church of Rome. Bute had pneumonia in April and recovered in Torquay. Difficulty in breathing is a symptom of pneumonia, and probably he had been severely frightened by this illness, which would mimic the way the lungs fill with fluid in Bright's disease, from which his cousin Edith was suffering, and of which his reckless cousin the Marquess of Hastings was by now showing advanced symptoms. Thoughts of an imminent plunge into the 'afterwards' concentrate the mind wonderfully on what (legend has it) Charles II, in similar circumstances, called 'fire insurance'. Bute told Sir James Fergusson that he intended to become a Catholic.

Massed and massive disapproval met him. Sir James Fergusson arranged for him to meet with the Lord Chancellor, as the Court of Chancery still had jurisdiction over Bute, who was not yet twenty-one. Returning to Oxford, Bute spoke of it to Liddon on 10 April.

Walked with Lord Bute to the top of Shelover. He told me that he had made up his mind to join the ch of Rome. He had never belonged to the ch of England: he had been brought up a presbyterian. He had refused to be confirmed in the ch of England because of Royal supremacy. He hoped to be admitted on Tuesday or Wednesday in next week & receive his first communion on Maundy Thursday at Edinburgh. I three times begged him to pause and to consider the claims of the ch of England. He said it was impossible. If he had been brought up a High Churchman he might have lived and died in anglicanism. As it was, he hoped on Thursday next to secure that which he has been hoping for all his life Viz.; his first communion.[7]

Bute then went to meet the Lord Chancellor who succeeded in persuading Bute to wait until he was twenty-one before taking this step. Sir James Fergusson thought that Bute had 'given in with a very good grace and I really think is glad to be helped by a gentle persuasion out of his imbroglio'.[8] To Bute it seemed very different. He had found another confidante at Oxford, another middle-aged literary lady of extremely High Church opinions, Miss Felicia Skene,[9] the cousin and biographer of the Tractarian Bishop of Brechin, A. P. Forbes. To her he poured out his feelings, describing Liddon as a Protestant, which would not have pleased him:

> On this day, which was to have seen my First Communion, I do not believe I should have the heart to write and tell you that it has all failed, if it were not for a sort of hard, cold, listless feeling of utter apathy to everything Divine which is new to me, but which has, as it were, petrified me since my fall.
>
> The long and short is that the Protestants – *i.e.* the Lord Chancellor and his Court; my Guardians; my friends and relations; and Mansel, Liddon and Co. have extorted from me a promise not to become a Catholic till I am of age. They are jubilant with the jubilation of devils over a lost soul; but I am hopeless and weary to a degree ...
>
> I know what my own position is. It is hopeless, and graceless, and godless.[10]

In Felicia Skene Bute had found a truly remarkable person. It was a friendship which, despite the disparity in their ages (she was twenty-six years his senior) was to last all her life. She was deeply concerned with 'outcast women',[11] working not merely to persuade them into refuges, but to lighten their lot when they got there. She was a vegetarian, an anti-vivisectionist, and a tireless prison visitor. She nursed those sick with cholera and smallpox during epidemics, and was a friend of Florence Nightingale. Bute was only one of the undergraduates to whom she became a friend. Perhaps it is a mark of her influence on him that he also became deeply concerned with the rescue of women and with the treatment of animals.

Bute's misery was real enough, but he could look forward to his majority in a very short time, and with it not only liberty of conscience but the freedom of a large fortune at his disposal. His cousin, the

Marquess of Hastings, was facing problems with no solution, and behaving with all the recklessness of a man who knows he is doomed. Bright's disease was closing its stranglehold on him. He had taken over the Mastership of the Quorn, the most prestigious of all the hunts, to which the position of the Hastings family seat, in the middle of Britain's best fox-hunting territory, almost predestined him. It was famous for its long, open gallops. Harry did not have the strength or the lung capacity for such exercise, nor could he blow on the hunting horn. It was not laziness or 'slackness' as his contemporaries assumed: with his lungs filling with fluid, it was remarkable the half-drowned Harry even attempted such punishing feats. Harry had lost nearly everything he had to lose, including the love of his runaway bride, whom he could never bed. He had also lost nearly all his fortune.

Next to the Bute inheritance, the Hastings fortune was a poor thing. Considered in its own right, however, it was substantial. Harry had gambled it away in his vain bid to break 'the [bookmakers'] ring'. With the Derby approaching, Harry saw his best chance. He had a wonderful horse, Vauban, and now the only real rival, Hermit, seemed to be out of the race. With the desperation of a dying man, he determined on one last-ditch attempt. He backed Vauban to the hilt. It lost. That the race became one of the classics of all time – 'the most sensational Derby on record, perhaps, with one of the most exciting struggles ever witnessed, throughout which each horse ran as straight as a line and as true as steel'[12] – and that the victor, Hermit, was one of the few racehorses whose name became immortal, was no consolation. The Marquess of Hastings had lost the race and his fortune. The added salt in the wound must have been that Hermit was owned by Henry Chaplin, the fiancé from whom he had stolen his bride, and whom his bride, it seems, still loved.

Bute, always aware of his Hastings heritage, did what he could to help. He bought Hastings's yacht, *Lady Bird*, and the Loudoun estate, which was the Scottish property of the line, having come into the Hastings family through Sophia's mother Flora, who was Countess of Loudoun in her own right. Bute originally hoped that Lady Edith, who was heir to the estate, would purchase it. She did not, most probably because she could not afford to do so. The estate had been heavily mortgaged in order to cover Harry's racing and gambling debts, and these sums had to be paid off before the purchase price could be found. Bute was warned that he would make a heavy loss, but in July that year, he made the decision to buy.[13]

The Loudoun estates, so near the countryside around Dumfries House and Dallars where he had spent much of his childhood, were a logical purchase for a sentimental young man who was already a great landowner. The idea of a chronically seasick boy buying a yacht is a little comic, but the yacht had compensations. Bute was still a member of the Church of Scotland, which provided a set of services for laymen to use at sea. 'On Sundays in my yacht . . . I am to conduct Presbyterian services. There is a book of prayers approved by the Church of Scotland for the purpose: instead of sermon, some immense bit of Scripture, e.g. the whole Epistle to the Romans.'[14] That same July he made a voyage with three of his Oxford friends on the newly-purchased yacht to Iceland, via Orkney. He kept his word on the services. His friends were, it seems, not very thankful for them: 'Bute gave us . . . some prayers whose only merit appeared to be that they had been composed by John Knox & about 10 chapters from different parts of the Bible . . . a tedious ceremony.'[15] They were better prepared for the next Sunday. Someone had a watch to time it: '86 minutes'.

Two diaries of this trip have survived, one Bute's own, and the other by John (later Sir John) Dasent,[16] son of the great Icelandic scholar and translator, George Webbe Dasent.[17] It was he who timed Bute's services. To him, Bute was a somewhat remote, even august, figure, quite unlike the impulsive, confidential person who emerges from his own writing. The two young men make an extraordinary contrast. Bute was interested in everything from wildlife to the picturesque, and, of course, everything of religious or antiquarian interest. He moved like quicksilver from delight to disgust. Dasent was only interested in sport, and the greater part of his diary is a record of what he either shot or fished, or failed to shoot or fish. The easy conversational style of Bute's diary, grumbling gently over hardships and tiredness, and recording interesting experiences and corn brandy with equal enthusiasm, hides just how epic the journey was.

The other members of the party were Addle Hay Gordon, his friend from Harrow, and Frederic Grantham Vyner.[18] The *Lady Bird* sailed up the east coast of Scotland from Leith to Orkney, where Bute occupied himself with the local antiquarian George Petrie, and the others roamed about getting bored. They then headed north to Iceland, still largely unexplored territory to the British. Lord Dufferin had visited in 1856, Sabine Baring-Gould in 1863. William Morris was to follow in 1871.[19] Like Morris, Bute was attracted by the romance of the Icelandic Sagas.

Again horribly sick during the journey, Bute provides the first glimpse of Reykjavik where 'most of the windows have white muslin blinds and flowerpots in them like cottages on the stage'.[20] The party first travelled from the capital to the famous Great Geysir,[21] and camped near it. Bute was inclined to favour the more reliable but less spectacular Strokkur geyser. However, after several days impatience was rewarded:

> Woke about seven, by Geysir going. Everybody rushed to see in various states of dishabilles, except V[yner] & me, who being quite undressed, lay with our heads out of the door of our tents.

The party set off south on their ponies, to Oddi 'in the middle of a great grass plain. It consists of a church and a manse.'[22] Oddi was associated with the saga writer Snorri Sturluson, and Sæmundur, a black wizard with no shadow, was fabled to have been its first inhabitant. Bute was offered hospitality in the traditional turfed house, which he accepted.

> All the household were asleep long before but they left the door open for us. It seemed like going into a cave, entering a door in the side of a green hill. The rooms are cased with wood, but the passages and under parts of the house are all earth and stone, with earth floors and moss on the walls, and as their [sic] is not a glimpse of light and they are really several feet underground the effect is very like that of a natural cavern.[23]

Oddi is near the south of Iceland and from there they turned north to cross the huge island. Their first stop was to ascend the volcano Hekla. They began to trek north, the cold growing more intense as they got nearer the glaciers. On Wednesday 21 August, they stopped for a day to rest the ponies. Bute and Dasent both recorded entries for 21 August.
First Dasent:

> The place is awfully cold with rain almost all last night and a good deal today.[24]

Then Bute:

> It was a regular Icelandic summer morning. Rain poured from the sky in torrents. Clouds covered everything, and through them one could occasionally see looming the green & grey sides of the glaciers. It was bitterly cold, with wind off the snows.[25]

They crossed the barren central area, passing between the glacial massifs Vatnajökull and Hofsjökull. They set off at 2.45 a.m., just before sunrise, riding 'for five hours through black shingle'. Even in the twenty-first century, travellers are cautioned to take precautions when travelling through this area, which is completely uninhabited. Black with volcanic rock, it is bitterly cold, with snowfall even in high summer, and almost no vegetation. Cold, wet, hungry and tired, Bute was not in any mood to be impressed by glaciers:

> The view of the black desert . . . bounded by large snow hills is not, at least so we all thought but D, worth any particular notice. V & I agreed we would as soon see the Malvern Hills covered with snow as Vatna Jokul from this point. After 8 we reached the small barren lake at Fjoroungsalda, in which centre the four quarters of Iceland and which is in the middle of the Sprengisandr. Here we changed ponies and the others eat a meal of which raw onions and raw bacon formed a part. It was nine when we left. At 2.45 we reached the first grass . . . In about an hour we started again, going down into the great valley.[26]

The first farm and a bed in a tent was a relief. They had done the crossing in record time, Bute noted, and had now been travelling for seventeen days. The next morning they set off again. Bute

> was in front with the farmer, who guided us. We talked a good deal in our respective languages, without understanding each other but found we had a common feeling about corn-brandy, of which he carried a bottle.[27]

All the young men learnt to drink the local corn brandy neat to alleviate the cold, Bute greatly preferring it to cognac. Snow fell and lay for a morning. They reached Reykjahlid on 26 August, and went on by easy stages. There was much game, and Bute, who did not shoot, recorded glumly that 'after a time we reached a river, but unhappily found some Ptarmigan'.[28] Finally on 29 August, they spent their final night on Iceland, Bute commenting he had never been so stiff and sore in his life. The next day they found Eyjafjord, and their yacht lying in it and 'the warmth of the cabins felt quite wonderful'.[29]

The trip was a distraction for Bute, but not a formative experience. Even in Iceland, with its new experiences and hardships, he worried at religious questions. He enquired into the state of its (reformed) Church, and the beliefs current, noting that there was no concept of Apostolic Succession, but they believed in the real presence of Christ in the bread and wine. He does not seem to have understood that such beliefs are common in Lutheran churches. He returned to Oxford to continue 'considering and reconsidering his position'.

That autumn was a significant one for Bute, but the details remain hazy. Somehow he got to know 'Mr Charles Scott Murray, a Catholic gentleman of Scottish descent and good estate'.[30] Scott Murray was a convert, and had a sympathetic wife to whom Bute could talk of religion, a house near Marlow called Danesfield, a beautiful Pugin chapel and a chaplain. The chaplain was the Rev. Thomas Capel,[31] later and better known as Monsignor Capel. Bute spoke lengthily to Liddon in October, after he had met Capel. 'Lord Bute sat with me in the middle of the day for nearly 3 hours. He followed his old line of praising the Presbyterians and deprecating the Scottish Episcopal clergy. He repeated F. Capel's arguments wh. I answered seriatim.'[32] For Bute, the Presbyterian church of his Covenanting ancestors was the only alternative to Roman Catholicism. Most of Bute's family would have been happy to see him take this path, but not Liddon for whom the Presbyterian option was a deeply flawed one. If there had been a single able and respected academic at Oxford willing to argue the case for Presbyterianism, he might have swayed Bute, but to the Anglicans, the Church of Scotland seemed alien and inadequate. Liddon had a great deal more sympathy with the Roman Church but he still rejected Capel's arguments outright. The year before Bute came to Oxford, Liddon had met Capel for the first time whilst they were both in Pau, and summed him up as 'an active, tolerably well-informed, and very gentlemanly man'.[33]

At some time in the autumn of 1867, Bute was in great distress. At Danesfield, 'consolation was given ... in the midst of sorrow'.[34] It was a significant event for Bute, and intensified his attachment to the Catholic Church. He made 'solemn promises ... at Danesfield to live and die in the Church of God'.[35] What the sorrow was is not clear. It could have been his continuing sense of guilt at not entering the Catholic Church. It might have been the illness and subsequent death of his sole remaining Hastings aunt, Lady Selina, or the knowledge that his cousin Harry Hastings was dying.

In November, Bute went to Lady Selina's funeral.[36] His sympathy for his cousins (Mabel Henry liked to sign herself his loving sister)[37] was real and deep. He had written earlier to another female friend that with her own mother's death she had 'lost ... what [she] loved most in the world'.[38] He was in his middle age before he assured those around him that he could now think of his own mother without pain. Nor did the Low Church Anglicanism of his cousins dismay him. He never had the least difficulty in sympathising with any views which were heartfelt.[39]

Above left. The earliest image of Bute. By the time this pen and ink drawing was made, he was already Marquess of Bute and Earl of Dumfries. (© The Bute Archive at Mount Stuart)

Above right. Young Bute stands beside his adored mother. His notorious shyness made him appear stiff before the camera. (© The Bute Archive at Mount Stuart)

Left. The young Bute stands before Cardiff Castle, showing the building as it was before Burges's re-development. (© The Bute Archive at Mount Stuart)

Right. One of the series of images of Bute discussed at the end of Chapter 3. These were taken at some point between his leaving Harrow and starting at Oxford. (© The Bute Archive at Mount Stuart)

Below. Marie Fox, later Princess von Liechtenstein, had a romance with the young Bute. (© The Bute Archive at Mount Stuart)

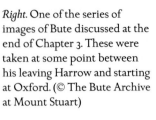

Above left. Lady Elizabeth Moore, a distant cousin of Bute's mother. Even as an adult, Bute was 'freely, justly and willingly devoted to her'. (© The Bute Archive at Mount Stuart)

Above right. This portrait of Gwen was released to the picture papers ahead of her wedding to Bute. It shows a bloom she never regained after her attack of scarlet fever. (© The Bute Archive at Mount Stuart)

Left. Gwen, standing to attention for the camera in her wedding dress. (© The Bute Archive at Mount Stuart)

Above left. With her beautiful bone structure clearly seen, this is Gwen as a young matron. (© The Bute Archive at Mount Stuart)

Above right. Bute as a young man, perhaps around the time Ethel Wilton fell hopelessly in love with him. (© The Bute Archive at Mount Stuart)

Right. Bute in an amateur photograph, holding a baby, probably Margaret. Both his tenderness and the fact that he was comfortable to be photographed in a pose so unconventional for a Victorian aristocrat tells one much about Bute. (© The Bute Archive at Mount Stuart)

Left. Bute's children: Margaret holds the baby Colum on her knee, while 'Nohn' (in breeches) gazes to one side, and Ninian (seated) looks cheerfully ahead. Owing to the gap in ages, Margaret always had a motherly role towards her brothers. (© The Bute Archive at Mount Stuart)

Below. Gwen's New Year pantomime productions were a feature of the family's winter celebrations. 'Alice in Wonderland' was produced in 1890. (© The Bute Archive at Mount Stuart)

Prince-of-Wales feathers in her hair, Margaret poses for her coming-out picture with her mother. (© The Bute Archive at Mount Stuart)

Bute in middle age, dressed in the tweeds he habitually wore. (© The Bute Archive at Mount Stuart)

Margaret in walking dress with a cairn terrier. (© The Bute Archive at Mount Stuart)

Left. A butler and four footmen pose on the steps of House of Falkland. Staff would have greeted the family when they arrived after an absence. The support of his staff enabled Bute to concentrate on his interests and to live a busy and varied life. (© Falkland Stewardship Trust)

Below. Curling was one of the few sports Bute enjoyed, and there were curling rinks at his Scottish homes. Sometimes lanterns were sent to the rinks to allow a game to finish after the daylight faded. (© The Bute Archive at Mount Stuart)

Right. Bute in his self-designed robes as Rector of St Andrews University. He took the job believing the role would be ceremonial and found himself heading a successful struggle for the survival of the University. (© The Bute Archive at Mount Stuart)

Below. Bute (far left) and Gwen (next to him) in the old Mount Stuart, a comfortable Georgian house. Bute rarely mentions the family dogs, but they were recorded in photographs and paintings. (© The Bute Archive at Mount Stuart)

Cranes raise the new Mount Stuart House, which is built around steel girders. (© The Bute Archive at Mount Stuart)

Margaret with her dog-cart and team of Shetland ponies outside Dumfries House.
(© The Bute Archive at Mount Stuart)

A kindly contemporary caricature of Bute. (From a photograph in The Bute Archive at Mount Stuart)

In September 1867, Bute was twenty. He was six foot tall, broad-shouldered, slim-hipped, with a handsome face made striking by its high-bridged nose and blue eyes. He was fit from his long walks and swimming, and his practice of the romantic sport of fencing. He bore the second-highest rank in the nobility, and he was very wealthy. In short, Bute attracted attention and admiration.

> No doubt you will be surprised to get a letter from a stranger but I have endeavoured to get an introduction to you but without success. If I told you I loved you, you would laugh at me for being so absurd, but it is the truth, my darling . . . what would I not give for one kiss of yr dear lips.[40]

The unknown one signed herself Ethel Wilton, and Bute replied at once.[41] On paper, Ethel was very bold, but she began to sense some of the difficulties ahead: 'If we met I am sure I could never tell you what I feel for one I love so dearly.'[42] The beloved in the flesh tends to be disconcertingly unlike the beloved in the mind. Nevertheless, she set up a meeting: 'I will be on the bridge on Tuesday . . . we must appear as friends in case I was seen by anyone so don't pass me by but speak at once. I shall be in mourning[43] & I will wear a bonnet. You cannot make a mistake.'[44]

Ethel ran full tilt into Bute's disconcerting manner with strangers. 'I don't think you liked your walk yesterday and you must have thought me awfully stupid but you looked so grave I felt quite shut up.'[45] Alas, so unpropitious a meeting did not cure her. 'I suppose you thought I was too slow. I am twice as spoony about you now than I was before.'[46] Lacking much response from Bute, her mind swung at once to another terrible possibility: 'Pray do not think I am a "fast girl" as no doubt you do! because I am as well born as yourself & my position in the world is very good.' The relationship concluded with a plaintive letter from Ethel: 'Why are you so unkind not to answer me?'[47] Bute had decided to end a relationship which, carried on in secret as it was, would have incurred the wrath of every respectable adult, and would indeed have labelled Miss Wilton as very fast. In addition, he was not good at answering letters, he was approaching a 'dreaded examination'[48] at Oxford, he was preoccupied about his religious position and he was beginning to form another relationship.

The fact that his new love was the daughter of a determinedly Protestant family known for its 'proselytising tendencies'[49] was greatly complicating his consideration of his faith. No letters to or from her survive, and therefore her identification cannot be absolutely certain, but Bute's courtship of his Protestant lady, carried on as it was in the eye of the small world of those days, could not but attract attention. She was Lady Albertha Hamilton,[50] the Marquess (later Duke) of Abercorn's sixth daughter, later Lady Blandford, 'the sixth of seven beautiful daughters of a well-known peer'.[51] Lady Abercorn was deeply religious, and the joke went that 'whereas other mothers of marriageable daughters invited desirable young men to their opera-boxes, Lady Abercorn would ask them to share her pew'.[52] This was a pew in the Crown Court Church, the Church of Scotland congregation in Covent Garden, where the great Presbyterian preacher John Cumming[53] was Minister. He believed Judgement Day was going to arrive by 1867.[54]

Bute felt bound to defend Catholicism, not least because many of its critics were unfair or biased. The idea that all Catholic priests were deceitful, manipulative and insincere was accepted almost without question by many Protestants. The note of hysteria in parts of the English Protestant establishment over the Church of Rome could only have disgusted him. Yet the fact that Bute could and did ably defend the Catholic Church did not necessarily mean he was convinced by all his own arguments. It is one thing to defend the beloved from hostile detractors, another to feel that she is wholly worthy of that defence. To become a Catholic convert was a huge step, with many disadvantages. A convert was not the same thing as a Catholic born, either to Protestant high society, or to the ancient recusant Catholic families.

Capel, to whom he may have voiced his uncertainties, does not seem to have been very confident that Bute would make the final change. When his family and friends had constrained him to promise not to enter the Roman Church, they had seen that there was a gulf between an attachment to that Church and actually joining it. Capel was concerned to bridge that gulf by stressing Bute's unity with Catholicism:

> Let me beg you to prepare yourself as though you were to receive the Bread of Life on Easter day. Begin by the thought of renewing these solemn promises made at Danesfield to live & die in the Church of God. Then prepare for confession ... Lastly, in humility & sorrow & love dwell on the mystery of the most Holy Eucharist ... In this way though materially out of the Body of the Church, you will be of her children united to her soul.[55]

It was an ingenious way of binding Bute to the Roman Church.

As if these were not pressures and difficulties enough, Bute's Hastings relations were in great misery. Edith, who had been reconciled to her difficult husband, lost the baby she was carrying, it was thought from worry caused by her brother, who was still dying slowly, and whose ruin had impoverished all his dependants. She recovered from her miscarriage 'very nicely', as their mutual cousin Mabel Henry told Bute in May, but:

> She feels so about Harry. He promised to pay our money by the 15th & did not, so I only hope it may not be lost in the general smash. Did you ever see anything more terribly true than the picture of his career in the 'Tomahawk'? [56]

The cartoon carried by the satirical paper shows the carriage going 'home from the Derby' with the Devil driving and 'Death in the rumble'. He is pouring champagne for a young man who flings 'honour' and 'dignity' overboard. A weeping woman, with a marked likeness to Lady Hastings, shares the landau, 'long lost to the path of virtue, and fast drifting to the shores of Hell'. [57] Poor Lady Hastings, and poor Edith, with her family pilloried in the press. Bute suggested that Lady Edith might go to Loudoun with her whole family over the summer to recover. It was, as Lady Elizabeth Moore remarked, 'a very wise and amiable plan'.

Bute had been sent to Oxford with hopes of his gaining academic distinction. Distracted by love and religion, and still fearful that the pressure of too much work would plunge him back into illness, he dreaded he would simply fail his examination, and told his fears to Lady Elizabeth. As usual, she cheerfully braced him up, quite sure in her own mind that a lack of courage and resolution were his chief weaknesses: 'I dare say it will prove less terrible than you imagine & that you will get through quite well if you only pluck up courage! If you do fail I shall ascribe it entirely to the distraction of thought occasioned by a fair lady, who I trust will make ample amends in the future ... I cordially wish you success at college & in London.' [58]

She was not alone in her hopes. Lady Edith Fergusson suggested that Bute 'might send ... a little line ... if you have any good news of yourself, which I hope you will have – perhaps I shall hear you have become a confirmed Cummingite' [59] (that is, committed to both his 'fair lady' and to her congregation, Cumming's church). Most of the others who had been aware of his religious struggles were unconscious of the increasing dilemma that love was posing to him. Understandably, he revealed his feelings to very few, and as he approached his twenty-first birthday, all the players in the game were aware of making a last bid. Liddon and Mansel both wrote to him, trying to persuade him. Emily Freemantle, an old friend of his mother, annoyed him with her letter, possibly a sign he was also moved. She recalled an injunction to her from Lady Bute to watch over her son.[60] Mabel tried to tempt him. The kind vicar of her home church 'is to have a confirmation ... it is a happy time to him always & I am sure it is to those so fortunate as to be his candidates. Dearest Bute, how earnestly I wish you were to be one of them!'[61] Lady Edith Fergusson also wished she 'could think you ever really look at our side of the question'.[62]

Yet to Capel, it still did not seem inevitable that Bute would take the final plunge: 'Surrounded by temptations and weakened by the falls of the past, it is not surprising you should feel almost an insurmountable difficulty in battling with self.'[63] It was not easy for Bute to voice publicly the difficulties of his position. His attachment to the Catholic Church had been both real and public. Moreover Capel had plans to proselytise in Oxford in May if Bute thought it would be useful just then. Bute considered that 'Mr Capel will find men here not unprepared to listen to him.' Two undergraduates had died of accidents within days of each other, plunging the university into a solemn mood. One of them was the twenty-year-old Robert Marriott of Christ Church, who died from falling out of a window. Hunter Blair quotes a letter of Bute's describing his death.

I had seen him lying in the ground-floor room where he died – totally unconscious, and breathing with great difficulty. The Senior Censor came in when I was there, and read over him the prayers for the dying. This was the very clergyman who told me a few months ago that he did not believe in prayer ... I went into the room again after the men had gone to the billiard-room. It was the room of a friend of his: the walls covered with pictures of horses and actresses, and whips and spurs and pipes. The body lay on a mattress on the floor covered with a sheet. It was all dreadful, and I tried in vain in that room to say a *De Profundis* for him.[64]

The letter is almost a statement of the major themes of Bute's obsessions: his concern with death, with prayer, with depth of belief, with right and fitting ceremonial. Only his love of art is missing, though this is reflected in his reaction to the worldly litter of the room. The actual funeral was to be at the boy's home, but parts of the service were read before the hearse took him to the Canterbury Gate on his last journey. The extreme gloom of the occasion struck Bute as godless, for however much Christians grieve for themselves, they should rejoice in one reborn in a brighter world. This was 16 May, and Capel finally arrived on 23 or 24 May. Scott Murray thought Capel was 'very timid about this visit & fearful about not doing the best for your friends'. Hunter Blair put a good complexion on this visit.

> Bute's hope, no doubt, was that [Capel's] earnestness, sympathy, and tact might have a soothing effect on the nerves of his friends, still quivering from the shock of the recent catastrophe ... Several undergraduates made Mr Capel's acquaintance ... One of them, he found, had been for some months resolved to make his submission to Rome; and by Mr Capel's advice he asked for an interview with the Dean and frankly informed him of his intention . . .[65]

In fact a miserable row ensued. The undergraduate in question was Charles Biscoe.[66] A friend told Bute:

> I never heard of anything so gratuitously brutal as the Dean's conduct towards him ... the Dean in his lecture gave it you hot, as having 'sown the seeds of this mischief far and wide'. Now this again any person who knows you will say is untrue ... although your opinions were well known among your friends, I am not aware you ever tried to proselytise.[67]

Biscoe's resolution was to fail him. He did not become a Catholic and wretchedly told Bute: 'I know I have been miserably weak and cowardly and nobody can think worse of me than I do of myself.'[68] He became a clergyman in the Church of England.[69] All the incident had done was to underline once again the price to be paid for becoming a Catholic. What is more, it had to be paid in the currency which cost Bute most dearly: rows with authority figures, pressure, and opprobrium.

Bute's state of mind is well shown by his masked ball. In June he sent out invitations to a *bal masqué* in *La Morgue*. It was a goodbye to Oxford, and a celebration, and a summing-up, of his time there. As Hunter Blair explains, the *'morgue'* of the invitation was merely a room adjacent to Bute's suite of rooms occasionally used as a resting place for a dead undergraduate. It was the room which had been used that very May. Bute needed neither to use this room, nor to describe it as a morgue.

The symbol of Christ Church is a cardinal's hat, for it was originally Cardinal's College (after founder Cardinal Wolsey): the hat still appears on college stationery. Bute reproduced it upon his invitation card, which as an undergraduate of the college he was entitled to do. Under this symbol he drew a face in a parti-coloured carnival mask, half in cardinal's red and half in death white.[70] It was no longer a hat, but a Catholic cardinal in an extraordinary and enigmatic disguise. It echoed the costume Bute chose for the event. He was 'his Satanic Majesty' in red and black, complete with horns and tail.[71] Whether he was the devil for choosing Roman Catholicism, or for rejecting it, he left his friends to guess. Maybe he was damned if he did, and damned if he did not. Then he left Oxford without sitting for his degree.[72]

He found his escape where it always came most easily to him, in travel. He spent his summer yachting and visiting Russia, taking Lord Rosebery with him. According to Henry Blyth, Harry Hastings was on board the *Lady Bird*. Newspaper reports speak of Harry being in Norway that summer, in a last-ditch attempt to improve his health, which would fit with yacht travel in that general area.[73] Bute travelled on to St Petersburg and other parts of Russia. If he and Harry were together on the yacht, then Bute once again had the chance to observe at first hand the horrible symptoms of Bright's disease.

The end of this summer is almost certainly the time when Bute argued theology 'with the Presbyterian minister of Auchenleck in the morning and with the Roman Catholic priest in the afternoon', according to Sir Herbert Maxwell. Maxwell's next statement has long been doubted. Bute told him 'in after years that he had very nearly decided in favour of the Presbyterian Church'.[74] Yet it is almost certainly correct.

The problem for Bute was in part not theological, but temperamental. It is well illustrated by his difficulty earlier that year in trying to present a stained-glass window to Cumnock parish church, the home church for Dumfries House. The Presbyterians took a strict view of the Second Commandment which forbade making an image of 'any thing that is in the heaven above, or in the earth beneath, or in the waters under the earth'. Just as Scottish Reformers three hundred years earlier had smashed what they thought of as 'images' in churches, so the stricter Victorian Presbyterians were firmly against making any pictorial image of God, which included Christ, as the second person of the Trinity, or allowing any images of his saints into churches, lest they attract the worship due to God alone. The minister of Cumnock, James Murray, could not have been kinder about the problem. It would be fine if Bute offered 'windows filled with mathematical designs', but Bute did not want mathematical designs.[75] *The Buteman*'s 'London correspondent' put it rather nicely: 'whilst professing the most ardent love for all that is advanced in ritual and aesthetic in religion, the Marquis, who was brought up as a Presbyterian, always gave it to be understood he had not joined the English Church . . . [but] Presbyterianism [is] scarcely . . . a home for a high Ritualist.'[76]

Not the least of the problems when trying to assess the reliability of accounts such as Maxwell's is their tone. Bute's interest in religion and his tastes were too eccentric to be taken seriously. Such accounts, often including Hunter Blair's, adopted a mocking tone, saying anything to raise a laugh, making it hard to weigh the evidence they present.

That autumn Bute was to celebrate his majority, and, as the many who wrote to him realised, he would be more than ordinarily glad to reach it. It would not just put him in possession of his wealth, but make him master of his own life; and in an absolute way that no young man with a father or mother living could experience. It would be his day of freedom: the day also when he would not be able to shelter behind his promises to delay his choice of a Church. There was nothing to stop his becoming a Catholic then, nothing except his relationship with the Duke's daughter, and his dread of the reaction of many of those whom he loved, including the staunchly Protestant Lady Elizabeth.

One possible solution which occurred to him was to marry without telling his bride of his intention to become Catholic. Capel was horrified, and insisted that the minimum required was to tell the lady he intended to convert, and promise that his children would be brought up as Catholics. Capel, having laid down the minimum, was firmly against the marriage: 'I know of no misery on earth so great as that two beings united by every bond of affection should on the sole thing necessary be separated.' He was doubly concerned, for Bute was not only proposing to marry into a Protestant family, but an exceptionally ardent one. The family would impede Bute's generosity to his chosen church.

Capel did not add that doubt must be raised as to whether Bute would once again be talked out of making his submission to Rome. His final plea suggests that he was only too aware of this but did not like to put it into words for fear of making the possibility more real: 'Let me again urge you to come at once to confession & decide once for all to make your abjuration the very day you are of age.'[77]

Before Bute reached his majority, there was a breach between him and Capel. Perhaps Capel's letter had caused it, or maybe Bute, who hated pressure, was simply avoiding him. Capel was expecting him to arrive and spend time at Danesfield with the Scott Murrays, but Bute did not come, and did not keep in touch with him. Capel could only blackmail that 'humanly speaking the salvation of thousands born and unborn depends on you . . . to prevent such great glory to God, the Evil Spirit will leave no effort untried'.[78] Yet again he begged Bute to make his submission on his birthday, or immediately afterwards, but that would have made a huge row in the middle of very public festivities.

The programme for the celebrations was on a massive scale, and poor Bute was to be centre stage at public events for more than a week. They began on the eve of his birthday with a public ball on Bute. On the platform with him, amongst others, were Sir James Fergusson, Lady Edith Hastings, Lady Elizabeth Moore and Rev. John Robertson, the local Minister. Bute had not changed his views on whom he owed debts of gratitude. The next day, the tenantry gathered at Mount Stuart, to present Bute with a formal address, to which he replied touchingly and tactfully:

> I feel towards the island all the proud affection which has for centuries bound my fathers to its soil, and I know how many there are among you whose attachment to it is not less hereditary than my own.[79]

Four days later, after a round of balls, receptions, addresses and dinners, the Marquess left for Cardiff, where a similar programme, complete with public ox-roasts and fireworks, swung into action. Cardiff was the scene of Bute's greatest responsibilities, and he made a speech typical of him. His new responsibilities seemed to crush him with their weight, he said, especially in light of his inexperience and his faults. He knew that it would not do for him to think like this, and he would endeavour to do his duty.[80]

After Cardiff came Ayrshire. With the festivities over, Bute was truly free to make his submission to Rome. He chose instead to place a paragraph in *The Times*: 'I authorise you to state that it is not true that I have joined the Roman church.'[81] If he was intending to do so in the very near future, there seems no reason for his statement. According to letters quoted by Hunter Blair,[82] he was reading as a preparation for reception into the Roman Church. Yet with Bute's omnivorous taste for reading, how much did that mean? Perhaps more significantly he began to keep (somewhat unenthusiastically) the Catholic rules for fasting. Not that Bute minded going without food, but to a chef of the period, meatless dishes meant fish dishes and Bute hated fish, however well-cooked.

At the end of October, six weeks after his birthday, he heard from the mother of his lady: 'It is very disheartening. Unless the woman *lies*, she will do everything in her power to prevent the marriage. She is, I think, too upright a woman to deceive.'[83] This can only mean that Bute had actually discussed marriage with Lady Albertha, and that he himself was bound to it, since at that stage, only a lady might break off the relationship; it was socially and indeed legally, impossible for a gentleman to 'breach' his promise of marriage. Lady Albertha was twenty-one, like Bute, and so did not legally require her parent's consent.

On 10 November, the Marquess of Hastings died of Bright's disease. The 'curse of the Hastings', the 'almost hereditary' and incurable disease, seemed all too real, and Bute was half-Hastings. John Boyle is said to have heard the wheels of the ghostly Hastings death-carriage at Cardiff Castle on the night of Harry's death, and that can only have emphasised Bute's Hastings inheritance. The original story was that the head of the Hastings family would hear the wheels of a carriage outside his house twice: each time, on looking outside, the carriage would not be there. It was a ghostly hearse, come to carry the head of the family away. Originally, then, it was a warning of death. With Harry dead, his sister Lady Edith was in theory the head of the family. But did ghosts recognise women as heads of families?

At some point that autumn after Bute had come of age, Capel wrote to Bute, mentioning 'special graces' Bute had received in the last four days. He begged Bute make a daily act of sorrow for 'whatever may have been sinful in the imprudent promise' and to renew his promises to become a Catholic and to look upon himself as somebody waiting for the right moment to make his submission to the church. Capel concluded:

> I leave here on Monday morning, and I shall be delighted to make any arrangement you may judge convenient. Hammersmith is quiet & easy of access, and in your present state of mind no very special preparation is needed.
>
> My address will be Charing Cross Hotel. Should I not find a note awaiting me there from you I shall go on to St Catherine's Villa, St Leonard's on Sea. May the Sacred Heart receive your good resolve.[84]

This, again, is not the letter of a priest who is certain his catechumen will make his profession. One would give a good deal for a date on it, and even more to know if the 'imprudent promise' which plainly figured so largely in Bute's life was the one which pledged him not to join the Catholic Church until of age, or some other promise given to his lady.

It is possible that in November Bute's beloved finally broke with him. She may not have formally promised herself to him. Equally, she may only have broken the relationship when she knew he was quite definitely going to become a Catholic. It is also possible that Bute went to his cousin's funeral. There is no mention of him in the press reports of it, but given the crowds of thousands who thronged to Kensal Green Cemetery[85] on 14 November, Bute could well have escaped attention. *The Morning Post* records that the Marchioness of Hastings was supported by various gentlemen,[86] and it would be typical of Bute to choose such a role, rather than travelling in his own carriage behind the hearse. The combination of greater anonymity and greater usefulness would have attracted him. Either the breaking of his relationship, or the trauma of Harry's death, would have been enough to make Bute reconsider his religious position. With the loss of the former, he would have far less to lose by becoming a Roman Catholic, and the death of Harry would suggest that he had more to gain.

Bute did indeed go to Hammersmith where there was a convent of the Sisters of the Good Shepherd and his conditional baptism, profession of faith and first Communion took place on 8 December 1868,[87] the Feast of the Immaculate Conception.

6 Lothair?

*'Extremely good-looking, highly bred, and most
ingenuous ...'*

Having joined the Catholic Church, Bute knew quite well a storm
would break. He ran away to the Mediterranean and spent the winter
there on the *Lady Bird* with Edith, who was mourning Harry. Capel
very conveniently found that his health needed some time by the sea,
and Bute's yacht was more appealing than St Leonard's. Sneyd, now
his secretary, came too. Bute spent Christmas with the Scott Murrays
at Nice. 'He was always ready to join in any fun, as long as he had
not to meet strangers.'[1]

In the early spring he went to Rome, where he was confirmed by
Pius IX in the Sistine Chapel. Capel complained about Bute's 'idleness',[2]
which suggests that during the religious turmoil of the autumn he had
become thoroughly exhausted. From Rome, he and his party went
again to the Holy Land. He wrote to Miss Skene, to assure her that
he was '*very* comfortable' as a Catholic and at 'perfectly at peace in
the Church', with his taste for controversy gone. He took a certain
pride in telling her that he was 'like the *slowest* type of old English
Catholicism'.[3] This aligned him with the recusant aristocrats, rather
than the newer movements in the Catholic Church, which enjoyed an
enthusiastic style of worship, and with it, a greater devotion to the
Pope, and more respect for the hierarch, but it was not mere posturing.
He disliked what he considered unnecessary display, as much as he
loved heartfelt devotion.

The newspapers broke the story of the 'perversion' of the Marquess
of Bute in January 1869. *The Glasgow Herald* doubted 'whether a
young man who has changed his religion with this facility is made of
the stuff which has much personal influence over other men'. But it
was shrewd enough to realise that the Marquess was not placing his

whole fortune at the service of Rome. 'A young nobleman in such a position and with such an income is not in the least likely to do more than give a liberal support to a few charitable institutions and subscribe handsomely to the buildings and clergy of his communion wherever he may reside.'[4] It took, however, a gloomy view of his future prospects, for it must show 'priestly influences acting upon a weak, ductile and naturally superstitious mind' and Rome would ensure those influences darkened around him all his life.[5]

The storm, coupled with the eccentricity of Bute's character, caught Disraeli's attention, which was possibly further excited by the No Popery furore aroused by the meeting of the First Vatican Council in 1869–70; he had briefly met Bute in 1867 when in Edinburgh.[6] Disraeli had climbed the greasy poles of both society and government, but he had begun as an outsider; and his attention was always caught by singular people (he had, after all, married one). Disraeli also had an axe to grind himself, for he had originally believed he had Archbishop Henry Edward Manning's support for his attempts to set up a Catholic university with lay control in Dublin. The attempt broke down. Manning failed to support Disraeli, and Disraeli lost office. Disraeli felt he had been deceived.[7] Bute's earlier romance and his conversion now became the starting point of his latest novel, an intriguing *roman à clef* with the eponymous hero *Lothair*.[8] It is remarkable as being a contemporary account of Bute more than a few sentences long.

The Protestant heroine, Corisande, is the alter ego of Lady Albertha, and the sixth daughter of a Duke.[9] Corisande is very young when her brother introduces his Oxford friend into the family circle. Lothair has been reared by the forbidding figure of his maternal uncle, one of his two guardians,

> a keen, hard man, honourable and just, but with no softness of heart or manner. He guarded with precise knowledge and with unceasing vigilance Lothair's vast inheritance, which was in many counties and in more than one kingdom.[10]

It is a generous description of Charles Stuart, though Disraeli makes the guardian deliberately unlike him in having him rear Lothair in the remote vastness of Scotland. The sport with a *roman à clef* lies in separating the real clues to identity from the liberally scattered red herrings. Disraeli's wife was the widow of 'the Glamorgan lawyer and industrialist Wyndham Lewis',[11] and he had therefore an excellent knowledge of, and contacts with, the Cardiff area, where Charles Stuart was Trustee. Lothair's other guardian is a cardinal, and unmistakably drawn from the emaciated figure of Manning (who was not yet a cardinal himself). Lothair, unused to the warmth of family life, falls in love not so much with Corisande as with her family. His every word reveals his immaturity and naïvety, and with good sense, and considerable self-control, the Duchess forbids him to speak to Corisande of his love. Self-control because Lothair, like Bute, is heir to a huge fortune.

In the early chapters, Bute's unease in society is wonderfully captured, with Lothair risking all sorts of social solecisms from his reluctance to approach strangers. Even more telling is the scene in which Lothair, still under-age, approaches his solicitor to ask for the money he has promised to a friend to help him out of difficulties.

'Your Lordship has an objection to apply to the trustees?' enquired Mr. Giles.

'That is the point of the whole of my statement,' said Lothair, somewhat impatiently.

'And yet it is the right and regular thing,' said Mr Giles.

'It may be right and it may be regular, but it is out of the question.'

'Then we will say no more about it ... Don't you think I could see these people,' said Mr Giles, 'and talk to them, and gain a little time. We only want a little time.'

'No,' said Lothair, in a peremptory tone. 'I said I would do it, and it must be done, and at once.' [12]

The combination of imperiousness and impracticality, and total lack of concern for the 'right and regular thing' is very like Bute. Even more like him is the ease with which Lothair is made grateful to Mr Giles, who lends him the money personally, and uses this as an excuse to manoeuvre him into dinner at his house, providing Mrs Giles with a huge social coup. [13] Throughout the book, Lothair feels gratitude easily, and Bute himself responded instantly to kindness and never forgot it. Perhaps most clever is the difference between the private, loquacious Lothair, who is full of confidences and of wit, and the public figure who is 'monosyllabic and absent'. [14] The contrast between the venality of the social parasite, and Lothair's seriousness, is beautifully drawn, as is his failure to realise that he is being toadied to.

Lothair is absorbed by the Catholic aristocracy, especially Lord and Lady St Jerome (Lord Howard of Glossop and his first wife). [15] Disraeli raises the old terror that all Roman Catholics are, essentially, traitors because of their loyalty to Rome, and introduces 'Monsignore Catesby ... a youthful member of an ancient English house' who has inherited the 'beauty of their form and countenance'.[16] He becomes Lothair's chief Catholic mentor. The suave priest, named for the Guy Fawkes conspirator, Robert Catesby, is a portrait of Capel.

In the interests of a good story and political point-scoring, Disraeli leaves the real life of Bute further and further behind, yet the social portrait is astute. One of the scenes most clearly based on Bute is of Lothair at the jewellers, buying pearls:

> what I want are pearls. That necklace which you have shown me is like the necklace of a doll. I want pearls, such as you see them in Italian pictures, Titians and Giorgiones, such as a Queen of Cyprus would wear. I want ropes of pearls.[17]

One of the few similarities between Bute and Disraeli was their genuine liking for female society, their ease in it, and their attraction to older women. It is impossible to guess if Disraeli gave Lothair this feature because he had heard of it or observed it in Bute, or because it was so natural to Disraeli himself. Perhaps it was one point where he could fully sympathise with the original of his hero. It is in the areas where Lothair is most conventional that he is most unlike Bute, and Bute's lively sense of the ridiculous would have prevented his jumping into a hansom, and then exclaiming as does Lothair, ''tis the gondola of London'.[18]

Disraeli makes Lothair a non-smoker, which successfully establishes him as a slightly antisocial oddity, but which was far from the truth, as Bute smoked heavily. It has been usual to argue that Bute was not very like Lothair,[19] partly because Lothair is pictured wavering. Bute has been drawn as a man of fixed purpose, yet he described himself as often vacillating.[20] Lothair is in fact a most revealing caricature of Bute. If Disraeli failed to get inside Bute, to understand the springs of thought and action, he nevertheless presented a telling portrait of the way he appeared to others. He puts into the cardinal's mouth an affectionate summing up of Bute/Lothair:

> Extremely good-looking, highly bred, and most ingenuous; a considerable intelligence and not untrained; but the most absolutely unaffected person I have ever encountered.[21]

Lothair was published in 1870, the year in which the Italian army finally occupied Rome.[22] The first edition was exhausted in two days, and eight editions were produced that year.[23] The book became the lens through which the world viewed Bute, and when he died, many obituaries carried headlines declaring that 'Lothair' was dead. There is no record of Bute himself ever referring to the book.

While 'Lothair' was being written, Bute's life was occupied in a somewhat more down-to-earth fashion than Disraeli was imagining for his alter ego. He had gone to Rome for the Vatican Council of 1869. He was in the 'inopportunist' party of those reluctant to see the Pope declared infallible, but once the decree was promulgated, accepted it as a good Catholic.

Work had started on Cardiff Castle in the spring of 1869, and Bute visited it to see the progress made in the autumn of that year. It was a project which had been suggested since at least 1866. The original building on the site had been a square Roman fort. The Normans built a castle there, and in the late mediaeval period the Earl of Warwick followed fashion by erecting a dwelling-house a little apart from the original castle. However, what had been a fair-sized building in the middle ages no longer gave adequate accommodation. Cardiff Castle had long been an inconveniently cramped house for a well-to-do man, and too small for entertaining. The second Marquess had found it so, and the first had rarely used it.[24]

In 1865, Bute had met one of the most original architects of the Victorian period, William Burges.[25] Both men were passionately interested in history. Bute had fallen in love with the Gothic style before his ninth birthday, and Burges invariably built in the style. It is not clear if they first met because Burges had already been asked to prepare a report on restoring Cardiff Castle, or if he was asked to make the report following a chance encounter; there is no reference to Burges in the few papers of this period which survive in the Bute archive. It is impossible to guess at what point shared enthusiasms deepened into the friendship which is apparent as soon as references to Burges appear, when it frequently sounds as if Bute is echoing Burges's words. Thus Burges refers to the building as having been 'restored over and over again' and Bute to its being 'by no means satisfactory . . . the victim of every barbarism since the Renaissance' which sounds like a version of same words before they were toned down to be turned into a formal report. Burges was known for his hot temper.

Burges's report was presented in February 1866. It dealt primarily with the castle as an antiquarian relic, and took as axiomatic that nothing must be done to damage the ancient remains of the mediaeval castle, which Burges pointed out had been built over the Roman original. It suggested three possible courses of action: the strictly conservative, designed merely to protect existing remains; the antiquarian, designed to explore them a little; and the 'modern'. This latter would ensure the preservation of genuinely old walling, 'all that the antiquarian can possibly care about ... the supposed work of Robert Earl of Gloucester', whilst allowing for new building which would recreate what might originally have been there. Burges argued passionately for the latter course, which would allow him the creative space for a superb example of the Victorian Gothic. He had to convince the staid trustees, especially the conventional Stuart, not the young Bute. To win them over, the argument was on traditional lines, with an appeal to the rank of his patron.

> In considering these three courses there is no doubt at all, that in any age other than the present the last mentioned one is that which would most certainly have been adopted in as much as it is the most suited to the circumstances of the case; for we must never lose sight of the fact that Cardiff Castle is not an antiquarian ruin but the seat of the Marquess of Bute.

Burges also needed to reassure the young Marquess that he would not be considered a vandal:

> were the remains of high interest in the history of architecture or precious on account of their art, I should most unhesitatingly advise the strictly conservative treatment but this is by no means the case. Every part of the castle has been restored over and over again.[26]

Bute's interest was caught, but before work could start, he had his bitter row with Stuart. Since Bute had accused his guardian and trustee of overspending, and cast doubt on his financial probity, it is hardly surprising that this plan for the Castle was suspended. The one exception seems to have been a private sitting room for Bute. Burges

> converted a dull Georgian bedroom into a splendid Gothic fantasy, a private retreat for his patron ... Burges banished the sash windows, lowered the ceiling, and commissioned from Charles Rossiter a deep painted frieze depicting the life of St Blaan.[27]

More usually St Blane, he is one of the Celtic saints of the island of Bute, and the considerable remains of the monastery he founded, among the most important in Scotland, were owned by the young Lord Bute. One of the first acts of his majority was to give the go-ahead for the ambitious new tower to be built and decorated by Burges. Work started in the spring of 1869.

To say that the work was by Burges is only to give half of the picture. Burges was the architect and also the designer. It was not just the architecture for which he was responsible, but the decoration, the interior joinery, the furniture and the glass, very often stained glass. There were exquisite pieces to set on the tables as well: jewelled cups, and dishes of precious metals. Lest one should take all this magnificence too seriously, jokes abounded, jokes wrought in stone and silver, rebuses, visual puns.

One man could not achieve this alone, and a team worked under Burges. The first sketches were by Burges; these were then realised by his team as models and cartoons, and finally painted, glazed or made in precious metals by others. William Frame[28] was an architect who worked as Burges's assistant, absorbing Burges's style, and repeating it. John Starling Chapple[29] was Burges's friend as well as his clerk of works, and it was he who finished another project after Burges's death: Castell Coch. Horatio Walter Lonsdale[30] was Burges's principal artist. He had trained as an architect, and could, and did, design anything, adapting himself to the demands of those who employed him, perhaps too easily. Fred Weekes[31] created splendidly blocky figures, realising all the masculine potential of Burges's first sketches, and his work in the Bachelor Bedroom at Cardiff is especially compelling. Thomas Nicholls[32] was the sculptor, a genius so irascible and independent he gained more freedom than most of Burges's team. Once the first sketches had been filled out by the team, other craftsmen then realised them. The principal painter was Charlie Campbell, who in 1873 left Harland and Fisher to form his own company, Campbell and Smith and Co. The principal silversmiths and jewellers were Barkentin and Krall, while stained glass was executed by Saunders and Co.

Managing such a long design process from first sketch to finished article, through the hands of so many talented and individual craftsmen, implies a very single-minded control. Burges's work has an astonishing unity to it, and his control was absolute. It seems that some of the artist-craftsmen he employed at times gave the genius a rocky ride. Others, like Lonsdale, when finally released from Burges sometimes produced works of much greater genius than anything they achieved for the master, and sometimes a dispiriting vapidity.

The first section of Cardiff Castle to be completed by this design process, and involving most members of the team, was the clock tower at the south-west corner, which contained a bachelor bedroom destined for Bute and two smoking rooms: a winter smoking room low in the tower, and a summer smoking room at its top. The theme of the lower room was the passage of time, appropriately for a clock tower. The seasons were evoked by the signs of the zodiac, and figures of the sun and moon. The dominating feature was the fireplace. Burges, who was 'so short, quite tiny', ugly and plump,[33] put a burning intensity into this fireplace. Youthful, tall, elegant lovers radiated on it. A girl warmed herself by a painted fire, her cheeks reddened by it, or by the words and the presence of a beautiful boy who leaned over her, his hand slipping down her shoulder. Another couple went skating, which gave the excuse for the supporting arm of the boy, the timidity of his girl. Couples hunted each other as much as their putative target while their bows and arrows echoed Cupid's own. Regal, the god himself stood to receive the homage Virgil demanded for him in the inscription, for he 'conquers everything and we all yield to love'. His support was Capricorn, the goat, which is appropriate for a room centred on the zodiac and for a god centred on lust.

From the beginning, the summer smoking room was to have two tiers, with an open gallery above the main room, and both with rows of windows. The design always was mediaeval, but, by the time Burges came to exhibit his ideas for the interior at the Royal Academy the following summer, it had also become oriental, in fact a recreation of the 'grand smoke' at Chios, on Bute's tour of Greece in 1866, just before plans for the new rooms were suspended. The seating is based on divans, the draught is blowing from the open windows, the company of youths and grown men are smoking chilbooks. Recreating Bute's experience, the older man is 'doing' a cigarette, anachronistically for the period suggested by the costumes and decoration.

The iconography of the summer smoking room was intended to be Christian. The top gallery had a mural of the Fall and Expulsion from Eden, whilst, appropriately for a room which echoed the East, the murals in the lower room told the story of St George, the saint the Crusaders are said to have brought back from there. Before the room was built, these plans were changed and the walls were decorated on the lower tier with illustrations of the stories of the signs of the zodiac, and on the upper tier with the four elements. It is impossible to be certain why the alteration was made. One suggestion[34] is that Bute had not been aware of the attention the new tower would attract. When he became conscious that it would be very much in the public eye, he wanted to remove from it everything that might draw attention to his still notorious conversion. Equally, a religious young man might well feel that the walls of a smoking room, dedicated to easy male socialising and 'loose talk', are not the best place for Christian iconography.

The signs of the zodiac came from Burges's imagination and not Bute's.[35] Burges was interested in Rosicrucianism, in which astrology is important. The upper tier plays a good deal with the idea of minerals, another interest of Rosicrucianism, since one of its roots was in the mining and mineral-working tradition of the Tübingen area of Germany;[36] Burges was fascinated by the fact that his patron was in real life the owner of mineral wealth. Introducing the elements sparked another idea. The pillars supporting the gallery had originally been decorated with wyverns, and then with angels, each pillar essentially the same. In the latest transformation, they became each of the eight winds, beautifully, individually and exotically personalised. This is an idea which appears in Bute's late buildings, and may be his own. They are very much a classical idea, with stories of the winds let loose to make storms for sailors, just the thing for a boy with a yacht.

Yet it is love which dominates this room, as it does the winter smoking room. Was it Burges or Bute who chose the theme? The mural of the zodiac exploits every romantic nuance; the end wall of the summer smoking room is covered with the erotic story of Psyche, and the fireplace itself is alight with courtly love transformed by sensuality. Again, Cupid dominates the fireplace. Burges had originally intended to depict him standing quite formally, but changed him into a much more approachable seated figure, absorbed in a pair of love-birds on his wrists. Below him is his summer motto, *aestate viresco,* or 'in summer I flourish'. Under him, couples court and hunt through a summer landscape.

Bute's 'bachelor bedroom' was between these two rooms, to give him a private suite of three rooms in the tower. This room too had been intended to have a religious theme, with a mural of a crucifix. That was changed, and instead the walls and ceiling were covered with images and mythology of mineral wealth and alchemy, very much Burges's themes. The furniture was of course also designed by Burges: massive, Gothic, and often decorated with inlays, fabrics and painting. At Cardiff, none of the pieces is painted; instead they

> rely for their decoration on high quality carving and marquetry. In choosing carved and inlaid rather than painted furniture, Burges made use of the excellent workmen available locally in Cardiff's Tyndale Street.[37]

Wit runs through his pieces, and although he has certain well-loved themes, each is carefully chosen as appropriate to its setting. Years earlier, Burges had drawn the Sleeping Beauty to illustrate Tennyson's poem *The Day-Dream*, where the poet quite explicitly viewed the fairy story as a parable of sexual awakening. A version of this was painted for Burges by Holiday upon the head of his own bed, where a luxurious demi-nude with auburn hair is about to be awakened by her prince. Burges had imagined a beautiful bed for her. He recreated this bed, complete with its cushions, for the young Bute.[38]

Bute finally returned in to Britain in August 1870, and most of that autumn and winter was spent at Cardiff, or on Bute. It is easy to imagine that in the rural beauty of Bute, the storm over the newly published *Lothair* passed Bute by. It was about this time that Bute at last did what Capel had been promising he would do since his conversion.[39] He made a new Cardiff 'house' for the order at whose Hammersmith convent he had stayed to be received into the Catholic Church. The idea was to create a refuge for fallen women, 'always so desirable in a seaport town',[40] with a laundry for the women to support themselves by their work,[41] together with provision for children and a school for them. It would be run by 'Nuns of the Good Shepherd' at Pen-y-lan, where a barn with an 'ecclesiastical appearance' was to be converted into a chapel. Two nuns came to Cardiff to look at the site, and the Marquess went out to Pen-y-lan to meet them, 'running towards [them] and leaving no time to take off [their] black aprons'. The bulk of the work was to be done by the Marquess's builder and clerk of works, Mr Barnett; decisions were left to him and the builders. Bute said he was 'confident' that they would not put him to any 'unnecessary expense'. The chapel he wanted 'fitted up in a very simple but somewhat handsome manner by my architect, Mr Burges'.[42] The picture of the impulsive young man running towards the nuns, and his concern with avoiding 'unnecessary expense' is somehow very typical of the real Bute, and very unlike his public image.

Jane Austen's famous opening lines from *Pride and Prejudice* suggest that society should have been well aware that Bute was very definitely in want of a wife, and his past experience had taught him of the heartbreaking difficulties attached to loving a girl who was a Protestant. In 1871 he became attracted to Lady Holland's adopted daughter, Marie Fox. The Hollands had converted to Catholicism in 1850. Marie was about twenty-one years old, petite with 'black hair and sparkling eyes'.[43] The only remaining account of the courtship is from the Fox family.[44]

Situated as she was, at the centre of society, Marie had many admirers; but Lord Bute was an outstanding prospect, offering not only his impeccable birth and title, but his fortune. Lady Holland was particularly concerned with engineering a good catch, according to the

Protestant Lord Rosebery, who claimed that Marie refused him on the grounds of religion before he had even contemplated marriage. Marie seemed in every way perfect for Bute. Then the expectation of an engagement was disappointed. Lady Holland felt quite sure that Marie had been wronged, and she gave her considerable energies to ensuring that her version of the facts was circulated. Time, and missing letters, have somewhat blurred her account, but a letter from a friend suggests how carefully it was managed: 'I have not hesitated to sketch the case exactly as it appears by your last letter to such people as I think you would like to know it ... I think if you could hear all that is said you would not be dissatisfied ... you would I think find much less is said for His side than you would expect.'[45]

The version told in the *Chronicles of Holland House* is that Marie's adoptive father being dead, Bute went to speak to her mother. He was, it seems, a little disturbed about the fact that she was adopted. 'Bute asked to see the papers which referred to Marie's birth. Lady Holland prevaricated. She replied that he should have made the request long before.' Bute wanted to marry Marie, but only if her birth was respectable. If she was a bastard, he was not prepared to make her his Marchioness, however proper her upbringing and adoption, and despite the fact that she was accepted by society, and had been presented at Court. When 'Bute went even further, and demanded to be put in touch with the girl's father, any question of an engagement was speedily at an end'.[46]

However, two letters from Bute in the Holland family archive suggest a different version. In the first, Lady Holland has 'offered' to show Bute papers and Bute explains he had pressing business in the Lords and at Cardiff, and would accept her offer and look at the documents on his return. He feels the inevitable awkwardness would be overcome by entrusting these to a third party and keeping matters on a business footing.[47]

Lady Holland had told a friend that it would take 'interference at the right moment'[48] to persuade Bute to make an offer to Marie. That would, of course, be the time when he might feel his courtship had not quite amounted to commitment on his side, but that there was a possibility that Marie had read it as such. Once a gentleman had deliberately engaged a girl's love, once it was plain to those around him that a proposal was imminent, he could not draw back. Lady Holland was attempting to manoeuvre Bute into an engagement before he himself had made a decision.

Bute's letter plainly caused Lady Holland offence, and the next letter, two days later, begins with an apology, in which he carefully implies that he did not believe the story that Marie was the illegitimate daughter of Lord Holland.

> I did not mean to imply that there could be anything to cause a feeling of awkwardness on your part. I meant that to myself it was painful, as it is, to make in relation to Miss Fox such enquiries as for the sake of possible children, in the event of marriage, I feel it my duty to make. The investigation of such a document as a certificate of marriage (which forms, I presume, one of the papers) appears to me to come within the description of a legal matter, and one of those which, especially in circumstances analogous to the present, are usually and best transacted in the most formal manner.

He said that he regretted she thought he had been slow in seeking this information but

> It is not 'long ago' since those circumstances arose which alone, in my judgement, justified me in claiming participation in a family secret to which you attached so much importance.[49]

Lady Holland took Bute's advice and placed what papers she had in the keeping of Mary Beauchamp, the young wife of the 6th Earl.[50] Bute found out, without actually seeing them, that the documents did not include those he sought and Lady Beauchamp had the unenviable task of telling her of the 'tone of disappointment wh. filled Lord Bute's letter'.[51] By the end of July Bute was telling Miss Skene: 'There is no engagement between Miss _ and myself, and nothing is less likely than that there ever should be ... here I am thrown out on the world again, feeling very lonely and desolate. My future, indeed, looks pretty blank just now.'[52]

Capel had reported that the breach was 'six of one & half a dozen of the other',[53] and later events and comment cast further doubt on the tidy Holland House story. The following summer, 1872, Marie was married to Prince Louis of Liechtenstein, who had seen all the papers relating to her. Some of the most crucial papers, including the birth certificate, appeared to relate to another girl.[54] Pressure was brought to bear on Lady Holland to reveal more, and she either could or would not do so. The official tale is that Marie then 'lost her head and accused Lady Holland of unkindness in her youth, which was certainly very far from the truth'.[55] Marie in fact went a lot further than this. What distressed Lady Holland most was that Marie 'accused her of "encouraging men in being immoral to [her]"'.[56]

Gradually, friends and employees came forward to admit that for years Marie had been making similar accusations. Lady Holland's niece reported that even whilst she had seen Marie 'overwhelmed with kindness and affection', the girl had been telling tales of her sufferings. Worse, the niece had borne 'the blame of many stories put on [her] most ungenerously by Marie'.[57] From Lady Holland's point of view, probably most damning was the evidence from her husband's former agent, who told of Marie having claimed to have seen some improper things relating to a footman through a hole in the wall 'which was all nonsense, as there was only an indent in the wall and no hole'. Lady Holland came to suspect that Marie had been sexually abused by a servant.[58] This would account for much. She made herself the heroine of dramas, especially sexual dramas, from at least her early teens.

Not only did Bute have a most punctilious regard for the truth; he also had a strong dislike of dramatic scenes. He was, in addition, hypersensitive to any suggestion of being deceived. One of the allegations now made against Marie was that she changed her love 'so easily' from one man to another and 'wrote love <u>letters at the same time</u>' to different men.[59] If Bute had suspected that she was behaving this way towards him, he would indubitably have considered himself 'thrown out on the world again, feeling very lonely and desolate'. The most probable candidate for the alternative suitor is Prince Louis whom she had met in 1870 and whom she later married. He had returned to England in 1871, the year of Bute's courtship. After Marie's tragically early death, the Prince was in the Mediterranean at the same time as Bute, and sought a meeting with him. Bute's tone suggests that he felt he was the injured party: 'It gently amused me to find myself a friend of Marie Fox's husband.'[60]

Marie may herself have rejected Bute when he showed that he was not happy with the lack of information about her birth, since a friend of hers asked if Lady Holland had 'dismissed that man as he deserved'.[61] Marie may well have been outraged that Bute seemed to need evidence for the romances she fabricated about her birth, which are suggested by a later letter from Bute to his wife, written when Marie had tuberculosis. 'I met a man, who knows Marie Fox well – & who told me she is dying . . . He told me more or less about her rows in Vienna & her . . . constant mania about being some kind of royalty – legitimate or otherwise . . . I suppose the whole thing is going to sink into a grave – hers – It was an odd mystery while it lasted.'[62] Lady Holland forgave Marie, but refused to meet her again, and Marie on her death-bed, with true histrionic ability, acknowledged her fault and expressed her sorrow and repentance.[63]

For the first time, Bute sought refuge in work. The winter of 1870, he began translating the Roman Breviary into English 'as good, plain, manly and idiomatic' as he could contrive. The Church of England had one prayer book, the *Book of Common Prayer*. It contained the orders for both daily prayer, and for Holy Communion and the other services and sacraments of that Church. The Catholic Church had several, including the Missal, which carried the order for Masses, and the Breviary, which contained the orders for the other services of the day. Both Anglican and Roman priests were expected to say their offices each day. Pious lay people also chose to say them. All the psalms, many passages of the Bible, and passages from the lives of various saints were in the Breviary. There was therefore a great deal to translate, and Bute later admitted that he had underestimated the scale of the task when he began it. It was to result in a two-volume work running to more than 3,000 pages.

Rev. James McSwiney[64] was one of the few people with whom Bute saw eye to eye. McSwiney was a learned Jesuit, and good company, though shabby and dirty. He was invaluable as someone with whom to discuss the difficulties of the Breviary project. All the Biblical readings in the Breviary were from the Vulgate, a fourth-century Latin translation (principally by St Jerome) of the Greek and Hebrew texts. Biblical scholarship had greatly advanced, and the problems of which 'reading' to follow where texts differed had been much discussed. Bute's old Harrow master, Westcott, was one of those most actively involved in such work. This presented Bute with a dilemma. As a scholar he did not want to follow an incorrect version, yet he was bound to translate the Latin before him. He tried as far as possible to compromise. Afterwards, it was generally agreed that the passages from the lives of the saints were especially successful, perhaps because most of them had not been translated before, and therefore Bute was able to be more original and idiomatic in his use of English.

Thus Bute provided himself with a long-term academic work to occupy the 'blankness' of his life. Not that it did remain blank for very long. In the winter of 1871-2 he fell in love again, this time with a young lady from a family both impeccable and Catholic. The Hon. Gwendolen Mary Ann Fitzalan-Howard was the granddaughter of the 13th Duke of Norfolk, and the eldest daughter of Lord Howard of Glossop, the same Lord Howard who had provided Disraeli with the model for 'Lord St. Jerome' in *Lothair*. Gwendolen was small, with fine eyes and an exquisite bone-structure, still only seventeen and a little plump, with a high colour and brown hair with golden lights. By February they were engaged to be married.

Capel was ecstatic. He wrote at once to felicitate Gwendolen, assuring her that 'None of your parents have prayed and wished more than myself for this happy issue. I am sure it is God's holy will.' As Bute's confessor, he knew him better than others, he said, and he added that 'his frank, earnest, generous nature needed but the affectionate heart of a spouse for its fullest expansion'.[65] Bute explained to Gwen that Capel had an allowance from him 'from which he administers beggars, and occasionally comes to act as chaplain for short periods and it is to him I generally confess, particularly in the case of long or delicate confessions. He is very clever and exceedingly useful to me, particularly in ecclesiastical affairs.'[66]

Bute returned to Cardiff, suddenly liking it better than ever. At first he worried a little over the disparity in their tastes, since she was not at all interested in art, 'which is one of the greatest pleasures I have'. Yet he was sure that 'your common sense will be a great help to me . . . for you know that I am myself often vacillating'. He enjoyed himself making preparations for his bride: 'I shall have a bedroom fitted up with red silk for you – as that will suit your complexion.'[67] He chose a room close to his own private sitting room, with its gentle religious theme. He hoped that he had not suggested that work on Cardiff was further advanced than it really was:

> Pray don't imagine, my dear, that the house is all done up as if we were living in the reign of Henry III. There is only my sitting room, the Oratory and the New Tower. The rest is by no means satisfactory and has been the victim of every barbarism since the Renaissance.[68]

He also looked out the family jewels for the first time:

> there is both a 'tiara' and a 'diadem' – one of which had probably better be altered, as you are not, I suppose, tall enough to bear much of that kind of thing . . . my mother apparently gave up the wearing of them for ever immediately after my Father's death.[69]

Bute towered over his contemporaries, whilst Gwen was very noticeably short.[70]

Both parties suffered a little from the misgivings of a couple about to be bound together for life. Would they make the other happy? Would they be happy themselves? Bute reassured himself that 'I don't think there is any woman with whom I am so likely to have [a happy home] as with you. I have been very happy with my bachelor life hitherto, and I know it will be your wish to make me still happier.'[71] Later, perhaps realising this was a little one-sided, he hoped that 'I may be able to make you happy with me! ... I hope and pray that nothing may be wanting in me to make us so, and I don't see how anything can be wanting in you.'[72]

Of course Gwen and her parents had to be invited to Cardiff Castle, and Bute, lacking a mother to act as hostess, persuaded Edith and her daughter Flora to come. This put rather a strain on the limited accommodation at the castle but Bute discovered that 'Edith and Flora want to sleep in the same room (for fear of ghosts)'.[73] Entertainment included visiting the new convent building at Pen-y-lan.[74]

Like many a prospective bridegroom, Bute found himself enmeshed in warring factions of family and friends. 'Edith and I have been looking up a list of my relations. They are a very queer lot, and she don't want some of them asked that I do, and vice-versa.'[75]

> I find Edith has quarrelled with many of her relations and says she won't come to the marriage if they are asked ... She can't see that if I forgive the Chas. Stuarts she may as well forgive Corry Marsham. Lady Elizabeth has not written to me – I cannot conceive what fault I may have committed. I am freely, justly and willingly devoted to her, but I do think she is rather hard on me. I hope your blandishments may have some effect on her. Query. Do all women who grow old maids get rather odd?[76]

He suffered the usual problems of hideous and unwanted wedding presents, problems his own tactlessness made worse.

> John Boyle's wedding present [a clock] had been brought up to my sitting-room without telling me what it was, and I thought it was something that the servants had bought. So Burges and Sneyd and I began to make jokes about the art ... and John Boyle there all the time.[77]

The next day, in some trepidation, Bute set about righting wrongs:

> Mercifully, I didn't say anything very bad, and so I promised to keep it in this room or put it in yours, and it's all right again ... the dial is a good size and the works are all right.[78]

The tenantry and townspeople at Rothesay had subscribed for a wedding present of a bracelet, pendant and earrings of pale coral, pearls and diamonds. The Ayrshire tenantry gave diamonds, though the gifts from Cardiff were to be presented once the happy couple were there. Gwen had not realised that it would be tactful to use one of these at the wedding. Bute, always very conscious of the feelings of others, especially those without his wealth and social position, had to use a little persuasion to get her to wear one set of these (the Rothesay set was chosen) to 'go away' in.[79]

A great many people would want to come to this ceremony, and St Paul's Cathedral was mentioned, but the Catholic religious authorities objected; marriage in a Catholic church had been legal since 1837.[80] Then it seemed for a time that the marriage would be at Glossop, near Manchester, but travel from there was demanding for guests. Bute, who found himself shrinking from the idea of a busy and sociable wedding breakfast, proposed hopefully, 'I should think ... we had better breakfast together privately'.[81] The idea was that they would then be able to make an early start to Cardiff. Eventually it was decided that the bride should be married from her London home, and that the ceremony would be at the Brompton Oratory.

Bute took great pleasure in designing the presents for the bridesmaids: lockets with the coat of arms that would be his and Gwendolen's.[82] Round the coat of arms was to be a girdle 'alternately rubies and diamonds, being your colours – red and white'. With a gold background, enamelled colours, and real pearls in the coronet, Bute thought they would be 'very well'. He had given the commission to an Edinburgh jeweller, hoping it would 'get his name up'.[83]

Bute made arrangements for his going away, anticipating gleefully the pleasure of having his bride alone with him. He was amused when it seemed the railway company carried that anticipation a little too far. The 'Great Western Railway is very civil – will be delighted to put on what is called a family (!) carriage for you and me'.[84] There was also the horse-drawn carriage, for 'going away'. 'I have been giving orders, or rather, taking them from the stud groom about carriages', remarked Bute ruefully. Gwendolen was happy to agree to 'our brown pair of horses', which would have looked virtually black, rather than borrowed and bridal greys, which would have been almost white.[85]

In the no-man's-land of engagement, social functions bothered Bute. He refused an invitation to a dinner-party at the Rothschilds 'for a variety of reasons', the most important being a fear that it was set up to make fun of him and his fiancée: 'If I talked to you, you know we should make a joke for the whole lot, and if I didn't there be no end to the ill-natured remarks they'd make. I do think it would have been in better taste if they had not so transparently invited us to act a scene for their entertainment.'[86] Bute was very sensitive to people's reactions to him, and he greatly feared being a figure of fun: not without cause. His interests were not conventional ones, and society then was more rigid than it is now. Hunter Blair's memoir of Bute preserves this mocking tone.

Gossip weighed the prospective bride in the balance of Society and found her wanting. She was 'quite without such knowledge of the world as might fairly be expected at her age, & in no way likely to be such a help as he wants'. Her natural mother was dead, which argued Gwen might well die in childbirth, and 'you know her brother is very wanting'. Frank Fitzalan-Howard, who was twelve at this time, was mildly learning disabled. In addition, the 'Foxites' suggested that Bute was inherently fickle in love, and that Gwen would soon discover the shallowness of his feelings for her.[87]

Bute dreaded most aspects of the ceremonial surrounding his wedding, and tried to impress this on Gwen: 'I fancy our entry into Cardiff will be very trying – more so than you imagine.'[88] Gwen was shy, but not only did she have a robust good sense about such things; she was also a little more ambivalent about the status which her new role brought her.

> Papa . . . said to me this afternoon that you said something about you hoped the nervousness at Cardiff would not take the shape of crying. Don't imagine that that is the least likely. It's most improbable. No! I hope I shall behave like a sensible person and look pleased (which it would be impossible not to be under the circumstances) and make my bows properly which will be quite new to me.[89]

Great popular excitement was aroused by the prospect of the marriage. The couple were to be greeted by the mayor and corporation on their arrival in Cardiff by train on the evening following the wedding. After speeches, they were to be escorted through the town in an open carriage, cheered on by crowds for whom the local railway companies were putting on cheap excursion trains. The town was to be decorated with triumphal arches, transparencies (gauze cloths) painted with such subjects as Hymen, the god of marriage, portraits of the happy couple and still more coats of arms. The *Illustrated London Weekly News* carried photographs of the bride and groom. The groom stared into the middle distance with the stern expression he always assumed under the intrusive gaze of the lens, and the bride looked becomingly demure.

In preparation, Bute made a retreat to Belmont, a Benedictine abbey just outside Hereford, easily reached by train from Cardiff. Bute very much needed the calm of such retreats, as his mercurial temperament was still liable to soar to fever pitch, which is just what it reached by the eve of the wedding.

Rosebery, who was to have been his best man, reneged the day before the wedding. Bute turned at once to his friend and cousin Charley, as a substitute: 'Never mind, Mauchline . . . will do quite as well.' But of course Bute did mind. As usual, his direct writing gives a vivid picture of his mood, feverishly turning over unopened presents, pausing to unwrap one, and then putting it impatiently down: 'There are a lot of things here – I haven't the patience to open them – Here's a smelling bottle from the Ryders.'[90] Gwen hastened to reassure Bute, and to comfort him as best she was able:

> My own darling don't mind. I'm certain its not unfriendliness on Ld. Rosebery's part, he's probably much taken up with his own affairs, & is thoughtless about ours. It's annoying for you I know of course, but I entreat you not to think about it.[91]

Outside the Brompton Oratory, temporary stands were erected in the road, so that the assembled crowds might get a good view. The wedding itself, on 16 April, was not only under the eyes of family and friends, but the curious gaze of the Protestant press. Bute had seen no objection to reporters getting into the Oratory.[92] All except the avowedly Catholic press commented on unfamiliar aspects of the service. *The Glasgow Herald* was quietly surprised at how similar the ceremony was to a Protestant one.

Bute was accompanied by Charley who cut a dash in 'full Highland costume'.[93] Bute crossed to one of the two *priedieux* at the front of the church. He rested his head in his ungloved hands, and remained there, praying for twenty minutes, while the church filled behind him, and the groomsmen and the eight bridesmaids arrived. They included Angela, Winefred and Constance (known in the family as Mary) Fitzalan-Howard, Gwen's sisters. Angela was just a year younger than Gwen, and the sisters were very close. Charley's sister Lady Flora, and Lady Phillipa Fitzalan Howard, Gwen's cousin and friend, were also bridesmaids.[94] They were dressed in white taffeta and muslin, with touches of pink, and carried pink May blossom and rosebuds.

Under the eyes of the astonished popular press, Bute remained praying, and therefore in a place safe from the crowds, until his bride, on her father's arm, arrived at the *priedieu* next to his. She was 'simply' dressed

> in the richest white satin, covered with magnificent *point à l'Aiguille* lace, and trimmed with wreaths of finest orange blossom. The

corsage, cut square, was ornamented on one side with sprays of diamonds and on the other by a wreath and bouquet of orange blossom. On her head a large tulle veil enveloping the figure over a wreath of the same choice flowers.[95]

From behind the veil, 'curious old diamond flowers', part of the Crichton Stuart family jewels, blazed out. The marriage was celebrated by Archbishop Manning, and Mgr. Capel preached the smooth and unremarkable sermon.[96]

Among those to sign the register was Benjamin Disraeli. One wonders (for there is no record of it) what his Lothair made of him. Afterwards, the two men being on the best of terms, it was widely rumoured that Bute had never even read the book.[97]

7   Marriage

'All that one could have hoped for or desired'

The honeymoon was deliciously happy. Three days after her wedding, Gwen wrote to her sister Angela with ungrammatical enthusiasm, 'Happiness don't half explain what I am, if Dr Johnson was alive he'd have to invent a new word with a stronger meaning.'[1] The only thing to dent her happiness slightly was the fear that she had lost an especially precious letter from the many Bute had written her, and she urged her sister to search everywhere for it, for she 'would be sorry for losing that letter'.[2]

The petty disruptions of social life were an annoyance when they began to make themselves felt, but no more than that. Gwen especially disliked having to spend many of her afternoons returning 'calls' which had been made on the couple, and she was downright nervous over her first dinner party, mainly over 'how these queer people are to go in, they do fight so over their precedence and as much/if any don't exist it is very difficult to manage'.[3] Gwen was, however, a much more trenchant personality than Bute, and she cared much less about the opinions of others, which made her life easier. She did not agonise as he did over the endless begging letters which were also part of her new life.

> B's doing the Beggars with his librarian down stairs, they are the most extraordinary sort of people I ever heard of. I get about ten also every morning & more come in during the day with the many posts. The sums they ask for are quite fabulous, from all parts of the world. I tell B he gives them too much and they tell others and come again themselves.[4]

Bute was only slowly learning how self-reliant she was. At a picnic for Catholic children in the parkland behind the Castle, one of the many public festivities to celebrate their marriage, they decided to separate and he suggested that she should find Fr Clark to protect her. As she told her sister: 'I naturally said I was capable perhaps of taking care of myself, which I succeeded in doing!'[5] Marriage brought her much-increased freedom, from her own bank account and chequebook,[6] to the right to read and send letters without supervision; Bute thought that a husband insisting on reading his wife's letters was 'intolerable'.[7] The cheque book was a little daunting at first, and she got minute directions on how to write a cheque from her father,[8] who was delighted to still have a role to play in his daughter's life, as, perhaps she had known he would be.

Gwen discovered that her accounts of social life, for instance 'a Catholic party – Mr Manning figures as one of my principal examples', could send Bute off into 'fits of laughter'.[9] She was dryly amused by Bute's slangy talk, regularly quoting his many uses of it: 'Bute insists on my wearing my lovely Elise's gown ... Bute does it for the fun of the thing I'm sure. He says "Why you'll 'fetch' the old women so." That word I used is not my usual way of expressing myself, but Bute always says it and I've heard it so much these last two days.'[10]

Bute greatly appreciated the contribution of Gwen's musicality to worship. She was too loyal to do much more than hint that Bute's musical tastes were not the most sophisticated.

> I play the oddest things for Offertory's that you can imagine 'Maryland, my Maryland' that style of thing. I'm quite ashamed but B delights in it so that makes me do it of course. He says he likes lively things during the Offertory. I 'cage my songbirds' every day at 5. B is pleased to describe my choir so, it's not my originality, so don't think so. I have 2 maids & 1 groom, all have good voices and ears happily for me. I shout at them at the top of my voice & play the harmonium at the same time, it's not altogether what one would call 'easy' but still I manage pretty well.[11]

At Cardiff the Butes worshipped in a small chapel created by Burges at the start of his work there. Bute told a friend, 'we venture on nothing more than hymns, and get along pretty well'.[12]

Gwen took her provision of music for the services very seriously. When her lady's maid was leaving she ruefully told her sister that it would not be easy to get a replacement. Like every other aristocrat, she wanted one neither too young nor old, good-looking and a good dressmaker (most clothes were made by the lady's maid). But Gwen also wanted her, if possible, to 'have a good voice, and be a Catholic. Her voice is for the choir, as you may imagine.'[13]

In June Bute was summoned to vote as a Conservative peer, and both he and Gwen begrudged the moments apart. Bute was not much interested in politics. He voted as part of his duty, that being for him, as for other Victorians, 'the operative word'.[14] Ruefully, Gwen told her sister that her tall husband was 'a horrid little person to leave me here alone for four whole days which I told him more than once'. It was only in his absence that she realised just how much she had given up in leaving her busy home life with a beloved father, a stepmother, four sisters and a brother: 'it's only the thought of Saturday coming and bringing him back to me that keeps me alive at all.' She was guiltily aware that she was flouting the conventions in speaking even thus openly of her love to an unmarried sister:

> you can't understand all this & I ought to keep it to myself but when my little duck is away, it seems so odd not to have a soul like oneself to speak to & for four whole days, after being accustomed to so many sisters & always Papa and Mama.[15]

Convention made meaningful conversation with the houseful of servants impossible. Bute told her that she realised 'so very much all that one could have hoped for or desired, that it grieves me, will I nill I, that you should be put to the least pain'.[16]

In August, only four months after the wedding, Gwen felt unwell. Next morning her symptoms were described as 'serious'. She had one of the most dreaded of Victorian illnesses: scarlet fever.[17] Queen Victoria sent a telegram from Balmoral, demanding news of Lady Bute.[18] Within the week, Gwen was improving, but her convalescence was long. Later that month Bute broke his arm.[19] To convalesce, they travelled to the island of Bute.

Bute enjoyed surprising his wife. She told her sister ecstatically: 'The one wish of my life I now have. Bute told me last night I am to have a pony carriage got for me (without telling me anything about it) as I liked driving. I am going to begin with one horse or pony.'[20] Her other great pleasure was rowing. Despite their numerous servants, it was difficult for her to get help to take her rowing-boat in or out of the sea, and of course, Bute with a broken arm could not assist a great deal. When 'Bute's men friends' came to stay, they were press-ganged into helping, compensating for her loneliness during the time they spent with him.[21] Gwen was uncomplaining, but probably both the rowing and the pony carriage were designed to help her back to full health, for she was still weakened by the scarlet fever. Before her marriage she had written that she hardly ever had a bad headache;[22] now they were a regular occurrence.[23]

Her sisters and friends came to stay with her, too, but increasingly she missed her big family circle, and such amusements as the acting they had enjoyed. She arranged to have her own copies of Shakespeare sent to her: 'I can't act – still I can pretend or now & then imagine myself to be acting Caesar or Ldy. MacBeth & those are my two favourite parts.'[24] She mixed with the limited circle of Bute's acquaintance on the island, especially the Stuarts of Ascog, children of Bute's factor, 'Bute's cousins about ten or twelve times removed . . . still they are his cousins'.[25] She fell in love with the Georgian house and the beautiful and peaceful surroundings, and they became 'my beautiful Mount Stuart'.[26]

Arrangements for Christmas, still not much celebrated in Scotland, mainly meant preparing for the various services in Bute's chapel. About the time that Bute converted to the Catholic Church, he commissioned Burges to create a chapel in the guest bedroom wing of Mount Stuart House.[27] Bute implied it was modelled on a portion of the Church of the Holy Sepulchre in Jerusalem.[28] In fact, only an arch in the vestry is an exact copy of any part of the building, and is a replica of the distinctive twelfth-century arch over the door into the 'Church of the Resurrection', as the Greeks call it. The chapel is not in Burges's usual Gothic style which is doubly puzzling because the Church of the Holy Sepulchre as it now stands is in large part in just that style.

Bute was well able to read the Greek account by Eusebius of the original buildings put up by Constantine. They were destroyed in the eleventh century by the Muslims, and new buildings were created by the Crusaders.[29] He had also visited the still standing Constantinian church at Bethlehem, and Sta Maria Maggiore in Rome. Bute was evoking a miniature, not of the church he had seen, but of the beautiful and cohesive original built by Constantine. This is why the chapel has a pillared colonnade running down the side of the tiny nave, whose columns (copied from many different capitals of the Crusader church) support flat Constantinian architraves and its coffered ceiling takes the form it does. Ornamented and coffered ceilings are typical of Burges, but his coffers are usually square, or rectilinear. The ceiling in this chapel is of narrow straight coffers, moulded and gilded, like sunlight on water, a regular up-and-down like stylised waves. They recreate the ceiling Eusebius describes as 'carved and coffered', stretching 'over the whole basilica like a great sea'. Burges echoed the angular shape of the outer roof of Constantinian basilica churches, rather than inserting a lower flat ceiling, probably to give a greater sense of space in this tiny building.

It is not, of course, a model of Holy Sepulchre. Burges had to work within the given confines of a guest bedroom. The double colonnade which divided the nave from the aisles of the original church[30] has become a single row. The number and size of the pillars is inevitably drastically reduced. The nave is relatively broader and the aisles narrower in order to accommodate worshippers. The walls are not marbled; instead they are a restrained and tasteful natural wood with simple Romanesque arches carved upon them.

Although the point is evocation, not recreation, many features of the first Holy Sepulchre have been imitated. The metal pillars have been painted to look like the 'polychrome marble' of Eusebius's description. The almost square space (some 5.10m by 5.30m) is very like the proportions of all Constantine's basilica churches.[31] The symbols in the chapel help identify it. On the altar, and at the point of the arch above it, there is set what today is called the 'Jerusalem Cross' but is actually the 'Cross of the Holy Sepulchre'.[32] Under the altar is a map of the Holy Land. It is split into three sections, and centres on Jerusalem. A mother-of-pearl model of the Church of the Holy Sepulchre stood there whilst Bute was alive: the heart of the heart.

The altar is placed on the longest axis, on the north wall. It is made of cast metal, with pillars, so that one can easily see under it to where there is an arrangement of pressed, dried flowers, now bleached white with age, carefully labelled as 'flowers from the Garden of Gethsemane'. Above them is carved a relief of Christ's agony in that same garden, with an inscription that tells that the stone for the carving came from the Chapel of the Agony. This at once links the Burges chapel to Bute's formative experience in the Gethsemane chapel as he recovered from an episode of depression. It marks his own agony and his own resurrection.

Now married and living at Mount Stuart, Bute continued work on the chapel. Constantine's great church was called the 'martyrium', which had a connection with those who died for their faith, but it also, as Bute knew, means that the church itself was a 'witness' – a witness to Christ's empty tomb. Bute played with the double meaning of the word. Down each of the walls of the central nave, above the colonnade, he had a procession of saints painted. They are not all 'martyrs', but they are all witnesses to the power of Christ in human lives. They walk in pairs, each with their own emblems. Lest one should miss the point, behind them are Elijah and Moses, those witnesses of the Old Testament who came to speak to and for Christ at the Transfiguration.

The saints are chosen with great care. Constantine himself is there. The Welsh and the Scots are heavily represented including St Magnus from Orkney, and St Winefred from Wales. As the inscription from the Book of Revelation makes clear, they come from every nation, every condition of life. These paintings, by Harland and Fisher, were created for this chapel, from December 1872 to August 1873. The invoice describes them as being 'from Lord Bute's design', which may just mean that somebody, perhaps Burges, designed them for Bute; but, more likely, it means that Bute designed them himself, and the firm scaled them up and painted them. Bute was a fine draughtsman.

Two years later Bute decided that he wanted Charlie Campbell (who had worked for Harland and Fischer and had executed many of Burges's designs) to add to the tympanum. He wrote the instructions to Gwen:

> what I wanted painted was a little mound, with four streams running out of it, and stags drinking thus. He had better sketch roe deer for the purpose but begin the rock first and I'll talk about the deer when I arrive.[33]

The deer are actually tin-tacked onto the mound below them. In Psalm 42 the desire of man for God is spoken of as the longing of a hart for the running streams. The psalm speaks of the procession of 'the multitude' to the house of God. Yet it also speaks of the suffering of the individual to whom 'tears have been my meat day and night'. It ends with advice to 'put thy trust in God: for I will yet thank him'. This image recapitulates the major theme of this chapel, the theme of suffering and resolution. Christ sits enthroned on the tympanum, surrounded by the apostles, whilst his mother Mary holds up her hands to intercede for mankind. As is right in such a Middle Eastern building, she is unmistakably a Jewish woman.

To make absolutely sure that the point made privately by Bute with the flowers from Gethsemane under the altar is publicly understood, he had a text put round the sanctuary: 'God will provide the sacrifice'. These are the words of Abraham to Isaac, the son he believed God was going to ask him to sacrifice. Bute, the only child of elderly parents, particularly associated himself with Isaac. But Isaac was not sacrificed. Instead, a ram was provided, and later, more profoundly, God himself was the sacrifice, upon the cross; yet his story did not end with suffering, but with rebirth. The circle is once again complete in the one building which encompasses both defeat and victory, death and resurrection. Layer after layer of meaning is built up in this chapel.

The saints to whom the chapel is dedicated are in the procession which dominates it. Not vulgarly taking pride of position, nor ignominiously in the rear, but decorously two-thirds of the way down the crocodile of 'witnesses' is Bute's name-saint, the passionate and mystical John the Evangelist. Exactly opposite him, in the procession of female saints, is the couple's other patron saint, Margaret of Scotland. There is a small mark above each, singling them out.

Small wonder they chose Margaret as a patron. Margaret was another English woman who had married a powerful Scot. Like Gwen, she was a highly independent woman with a mind of her own. She was one of comparatively few female saints who were notable as wives and mothers. When the chapel was being completed in 1875, Gwen had been married for three years. Despite the fact that her marriage had been happy and close from the start, there was still no sign of a baby for the Butes. Bute had got two relics of Margaret for Gwen, using Cardinal Manning's good offices, and a splendid reliquary had been made for them. Who better to intercede for them than an English saint and mother? Making the point that chapel had a double dedication, the end wall was stencilled with a diaper (repeating pattern) of gold motives: St John's eagle, and St Margaret's marguerite. It is not the Burges chapel, it is the chapel of St Margaret and St John, and its history is on its walls, for those with eyes to see.

In the new year of 1873, it was plain that Gwen's health was still poor. Her alarmed family had learnt she was 'very thin & pale, & had frequent fainting fits',[34] one lasting nearly two hours. They hoped that a natural explanation of this might be that Gwen was expecting a baby. On a visit to her old home she consulted the family doctor. Bute told her that

as to Dr Noble, you know, my own darling, that if you never had a child in your life, I hope it would never make any difference in my affection for you. Of course, all the same, if you have – or are even now pregnant – it wd. give me great pleasure.[35]

Gwen slipped back for a few days into her girlhood, sleeping at her own request in her 'little room' instead of the 'room of state' with 'the pink curtains that we all made such a to do about for dear B last year!'[36]

Bute was away in Cardiff while Gwen was seeing the doctor:

I do hope and trust you are taking care of yourself, and will mind and tell Dr. Noble everything. The points may be chiefly divided into 1st. Back. 2nd Legs. 3rd. Squeams. 4th. Faintness. 5th. Headache. 6th. Weariness and 7th. & 8th which latter need not be put on paper.[37]

When they had been married a little longer, both the Butes wrote openly about Gwen's irregular monthly cycle, and the heavy bleeding that accompanied it.[38]

Despite the fact that he adored Gwen, Bute could not hide from her his longing for a child. Dr Noble suggested that she should take up riding again, which he hoped would give her 'enjoyment and exhilaration without the fatigue of walking'. Gwen was an accomplished horsewoman, and her family thought she should follow the example of the Queen and ride until she was sure she was pregnant, and then resume after a gap for the first couple of months. Bute was not fond of horses or riding himself, and he hated to see Gwen take the slightest risk.[39] It was beyond him to see that she might genuinely benefit from something that would have done him no good at all.

Meanwhile, Bute was indulging in his favourite hobby of building, which still meant one architect: William Burges. Calling him 'soul-inspiring Burges' or 'the soul-inspiring one', was a joke between Bute and Gwen, a joke with a foundation in reality. Not only did he create his greatest triumphs of architecture for them, but his company charmed them. Bute reported time spent with him as an especial treat, almost objectively, as though he was noting a fine performance in the theatre, or a good vintage of wine. The state of Burges's temper was usually worth recording, especially the comparatively rare occasions when it was good.[40]

At Cardiff Castle, the clock tower was completed 'except for the tiles in the top room'. Seeing ideas realised which before had only existed on paper, such as the moat around the keep, was 'quite astonishing. It causes the mound to look more like a large natural hill than anything else.' Bute was full of enthusiasm for his latest project, the creation of a proper Great Hall: 'The effect of the lowered floor between my room and the hall is hardly perceptible below, but so very good above that I think of having the dining room immediately treated likewise. This will give some idea of the effect of a restored Great Hall above, and only necessitate a partial change in the pictures below.' Gwen was working embroideries for the project: 'I saw the coloured drawing for your work – it really is quite charming.'[41]

Burges was not only axiomatically inspirational, clever and endlessly creative; he was also something of an autocrat and decidedly impractical. Bute, growing more confident, prepared to tussle with his architect: 'I think hardly anything can be done till a few new rooms are added, wh. in my opinion they may easily be, towards the water tank – when Burges comes I shall fight him at once on this point.' The new plans were extensive with new rooms for the use of servants over the kitchen, and a bedroom for himself above his sitting room, a library in what had been the dining room, and the exciting Great Hall 'blossoming' into being.[42]

Bute travelled on to his friend Addle's wedding. He could be relied upon to send Gwen a full description of the dresses of other women. Young and very much in love, Bute also took great pleasure in advising his wife on her dress and especially her jewels:

> I have been thinking that if the diamond stomacher is too gorgeous, you can put my ruby-and-diamond cross of the H. Sepulchre on yr. breast with three diamond stars in yr. ears and two on your head – with the Cardiff bracelet like a tiara, between your hair and yr. chignon.[43]

He loved to create suitable backdrops for her, as she told her sister:

> I am going to have my sitting room redecorated. Bute says it must be done with yellow to suit my complexion – not that I should have thought is worth while suiting, however.[44]

Gwen's father fretted, although he knew that Bute would 'love & protect'[45] her. Now she was married, Lord Howard had 'no business to advise'[46] her, which did not, of course, stop him doing it. Sending her back to Bute after her holiday in Glossop, he put her (and presumably her maid) on the train. Because she was travelling without a male escort, for the first time in his life he tipped a guard, asking him to keep an eye on her. He pondered on the morality of it: 'I do not grudge the poor people, but I do think, like other bad habits, it is now an acknowledged thing – & if it profits darlings like you ... it's not far wrong.'[47] Neither of the Butes indulged in grand behaviour, and the pretensions of others made them laugh. Gwen told Angela that they had gone to a wedding where Lord and Lady Stafford had their footman who carried all their belongings, including their prayer book, but the Staffords 'didn't get served first, as they thought they should ... In short their what Bute called "swagger" was odious.'[48] In contrast, the Butes carried their own waterproofs, umbrella and prayer book.

Meanwhile Bute was about to use his immense knowledge of mediaeval architecture in an attempt to save an ancient building which he had loved since childhood. Paisley Abbey was one of the oldest of Scottish religious buildings still in use, and a tomb there had long been described as that of Marjory Bruce, who, through her marriage to Walter Fitzalan, commonly known as the Steward or Stewart, had founded the royal Stuart dynasty, giving Bute a family attachment to the building.

Paisley had prospered through the development of the textile industry, and now there were plans to improve the cramped and insalubrious streets by widening them and building sewers. These plans also included demolishing part of the Abbey. This portion, to some Victorian eyes, sat at an infelicitous angle to the main building, and was an indubitable inconvenience to the proposed new street plan. The town's historian, Mr David Semple, assured everybody that it was a modern addition to the Abbey, put there by the Earls of Dundonald 'in the beginning of the eighteenth century'.[49] Semple passionately advocated the demolition of this part of the Abbey, wishing the building to stand out unencumbered by its curtilage, dominating the surrounding area.

Bute was horrified. He believed that the area in question included the ancient cloister of the Abbey. He employed the Scottish architectural firm of Bryce, Anderson and Bryce to prepare a report on the 'Abbey Close'. The job fell to Robert Rowand Anderson,[50] who concluded that the work was of different periods, but that the oldest part was actually older than any other part of the Abbey. He suggested an alternative route for the new street, which would avoid demolition. Changing the plans would be expensive, not least because houses had already been purchased for demolition. In the summer of 1873, Bute offered £1,000 towards the increased costs if the Abbey Close was saved[51] and, to his credit, the Provost of Paisley offered a further £500. Semple continued to assert that the building was modern, and his assurances were accepted. Work started in January 1874. By February, the local paper was reporting, smugly, that 'in a few days more the effect of the improvement there will be fully seen and cannot fail to be appreciated'.[52] However there was also growing consternation, and objections were on the increase; the improvers dealt with this in time-honoured fashion. Lord Blantyre, one of the feuders, had objected to the removal of the wall of the burial ground. He awoke to find it had been taken down illegally in the night.[53] Apparently, Semple could hear voices that others involved in the struggle could not. He wrote that he asked the 'arching' in the rest of the Abbey if the arch revealed as the cloister was demolished was genuine, and heard the Abbey cry out 'a resounding "No!"'[54] The voices so clearly heard by him were dumb before everyone else. A furious correspondent to the paper delivered what was to be the judgement of history:

A single glance will convince anyone that the row of arched buildings forming the side of the cloister court which is now in course of demolition are ... part of the Abbey Church properly ... and which the Duke of Abercorn could no more sell or make merchandise of, than he could sell the transept of the choir ... or the Abbey itself.[55]

The Duke of Abercorn owned part of the cloister, and received £500 for something of no personal use to him. One can only wonder what Bute made of the involvement of the man who might have been his father-in-law. Nothing Bute could do was able to save the oldest part of Paisley Abbey from being demolished.

Bute's concern to save the Abbey Court was most certainly not born out of a desire to cross Abercorn; it was a part of his dislike of the wreck of old and beautiful things, and his unwillingness to subject them to the Victorian urge to tidy up. Throughout his life Bute continued to be saddened by the prevailing habit of turning buildings into a uniform Gothic style, including a Yorkshire church 'being ruined, as most of them have already been, by what is playfully called "restoration". There is a rather good Georgian ceiling in plaster work with a curious bas-relief of an angel wh. is, it appears, to be destroyed.'[56]

Nor was it religious buildings alone, or even especially, that he desired to protect. He had learnt from his experience at Paisley that a secular building, or a building partly in secular use such as the Abbey Court, was especially vulnerable.

While I applaud the zeal of persons who investigate churches, I myself tend to take at least equal interest in domestic and secular buildings which are also much more likely (as at Paisley) to be destroyed, and might suggest as curious the castles in little Cumbrae and in the south of Arran (don't know the name of this last which is said to have once belonged to my family) and the defensible farmhouse at Wester Kames[57] & the remains of a similar one at a farm somewhere on the West side of the Island[58] – and specially the table in Brodick Castle at wh. Robt. Bruce is said to have eaten.[59]

Conservation was, however, only one side of Bute's love of architecture. As well as rebuilding Cardiff Castle, he was also working on the Georgian Mount Stuart. With work well under way on the chapel, he moved on to the dining room, for which vines and 'oak for festoons on frieze etc.'[60] were drawn from nature. Bute engaged two of Burges's top craftsmen to work on this project. These vine leaves and heads of grapes were carved by Thomas Nicholls[61] and painted by Campbell, Smith & Co. In all there were fifty-eight panels for the ceiling 'including 100 swallows, painted raised vine leaves & about 100 bunches of grapes to imitate nature'. The drawing room was lavishly decorated with 'birds, squirrels and butterflies',[62] which were always Bute's favourite decorative themes. In addition, Nicholls created the originals for a 'horse and stag ... finishing same for casting in bronze for fire dogs'.[63] Beautiful, nervous creatures, with all the flightiness of the live animals, they still grace the family's firesides.

Bute was far from being the only aristocratic builder of the period. The Duke of Sutherland virtually rebuilt three of his houses, giving Sir Charles Barry a handsome run of commissions. The Marquess of Westminster remodelled Eaton Hall, as did the Duke of Northumberland Alnwick Castle. Projects like these could cost £400,000, and 'displayed the taste and the modernity of the noble builders'.[64] Nothing about Bute suggests he had much taste for personal grandeur; it was the pleasure of working on the designing and building of his projects that impelled him. He once famously remarked that he had 'comparatively little interest in a thing after it is finished'.[65] He was deeply and personally involved in all his projects; Burges was more of a collaborator than an employee. Lesser crafts-people awaited Bute's visits, ideas and judgements with a mixture of pleasure and trepidation.[66] He was also extremely price-conscious.[67]

A childhood taste Bute also indulged was a delight in animals, and he made a small collection of favourite species. There were beavers, first at Cardiff; and soon the original pair were joined by two 'wretched little things – I suppose young ones out of a nest ... One dare not put them with the old ones, who have been in a horrible temper ever since the new ones were put in sight of them.'[68] There were also beavers at Mount Stuart.[69] Gwen hit on the perfect present to give to Bute, in return for those he was so easily able to shower on her: 'kangaroos' (actually large wallabies) went to Mount Stuart. They arrived whilst she was away:

> to begin with, Ma'am, I must wait till Tuesday to thank you anything like sufficiently for your excellent present. The beasts have not arrived yet, but I hope they will come in an hour or two. Churchman has gone up to Glasgow to meet them.[70]

Gwen herself was not without reservations about them, as she joked to Angela:

> they are to run wild in our woods ... I shall have to give up going out. The kangaroos may be 8 feet high, they are tame creatures or at least may get so & they are very fond of jumping on top of people.[71]

It was not just wallabies and beavers that filled his grounds; there were rabbits, too. Not only did he forbid the hideous cruelty of gin traps, which were still common at this period, but within his gardens and policies, rabbits were protected. Amazed guests saw them washing their faces on the lawn before the drawing room windows. 'There are really quite a large number of plants that rabbits don't injure', Lord Bute would say when a visitor deprecated their appearance in his beautiful gardens.[72]

Bute was delighted at the progress of Cardiff Castle, but Gwen, arriving there in the autumn of 1873, was not: 'Here we are again at this ruin. I don't know when it will get the least into shape, not for 2 or 3 years I'm afraid – but it will be worth seeing when its inhabitable. We had lunch today for the 1st time in the lower room of the Tower. Dear Burges was present & quite content with his work.' Gwen drew him for her sister, a squat figure 'with his absurd glasses ... he is so short, quite tiny'.[73] Her judgement on him has become part of his biography: 'ugly Burges who designs beautiful things'.[74]

The Butes spent the whole of the winter and spring in Majorca. Socially, Bute had gained by his marriage. His range of contacts was no less. His 'men friends' came to visit as often as they had before, and in addition, he had the company of his beloved wife. Burges was happy to spend time abroad with him, and he was in touch with those at home through his letters. Gwen, however, was in a different position. She felt the lack of easy daily social contact with a wider circle. However much she enjoyed trips out behind 'our pair of mules', she missed having people to talk to. Her valiant attempts to learn Spanish from a book were not very successful. Suggestions to Bute that she ought to have a tutor fell on deaf ears.

He says what I suppose is true 'why can't you teach yourself?' – I say I don't know where to begin & then he says calmly, read the grammar through and through – he does that with his Hebrew, but I fear there is a slight difference between my husband & myself in the brain line.

So when her maid began to reminisce about a visit to Glossop, Gwen became upset. 'I let her talk a little of it, then I cd. not bear to think of that happy day, & I said don't talk of it to me, stop. The servants hate this place you know.' It was another way of saying that Gwen herself was feeling isolated. But she admitted to her sister that 'I am looking at things in rather what Bute calls the tragedy light. The fact is he always looks at things in the comic light & I get sometimes tired of it. However he's wiser after all.'[75] Perhaps he was, for when Angela herself came to marry, and Gwen wrote her a letter of sisterly advice, she thought it impossible that her sister would be quite as happy as herself. However, Gwen was alive to the real difficulties and strange demands that might face a young Victorian bride, and lest her sister enter on marriage unprepared, she told her a story to illustrate possible problems ahead.

Whilst living on the Isle of Bute, and visiting her tenantry, she had seen a baby just a few weeks old in a cottage. It was delicate, and the parents told her 'in a careless way' that because of this they had not taken it to church to be baptised. As a good Catholic, Gwen was naturally horrified, since she believed they were putting the baby's eternal welfare at risk. She made the couple promise to have it baptised, but although she visited them twice after this, they still did not act. She told her husband

> and now my little difficulties arose because he told me to go the next day to the Minister or his wife and tell them about the child and not come away without in some way getting it baptised either take the child to him or he to it or else if they being Presbyterians could not do it without preparation I was to go in the meantime and baptise it myself, had all this been to a priest about a child who was to be a 'cat' it wd. have been easy enough – but to a great fat minister, about one of his own kirk it was difficult as you may imagine.

Poor Gwen was trapped between two different churches, for the Presbyterians put a different emphasis on baptism, and would not have considered it valid if administered by a woman. She knew she would be thought very strange for this incident. Bute, typically, did not heed the usual social conventions which would have left the baby unbaptised (and Gwen unembarrassed). It was this kind of incident that exemplified to her the downside of marriage. The story, however, ended well. 'I went and made it all quite clear & satisfactory and it seemed to come so easily when I did it all because Bute wished it done and had told me to do it.'[76]

The conventions of the day did not allow Gwen to write to her unmarried sister about what lay behind her seeing life in 'the tragedy light'. Although Gwen was well again and the couple had now been married two years, there was no sign of a baby. As if childlessness was not enough, 'iniquitous calumnies'[77] began to spread that this was due to a failure in the relationship between Bute and Gwen. Presumably Bute's reputation for eccentricity, and the fact the young couple did not much appear in London society, made them an easy target for such gossip.

In 1874, two events reminded Bute that he might well die young, and childless. At the end of January Edith Hastings died of the Bright's disease which had plagued her for years, and Bute was much saddened. He had known her since the age of nine, and her children were nearly enough his age for them to be his friends. Then in June, whilst he and Gwen were cruising on their yacht, a steamer suddenly altered course, ignoring the rule that steam should give way to sail, and ran the yacht 'so close that the steamer carried away a portion of the rigging of the *Lady Bird*'.[78] As his friend Addle wrote to him: 'It must have been a very narrow shave.'[79] Bute wrote to his father-in-law Lord Howard to make arrangements for what would happen in the event of his early death. Lord Howard, despite his own childless second marriage, remained resolutely optimistic:

> I trust and hope, most sincerely, that the contingency alluded to, will never occur. Yourself and Gwendolen, will, I fervently hope, live long and that Providence will bless you with a family ... I much regret that Mr Boyle has done some ill judged, or perhaps, hasty thing. I do hope you will not stand to lose £35,000.[80]

Bute stood to lose a great deal more than that. The Cardiff estate was still run by trustees, as it had been in Bute's minority. One of these was John Boyle, the other, less active, William Stuart. Davies records of this period that

> Boyle remained dock manager and chief trustee, his salary rising to £2000 a year after 1868, and under him the agents of the various departments continued to operate. A marked feature of the 1870s was the increasing prominence of the mineral agent, W. T. Lewis, who in that decade became an industrialist and a public figure in his own right.

Although consideration had been given to winding up the trust and allowing Bute to run things himself, the legal position was not clear, and Bute did not have his father's interest in business. The Glamorgan estates, too, had grown so much that, as Davies points out, it would have been hard for any one person to control them.[81] John Boyle had a policy of expanding the docks, and he overspent very considerably. Bute began to perceive that all was not well in the autumn of 1874, but the full storm broke in the early spring of 1875. The increasing amount of coal being exported from south Wales created a demand for larger docks at Cardiff.

> With the commencement of the Roath Basin in 1868, annual expenditure soared to around £150,000 and on its completion in 1874 the Bute investment in dock construction had reached £2,285,000. In that year, when £133,000 was spent on new works and a further £29,000 on loan interest, the Glamorgan estate produced a net income of £114,000. Further loans were therefore obtained, the rise in interest paid suggesting borrowings in the region of £475,000 between 1868 and 1874. In 1874, when net dock receipts stood at £62,618, the return on investment was 2.7 per cent, while rates of up to 4.5 per cent were being paid on money raised to finance dock construction.[82]

Boyle had borrowed heavily to find the capital to build the new dock and the income from the dock did not cover the loans taken out. Hardly surprisingly, the banks became alarmed.

Bute went down to Cardiff, leaving Gwen at Mount Stuart with Edith's daughter, Flora. She had been staying with them a great deal since their return to Britain, and she was not in good health. Gwen, who loved acting and reading aloud, spent much of her time entertaining Flora, who was often confined to bed.[83] Bute's regular letters to Gwen are the only record of the crisis. 'Affairs are, I must say, looking as black as night – and, if we can still cash up to the butcher and bakers, we can't to other tradesmen employed by McConnochie.'[84] McConnochie was the dock engineer.[85] However Bute was still optimistic:

> John Boyle has been with us nearly all day. He is in good spirits enough now, quite jesting. I can't help hoping we may raise the wind by selling some of McConnochie's plant which cost £70,000.[86]

This optimism was not to last. In early March, it became clear to Bute that he was in the middle of what he hated above all things: a crisis.

> My own darling wife –
> John Boyle and McConnochie have just gone, and the result of their interview with me makes me feel just as if somebody had knocked me on the head – I hardly know what to say or do.

Bute believed his property was much more valuable than the mortgage owing on it, so even if the banks foreclosed the end would not be

<u>Bankruptcy</u> – but that is the word, and the fact perhaps, that is to be faced ... We have at least however, among other mercies, so undeserved by me, to thank God for our affection one to the other, which will always remain, remain to us amid any hardships. It is also well for us that the tastes we have – at least as regards pursuits – will be able to be moderately indulged, being inexpensive.[87]

The situation gradually worsened. Boyle went to London to try and borrow further money. The financial position was so tight the workmen labouring at the dock would have to be paid off if the money was not forthcoming. The question was how far Bute money was distinct from Trust money. Since the docks were run by the trustees were they liable for the losses? Was Bute personally liable? Bute himself blamed Boyle wholeheartedly: '. . . the horrible crisis seems to require my presence to keep some watch on matters, such as John Boyle'.[88] Bute summed the situation up in his own clear and dramatic words. He had his mother's disastrous gift for outspokenness.

Telegram from John Boyle, indicating what a letter more fully tells this morning – viz. – that he cannot borrow any more money, and they demand some security for what they have lent already – I had a conversation with Shirley[89] last night who says in effect

1/ No security exists to be given.
2/ My Scotch property, and the Castle cannot be seized for the debts of the Trust.
3/ John Boyle and William Stuart are the persons open to the legal proceedings of the Creditors and as
4/ Everything that can be pawned is pawned already
5/ The creditors will have nothing to seize and can only, if so disposed,
6/ Put John Boyle in prison!!!

I have telegraphed to Pitman to come here if he can on Saturday night.[90]

Frederick Pitman had been Bute's man of business and lawyer since his minority, and he trusted him fully.[91] That Bute had to attempt to reassure Gwen in his next letter is not surprising: 'I think from your letter received yesterday that you are more alarmed than the state of things absolutely required.'

Bute thought that he would receive no more money from the Cardiff estate for the time being. He did not think the trustees would be made personally bankrupt, but there would be 'a most infernal row, scandal and uproar' and he and Gwen would need to live for some time on the income from the Scottish estates and other non-Trust properties.

> I suppose we shall have to retrench very unpleasantly and the works on the house here will have to stop. That the Trustees will in the long run be able to pay their debts I think there can be no doubt – but the policy in general which Mr. Boyle has for years so disastrously pursued will smash, and become for ever (almost without doubt) impossible.[92]

This was in fact the blackest point. Bute was terribly dismayed at the prospect of rows. He was not all that dismayed by the prospect of being much poorer. Though he very much regretted having to cut back work on the Castle, he was sanguine about the 'retrenchment' in his private life.

In mid-March 1875, things were beginning to look a little better. The trustees succeeded in borrowing £100,000 from 'the Equitable' on the grounds that the mortgaged property was worth a good deal more than the sums already lent on it. The income from the Glamorgan Estate might not exceed the expenditure, but the capital value of the whole area in Bute hands far exceeded the debt John Boyle had incurred on Bute's behalf. Bute proposed to pay the bank half of the borrowed money, and persuaded them that the estate was property-rich. He hoped (correctly) that they would then refrain from issuing a writ for John Boyle's property and that the weekly income would cover the wages of dock workers, and that the other £50,000 would enable other tradespeople to be paid something on account, until things improved.[93] Typically, he asked for arrangements for Passiontide at Mount Stuart: 'Please see that the Chapel is veiled by next Saturday evening. You had better use a dead greyish purple – say, the unglazed side of purple calico.'[94]

It has been considered a mystery that Bute did not carry forward the work on Cardiff faster. Mordaunt Crook remarks on the proposed and nearly-completed stables,[95] that Bute did not care for horses. Bute's once-made, off-the-cuff remark that he took his chief pleasure in building and that he was not interested in a project when it was once finished has been quoted and re-quoted to try and explain why he denied himself precisely the pleasure of seeing work in good and vigorous progress, and plans coming into fulfilment. In fact what caused some projects to be abandoned, and others to be scaled down, was this crisis: 'Burges is here, and we hope to reduce all expenses to about £25pw.'[96]

There was another project shared between Bute and Burges that was perhaps even dearer to Bute's heart. In 1872 Burges had prepared one of his meticulous reports on Castell Coch, a wholly ruinous castle five miles outside Cardiff. The plan was to recreate some of its original features, such as the portcullis, whilst making a simple retreat with bedrooms for the family, a dining room, sitting room, and minimal kitchen and servants' quarters. Bute had been abroad, Burges busy with Cardiff. For whatever reason, work had not started in the spring of 1875. Before the full force of the storm broke, Bute took his former guardian, Sir James Fergusson, to see the site, and was utterly astonished at his lack of interest.

> I walked with Sir James to Castell Coch on Saturday. I don't think he either knew or cared a bit about it, being on the contrary entirely absorbed by the fear of getting a chill from being in the open air.[97]

So much for the image of the tough sportsman Fergusson and the soft townie Bute.

As well as rebuilding the castle, Bute was planting a vineyard on the sunny south-facing slopes below it. The project of rebuilding Castell Coch was a pleasure he could not bring himself to abandon, and he intended to lease it from the trustees, and continue work on it from his own pocket. That it was Bute's own particular pet project perhaps explains its perfection. That he carried on building it in his circumstances tells one a lot about Bute. He warned Gwen:

> I think that our income will be reduced for 5 or 6 years to about £15,000 a year. This will of course make it necessary to reduce our expenditure to something under £10,000.[98] Compared to other people of our own rank we shall be very poor. I think that the time for making our retrenchments will be when we leave Mt. Stuart after Easter ... I think also that we shall have to consider, no longer as a joke, the idea of living abroad, at any rate for some very considerable time ... rather than to live in a corner at some place of our own with 3 or 4 maidservants and nothing of a stable to speak of, and a continual wretched struggle to keep up appearances.

Despite his anger at the way he felt others had got him into this trouble, he had come to a 'sort of agreement between myself and the Trustees'. It is difficult to be absolutely sure of the income from the Scottish estates at this time, but during the custody battle more than ten years before, it was estimated at £17,000. The English (as opposed to the Welsh) lands, which included some mines in County Durham, must also have brought in some revenue. Bute was not drawing at all from the Welsh estates, and it looks as though he was paying out of his pocket to keep the Trust afloat. Of course, in comparison to the great majority, he was still a very rich man, and John Boyle was drawing a salary of only £2,000. As he admitted, it was only by the standards of the wealthy nobility that he had suddenly become poor, and as he reassured Gwen 'this need not, I hope, last many years'.

Perhaps guilt is too strong a word for the way Bute felt about his wealth. The word he had chosen to describe his responsibilities when he came of age was 'burden'. He was all too aware of being privileged, and privilege in the face of want is an uncomfortable position. Bute spoke of his hopes to Gwen, words belonging to the deepest and most private places of their relationship, and only overheard because, being over three hundred miles apart, they were confided to a letter.

> One is always dissatisfied with the particular cross that God chooses to lay on one, and I am sure both of us have prayed very much to have another one than the one we have hitherto had – One cannot speculate on the hidden counsel of the Divine Will, but I cannot help indulging the first glimmers of a hope that if this new cross is to be laid a little grievously on us, the lightening of the present one may perhaps be contemplated by Our Father who is in Heaven. Come or come not what may, or may never be, I am always, my dearest Gwen, your affectionate husband.[99]

Bute returned to Mount Stuart for Holy Week and Easter, which was in March that year, and they then left for Angela's wedding to Marmaduke Constable-Maxwell.[100]

The Butes did not go abroad. By the time they returned to the Isle of Bute on 5 June, Gwen was looking fragile.[101] She was plainly not fit to travel. The cross had indeed been lightened: Gwen was expecting a baby. Because of her pregnancy, they spent that summer in Britain after all. Living quietly in the Scottish countryside at Mount Stuart was comparatively inexpensive, and it was a peaceful and healthy place for an expectant mother.

They continued to welcome visitors. Lady Edith's death had made a serious gap in Bute's extended family. Edith had never been a Catholic, nor had Charley but Edith's daughter Flora had been attracted to Catholicism for some years, and Bute had thought it 'certain'[102] she would convert, which she did in the summer of 1875. Her father had been considered to be a very difficult man since the early days of

Edith's marriage.[103] No longer having a wife, he embarked on making his daughter's life miserable. His tactics included reducing her food to starvation point. She was twenty-two, and her brother, now Lord Loudoun, a year younger. She endured her treatment with 'admirable patience, being reinforced and supported by the remarkable kindness of her brother . . . Norfolk has been kindness itself to her, and so, too, have others.'[104] The irony was that Flora's father came from a Catholic family, and was to convert to Catholicism himself a few years later.

Bute made occasional necessary visits to Cardiff. As well as business, he was heavily involved in ecclesiastical matters. There were problems over which religious orders should be active in the Cardiff area, about which Bute was frequently consulted. He had a particular dislike of the Italian Rosminians,[105] because he thought 'they want to make this whole great town and mission with its thousands of Catholics a sort of "garden enclosed" for their own order'.[106] He was also promoting monasticism in Scotland. He wanted to see Benedictines established there, and had 'engaged . . . to support certain subjects at St Michael's Hereford [the abbey at Belmont] to be employed in Scotland in due course after their promotion to the priesthood, and eventually to found a monastery'.[107] He also bitterly criticised Charles Eyre,[108] in charge of the Western District of the Catholic Church, over his lightening of the rules of the Lenten Fast. Eyre explained kindly that, 'the fact that nearly all of our people are of the poorer and working classes . . . who cannot do their work on an abstinence diet'[109] had led him to take this step. In addition he had taken account of the especially unkind climate of Scotland, where Lent is usually in the harshest part of the winter. Bute was quite unappeased. He did not grasp how hard life was for poor Catholics, although he entrusted monies to help the really deserving to priests or nuns working with them.[110] A priest was to remonstrate: 'I try to help only the really deserving tho' I am afraid that if God were to serve some of us so, we should be very badly off.'[111]

Later when he was invited to take part in 'some tribute of respect to his Grace Archbishop Eyre', Bute refused to contribute. Despite his respect for him as the representative of the Pope, despite his unremitting attention to his 'difficult position', and despite Eyre's 'personal goodness and kindness . . . his personal piety and self denial', nonetheless, Bute concluded that 'the unprovoked attack made within the last few years upon the observance of Lent in Scotland must (as I think) have inflicted . . . upon all the Catholics and probably all others in Scotland, injuries whose full extent is known to God alone'.[112] Scotland had been deprived of 'a vast means of grace'. This was in another unposted letter. Bute annotated it himself 'not sent, as I saw the people'.

By the end of August, it was generally known that Lady Bute was expecting her first child. It was the convention that matters such as pregnancy should not be spoken of before the unmarried. Bute was more than somewhat amused by the reaction of the nuns at Pen-y-lan:

> All the nuns began at once with one voice to say how glad they were at the condition you were in &c. &c. &c. I really think they were not as shy of the subject, and apparently knew as much about it as the old bags themselves.[113]

The nuns, of course, ran a refuge for 'fallen women'. The monks at Belmont were a little more reserved: 'Fr. Jerome's compliments: & that they are leaving St Benedict no peace in yr. regard.'[114] It was clear that the worst of the financial crisis was over: 'They have got together some £85,000 wh. is to be applied mainly to the payment of debts.'[115]

Bute also worked on the history of William Wallace that summer. Scottish independence, especially the doomed figure of Wallace, was one of his passions. He combined it with his Toryism, by simply declaring that the issue was above politics. The work started with Blind Harry,[116] the poet who provides Wallace's history in much the way Homer does the Trojan Wars. As Bute explained, Blind Harry wrote about 150 years after Wallace's death. However, Blind Harry had allegedly based his tales on a work in Latin prose by Rev. John Blair, 'a personal friend of the hero'.[117] It was likely that somebody else had translated this Latin into Scots first, adding to the possibility of error. Bute turned the somewhat allusive original back into a plain English prose version, adding his own notes on obscure passages.

He moved on to a recreation of the childhood of Wallace for a lecture he was to give in Paisley that autumn. It reveals his approach to history. He admitted that there was too little material on the actual life of the hero. Yet, 'if we look upon the scene into which the hero must have been born, and the things which must have surrounded his childhood, the matter becomes superabundant'. They might look at political history, or discover from archaeology what kind of house the hero would have lived in, and 'An essay, or a series of essays might be written on the games of his childhood.'[118]

From this admirable blend of documentary history and archaeology, Bute recreated a vivid picture of the early years of a moderately well-born boy living near Paisley in the thirteenth century. He evoked the image of a simple tower house surrounded by a huddle of lesser buildings, all with painted walls.[119] Bute imagined that the house was probably stone, which today seems less likely. In fact, very little is known of the housing of the gentry of this period, and the picture Bute created is probably truer of buildings one or two centuries later. But he was using the very best research of his own day, and using it creatively. When he came to consider the garden, he turned to evidence from illuminated manuscripts and early poems to create the image of a tiny gem of flower-scattered grass without formal beds, an image which holds true today.

As for religion, Bute was well aware that he, an adherent of the old faith, had the advantage, and he enjoyed gently teasing his listeners. He spoke to a Scottish Presbyterian audience of Wallace's devotion to the psalms, and this at a time when the singing of metrical psalms was still the principal form of praise in a Presbyterian service. He told them that the Wallace family would have had

> one or more of the [manuscript] Psalm books which may now be seen in museums and which are sometimes stupidly and ignorantly called Missals, though they are much more like to the Psalm-book of the Church of Scotland than to the Missal or Mass-book.[120]

He reminded them that the dying Wallace had had a Psalter held up before his eyes. He spoke of worship for the majority of the population, who could not read and 'the forms of prayerful meditation on the gospel history called the Rosary'.[121] It is perfectly correct to speak of the Rosary as an aid to meditating on the Bible, and it is perfectly certain that this aspect of the Rosary had never crossed the minds of his Presbyterian audience before.

Bute became serious again as he described the demolition of those parts of Paisley Abbey which were certainly old enough to have been seen by Wallace, recalling his great battle to save them. He ended his lecture with a reflection on his own line, and that of the Wallaces. He had started his lecture by explaining that the name Wallace is derived from 'Welsh'; the Wallaces were a Welsh family in their origins.

> The Stuarts ... belonged essentially to the conquering Norman race ... not so the Wallaces, ... the savage injustice and cruelty of the Plantagenet conquest of Wales ... must have struck them with peculiar horror and indignation ... The Wallaces had found shelter from English bondage in Scotland ... when they found [they were liable to come under English masters there as well] they determined to resist for themselves to the uttermost of their power.[122]

The English were tyrants, and the Stuarts were, in origin, English. This lecture is perhaps the most perfect of all Bute's scholarly works. It played entirely to his strengths and his passions: literature, social history, noble inspirations. Above all, it was centred where he was strongest, not in hard fact but intuition and allusion.

Bute might have been happier if he had spent more time in historical research and writing, for ecclesiastical matters often drove him to fury. Plans to re-establish monasticism in Scotland were not going smoothly. The Rt Rev. Abbot Richard Burchall,[123] the powerful, long-serving President-General of the Anglo-Benedictine congregation, and the only English mitred Abbot, was in charge of the project, and Bute did not find him at all sympathetic. Burchall failed to attend prearranged meetings, and refused to listen to Bute's advice.

> As there is no feeling or opinion of mine touching this matter wh. has not now been disregarded I naturally feel a reluctance to meddle with it any more than I can help in future ... I am weary of saying that if the monastery is started at Lanark or any parallel place two results will as I believe certainly ensue.
>
> 1) a collision with the secular clergy, the full misery of which cannot be gauged and
> 2) The failure of the school and probably of the monastery.[124]

The Abbot's reply was more than a little condescending, and he missed the point that Bute was arguing for a site where monks would not come into conflict with parish clergy, and blithely assumed Bute wanted a site to which he had a sentimental attachment:

> I presume that you consider the vicinity of the ancient churchyard of Loudon an eligible site, and that your Lordship has a preference for it ... as I have not a Bradshaw to hand, I shall feel obliged if your Lordship will kindly inform me what is the best way of getting to the spot in question from Carlisle.[125]

Bradshaw listed the departure times of every train in the United Kingdom, then nearly at the height of the railway boom. Bute was incensed:

> I must take this opportunity formally to protest & disclaim any kind of responsibility for such a decision or any consequence wh. may or may not ensue. To know the pages of Bradshaw by heart is not an acquirement of mine, & I cannot understand why you should

imagine me able to prognosticate the contents of his issue for the month of November.[126]

After that, no doubt Fr Burchall realised that he had lost his patron's confidence and respect. In some ways, it was an untypical outburst. Bute's natural ability with words and his inherited forthrightness could make him extremely cutting, but it was an ability he normally restrained. Many letters, originally written with all too telling invective, were later corrected and much toned down before being sent. He was not of a quarrelsome disposition, and he frequently mollified his much more pugnacious wife. Perhaps the natural anxiety of a prospective father was irritating Bute's temper, for Gwen was now in the last month of her pregnancy.

Bute was to remember his wife in a

cheery condition, swollen to a preposterous size, with a large child jumping about inside, and a gentle flutter of monthlies [midwives], pill boxes [doctors], nurses, tradespeople and sympathising friends.[127]

They prepared carefully for the occasion. Bute asked for an especial cross from the convent at Taunton, which Gwen's mother had held in childbirth, and there were blessed candles to burn. Gwen was not afraid.[128] Dr Noble, from her family home at Glossop, came as her *accoucheur*.[129] Did the couple predetermine that Bute should stay at his wife's side for his child's birth, or was the decision made spontaneously because she naturally clung to him for support during her labour? The baby was a breech presentation, and Gwen was a small woman. Either way, the fact that Bute was there[130] shows their intimacy and how little Bute was interested in conventional male roles.[131]

In the early hours of Christmas Eve, Gwen was safely delivered of a daughter, Margaret, who was christened that evening in the little Burges chapel, packed full with local friends, notables and farmers. Bute had especially asked for the family gamekeeper, Wilson, to be present. This was the same 'Jack Wilson . . . [who] knocked a writ-server down the stairs of a Rothesay hotel'[132] and had accompanied Bute on his flight with Lady Elizabeth. Bute made sure the local paper recorded that Wilson's 'presence greatly gratified his Lordship'. In the hierarchy-ridden world of a Scottish island, and the even more hierarchy-ridden world of Bute servants, the note in *The Buteman*, which neatly and wittily inverted their social importance, must have meant much. To the best of his abilities, Bute paid his debts.

Mgr. Capel sent Bute a little note of congratulation on 'the happy events of today. God has indeed blessed you.'[133] One might think the formality of the note a little strange from the chaplain who had baptised the new baby. But the relationship between Bute and Capel was already strained to the uttermost. Bute had found out that Capel was cheating him. At the beginning of 1878, when he feared that Capel might be made a Scottish Bishop, Bute wrote in French to Cardinal Franchi, Prefect of the Congregation of the Sacred Propaganda in Rome.[134] Bute explained how much of his social position Capel owed to Bute, and that he had enabled Capel to get the position which had earned him the title of 'Monsignor'. Bute had used Capel as his chaplain and almoner.

> He had 7,500fr. (£300) [Bute's figures] for very little trouble, since I only rarely made him work as Chaplain. He had a further 7,500 per annum to distribute among some of the poor who sent me begging letters.
> After some years, never finding a single pauper who has received alms at his hands, I began to have some suspicions. Specially (for example) I had asked him particularly to give £50 (1,250fr) to the Pères Servites of London. Nobody ever saw the money.

Bute asked him to account for the money given him for charity, and Capel promised to give an account but never did. Bute felt obliged to end 'the previous arrangements'.

> Your Eminence, no one but my wife, my secretary and one of my agents knows up to now what I dare to write to you. I find myself driven by duty to His Eminence, to my country and to the Holy Apostolic See, to write what I have just written. It is to be taken as a personal confidence.

So far the letter is restrained, painful, careful. This fraud showed Bute as a credulous dupe who could not expect to be valued for himself. Once more he could say 'I can trust nobody'. No wonder Bute had found difficulty in writing this part of his confidence.

By contrast, in the last section, he wields his knife with panache. The pain is less personal, and Bute is free to attack with some pleasure.

> I shall not add a word, except to say that I have heard things said by Mgr. Capel that in my personal opinion, cannot be reconciled with either Catholicism or Theism itself. It is true that it was only through his ignorance of questions often enough discussed by ancient

and modern thinkers that he brought these latest idiocies to light
– but the effect would be no less scandalous for that in a sceptical
country like mine.

He has not made such a success of his school at Kensington that
the English would not probably be glad enough to be rid of him –
but let them not do so by giving him to us . . .

Yet even the discovery of Capel's very limited intellect must have been
painful. It was not Capel alone who had steered Bute into the Catholic
Church but he had been a key figure in that process. Now Bute had
found Capel to be utterly wanting in human decency and intellectual
competence, let alone Christian virtue, or Catholic teaching. The letter
is marked in Bute's own hand 'not sent'. Yet Bute carefully preserved
it; perhaps it had fulfilled its real purpose. It had given him the chance
to formulate and express his feelings.[135]

Capel was in trouble on many fronts. He had been Manning's choice
as Rector for the Catholic 'University College' at Kensington, which
was opened in 1875. The scheme was a failure. Manning was to some
degree to blame for the weakness of the pro-university's academic
side,[136] but Capel, who had not kept any accounts, was responsible
for the large sums of money which simply vanished. Manning was
too late in noticing. In addition, the college was suspected of reckless
irregularity and immorality.[137] Capel was suspended from the office of
priest in the Diocese of Westminster. In 1879, it was determined that
he should go to California. When Bute heard of it, he wrote a note
wishing him well: 'in case we should not meet before you leave, I write
to say I hope God may give you the happiness of promoting his glory.
I am about having some masses said for you.'[138]

Gwen had been right when she commented to her sister about their
only brother: 'fancy poor, dear Frank going to school at Capel's, I
don't tell Papa so, but I don't like it.'[139] Nevertheless, Bute's money
had not been spent in an attempt to make the pro-university viable.
He had severed all links with Capel before then. Money entrusted to
Capel had a habit of vanishing. He had completely betrayed the trust
put in him by a man to whom he not only owed much, but whom he,
as his confessor, knew to be particularly vulnerable. The ceiling of the
tiny chapel that Burges had constructed in Cardiff Castle out of the
dressing room where Bute's father had died is decorated with angels
holding the instruments of the passion. They all look sorrowfully at the
humanly devised instruments of torture, except for the angel holding
a picture of Judas's kiss. He veils his face; treachery is too grievous a
sight for the angels.

8   Purgatory

'I do not dare to say ... "Send me here my purgatory."'[1]

There had been little contact between Bute and the royal family, despite his wealth and status. It is tempting to speculate that the visit of Prince Leopold[2] to Mount Stuart and the Isle of Bute in 1876 was intended to bring about a rapprochement. Bute might have felt it disloyal to his mother to entertain the Queen, but her children were a different matter. The attack on Flora had been a personal one, not one by the monarchy. Bute was now a father, with his daughter to consider, and, perhaps, other children as yet unborn.

A tremendous amount of preparation went into the visit, and a whole suite of rooms in the north-east corner of Mount Stuart House were fitted up very lavishly. Space was at a premium in the house, with Bute giving up his personal sitting room for a nursery, and all pretence being abandoned that Gwen had a separate bedroom; that room now became her dressing room, and the couple had a 'family bedroom'.[3]

In the same flurry of work for the Prince's visit was included a making-over of the stairway area and 'designing & painting and gilding on the dome'.[4] Details of the decoration are lacking, but it was based on a starry sky. Bute had been enormously impressed with the glittering stars in the ceiling of the summer smoking room at Cardiff, but Burges had set them out formally, evenly spaced. The new decoration was to be a realistic depiction of the night sky, for the invoice included moneys for 'making model and getting it properly set to scale at Greenwich Observatory' as well as 'providing and fixing stars at 1/6 each made of cut glass & fixed with metal settings'. Nicholls's figures of morning, noon, evening and night from Cardiff were recreated, and the staircase was decorated with flowers representing the seasons. None of this was cheap, perhaps indicating that Bute had now largely recovered from his financial crisis, or more likely that he simply could not resist spending on his houses.

Bute took a villa near Nice for the winter of 1876 and the early spring which followed. Gwen, who did at least have her baby for company, got rather bored whilst Bute went into Nice each weekday for 'Hebrew and fencing' lessons.[5] She waited eagerly for word of her sister's first baby, which was born in January and named after her Aunt Gwendolen. In the spring, leaving Gwen in her villa, Bute went with Sneyd by a P&O steamer for his first visit to mainland Greece. 'We had a beautiful view of Capri in the evening as we left – but it was as cold as if it was night. Tiberius must have been crossed sometimes in his pleasures. He had 12 villas in it.'

Bute fell immediately and lastingly in love with Greece, and especially Athens, an Athens without pollution to stain the clear air. Set in a green, well-watered and cultivated land, it was more overlooked by hills than he had expected. It was a 'small new town' with 'some very quaint small old churches'.

> We have been all day looking at antiquities . . . – set in the midst of a lovely landscape, canonised, beautified, transfigured, vivified by the most xquisite poetry and history, they quite exceed anything at Rome. It is something like the difference between opera and the conversations in a dialogue book. The pure Greek art is totally by itself, and I shall have to go again more than once before I can fix what it is first and then try to conceive (wh. I suppose cannot be done) what it must have been. It is a dream of intellectual sensuality.[6]

He had begun to revise his harsh judgement of the Orthodox Church: 'On the whole, the state of the schismatic church is a favourable contrast to much one sees at Nice.'[7] He was deeply struck by Eleusis: 'I had not known that the place was so situated as to apply to the imagination every stimulus wh. it is possible to think of.'[8]

The Butes returned home by way of a sightseeing trip through Italy. Gwen was enchanted with Assisi, and especially the body of St Clare: 'she must have been good looking I should think. I never saw a corpse so sharp featured as she is still.'[9] Bute was in his element on journeys, sightseeing, changing his plans with a glorious sense of freedom, and reading French novels so silly that his wife could not be bothered with them. She on the other hand, was becoming increasingly impatient. It was not just that they had sent Margaret on ahead to Lago Maggiore, to wait for them in comfort and safety, and that Gwen was missing her dreadfully. Gwen wanted the usual occupations of life in Britain:

family, friends, pets, riding, amateur theatricals. Angela was going to a meeting of the extended family at Arundel, and Gwen longed to be there too. 'I envy you arriving so soon at Arundel. Bute can't imagine why I want to hurry home as he calls it, he looks forward to going back to England after being abroad as boys returning to school.'[10]

Gwen was envious of her sister's pastimes, and chafing at the restrictions that Bute's tastes placed on her.

Imagine my never once having been on horseback for five years, soon I shall be getting too old for all these youthful amusements: I don't myself see the fun of passing all one's youth abroad, though this is only for you, once I am back, tho' fond as I may be of doing what Bute likes still he can't have all the fun and I shall be careful how soon I come abroad again because after a stretch of seven months a good interval may be allowed.[11]

She soon set about satisfying her desire to ride again. That summer they intended to spend time at Cardiff, and prepared accordingly: 'We have just bought for our Victoria [carriage][12] at Cardiff a lovely pair of horses and Harris assures me that I cd. ride one of them beautifully so I shall insist upon being allowed to do so.'[13] Since a carriage horse and a lady's hack look quite different, there is something slightly comic in the image of the beautiful, tiny, and wealthy Lady Bute riding out on her driving horse, the more so as the financial crisis seems to have been largely over.

She kept up her own driving, too, having her ponies and carriage sent to Cardiff, 'as if I am to be victimised by being made to do a most prodigious amount of calling, I don't see why I shd. not do it in the way wh. pleases me most & I like driving'.[14] 'Calling' was the bane of Gwen's life, part of the social straitjacket imposed upon upper-class women which so infuriated Florence Nightingale. A 'morning call', took place in the early afternoon. One might make a call on foot, or from a carriage, but in the latter case, it was assumed one had a coachman to drive one, and a footman with one, who would walk up to the house and ring the bell. It was nowhere suggested that the lady might drive herself, and in doing so, Gwen must have raised eyebrows. If her hostess was 'in', the visitor was condemned to talk on light and harmless subjects for some fifteen minutes, after which she left. It was exquisitely boring, but necessary, as the failure to do it caused offence to the local notables, who might not realise its omission sprang not from Gwen's belief that they were below her, but from her dislike of the activity.

Bute had exempted Castell Coch from his economies, and was delighted with its progress.

> I went yesterday morning to Castell Coch with Burges. I believe it will get on fast, and that the two halls, cellar, ground floor room, kitchen & great, lesser & least bedrooms with the wall-gallery will be done by the autumn.[15]

Coch had many advantages for Bute. It was a small enough project for him to see rapid progress on it. It made a convenient focal point for one of his daily long walks, and it was in the country, away from the city, and its associated 'rows'.

In November 1877, Bute's cousin Flora married Gwen's cousin Henry, Duke of Norfolk, who had been so kind to Flora following her conversion. The Butes' wedding present to her was a pair of jewelled ivory hair brushes designed by Burges.[16] Gwen reported to Angela that the bride 'insists on having the sleeves of her chemises all lace'[17] which seemed an unpardonable extravagance to Gwen. However, she was pleased to announce that the wedding had been successful and 'Flora looked quite pretty'.[18] Flora's health continued to be poor, and not long after the wedding, she was showing signs of the dreaded Bright's disease.[19]

The Butes had intended to spend the winter at Mount Stuart. On 3 December, with the Butes still in London, Mount Stuart House caught fire, caused 'by the over-heating of a copper flue, 12 by 8 inches, leading from a furnace on the ground floor', Due to lack of space in the house, Gwen had had the former servants' bedrooms in the two wings redecorated as guest bedrooms, and moved the servants to the loft. This necessitated insulating the underside of the roof with thick felt, which had caught fire. The fire was discovered at 10 a.m.[20] There was plenty of water, but 'fire extinguishing apparatus was found to be practically useless'. The servants began moving pictures, furniture and books out of the building and were later joined by the forty men of HMS *Jackal* and by men from Rothesay, including all those in the employment of the burgh. At times it seemed the fire-fighters would win the battle but then fire got a renewed grip, and it became clear that the only possible areas to be saved were the two wings. The lawns were dug up and

> turfs were placed against the doorways of the long narrow corridors which led from the main building ... The flames reached at least 50 feet high, and all around was illuminated as clear as if it were daylight. As the flames came shooting out of the windows, the

firemen turned the hose upon them, and the water hissed upon the frames.

Most of the more valuable items were saved, but there was much damage, some of it done by 'roughs'[21] who came out from Rothesay attracted by the food and wine distributed by the maids to the workers. The two wings were indeed saved and the Burges chapel unharmed. However, the central portion of the house was a shell.

There was nothing for it but to spend Christmas at Dumfries House, which Bute loved, but Gwen disliked: 'Here it will be very dull, I find it a very depressing place, but we are hardly settled and the house tho much prettier than when you saw it last is still not as I could wish.'[22] She envied her sister a Christmas with her two children, Angela having had a second daughter, named after her mother, at the start of December. Her regrets were made more poignant as she had had an early miscarriage in November.

Moving his main Scottish home from Mount Stuart to Dumfries House focused Bute's attention on the Catholic Church in Ayrshire. He believed in keeping the religious authorities up to the mark:

> Spent a lot of time with the Abp. to whom I gave a good talking to about those two priests ... as to McGinnes [he said] he was such a scandal he had to be got rid of somewhere & so he sent him to Cumnock, out of the way![23]

Since Cumnock was Bute's home church at Dumfries House, it is hard to know whether to pity McGinnes or Bute more. Determined to celebrate Holy Week with the correct ceremonial, Bute ordered a cassock in a larger size, and served Mass at the local church. Gwen reported to Angela:

> Our services here have been a great success, Bute trots about in cassock and surplice and keeps them all going, of course if it were not for this there would be a mess as the priest knows absolutely nothing about it & has to be shown how to do everything. You or anybody else would be surprised to see how much we do &, though in a humble way, so well.[24]

There was the dilemma of the clergy in a nutshell. Bute was clearly usurping their authority, and of course the priest was liable to become Bute's chaplain in exactly the style that the hierarchy most understandably disliked.

There was a genuine problem with the clergy at this time, especially in the diocese of Galloway (which covers Dumfries House). Priests sometimes had woefully low standards, some drank to excess, and there was an unholy stramash in Irvine[25] between clergy and Bishop John McLachlan over lax standards.[26] Bute's attitude to the clergy was a reflection of the situation he and the Bishop found in the parishes.

The academic work Bute had in hand was Ayrshire-based as well. It was an attempt to untangle an episode known as 'the burning of the Barns of Ayr'. This grew out of his interest in 'Blind Harry' who is one of the sources for the incident. Bute first laid out very concisely the undisputed background to the event:

> In the winter of 1296–7, the English Government appeared to be firmly and, on the whole, peaceably established in Scotland. Early in May 1297 . . . a riot took place at Lanark. The same day William Wallace's wife was hung there . . . and that night insurrection broke out in the burning of the English quarters at Lanark.[27]
>
> Immediately after the burning of Lanark, William Wallace and his friends successfully attacked the English Justice sitting at Scone, where he had been acting with great severity.[28]

Later, at Irvine, the two armies, Scots and English, met, and the Scots cavalry being much weaker than the English, the aristocratic leaders of the Scots decided on surrender, amongst them Robert Bruce. 'William Wallace appears to have entirely dissented from the conduct of the great people at this "capitulation of Irvine", as it is called.'[29]

Bute was whole-hearted in his respect for the comparatively humbly born Wallace, while his contempt for his own ancestor, Bruce, is plainly and beautifully expressed.

> It would seem that the battle [of Falkirk] was preceded by a violent quarrel between William Wallace and the leader of what must, perhaps, be called the aristocratic party, in consequence of which Wallace retired from the army, to which he only returned when the sight of the misfortunes of his country became more than he could bear. As the shattered remains of the national army retreated over the common, Wallace had an altercation across the stream with Robert Bruce, who was fighting on the English side. Robert never again bore arms against his country.[30]

He later remarked of Robert that he 'was finally elected Guardian of the Kingdom, in which capacity he wrote a most insolent letter to the

King of England . . . and did not change sides again for quite a little while'.[31] However, Bute concluded that this event can have had nothing to do with the executions of Scots gentry in the barns at Ayr that Blind Harry records, which in turn led to the 'burning of the barns'. Bute surmised compellingly that this event took place much later, in 1306 or 1307, when the ageing King Edward had lost his accustomed patience. Bute omitted to comment on the fact the English soldiers were burned alive in their beds.

Mainly, however, *The Barns of Ayr* displays the objectivity of which Bute was so proud in his historical work. He was not remotely tempted to whitewash his ancestor Bruce, rather the contrary (today the judgement on him would take a better account of the political realities of his situation) and he was completely fair to Edward I. He picked an episode concerned with Scottish independence, always close to his heart, and revolving around issues of death, justice, and cruelty. The wars of independence were not attracting proper scholastic attention at this time, and Bute was, once again, very much a trailblazer in his interests.

Early in 1875 Bute accepted a knighthood of the Order of the Thistle from Queen Victoria. He knew well how his Aunt Selina's children would view this, and he wrote at once to Mabel to explain. She was mollified:

> The contents of your letter received this morning are a source of mingled surprise and joy to me . . . I tell you frankly that I have been very angry with you, for I fully believed you had . . . condoned her Majesty's conduct to our family by accepting the Thistle from her . . . you voluntarily assure me that you have never sought the Queen, except at her royal <u>command</u> & I am most thankful for it . . . your letter has raised my warmest sympathy & the old sisterly feeling.[32]

Mabel had stored all the old material relating to the pitiful trouble between Queen Victoria and Lady Flora Hastings, and she sent copies to Bute. She also sent an account of the origin of the Curse of the Hastings,[33] which went back to the time of the death of 'the last Hastings Earl of Pembroke' (in 1389) when there was a bitter dispute between the heirs through the line male and the line female. The rightful claimant was set aside for the descendant of Grey de Ruthyn, and because he refused to pay the costs of the legal action, he was jailed, and died, cursing any of his own heirs who married into that family. Alas, the 2nd Marquess of Hastings had, in 1833, married Barbara Grey de Ruthyn. Mabel catalogued the deaths. Flora Hastings, 'the innocent victim of a vile conspiracy headed by the Queen herself', then her mother, 'of a broken heart', then George, whose marriage had allegedly sparked this disaster, and his eldest son at the age of nineteen. Then Harry, only twenty-six, and Harry's sister, Edith, aged forty, having already lost her sight. 'Some Welsh gentleman hunted out all this about the Curse, in an old History & wrote it down for Lady Selina Henry.'[34] George, Harry, Flora, Bute's mother Sophia and Edith undoubtedly died of Bright's disease, an impressive roll call.

For the moment, however, psoriasis was the only ailment troubling Bute. He travelled to a 'water place'[35] at the end of May, and he and Gwen spent six weeks there, which she hated. In August the family went to Harrogate. Her sister Angela was staying nearby, and she and her husband called into the Butes to propose a trip to the races. Bute made a fuss. He did not want to go, and refused to consider the possibility of entertaining himself with looking about York whilst his wife joined her sister and brother-in-law. He seemed to have no idea how his own dislike of company frustrated his much more sociable wife, or the sacrifices she made for him. She spilled her anger and disappointment out to Angela. Bute 'tried to show he was a martyr and as he didn't choose to see that he cd. have gone sight seeing . . . why it was better I suppose to have done with it and give it up. Of course I never see people and it gets me out of the way of junkets but I like them when I am at them on rare occasion.'[36]

Some of the summer of 1878 was spent on the Isle of Bute, in a rented house Balmory, at Ascog. After careful consideration, it was decided that Mount Stuart could not be restored,[37] and that Robert Rowand Anderson should build a new Mount Stuart, incorporating the surviving wings of the old house. The question has always been raised of why Bute did not turn again to Burges, and the answer most usually given is that the latter was already very busy, as was true. It is also true that when Burges was shown the drawing room at Mount Stuart, which Bute had designed in accordance with his own taste, he 'looked up, shrugged his shoulders, muttered "I call that damnable," and walked on'.[38] Perhaps for his most beloved home, Bute wanted a craftsman who would be a little more sensitive to his feelings.

Cardiff, however, continued under Burges's care, and Bute's new bedroom was nearing completion. It had the very personal theme of Bute's name-saint, John, and the Book of Revelation. The windows embodied the 'seven churches', amongst the least comforting of all possible scriptural themes. The churches addressed were struggling in a time of persecution, but the last church, Laodicea, is blamed for being 'neither hot nor cold'. Beautiful and peaceful as the room is, it must have served as a perpetual reminder to Bute that lukewarmness is amongst the greatest of sins. Looking at his life from the outside, it does not seem he was much inclined to this failing, or to the idleness of which Capel accused him. The view from inside may have been different. When furniture was installed, the only bed was a modest single with a metal frame.[39] It is highly likely, however, that Bute used this room as a sitting room and dressing room, and Lady Bute's room was the family bedroom.

Climbing the stair from his bedroom brought Bute to a roof garden. The architecture, Roman-inspired, conjures up memories of the Mediterranean, but the walls are covered with scenes from the life of Elijah, and the memory, more immediately, is of the roof garden of the bishop's palace in the Levant, which had been such an oasis of peace in a troubled time. Perhaps, too, its smiling Madonna reminded him of his intensely personal experience in the same palace.

Work was also under way on a small dining room, which was based around the theme of Abraham and Isaac. The fireplace was carved with the three angels who visited Sara and Abraham, who 'entertained them unawares'. She is laughing to one side of the fireplace, at the improbable news that she will bear a son. Beautifully realised by Nicholls and painted by Campbell, she is an older woman, not a crone. In this same room hung the portrait of Lady Sophia, who, also against the odds, bore a beloved son. Given the themes and puns at Cardiff, the allusion is surely to her, and to her late-born son.[40] The windows continue the story of Isaac, who became the founder of a numerous family. This room only made slow progress in the late seventies; did Bute try to avoid thinking that in his own family the descendants might be few indeed?

Lady Margaret was a delight to the Butes, but they wanted more children, and especially a male heir. The 2nd Marquess had left the estates entailed, so Lady Margaret would not be able to inherit the bulk of the Bute wealth, and although she might inherit the Scottish Earldom, and become Countess of Bute in her own right, she could not inherit the Marquessate, which was a British title.

In late 1878 Gwen became pregnant for the third time. She was in London, and Duncan was her doctor. The record does not give a Christian name, but this was probably James Matthews Duncan, a Scotsman who was one of his age's most advanced and respected obstetricians.[41] From the beginning, things did not go well with Gwen's pregnancy.[42] Almost certainly, Gwen suffered from intermittent bleeding. Duncan could not offer her any reason for this, and she was in an agony of terror, since she believed he was hiding some dreadful truth from her:

> I believe [Duncan] can't say what is the matter with me – but I am afraid it is nothing natural – he hoped to tell me in about a month ... I can't explain dear in a letter all about myself. I may have a miscarriage at any time of something, no one knows what – & I may not. Duncan wd have it away at once he says if I were his wife or daughter – but as we won't in case it were all right I must just wait for apparently an indefinite period.[43]

In February 1879, she miscarried. Her fears that there was something seriously wrong with her child were completely unfounded: 'It is all over – I had a miscarriage last night about 11 of a girl three months. Duncan did all for me & tho it was a quite properly formed child still he says it wd. never have gone on right.' A melancholy 'little deposit'[44] was made in the garden at Chiswick. There was concern about Gwen's health, but what had been shaken most was the confidence of both parents. Bute could think of only two possible cures for the grief Gwen was experiencing: jewellery and travel. He applied both. For her birthday two weeks later he gave her 'a lovely bracelet . . . a big cats eye & diamond snakes with ruby eyes on either side all on a gold band'.[45] Then he took her off for a trip by P&O. For once, travel worked to lift Gwen's spirits, more because she was able to mix with a wide range of people on the boat, in a way impossible to her at home:

> there was a young married couple going out to settle in Australia – & the Australian sheep farmer having come over to see England & Scotland ... there was the young husband & the old wife going to Malta for reasons of health – there was sweet seventeen having just come out of her school & going to her Father at Madras etc. oh it was a very funny thing for a fortnight with the same people ... the sun and warmth are very nice but it does not make up for the want of home and child.[46]

Gwen had a strong tendency to want to have her cake and eat it. Bute himself was always badly affected by stress, and was feeling less than well, and much troubled by his skin. There were large red patches on his scalp, chest and back. In September he went to Harrogate, taking Margaret with him. This time, Gwen stayed behind in London, because she was once again expecting a baby. Paradoxically, the times that Bute and Gwen spent apart give the clearest picture of their life together. Bute wrote daily, or almost daily, and most of the letters were preserved.

Bute was given a new diagnosis by his doctor at Harrogate: 'it was not eczema (which is an affection of the blood) but sorysis (I think he called it) – wh. is a slight derangement of the skin-nerves'. The Harrogate doctor was correct. The site and nature of Bute's 'spots' as he called them, suggests psoriasis, which is an over-growth of skin. The condition has a strong genetic link, and is common among Scots. The condition responded well to the treatment prescribed in Harrogate, the application of tar. To this day, tar-based shampoos are used to treat psoriasis of the scalp.

After Gwen's miscarriage in the early spring of that year, Bute was full of concern for her:

> I suppose I needn't impress upon yourself the necessity of caution as to yourself. But at the same time, open air – when possible, is a great thing – the creature must now be about as big as a grape.[47]

Bute had Margaret with him because it was thought that her health, too, would benefit. She was now four and they were beginning to be concerned about her. Although there was nothing obviously wrong with her leg or hip, she walked with a slight limp, which only became obvious as the naturally unsteady gait of childhood wore off. Hew, his manservant, was also there, and Margaret's nurse, Campbell.

They stayed in a suite of rooms in an old hotel. Hew was a great favourite with Margaret. Her father welcomed this, often leaving the room, rather than remaining when to do so might have made Hew feel awkward because he and not his employer was the chief object of Margaret's hero-worship. Hew, whom he trusted greatly, could be relied upon not merely to pack and care for Bute's clothes, but to remind him who would be expecting presents, and other such practicalities, which those of Bute's turn of mind are only too liable to forget.

Bute valued his servants, with whom he had a very easy-going relationship. He was always conscious of their vulnerability. It was, perhaps, the more remarkable in Hew's case, for on occasion there would be an outbreak of 'Hew's unfortunate failing'.[48] Hew would get drunk, sometimes simply tipsy enough that Bute did not care to be served by him, and sometimes too drunk to be capable of work. Bute also endured for a long time a cook whom his exasperated wife reckoned 'no better than a kitchen maid who had lived in a 2nd. rate inn'. Gwen finally dismissed her for 'gross impertinence', adding that she would have sacked her earlier for 'vile cooking' except for Bute's 'kindness of heart'. Even then, Bute would not send the damning reference his wife composed, preferring to create a kinder one of his own, though ringing in his ears were Gwen's instructions not to say the woman was a good cook and 'make me out an idiot'.[49]

Physically and in character, his daughter was very like him. Margaret had a happy but somewhat wilful disposition: '[Margaret] is very affectionate with me, but I am not sure, from the things she says ("I will not" and so on) that she isn't rather spoiled.'[50] With Gwen missing Margaret, Bute reassured her by telling her of Margaret's games and her health.

> Margaret and I get on excellently. Her colour is really generally very good. Her legs are hard and her arms, I hope, somewhat better. Her spirits leave nothing to be desired.[51]
>
> Margt. spends a good part of every afternoon now in playing at being a kitchen maid in concert with Campbell. She arranges rowan berries, hips, and hauchs (haughs? haws?) in toy dishes and serves them up. When this is done, she makes believe either that it is another day, so that a new dinner is required, or else that suppertime is arrived. This generally lasts until the bath comes, when there is a frightful excitement swimming tin fish and walnut-shells (wh. are named severally after the principal steamers of the Clyde) in it. I find that she still cannot pronounce L or R though in some words such as 'Rothesay' she gets pretty near it. I heard that the little Mowbray girl, who is the same age, is a good deal bigger, but cannot speak so well.[52]

Bute dined with the Catholic Lord Mowbray.[53] He was 'certainly fond of eating, and a little inclined to coarse language and risqué double entendres. However, as he rather led me into it, the least said, the better.'[54]

Bute also tried to raise his wife's spirits by telling her of his daily activities. He was working on learning Arabic, and he had a visit from Burges:

> whether it was the consequences of the champagne (the only night I've had anything but St Julien) or what, I don't know, but the soul-inspiring one was a martyr to the colly-wobbles this morning. He told me, about 10 a.m. that he had already visited his aunt[55] 6 times. Pill box had to be sent for, who complimented him on his boyish appearance, considering his age, and gave him medicine and

chicken broth etc. He was supposed to be fit to start (and did so) for London abt. 4 p.m. His own remedy seemed be eating very strong peppermint lozenges, so that the room smelled of them even more than it does of tobacco, wh. is saying a good deal.[56]

He also heard from Anderson, who sent plans for the new Mount Stuart.

Anderson's plans are exceedingly nice. The house seems to bid fair to be a splendid palace. There were only a few things, partly in regard to the picturesque and partly the luxurious, wh. I suggested alterations to him. And these I shall see better in the model which is in Edinburgh on my way back from Glasgow. I think I will have the model brought to Chiswick for you to see, only it is very large and heavy.[57]

Bute's own treatment continued, with applications of tar to the 'spots' and daily baths in the spa water. The 'spots' began to fade: 'The ones on the head are become only faint rose-coloured spots, and the two big ones on the body are rapidly working in the same direction.'[58] Bute was anxious to stay in Harrogate until his treatment was completed, and the spots cured, although he was realistic enough to know that he would have a recurrence later. But his anxieties about Gwen pulled him in two directions, for she was in a 'low, moping, solitary, jumpy beastly state', and he longed to comfort her.[59] Her confidence had been badly shaken by her miscarriage. Bute, at a distance, tried hard to find her occupations, suggesting friends who might come and see her, including Burges, and activities for her. She was studying Classics with her unmarried cousin Phillipa, who, being two years older than Gwen, was now twenty-seven.

As you are at Latin, I think you might try Horace's Odes or Ovid's Fasti. The only draw-back in these (except Horace's Odes) is that certain natural things (e.g. the relation of husband and wife in certain circumstances) are spoken quite plainly, and, in Ovid, rather sensual. I should think however you wd. smell this rat soon enough, at least before Phillipa had caught the unhallowed fire.[60]

Bute seemed just a little entertained at the prospect. Yet, however he tried to cheer his wife with news and with positive images of her later in her pregnancy, and plans for her amusement, he shared in her worries. When a letter came late, he had been afraid that, yesterday being the monthlies' own day, they might have taken it into their heads to come on, and perhaps the whole thing gone shipwreck and you too ill and wretched to write. On the contrary, I am delighted to hear you are so well.[61]

He began to question his doctor in Harrogate about the times most likely for a miscarriage, and spoke to Margaret's nurse as well. He was dismayed to learn that his elder brother had been 'born dead from an accident in the <u>seventh</u> month, when one thinks everything safe'.[62] He found he could not even pray about Gwen's pregnancy.

I confess that I prayed so much about the last thing, and with so little effect, (but rather the contrary) that I feel rather shy of exposing this one to the same circumstances. Perhaps it's very wrong, but I do not dare to say in every sense, 'Send me here my purgatory.'

He struggled to hide his own fears and depression, revealing just enough to make it clear to her that he was sensitive to her position. Her fears, his worry about her, and the comparative solitariness of his life at Harrogate sometimes oppressed him. Occasionally the mask slipped: 'In the afternoon I felt so low, I went and asked O'Donnell to take me for a walk, wh. he did. He really is a very nice old man.'[63] Bute continued to reassure Gwen: 'Do try to realise that it is all physical and that there is not only nothing to be sorry about, but everything to be happy about.'[64]

There was 'everything to be happy about' only for a short time. Later that winter, Gwen lost her baby. Three miscarriages and countless disappointments did indeed give the Butes a purgatory on earth. Even leaving aside his own longing for a son, Bute was too close to Gwen not to be devastated himself by her grief. To lose a baby is distressing for any couple. Many Christians comfort themselves with the thought that their baby is safe with God. But for Victorian Catholics, the baby could not be with God unless it was baptised. The unbaptised child would not go to hell, but remain in a state of twilight being, limbo, neither experiencing bliss nor pain. If the child was born alive, even if it could not live, then it could at once be baptised (and any one could perform this baptism) and then it was assured of heaven. Bute was most insistent that any child born, unless it was quite certainly dead long before it was born, should be at once baptised.[65]

Flora, Duchess of Norfolk, bore a son. It quickly became clear that he was blind and epileptic and his mind never developed beyond that of a child. He was deeply loved by his parents who continued to hope for a cure. The Butes greatly pitied them, and the tragedy did nothing to lift their own hopes.

That same autumn of 1879, the Breviary translation was at last published, with much interest being taken in the press. Most of the reviews were positive. They admired the clarity of Bute's English, and the size of the undertaking. Many reviewers were High Church clergymen pleased to have an English version of the Breviary. The publishers, Blackwoods, had hoped for a degree of controversy, which they thought would help it sell. Bute was not very happy about this.[66] When the reviews began to roll in, there was only a minimum of fuss. 'Mr T. G. Law, Librarian to the Signet Library, Edinburgh and previously of the London Oratory' took the purist Roman view that Bute should have translated the Latin Vulgate instead of straining to get his translation close to the Hebrew.[67] 'Bishop Wordsworth (*Edinburgh Courant*)' took a staunchly Protestant line of criticism. He felt that Bute had watered down the Catholicism of the Breviary, and was therefore in danger of persuading his readers that it was less objectionable than it really was.[68] Others reflected that his translation of the psalms was much influenced by the Book of Common Prayer, as indeed it was. Personal letters also came in, some requesting copies of the Breviary. Perhaps the kindest, and the most full of insight, came from Cardinal Newman. The Catholic convert and learned churchman was himself an author and translator of substance.[69] 'I know what a laborious work it must have been, and, as well as anyone, how little a translator can, after all his endeavours, satisfy himself. But others will not be so unfair to the work as you are likely to be from what you say.'[70]

Probably the most pertinent criticism was that the Breviary would have little use. By and large, the Catholic clergy were well enough educated to understand the Latin they were required to read, and so were the Anglo-Catholics who were interested in it. But it was popular amongst orders of female religious, especially in the colonies, who could not read Latin fluently. Perhaps it was most successful as part of the movement that was to push the Catholic Church into finally authorising worship in the vernacular. Bute himself certainly favoured this. The Mass, of course, could only be heard in Latin, but Hunter Blair records that all other services in his homes were said in English.[71] Bute wanted to make the wealth of worship he enjoyed accessible to everybody, and he knew how little able to understand or enjoy the Latin original others were. Catholicism, despite its ancient families and well-born converts, was largely a working-class religion, indeed a religion of the poorest labouring classes. His own servants could not follow the Breviary. It was not a dislike of the Latin, whose sonorous and economical phrases he loved, but a desire to make worship accessible to all, even to his own loss, that impelled him.

It was now five years since the great financial crisis of 1875, which was the time Bute had originally thought it would take for his south Wales estates to work their financial position around to solvency. Indeed, there were the kinds of changes which would indicate the resolution of earlier troubles. Davies records:

> Boyle retired as dock manager, the pill being sweetened for him by an annuity of £3000. He was succeeded by Lewis, who became manager of the estate as a whole ... In 1881 Boyle and Stuart resigned as trustees and the trust was reconstituted with three members H. Dudley Ryder, a Bute kinsman and a director of Coutts Bank, E. B. Talbot, a relation of Lady Bute's mother, and Frederick Pitman.[72]

There was once again considerable pressure from the town for Bute to expand the docks, which were proving inadequate to the demands upon them. Bute now endeavoured to separate the docks from the rest of his property. It was not so much that he wanted a solution which would recognise the vast sums of money his family had ploughed into the docks. Rather, he did not want to risk pouring more money into the docks without any guarantee that the returns would even cover the necessary borrowing. A meeting was held *in camera* between Wyndham Lewis and Shirley (representing the Trust), and representatives of the Chamber of Commerce and the town council. Lewis reported to Bute that he had told the meeting that while Bute was unwilling to spend more on the docks, he wanted to see Cardiff trade grow, and would be happy to see a scheme which transferred the docks to the town.[73] The initial reaction of the town's leaders was to form a Harbour Trust; however, the plans came to nothing, and Wyndham Lewis presided over another expansion of the Cardiff docks.[74]

As always Bute's real enthusiasms were far away from the world of business. He had just begun to explore a new one – astrology. The signs had long decorated his rooms at Cardiff, but he first came across a contemporary written account of astronomy where most contemporary readers discover it: in the popular press. Francis Condor wrote regularly for the St James's Gazette 'where you will not be surprised to hear that his chief astrological labours are dedicated to trying to forecast the successes or otherwise of the eminent statesman whom he blasphemously describes as "the Catiline of Downing Street"'. Condor was Bute's first, and most regular correspondent on the subject.

Bute did not have a mathematical mind, and he struggled with 'the papers of figures & diagrams of triangles &c'.

Bute was caught between his enquiring mind, which was always seeking a much better understanding of the rules of cause and effect in the world around him, and his natural scepticism, which made him hard to convince. He had read enough of astrology to scare him away from 'any dogmatism one way or the other'. He tried experiments where he set up 'schemes' (charts) for past events, and found that his predictions, 'have an indication reflecting them in the scheme. But this may be merely because the rules are so vague that almost everything may mean anything'; on the other hand, no forecast was simply and clearly realised in an event. However, to a degree this was explained not only by his own 'incapacity as to both mathematics and astrology, but the incapacity of the ... people who draw up Ephemerides &c and the abject manner in which geocentricism and everything else that Ptolemy believed in are clung to for these purposes'.[75] Nevertheless, the fascination with it was real enough, and Bute turned to astrology for indications when advice from more usual quarters was uncertain. By the spring of 1881 he was seeking advice from any area he could get it.

In October 1880 Bute went away for a country house weekend, whilst his wife pleaded ill-health, an all-too-transparent euphemism in Victorian times. Bute tried hard not to add to Gwen's burdens by undue solicitude for her: 'I know if there were anything serious you would have telegraphed. If the things have come on, I should not think it would be a miscarriage, only the things at their tricks.'[76] Above all else, he wanted to reassure her that she was not doomed to perpetual miscarriages.

But 'the things' did not appear, and by the spring of 1881, it was clear that Gwen was expecting a baby, due in the early summer, and that the most dangerous time was over. Bute longed to take Gwen to Bute or Dumfries, so that the baby could be born in Scotland. The family doctor thought in March that travel would be safe. Bute was still unsure. He turned for help to Francis Condor, who was dubious. Some astrological aspects raised a question. In particular, 'an unusual coincidence' in their birth charts indicated that Lord and Lady Bute should not travel together. 'If I remember aright, you met a carriage accident on your wedding journey.' He added that after a series of miscarriages, his own wife had only borne her children safely to term by resting in one place for the whole of her pregnancies. It was best not to take the smallest risk: 'If it should be a son, you will be too proud and happy to welcome him to have room in your mind for a brief regret.'[77]

Whether astrology or personal experience prevailed, the Butes decided to stay in London at Chiswick House, whose extensive grounds had not yet been sold for development. There was space for Bute to take the walks so necessary for his health, and easy access to the best medical advice for Gwen. In addition, there was a wide circle of friendly relatives, despite a growing tension between Bute, Gwen and her stepmother. In 1880, Gwen's third sister, Alice, had married Bute's cousin Charley, who was now Earl of Loudon. Charley had always been a friend of Bute's. He was, at this point of his life, everything Harry Hastings had not been: reliable and full of good sense and kindliness, but with that touch of wit, charm and liveliness so necessary to Bute in his friends. Angela, Gwen and Alice were close, and the brothers-in-law good friends. Despite blood ties, the Butes were not close to the Norfolks. Bute felt that the Norfolks had 'quietly dropped them'.[78] Nevertheless, relations were cordial and they were heartily sorry for the Norfolks, whose only son continued to be an invalid whose only hope of a cure was a miracle.

While he waited for the baby, Bute was enjoying the various libraries for his current academic and religious enthusiasm, the making of a proper calendar, or Proprium, of Scottish saints. This work followed on logically from the Breviary. The 'home saints' of a country are remembered on weekdays, along with less important but still internationally renowned saints. Depending on the perceived importance of a saint, she or he may just be remembered on her own day, or he or she may be given an 'octave', which is to say the saint will remembered on their own feast day and each successive day after for a full week, making eight days in all. Thus, they are rarely remembered on Sundays, and only those interested enough to follow an organised pattern of prayers will encounter the 'Proprium', the proper calendar of saints and their days.

For Bute it was a delightful and engrossing study, involving many aspects of his life he loved best. There was the constant pleasure of academic research, designed to find the names and death-days of the saints, and to attempt to track down some actual historical facts about them. This could be a challenge, as Bute commented on St Bridged [*sic*], whose 'Lives bristle with the most alarming miracles, like hedgehogs':[79]

Fr. McSuibhne is here, and I am making him read the Lives of St. Bridged. As he does so, the word "impossible" occasionally escapes his lips, and he has not, I believe, yet met with anything which he regards as fit to be put forward in the guise of a historical fact.[80]

Then there was the religious aspect, the consideration of the virtues of those saints who, unlike Bridged, were historical figures. It must have been while working on the Proprium that Bute committed a social gaff which was remembered long enough to find its way into his biography. At social events, Bute was frequently 'bored to xtinction' as he so often wrote in slightly different forms of words in his diary. Small talk was polite, but 'tedious'. On one occasion, presumably either thinking his own thoughts about study in hand, or valiantly attempting make the conversation more interesting he remarked to a startled lady: 'Don't you think it monstrous that St Magnus does not have an octave?' The remark was not as random as it sounded. Bute was talking shop, and it was as little appreciated as such conversations usually are by outsiders.

The other huge advantage of this study for Bute was that it brought him into contact with those whose lives were not confined by party politics, 'sport', or the weather. One of these, who would become one of the closest and most confidential of all his friends, was Colin Grant.[81] Grant was a Gaelic-speaking, highly educated, cultured and interested priest from Aberdeenshire. At some point the two men must have met, for Grant first appears in an undated letter in which Bute thanks him for a Gaelic New Testament. At the date of this letter, Bute spoke no Gaelic (he was later to learn at least some), but he responded with interest and typical generosity:

> It is so pleasant to meet with one who takes a critical interest in the sacred text that I hope you will allow me the pleasure of giving some book in return – Perhaps you may not have a LXX[82] or Alfrid's Greek Testament? Or the Hebrew-English OT published by the Bible Society, a work I find very convenient for scriptural reference?[83]

It is only too apparent[84] that Bute had to work hard to talk the Scottish priests and bishops into the project, but they were forced to acknowledge, that, due to their long suppression, they did not have the calendar other Catholic countries and provinces enjoyed. So a committee was set up, consisting of the Scottish Bishops, a few educated clergy and Bute. As Bute gleefully told Grant

> A good deal of the rough work (the drudgery, if you will, only I approach it with anything but distaste) of preparing the Proprium is expected to fall on me. I mean that I shall have a good deal to do in preparing matter for the committee's consideration. And I am

quite willing to do my best on it. It seems quite natural to me that this should be the case, as I have more time for such study than the other members of the committee . . .[85]

One of the real charms of Grant for Bute was that he was somebody with whom he could exercise his impish humour:

We shall have to encounter a kind of vis inertia somewhat such as you might experience if you tried to make me get up at 6am, although I acknowledge that it would be on the whole desirable for me to do so.[86]

It was as well for the Butes that they had the hope of a child. In March Burges had visited Cardiff, and caught a chill. He returned to his London home ill, where he died on 20 April 1881.[87] Gwen reported sadly: 'Bute & I feel the loss very much . . . in more ways than one.'[88] They lost a friend who could be relied on to charm and to cheer them. Burges had taught Bute an enormous amount about style, art and architecture.

Gwen had also lost a source of birthday presents for Bute. Answering the problem of what to give the man who has everything, she had commissioned a series of delectable, useful gifts from Burges. The most charming of these was also the most revealing. Burges described it as a 'pepper pot', though it was in fact a cruet set. The design process for the Bute cruet is more than usually well-documented, as Burges made the sketches in his small notebooks. The salt and pepper are carried on a stretcher between two figures, who feel the weight of their burden very acutely. That idea came early. Burges played with the figures carrying the stretcher. There might be two ladies, one in a tiara which suggests that she might be a marchioness, carrying the cruet between them, or a jester in a cap and bells as one of the figures. The jester was Burges's alter ego, and there is a photograph of him dressed as one. The image speaks volumes for his sense of being on the margins of society, for mediaeval jesters were often distinguished by being dwarfs or in some other way physically different. Burges himself was abnormally short, and of course, also a joker. Should Gwen or Burges serve Bute? Icons can easily show too much. The final design is of two ordinary serving-men. The last September of his life, Burges had again made a gift for Gwen to give to Bute. It was perfect for a traveller: a 'pilgrim bottle' with a fish with jewelled eyes at the bottom of the accompanying cup.[89] When Bute travelled, Gwen worried over bandits, and this was just the very thing to convince them that the traveller was not worth a ransom.

Now Bute carried the work on the Welsh properties forward, ably assisted by Burges's team and the painter Nathaniel Westlake.[90]

Westlake picked me up. He does everything he can to make himself amusing. His prevailing traits are ultramontanism and horsiness, the former according to zeal rather than knowledge. I think we shall get on very well as to artistic things. Castell Coch is very comfortable and we get on very well – at the same time, it still wants a lot doing to it. There has been a good deal done down here, and some of the rooms, e.g. the library, look beautiful. The heating appears to answer, as Westlake finds nothing whatever the matter with his pictures. He pointed out to me your portrait put into Limbo as Esther.[91]

Spring lengthened into summer, and Bute longed for the clean air of the Scottish countryside,[92] or the bright colours and real heat of the Mediterranean, but kept it resolutely to himself,[93] and busied himself with his academic work and with caring for Gwen. She would walk a little in the grounds and sit in the shade of the trees, embroidering blue and red parrots on a bed covering destined for the baby she was carrying. On the morning of 20 June, Gwen had 'the show', but the doctor, Lawrence, was non-committal. Gwen had breakfast with Bute but felt ill in the afternoon. Her father and stepmother came to call, and Bute invited them to dinner. Gwen was not sure whether to come to dinner herself, and in the end dined in her room, eating very little. Then Lawrence arrived, and decided to send for Duncan, and Lord and Lady Howard had to be told their daughter was in labour. The doctor and Bute and his parents-in-law all dined together 'in solemn manner, and Ld H made small talk to Lawrence abt. anything that wasn't interesting & Ldy. H. cdnt. restrain herself from talking insides to me sotto voce'.
Then Gwen sent for Lawrence and Bute and

everything was very much the same as usual in such cases, until Lawrence was called out to introduce Duncan, & I had to scream for him & John was born. I remember so well going into the dressing-room & finding Porter & saying 'She has a son.' Do you remember John crying, & trying to curl up under you & Duncan slowly detached him & Lawrence looked and said it was a son? He was carried in to Porter, who held him in a blanket. I remember the shock of adding to my prayers the words 'and my dear son.' I have a vivid recollection also of George beginning to play the bag-pipes outside. I went and told Ld. H. . . . He insisted on coming into the chapel at once to give thanks & I said 7 (I think) Gloria Patris – wh. he and Ldy H. answered (I pity that poor woman for her barrenness, very much).

Do you remember the xposition & blossoming of the withered rose from the Holy Land, put in hot water before the picture of the B. virgin?[94]

It is typical of Bute that in the midst of his own great joy, his thoughts turned compassionately to a woman he cordially disliked. It is also typical that his first act was to give thanks to God, and honour to the Virgin, with a simple and symbolic ceremony. After all the dry and withered days of barrenness and loss, his and Gwen's hopes and love could expand with the birth of this child.

9   Family

'The common natural instinct of the male animal which defends its female and young'

The Butes showed their delight in ways typical of them. Bute, by commissioning a church and giving Gwen a beautiful new piece of jewellery, a 'large diamond bracelet with a ruby ... in the middle perfectly splendid'; Gwen, by pouring out her joy to her sister:

> as John was my present I can't quite make out why I have [the bracelet] ... Well it's all over & seems like a dream and I must be the happiest woman that ever lived and I am equally thankful for God's immense reward & goodness to me.[1]

Gwen was a devoted mother and this time her health was good, so she was able to breastfeed her son. As soon as Gwen was once again out of her bed, the whole family went to Harrogate. Bute was suffering a severe reaction to the anxiety of waiting for John's birth and psoriasis is a condition which flares up in reaction to stress. As soon as he started taking the waters, he again suffered a bout of depression. He told Grant: 'the shock of beginning the course here has so upset me that I do not feel able to ask you to make any definite arrangements for coming here after the Assumption [of the BVM]'. He took a 'solitary and nervous constitutional' and 'tormented' himself with 'the difficulty of finding a proper hymn for the mattins of St Columba', upon whose offices in the Proprium the men were working. To his surprise, he found himself easily able to compose a 'jingle' in Latin which he thought would be adequate if they did not find anything better.[2] Despite emotional ups and downs (the latter caused mainly by Gwen's being 'suddenly laid up with an alarming approach to what is called "white legs",[3] all danger of which we had hoped had passed over') his spirits gradually improved. His librarian had got together a

> very great number of Propria – perhaps 50, including Mexico & Algeria & all sorts of places. If I am able, I think I shall write an analytical essay on them, wh. will make the committee's hair (as far as is left on the verge of the coronal tonsure, that late and objectionable novelty) stand on end, and prepare them to swallow anything.

He added that he was working on the 'hymn on St Comgall. It is a long ABC Darian poem. I think we must lick it, or some of it, into his office. It is all in what McSuibhne calls that "he-was-a-good-father,-and affectionate-husband,-and-all-the-rest-of-it" epitaph style.'[4] Bute was also making a translation of the 'Altus'. This Latin poem, attributed to St Columba (correctly, Bute believed) is another long ABC Darian poem, where each set of verses begins with a letter of the alphabet. He divided it into each of its alphabetical sections, and offered a prose translation and notes.[5]

In September, Bute was 'rather better' and Gwen was 'pretty well' and young John was 'exceedingly well'.[6] The family went to Balmory on Bute, where Grant visited them, and the men worked on the Proprium. In the evening there were readings from the Quran.[7] When Grant left, Bute wrote a paper on David II of Scotland for the Society of Antiquaries. After that he 'took St Kentigern in hand':

> I . . . am up to the eyes in him, having completed about a quarter of the work. He may be uninteresting, but then he's Glasgow. I doubt if the Caledonian Assoc. will find him interesting as he turns in my hands into a kind of cabinet of shelves to be filled with the most unflinching application of the chronological method, varied with a little comparative philology . . . I think you hit the right nail on the head in identifying the peculiar (and less attractive) features of the Kentigern school with British as opposed to Gaelic blood. These distinctions are real ones, and seem eternal.[8]

The British peoples who had lived all over the isles which derive their name from them were finally driven back to Wales, Cornwall and Brittany. The Gaels were Irish adventurers and colonisers who became the Scots. The 'chronological method' attempted to evaluate the existing biographies of the saint by taking into consideration the dates of older manuscripts which their authors had before them. It also uses known dates from one life (in this case, Kentigern's) to establish the dates of others (in this case, St David of Wales, whom Bute calls by his correct Welsh name, Dewi). In much that he wrote on Kentigern, Bute was following Skene.

Bute had hoped to leave for the Mediterranean after giving this lecture. The misery of the cold and dark of the British winter filled him, not just with the gloom with which it is generally greeted, but with that lack of all energy[9] which is the sign of real depression. His psoriasis had been only temporarily improved by his summer at Harrogate. In January, Gwen realised what she was once again pregnant. She was miserable:

> As far as I can make out I am not to leave for months – Bute goes for two months on 15 February to after Easter – and I stay here as I cannot move – I hope I shall not retire to bed shortly – if I can keep on as I do now I shall indeed be thankful – but going to bed or perpetual lying up – even the thought pretty nearly does me up.

Her feelings exploded in trouble with the servants:

> I have had two rows with Campbell – fearful impertinence. I finally told her next time she will go. She is so flabbergasted at this, that she has been better since. I think she thought I could not do without her. She is quite mistaken.[10]

The shackled Gwen was only too aware that Campbell could do for the children what she could not.

Despite at once giving up driving, and sitting 'hands folded and almost legless',[11] in February she haemorrhaged. Bute told Grant that she was 'seriously and distressingly, though not dangerously, ill'.[12] McSwiney commiserated with the Butes on her 'sentence of indefinite confinement (imprisonment, [one] may call it)'.[13] Everyone had hoped that after the relatively straightforward pregnancy with John, all subsequent ones would be successful. The doctor swore that she had not miscarried. She was sure she had, and that the precautions she was taking were a waste of time. Bute at once postponed his trip.

By March she was a great deal better, though still on her couch. Somewhat distractedly, she made arrangements for Bute, who left for his Mediterranean journey on 6 March with his impoverished university friend and co-religionist, Woodward:

> I have got Woodward to go and take care of him & look after the

money wh. I sd. not like to leave to the tender mercies of Hew . . .
it was a horrid parting, me lying, lying, lying.[14]

She had indeed miscarried in February, and was soon released from
her sofa.

Whether Bute was too ill to look after the money himself, or lacked
the desire to do so is unclear. He certainly felt sure he was most unwell.
He had not been abroad since June 1880.[15] As usual, he wrote to Gwen
every day. Woodward was to act as his secretary and companion as
well as his treasurer, and as Woodward was bankrupt, he was glad of
the employment.

He has no assets but his clothes and watch. His present favourite
scheme is a sort of coal delivery speculation at some unknown place
on the African coast . . . I can't say I feel very cheerful at the idea
of putting £1000 into it, especially as the other people are Capel's
brother and a Cardiff Spaniard.[16]

Bute, as usual, was plagued by seasickness. Hew thought the boat
rolled so much that her gunwales dipped under the water. She was not
at all luxurious:

There isn't a bath on board. We wash our necks, armpits, hands &
feet and the aunt and the other region before and behind, in basins
and footpans as best we can, & some of the men come up in despair
about 6 am. and get the sailors to turn the hose on them when the
decks are being cleaned . . . there is only one aunt for about 30–40
people, and she's a kind of box . . . without enough room to let one
stand up comfortably to button one's trousers.

'Visiting Auntie' was common Victorian slang for going to the toilet
and, by extension, 'aunt' could also refer to the parts of the body used
in it. Despite the discomforts, the sunlight almost at once worked its
magic on Bute:

I must say I am feeling very much better and happier. The sight of
what St Francis calls 'Messr. Frater Nostro Sole' seems quite home
to me. I don't think I can live so long without him again.

He was, however, longing for a good café-au-lait. His fellow passengers
as usual interested him. There were 'swells' called Henderson. It
appeared that Mrs Henderson had been an actress.

She dresses much better than most English women . . . Close to, she is, as Woodward says 'Laide comme un peché mortel' [as ugly as a mortal sin] but when nicely made up, in a good light & at a distance, with veil &c. she's quite beautiful.[17]

His destination was Italy, where he was to stay with his old friend Grisewood, who was married to an Italian. Bute and Woodward stayed at a hotel, but passed their days, and took most of their meals, with the Grisewoods. Mrs Grisewood was expecting a baby, not her first. Unlike Gwen, she enjoyed robust good health, walking freely, and scrambling up hills. Bute, conditioned by Gwen's problems to regard all pregnancies as potential miscarriages, was astonished: 'I can't imagine how Mrs Grisewood can do these things, as she is, without hurting herself.'

It was Lent, and the local rules for fasting were for nothing but bread with a little salad during the day, and a meal at night.

We get so hungry that we eat up everything the Grisewoods have for dinner and are still famished. Last night I had lentil soup, liver with oil and herbs (two large helpings), 4 large veal cutlets with heavy sauce, and 2 helpings of chicken, besides the dish of vegetables & had to have several helpings of ham fried in addition.[18]

The next day he remembered that he had also had two helpings of dressed calf's head, and a large serving of vanilla ice cream. It is not surprising that Bute's slender figure was filling out, despite the regular walks he still took, at least two hours each day. When on Bute, he usually walked to town over the moor road, which he loved, and back to Mount Stuart by the shore road, a round walk of ten miles. Abroad, while his companions wilted, he walked on, rejoicing in the heat.

Bute was much perturbed by the atmosphere at the Grisewoods. He himself was very even-tempered with his intimates and hated rows; not so Grisewood.

The main xcitement at this moment is Grisewood's temper, wh. was beastly yesterday, as he went to confession. He was boiling over all day and very nasty to his wife before us. And after confession, being in the sacristy with an old man, he said 'Damn his eyes' and struck him down. I don't wonder there are rows.[19]

Bute was especially concerned at Grisewood's 'brutality' to his wife, whom he abused and bullied, regardless of anyone present, 'with less self control than a beast'. Bute, who was naturally inclined to side with women, in the end

> told him I could not stand it, and must beg him not to go on so before me, or I must go. He received it with cold-blooded and lying hypocrisy, saying that he liked to be told his faults ... He talked about his intense affection for her and my being almost his only friend – and so on. You'd have thought he was a martyred angel. It really is very disgusting. I think his brutal temperament makes him take pleasure in making her suffer and seeing her suffer, and he is too degraded to feel the common natural instinct of the male animal wh. defends its female and young.[20]

Despite Grisewood's temper, there were lighter moments: 'The Grisewoods had a dinner party last night. Grisewood sang in the evening. It's curious how incapable some people are of seeing their own incapacity.'[21]

When Bute heard from his wife that 'the monthlies' had come on again he had mixed feelings. He was sorry that they were not to have another child, but relieved that Gwen did not risk another miscarriage at present. Their tenth wedding anniversary was approaching, and Bute began to search for a present for Gwen, to remember 'the most fortunate' day of his life. He sent her a bronze statue of Mars, and she was ecstatic: 'It is the only bronze of any sort I possess and it is more lovely than I would ever have thought possible, especially as my own possession. Thank you again and again.'[22] She had moved from Bute to Dumfries House. Bute cajoled her to call on her neighbours, knowing that the attention would be appreciated, and its omission would cause offence; though Gwen had not come to enjoy calling any more over the years.

Bute still sent Gwen her daily letter, and, lacking much real news, he filled sheets with descriptions of masses and ceremonials, approving of some and criticising others. In general he found the state of the Church in Italy deplorable. The clergy were sloppy and lacked real feeling. There were exceptions.

> We were lucky in the Priest for once. He is a wretched little thing with St Vitus' dance but is serenely reverent and pious & was really impressive despite his compulsive grimacing, jumpings & grabbings, & also knew the ceremonial.[23]

He was beginning to miss Gwen very much, and begged her to consider coming out to join him. He could show her Athens. He flirted with her, implying both his own recovered health, and how much he was missing her. He was sure she would become pregnant again, and if she did, could remain in the Mediterranean for all of her pregnancy. He thought it would also be good for Margaret, too, who, he was sure, had inherited his constitution. For Gwen, the idea of being tied to a sofa in a foreign land without even the amusements offered at home must have been enough to ensure she remained in Britain. Yet she was miserable without him.

> You can't think how awfully lonely and aimless life seems to be without you & yet I have the two here & John is so like you – & Margaret is such a blessing – I seem sometimes to wake up & remember you are in the world and will come back – but then the gt. blank seems greater that you are not here now, and the days have to be got through without you, come how.[24]

The pain of missing Bute was less in London where there was more to distract her, and her friends, and especially her cousin, Phillipa, to be a companion to her.

> Last night I took Phillipa to the Academy evening entertainment and we enjoyed ourselves as it was very amusing to see the remarkable dresses of some of the women – why because you are the belonging of an artist and dress esthictically [sic] shd. you be dirty, I cannot see, but they certainly were filthy and so were the clothes they wore ... MacSwiney ... looks a good deal dirtier than usual and a vy. shabby coat on. It reminds me of the good old days so seeing him, and it makes me long so for you.[25]

Her main motive for a visit to London was Margaret's leg. She was now six-and-a-half years old, and she walked with a limp. The Butes had already been told that one leg was slightly shorter than the other. With Bute away, Gwen consulted London doctors who confirmed that there was 'no disease in the bone of either the spine or hip – and that the whole thing is that one leg is nearly ½ an inch shorter than the other'.[26] Problems with the hip are a common result of a breech birth.

There was a three-week wait for a built-up boot. Bute agonised, more especially when the boots proved uncomfortable; 'surely something must be done to enable her to wear shoes. What is she to do in the evening? Or to dance?'[27] He never resigned himself to limitations imposed by lack of human imagination or enthusiasm. He casually wrote Margaret a couple of letters and failed to realise how much these meant to her. When no more followed, she was devastated. Gwen explained to her husband, and, conscience-stricken, he began to write regularly to Margaret.[28]

On the advice of his doctors, he left for Sicily. He enjoyed the sail, sleeping out on the deck in the open air, which he had not done for years, and which reminded him of his summer voyages as a boy.[29] In Sicily, bandits were a real risk. Gwen was inclined to panic. Bute assured her that he was taking every precaution. He travelled under the name of 'B Crichton Stuart – the B being in case anyone should notice the B on any of my things'.[30] He addressed all letters to her as 'Mrs Stuart' and then constantly worried in case, as she travelled about, some servant should fail to realise for whom they were intended. When she went to stay with her family rather than going to Chiswick House he 'tried to show he was a martyr',[31] as she had earlier put it: 'I suppose my telegrams and my voluminous letters are all wasted and gone – Heaven knows where! I can't repeat them – pages and pages – worth very little I dare say – I won't say anything but it is a little thoughtless, isn't it?'[32]

Woodward was made ill by the heat of Sicily, and left. Bute was alone with Grisewood. He wrote home, a little plaintively, saying he would love Sneyd's company, only he could not possibly demand that he come. Sneyd had married the daughter of Bute's cousin and factor, Henry Stuart, in 1880, and a married man was tied in the way a single one was not. But Sneyd, too, loved travel, and somewhat to Bute's surprise, and wholly to his delight, jumped at the chance. Meanwhile Bute filled in his time with astrology.

> I have been drawing up a lot of astrological schemes. They seem all to indicate a row in Ireland of the most frightful kind. I have a sort of idea that Gladstone may go out of office towards the middle or end of June and ... about the middle of November, there may be a general election replacing Gladstone in power.[33]

In the first part of this he was very nearly right. With opposition to his handling of affairs in both Egypt and Ireland, on 7 July Gladstone told his colleagues in private that he intended to resign, but did not do so.[34]

What really distressed Bute in Italy and in Sicily was the casual cruelty to animals which he could not help witnessing. Mostly, he hid it from Gwen. Occasionally his need to write it out of his system overrode his desire to protect her: 'I have got the blues. There was such

a row last night about burning a toad alive with petroleum – horrible
to think of & still more horrible to see, wh. I'm glad to say I didn't but
I think G might have interfered with less violence and more tact.'[35] It
was only later, when there was a real chance of her travelling abroad
again, that he spoke of 'the cruelty to animals, wh. sickens one's heart
and haunts one's memory and dreams'.[36]

Even on holiday he was fielding requests for charity too large to be
sanctioned by his almoners. The Roman Catholic Church in Scotland
was largely a church of the very poor. In the Ayrshire weaving and
mining villages, many of the women at Sunday Mass would not be
wearing shoes. The few rich patrons had to assist generously in school
and church building projects and Bute was giving help towards '14
schools built at the cost of £500 each' for the Bishop of Galloway.
Some would have additional sponsors, or be refurbished, or housed in
existing churches. Bute intended to give a sum 'not less than £1000
and not more than £2000'.[37] The Scottish Education act of 1872 had
made education compulsory. The state provided free schools, but they
were in effect Protestant. The Catholic Church began to open schools
in almost every parish for its children. 'A poor community voted, in
effect, to tax itself even more heavily to sustain Catholic education.'[38]

Architecturally, his main interest was in building a chapel in the
Byzantine style. He thought he had discovered

> the secret of altars in apses ... You first draw a square, and then
> a circle in it, & the east half of the circle & the west half of the
> square form the sanctuary. Then 3 concentric squares rising by a
> step each, inside the circle which forms the steps of the altar, the
> steps being returned to the sides, allow a sort of platform behind.
> The altar itself has its front of middle coinciding with the diameter
> of the circle.[39]

Since he intended building a chapel at Troon, he was suggesting his
Byzantine church for there.

> I insist upon building the Byzantine chapel at Troon. It will be built
> of brick or whatever is the cheapest material, as these buildings
> depend for effect upon the decoration ... What I want is to locate
> my dome. I must ask you to take up and go on with the whole thing,
> and judge for yr. self if it's to be Anderson, or Pullan, or anybody
> else – ask anybody's advice that you choose. Pullan[40] seems rather a
> brute personally, and Englishmen are a-sea with Scottish tradesmen.
> But who knows how to do the thing? Of course I must see any plans

first.[41]

He intended dedicating it 'either to the Eternal and Uncreated Wisdom of God (Patronal feast Xmas Day)' since it would be the first church built in Scotland in the 'style of which the Σοφια [Sophia] of Constantinople is the chief type, or to St John of Neponne in allusion to a remarkable incident in the life of Mr McLaughlin. I have so deep a respect for him that I rather incline to the latter.'[42] Patrick McLaughlin[43] was in charge of St Margaret's, Ayr, which was the mother church of the one proposed. Gwen engaged Anderson and plans were quickly sent out to Bute, who returned them with 'two sheets of remarks'.

> The chief drift of it is that I think it had better be made a little longer, as it would be barely big enough for the congregation as it is, and natural increase must be looked to.
>
> I should think that, internally as well as xternally, the brick had better be xposed, & the floor tiled. The apses or any other parts of the chapel can be decorated at any time – however I suppose the apses had better be plastered all over inside at once, as the semi-domes won't be brick ... I rather think the clerestory windows under the dome might be glazed with ruby glass – it's a real Russian dodge.[44]

In Sicily, he found the Church had a 'style of richness and simplicity',[45] though he was a little disturbed by the anti-church feeling in sections of the people. He also made the classic mistake of the Scottish visitor to the Mediterranean.

> It occurred to me yesterday that it would be a good thing to get my face well tanned at once, and I accordingly sat with it uncovered in the sun for three hours. The consequence has been that it has turned the colour of red coral, except around the eyes, which have, as it were, white spectacles, and that the upper part of the forehead is quite raw this morning.[46]

He was in Sicily for Corpus Christi and the real piety awakened by the processions of the Blessed Sacrament moved and delighted him. However he was perturbed that they 'set them all so at us against priests & religion, & Bourbons & all the rest of it'.[47] In comparison to that, the official mourning for Garibaldi was half-hearted:

> A sort of procession gathered a little way up one of the chief streets . . . It was accompanied by a small mob of the less respectable classes

and gazed at in silence by a scanty crowd – very scanty. Everybody kept their hats on, xcept for one man of singularly unprepossessing physique, in the procession itself, and there was absolutely no sign of respect or sympathy of any kind.[48]

Quite unexpectedly, Bute found himself the hero of a real drama.

About 3 this morning, Sneyd came into my room wh. is next to his, and said – 'the house is on fire but there is plenty of time.' I accordingly got up and went into the passage, where I saw that the wooden stair leading up to the attics where the men servants sleep, was in a bright blaze. I . . . put on my Egyptian slippers, a casual pair of trousers & my frock coat, the first things I could find.[49]

He then set about systematically carrying containers full of water from the tanks in the garden up the stairs to where it was needed.

This was not an easy task from the passages & stairs being pitch dark. . . . the kitchen on the ground floor, the back stair on the 1st & the attic stair were all blazing . . . Some people showed great presence of mind & acuity, especially the eldest son of the Director, who got his hand hurt and above all the Neapolitan waiter, named Michale who went about stark naked (and hurt his feet, poor man, especially running down the burning wooden stair from his room) and did more than anybody else to put the fire out. He formed a most ludicrous contrast to the other waiter, Fritz, who seemed to do nothing, and was completely dressed in evening clothes . . . And what do you think it was all about? Wilful fire-raising. The cook's brother, who was employed in the house, had been for some time suspected of stealing the men-servants' money. He was caught in the act yesterday evening . . . Either in revenge, or to burn alive those who might witness against him, he had laid a trail of oil and petroleum-soaked rags through the house, up the wooden stair to the attic where the men slept, and set it alight. The attic windows were barred.

Bute played down his part in putting out the fire, but could not resist sending his wife a newspaper cutting, from which it appears he had a major role. For once he could be quite sure that neither his rank nor his money slanted the reporting, for here he was simply Sig. Stuart. When Gwen responded with praise and alarm, he said that he had only performed what was 'I won't say, one's duty, but one's simple instinct to do, and what everyone would naturally do'.[50] In fact he had done what nobody else did, and with commendable courage and promptness.

The next day was John's first birthday, and Bute recalled the birth in minute detail, reliving all anxieties and the joys of that day. Then he collapsed into reaction, exhausted by the fire and overwhelmed by the stress of the past.

> I tell you frankly that I have only one motive in returning – viz. not to pain you any longer by being away from you. My health, as you know, has been bad for so long, and now I shrink from coming back to the north ... I feel anything but well & it seems only the air & the light & the heat that keep me going. I cling to the hot climates as a wounded beast tries to shelter itself in a hole ... I think it is not impossible that it may have something to do with the heart (of which my father and Uncle died) which requires for comfort the stimulant of these hot climates ... I feel so different in these places from what I do at home. And it keeps floating through my mind – Is it impossible you shd. come out to me? ... However I suppose its no use thinking & I shall be starting homewards. I must say the prospect of passing another winter with you laid up; the sickening anxiety & then hopelessness, in the middle of darkness, cold and wet. And Mgt. [Margaret] possibly falling ill again.[51]

In the winters of 1878–9, and 1879–80 and in the spring of 1882, Gwen had miscarriages, and the winter of 1880–1 must have been one of almost constant worry. Gwen was understandably upset by his outpouring, and Bute was only a little apologetic: 'I am very sorry you are put out by mine of the 20th, but "anything that a man hath will he give for his life" and I can't help feeling the need of light and warmth'.[52] Psoriasis is a condition which can be radically reduced by exposure to ultraviolet light so Bute was probably not mistaken. He asked Gwen to see that all the matters with 'the Padres, including the Bishop and his school' were settled before he arrived. He thought that, perhaps because she was a woman, or because she was not a convert, she could manage such things better. He added, pathetically, 'besides, I don't feel up to a struggle'.[53]

The party left Sicily for Greece, and Bute's spirits recovered with the beauty and the clear air:

> the sea like an ocean of blue oil & the moon & stars more beautiful by night than the sun by day. The setting Venus threw a track of light over the sea at night at right angles to the almost full moon.[54]

Athens was all clear colours and looking at archaeology. There was another bout of sulphur baths, then he headed for home. This time, he was very, very careful not to give any hint that he felt desolate at leaving the sun and the warmth. He told Gwen, instead

> I suppose one never feels much pain in leaving the place where one has been taking sulphur baths. This, however, is certainly a particularly nice place, and someday or other, when we may be about this part of the world, I must bring you here.[55]

She replied with typical warmth: 'My darling you certainly will <u>not</u> have lemon groves or orange flowers here, but you shall go away again if you will only come that I may look at you and give you a kiss, & hear you speak.'[56] But in fact Bute was content enough with Scotland in high summer.

The family returned to Dumfries House, Bute being anxious that his children should come to know and love it. As he had predicted, Gwen became pregnant again almost at once, and so they were fixed there for nine months. It was more pleasant for Bute than being at Chiswick, as he disliked long periods of time spent in London. Gwen, and the doctors she consulted, might and did argue that Chiswick House with its extensive parkland was as good as the countryside,[57] but Bute felt the London fogs which enveloped it must be unhealthy. The main awkwardness for him was that the bulk of his library was on Bute, and he felt that he could not leave Gwen long enough to consult it. The anxiety he felt every time Gwen was pregnant was inescapable wherever he was. He delayed a proposed visit from Grant, with whom he was still labouring over the Proprium:

> In the meantime, I wish to remain free to spend all my time, except when taking needful exercise, in . . . my Lady's room, should she be laid up, which is at any time possible, and indeed must be the case to a certain extent, for precaution's sake . . . Of course, I'm very anxious, and have got the blues, and the eczema foaming out over my body doesn't conduce to cheer me up. Besides, I am beginning, in the almost unceasing rain and darkness of this climate, to feel the symptoms of neuralgia in the neck and head, which frightens me, for the pain is sometimes with me so bad that 1/2 hour makes me fit for nothing for the next 24.

Despite this, he found plenty to laugh over. Considering the saints Maura and Brigida, he asked:

Is their father Alla the one on whose name St Gregory perpetrated his shocking pun of ale-luia? (Bless us! What a hand he'd have been at writing the libretti of pantomimes & comic extravaganzas, if he hadn't been almost sub\supra humanly dull & heavy)[58]

In Grant, he had a confidential correspondent, with whom he could share his amusement at his fellow men, such as a 'cross P.S.' from Hunter Blair, his future biographer.

I had a letter from Hunter Blair, who seems to be in charge of the Ft. Augustus [Monastery] library ... His letter contained a very rude & cross P.S. because I had addressed him (in the innocence of my heart, but which he says 'can hardly have been through inadvertence') as 'Esqr.' whereas he is 'a cleric and professed religious'. It is the first time I ever heard of an acolyte (if he has got so far) wanting the dignity (or first tonsure if it's that) expressed outside his letters ... Isn't it funny? But I am quite ready to address him as 'His Holiness' or anything else that may soothe his nerves.[59]

Grant told Bute that the Benedictines thought that Hunter Blair did not have a vocation, and that he was intending to become a secular priest: 'The end will be that you will yet have to return to the forbidden Esq.!!!'[60] The 'Rev. David' went to Belmont ostensibly to continue his studies, and in fact to allow tensions with his superiors at Fort Augustus to be sorted out.[61]

Dumfries House was also reasonably near Paisley, where an exciting new venture was engaging Bute's sympathy. This was a quarterly periodical, designed to replace the *North British Review,* to support the cause of Scottish Home Rule, and to 'protest against the idea that London is the centre of Scottish life'. Its editor was the Rev. William Metcalfe, and the publisher was William Gardener of Paisley, who was to publish much of Bute's work. Such a project must interest Bute, and from the beginning he wrote for the new magazine. His first article was on ancient Celtic Latin Hymns, 'those of the golden age of the Scoto–Irish church'. He admitted at once that 'some few of these curious poems were clearly not themselves of Celtic origin, but their interest is well nigh the same, as throwing light upon the feeling, practices and beliefs of the school by which they were assimilated'.[62] Like the life of Kentigern, and the later essay on St Patrick, this was a product of his work on the Proprium. He had acquired much new knowledge in his researches, and he enjoyed writing it up into articles.

Troon is also within easy reach of Dumfries House, but Bute did not have the expected pleasure of building his new church there. He arrived back to find that work was well under way and on a design about which he had not even been consulted. To add injury to insult, he was expected to pay for the whole. He was both furious and hurt but decided he must still contribute to the strictly functional building.[63]

Gwen's pregnancy was progressing well. In November, she was 'in the dining room and B's room'.[64] He had left her for a few days, to visit his old friend Lord Rosebery at Dalmally, and attend Rosebery's installation as Rector of Edinburgh University, receiving an honorary degree from him. Lord and Lady Howard came to keep her company. After that, Bute once again spent most of his time with her.[65] By the end of the month she was able to get 'as far as the drawing room, where [she] installed [herself] after breakfast' and stayed till dinnertime.[66] Bute was meantime adding Syriac to his stable of Semitic languages.[67]

That winter, the extended family was involved in one of the domestic squabbles that Bute detested so, but in which his calming and moderating influence was most useful. Gwen's brother, Frank, was engaged to a Miss Clare Greenwood. Lady Howard took an immense dislike to her.[68] Bute himself considered that the match was an unwise one, not because he disapproved of Miss Greenwood's birth, as the Howards did, but because he thought that her intelligence was so far superior to Frank's, and her disposition so masterful, that there was quite likely to be trouble. He knew, however, that Frank was very likely to have a wife who was his intellectual superior.[69] He refused to join all the plots to undermine the relationship, repeating that if Clare Greenwood decided to call off the marriage of her own volition, it was one thing, otherwise Frank must be supported in his choice.[70]

Suddenly in February 1883, Lord Howard became very ill. His doctors and family all believed he was dying. Gwen was in agony:

> I have always dreaded this very thing – being unable to be beside him at this very moment – but I always thought I should be abroad, oh it is so hard you can't think – but of course if the journey brought on the baby – I shd. be laid up and equally unable to see him, and the child would not live – but you may imagine how I feel.[71]

At first she imagined that Lord Howard was barely conscious, but she soon heard that he was 'awake to everything'[72] which made her desire to be with him even greater. Bute urged her to stay where she was, McSwiney pressed the same thing. Lord Howard was surrounded by his family, and the 'eternal welfare' of the baby was paramount,[73] however miserable it was for Gwen to be far from his side. Bute spent almost every minute with Gwen, so that she complained of a 'dreadful day' when he went to Mass from ten o'clock in the morning to half past one in the afternoon, and again to church from five o'clock in the afternoon to 'past 8'.[74] Against all expectation, however, Lord Howard began to improve. He did not regain his former health, but he was out of danger, and plans for the wedding of Frank and Clare continued. Margaret was to be a bridesmaid, and her father went with her up to London in April. Lady Howard was still unable to accept the forthcoming marriage. Gwen's sister Alice, now married to Charley, was picked on, and Bute shuddered that

> the rows seem to have been terrible. Charlie [Charley], in his usual good nature, makes fun of a great deal, but I think that he _feels_ the insults to wh. his wife has been subjected . . . I understand from him that when yr. Father was supposed to be dying, the scenes between Lady H. and Frank were fearful.

He had the tricky job of reporting back to Gwen on the state of her father's health. He did not want to lie to her, but neither did he want to make her anxious in the last days of her pregnancy over a situation she could do nothing at all to improve. He spoke of Lord Howard being up, and sitting in a chair, or walking round the room, to show how far his strength had increased, but added 'I thought his head not perfectly clear at one or two moments just after M. and I came into the room, wh. I attributed rather to the nervous xcitement of seeing us.'[75] Later, when Gwen saw her father again, he admitted that he had known she would be shocked by his appearance.[76] Bute was dismayed by the lack of generosity in the presents given by the family to the bride: 'The display of jewellery is miserable, and yr. Father's present seemed to me a disgrace. It was almost invisible to the naked eye. The dressing case is barely decent.'

The wedding followed, with Bute very proud of his little daughter's appearance and her behaviour. 'She instinctively arranged the Bride's train, very neatly and skilfully.'[77] Lord Howard was not well enough to go to the church, so the bride and groom visited him after the ceremony, and before the reception. Afterwards, Bute took Howard's granddaughter in all her finery to visit him. Concerned that the bride should be made welcome in the family, Bute had lent Cardiff Castle for the honeymoon, reluctantly extending the invitation to Clare's dog, and fearing for the silk chairs and Turkish rugs.[78]

Although convinced that Lady Howard had behaved very badly towards Clare, he was not entirely uncritical of the marriage, as he told Gwen.

> How Frank wd. manage what he should have tried last night seems to have been the subject of general & almost incredibly indecent discussion – Charlie [Charley], with whom I have talked the most frightful things on the subject for the last 48 hours, says even he was taken aback when he went to William Maxwell's rooms, & found a collection of men . . . asking Walter if he had taken care to supply Frank with a pot of cold cream (if you don't see the allusion, ask me).

Even his daughter had heard half-understood allusions:

> Margaret observed this morning at breakfast before all the men-servants that she had been asking herself all night what Frank and Clare were doing. Silence. Then I said, as soon as I could collect myself, that I remembered that the day after our marriage we took a walk on the walls in the forenoon. Mgt. then asked me what it was we did before the forenoon?[79]

Silence again, one imagines. The rest of his trip was taken up with less joyous matters. He was very grieved at the 'destruction'[80] of the grounds around Chiswick House, which had been sold for building. He took Margaret to the doctors, for another check up, and was reassured that as long as she continued to wear her surgical shoe, there was 'no reason to apprehend either curvature of the spine or disease of the hip'.[81] Then he began to make preparations for his trip north, and for the birth of another child.

He had already begun a discussion of possible names for the baby with James McSwiney, whom he was by now addressing in the Celtic form of his name, 'McSuibhne'.[82] Born in London, McSwiney had received most of his education in Belgium at the seminary at Roulers (Roeselare) and in France. He had learned Breton from a fellow student, which enabled him to pick up Welsh later. He was an invaluable friend for a man working in the Celtic languages.

Bute had his heart set on a Celtic saint's name for the unborn baby, preferably one with local associations.[83] If the baby was a girl, he was considering the name of Vey or Maya,[84] a saint who had lived on the island of Cumbrae, which lay between Ayrshire and Bute. He brought back the font, and the relic of St Margaret, and the dried roses from Chiswick House, where they had been since John's birth. Gwen sent to Mount Stuart for the picture of the Virgin.

He also ensured that the Bishop of Galloway was free to come at

Bute's sitting room was the first room created by Burges at Cardiff, and it has the only painted door in the Castle. It shows Sapientia (Wisdom) presiding as the virtues battle the vices. (© Cardiff Council)

A sorrowful angel holds the church of Laodicea; the windows in Bute's bedroom at Cardiff Castle are far from comforting, but Westlake creates the most sensuous of wings for his angels. (© Cardiff Council)

The Bachelor Bedroom was designed before Bute's marriage. It is in the Clock Tower at Cardiff Castle, situated between the Winter and Summer smoking rooms, with murals by Frederick Weekes and centring on the theme of mineral wealth, on which, of course, Bute's fortune was founded. (© Cardiff Council)

Bute's bedroom at Cardiff explores themes from the Revelation of St John, Bute's name-saint. In fact, Bute probably followed his practice elsewhere and slept in his wife's bedroom. (© Cardiff Council)

The perfect illusion of a mediaeval hall was created in Cardiff Castle, the frieze of which shows parts of the story of the Empress Maud, whose story had delighted the child Bute, and the Earl of Gloucester, who was Lord of Glamorgan at the time. (© Cardiff Council)

Architect William Burges's genius for asymmetrical grandeur is perfectly captured in this view of Cardiff Castle. (© Cardiff Council)

Burges created a beautiful and peaceful haven for Bute and his books in the library at Cardiff Castle. It is ornamented with poets and sages. (© Cardiff Council)

Only Bute's daughter Margaret had been born when Burges died. The tile frieze of the nursery at Cardiff Castle is filled with characters from fairytales, a reminder of Bute's delight in reading to his children. Some of the toys and furnishings are not original. (© Cardiff Council)

The Bute Tower at Cardiff ends in a roof garden which directly recalls Bute's adolescent experiences travelling in the Levant, where he found the Maronite bishop's roof garden 'the most perfect apartment.' (© Cardiff Council)

The exterior of the Clock Tower at Cardiff Castle, with its figures representing the planets, created long before Bute had any interest in astronomy. (© Cardiff Council)

Left. In a detail from the Small Dining Room fireplace, a young man entangled in stylised undergrowth hunts a wyvern. (© Cardiff Council)

Below. So many of Burges's trademarks surface in the Small Dining Room at Cardiff Castle: the jelly mould ceiling, ornate fireplace, and the unified theme, in this case the Genesis story of Abraham and Sarah, who not only entertained angels unawares, but also had a late-born beloved only son. (© Cardiff Council)

It is in its detail that Cardiff Castle is most convincing. Here the sun lights up Weekes's murals and the carved and inlaid panels created in the Bute Workshops to Burges's designs. (© Cardiff Council)

The Summer Smoking Room at Cardiff re-creates something of Bute's experience of the 'grand smoke' at Chios. It also plays to Burges's themes, with the legend of Psyche round the walls. (© Cardiff Council)

The Winter Smoking Room at Cardiff is again themed around the pursuits of love. In 1873 the Butes lunched there and 'dear Burges was present & quite content with his work'. (© Cardiff Council)

short notice for the baby's baptism. Bute tried hard to persuade him that it would be a good idea to confirm the baby soon after birth, but to no avail. Not for nothing did the Butes call him 'Grandmother' in private.[85] The conservative cleric was polite but unconvinced. The preparations made, the Butes settled down to await the new baby. On 9 May, Bute confided to Colin Grant

> I xpected my Lady's confinement before now, & it may happen any time. I have been feeling more anxious than perhaps I need, and the constant anxiety day after day & night after night has got rather upon my nerves. I am told that by a provision of nature these things do not usually happen in a strong, cold, bitter wintry east wind.[86]

Bute had to wait until 15 May for the birth of his second son and the next day 'our rt. Rev. chairman baptised him . . . by the name of Ninian. He (N.) and his Mama are both exceedingly flourishing.[87] The great Saint Ninian had founded the first of Scotland's Christian settlements at 'Candida Casa' or Whithorn, and a chapel dedicated to him was founded on Bute. It was also a name from the early years of the Stuart of Bute family.

When the strain of the pregnancy and birth was over, Bute went to Harrogate for treatment for his skin.[88] After the stress of his father-in-law's illness and his wife's pregnancy, he again suffered a reaction. His worst moments coincided with a spell of very wet weather: 'Down it pours, down it pours, never ceasing, or when it does, for a few minutes, never hours – and it is still always dark.'[89] His feelings of irrational, or partially irrational, gloom or depression coincided either with winter or with very dark and wet summer weather. Bute may well have been right in thinking that the winter made him ill; it is only a hundred years later that seasonal affective disorder has become a recognised diagnosis.

He was summoned by telegram to speak at the Eisteddfod which was in Cardiff that year. He got into a state of disproportionate anxiety about this, recalling over and over again his panic on reading what seemed to him terrible news. It was not so much the speaking that alarmed him, as the necessity for entertaining. He remembered every row and difficulty from Cardiff in the past:

> It isn't the business I mind. It is the certainty that I have learned by so many years experience that it is impossible for me to do anything there without a row, so that every visit of mine there does much more harm than good.[90]

Miserably, he accepted the social necessity of going.

He was disinclined to make the effort to talk to Jack Stuart, who was his Factor's son and George Sneyd's brother-in-law,[91] or to send for Woodward. It is not surprising, as neither shared his interests. Jack Stuart left, and Bute was able to occupy himself with work, including writing his hour-long speech for the Eisteddfod, and as the weather improved, he gradually became more sanguine. Gwen still felt he should have a companion, but his habit of being tongue-tied with all but his intimates troubled him: 'for instance this afternoon, when . . . with the Priest Nath & young Redcliff, I felt quite awkward at having nothing to say'.[92]

He was cheered to discover that the Eisteddfod was an earnest matter and:

> a dance wd. be a kind of insult to it – or a heavy feed either. Besides that, several evenings of the week will . . . be occupied by concerts – doubtless of a solemn and national character – wh. one had better attend in state . . . But you must remember that of all things pregnant with infernal rows – & of which they never go wrong – invitations & entertainment are the most prolific.[93]

He began to make quite cheerful plans for the concert and the visit. What he never learnt to do was to take the 'rows' over precedence and hurt feelings, in short all the paraphernalia of social climbing, with the amused detachment of a Disraeli.

Gwen travelled to Chiswick to see her invalid father. She was shocked at his appearance. Both she and Bute felt that his health was being further damaged by his wife's heartlessness. Howard would have been far happier out of town, but Lady Howard was reluctant to leave. The Butes felt that, if he could not leave town, he would at least be happier at Chiswick House, but Lady Howard was reluctant to allow him to go there. Bute wondered if she was afraid that 'people' would persuade him to change his will.[94] More likely she was simply afraid of the gossips saying that her husband was much happier with his daughter than his wife, a possibility that did not seem to occur to the Butes. They were distressed and outraged to discover that he had not been allowed enough ready money out of his considerable fortune for the fare for a cab to visit Gwen, and debated a way of getting him transport that would not wound his feelings.[95] Relations between Gwen and her stepmother, and indeed her sister Winefred, who was at home unmarried, were at a very low ebb.

Bute sent supportive and consoling letters to Gwen, but he made no move to join her. He needed, of course, to prevent his psoriasis getting out of hand, but perhaps he needed just as much to escape the rows and difficulties in Gwen's family. From Harrogate it was easy to walk the rolling Yorkshire countryside, and to visit such places as Ripon, where the Minster had been 'much injured as well as improved, by restoration'.[96] In fact, he began to consider having a house built for him at Harrogate.

The family were reunited in August at Cardiff, and Bute made an utterly anodyne speech in English at the Eisteddfod. Gwen's father was still unwell, and after the Eisteddfod she decided that the only thing she could do was to wean Ninian, who was now five months old, and go to Lord Howard, to protect him from his wife. It was a considerable sacrifice, for Gwen loved to be with her babies, whom she carried with such difficulty, and to feed them herself.

> I do hope dear Ninian will have done well that 1st night with Campbell. I do not get rid of the milk at all easily, and I feel almost wicked whenever it comes up, that I do not give it to him, but I cannot do everything – and I think it did not nourish him much.[97]

Bute returned alone to Harrogate. Of course, he was never quite alone; he always had his manservant Hew with him, which was sometimes a doubtful blessing. They moved to another hotel, the *Prospect*: 'My installation here was inaugurated by an outbreak of Hew's unfortunate failing'. Hew was sent to fetch a morning paper, some cigarettes, and some books which Bute wanted to discuss with Anderson, who was to visit him. Hew then vanished. Anderson came to visit 'but no Hew – and no cigarettes'. Bute bought his own paper and cigarettes, and Hew turned up drunk about half past five. By the evening, he was sober and blaming 'fatigue' for his lapse. Bute accepted the excuse but ordered him not to reappear until the morning.[98]

He continued to worry over Gwen's father, and also the miserable state of his brother-in-law's marriage. With Clare pregnant and vulnerable, Frank was treating her abominably.

> He ought to have felt the luxury of having everything done for him by an able person, who was both willing and able to put him in the best light, and she ought to be contented to bear with a little annoyance, and the need of some exercise of tact, by the possession of absolute actual power.[99]

At first he thought that perhaps the worst aspect of Frank's behaviour was his insistence on seeing all 'the letters that C writes, even to her mother if I understand this rightly; it is certainly intolerable. Just think if I had had the folly to insist upon seeing all yours to your Father, sisters and friends'.[100] He came to realise Frank had been controlling and verbally abusive. Bute considered storming off to the young couple's home in Doncaster but 'the deliverance of this poor woman must be by her husband's family ... I am only the brother-in-law.' He warned Gwen to remember, too

> that if a third person interferes in a quarrel between husband & wife they both leave off fighting in order to fall on him ... I agree with yr. suggestion that the best thing that cd. happen wd. be a separation till, say, Feb, when he ought to go to be present at Chiswick at the confinement.

Bute dodged inviting Frank to accompany him to Greece, but thought he should visit his other brothers-in-law, adding pointedly 'the society of gentlemen might possibly do him good & cdn't do him any harm'.[101]

That autumn Bute had agreed to stand as Rector of Glasgow University. He had been nominated by the Conservative students. The Liberal students put forward their candidate to oppose him, and unfortunately launched a series of nasty personal attacks on him. Conveniently ignoring his recent scholarship, they remembered that 'His Lordship had been distinguished at Oxford, but not as a scholar (laughter and applause). He was distinguished because he spent £11,000 a year while he was there.'[102] They went on to accuse him of having tried to buy this election by his much earlier gift of the Bute Halls to the University. It was not so much the defeat as the personal abuse that hurt him. As *The Glasgow Herald* commented, the students might have spared him. He was not active in party politics at all, except occasionally to vote in the Lords at his party's call.[103] To ensure his cup was full, the chairman of the Conservative students told him in private that while his opponents never made public use of Bute's Catholicism, it had nevertheless affected the minds of many of the electors.[104]

Bute was consoled by plans to spend the winter abroad. He had the prospect of a new secretary for the trip, a Mr Gatty. Bute's first interview with him was 'quite exciting ... He was quite frank and dealing with him was agreeable ... my impression is that his Greek is at least as good as mine. His Latin is much weaker.'[105] Bute told him that he did not wish for a regular secretary, but would employ him for occasional travels. Bute was trying to rattle through the work he needed to finish first. As he told Margaret, now seven years old: 'I write a great deal more than I used to do at Stafford House as I have not got you and Mama to talk to.' This time, he was determined to take Margaret with him. She, with her questioning mind, and her lively intelligence, was much more of a companion to him than any of his secretaries. Despite inheriting her mother's high colouring, her broad shoulders and high-bridged nose made her look a great deal more like her father. He told her, ruefully joking, 'I am sure it will be great fun – even to see me being sick.'[106]

Then it became plain that Lord Howard was failing, and the Butes could not leave. Howard finally died on 1 December. The Duke of Norfolk arranged the funeral, which involved the coffin travelling by train. For Bute this brought back painful memories of his mother's funeral. He protested to the Duke and got a decidedly dusty answer.[107] With the funeral over, the Butes went to Dumfries House for Christmas 1883. Gwen 'immediately fell ill. They called it measles' but Bute thought it was 'nervous reaction and misery'.[108] He was convinced that Margaret, too, was 'pining' from lack of sun and warmth, and, as soon as he could arrange it, he swept his whole family off to the Mediterranean and Athens.

Bute had been sure that they would all be healthier. Instead, the children caught a fever, and were seriously ill. In late June they had recovered enough to leave for home with their mother. After the fever, Margaret's weakness made her limp much more pronounced. Dr Adams explained to Gwen that Margaret's birth had caused the problem. The baby had been delivered with forceps which had damaged one hip,[109] and this had caused the leg to fail to grow properly. He reassured Gwen that it was in fact 'a common thing'.[110] Margaret was 'much pulled down by the fever and as a consequence terribly slouched in walk, limping a great deal and with one shoulder much pushed up & the opposite hip much thrown out'.[111] She was to work with a trapeze, in order to strengthen and straighten her shoulders and back, and to work lying on her front on an inclined board, and to ride for exercise. Gwen, who had been horrified at earlier suggestions of irons, exclaimed thankfully that this advice was 'the most sensible and practical I have heard yet'.[112]

Margaret's compensation was her lively brain and her ability with languages. As Gwen told Bute: 'Margaret . . . is your own daughter and no mistake. I am sure she will have tastes exactly like you and poor darling I hope she will grow up strong and be a real companion to you – but she must be made to walk better and grow straight before anything else.'[113] Despite treatment, every photograph of Margaret from childhood to adulthood shows her standing with one shoulder characteristically drawn up to compensate for her short leg. Margaret, now eight years old, had a governess called Jones. Bute had decided that Margaret should learn Latin, which Jones did not know,[114] and, typically, Gwen was all for sacking her and hiring a different governess. Bute suggested it would be better to encourage Jones to 'teach herself enough Latin to keep a few lessons ahead of Margaret'.[115]

In fact, Bute always had to devote a certain amount of time to preventing Gwen getting into quarrels. Gwen wanted to avoid inviting her brother to Mount Stuart, but Bute urged her to at least ask them. He decided, realistically, that Frank and his wife were 'the kind of people that we are not likely to be very sympathetic with', but that if Gwen asked them to visit, they probably would not come 'and anyhow the thing wd be soon over and need never happen again. I think it'd be better to do it, & we cd. drop them quietly, like Flora has us.'[116]

At times however, Gwen's downrightness was an advantage. This summer she returned to Balmory on the Isle of Bute to superintend building works at Mount Stuart and to harry the workers there.

> Here I have been since Friday, and I find Anderson (who came today) Jack Stuart and indeed all the people very difficult to get on with, but I was very firm with Anderson today, in going over the house and I have gained the day in most ways.[117]

Bute continued abroad, seeking improvement to the psoriasis. He was at Sorrento,

> one of those places . . . where mere existence seems a keen luxury . . . the Hotel faces north and stands directly over the sea. If I were to throw a stone out of the window, it would fall several hundred feet into the sea. I can see the bottom of the sea, and when the boats pass, they seem to float through the air, so clear is the water, and so great the distance between them and the bottom.[118]

Apparently, he had been advised by some 'pill box' that swimming in the sea would be bad for him, but the beautiful water tempted him, and he began to swim again. To his delight, the psoriasis began to disappear 'as if I were taking Harrogate waters . . . The sea-water is salt like brine, it smarts one's eyes and nose; and if you only keep your head back and your arms under the surface, you float like a bit of wood.'[119]

The beauty of Sorrento was somewhat damped as the sirocco began to blow, and he became impatient to leave. He was to travel to Greece in the Norfolks' boat – as soon as it was ready. He had been promised that it would leave on 21 July, but on the day before he reported that:

> The stores for the yacht have not arrived. The second engineer has not arrived. The head steward has not arrived. The men's clothes have not arrived. The men themselves are three short. I fear we cannot leave tomorrow.[120]

He was not free from family concerns even when travelling. That summer, a main worry was Gwen's youngest sister Winefred, who was considering becoming a nun. None of the family believed she had a true vocation. Bute reviewed the situation. She had had

> numerous love affairs – Mr Stopford, the man who had been a Catholic and became a Protestant, and Lord Feilding ... It is perfectly obvious that W wants to marry and is extremely amatory in disposition. Her past adventures show she is as inflammable as a hay-stack. The nun-dodge is a mere *pis-aller* [worse than second-best substitute] (Our Lord a *pis-aller* from Mr Tom, Mr Dick and Mr Harry!!!) in a fretful moment of disappointment.

Bute was also made very uneasy that Winefred was being pressed by her priest to join an order for which she had no liking:

> the money object is evident from the consideration that Beste selects the order he has control over, as opposed to the one she wished. It is monstrous and outrageous that a person should not choose for themselves the Order they are to enter – and to say that a person has a vocation for such and such an Order, when, as a matter of fact, they want to enter another is a formal contradiction in terms.[121]

He suggested that Gwen should lay the whole case before Manning, 'only ... take care he hears you, for he's very deaf'. Winefred did enter a convent, but only very briefly.

Meanwhile, Bute was travelling in the Norfolks' yacht through the Greek islands, full of sunlight and vivid images.

> The currants seem to be drying in beds on the ground all over the country, and the colour of these beds of dying black grapes is the most marvellous deep dead purple I think I have ever seen, especially

when it is set off by the marvellous living green of the vines close to or through wh. one sees it. The beds these currants are laid to dry on are thickly smeared with dung, not fresh, but the real cess pool business, including, I think, our own aunt as well that of other animals in an advanced state of corruption. It is brought in tin cans and the stink while it is being laid on is quite startling. They say it keeps the currants hot below, and I daresay it does – but it don't stimulate one's appetite for plum pudding.[122]

He visited the Island of Patmos, the traditional place of the vision of his name-saint St John, alleged author of the book of Revelation. For Bute it was a moving experience, and he wrote about it in an article published in the following year. He found the island 'belonged to that class of Greek landscape strongly suggestive of the north-west coast of Scotland'. Bute felt that no better background to the tenth chapter of Revelation could be imagined than the view from the actual island.[123]

Gatty was with him and also Hartwell Grissell[124] and an (unnamed) Apostolic Legate who alternately amused and exasperated Bute with behaviour common to a certain kind of tourist: 'while we pass a place, he don't look at it but reads somebody's description of it'. Also with the party was a young Greek called Panagiotes Kaloguopoulos, whose name, in writing, Bute usually abbreviated to 'K'. He was Greek Orthodox, devout but intelligently critical.

One of the reasons why K was so important to Bute was that he was one of the few friends Bute made who was his equal in alert intelligence. Gatty, of whom Bute had had such hopes, turned out to be disappointingly pedestrian. He had worked in the Liverpool Museum, and he was to work for the British Museum, but he lacked that spark of originality which set Bute's sympathies on fire. Also, he was not fit enough to accompany Bute on his walks. Hartwell Grissell was in some ways even more unsatisfactory than Gatty, being less intelligent and hardly more athletic. He was Bute's co-religionist, but with none of Bute's questionings. Bute increasingly lumped them together on this voyage as 'the Gs'.[125]

There were so few people able to offer him a truly equal friendship. He still had Sneyd, but Burges was dead, and he would have to leave K behind to his own life in Athens. He had his growing family, and in particular Lady Margaret, and his much loved wife, but he badly needed friends, people of his own age and abilities; but there were few his equal in originality and intelligence. Bute realised that 'I don't think that the company of the G's is very good for me, on several grounds, including making me idle and conceited'.[126] Conceited because he so easily outclassed them physically and mentally, and idle both for that reason and because he stopped walking and swimming at his desired level to accommodate them.

He had another problem, too. His disenchantment with the Catholic Church, or more especially with its clergy, was growing. In Continental Europe, anticlericalism was part of life. He could not but hear the comments on every side. He would doubtless have found them a great deal easier to ignore if his own experience had not backed them up. He might have dismissed Capel's betrayal of his trust, and exploitation of his wealth, but he could not dismiss so easily his troubles with his own parish clergy.

For the clergy, Bute was a nightmare. Ordinary parish priests were, technically, his religious superiors, but they not only lacked his background and wealth, they lacked his education in all religious matters. It was not simply Latin or theology he knew better than they, it was church protocol. For a poorly educated Irishman to have as one of his parishioners the Most Honourable, the Marquess of Bute, Knight of the Thistle etc, would have been difficult enough. For the same Irishman to have the Marquess in his own vestry, the tall, broad frame dressed in a cassock and surplice of his own providing, looming over the poor man, or standing silently beside his altar, immensely knowledgeable about the minutest details of the ceremonial of the day, and ready to offer an instant prompt at the slightest sign of fumbling must have stretched the nerves of his priests to screaming point. The fact that the prompt was kind and gentle and utterly guileless must frequently have added to the irritation.

The parish priest at Cumnock was to be Daniel Collins.[127] Bute had built a new church at Cumnock in thanksgiving for the birth of his first son. It was a barn of a building by Burges and lavishly decorated. The Butes were providing a paid choir (a logical extension of Gwen's early work in providing a small choir for Bute's services) and also a choirmaster and organist. There had been a struggle to get a priest for the chapel. Cumnock was a desperately poor community with many Irish immigrants. It needed all the help it could get. In the summer of 1882, with Bute away, Gwen had undertaken to ask questions on Bute's behalf, largely to save him a 'row'. She wrote resignedly:

If I can get to the bottom of what all the Bp's intentions [are] that will be something ... & I know he hates women, I don't think he will like me very much when he is done with me, however I can't help it ... what I want to get at is – what I mean to ask the Bishop point blank is why is there not to be a priest attached to the

Cumnock chapel.[128]

Gwen fought the good fight and prevailed. Daniel Collins was appointed to Cumnock,[129] and complained bitterly that when in Cumnock, Bute had not been to the Friday service. Bute replied that this was because it largely consisted of 'the Rosary, wh., in public, wearies me to irritability. If Collins had stuck to the service at the end of the little prayer-books ... & given a wee reading at the end of it, it wd. have been all right, I think.'

The latest problem was the provision of a servant for Collins. Bute had offered to pay for a man servant for him, and Collins was insisting he should have a live-in female housekeeper. Bute thought there would be 'what's politely called a "clerical scandal" within twelve months' of her installation. Then he exploded: 'Perhaps it won't be a scandal, though, because it will be kept secret. I confess the longer I live, the more indications I find that the Padre's chastity consists very often in not being found out, or else not being talked about when it is found out by their flocks.' If there was a pregnancy, then 'all the others swear their great gods it wasn't that unless he marries or becomes a Protestant, and then they tell the truth sharp enough, – and sometimes lies in addition'. He added that if Collins wanted a woman he would need to pay her wages himself.[130]

K in contrast was able robustly to defend his Orthodox church, and, paradoxically, this seems to have comforted Bute, and given him hope for the Catholic church:

K is very amusing. I hope I shan't become an anti-clerical, though I am sure the behaviour of the Padres is enough to produce the result. K says there's no such thing as anti-clericalism in Greece, because the Padres being married brings religion home and don't create a separate, anti-social caste. He labours under the delusion that the A[postolic] L[egate's] obvious imbecility is the depth of Jesuitical art.[131]

K and the Gs were his companions on hilarious adventures, like the trip to Sparta where the accommodation was more than Spartan, and where Gatty had a migraine that laid him up. It was K who enhanced his pleasure in the ridiculous:

we arrived at Sparta at 1-45 ... and found G and K at a singularly feeble shadow of a hotel, like an open shop. The lower story was a restaurant, the upper had one furnished (?) room with beds full of bugs (the landlord himself put in the flea powder formally and publicly over night, & in the morning there was quite a spoonful of the creatures) & one wash-hand basin, in the passage. Aunt was quite indescribable – a triangular hole in a wooden floor, in a lean-to with part of the wall wanting towards a downstairs chamber.[132]

The party reached Athens on 1 September, and Hew began drinking and hadn't 'been sober, to speak of'[133] until 4 September. He was too drunk again on 5 September to help serve dinner, leaving another servant, Tom, to manage serving a large party alone. 'I am very angry with him', said Bute, especially enraged at the lack of consideration to Tom, '& shall give him a talking to one of these days'.

K's ability to steer a way between the Scylla and Charybdis of being a prude and indulging in 'loose' jokes and conversation where Bute felt his all-too-lively sense of humour sometimes led him astray, stood in sharp contrast to another set he met in Athens. 'We went to the Schuylers to breakfast, nobody but us, his friend Fisk, the Bakhmetieffs, & Lyon.' First came the disillusion of drinking his first 'cocktail' and finding it was not 'a kind of refreshing fizzy drink of the brandy-and-soda type' but instead a mixture of spirits and bitters 'more like a dose of medicine'. After that they breakfasted in the garden. Bute would have thought the conversation 'loose if the party had consisted entirely of unmarried men', but the two married ladies joined in happily; it 'seemed to have occurred to them that indecent talking wd. form a nice amusement and accordingly they had resorted to it, and coined an xpression to describe it. They called it 'XVIIIth Century'.[134]

Bute's psoriasis was not markedly better. He had to a large degree learned to live with it, and was doubtful of taking some of the cures he was offered, fearing that the treatment would be worse than the condition. As a common treatment was arsenic, he was probably wise.[135] He was more concerned about the cough he had every morning which he thought was part of the psoriasis. 'There is hardly a morning I don't cough up something when I get up, though I'm all right after that for the day'.[136] Nobody was aware of the link between smoking and lung disease, so Bute did not change his heavy smoking habit.

He suggested to Gwen that it might be a good idea to spend Christmas in Athens. She exploded. She had been working hard on Mount Stuart hoping to have it ready for him for Christmas, and then came home to find letters from him proposing he spent the festival abroad. Did he, she enquired, expect her to spend Christmas alone with the children, or was she to abandon them?

After a hard day at work at Mount Stuart, hoping to have the place ready for you in 2 months time I came home ... & found two letters ... you say if I stay abroad this winter I shall stay at Athens but what a Xmas what a Christmas indeed – and do you xpect me to come out to you & leave the children without a <u>Christian</u> Christmas – & do you xpect me to be with them and away from you? I cannot see what possible excuse you can make for staying out of the country so long a time, & never had I xpected this staying out for Christmas even in yr. wildest moments this calm way you say you may be away at Christmas when you have children and a most beautiful home waiting for you here.[137]

After this, it is surprising that Bute could still grumble a little, 'If it wasn't for seeing you and the babies, you know I shouldn't be very cheerful',[138] as he left Athens in October, to spend Christmas in the Mount Stuart upon which Gwen had been working so hard.

'I should like Lord Bute's ideas to be carried out'[1]

Gwendolen, Lady Bute, seems an improbable clerk of works, but while Bute was away in 1884, her love for him, her innate perfectionism, and the desire to achieve all that he wished her to, gave her a pretty much full-time job in this line. Bute had always regarded Mount Stuart as his principal home, and progress on building a new house on the original site after the fire of 1877 had been slow.

The initial delay had been caused by Bute's hesitation over whether to rebuild in the shell of the Georgian house. The fire had gutted the internal structures of the house, but left the exterior walls standing. The east, sea-facing façade of Mount Stuart House had been built according to McGill's design from 1716,[2] and had been left pretty much untouched, as shown by photographs taken after the fire. The west face had been considerably altered, and photographs show a modest extension with balcony, pillars and decorative features which were not there at the time of Bute's coming of age.[3] This is not surprising, as the 'barrack-like' exterior of the building had been much criticised, and space within was always at a premium.

The plans for restoration by Anderson preserved the whole of the exterior to east, north and south, but threw an extension towards the west, producing 'a rectangular block larger than the old *corps de logis*, nearly symmetrical, with two bay windows to the landward [i.e. west] side of the house'.[4] However an oriel window was to be added to the east which, as Andrew McLean points out, is very similar to the window at Balmory House, the small rented property on the island where the Butes were staying at the time, and which would have sat incongruously on the austere façade of the old Mount Stuart, even in its refurbished form.

Over these plans for the reinstatement of the old Mount Stuart with selected additions, including a block of kitchens to the north, is drawn in a sketchy hand a radically different plan for a new building. The basic form of the new house is a most ungothic block. It takes as its starting point the line of the west façade of the old house, and extends it slightly, so that it meets the north wing of the old house square on, and takes a small slice of the south wing.

Then it flings boldly backward, projecting beyond the two wings, instead of lying recessed between them, and, at this stage, envisages two towers on the new east face. A tiny pencil drawing towards the bottom of this plan offers a projected elevation of this. It is nothing like the final smooth façade of the new Mount Stuart, being much more church-like, Burgesian in all but its symmetry, rather than the 'lean and spartan functional lines preferred by Anderson'.[5]

The sketch in its very roughness suggests strongly that it was a spontaneous creation, surely between patron and architect at a single meeting. Ian Gow speaks of 'a ghost' of the old Mount Stuart in the arrangement of rooms in the new one.[6] It is indeed remarkable how far the internal arrangements were preserved. Instead of a large vestibule, we now get, over the very same spot, a square 'atrium'. Because the front wall has moved so far forward, this is now at the centre of the building, as cross-marked lines point out.

The new drawing room is designed to be larger than the old, but is in the same position, giving the same views. The library is again to one side, and once again, the bedroom is placed over it. The dining room again is to the west. Every room is slightly larger, and there are more rooms, but each important or family room comes home to the same spot. The new proposed oriel window metamorphosed into bay windows in the personal sitting rooms, and study and library.

Given the apparent emphasis on the Gothic in the new building as it was completed, the sketchy ground-plan, later executed very faithfully, is quite extraordinarily square and blocky. It is very much the design of an Italian *Palazzo*, or perhaps the original of that, the Roman villa. It was a late flowering of the 'Gothic dream' for as Mordaunt Crook points out, its greatest flowering was over by the 1870s,[7] and the 1880s were the period of the Aesthetic movement, typified by Oscar Wilde, and satirised by W. S. Gilbert in *Patience* (1882). Bute still loved the Gothic style, and Anderson had undoubted mastery of it.

Anderson had been faced with a serious limitation. Bute wanted to keep the surviving two wings of the Georgian house. This may in part have been nostalgia, for Mount Stuart was associated with Bute's childhood, and his mother. Of course, he was also a great conservationist, and generally deplored the Victorian habit of despising Georgian elegance. More likely he was determined to keep the emotionally charged Burges chapel in the one wing, and the room known as the Prime Minister's room, commonly, though probably erroneously, associated with the 3rd Earl, in the opposing wing. Faced with the necessity of building a much larger house while keeping much within the east frontage of the older, smaller house, and an extension to the west, Anderson had but small choice of further directions in which to go: up, and down. He chose to do both.

The house is built on a slope (it is doubtful whether there is a house on the Isle of Bute which is not) and only enjoys its full seven floors at the eastern face,[8] looking down over a lawn to the Firth of Clyde, then even more than now busy with shipping. The sea opens towards the south, and there lie Bute's smaller sister isles of Big and Little Cumbrae. On the other shore roll the hills of Ayrshire, and hidden in their folds, the Marquess's seat at Cumnock. On this seaward face Anderson created the more interesting façade. There are regularly spaced Gothic windows, differing in their detail, but most with two arches, with a quatrefoil between them, set in a larger arch. The surface of the wall is then further broken with balconies and bay windows, designed to allow enjoyment of the pure air and outstanding views.

In the attics lay a warren of servants' bedrooms. Under them come a circle of handsome bedrooms designed for visiting guests. When the house was built these looked onto an open balcony. In the early 1880s a portico or colonnade was added, so that when it was wet Bute could walk here, and get exercise without being soaked.[9] These bedrooms sit above and to one side of the covered square, which forms the centre of the house and its Great Hall. They rise above the well of the central hall and shield it from wind and rain, which is a significant matter on the westerly situated island, raked by Atlantic gales and storms, where winds reach hurricane speeds once or twice in each generation. Unfortunately, they also prevent sunlight reaching its windows in winter.

This Great Hall is the glory of the house, its innermost dimension a square 32 foot 8½ inches. It rises in three storeys, each framed with Gothic arches, the topmost two being variations of the double arch within a single larger arch that Anderson used on the exterior of the building. On the top tier, these frame clerestory windows. On the second, slightly larger arches lead to a groined gallery (one where four intersecting arched vaults meet in a central cross) repeated down the length, producing a design of pleasing simplicity and great strength. From this gallery, doors open to family rooms, except on the south side, where a grand marble staircase rises with shallow treads in three short flights with two quarter-landings from the principal floor, the *piano nobile*. Here too, are pillars, now supporting single massive arches, of similar proportions to the encompassing single arch on the floors above, but so scaled as to suggest through cunning use of perspective that the eighty-foot-high hall is in fact even higher.

At this level, the north side is occupied by a spacious ante hall, lit by three windows, and with a beamed ceiling. Another flight of stairs leads down to the main door which is at actual ground level to the west. The staircase to the south is equally well lit by a window running the height of the building. The dining room is a bright and open room, not pillared at all and looking onto the garden. It lies behind the shadowy colonnade to the west of the hall. The drawing room is set to the east side. It is divided into three bays by marble pillars, and is probably the least pleasing room in the house.

The pillars in the house are formed in various ways, according to their size and structure. Some are square, or multiple squares, with single narrow columns in their interstices, others are single or twin columns, and perhaps the most spectacular are the massive, simple, single columns some 6 feet 5 inches in diameter, sitting on larger bases, which run round the Great Hall at its foot. A wide variety of marbles is used for the columns. Bute had at first considered using granite for the work, although given his usual careful approach to spending money, his reported comment that the extra projected cost of £20,000 did not weigh with him should perhaps be taken with a pinch of salt. All the columns have a white Carrara marble capital, designed to be carved; and not merely with formalised acanthus leaves, but with naturalistic leaves and flowers and additional details, such as the spider and spider's web in the drawing room, and the limpets and whelks in among the seaweeds of the Great Hall. In the whole house, only two capitals repeat a design, and the folklore of the house is that the carver guilty of this slip was sacked. The quantity and quality of carving demanded many man-hours from the most skilled craftsmen, and the work was never totally finished. It revealed the need for a fairly constant supervisor for the building as early as 1883. In an effort to speed work along, a second team of carvers had been introduced to work on the marble capitals. The original team had taken great offence, and the chief of them wrote to Bute, full of indignation:

Another firm has orders to send men to undertake this work & their representative has arrived for the purpose ... In any case my Lord this rivalry which it will cause will not produce the highest class of work for it requires a person not to be disturbed and agitated to carry work out to a successful issue.[10]

Plainly, everyone knew that the suggestion that the quality of the work would be affected was the one most likely to get Bute's attention. Bute left Harrogate, where he was taking the waters, and travelled to Mount Stuart to sort out the matter.

Now, in the summer of 1884, Gwen devoted herself to the work of harrying, inspecting, and inspiring the workmen who were labouring in the uninhabited shell of the new Gothic extravaganza. She installed her 'babies' in Dumfries House, an easy day's journey away. They continued to recover from their fever in the unhurried country atmosphere, while she went to live in the much smaller, rented, Balmory House, to work on the creation of one of the most extraordinary domestic interiors of the Victorian age. She undoubtedly only saw herself as a poor second-best to Bute and often found it a very difficult role to fulfil:

> It is not pleasant work altogether although the head men are civil and bear with me ... still I am always grumbling & I cannot be a pleasant sight for them – if it is to give you the pleasure of finding the house got on & the place in order for you I don't mind how much I slave but if you are not coming pray say so.[11]
>
> I do wish you would come here and see to the stocking and arranging of your new conservatory, it is very large, as large as the sitting room and you ought to be beginning to fill it. I am sure you would find work enough – and here are rooms in wh. you cd. have friends for all the guest rooms are really done and dry and only want doing up – wh. of course I can't do alone.[12]

In fact she stayed at work on the house till Bute returned in September 1884, and seems to have been very effective in her chosen role. The work at hand in this period was the fitting out of the guest bedrooms, and the family rooms, and of course the essential nursery. This, along with the libraries, lies in a wing to the south, which runs behind the Georgian kitchen. The carving of the marble in the drawing room must also have been well advanced, although the woodwork was not yet installed in the dining room, the floor was not laid in the Great Hall, and the present elaborate decoration of the family rooms was not yet embarked upon.

This was not merely a mediaeval extravaganza. Burges had been laughed at for the lack of comfort in his houses. This home was designed to be heated centrally from the start. The beautiful open fireplaces were only to add to the comfort derived from the background warmth. However sympathetic Bute was to aspects of Gothic idealism he was a realist, as was his architect. The building looks as if it is supported on soaring marble columns and stout timber beams. In reality, the framework of the house is the metal girders which support it in all directions: in walls, between floors and within pillars.

There was also electricity in the house. Bute had had a simple temporary lighting system installed in Cardiff Castle before October 1883,[13] and now he returned to the same firm, W. Massey of Twyford. Massey, hearing that Lady Bute intended to finish some of the rooms at Mount Stuart, had moved with commendable commercial good sense to convince her of the need for electric light, and had 'ventured to fix a few lamps in order that her Ladyship might have a light of some kind when she came'. The Butes, especially Lord Bute, for whom electric lighting was to become a hobby, had been delighted by the arrangement, leaving poor Mr Massey to worry that his very provisional first fix would be taken by the Butes for the best he could do. The final system was to have 'duplicate or reserve',[14] presumably in the system which powered it, the Butes having opted for a simple and unpicturesque generator.

The result was that by the time Bute returned home in the autumn of 1884, such progress had been made on the house that the family were able to spend their first Christmas in it. Bute's long-time friend Rosebery congratulated him 'on being in your new house. Rumour paints it as something beyond the Arabian Nights.'[15] For once, rumour did not exaggerate.

When Bute returned from abroad, the building lost its most able project manager, and Gwen reverted to the role of Bute's companion and occasional hostess at her various homes, as well as continuing to mother her children. Bute to some extent stepped into her shoes, but he always had irons in so many fires that supervising his buildings could easily be sidelined. In fact, in 1885 Bute was not in a position to do much personal supervising, and it seems that in 1885–86 very little progress was made at Mount Stuart. Another pregnancy anchored both Butes in London and this did little or nothing to advance work at Mount Stuart. Poor Mr Massey, in charge of the electric lighting, was left bemused, as Lady Bute gave a command to 'stop the lighting'. Massey blamed the architect:

The architects can never tell me anything – although they can most effectually prevent me getting money on a/c of work done, – and it is not easy to know exactly what to do to please everybody – ...

but I shall certainly be sorry if Lady Bute does not approve of what has been done with the best intentions in the world.[16]

As late as 1887, Bute was still pondering the options. It did not help that he had developed a huge enthusiasm for electric lighting, and was calling into every electric lighting shop he passed on his walks in London. In fact his passion for it became so intense, that his wife gave him an 'an electric-light button-hole flower' as a present for his forty-seventh birthday.[17]

It was left to Mr Pitman to pacify Mr Massey, eager to get rid of the temporary lighting and replace it with 'a permanent scheme':

> Long meeting with Mr Massey in regard to Electrical Lighting – Explained to him what Lord Bute's position was and that he must be allowed to take his own time in deciding as to what scheme should be adopted. Mr Massey pointed out difficulty of position he was in owing to delay but told him that this could not be avoided. Arranged that Mr Massey should send us copies of the Reports which he furnished a few years ago in regard to relative merits of Steam and Water Power.[18]

Bute had been alive to the challenges of housing the bare bulbs in something which would be aesthetically pleasing from the beginning. In July 1885, his friend 'K' sent him various 'hanging glass lamps'[19] which provided an inspiration realised so magnificently by Weir Schultz,[20] who created his own version of little Greek and Turkish hanging lamps in glass – sea shells, and globes supported by swans, or by brazen bands hung from tiny jewelled crowns, or little urns, clear, frosted and ruby.

With the Butes preoccupied with parenthood, there was a problem of whom to ask to carry out the work. It would not be the architect of the house, Anderson. There is no doubt that, while Bute continued to like Anderson, the two men were not well placed to understand each other. Bute was an anxious perfectionist: Anderson was concerned with the wide sweep and the overall effect. Bute cared for nature, trees and all things living in a way into which Anderson could not enter. There is something of a sneer in his comment to Bute's factor that 'I got your note about the trees. I will take care that nothing is done that will rouse his Lordship's sensibilities & tenderness for trees.'[21] If Bute had ever caught that note on Anderson's voice it would have wounded him so much that he would have retreated into the distant, magisterial presence which he used as his mask and his shield from hurt. It seems likely this happened. Anderson seems not to have been very well able to understand his greatest patron at all, and when Bute famously commented: 'But why should I hurry over what is my chief pleasure? I have comparatively little interest in a thing after it is finished',[22] Anderson believed the excuse.

Since Bute's public image is indeed of just such a ponderous, calm aristocrat, remote from the pressures of everyday life, this saying has been accepted without question and gleefully repeated. Bute was in fact impulsive, quick-witted, anxious, mercurial and chronically, almost morbidly, indecisive, and it is to be doubted if this was much more than an off-the-cuff remark designed to dispose of an architect demanding final decisions where he still wished to consider his options and press for something more perfect. The indecision could drive his employees mad, as it did Mr Massey, but it was in part the mark of a true artist. Bute would consider his options and change his plans, but only because new, and better ideas came to him as he worked. He hated to be pressed and harassed, but he loved to see work advancing. It is a small town newspaper report which has left us the best image of Bute working on a building: 'Lord Bute, in the quiet way indicative of strength and knowledge, moves about and sees if the whole work has been carried out to his mind.'[23] He did not have the disposition which finds ideas most easily in solitude; his best responses were made in company with others, and in answer to situations which arose spontaneously. If he was not really at ease with Anderson, then he would not be a ready choice for the intimate of interiors of the beloved new home.

There is no doubt, either, that Anderson's imagination was at the best of times limited. He himself tells the story of how he designed a set of railings for gallery of the great hall at Mount Stuart:

> I had proposed, in accordance with my duty, a design strictly in keeping with the mediaeval character of the building. Lord Bute, however, had seen and remembered the ancient and curious bronze railings which stand round the tomb of Charlemagne at Aix-la-Chapelle.[24]

Bute sent Anderson to make detailed measured drawings of these railings, which he had seen as a child, thus sparing Mount Stuart's gallery from the vacuity of yet more of railing in the style of that already beside the marble stair, and replacing it with a design that Anderson admits is appropriate 'sentimentally'. In fact, the note of aged bronze is just the thing to break up the marble rise of the hall; the intricate detail of the railing gives a relief of the plain surfaces around. Where Anderson had gone wrong was in assuming that it was his 'duty' to suggest the ordinary.

Neither Bute nor Gwen had been very impressed with the work carried out by Anderson. It is difficult to reconstruct exactly where the problem lay, but it seems as though they approved of his grand designs, but felt that the execution of details did not live up to his overall plans. Bute unburdened himself to his old friend, Sneyd.

> The trees are not cleared away at Mt. Stuart, and the house is just like a carpenter's shop. Perhaps the men may be out in a month or six weeks. Anderson has been very careless and the work's very ill done. There will have to be a perfect revolution once I'm clear of him.[25]

Admittedly this letter was written when Bute was in a state of great exasperation over other matters, and indulging in the pleasures of invective of the most incendiary kind to a trusted confidant, but there is no reason to doubt it reflects his mind. However, he was tied up with other building projects: among the major ones, Cardiff Castle, Castell Coch, the outfitting of Oban Cathedral, and the building of St Sophia's, Galston. He was also involved in trying to get a Dock Bill past Parliament, to separate his personal finances from the more problematic ones of Cardiff Docks. If one adds to this the constant drain of 'the beggars' whose letters he reviewed personally before his secretary responded, and his academic interests, it is easy to see how time slipped round to the autumn of 1886 before an excited and excitable new artist-architect became what today would be called the project manager for Mount Stuart House.[26]

Creative, lion-hearted, irascible, William Frame was only too happy to fight Bute's battles for him, coaxing and cursing work from the team of artists who laboured on Bute's houses. He was, in his own way, as doggedly loyal to Bute as Gwen. An architect in his own right, he had been for years William Burges's deputy, and that was a role liable to teach the meaning of perfectionism. After Burges's death, he had continued to build Cardiff Castle and Castell Coch to the great man's designs.

Frame's biggest single preoccupation was that Bute's ideas should be put into practice, and that his wishes should be obeyed. What the buildings lost from the hard-edged genius of Burges, they gained from having the impress of Bute's mind placed more clearly on them:

> In reference to the Dragon Lord Bute mentions (as far as I recalled) that Homer speaks of one. Will you kindly let me know if you can

find any mention of it as I should like Lord Bute's ideas to be carried out.[27]

He was especially anxious that the work should be of the highest order in all Bute's houses, and it was over this that he had many struggles, especially with Campbell, Smith and company, whom he regularly accused of putting inferior workmen onto Bute's most sensitive projects:

> In reference to the painting of butterflies in the ribs and boss of ceilings I certainly shall not agree to Wallace or either of the men at present working there doing them. Our arrangement from the first was that your cousin should do them.[28]

These particular butterflies, at Castell Coch, remained a source of contention, Frame writing in exasperation nearly a year later:

> The butterflies in the ribs still remain to me a very great eyesore. They look dirty & far from what I anticipated they would look, there is one thing I am fully determined upon, & that is in all future work where an artistic mind is required an ordinary decorator will not be allowed to put in the colours. This has caused the failure in this case.[29]

Frame thought the Campbells were always trying to cut corners.

He was also engaged in a perpetual struggle to keep costs down. The idea that Bute simply threw money at his buildings is a very mistaken one. He was in fact very cost-conscious. The need to balance the cost of sending workmen to and from Scotland, as opposed to keeping them idle while Bute used his beautiful rooms, always caused some concern for 'the expenses to and fro will cause him to complain'.[30] Less than perfect work also had him grumbling about cost: 'In Lord B's bathroom the sea weed is very very bad & I am afraid he will make great complaint. Of course £50 is out of the question for this work.'[31] After a lifetime's experience, Frame knew almost every trick of the trade, and none of them slipped past him:

> I submitted your est. for screen to Lord Bute. It frightened him. I do not think he will spend the money on it. The fact is:– Peter in this amount has tried to make up whatever has been lost on other work.[32]

It was only because he was writing to a tradesman for whom he had great sympathy and respect that Frame expressed himself so mildly.

Antill was a cabinet-maker who produced fine work, but he seems to have bounced along the very border of financial solvency. Frame knew this and sympathised with his plight. He was one of the principal contributors to Bute's projects; when free-standing furniture was called for, the contract usually went to Antill.

Frame's sympathy only went so far. One of his major projects in the early 1880s was the fitting out of Oban Cathedral. This was a basic oblong built of tinned corrugated iron, but fitted out inside with all the skill and verve of which the team which had worked for Burges was capable. Antill over-charged.

> Lord Bute will see the extraordinary difference in these two items at once. I am perfectly willing to pay a fair price but not exorbitant charges. Lord Bute ... calls it 'the hideous expense he is being put to'.[33]

He did not, however, fail to give honour where it was due. Antill supplied the rood screen, confessionals, and the rest of the fittings for a complete cathedral, and Frame noted that it had 'been carried out in a most efficient & workmanlike manner to my uttermost satisfaction'.[34]

Perhaps understanding that Antill was a better craftsman than businessman, Frame told him:

> I am very pleased to learn that you have made the table for Lady Bute. Would you mind letting me have privately your charge for making. I expect there will be several more to make & in giving estimated cost I will allow you an ample margin for extra profit above your price to Maples.[35]

Frame knew the difference between sensible profit over a number of items and a totally unreasonable charge for one of them. Contractors who for no very obvious reason bumped up their costs got scant sympathy. Frame had a good deal of trouble with the invoice for glass stars, used to decorate the Great Hall. They came in three sizes, to express the different magnitudes they represented. Created by Hall of Bristol, the original estimate was for twelve shillings and sixpence for the medium-sized stars. When the invoice arrived these were charged at fifteen shillings, with twenty-one shillings (a guinea) for the larger size. The naturally exasperated Frame commented: 'Of course I shewed your estimate to Lord Bute and he accepted it. I cannot again open the matter with his Lordship. Will you please explain this discrepancy?'[36]

While costs had to be watched, Bute's feelings were of paramount concern to Frame, and as he ordered carved heads from Nicholls, he told him:

Make them as nice as you can but not very grotesque as they are for a religious body & Lord Bute objects to anything touching the vulgar. Can you give them a sanctimonious expression?

Devoted to Bute's interests as he was, Frame was not above manipulating him to achieve his own ends. Frame had some difficulty in getting permission to leave Cardiff and help the work along at Mount Stuart. He sent a letter to his personal subordinate:

Send me a telegram tomorrow that will reach me about two o'clock worded as follows – Come to Mount Stuart at once, nearly finished, waiting for you.

P.S. When Lord Bute sees above telegram perhaps he will let me come.[37]

The reply to that telegram was: 'At Rothesay tomorrow. Send man and cab to meet me. Frame.'[38] He was also continuing to work upon Castell Coch – pressing Campbell to return the model of Lady Bute's bedroom, with the proposed decoration shown on it, and asking Nicholls, anxiously: 'do you think a shield in the form of a heart would be correct, or, would Mr Burges have done it? I think a shield similar to what was upon his rough drawing had better be used. Thus.'[39] Despite Frame's anxiety to put an oval-topped heraldic shield in the hands of the fairy-winged Psyche, Nicholls let her have her enchanting heart.

One piece of Burges's inspiration that was causing concern was the animal wall at Cardiff. The animals had been drawn by Burges, climbing from behind the wall, and seating themselves on little hogs-back turrets spaced along it, but they still had to be executed. This was a job which only the master sculptor Nicholls could successfully carry out, but he was slow with them, not helped by the fact that he was having periods of ill-health. The animals went through several stages. First came the walks round the London Zoological Park, to look at those and possible further species: '... will you try to arrange to go with me to the Zoo Gardens on my next journey for the purpose of choosing the other animals we might require'.[40] Then came the clay models. After that the beasts were inspected by Lord Bute, and then carved. Finally, they went to Campbell and were painted. The painted finish, which Frame disliked, refused to stay in place, and was eventually abandoned. As he told Nicholls:

> I thought I would try and find out what the Cardiff people thought of your works of art. The animals are all fixed & as you may imagine the comments passed on them are very funny, some in the highest terms of praise, others just the reverse. As far as I am concerned they meet with my approval – respecting the painting we have always agreed that it ought not to have been done & I still abide by this opinion especially as the lion shews at once the difference between the two – however it was Lord Bute's wish & I had nothing further to say in the matter.[41]

Horatio Walter Lonsdale, artist and stained glass designer, was Frame's equal, and his friend, and the two worked together in the greatest harmony. Thomas Nicholls, who designed and executed carvings, was also his equal, but Frame had a somewhat difficult relationship with him. Nicholls was touchy, and Frame short-tempered, and there were many small flare-ups. Everything was complicated by the distances involved. Nicholls was based in London, where he and his son carried on the business. Frame was in Cardiff, Campbell was again in London, and Dan Macfarlane was the head carpenter at Mount Stuart. Mistakes were bound to occur. Frame snapped at Nicholls:

> You had the timber sent you to carve – when you found it was not correct you ought to have returned it, and refused to have commenced carving until your requirements had been satisfied by Mr Antill ... Now I am as sorry as you are after so many years friendship that one single unkind word should have passed between us.[42]

One principal means of keeping all the artists, craftsmen and the patrons in touch with the work on Bute's buildings was the architectural model. One of the many models used by this team still survives: the model of Lady Bute's bedroom at Castell Coch. Matthew Williams has shown how this not only has the architectural detail, but the decoration, 'painted on paper and glued onto the model'.[43] The finished room followed the general line of the model but with significant changes. 'Certainly Lady Bute would have found it easier to envisage her new room with the aid of such a model, and might therefore make informed comment.'[44]

The 1901 inventory of Cardiff Castle refers to the 'Model Room' in the Black Tower, which contained not only a trunk full of Burges's original drawings, but also 'a quantity of plaster mouldings and models' and 'various wood and other models'. None of these appear to have survived the departure of the Bute family after they gave the castle to the city of Cardiff in 1947.[45]

Despite having been involved with their buildings from their first inception, and followed the artistic process on models and through specimens of it drawn on paper or executed on linoleum, the Butes were occasionally unhappy with the finished result. Frame told Campbell that: 'Lord Bute having occupied the whole of my time during his stay here, prevented my writing to you before. He visited Castell Coch yesterday and saw some of the panels fixed with monkeys in them & he does not like them.' Bute apparently had said he would prefer birds upon the ceiling.[46]

There were models for Lord and Lady Bute's sitting rooms at Mount Stuart. Both of these exquisite rooms, with marble pillars framing bay windows, and each with its own bathroom, bracketed the centrepiece, known to Frame as Lady Bute's bedroom, and to future generations, since the room was shared by the couple, as the Family Bedroom. The first plans for the decoration of these rooms were drawn up when Frame and Lonsdale met Bute at Mount Stuart in December 1886. 'Frame & Mr Lonsdale came. With them about the decoration of our rooms, etc.'[47] remarked Bute laconically to his diary. The decorative carved wooden ceilings in these rooms were created in Cardiff, shipped to Mount Stuart, and fitted by the carpenter up there. Before the ceilings were finished, roughly finished trial pieces were fitted, Frame sending

a full sized rough piece ... it will go in the corner where we tried the pictures up ... The half piece of beam fits against wall and the other will fit round the present beam as per the enclosed tracing. You can fit it up in any way you like, but as soon as it arrives you had better ask Lord Bute's permission to do so at once as it will take you some little time, & if possible I want Mr Lonsdale & I to be at Mount Stuart next week, & if the ceiling is fixed Mr Lonsdale will not be delayed.[48]

Frame directed Campbell to carry out work, partly based upon instructions from his employers, and partly on what he knew of their tastes.

I have sent you per G.W.R. two models, one of Lord Bute's sitting room, the other of Lady Bute's sitting room. The former as you know is the Astrological ceiling – the centre of which will be filled up as I have shewn with glass stars, & coloured glass globes to represent the planets, the other part I think I should decorate with birds, flowers etc in bright colours as Lord Bute seems to have a failing for it.

Lady Bute's ceiling will be gold ornament upon cedar & nothing else, no other colour. Will you get these models done as quickly as possible & can I have them by 21st May? I expect Lord Bute some time this month, & I should like him to settle the whole affair.[49]

The astrological centre showed the major stars and the planets as they were at the moment of Bute's nativity. A good deal of effort went into determining the exact time of this. A search of the Kingarth Register did not reveal the hour of birth, and in the end enquiries were made of those still alive from that day:

Duncan McCallum, who was valet to your father at the time of your Lordship's birth, says that the hour was about five o'clock, and that no nearer approach to the exact hour can be made. If, as now, Greenwich time was followed in Bute, 5 o'clock Greenwich time would be 20 minutes before 5 Bute time.[50]

How best to execute the chart was a worry from the start. For once dropping his exasperated banter with Campbell, Frame confided in him:

I really do not know what to say with reference to the stars & planets, you after all have had far greater experience in these matters than I have, & if you think polished white metal enamelled to be the best, estimate for it accordingly. The effect I want is this; when the stars are fixed they must have a brilliant appearance so as to mislead or deceive the uninitiated & make them believe they are real stars.[51]

With so many ambitious projects, sometimes things came unstuck and the plan for the centre of Lord Bute's sitting room was one such. Not only did it prove impossible to fit the model planets, due to the fact that there was no access from behind the ceiling,[52] but they turned out to be clumsy things, hung on substantial chains.[53] The plan for the ceiling, painted on linoleum, was put into place and never removed until its decay led to its replacement by a painting in the twentieth century. The rest of the ceiling also gave rise to a dilemma.

In reference to the model of Lord Bute's room, I am sorry to say he made hardly any remarks, but from what I could get out of him, both he & Lady Bute disliked the white ground. I quite agree with you a blue ground would not do, or he will be under the impression we can do nothing else but <u>blue</u>, yes, I think the large beams red & gold would do, & no doubt you will be able to manage the other parts. We must bear in mind the centre is a mass of blue . . .

Campbell created one of his most beautiful works, a dull red and gold ceiling, with the beams and jelly-mould domes decorated with leaves and flowers, while on the flat panels, parrots fly through naturalistic foliage, beautifully realised, as they would be seen from below.

Lady Bute's sitting room was altogether more restrained. The ceiling was a mixture of heavily carved deal, which was painted white and gilded, and cedar, which was left in its natural colour, and then decorated with a little gold. Frame sent a flutter of anxious letters from Cardiff to impress on the workmen at Mount Stuart that 'none of the size or other preparations shall cover <u>any</u> of the cedar wood, except that upon which the gold shall be put'.[54] At Castell Coch, Lady Bute had thought the gold was overdone: 'What Lady B wants is for the wood to be the decoration in itself & only a small quantity of gold to be used upon the work.'[55]

The problem in Lady Bute's room was the stained glass. Although elaborate designs were by an artist, usually Lonsdale, smaller commissions were worked directly by Worrall, the manufacturer who was actually responsible for making the stained glass, who did not always rise to the heights demanded by Frame, and there was a problem with the heraldic lions in Lady Bute's sitting room: 'You will have to alter the heads of the lions – they are too modest looking. More like pets than roaring lions.'[56] Frame got Lonsdale to inspect the next version: '[Worrall] has to draw a small lion to replace the one that I condemned . . . will you kindly for me see that it is all right?'[57] In all of these matters there was an added anxiety. These things were being created for Lady Bute. Not only were Gwen's tastes very decided, but she was far less tolerant of mistakes than Bute. This made the creation of the Chaucer Room at Cardiff an anxious business.

re the Chaucer Room – what I meant by delicacy of work is, that the foliage, birds, diapers &c will have to be small, nothing in comparison to what is shewn upon the model. These matters I mentioned a long time since to you. The whole must be most carefully done as it is <u>Lady Bute's Room</u>. I think the best way will be to execute a panel & as Lord & Lady Bute will be here in Sept. they will be able to see at once if they like it or not.[58]

In September 1887, work at Mount Stuart was too slow. The Butes were to visit Mount Stuart in October, and Frame had piled the pressure on his own deputy, Thomas Earl, whom he had sent to Mount Stuart to see the ceilings fitted into the Butes' sitting rooms:

> The domes in Lord Bute's sitting room and the centre point in Lady Bute's sitting room must be fixed by Thursday next, it is of no use to say it cannot be done, for it must and shall be, if the men have to work night and day.[59]

It was as well the Butes were resigned to inconvenience during building works, for the next instruction to Earl was: 'Lord Bute will use the bedroom & dressing rooms but the sitting rooms you can still continue to work on.'[60]

With work genuinely under great pressure of time, one way of speeding it up was to ask Nicholls to design carvings, which were then executed by Frame's workmen. All the tiny square panels (carved with themes such as winged time, or musical animals) in the Horoscope sitting room were executed in this way: designed in London, carved in Cardiff, shipped to Mount Stuart (changing ship at Greenock) and fitted at Mount Stuart. No excuse for delay impressed Frame: 'I am very pleased to hear that you have a lot of work for the Queen in hand, but I want mine as well.'[61]

The two sitting rooms are designed simply to give pleasure. Their decoration reflects their occupants' tastes, and their interests, but no more. The Family Bedroom has a story to tell. Only Burges, long dead before the bedroom was conceived, or his pupil Bute, could pile up meaning and image as they are laminated here. The concept behind the room is nowhere recorded by Frame, and while much of the decoration is by Lonsdale, his skill was in executing the ideas of those who commissioned him in whatever style most suited the idea and the design.

The centrepiece of the room is the life of St Margaret of Scotland, portrayed round the walls in a frieze executed on canvas. Her early piety, her marriage to Malcolm of Scotland, her charitable works, and her holy death are portrayed, with captions taken from her 'Life' by her confessor Turgot.[62] The central, and dominating, image on the principal wall is of Margaret teaching. The diminutive figure of Margaret is a likeness of Gwen. There she stands, teaching with the book in hand, while her big husband ponders, and the Culdees (monks) of the Celtic church are argued out of court. She is at one time several different things, piled upon one another, as meanings pile up in poetry. She is Gwen, illuminating Bute. She is Margaret, the ancestress of Bute, whose prayers he will seek to ensure her line is continued in his Catholic family. She is the Holy Mother Church, spreading her light in a world of doubt, error and perversity. She is Woman, who may teach, and to whom Man must listen, or lose much wisdom.

At first sight, the coats of arms in the stained-glass windows of this house have no relationship to the frieze, and it is only through inspired and diligent research by the present archivist at Mount Stuart, Andrew McLean, that the meaning of the room has been decoded. The windows show each marriage by which the blood-line of Margaret passed down through the Kings of Scotland, till they reached Marjory Bruce, and, through her marriage to Walter Stewart, the line of Stuart kings. And not just Stuart kings, for the line of the Stuarts of Bute springs from Marjory's son, Robert II. He, and he alone of the Bute ancestors, is not recorded in this room, because this room celebrates marriage, and Robert II was not married to Bute's ancestress.

Thus the theme of the windows ends, and the story jumps onto the ceiling. Here, the shields are all connected by a rope – a rope which starts with a knot, where there should be a shield. It may be because marriage is 'tying the knot' and Bute wanted to ensure the point was not missed, or else because there had been a break in the thread from Margaret which needed mending (the Duke of Wellington used to refer to his campaigns as ropes; when something went wrong he would tie a knot and go on). Then the series of marriage-shields takes off again, this time with those of the Stuarts of Bute. Each and every marriage in the Bute line from which children sprang (poor Maria North is not represented) is a carved and painted shield on the ceiling, linked by a gilded rope until, large and splendid before the fireplace, comes the marriage of Bute and Gwen, and the rope vanishes into the future through the fireplace.

A reflection of the importance of this room to Bute is the anxiety Frame felt about getting the decoration up in place both correctly and fast. He warned the workman doing the job: 'If there is one single picture wrongly fixed, you will have to take it down and refix it at your own personal expense, so take care.'[63] Frame was scrabbling to get the Family Bedroom finished in May 1888, for he expected Bute to arrive back from Italy in that month, though in fact it was June before his return.

The final stage of any major work like this frieze was for the artist who designed it to come to the site, inspect the work, and pass it. Then the final payment was authorised, although staged payments 'on a/c' would already have been made. Payment was actually made by Frank Anderson, who had become Bute's secretary, and occupied the role until Bute's death. Anderson's apparent lack of understanding of the processes involved in these elaborate decorative schemes drove Frame near the edge of his (never very extensive) patience and courtesy.

> In a conversation I had with Mr Stuart [Jack Stuart, the Bute Estate Factor] he casually mentioned that he believed you had at last received the drawings of Mount Stuart from the architect. If so will you <u>kindly send them on</u> as at present I am placed at a great disadvantage in as much that every design I make entails a journey to Mount Stuart to make the requisite measurements.[64]

Anderson had plainly failed to appreciate how much the structure of the house determined what was possible in fitting it out. As usual, Frame relied on the donkey-work of the chief carpenter at Mount Stuart, Dan Macfarlane, when it came to designing and fitting a wooden ceiling for the Blue Library.

> I have to design a ceiling for the blue room. I believe it is called the library. Will you get me all the rods together with sections of the beams by the time I come. You had better uncover one of the present girders so that you can see exactly what the woodwork is below, also how much we have to spare from the present line of boarded ceiling to the pegging above. If you do this I shall be able to design and settle this ceiling.[65]

At about the same time, work was beginning on the crowning glory of Mount Stuart, the zodiac windows and the celestial ceiling, both designed by Lonsdale, which carry Anderson's Great Hall to a triumphant conclusion. Even at the earliest design stage in 1888, the project filled Frame with enthusiasm, and he excitedly told Worrall, 'Mr Lonsdale is making a lot of sketches for glass for Mount Stuart that you are to make. I shall be in London shortly when I will call on you and explain everything.'[66] Templates of the windows, which the glass was to fit, and 'a roll containing mounted tracings shewing plan & elevation of Hall at Mount Stuart the panels'[67] of the vaulted ceiling were sent to Lonsdale. The ceiling stars and the windows were designed together.

There is a problem with this design. Although a perfect star map, the map reads backward. There are two possible explanations. One is that the original intention was to allow the magnificent star map to be reflected in a mirror either on the floor or the table. There are indications that this might just be so. It is usual in Bute buildings for sustained games to be played with a theme. In the case of Mount Stuart there are not only the mirror-glass stars, but also large mirrors set in each arch behind the corridor, creating ever-retreating images and illusions. It would have been very like Bute to have continued the mirror theme with a mirror table, centrally in the Hall, which would have allowed an easy view of the magnificent ceiling, and created a perfect (because a mirror reverses an image) star map. Such a mirror would have imitated the central pool, the impluvium, of the Roman atrium upon which the great hall is loosely based.

The other possibility is that a mistake was made. Lonsdale did not understand that the zodiac in the sky 'reads' from right to left. Because each year we experience the zodiac in the opposite order, which we would write on a page as the familiar order Aries, Taurus, Gemini, etc. he therefore created his zodiac to read from left to right, and the mistake was only discovered after the windows had been created. It would be impossible to reverse them, so the only thing to be done was to put in the sky in an equally reversed manner. We have one tantalising clue as to the process. In September 1890, Bute, who was staying in London, recorded that he met 'Mr. Lonsdale abt. the Mt Stuart windows. Determined to put ♋ [Cancer] to the south instead of ♑ [Capricorn].'[68]

Lonsdale had already produced series of stained-glass windows under the direction of Burges, including the lords and ladies in the windows of the Banqueting Hall of Cardiff Castle. In each case the draughtsmanship is excellent, but the individual figures are unexciting. The line is a little more fluid than some of Fred Weekes's marvellously concise figures, but it is also less muscular. Mordaunt Crook judges that whilst Lonsdale was 'undoubtedly a draughtsman of exceptional precision, and a fluent designer of occasional power ... without [Burges's] control, much of his later figure work tends to be mechanical and vapid'.[69] More recent appraisal has concluded that 'his contribution should perhaps now be given more credit than has hitherto been the case' and admitted that his career after Burges's death 'is still much under-researched'.[70] Little attention has been paid to what is admitted to be the 'apogee in quality of [Lonsdale's] interior design work',[71] his 'Astrological windows' for the Great Hall at Mount Stuart.

It is difficult to find direct comparisons for the 'zodiac windows'. It is tempting to compare them with the roundels in Cardiff Castle's Winter Smoking Room. There each zodiacal sign, executed by Weekes, is compressed and stylised in a roundel. A more direct comparison with Lonsdale's glass is that designed by Burges himself for St Fin Barre's Cathedral, Cork, for which his own cartoons survive. There is no doubt that these were a great influence on Lonsdale's designs for Mount Stuart, but the differences are large. At Cork, as in the Mount Stuart windows, the stars of the constellations are shown within the figurative creatures of the zodiac. In Burges's design the need to fit them into his concise drawing has caused them to be so highly formalised that they are not easily correlated with the stars in the sky. But in Lonsdale's windows they can be recognised at once. The style of the windows is dissimilar too. Burges's are Gothic: 'The main ground of the lancet is filled with a lattice pattern with two coloured panels in the centre.'[72] In the Mount Stuart windows, the ever-changing background is a major feature of the composition.

Bute devoted a good deal of time to discussions with Lonsdale about the windows, especially in January 1889: '4 Jan. ... with Lonsdale about zodiacal windows in hall. 5 Jan. After luncheon with Lonsdale till after dark. Fixed experimental paper window.'[73] The band of the zodiac is represented in colour in the windows. A complete set of preliminary sketches (three-quarters of an inch to the foot) in watercolour survive.[74] Although they have much of the movement of the final windows, they are more hesitant, and the figures are weaker. Hercules (in Cancer) is a rather aesthetic figure in the sketch. In the cartoon, he has much more muscular tone, his head is bigger, his calf is broader and above all, his neck is thicker. He has become a hero. The windows are emphatically not Gothic, and they disregard all earlier precepts of containing subjects within the frame offered by the architecture.[75]

An unbroken, swirling chain of figures streams around the hall. Each window leads into the next. Scorpio leaps across to set Libra's scales swinging. Venus rises in Pisces, and below her Cetus moves in muscular curves into Aries. As well as the signs of the zodiac, others appear beside them, figures from myth, whose stories connect with the themes of the windows. Capricorn is surrounded by nymphs, who milk her for the infant Zeus. Taurus, the bull, is shown garlanded by Europa, whilst he is challenged by Orion. Bute himself may appear as a portrait in the window devoted to his own birth-sign, Virgo.

Embedded in the windows are stars of cut glass. They are fixed there using the technique by which gemstones were embedded in mediaeval glass. These stars are clear, not coloured, although they do add glitter to the window. When the sun shines, their other purpose is revealed. White in themselves, they shed colour in pools over the walls and floor of the hall, for they are prisms. The Victorian child's trick of hanging a prism in the window to create a spot of rainbow in the room is used to great effect on a large scale. They pick up the theme of the spectrum used in the windows themselves. These stars are those of the constellations of the zodiac, each one in its proper place. Above the windows, the constellations continue to climb, still in cut glass, this time mirror-glass, to reflect back light as they are fixed to a solid surface. In ghostly white behind them are painted the figures of the constellations, the swan, the bear and the others, so that the untutored eye knows what it is looking at.

Below, behind each zodiac figure, shading into one another around the hall, flow all the colours of the rainbow, articulating the full spectrum as they go, each evoking a season: clear, cold blue for the Scottish winter skies, shading through aquamarine to green for spring, yellow and red for the heat of a southern summer, so loved by Bute, and back to the soft purple of heather and autumn mist for the fall of the year. The risk of cloying is avoided by what is, to borrow from musical terms, dissonance and atonality. The finest windows are Scorpio and Libra. The scorpion's pincers are orange-red, set against a series of small red-purple panes. Below them a peculiar dead blue provides a further contrast. The first sketches for the windows only offer very simple backgrounds, of more or less unbroken colour. In the cartoon the colour changes begin to be a feature, but only in the window itself are these suggestions brought to maturity.

By this period, Lonsdale's way of working was a little old-fashioned. He was, it is true, responsible for everything from the first sketches through to the final cartoons, but he does not seem to have superintended the work, or participated in it, as the new generation of Arts and Crafts workers were doing.[76] That the window is exquisitely leaded, with none of the infelicitous cutting off of hands or feet by the black bars of lead that so often mars Victorian painted glass is not unexpected, for this is always a strong point of Lonsdale's work, perhaps learned from his master Burges. For the rest the windows are a surprise, even a shock. The makers of the windows were Worrall & Co, who had

operated for about twenty years from 1880, when William Gualbert Saunders (1837–1923) was obliged to pull out of his own firm Saunders & Co. His glass painter William Worrall then took over and took the odd decision to change the name of the firm.

In David Lawrence's opinion, 'the quality of the work rapidly declined'.

The most graphic illustration of my point can be seen in a particular window at St. Fin Barre's Cathedral, the execution of which bridges the changeover from Saunders to Worrall. The Saunders half is, as with all his work for Burges, truly inspired, but the Worrall half is clumsy, dull and unbalanced and this, despite the fact that both are working from the same design (by Burges/Lonsdale) and the same cartoon (by Lonsdale).[77]

Frame had told Lonsdale that 'His Lordship mentioned that the glass for the Hall windows at Mount Stuart he hoped would be brilliant.'[78] It is both brilliant and subtle, with nothing muddy and nothing garish. The Worrall ledger shows that a 'specimen window' was fixed, and continues, 'meeting Mr. Lonsdale for inspection. Taking same out again and returning to London for alterations.'[79] There is no indication as to the changes made.

Far from being 'mechanical and vapid' this work is the strongest of Lonsdale's career. More than that, it has a good claim to be the finest glass of the Victorian period. Certainly, in energy and vigour it is not surpassed. Something occurred at Mount Stuart which turned into a masterpiece the work of an artist usually dismissed as not much more than a really good draughtsman, collaborating with a firm of stained-glass makers whose work too easily became 'clumsy, dull and unbalanced'. In this instance, 'something' could only be the 3rd Marquess of Bute.

There are none of the proverbial jottings on the back of envelopes to suggest his hand in the work. The few of his sketches which survive show Bute was a fine draughtsman himself. Even supposing that his were the initial drawings, and his was the suggestion for the unbroken line of design, this alone could not account for the ever-increasing strength and confidence of the work, which grows immeasurably from sketch, through cartoon, to finished window. It is known that he met with Lonsdale at every stage in the development of the design. It must have been he who gave permission, indeed encouragement, for the extraordinary path this series of windows took.

The conditions imposed on the Victorian stained glass artist, and the compromises he would have to make on behalf of the architect, donor of a memorial window, incumbent, or whoever the client may have been, are frequently all too apparent from the finished result.[80]

Bute did not ask for compromise; instead he was able to give his artists and craftsmen a freedom which Burges never could. Sometimes this led to a lack of unified design, or even to downright weakness. It did not create the density of Burges's interiors. Yet Bute could, on occasion, conjure from his collaborators something of exceptional quality. Lonsdale was able to create the dynamic zodiac windows because Bute encouraged excess and individuality.

Partly by chance, and partly because they required more attention to detail, and less artistic inspiration, the best insight into Bute's input into his buildings is offered by the staircase windows. For many of the craftsmen, Frame was their chief point of contact for work they undertook for Bute. This was most certainly not so for Lonsdale. Although Lonsdale was in regular and friendly communication with Frame, most of his discussions were directly with Bute. Unfortunately, many of these were face-to-face meetings, and so lost. But occasionally they were by letter, and from these rare letters we get a picture of Bute's involvement with his buildings.

In accordance with your wish I forward herewith the sketch of scheme for the Mount Stuart staircase windows. In all essentials I have adhered to your Lordship's arrangement, but suggest an alteration in the stems in the side windows, to obtain a more balanced distribution of the shields. The centre window having fewer of these, I have shown them larger, and have introduced the old Bute supporters into the lower lights. The horse, being white, encases the shield in front of him, while the stag proper would supply the colour required to balance the shields, and could be cut up by overlapping branches, so as not to present too heavy a mass. I beg to return with many many thanks the seven sheets of notes you kindly sent me for my guidance. Enclosed is also a list of names for mythological personages in the Hall windows, which I will ask you to be good enough to look over and inform me if they are correct, also what style of lettering you would prefer.[81]

The staircase window embodied Lord Bute's passion for heraldry, and for his own family history. It took the form of a wild rose tree, upon which grew, as well as roses, the shields which represented all his direct ancestors. The central and largest window has the Bute family tree, with all the Earls. The Crichton family, the Earls of Dumfries, are to one side, and the Earls of Pembroke, from whom the Windsors descended and through whom his Cardiff estates had come to him, are in the other, flanking the Earls of Bute. At the time of its creation, it looked as if the Marquisate might become extinct, while the Earldom lived on through Margaret. Earls had an enhanced significance just then. It is a delightful, airy window, which successfully hides the fact that the grand staircase backs onto a wall, whilst allowing plenty of light to stream down onto the marble staircase beneath.

The wonderfully illuminating series of Frame's letters ends abruptly at the end of 1889. The letter book was simply full, and for the new year Frame moved onto a new letter book, now lost. The last entries concern the animal wall at Cardiff – the paint on the sea-lion was 'going wrong',[82] the bear was roughly modelled in clay, and the lynx was almost ready for painting. Tantalisingly, Frame was on the point of commissioning models for the dining room at Mount Stuart 'just to your taste – foliage and grotesques all referring to dining'.[83]

Sadly, the carving in the dining room is not Nicholls's inspirational best. In the dado, which tops the half-panelling of the walls, various birds feast on insects who in turn make a meal of the oak leaves. It is pretty, restrained and pleasing. The birds, although not coloured, are easy to identify as particular species, and the insects are varied and accurate, but it has nothing like the punch of which Nicholls was capable. Even the built-in sideboard is disappointing, and there are none of the larger pieces or grotesques at which Nicholls so excelled. This work indeed may not be by him. There had already been frequent references to Nicholls's ill-health in the last years of the letter book. He died in 1896. It is possible that he was simply not well enough to carve for this room. Perhaps the models made for the Bute workshops at Cardiff were weakened by his ill-health. The very uneven nature of the execution of the lower frieze show it was executed in a number of different hands, therefore at the Bute workshops. The carving consists in a number of motifs, which are repeated in different arrangements around the wall, thus deceiving the casual observer into believing that there are no repetitions. The cornice in the dining room was carved by Rhind, who was paid £12 for it in 1903.[84] He had worked on the Scottish National Portrait Gallery for Anderson. Despite the nice conceit of squirrels dining on acorns, the family crest of the Stuarts, it has no impact at all.

Without the letter book, it is hard to be certain of the dates for all the projects undertaken. The gallery is decorated with stylised 'tree of life' decorations supporting the heads of mythological minor goddesses, each named in Greek uncials, except where the heroines of German literature, familiar to Bute through Wagner, are evoked. The cartoons drawn by Lonsdale are still extant, but undated. They can putatively be allocated to the early 1890s when Margaret was working hard on her Greek. Once again, the status and power of women was affirmed.

It is tempting to allocate the mirrors which fill in the arches either side to the same date. New visitors to the bedroom floor of the building, where an arched colonnade with the decoration of trees and goddesses runs round the outside of the central atrium, are dazzled by the sight of other almost endless colonnades stretching away behind the oak panelling and doors. Grand as Mount Stuart is, it does not in fact run to a labyrinth of arches and corridors. The visitor is deceived by mirrors, which seem to continue the joke of the mirror image of the sky.

Bute's house continued to embody his interests. In 1895 there was another spurt of activity, this time embodying his involvement in education, and his concern for his younger sons. Lonsdale was once again summoned 'about drawing-room windows & hall ceiling'.[85] Although the hall mirror-glass constellations were put in place under the aegis of Frame, the actual painting in of the decoration was done at this time. The dated sketches for them still survive in Lonsdale's hand. This confirms the impression that the inspiration for the ghostly figures came from St John's Lodge.[86]

The main interest, however, was the decoration of the drawing room. Bute now had three sons and the younger two were old enough to begin to feel the difference made by being a younger son. Now a ceiling was created which embodied (in the form of a shield shown on a growing vine) each son of the house of Stuart, and their marriages (or in the case of those with bishoprics, their dioceses). Each son matters, says the ceiling, not just the oldest. It is, however, a singularly ugly creation. The background of polished mica fails to sparkle, and the stylised bunches of grapes are clumsy. Perhaps aware of how dark the ceiling was, Lonsdale had kept the stained glass in the window very light. The subject is charming and suitable both for a drawing room and for a University Rector.[87] It shows Apollo and his daughters, the Muses. It contains nice tricks – for instance the frogs and wasps in the background of Comedy. Sadly, however, none of the ladies is inspiring, and they all appear to be suffering from melancholy and consumption. It has nothing of the dynamism which many even second-rate works by Lonsdale possess (for instance the figures, possibly his, in the windows of the Wallace Monument at Stirling). But by the time these windows were created, Bute himself was no longer feeling inspirational.

11   Hierarchy

'Angus of Argyll seems one of the worst Padres in some ways' [1]

Bute was probably correct in feeling that Gwen dealt better with the Catholic Church than he did. [2] She was not burdened by his intimidating level of knowledge, and she never omitted to sign herself 'your obedient daughter in Christ', and manage a deferential tone. Also, she did not find being disliked a personal grief to her. She was, in short, a much more typical aristocrat, and the bishops seem to have found her more expected mixture easier to deal with. All Bute's letters have very much the same air of addressing an equal, regardless of his correspondent. He wrote more flamboyantly, with more humour, and on more personal topics, to his intimates, but otherwise the tone of his letters was exactly the same whether he was replying to a beggar or a prince of the church.

Yet Bute was generally more aware of the sensibilities of others than Gwen, who was much less shy, and therefore much more outspoken than Bute. She was also even more concerned to get what she was paying for. During Bute's absence during the summer of 1884, all contact between the Butes and the church choir had been in the hands of the outspoken Gwen. The wound of her beloved father's death was still raw, her children had been seriously ill, her husband was abroad; she was stressed, sad, lonely and in all probability more acerbic than usual.

Consequently, by the time Bute arrived back in the winter of 1884, feelings were running high in Cumnock. The Butes had spent the two preceding Christmases at Dumfries House, but now they returned to Bute, to spend their first Christmas back at Mount Stuart, in the palatial but barely half-finished new house. Meanwhile, across the water at Cumnock, trouble between Collins, the parish priest at Cumnock, and the choir boiled over. The choir were working men, drawn from what was, and is, a very poor district.[3] The main industry was mining, for coal and ironstone, and a strike in 1880 led by Keir Hardy had lasted ten weeks, impoverishing the miners and failing to win them better conditions. Bute funded soup kitchens throughout the strike.

The Bute choir were paid, but very conscious of their fringe benefits. They were also ably led by the educated organist, not a Roman Catholic, but a High Church Anglican, Henry George Clements. Clements was a protégé of Bute's:

> I sent for Mr Clements, whom I of course know to be poor, and offered to pay the fees if he would like to take the University degree of Bachelor of Music. He was grateful, and told me the degree had been an object of ambition to him, and he had even begun to try and compose the cantata he wd. have to send in . . .[4]

As an Anglican, he was a constant source of irritation to the Catholic clergy, who felt that with Clements, they were merely an employer, not a superior. Although Bute did not realise it, Clements was a troublemaker. Worse, he was a troublemaker with Bute's ear. It was very simple to appeal to Bute. He was utterly unmoved by birth (he considered Gwen's brother, grandson of the Duke of Norfolk most ungentlemanly) and many of modest birth became his closest friends. Wealth also left him unimpressed, but he warmed at once to those with wit, intelligence and like-minded views.

When Bute funded any project, he always asked for regular letters from those involved in it. Many found this a real difficulty, something that Bute could never understand, for he wrote easily on the minutiae of life. Clements shared his gift. Here, for instance, Mr Clements animadverts upon an unfortunate chorister:

> Mr Hickey sang the 'Exultet jam angelica'. He is a very young man, but had anybody closed their eyes during the singing of this, they would have imagined the singer to be an exceedingly old gentleman . . . who in days long gone by had gloried in the music and the functions of his church and now in his old age, perhaps for the last time, was struggling against physical difficulties, to give to the words and music the effect to which he had been long accustomed.
>
> It seems a shame to write like this about one who was so willing.[5]

Such ease and wit, coupled with the ability to raise a laugh, and undoubted competence at his job, gave Clements an unparalleled chance to gain Bute's sympathy.

The choir had expected the chapel to be decorated for Christmas 1884 with flowers and greenery, as it had been in previous years. It was not. They had also practised their music for Christmas. The Midnight Mass was sung most successfully in the undecorated church, but 'Mr Collins was not well enough to sing Mass at 11am so it was said, the choir singing English hymns.'[6] Bute always kept the festival of his name saint, John, which falls on 28 December. The choir were usually given a dinner on this, the feast of the saint to whom their church was dedicated, in recognition of the extra Masses at Christmas, St Stephen's day and St John's day. But this time, no dinner was arranged. The choir went on strike.

Collins had been genuinely unwell on Christmas Day, and coughing blood. In all the troubles that followed, it is necessary to make allowance for a sick man. The two previous years, the Butes had been at Dumfries House, and had sent gardeners with greenery to the chapel to decorate it.[7] The dinner had simply slipped Bute's mind. It had also slipped the mind of his factor, Charles Shaw. Not understanding that the two sides had been spoiling for a fight for some time, Shaw thought it 'really extraordinary that neither Mr Collins nor Clements took any steps about the decoration of the church, or the choir dinner'. Bute sent Shaw to sort the situation out: 'The choir appear to have been disappointed partly as to the decorations and more so, as to the dinner. Their conduct in refusing to sing on Sunday was childish, but I dare say very natural.'[8] If Collins had been prepared to meet the others half way, the whole thing would be ended. Instead, he was determined to pick a fight.

Shaw had mentioned among other matters his failure to sing the Mass on Christmas Day. The services a priest provides in his church are a matter for him and for his Bishop. Collins was quite right in thinking that the factor of a rich Lord had no business interfering. He went further:

Indeed I may say that it is this sort of thing, coupled with several other matters that have come to my ears lately, that is making my life in Cumnock well nigh unbearable and I shall never rest content, though it should take me years, until I sever all connection with a place where I am so little trusted.[9]

Bute was understandably upset. He really did try very hard to get on with the clergy.

I need not say that your letter much distressed me. To keep me in entire ignorance and then to blame me for not knowing & acting accordingly is not I venture to think to act fairly towards me. You designate it as 'this sort of thing' ... 'several other matters that have come to your ears lately'. They have not come to mine. I do not know what you mean.[10]

The choir were persuaded to resume their work, but Collins proclaimed that having gone on strike, they might stay on strike.[11] Bute had hoped to sort the 'row' out by himself,[12] but in the end he had to involve the Bishop, who helpfully reported that Collins was alleged to have said: 'Fr O'Neill fought and conquered the Butes, Fr Murphy fought and conquered the Butes, and I'll show them that I'll conquer them too.'

Collins finally provided an account of why he did not contact the Butes when the expected decorations failed to materialise on Christmas Eve:

It at once occurred to me that it was so ordained by Your Lordship as a mark of displeasure whether towards myself, the choir or the congregation. And I think you must admit that with this idea in my mind I was not likely to write to anyone on the matter with the expectation of being told to mind my own business.[13]

Since this represented Collins's idea of an appropriate conciliatory gesture, it is not surprising that more trouble was in store. It once again boiled over after Palm Sunday that year. Bute asked Collins to send a blessed palm to his old tutor Dr Westcott, with whom he enjoyed an occasional but warm correspondence on academic matters, such as ancient images of the saints.[14] Collins replied provocatively: 'I cannot see my way to send a Palm "with my compliments and best wishes" to one of whose very existence I was ignorant till Saturday morning.'[15] Bute's reply got the kind of apology which, by its very excess, is designed to give offence:

I am very sorry that the tone of my last letter should have been so disrespectful. I did not mean to give offence. I can only therefore consider myself the most unfortunate of men.[16]

Bute answered with the calm of a very cross man:

I cannot help replying to your last. Forgive me for pointing out that I said nothing whatever as to the tone of your letters having been 'disrespectful' or not. I really am at a loss to conclude how such an idea could be ascribed to my words.

What I said was, that the tone seemed to me intended to make me feel that I had offended you, and that I thought it would be fair to let me know what it was, as I am quite unconscious of having done anything to justify such a feeling. That was all.[17]

Bute referred the whole matter to the Bishop of Galloway, who, as part of a general move of the clergy, transferred Collins to Stranraer at the other end of the diocese and moved Mr Hourigan, 'the junior priest at Kilmarnock' to Cumnock. He was, said the Bishop, 'not so touchy nor so fiery as Mr Collins'.[18] The tone of Hourigan's letters to Bute is at first somewhat timid and defensive, as though Collins had left behind a myth of Bute's unreasonable demands, but through time, it relaxes into informality.

The ever-helpful Clements sent Bute a splendidly catty account of Fr Hourigan's first days in Cumnock:

I fancy we are more advanced than Mr Hourigan expected to find us, but things are going on much better – the ritual seems to trouble him – if the choir had not been well up we should have had muddle on Candlemas Day for he had the Missal in one hand and Baldeschi in the other and being naturally nervous his uncertainty was more plainly seen, but the choir went straight ahead, and so any unseemly pause did not take place.[19]

No wonder that the hierarchy generally struggled with Bute. He was a generous donor. He had funded schools, and churches, and soup for the poor. Excellence in liturgy was one of the passions of his church, but the clergy saw the liturgy as their concern and there is no doubt that Bute was committed to his own agenda in church matters. He was fortunate that the Bishop of Galloway, cautious 'grandmother' though he might be, was largely like-minded. He was happy to balance the needs of charity, teaching and the provision of basic facilities for worship with excellence both in liturgy and church building. In this area Bute had much to offer his church that it would otherwise never have enjoyed.

Between 1884 and 1886 Bute was engaged in the delightful process of collaborating with an architect on building a church. Thwarted in the desire to build a 'dome', a church in the style of St Sophia, Constantinople, at Troon in 1882, Bute decided to offer a new church to Galston.[20] Henry Laverty,[21] the local priest, was enthusiastic over the prospect of a church for Galston, where the congregation were meeting in a weaver's shed which was already too small.[22] He thought that 'there would be great use in building a church at Galston, to accommodate even two hundred', but he pressed discreetly for a larger church.[23] Gwen therefore advised Bute that the church should be built to accommodate 400.[24]

From the point of view of emotional geography, Galston could hardly have a more significant set of co-ordinates. It is a small town set on a hillside, and it dominates the view for miles around. It is within easy walking distance of Loudoun Castle, which was Bute's mother Sophia's home during the years of her spinsterhood. In another direction, it is near the small gentleman's house she hired at Dallars to make an Ayrshire home for herself and her little son. A little further on is Dumfries House, the Ayrshire seat of the Bute family. It was irresistible that this church should be called St Sophia.

The plans were for a classic Greek-cross church. It has a dome inside, and outside a curious little turret, Armenian style, designed to defeat the pervasive west coast rain. Gavin Stamp describes it as 'hard dark red brick'[25] but, like Hagia Sophia as Bute first saw it, growing ever clearer through the early light, it glows orange, brighter than the similarly coloured but lighter-toned red sandstone. Brick, rather than the local stone, was chosen on grounds of economy, even before the choice of architect; but Bute provided many mission churches, including a Cathedral at Oban, built of iron. Brick was, by these standards, luxurious.

Striking as the exterior is for south-west Scotland, in both design and material, the interior is more noteworthy, remarkable for the light, white domes. Behind the four piers supporting the main dome spring four smaller domes, which, by contrast, increase the apparent size of the central one. Light streams in from eight small clerestory windows. Either Anderson had persuaded Bute to drop the idea of red glazing, or else the latter came to realise that stark white light would be more effective in creating a sense of space. Indeed, the light and height gives an impression of immense space, and of overwhelming calm.

Calm was something Bute was currently lacking in his relations with the church. He was involved in a battle to right a major wrong which would have profound consequences for his subsequent standing in the church. His great struggle over the Carmont affair altered attitudes to him among the hierarchy for all time.

John Carmont was a Catholic priest living at Blairgowrie, Perthshire.[26] Ill and unable to work, he applied for relief to the Mitchell Fund. Captain Thomas Peter Mitchell who died in 1865 left much of his property in trust to provide an 'asylum' for sick, incapacitated or aged clergymen. Before 1878, when the Scottish hierarchy was restored and diocesan bishops were consecrated, Scottish Catholics were cared for by three bishops acting directly for the Pope. The trust was to be administered by these three Vicars Apostolic.

Times changed, and the bishops knew that Catholic priests would not want to live in an institution. Having made that decision, however, they did not take the prudent course of getting a legal opinion on what should properly be done to carry out the intentions of the benefactor without actually implementing the strict terms of the bequest: for instance providing individual houses scattered throughout Scotland. They decided instead to divide the money (running contrary to the terms of Mitchell's will) unequally between the three districts, and instead of arriving at joint decisions, in accordance with the terms of the will, decided each would make unilateral decisions about the money in their charge. Thus any priest wanting relief under the terms of the will had to apply to his own bishop, and the natural result was that his bishop's opinion of him tended to colour what, if any, relief he got. Any monies derived from the capital left over at the end of the year were applied by the Bishops to whatever cause they favoured. The Catholic church was notoriously poor, and the good causes the Bishops needed to fund were numerous. This added to their disinclination to use the money left by Mitchell for anything like the purposes intended, and as the capital alone was left for investment, it gradually dwindled.

Two of the bishops put the money towards new missions, and not relief of the clergy at all.[27] As if all this was not bad enough, one of the bishops lent the capital of the Trust to several priests on no security. When the hierarchy was restored, the new diocesan bishops took legal opinion. This condemned the past action of the trustees. The new bishops then refused to take responsibility for the Trust, and appealed to the Cardinal Prefect of Propaganda – the body charged with the oversight of Catholics in countries without a formal hierarchy of diocesan bishops, and responsible for the spread of Catholicism – 'who as is clear, was powerless to remedy the grave illegalities of the trustees which were not otherwise remediable than by the intervention of the Supreme Court'. Two of the original trustee bishops were dead, and the third approaching the end of his life. At this point 'the priest John Carmont having acquired on account of infirm health, an immediate interest in the Fund thought it his duty to intervene to protect his right and that of all the beneficiaries, already so gravely prejudiced and threatened indeed with total ruin'.

Carmont was offered money for support, but he knew it did not come from the Mitchell fund, and refused it, believing that accepting it would make his motives look suspect. In other words, he refused what clearly could be interpreted as an attempt to buy him off. Carmont took the trustees, that is the bishops, to the civil courts, and won. The courts demanded the Fund be reconstituted and used to support infirm priests. The case finished on 15 January 1885. As soon as he got news of Carmont's action in the Scottish courts, John Strain, by then Archbishop and last of the original trustees, alleged that the Cardinal Prefect of the Holy Office, Simeoni[28] (head of the church's official guardian of faith and morals) had given an opinion that if Carmont went ahead with his action against his Church's bishops, he would be excommunicated by the very nature of his act. His offence was using a civil Scottish court against his religious superiors. In matters relating to the Church, they said they were only subject to the Church. The hierarchy had Privilege of Clergy.

Carmont's address was known to the hierarchy, but this threat of excommunication was sent to his agents. The first Carmont knew of the threat of excommunication was a forwarded letter telling him that he was already excommunicated. Carmont wrote to the Sacred Congregation of Propaganda and to the Pope, trying to get himself rehabilitated. A number of priests got up a petition to help him. However, in the hierarchy anger against him was great. William Smith,[29] a senior priest who in the autumn of that year would be consecrated as Bishop of Edinburgh, told him:

> I am afraid that these efforts [writing to the Pope, Propaganda and presenting the petition] are doomed to failure from want of the necessary condition of success – an expression of regret on your part for having gone about what was a good work in a wrong way ... Without an indication of regret on your part your case is hopeless. But with that in my hand I am sure to succeed.[30]

Before the final resolution of the case at the start of 1885, Bute had become interested in it. He instructed his solicitor, Pitman, to make enquiries about it, because he doubted if a priest could be excommunicated for taking action through the civil courts.[31] Inevitably, Pitman was soon out of his depth in the field of Canon Law, as were Carmont's agents, and the former suggested that Carmont needed to approach Bute direct. The result was that Bute himself entered the lists. He had far more experience of Rome, and where he lacked knowledge either of the law or of the labyrinthine processes of influence and patronage at the court of the Vatican, he had friends who knew who to speak to, when, and what about. In the end, he wrote, in his own hand in pencil for transcription by his agents, the final appeal which Carmont presented to Rome.[32] It combines his methodical and logical approach to facts with his typical verbal pizzazz.

> Dr Carmont denies that he has incurred the excommunication, because, *inter alia*:
>
> It is plain that the Privilege of Clergy with regard to worldly matters presupposes a state of things such as that which prevailed at Rome before the events of 1870, viz., one in which the Church Courts exist with the power of enforcing their decrees, and thus affording redress against clerical offenders. It cannot possibly be intended to secure immunity to all tonsured criminals ... If, for instance, a little girl were abducted by a cleric for the purpose of prostitution, her relatives would be unable to appeal to the Civil Power to rescue her. This is a <u>reductio ad absurdam</u>, and causes the principle upon which alone Dr. Carmont is held to be excommunicate, to fall to the ground ...

Bute then brandished before their faces a number of flagrant breaches of justice perpetrated by the bishops and clergy, from Archbishop Strain's refusal to pay wages due to a workman, to a girl threatened with excommunication when she attempted to get redress against a priest who had defamed her. In all cases, the church had taken no steps to enforce justice. Since the Church courts could not enforce the law, good Catholics must go to the civil courts. Justice must be done. There followed some pages of argument over why the excommunication was not valid including that there had been no formal trial and the idea that possibly, given that the words were hearsay, Simeoni had not actually given this opinion at all. This suggestion appears to be a graceful way of allowing the cardinal to back down without loss of face. The appeal concluded with the request for a proper trial, if Carmont was indeed to be excommunicated. One may well imagine the delight the Protestant press in Great Britain and the anti-clerical press in Europe would have taken in such a trial.

Bute and Carmont won: 'the Cardinal Prefect of Propaganda denied that he had ever sent to the Bishops or ever authorised any one to send, such a message as that contained in Mgr. Campbell's letter'.[33] Carmont was not rehabilitated; instead, he was declared never to have been excommunicated. Yet, although it yielded in this instance, the Catholic Church did not take on the key lesson, that it could not safely or properly manage justice in all matters relating to its priesthood, and the attempt to do so might lead to flagrant injustice and distress. Had it done so, the scandals of the late twentieth century might perhaps have been avoided and the church have understood the need to hand child abusers and IRA bombers over to the state for trial and punishment.

The cost of the victory for Bute personally was high. It is doubtful that the bishops liked being compared to those abducting children for prostitution, or having it made very plain to them that they had on a number of occasions acted contrary to natural justice. Even Bute's friend, Colin Grant, articulated the common perception in the church: 'Dr Carmont's case has always seemed to me like that of children fighting their parents; even if in the right, they are wrong.'[34] Grant was too good a friend of Bute for there not to be a full rapprochement, but those like Angus Macdonald, the Bishop of Argyll, who had for some time cordially disliked Bute now bore him serious ill-will.

Macdonald,[35] an Ushaw-educated priest, was, as Bute admitted even when relations were at a very low ebb indeed, a gentleman. He was one of the two recipients of the Burges mitres.[36] Bute's two Scottish seats lay in two different dioceses. Dumfries House was in Dumfries and Galloway, and Mount Stuart was in Argyll. One of Bute's first acts after the restoration of the hierarchy was to commission Burges to design mitres for both of them. Typically, much of the design came from Bute:

There is our mitre. It is not as showy as the Bp. of Galloway's but it is almost the same in value, as the precious stones, though fewer, are more valuable viz. emeralds and rubies &c instead of beryls & the like – and, as a matter of artistic taste, I confess that I rather prefer it ... The idea of it was suggested to me by the custom of the Greek Bishops, whose vestments are often woven or embellished in wavy stripes, to typify the rivers of grace which flow from the Pontiff. Hence you have the four Rivers of Paradise, with the tree of life rising between them, laden with precious fruits, and with the birds of the air taking refuge in their branches, while the living streams flow round the head. Of course, all the stones, gold, pearls etc. are real.[37]

Of course. In addition, he was able to tell the Bishop that Lady Bute 'had got something into her head about trying to build you a little Cathedral'.[38] It is possible that collaboration on the Scots calendar did no good to relations between the two men, but in 1882 Bute was still consulting him as one might a respected and slightly senior colleague.

In 1884, the question of a Cathedral for Oban was finally seriously discussed, an idea with which Bute 'perfectly sympathised'. As Bute told the Bishop, he had originally intended to offer to pay for the plans for a cathedral and clergy house in Oban, and to build a considerable portion of it himself, subject, as he ominously added 'to certain arrangements as to Trustees &c and the ways of carrying on things'. The unexpected expense of rebuilding Mount Stuart now prevented that. However, he confidently added that the bishop 'seemed to be of an opinion' which Bute himself held strongly. Bute believed that a Cathedral without the regular performance of the daily offices 'is a mere sham and mockery, a nut-shell without the nut, whereas the services without the Cathedral are really the nut without the shell'.

He seriously informed the Bishop that once started the office must 'never be dropped, in whole or part, for a single day'.[39] The Bishop took immediate umbrage. Bute wriggled out of it by suggesting that he had not really meant that the bishop would be compelled to keep up the unremitting round of daily services but that he would naturally want to do so as

> it is a continual daily offering of public prayer and praise. This arrangement would be an example not only to Scotland but to England, it would be the liturgical model and centre of the diocese, it would be a distinctive feature of the town of Oban and would enter the daily . . . life of you and your own people, whose devotion would form itself into ecclesiastical moulds. To drop it would be impossible.
> But your letter gives me the idea that you would rather not have it. Am I right?[40]

He was resoundingly right. Exasperated, Bute told his wife that Macdonald seemed 'one of the worst of the Padres in some ways'.[41] Yet, in the face of the Bishop's lack of enthusiasm, amounting almost to downright hostility, Bute pressed ahead with the scheme. As seen above, he decided to give a 'tin tabernacle' to Oban, a temporary structure, but to fit it out with beautifully carved wood, and with paintings, which could be transferred to the permanent building. Bute would then have the money free to provide the kernel of the nut: the school and the services. He explained enthusiastically how well it would all fit in with the natural pattern of life and the school day. The services would be introduced gradually. First Compline, then the Mass, then Vespers, then Lauds, Terce, and lastly Mattins:

> as to being occupied, no one is occupied (or very few) at 8 p.m. and Vespers and Lauds are just when the boys come out of school & before they go in. Mattins and the Hours (or the rest too) you can have as long as there are say two people who can read.

To the Bishop's complaint that he did not have a priest free, Bute replied crisply that 'there is nothing sacerdotal about the Office. The only sacerdotal thing is the oblation of the incense on certain days.'

Bute had been thoroughly exasperated by the way Macdonald was dragging his feet and making difficulties, and he now allowed his pen to run away with him. It did this very easily, but usually, his policy of revision ensured that the end result was polite. On this occasion he posted a letter which had very definitely slipped into a rude and bullying tone:

> To your remark as to figured music being quite allowed (within certain limits) I quite agree. It is a matter of taste. But my taste is the other way, and anybody provided by me would be for Gregorians only. I shd. not allow him (the organist) to help directly or indirectly any service of the church, even on a private domestic level where anything else was used ... But of course I should not stipulate against the use of figured music in the services – e.g. the choral office wd. be over by 11.30 or thereby, if a shady theatrical company, or other body, chose to give a performance at 12, why should I try to impede you from allowing them?[42]

The astonishment is not that Bute roused hostility, but that despite his serious misgivings, Angus Macdonald finally agreed to let Bute go ahead with his scheme. Understandably, with a large, geographically awkward and very poor diocese, he would have preferred that Bute spent his money on other projects. If he had either refused to let the project go ahead, or decided to offer it a little support, he would have simplified things for both himself and Bute. He did neither and the result was to be protracted misery and anger.

Meanwhile work on Oban Cathedral was so poorly advanced that there could be no question of any services taking place in it at all, and Gwen was once again expecting a baby. This time she had fallen pregnant in Chiswick House, which did at least have the merit of being reasonably central for family and friends, and for libraries to provide Bute with books to further his various pieces of research. Because of fears for both Gwen and their unborn babe, her pregnancies were a nightmare to her, and hardly less so to Bute. These days, he was only a little freer than her during the pregnancy, and many pregnant Victorian women allowed themselves more travel and excitement than Bute enjoyed during this time of waiting. He filled in his time with various matters. There was the steady advancement of work on the Scots calendar of saints. There were articles for *The Scottish Review*.[43]

This year he published his previously written account of the island of Patmos, and *Some Christian Monuments of Athens* which arose from his stay there in 1884. The old churches in Athens had had their interiors whitewashed, destroying all the old iconography, or else were in ruins. He hoped by describing the ruins, he was in a way preserving them for the future.[44]

He was even more amusing and discursive on the lighter subject of *The Scottish Peerage*, which he was writing at the time, recounting tales of the courage of the Douglases:

> It is a striking instance of their character, that when James, ninth Earl of Douglas, was brought into the presence of James II, in 1484, and could have had little but death, probably by torture, staring him in the face, he simply manifested his contempt for the crowned destroyer of his race and personal assassin of his brother, by silently turning his back upon him. The king, probably awed by his courage, allowed him to retire into the monastery of Lindores for the rest of his days.[45]

The article took a ramble though the Scottish Peerage's religious affiliations (most were Episcopalian from the influence of English wives), and the ability of its daughters to inherit in many cases (which could and did lead to peerages re-emerging from where they had been subsumed in other titles by marriage).

There were also translations of two of the articles by the Greek scholar Bikelas on Christian Greece, a project dear to Bute's heart, which covered the history of the newly independent country. These are worthy and ponderous, but must have done much to raise awareness of a country beloved by Bute which was just struggling into the mainstream life of Europe. Bute worried over his 'free-thinking' paragraphs, which he 'cooked' (his own word) and which Bikelas then 'scepticised' again.[46] Bikelas was to remain a dear friend.

The other work for the *Scottish* was an account of the Bayreuth Festival, and of the two works, *Tristan and Isolde* and *Parsifal* which Bute had heard there. It is difficult now to conjure up again a world so large that few people could go to the small German town which was the only place *Parsifal* was to be heard, and to imagine a world so proper that the theme of the adultery of Tristan and Isolde required careful circumlocution and assurances that a duet and a kiss was as close as they got to any representation of love-making. Bute was at once irritated by the artificial elements in the story (death potions and love philtres), made uncomfortable by the theme of overwhelming and yet illicit love, and awed by the music 'of such exquisite beauty'. His writing was at times broken and laboured as he struggled to get into his theme. He relaxed into the story of *Parsifal*, of which of course he could thoroughly approve. He wished it were possible merely to hear it, as the production, though enjoyable, did not rise to the level of the music. Yet he was acutely conscious of the role that the experience of attending the theatre has on the whole. His article ends:

> The hearer joins the crowds which are streaming up the little hill towards the great dull-red building. Presently he is in his place in the large plain auditorium. A while and the lights are lowered. The audience settle themselves and the buzz of conversation dies away. Darkness ensues. The closing doors shut out the last glimpses of daylight. There is a hush, followed by silence and stillness. And presently the first notes are heard. Another six hours of intense enjoyment has begun.[47]

Bute was also writing an article on the so-called 'Prophecies of St Malachi'. These were attributed to the twelfth-century saint by a Benedictine of the sixteenth century. (Their historical material indicates they were composed in the latter century.) They offer a short tag or motto on each Pope, the list of whom extends nine popes past Bute's date. As Bute implies, they are almost certainly not the work of Malachi, but their accuracy as prophecies did not depend on their origin. They had excited a good deal of interest in 1878, the year of Leo XIII's election, as 'many were, and are, quite satisfied that the fiery star on the dexter chief of the arms of the new Pope fulfils the prophetic motto "*Lumen in coelo*"'. As usual Bute strove to be absolutely equal-handed.[48] The prophecies suggested the world would end in 1996, which current readers may not feel adds to their credibility. It is not perhaps surprising that Bute chose to publish this essay far from home in the *Dublin Review* of 1885.

Writing was not Bute's only entertainment. There were walks in London, and visits to friends, and 'turns' in what was left of the park at Chiswick, and the inevitable letters. One touching and unexpected letter came from his old guardian, Charles Stuart with whom he had not kept in touch. Stuart was now blind, and wanted to pass on to Bute his library, largely drawn from their mutual ancestor, the 3rd Earl of Bute. The old man spoke of his pleasure in hearing of the birth of Bute's sons. Bute took Margaret to the circus at Covent Garden, which was 'no duller than other circuses',[49] and he himself went to *Faust*. There were minor excitements in the form of ghost stories told to him by various friends, including Fr McSwiney, and experiments in thought transference.

Then late in the evening of 2 April Gwen went into a labour which lasted much longer than that with her first son. It was 7.21 a.m. before her third son, Colum, was born. 'My Lady suffered horribly',[50] Bute recorded sadly. But he was overjoyed with the baby, 'the finest child we have had yet', he told his friend Grant.[51] He thought babies were stronger when the parents were older. Bute was thirty-eight now, and Gwen was thirty-two. The baby was actually baptised Columba, but with the intent he should be known by the Gaelic shortened form of the name,[52] and Bute told Grant he knew that his friend would 'take pleasure in the name. I am regarded as extremely eccentric for having given it. But the only thing I wonder at is that it should not have been done before and I trust I may set a good example.'[53] He added that he had been at Chiswick House for a year, and was getting very tired of the place.[54]

Then the most horrible of medical conditions caught up with Bute. A tooth which had begun to 'torment' him in 1883 once again flared up, leaving him in such agony that he rushed round London looking for a dentist to agree to abstract it.[55] The best he could find was one who agreed to put a leech on the swollen gum. The infection spread, and putrid pus began to descend his nostrils,[56] meaning that his sinuses had in turn become infected. It was a fortnight before his pleading persuaded his dentist to pull the tooth out: It came 'almost instantaneously and painlessly',[57] but the discharge continued: 'It is not nice to write about, but it's worse to experience',[58] he commented wryly.

It is highly probable that this episode led directly to Bute's eventual death, as later events reveal.[59] He and his dentists failed to realise just how serious the condition was, and no sense of foreboding darkened his trip back to Scotland and Dumfries House, which was within easy reach of Glasgow: the more so since it had its own railway station, installed (one feels it was no coincidence) in the year of Bute's marriage. Bute's psoriasis had also flared up once again with stress, and he put himself

> entirely in the hands of Prof McCall Anderson of Glasgow, who doses me and diets me, and washes me with lotion, and keeps me smeared all over with something called chrysophanic acid and, till the skin peels off, the irritation drives me nearly wild.[60]

At Dumfries House Bute had a range of family and country pleasures to enjoy. He walked extensively with his wife, his children, the visitors to his family, his secretary, and the governess: in short any present who could walk. He also entertained his friends.

One of these was the Benedictine monk, Brother (later Father) Oswald.[61] He had been born in 1853 the eldest son of Edward Hunter Blair, and heir apparent to the Baronetage. The family estate was (and is) at Blairquhan, Ayrshire, some thirty miles from the Bute home at Cumnock, and Bute's younger contemporary went to the same prep school, then to Eton and Oxford. Like Bute, he converted to Roman Catholicism, to the dismay of his family. But instead of settling down to marriage and the life of a landed gentleman, David Hunter Blair took the cloth as a Benedictine monk. Bute and Hunter Blair have always been represented as friends. In a sense, they were, but it was a somewhat troubled and uneven friendship. The first discord had been brewed by an over-frank letter from Bute to Hunter Blair when the latter was about to take his profession, the 'final and irrevocable step' of vowing himself to follow the Benedictine life of poverty, chastity and obedience. Bute told him, apparently not for the first time, 'you know what I think ... as to the injury which will be inflicted on the Church and the desertion of duty which it will be in yourself – in my humble conviction':[62] stinging words which were never quite forgotten by Hunter Blair, who later commented on 'the curious displeasure with which, notwithstanding his theoretical and archaeological admiration of monastic institutions, he always received the news of any friends of his own entering a religious order'.[63] Bute had felt, of course, that Hunter Blair's first duty was to his family and his estate. He should find his religious fulfilment in marriage and children. Had Bute appraised his friends somewhat more realistically, he might have realised that this was unlikely to be a successful course of action for Hunter Blair.

Both men came from similar backgrounds and enjoyed the same kind of learned pursuits, one of which was liturgy. As a treat, therefore, Bute arranged a High Mass. Br Oswald was a deacon, not yet able to celebrate the Mass. Bute had a visiting priest, Fr Moverley, and the young parish priest, Fr Hourigan. He had, therefore, the necessary set of three clergy for a High Mass, which requires a priest, deacon and subdeacon. The drawback was that only the deacon, Br Oswald, and the server (Bute) actually knew how to enact the dignified and complex dance that is the ritual of High Mass.

Sunday June 13 Fine Mr Hourigan said Mass. Communicatus sum. Walked with Miss B[ayliss] to Cumnock. High Mass. Mr M[overley][64], who had not sung Mass for 20 years celebrated, said 'I beg your pardon?' the first time Br Oswald (Deacon) said 'Benedicite

Pater Reverendi' with the incense. Hourigan, who had only seen High Mass twice in his life, did sub deacon with desperation.[65]

The mixture of hilarity and reverence is utterly understandable to those of a religious disposition; but the story must go some way to show why this laughing giant of a man by turns delighted and exasperated the clergy.

It was the level of education of most Catholics which exercised Bute, however, not that they had rarely seen the beauties of High Mass. Bute wanted to see Catholic laity and clergy taught to the highest possible level. He had been concerned in 1882 by 'the Bishops' condemning an Oxbridge education for Catholic boys. He had comforted himself with the thought that 'It is some 17 years before such a question can arise about John (if he is spared) & much will happen by that time – probably including Manning's going to heaven.'[66] As the comment shows, it was Manning himself who resolutely opposed permission for Catholic parents to send their children to Oxford or Cambridge, where he considered there was a high risk of their being infected by 'Rationalism'. He also disliked the lack of provision for middle-class young people and the out-of-date syllabus, based heavily on Classics.[67] However upper-middle-class and aristocratic parents wanted their boys (and it was boys these parents agonised over, despite the newly founded facilities for women's education at these universities) to be able to enjoy the standard liberal education and gentle initiation into adult society. The experience of Oxbridge was the important thing, not the education. Bute, however, was not a man to accept the status quo when it might be amenable to change.

In 1885, he discussed the matter with Fr McSwiney, who as so often sympathised with him:

> I have met F. Humphrey, S.J. ... [who] tells me that the morality of young men is far safer [at Oxford] than it would be in most other places to which young men are sent to prepare for their professions ... the Catholic undergraduates are (for the most part) exact in attending Mass and in frequenting the Sacraments. As to the dangers to faith, he says there are two categories – the far larger are those who are not exercised with deep problems, et puis the 'thinkers' who, says he, as the world now wags are not in greater danger of a collapse of faith at Oxford than elsewhere ... He further confirms my view that the circular of the English Episcopacy ... cannot ... restrain the action of Irish or Scotch parents ...[68]

Bute was surely right in that one cannot safeguard faith by keeping it apart from all questioning.

In the summer of 1886 a major project occurred to Bute. He had become aware of grumblings amongst the hierarchy concerning the training of the clergy at the college of Blairs. The history of education for the Catholic priesthood had been long, troubled and romantic. For some years, while Catholicism was a proscribed religion, Catholic boys intending for the priesthood had been educated abroad, at various colleges, including Valladolid and the Scots College at Paris. Then the need for education based in the home country had become pressing, and a 'secret college' was opened in 1716 at Scalan, in the north-east of Scotland, not far from Glenlivet, famed for its whisky. The little turf-built dwelling was in time replaced by a larger one, and the school survived the '45 rebellion, and prospered.[69] Catholicism became legal, and even accepted, and the seminary moved first to Aquhorthies, near Inverurie, and then to Blairs, near Aberdeen. Now Bute thought 'the Bishops . . . [were] seriously dissatisfied with Blairs, both as regards site, accommodation and the assurance of efficiency in the instruction'. He was certainly right about the building. It had been built to accommodate fifty students, and the numbers were steadily climbing. It is harder to be sure how discontented they all were with the level of education. The Bishop of Galloway certainly had reservations.

At the same time, Bute who always had an enormous sentimental attachment to any place connected with his childhood, was concerned about the future of St Andrews University. Numbers were at a very low level, 'about 200 students (undergraduates)'. The other three universities of Scotland (Glasgow, Edinburgh and Aberdeen) were situated in the centres of bustling modern towns. This was their strength, since there was a tradition of Scottish students attending the university nearest their homes. The strength of St Andrews was the beauty of the place and its history. Bute said that St Andrews was the only place in Scotland that was anything like Oxford. True, it did not have the quantity of good architecture, but the quality was excellent, and the situation on the magnificent Fife coast was incomparably better than the swampy situation of Oxford.

He proposed that a Catholic college be established at St Andrews, and that Blairs move there as a college. This would, in a short time, ensure a Catholic majority and see St Andrews become a Catholic university. All the Catholics intending to go to any university would go to St Andrews:

It would be practically impossible ... to resist the desire of the great majority of the University in religious matters. St Mary's College would become a Seminary for the final training of priests, and the University church be returned to Catholic uses ... Neither your Grace or I, I fear, would live to see the Cathedral and the Castle re-apportioned to the Archbishopric, but that time would not be very long after us.

So many of Bute's pet themes came together in one project that it is no wonder that it was irresistible to him. What the world has lost, in not having the Cathedral at St Andrews returned to the full, glittering, painted splendour which Bute would have created in it! More soberly, he moved on to consider the impact of training the young priests in a more open university. Since they needed a good general education, followed by a vocational one, his idea was that they should first sit an arts degree in his Catholic university, before moving into the seminary. For years, Bute had been distressed and embarrassed by the sexual and financial failings of some priests. At Oxford, he knew that the potential Anglican clergy used their time in the University as an opportunity to discover if their own conscience or the judgement of 'those who controlled them ... showed that their calling was for the world'. Now he saw a chance of establishing a method of sorting out at an early stage which candidates for the priesthood had unacceptable weaknesses, and which did not.[70]

In a way typical of him, Bute totally failed to take on board the way that his simple and straightforward plan to Catholicise St Andrews might raise a storm of emotional difficulties for others that would, in turn, shipwreck the desired end. It was left to the Society of Jesus to marshal a response to Bute's stunningly impractical suggestion. Some of the objections raised were mere excuses. It was alleged by the English Jesuits that the university courses were 'not really above those of good secondary schools' and that the students were not drawn from the kind of background likely to attract Catholic parents.[71] All the Scottish universities had for centuries attracted a wide mix of students, including those from quite poor backgrounds, of which they were justifiably proud. In addition, some students came from remote areas with no access to a good school, many, indeed, coming straight from elementary schools. Because of the need to even out all these educational levels, the first-year classes at all the Scottish universities, not just St Andrews, were taught at a standard no higher than the upper classes of a secondary school.[72] This did not mean that the higher classes were not of a good standard. The real fear, rightly, was of a

Protestant backlash, that 'the very first step towards invasion would rouse the Protestant feeling of the body and probably the whole of Scotland' and the authorities would take action to prevent Bute's plan being fulfilled.[73] As Bute should have known, it would have awoken the kind of fear of Catholicism which was only just dying down.

In England the steady trickle of aristocratic and middle-class Catholic converts was changing perceptions. In addition, the strong Anglo-Catholic movement in the Church of England also made Catholic theology respectable. The Church of Scotland, and even more, the numerous schisms from it, had always been calvinistic. The seventeenth- and eighteenth-century history of Scotland had involved the most disastrous mixing of politics and religion, and bloodshed and oppression in the name of faith had not ended with the Civil War of Charles I but had continued with bitter fervour up to the accession of William and Mary. A gentleman priest whom Bute was supporting in a mission in St Andrews pointed out that Scottish denominations were supported strictly along class lines. 'The middle class are all Presbyterians: the aristocrats are Anglicans but don't do much in the church going line. And the very poor, except my 70 or 80 Catholics, go nowhere.'[74] In the towns, there were large numbers of the Irish poor. They were ill-educated, ragged, frequently drunken, and Roman Catholic. To the bulk of the Presbyterian middle class they represented the myth of Roman Catholic rejection of truth, and, along with it, true education, in favour of indoctrination and misinformation.

Bute was not inclined to see the problems, and as usual when his ideas were thwarted, he reacted by withdrawing his funding. Failing his grand plan of 'Catholicising' St Andrews University, he wanted to ensure that priests were educated to University level, as he told the Archbishop of Edinburgh when refusing to help fund a wholly religious seminary:

What I said to your face as to the Archdiocesan seminary was that I thought that it would be a very good thing if such an establishment took the form of a college at one of the National Universities & the seminarians were all made to take their degree in arts. St Andrews seemed to me to be admirable adapted from every point of view for such a purpose, & that if such a plan were to be carried out I should be inclined to subscribe something to it. Perhaps I need hardly remind your Grace that at Glasgow I did subscribe something to the seminary, I understood from the archbishop that he shared my opinion as to the making use of the university in the way suggested.

But no one of the seminarians has ever matriculated there. A priest once suggested to me that the educational level in the seminary is so low that no one of them has ever been capable of doing so. I should be sorry to think it were so, but am not in a position to rebut my Rev. friend's suggestion.[75]

The hierarchy was still too concerned with its authority to find it easy to co-operate with learned and secular men, as it would need to do to create a college at a University. Bute had personal charm, undeniable profound learning in many areas, including theology and liturgy, both the wealth and the will to fund their projects, natural authority, and he commanded the additional respect the Victorians accorded a title. Yet the clergy struggled to keep an easy relationship with him because he was neither ordained nor wholly subservient. It is both laudable that they were not blinded by his title, and regrettable they could not see he deserved to be heard on personal grounds.

Now that Oban Cathedral was well under way, Bute was pursuing with renewed enthusiasm his plans for the Oban choir school. The original plan was to set up a small school for middle-class children, whose parents would subsidise the education, while Bute made up the shortfall.[76] It was rapidly apparent that there were simply not enough Catholic parents of the right class and financial circumstances to make up the numbers. Bute decided that the best thing would be to kill two birds with one stone, and sent to the school a number of bright but poor children whom he was, anyhow, considering educating at his own expense. He had 'at Rothesay at present, such a nice bright boy [Thomas Mitchell], son of a miner near Cumnock – who I had already made up my mind to experiment on with a liberal education, so that he might be able to follow a learned profession – or take to the priesthood – if he felt inclined'.[77] He had thought such boys would be easy to find, but his first excursions discovered one who had 'no more voice than a hedgehog'.[78]

A much more serious problem than providing the boys was providing the staff. Bute's first choice was 'a D.D. – not of the honorary kind, but by the result of examinations'[79] who suddenly 'threw [Bute] over'[80] ten days before he was due to start. Bute provided a French couple, the Duhamels, to provide housekeeping for the boys. He had still had to find somebody to teach them, and a priest to say the mass. The simple way of squaring the circle was to employ a priest to teach the boys. Unfortunately, his next choice, the Rev. Francis Moberly had no sooner arrived in Oban than he created a scandal by getting tipsy in the hotel. He had to be removed.[81]

The problem was that there were almost no free priests. Clergy were few in number, and mostly working very hard, and those priests available to take up a position at the choir school were nearly all in poor health. The latter was an immediate problem. The Bishop's Mass was at 8 a.m.; Bute's Mass was to be at ten o'clock. The rules on fasting made it impossible for the priest to breakfast first, and this put their first meal of the day to a time which a working man would think more suitable for lunch. So a man in poor health, if he were to both teach school and sing Mass, would need to have the care and teaching of half a dozen boys from perhaps seven until ten o'clock in the morning without as much as a cup of coffee to comfort and sustain him. Moreover, as Bute was to discover to his cost, a good number of free priests had flaws which meant their bishops would be only too glad to see them re-deployed. For this reason, he decided on a schoolteacher to educate the boys, and a priest who could then rise later, sing Mass, and then break his fast before helping with the boys' education in some way.

So when Bute saw a promising advert in *The Tablet* he responded.

F. R. Experienced in Tuition and school keeping, will be glad to hear of a Vacancy in a Catholic School or Tutorship in a private family.[82]

Bute checked F. R.'s testimonials and hired him. In a run of the ill-luck that dogged the Oban Choir School project, he had hired the brilliant Frederick Rolfe, later known as Baron Corvo.

Rolfe was the son of the last, and least successful, of a long line of piano manufacturers.[83] To fail at this must have been something of a feat, for the genteel would-be middle class practised considerable economies in order to invest a capital sum in the longed-for instrument: an activity ridiculed in Edinburgh as 'kippers and pianos'. Despite the demand, Frederic's father suffered ever-falling income, and the knock-on effect on the family was inevitable: 'his brother Herbert declared that Frederick had hardly more than a year at a decent school'. He was able, through study and intelligence, to make up whatever was lacking in the education. Yet despite his brilliance, he was not a happy man. He experienced adolescence as a terrible thing, and whatever the cause, it is arguable that he never outgrew or overcame this.

Afterward he characterised as the most awful period in the life of a young boy the point 'when he must watch the death of his own boyhood and assist at the birth of his own youth'. Rolfe's analysis of the pains of puberty emphasised the terror of the 'mind-rending body-tearing pangs' with which 'youth is born'.[84]

Unfortunately this kind of trauma seems a good prescription for an enduring fascination with pre-pubescent boys which only too easily translated into sexual desire for them. Rolfe had turned to teaching to earn a living, and was acting as housemaster at Grantham Grammar School when he became convinced of his own call to both the priesthood and the Catholic Church. Neither was compatible with his position, and he resigned and advertised his services. Bute wrote to him from Dumfries House, and Rolfe replied 'sending . . . copies of my testimonials together with an original one from my last Head Master'.[85] Bute 'interviewed and engaged'[86] Rolfe, who then travelled on to Oban, where Angus Macdonald received him 'most kindly'[87] and showed him the house where the school was to be kept, in Loyola House, which belonged to the Jesuits.

To be appointed to run a tiny school of boys who were to sing the office daily in a miniature cathedral, and to receive a basic liberal education for the rest of their working day must have seemed an extraordinary stroke of luck to a man in Rolfe's position. Bute had ordered him to write to him every two or three days with news of this school which was so close to his heart. The first steps towards the school were taken at the start of August. Four boys had been gathered at the school kept by the monks at Fort Augustus, where Brother Oswald was one of the teachers. There, they were learning some of the rudiments of their new job of singing the Office. Rolfe collected them on 4 August, and found another boy already at the school. Rolfe wrote on 4 and 6 August to Anderson, Bute's private secretary. Rolfe wrote one letter to Bute on 11 August, full of the kind of news that Bute longed for.

Frank Daniels cried at intervals for the first three or four days because he wanted to go home. He is better now I think. Edgar Bates has found it difficult to get up in time for the morning Mass. He does not seem to be on very friendly terms with the other boys, I think because he is not a Scotsman. At least I have heard a rumour it is so.[88]

He sent the letter to Anderson, to be forwarded to Bute, and then did not write again until 31 August.

Meanwhile, the Marquess had been ordered to Carlsbad by his doctor, to take the waters as a treatment for his psoriasis. Prof. McCall

Anderson had been treating him all summer, ordering a 'strict system of diet',[89] hot baths, rubbing with a pumice stone, and having the affected areas covered night and morning with chrysophanic acid. Bute hated Carlsbad, calling it 'one of the most odious places I have ever seen'.[90] His only pleasure there was attending the Synagogue on Saturdays. Beforehand, he had gone to Bayreuth with Gwen. To spend a fortnight listening to his favourite operas alleviated the pain somewhat. He alternated seeing his beloved *Parsifal* with *Tristan und Isolde*, seeing each of them four times.

In Carlsbad, feeling under the weather, stifled by the atmosphere, and miserable at drinking the waters, Bute was becoming very irritated at the failure of Rolfe, his personal employee, to follow the simple instruction of writing at short intervals. Far from writing every two or three days, neither the headmaster of his new school, Rolfe, nor his organist, Clements, seconded there from Cumnock, had managed more than one letter. A letter from Bute at Bayreuth to Rolfe was not answered quickly, and by early September, Bute, not yet having received the forwarded 31 August letter, was getting more and more worried: 'I hope Rolfe is not an idle, useless fellow. When you go to Oban, look after him, and give him a strong word of advice. And have your eyes open, to let me know what you think.'[91]

When the letter finally arrived, it set Bute's mind at rest to a large degree.

> The letter is perfectly clear-headed and interesting. He writes as if he had no idea of the offence which he has given me. If it had come sooner, it would have given me a feeling of satisfaction, confidence, and assurance of his fitness for his post . . . He appears properly on his guard against the dangerous priest A. Macdonald.[92]

Rolfe had been given the Bute line on the Bishop, and he adhered to it. He prevented contact between the Bishop and his staff and the boys as far as possible, creating a closed world in the tiny school, where it seems the line between fact and fantasy became blurred. Rolfe insisted the boys called him 'Rev. Fr. Rolfe'.[93] Bute was worrying that the boys had still only learnt to sing certain of the offices, and the time for Compline was not yet fully agreed. Bute wanted this fixed when it would be most likely to attract a congregation during the summer season (Oban being a popular holiday destination). He should have worried over some of the other information Rolfe had included in his letter. He claimed that 'Daniels will cause trouble, I fear. He is not truthful and will organise a really clever lie when occasion demands. I found him out in one last night.'[94] Rolf had made Daniels sleep alone in the upper dormitory, and Daniels wanted to join the other five boys who slept downstairs. The boy said he had had a nightmare and found himself sitting on a window sill of an upstairs window, which Rolfe knew had been covered with objects left to dry after a swimming trip that day. The question immediately arises of why one child had been separated out to sleep in a different room, alone, next to the room of a man whose fantasies were all of boys, and why Rolfe then branded that child as a liar.

Benkovitz leaves it as an open question if the explicit pederastic pornography which Rolfe wrote in his final years is fact or fantasy. The passages are written as though fact, naming particular boys. Yet Rolfe had told a fellow pederast and former pupil that he was 'innocent of pederastic experience',[95] and he had vowed twenty years of chastity in 1890, four years after his time in Oban. Given Rolfe's obsession with boys bathing, demonstrated in paintings, photographs and poems, it is concerning to read that these boys: 'shiver a good deal over their morning tub but I always superintend the operation myself & see that they get just a splash, a thorough ducking & a good rub'.[96] Donald Weeks thinks that Rolfe records the fact the boys all wore bathing drawers from 'innocent sincerity';[97] it is possible to doubt this. Bute did. The account of the boys taking a bath in their bathing drawers is 'in answer to some portion'[98] of Bute's comment in a now lost letter.

Others, too, were reading the situation in a similar way. Bute had appointed a 'stop-gap'[99] priest, the Belgian Fr Francis Beurms,[100] in receipt of monies from the Mitchell Fund, and he was followed and in time replaced by the Abbé Bérard, who had been tutoring in England.[101] Beurms seemed at first to acquiesce fairly well in the regime that Rolfe had set up. He told Anderson that Rolfe 'will do . . . he teaches well and . . . there has been a great improvement in singing'. Anderson had been sent to Oban to be Bute's eyes and ears on the ground, as Bute became more and more worked up over the non-arrival of letters. Anderson sent a letter of reassurance. At first 'Rolfe had little or no influence over the boys, now he has them well in hand . . . I have not been given the idea he is idle, & there are no grounds for any of your other fears.'[102]

One of Beurms's first acts was to teach the boys the Litany of Loretto, and, as Rolfe informed Bute,

we are singing it after Compline. He has also taught us to sing 'Magnificat' 2 boys stand in the middle of the Quire & sing a verse &

the choir responds to each verse 'Magnificat anima mea etc' [My soul magnifies the Lord, etc.] We have a harmonium to accompany this.[103]

Bute yearned for the pure and unadulterated traditional 'office' of the church and he exploded.

[this] is enough to make me think that [Rolfe] is half-witted or else that my express orders have no more effect on him that they would have on Charles' Wain [a constellation of stars] . . . If I ever explained anything clearly in my life, it was telling Rolfe that the object was the performance of the Church office, and that the boys were to be taught how to read and sing it. He now informs me that they have learned the Litany of Loretto, and sing it after Compline. The Litany of Loretto is no more part of the Church Service than Spohr's Last Judgement is part of the Book of Common Prayer. It must never be sung again. (I am not speaking of Benediction, wh. is not a Church Service, either.)

I told him the Ratisbon books were to be the usual standard, and all the rubrics strictly kept. He now says that at the Magnificat, he puts 2 boys in the middle of the choir and they sing it as a duet . . . of course this must be put a stop to.[104]

But it was not Rolfe who had taught the boys this, it was Beurms. For once one feels sorry for Rolfe, a new convert to the Catholic Church, still somewhat unsure about what services were and were not part of the Office, and facing a priest many years his senior in age and experience. There was no way that Rolfe could have successfully challenged Beurms. As it turned out, Bute's challenge to Beurms raised great hostility. Beurms complained bitterly, in broken English and the third person, that: 'Beurms knows as well as L Bute that the Litany of the B. V does not form part of the Officium Divinium, but he knows better than L B that it forms part of the night prayers in every Catholic community.' It was the old sneer at the convert and layman. Bute did not want what communities actually did, he wanted a pure ideal from the middle ages.

The Abbé Bérard arrived in this gently swelling sea of hurt feelings and dissatisfaction on 16 September. It seems that on his arrival, he mistook Rolfe for the Bishop, or it suited him to pretend that he had done so, 'when he found us at dinner on the night of his arrival . . . For Fr Bérard was misled by the display of rings, biretta and gorgeous cassock with a train requiring at least six boys to carry it.'[105] Beurms also told Dean Turner of Galloway, who had put him in the way of being appointed as chaplain to the Oban choir school:

Dumfries House: To Bute this Adam gem was the homeliest of his homes. (With kind permission from The Great Steward of Scotland's Dumfries House Trust)

Mount Stuart viewed from the lawns that run towards the sea. The exterior by architect R. R. Anderson is not as compelling as those of which Burges was capable. (Photograph Keith Hunter)

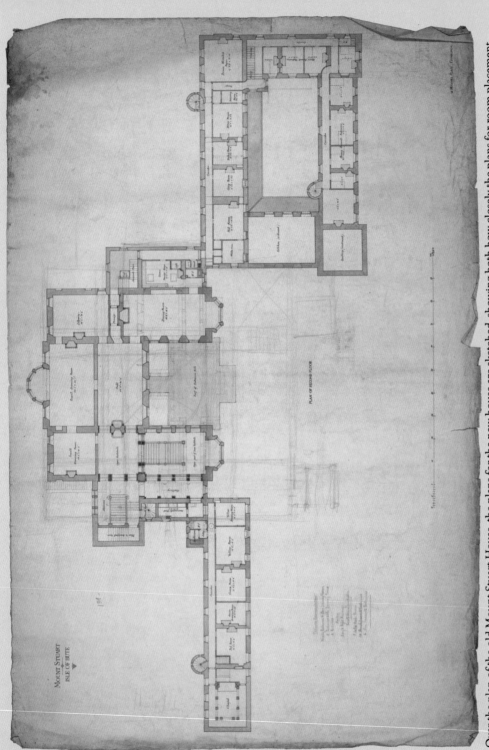

Over the plan of the old Mount Stuart House, the plans for the new house are sketched, showing both how closely the plans for room placement follow those in the old house, and how the inspired central atrium was part of the original concept. (© University of Edinburgh)

From all nations, tribes, peoples and languages, the saints stream along the walls of the chapel, towards the new Jerusalem. Martyrs, the learned, kings, the married and virgins, all together. (Photograph Christoph Kicherer)

St Margaret of Scotland processes opposite St John the Divine, Bute's name saint, in this chapel dedicated to them. This chapel is a monument both to Bute's pain and to his hopes. (Photograph Christoph Kicherer)

The chapel created by Burges at Mount Stuart: a servant's bedroom transformed. The mirror floor is an installation by artists Langlands & Bell as part of Mount Stuart Trust's Contemporary Visual Arts Programme. It provides a wonderful opportunity to enjoy the ceiling. (Photograph Christoph Kicherer)

The corridors run round the gallery of the Marble Hall at Mount Stuart. Anderson failed to see how much stronger a design feature the bronze railings were than the regulation marble balustrade he had planned.

The roundels of the Days of Creation at the head of Mount Stuart's main staircase were created by artist H. W. Lonsdale; seen here is the sixth day, when the vertebrates and Man were called into being. (Photograph Keith Hunter)

The Marble Hall is the atrium at the centre of Mount Stuart: tier upon tier of beauty. The topmost tier frames the incomparable Zodiac windows. Anderson has the ability to create an impressive open public space, an ability Burges lacked. (Photograph Keith Hunter)

Lonsdale's sketches for the Zodiac windows at Mount Stuart show how, from the beginning, it was planned that they were to be a continuous swirl around the building, with those portions which would be hidden behind the walls simply omitted – a staggeringly innovative and successful concept. The windows shown here are Libra and Scorpio, but aggressive Scorpio leans across to clutch at the Scales. (© The Bute Archive at Mount Stuart)

Here is the realisation of the sketch of the Libra window at Mount Stuart, with the coloured glass background now become a vibrant feature in its own right. Here Day and Night swing in the balance, for we are seeing the equinox.

The moon is in Scorpio. Note how the colours of the background have become more adventurous than in the sketch, introducing notes of dissonance. These two windows are in fact the least changed through sketch to cartoon, and finished window.

Lonsdale's celestial ceiling at Mount Stuart, studded with crystal stars, leads directly up from the Zodiac windows. The ghostly figures of the constellations were added after the success of the same concept, also by him, at St John's Lodge. (Photograph Flora Wood)

In the ceiling of Mount Stuart's Horoscope Room, William Frame's comment to Charles Campbell that Bute must not be left thinking they could do nothing but blue ceilings resulted in this splendid view of birds sporting through vines and pomegranates against a dull gold background, some of Campbell's finest work. (Photograph Tom Errington)

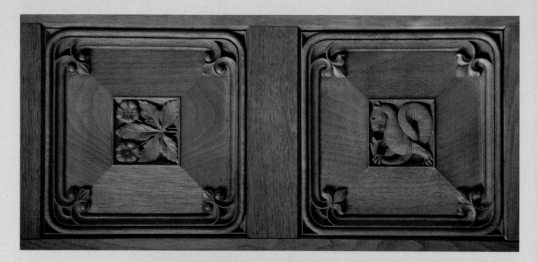

Above. Flowering buttercups and a wyvern intimidated by its own tail are just two of the fresh little carved panels in the Horoscope Room. As with so much of the Mount Stuart woodwork, they were carved in the Bute Workshops in Cardiff and shipped up to Scotland, already cut to size and ready to be fitted. (© The Bute Collection at Mount Stuart)

Right. Mount Stuart's Family Bedroom traces the descent of the Butes from St Margaret of Scotland. It is a hymn to married love; each marriage, from that of Margaret and Malcolm Canmore to that of Gwen and Bute, is celebrated in a shield.

CONCILIVO · SCHCHVIG · IN · OVO · SOLA · QVO · PAVCISSIDIS · SVORVO · CONGRE · PERVERSAE · CONSVECVDINIS · ASSERTORES · GLADIO · SPIRICVS · QVOD · EST · VERBVO · DEI · GRIDVO · DIOICABAT · PA · PII

Lonsdale's frieze of the life of St Margaret dominates the Family Bedroom, and the image of St Margaret teaching dominates the frieze. A portrait of Gwen, Margaret here represents both Bute's ancestress, St Margaret, and Holy Mother Church and Woman.

The Gothic Drawing Room is possibly the least satisfactory of all the rooms at Mount Stuart. (Photograph Keith Hunter)

Bute loved swimming and was surprised when attempts to introduce his sons to the joys of open-sea bathing in Scotland's icy waters were not wholly successful. The indoor waters of the heated Gothic swimming pool at Mount Stuart were better received. (Photograph Paul Jordan)

In Mount Stuart's Marble Hall, the capitals of the pillars are each carved with a different design of flowers, plants or seaweeds. It is intricate and delicate work. (© The Bute Collection at Mount Stuart)

The Dining Room was intended as a room of simple grandeur, but the quality of the carving in its dados and cornice is not as good as that elsewhere at Mount Stuart. (Photograph Keith Hunter)

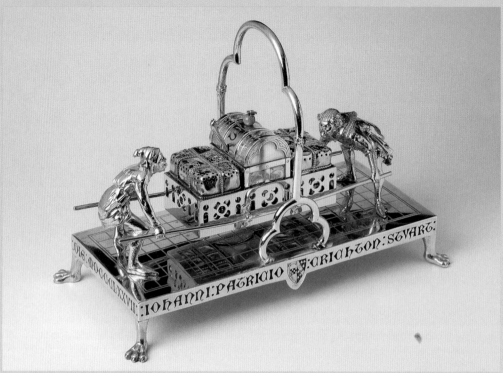

Burges supplied Gwen with answers to the question of what to give a man who can afford everything. Her birthday present to Bute was this 'pepper-pot' where two mediaeval retainers appear to strain to lift their burden for their noble master. (© Jarrold Publishing 2003)

If Nathaniel Westlake never had the inventive edge of Lonsdale, at his best he could create images of great beauty and wonderful sensuality. Here the angel of the setting sun blesses the end of Moses's long life in a set of windows to one side of Mount Stuart's entrance hall. (© The Bute Collection at Mount Stuart)

neither Fr Bérard nor Frank thank you for putting them in an awkward, ridiculous and untenable position. We have both been deceived. Father Bérard when arriving here did not expect to be made a footman to an unconverted boy.[106]

This last was a complaint about the organist, Clements, who had been moved by Bute to Oban. The same old arguments about priests taking orders from a Protestant were surfacing, as though ordination conferred an intimate knowledge of church music.

Bérard complained in very similar terms:

I think there is no possibility of remaining here. Everything is upset in the house – and everybody pretends to have the authority. I have been shamefully deceived. I wrote Lord Bute the very truth, but his Lordship sticks to his man Mr Rolfe, and does not believe any word of the two priests . . . The letter Lord Bute wrote me is simply absurd and insulting for my dignity of priest.[107]

And yet, the fear is that what Beurms saw was also true, that Bute was wrong to entrust

the care of six innocent boys and the direction of this house to a young man who does not understand the most elementary principles of Christian modesty and morality. I have given you a strong hint when you were here. I do not wish to write what I have discovered since.[108]

Tragedy now became farce. Bute had been told that Beurms drank beer rather than wine, and that he was a large man. Ever the gentleman, Bute determined to provide him with an adequate supply, and ever economical, he found out that larger quantities attracted a discount from the breweries. He bought in eighteen gallons a month, or five pints a day, every day. Ever the optimist, he trusted to Beurms's good sense to spin the supply out, at the same time admitting: 'I confess I feel a certain amount of trepidation on the beer question.'[109] Well he might! The two priests 'drank themselves drunk on beer out of decanters, chased each other round the refectory tables in a tipsy fight'.[110] The description is Rolfe's, but certainly accurate. So too was Bute's reading of the situation:

An internecine war has broken out at Oban between the Chaplain and the school-master whom I keep there to perform the Cathedral services, and I propose going there on Tuesday to sort them. I expect it will be a case of solutudinem facere, pacem appelare [to make a desert and call it peace].[111]

Bute sounds as though he was fairly sanguine about the 'Oban rows'. This was far from the truth. He was, as he put in his diary, 'absolutely possessed by beastly Oban row'.[112] He and Gwen reached Oban on the evening of 5 October, and spent the next two days in various conversations with Clements, Bérard, Beurms, the Bishop, and the Duhamels. The accounts of everybody and everything were most unsatisfactory. Bérard had ridden roughshod over Bute's wishes, and had insisted on the Litany of Loreto, and taking the boys to the parochial Mass. He had undermined all Rolfe's attempts to implement Bute's wishes. He 'refused to say Mass at 10'[113] because it was too much for him to fast till that time. Rolfe had proved a weak head of the school easily bullied by the older men, and, most seriously of all, his dealings with the boys were at best sexually suspect, something Bute would not have tolerated on any account. The upshot was that Bérard was 'to leave' and 'Rolfe gave up his place'.[114]

At the end of his time there, Rolfe had asked Bute to use his influence with the Bishop to have him ordained into Minor Orders (those below a deacon, doubtfully entitling him to the 'Rev.' he was already using) as 'it would perhaps be enough' to make him a cleric, and so set him on the path to ordination.[115] He had backed the wrong horse, for relations between Bute and the church establishment were in a downward spiral. Had he sided with the Bishop and Beurms and Bérard, his chances of ordination would have been higher.

Twenty years later, Rolfe wove the incident into his *apologia* in *Hadrian the Seventh*, where he allows his alter ego, George Rose, the pleasure of a long self-justification. The account he gives of the impossibility of the situation in Oban seems entirely fair.

the eccentric party who offered me the post, to accept what he called the Head-mastership of a Cathedral Choir School ... did not tell me that he was forcing the establishment on the bishop of the diocese, nor that the Head-mastership had been refused by several distinguished priests simply on account of the impossible conditions. I brought my experience. That I quarrelled with the chaplains is quite true. I did not quarrel effectually, though. They ... defied my authority and compelled the ragamuffins of the school to do the same.[116]

One recurrent difficulty experienced by those who employed Rolfe was getting him to leave after they had sacked him,[117] or persuaded him to resign. Bute had similar problems, but he prevailed; or maybe the trenchant Gwen managed the job. Rolfe left 'after some difficulty'.[118]

The rest of Rolfe's life was a story of quarrels and increasing financial misery. He worked as an artist, creating banners in an iconic style, and was an innovative photographer.[119] In 1887 he wrote to Bute begging for some employment,[120] and again begging for support in becoming a priest. Bute was certainly not moved to help him in this, but he did sometimes offer employment. According to Weeks, Rolfe approached Bute, requesting that Bute buy some of his paintings, through two of his friends. Bute replied that Rolfe was not a person he wished to have anything more to do with. It was only when he despaired of making a living from visual art that Rolfe turned to writing, and it was only posthumously that his books found fame.

*'I do not think I am in any way to blame, unless it were
not sufficiently searching out needs'*

Just before Bute left for Oban, his beloved Margaret, now ten years
old, had been taken ill with jaundice. She was slowly improving when
he returned. There was little Bute could do for her except to worry,
and to spend hours each day reading aloud to her (*Count Robert of
Paris*, the novel by Sir Walter Scott).[1] There is a link between psoriasis
and stress. At the end of the month, as Margaret began to get better,
Bute had once again to take action over his maddeningly irritating skin
condition: 'The application of the chrysophanic acid began again'.[2]
Two days later he recorded that his eyes were rather sore, and a week
later when he made the crossing to Bute, he had to be blindfolded.
He was returning to his still only half-finished home after an absence
of eighteen months: 'House very cold, a bare resounding desert'.[3] The
Butes once again set about a jolly Christmas season, which stretched
into the Scottish New Year celebrations, with the first ever Mass in
the refurbished chapel by the shore to celebrate Ne'er Day (New Year's
Day).

The little church had been Presbyterian. It was in the family
gallery here that Bute had listened to the sermon commemorating his
mother's life. Now it was a Catholic church, and, for one of Bute's
chapels, the interior and decorations were very simple. It was beloved
by him for its wild and romantic setting. In stormy weather, spindrift
washes its walls. With a lively and growing family, Christmas was
not all weighty matters of faith. Gwen's memories of happy amateur
theatricals and her love of theatre saw her flowering as producer of
a family pantomime: 'My Lady very busy with "Sleeping Beauty"',
Bute recorded on 11 January 1887. Five days later the production was
staged: 'to the Sleeping Beauty at 5.30. Mgt. very well as the princess,

John as Polly the Cook'. The children of his cousin, friend, and factor, Jack Stuart, also acted in it. As usual, family celebrations only ended in mid-January.

Christmas was barely over, when Fr Oswald (ordained priest since his visit to Dumfries House the spring before) came to work in the library of the new house. Things began well, with Fr Oswald saying Mass in the 'very pretty little' Burges chapel. Later, they went to the chapel on the shore where 'Lady Bute played the harmonium: the music was plain chant, but painfully diluted.'[4] On the next day Bute recorded cheerfully enough that Fr Oswald was 'working at history all day, in the afternoon in the Blue Library, first time so used'.[5] Then the two men had a serious difference of opinion over *The Scottish Review*. Bute had just agreed to take over ownership of the failing periodical. He told Grant that he would have liked to run a Catholic periodical, but knew that such a periodical would need to be 'entirely printed by the proprietors, for gratuitous distribution. But I do not like the only Scotch quarterly to expire, so I shall I think struggle on for a year or two yet.'[6]

He continued with the publication for the rest of his life. In a sense the *Scottish* was a strange periodical for Bute to support. Its editor was a Church of Scotland minister who became one of Bute's closest friends. Its tone was always described as liberal, and its aim was to appeal to a general Scottish audience, so its religious articles were for a Protestant readership. Bute ran it 'at a heavy loss',[7] and never lost an opportunity to promote its circulation. Hunter Blair takes up the story.

> During my visit ... Lord Bute had expressed his surprise that we [the Benedictine community at Fort Augustus] did not subscribe to the 'Scottish Review' [Hunter Blair was the librarian for this monastery] ... I told him that I did not like the tone of much that appeared in its pages, and afterwards wrote to him in detail on the subject, particularising various articles and reviews to which I objected, and designating the literary criticisms of the Review, generally, as consisting frequently of 'anti-Catholic twaddle'.[8]

Hunter Blair was 'disappointed' that, as proprietor of the *Scottish*, Bute could not 'do more for it than contribute an occasional article'.[9] The 'anti-Catholic twaddle' he lambasted consisted in reviews approving of books, which, *inter alia*, suggested that the 'publications of the Religious Tract Society are "pervaded by a devout and Catholic(!) spirit."' and that 'a set of "Sermons on Liberalism in Religion" are "just the thing to confirm the wavering and to strengthen the believer"'.[10]

Hunter Blair had taken just that superior tone which Bute most detested in the clergy, and a 'tit-for-tat' correspondence followed. Bute defended the breadth of views expressed in the *Scottish* in general, and said that as Hunter Blair had not read the sermons he was not in much of a position to criticise them.[11] Hunter Blair remarked cattily that:

> I adhere to my opinion that the passages . . . are false and misleading in themselves and calculated to do harm to religion, were it known that the review in which they appear is owned (and presumably controlled) by a prominent Catholic. I hope my plain speaking will not offend you.[12]

As Hunter Blair comments in his diary, Bute was quite plainly offended. Hunter Blair was just as hurt, and chronicled the whole row minutely in his journal, complete with copy letters. He also recorded he was: 'comfortable here, but they, one's host and hostess are shy, and do little to make one at home or put one at one's ease'.[13] (He later added that as the children grew up, the Butes became 'less unlike other people'.) This is the exact opposite of what so many of Bute's other friends said. All remarked on his graciousness as a host and how he set others at their ease. It seems that when Hunter Blair expressed his views on the *Scottish* he caused such offence that Bute withdrew into himself to avoid expressing his anger to his guest. The hurt and anger from this row lingered on for years and coloured Hunter Blair's judgements of Bute when he came to write Bute's biography. It is the only serious breach between Bute and any one of his friends to leave any trace in the record, so greatly did Bute value harmony in his relationships, and Bute took it the more seriously because it was so rare.

Holy week of 1887 was shadowed further by the message that Flora Norfolk had received the last sacraments. She was dying of the Bright's disease which had overshadowed most of her life, and fatally damaged her son. On Easter Monday the Butes

> received telegram announcing that Flora Norfolk died quite peacefully at 4.30 this afternoon. It was on an Easter Monday, after passing Holy Week here, that she originally announced her intention of becoming a Catholic.[14]

The next Saturday a telegram came from Gwen's brother Frank (now Lord Howard) in Paris, announcing the sudden illness of his wife, Clare. She was young, and strong, and given Frank's mental capacities, nobody took the warning seriously. The next day she was dead. The

Butes went straight from Flora's funeral to try and comfort Frank. Bute told his friend and editor, Metcalfe:

> It is almost heartbreaking here – the grief of my brother-in-law is so great that had not God mercifully accorded him the grace of submission to His will, it would amount to despair – and the appalling gravity of the loss to everyone who was closely connected to her seems to come out more keenly every hour. And will do so still more when the numbness produced by the blow and the additional occupation of the funeral have passed away.[15]

They stayed with Frank a week, and then returned to Bute and their own family. Bute as usual continued walking with his wife, and his sons and his visitors. Margaret was forbidden to do much walking, as it was feared her back would grow crooked, and Bute no longer rode, so could not join in her usual form of exercise. But he continued to read to her, sharing with her books which had been important to him:

> Began James Grant's *Memorials of Edinburgh Castle* with Mgt. Well remember reading it (same copy, now bound) as a child, & its first raising in me a strong Nationalist feeling.[16]

His own nationalist feelings continued as strongly as ever. He had become a member of the Scottish Home Rule Association, which was founded in 1886, and he chose to associate himself with the icons of Scotland's independent past.

On 25 June 1887 – 'a very hot, fine summer's day',[17] as he recorded in his diary, John Patrick Crichton-Stuart, 3rd Marquess of Bute was met by cheering crowds and a civic deputation at Stirling railway station. After lunch the deputation, with Bute at its head, left in a procession to the National Wallace Monument which had been looking down on the town from its perch on the Abbey Craig for almost 20 years. Once at the monument the Marquess performed the task for which he had come: the unveiling of a bronze statue to the great Scottish hero Sir William Wallace. In his accompanying speech Bute talked of Wallace's legacy to Scotland and how he was still of relevance to the Scotland of the late 19th century:
'His glory is that he was a noble example of obedience to [Scotland's] laws; and we who have a past, have a present, and must look to have a future. If it is to be a healthy development, the development must be a natural, that is a national one. The act of

homage which is here performed towards his memory this day is but one incidental acknowledgement, not only of his unselfishness, of his greatness, and of his goodness, but of the living and abiding truth of the principles by which he was actuated. And may it be so that all Scotland may be ever worthy of him who gave for her his toil, his sufferings, and his life.'[18]

The 'cult' of William Wallace had grown in Scotland during the nineteenth century and the choice of Lord Bute for the unveiling ceremony had been quite deliberate.[19]

Bute began this new year with a major new acquisition behind him. At the end of 1886 he finalised his purchase of the Isle of Cumbrae. Cumbrae is a very much smaller island than Bute, about four miles long and one-and-a-half miles broad, lying a mile off the Ayrshire coast, most of which[20] had belonged to the Boyles, the Earls of Glasgow, distant relations of Bute's. Bute's childhood mentor, Nora Boyle, had been one of the family. George Frederic, 6th Earl, succeeded his half-brother on 11 March 1869. Despite the 5th Earl's excesses, he had left a considerable estate. The 6th Earl was a committed Scottish Episcopalian. He had founded a seminary, with a tiny cathedral designed by the great Gothic architect William Butterfield, on the Isle of Cumbrae, built a cathedral in Perth and spent all the family money. In 1886 he broke the entail on his lands.

Bute had been concerned about the plight of the family for some time, worrying over rumours that they were living in wretched circumstances in lodgings on the south coast of England, and that they might lose possession of their estate, Kelburn.[21] The notebook diary kept by Mr Pitman, which reveals so much in so few words, shows that in March 1886, Bute's agents decided beforehand that it would be appropriate for Bute to help both the Glasgows and himself by buying land from them.

Discussed also with Mr Shaw [Bute's Ayrshire factor] certain questions affecting Lord Bute in regard to certain portions of Lord Glasgow's property which might be probably for sale and arranged as to a communication which he was to make to Lord Bute on the subject.

Meeting with Lord Bute in the afternoon when he stated he has seen Mr Shaw but had no special wish to acquire the lands which had been referred to but would be glad to consider further the matter after hearing what course was resolved to be followed by Lord Glasgow's Creditors. Lord Bute stated that he understood that there was some difficulty in the Glasgow family retaining Kelburn and it had occurred to him that he might help in this by guaranteeing a loan. Explained to his Lordship that I did not think that this proposal would effect the object which he had in view.[22]

In June, Bute agreed to buy Cumbrae, and his advisors breathed a sigh of relief and acted as soon as they could: 'Meeting with Mr Shaw again today when he reported interview which he had had with Lord Bute and stated that his Lordship was anxious to purchase the Property of Cumbrae and was willing to act on our advice as to the price.'[23] By November, Cumbrae belonged to Bute.

Bute had bought the island more in order to help his fellow aristocrats out of trouble than for the pleasure and personal advantage of owning more land, but it was not an act of true charity. Bute, however, was constantly involved in charities, and was faced with the sheer scale of need, not least the innumerable small gifts and donations made to the 'beggars' who wrote to him pleading various degrees of destitution.

Victorian society had few financial safety nets. 'Only the most fortunate and best established professional men' could take out effective insurance to protect themselves or their dependants from becoming unable to work or dying.[24] One advantage of 'service' was that those who had been faithful servants could expect that if they got into real difficulties later, their previous employer would make some provision for them. The annuities of which Sophia had grumbled during Bute's minority were in this category. In addition, any former Bute family servant who wrote to Bute in distress, making a reasonable case for having fallen on hard times, could expect Bute to meet their request for money. Many others had neither private means, nor a history of service. The poor lived on the edge of an abyss, at the bottom of which lay the workhouse with its prison-like conditions. Almost any single month of any daily newspaper covering an urban centre in the mid-1800s will reveal one case of death from starvation, coupled with the failure of the person or persons concerned to seek the help of the workhouse.

Men trained to a trade were in a better situation, though slumps could easily rob them of their means of making a living. Should they become ill, or die, their wives and daughters were in a terrible position, for there were few posts for which they could even apply. Even the middle and upper classes could find themselves penniless due to sickness, or offering loans to friends, or standing surety for defaulters, or just plain mismanagement of their affairs.

Usually, the sums such people applied for were not large – five or ten pounds. They rose from an inexhaustible well of misery. Even in the twentieth and twenty-first century attempts to dry this well have partially failed. Like many in his position, Bute endeavoured to give only to the deserving poor, an attitude richly caricatured by his younger contemporary, George Bernard Shaw, in his *Pygmalion*, where he puts the complaints into the mouth of the dustman Doolittle:[25]

> I'm one of the undeserving poor: thats what I am. Think of what that means to a man. It means that hes up agen middle class morality all the time. If theres anything going, and I put in for a bit of it, it's always the same story: 'Youre undeserving; so you cant have it.' But my need is as great as the most deserving widow's that ever got money out of six different charities in one week for the death of the same husband. I dont need less than a deserving man: I need more. I dont eat less hearty than him; and I drink a lot more.[26]

Bute did not want to be exploited, or to give to those who made a comfortable living from begging letters, or appeared to do so, when enquiry was made by a reputable agency. The position was impossible.

Over the years Bute learned to harden his heart. It was fatally easy for him to do this on the wrong occasion and provoke a tragedy. In February 1885 he had yet another begging letter from George Thompson, an educated man in his late fifties, who had applied to him before.[27] Exasperated but well-intentioned, Bute decided that a new start was the only way forward for Mr and Mrs Thompson, and said that the only help he would offer was a passage to America. The Thompsons arrived in America, and advertised for 'a handy man with a few hundreds' to accompany them to Los Angeles. The Wotherspoons, a married couple, responded, and both couples travelled together to the grape-growing area of Lancaster, where they staked their claims. Then their troubles began in earnest. The Wotherspoons had a little capital, the 'few hundred' dollars to enable them to subsist until they began to get returns from their claim, and to sink a well to irrigate the vines. The Thompsons were virtually penniless. They told Wotherspoons that they had means,[28] and borrowed twice from them. In October 1885, Thompson wrote to Bute, promising that a little capital to enable him to cultivate his vineyard would 'result in happiness'. Thompson tried to throw all the blame for his situation on Bute: 'I spoke against the scheme might and main, prior to our departure from Europe – in vain'.[29] Bute was tired of Thompson even before the emigration, and he reacted badly.

Bute could have given the £250 Thompson pleaded for without noticing it, but Thompson did not spend what he had wisely. He had his letters to Bute printed out. He wrote not only to Bute, but to his factor, and cousin, John Windsor Stuart, who remarked acidly to the other man with Bute's ear, his secretary Frank Anderson: 'I have received continual letters from Thompson, if he is starving how does he manage to find stamps for the letters?'[30] There were over thirty begging letters in all.

> On Christmas Day what Joy there must have been in your Lordship's ancestral halls. On that blessed day I read accounts [of the new Mount Stuart] and had no dinner of any description. I wrote to your Lordship on Christmas Eve to state that all we had was a little milk & water and a small quantity of bread, and, our flour was nearly exhausted.[31]

Moral blackmail and pleading both failed. He borrowed again from the Wotherspoons, who lent him enough to buy essentials, fearing that he would starve.

On Saturday, 5 February 1887, Thompson set off to walk to the post office at Lancaster. It was an eighteen-mile round journey, which he had made sometimes three times a week. His wife expected him back that night. He did not return that day, or on Sunday. On Monday, 'in a terrible state' she went to beg help, yet again, from the Wotherspoons. Mr Wotherspoon set out at once. Slightly further from the breadline than the Thompsons, he was able to afford a 'team' of horses. He found that Thompson had left Lancaster on Saturday. They finally tracked him through the bush to within a mile and a half of his own home. He was still alive, but not conscious. In the bitter cold and the rain he had succumbed to exhaustion and exposure. He was taken home by the Wotherspoons, and lived for an hour and a quarter, while they tried desperately to revive him. He 'seemed to be conscious just before he expired, but he was frozen, with no power to make a motion'. He left his poor wife nothing but the burden of their debts. Jeanie Wotherspoon pleaded on her behalf:

> My Lord, poor Mrs Thompson has not a cent in the world. The valley people are like ourselves, come here with a little means struggling to make a home in a new place and not having any returns yet, really have it not for their own wants . . . I am sure if your Lordship were to see the misery and distress of Mrs Thompson, your Lordship could not stand it.[32]

It was not only the Thompsons who had been ruined. With no capital left, the kind-hearted Wotherspoons were in a bad situation. Jeanie was forced to write to Bute, ending desperately: 'My Lord, I do beseech you, 'tho I know you have many claims on your goodness if you do not see your way to help here, if your Lordship would be so good as lend us £100 for three years to fund our well and go on, my Lord, it is not only the £124 Mr Thompson owes us but the want of it to go on that will cause us to lose our all.' Mrs Thompson was found a job as a housekeeper in Los Angeles by a philanthropic society.[33] The only positive note in all this misery is that when Bute's advisors finally ascertained that 'Mr Thompson really is dead and ... Mrs Wotherspoon has suffered considerably through him', they were ready to advise that he send 'some little sum'[34] to her.

After this, more and more 'reports' on beggars appear in his correspondence, compiled by the various societies, especially St Vincent de Paul, which specialised in advising donors on who were, and who were not, the deserving poor. The most pathetic of appeals came from those who knew Bute personally, and who were acutely aware of the disruption in their relationship with him that a begging letter could cause: moving Bute from the role of equal to that of patron. Of all these, the most touching was by his old friend James McSwiney. The family were educated but poor. James's sister Miss McSwiney had had a position as a governess (one of the few jobs open to a well-bred, educated woman) until her health broke and she retreated to a convent. The low returns from the family farm left her destitute. McSwiney said bitterly that he had put off writing as long as he could, because he felt his relationship with Bute gave the strongest reason for his never troubling him for money. If Bute decided not to help Miss McSwiney, he begged him to behave as if the letter had never arrived.[35]

Bute's response was swift and generous. McSwiney called it 'munificent' adding:

> Heaven only knows what it cost me to make it. It had been easier, so it seems to me, to have knocked at any other door but yours. To say I thank you from the bottom of my heart is so easy and commonplace that I hardly like to pen the words.[36]

Bute knew how to value his friends. He never allowed this gift to make a hint of a change in his friendship with McSwiney. Yet, because of his wealth, and also his other abilities, Bute's friendships were at constant risk of being overwhelmed by their inequalities. Some managed the balancing trick of working for him without ever becoming indebted to him, or behaving as less than an equal. His pugnacious friend Sneyd was his secretary for a time, and married his kinsman and factor's daughter. Bute gave Sneyd an incomparable dessert service by Burges as a wedding present[37] and Sneyd remained his confidant, one of the very few men with whom Bute totally dropped his guard. Bute recorded the death of Sneyd when it occurred early in 1894, linking him at once with Addle, though with no conscious foreknowledge that Addle too would die in July of that year:

> Heard of the death of George Edward Sneyd. It is difficult to say what this is to me. He had been an intimate friend since we were in Westcott's big house at Harrow – one of the very few at all, the most intimate (unless Addle Hay-Gordon), & the most trusted I have ever had . . . For these I had prayed by name so regularly at every Mass I have heard for many, many years that I did so almost automatically, unless absolutely distracted.[38]

Bute had remained intimate with Sneyd, but his relationship with Addle had faded, perhaps because of the large-scale help Bute had given to his friend. Addle had been involved in the failure of a business, and this always gave rise to greater problems over the rescue of friends from their difficulties. If Bute poured in his own money, he took the risk of encouraging bad business practice, which would in turn draw ever more of his money into propping up doomed projects. What Bute usually did in the case of failing businesses and debt-encumbered estates was to insist that an experienced businessman of his own choosing run the business, with the debtor only drawing a small regular sum from it until it was running smoothly. Bute might write off some debt, but he never made loans.

In 1882, Addle had written to Bute confessing that the firm in which he, his brother and his mother had invested money, and which had been their work, was 'in difficulties' but 'now contracting to show a profit on next year'.[39] He asked Bute to offer the bank a guarantee of £8,000. He added, pathetically, 'It has been very difficult for me, to ask you to do this.' Bute did what he always did in such circumstances, and refusing to give the £8,000 directly, asked Addle to 'let me have the address of your solicitors and ask them to make a clean breast of it to Mr Pitman in regards of your affairs'.[40] After the debts had been paid, a trust was set up for Adam Hay Gordon, securing his capital and realising him an income,[41] but this seems to have made true friendship with Addle impossible. For whatever reason, when Addle died in the same year as Sneyd, Bute recorded sadly:

Heard of the death on Thursday of one of my dearest friends, Addle Hay Gordon. Though at Harrow together, & very intimate at College, we had not met for many years. In our Oxford time, I several times stayed in Edinburgh with him & his parents (Rutland Square – 18 I think) during vacation. We were as brothers.[42]

The Maxwell Scotts, old friends and descendants of Sir Walter Scott, also ran into debt. Mrs Maxwell Scott, a very learned lady, was definitely one of the ladies Bute described as his 'nosegay of female friends'.[43] It looked at first as if the couple were going to accept his offer, and Pitman reported that

[Mr Maxwell Scott] seems grateful for your kindness and although at first rather taken aback at the idea of giving up the management of his affairs, I think I pretty nearly convinced him that it was the right thing to do and that it was the only possible way of his eventually being relieved of debt.[44]

However, the indignity of not only being unable to manage his affairs, but being assigned a fixed sum on which to live, and being obliged to accept the man of affairs nominated by Bute told against the scheme, and he refused help upon the terms offered. Nine years later, he again approached Bute:

Wrote to J Maxwell Scott abt. imminent bankruptcy – years ago he applied to me, & I consented to depart from my rule against lending money, under scheme of Auldjo Jamieson, who undertook to give the MSs £1,000 a year, and free the estate in 16 years, involving Mrs MS hardly at all, but JMS objected to his terms as too rigorous & preferred to decline them.

The smooth path of friendship was once again disrupted.

Not all Bute's friends found it so difficult to let themselves be helped. Woodward became a partner in a firm of timber merchants, who in 1882, ran into difficulties. He contacted Bute, who ordered his employees to extricate him. The firm was liquidated without his being formally declared bankrupt, since Bute himself provided the funds to repay the private creditors.[45] It was a gift not a loan, so Bute was not breaking his self-imposed rule.

Everybody involved in the troublesome business, everyone that is except Woodward, hoped that he would find himself some paid employment, but he did not, being more than content to be one of

Bute's less-well-paid supernumeraries. Bute paid Woodward £200 a year as a retainer, to act as a travelling companion when needed.[46] It was a small sum for a gentleman to live upon, but the duties were occasional, light and pleasant. Woodward offered assurances

> that he would be extremely grateful if this could be done and that there would be every desire on his part to meet Lord Bute's wishes and make himself useful in any way that may be suggested.[47]

By the New Year of 1886, Pitman was patiently explaining to Woodward that he needed to go and visit Bute at Chiswick, and that if he did so, then His Lordship might invite him to Dumfries House.[48] Now, in 1887, and with an engaging honesty which perhaps suggests why Bute tolerated his friend's gentle and systematic exploitation, Woodward reported that he had solved his financial problems by the most traditional of all routes open to impoverished and presentable gentlefolk: he was to marry money.

> I know you will be glad to hear that I am engaged to be married. I congratulate myself firstly, naturally I suppose, & secondly you, for getting rid of me, for I fear, my dear Bute, I have been a very bad bargain for you. I must take this opportunity of thanking you most sincerely for all you have done for me, & your great kindness & generosity for close to 20 years. I also express my deep gratitude to Lady Bute & yourself for your excessive thoughtfulness & consideration in every possible way whilst I have been staying with you; in no house, not even my mother's, have I been more considered, & never for one single moment have I felt that I was in anyway, in a dependent position. This could not have been so, unless Lady Bute & yourself had shown me the great kindness and consideration that you have, & I want to say how truly grateful I [am] to you both. I am engaged to a Miss Whitley,[49] an orphan and only child of a partner in a large brewery in Lancashire. She is very well off. Of course I think she is charming & I hope you will soon see her & think so too. She is not a Catholic & all I can say about her Religious views is, that she was baptized in the Church of England. She has a great leaning towards Catholicism, although knowing nothing of it, & I don't think it will take me long to have her instructed. We are to be married very shortly & very quietly, as she is in mourning for her Uncles.[50]

Bute's private charities involved relatively small sums. His public ones involved large sums and no less acrimony. Since there was, and is, no moral consensus on what percentage of their income a person should give, and how, and where, he was frequently criticised, and he was defensively resentful of such criticism. Most of such criticism was articulated in Cardiff, and this more than anything else soured his relationship with the town. Being the intensely private person he was, he did not often write of such things, but just once he poured out his heart on the subject to one of those he trusted most, 'dear and Rev'd Professor' Westcott, his former headmaster. He said his intentions towards the city could not have been better, although the road to Hell was notoriously paved with such intentions. He was 'by nature very timid & shy, with a nervous and melancholy temperament, very much alive to kindness & the reverse'. He felt he had been persecuted in the town for no reason, and that convinced him that 'it is better for everyone that I should keep out of the place, and have as little to do with it personally as possible'. Then he listed some of his charities to the town:

> I will tell you plainly that I do not feel myself in any way to blame with regard to Cardiff, unless it be that I do not take sufficient means to discover its needs which do not come before me — e.g. my wife suggested the other day, & I applauded it, & shall very likely do it, but had not thought of it before, to establish a lying-in hospital there ... I do not think the town has ever had anything like such a benefactor as myself. There are very few schools or charities in it, I think, of which I am not the chief subscriber; I may say that two-thirds of the penitent women owe it to me, if not more; the Infirmary, as it is, owes its xistance to me; I offered £10,000 to obtain for the town the benefits of the future South Wales University. I don't like saying these things – though I could say more of them if I did.[51]

Bute knew himself very well, and this letter is a most revealing summary of aspects of his character. It leaves out the light-hearted, impulsive, side of it, for the summary was written whilst Bute was at a low point, just after the fire in the Sicilian hotel, when he had briefly relapsed into depression. Nevertheless, it sums up perfectly his strengths and weaknesses when faced with the need for expending his wealth for the benefit of others.

He was indeed alive to kindness. His lifelong devotion to Jack Wilson, which made that man into a sort of celebrity, courted by all on their visits to Bute, was typical of him. Bute's friends all comment upon his utter lack of condescension. If he was aware of their kindness to him, he went out of his way to ensure they knew he was in their debt. McSwiney encapsulated it thus after a visit to Dumfries House: 'you so deliberately inverted our respective roles by thanking me!! for my! visit'.[52] When the great scholar Westcott appealed for the help on ancient holy images that Bute's wide travel and reading made him easily able to offer, he not only replied in detail, but added that he was 'very much gratified at your having thought it worth while to hear what I think'.[53]

Once he was aware of a need or a problem from his own experience, or because it was forcibly brought to his attention by others, he would campaign with money and energy to change the situation. Aware from his own family of the talents of women, and from the begging letters of their desperate plight when destitute, he actively sought to employ women in work for him, ranging from artistic work to gardening. His great weakness was that he simply could not think creatively about the difficulties of others, or step outside his own experience. His excessive sensibility to slight and unkindness was a fatal weakness which made him lump all complaints together as unjust.

Complaints in Cardiff were of two kinds. One was the usual small-town wrangling over precedence, and it was inevitable and unimportant that some were offended by not gaining as high a place in the social world as they felt they deserved. On one occasion, a local Cardiff paper devoted more space to the question of who had not been invited to a ball being given by the Marchioness of Bute, than to a serious strike in the docks, which inevitably involved her husband the Marquess, who was also Mayor at the time.[54] It is the other complaints which give one pause. The Bute family had grown rich from the town of Cardiff and their south Wales land; yet Bute never seemed to be aware of how much of his wealth he owed to the struggling poor, and to those who worked in the mines.

The ethics of economics are complicated. Miners went into the pits to escape grinding rural poverty. Just over the Black Mountains, and past Hay-on-Wye, Bute's contemporary, the Rev. Francis Kilvert, handed out blankets to families who had none,[55] and visited cottages where the bitter winter's cold was unrelieved by any fire.[56] The dangers of accident and dust down the mines have to be balanced by the comparatively comfortable lives lived in the miners' cottages. Over a hundred years later, miners would strike for the privilege of continuing to die from silicosis brought on by their work. Bute himself was not a major mine-owner. His money came in the main part from leases of mines, and of property in Cardiff, and from the penny a ton duty on the coal which was paid by those who leased his mines. He was not the only man to become rich on the backs of the miners, and the industry that they in their turn created. In this period, most simply accepted the reality that wealth was unequally distributed, which makes it singularly unfair to blame Bute in chief for failing to recognise the injustice of his great wealth.

Thus, his friend and colleague, Wyndham Lewis, who had also become wealthy from the industrialisation of Cardiff, was widely respected in the coal industry. The renowned miners' representative Mabon[57] wrote to Bute imploring him to help 'getting our Welsh coal trade recognised by giving its Chairman Sir William Lewis a Baronetcy' and speaking of Lewis as preventing 'the owners driving matters to extremities and breaking down the sliding scale arrangement which has been such enormous benefit to South Wales'.[58] Lord Bute met Mabon in 1894, and liked him 'much'.[59] Bute was not hostile to the miners' representatives. In Cardiff, a substantial middle class also grew up, occupying the town houses in the broad streets laid out by the Bute estate. The wealth coal produced was distributed very widely, although very unequally. Yet at no point did Bute indicate the slightest awareness that it was south Wales that generated his tremendous riches, and that he owed it a debt of gratitude. If he cannot be uniquely blamed, nor can he be wholly excused by the fact that he was surrounded by those equally blind.

Bute fell foul of popular opinion in Cardiff somewhat later, though it did not contribute to the dislike of the town he catalogues in his earlier letter to Westcott. As a child, he had been made 'president' of the 'Cardiff Savings Bank', and he had continued as its nominal head as an adult. It was, like numerous other small Victorian banks, born from a desire to encourage the poor to save against 'a rainy day'. As was usual, it had sought the great and good as its patrons and the Bishop of Bangor and Dean of Llandaff were trustees, and thirty-two of the 'leading gentlemen of Glamorganshire'[60] were managers.

Unfortunately, clergy and Marquesses are not necessarily good at figures, or wise supervisors: they accepted the sums presented by their actuary without question. He defrauded the bank to the tune of £40,000–£50,000. The bank closed in 1886, and it was estimated that savers would get 17/6 in the pound (that is, approximately 87.5 pence in the pound). *The Western Mail* reported that:

Public feeling runs bitterly against managers of the concern, under whose terribly misplaced confidence and easy way of doing things the late actuary was enabled to continue his swindling. Whether or not they are legally liable for the acts of their servant is a point which has not yet been decided ... In the first place it was a mistake to allow the actuary ... to live on bank premises ... the second mistake was to pay this man, placed ... in charge of the books and a turn-over of sixty thousand a year, a miserable stipend of two hundred and fifty pounds per annum, or considerably less than five pounds a week.[61]

Bute recorded defiantly in his diary: 'With regard to [the failure of the Cardiff Bank], my conscience reproaches me with nothing, nor do I regret anything which I ever did.'[62] In a sense, and although he was the President, it would not have been fair to ask Bute to carry the whole cost himself. He was not the only businessman, nor yet the only wealthy man who was responsible for the bank, and it did not fail because of any fraud on his part. Even for him, £50,000 would have been a colossal sum of money. Yet he could have found that sum, and not have been impoverished. Those who lost their money were not in that happy position.

The other trustees and managers had civil actions taken against them, and some agreed to pay a proportion of the loss while some fought. The action against Bute found him not liable. He paid his own costs. It was not about money, but guilt or innocence. Finally in 1893, Bute decided to give £2,700 to be applied to the friendly societies, the poorest of the bank's customers, people clubbing together to save for such objectives as their own funerals. *The Western Mail* pointed out, much money had been wasted in court to prove he did not actually owe a penny, and he had lost the chance to appear generous by making a large donation at the start.[63] He was sent a more favourable reaction in the form of a cartoon, showing him as a benign doctor, voluntarily dosing a poor saver of the bank with the donation.[64] Bute finally added another £500 so that clubs and friendly societies could have all their claims met. It finally swung the opinion of the *Mail* behind him.[65] In the end, all the regular investors had their claims met in full. It had taken nine years to get to this point, and as the *Mail* commented, it was an object lesson in how not to react to a banking failure.[66]

One can say in defence of Bute, that, like W. T. Lewis, he did at all times try to moderate the inflammatory actions and words of other rich men. At the time of the strike referred to above, he only attended a dinner attended by those in favour of breaking the strike after extracting a promise that the occasion would not be used to inflame the situation. He left early to avoid any conflict between his position as Mayor and the political posturing to follow, and when he heard the main speech had been provocative, he was understandably furious.[67]

This was not just prompted by his regard for the impartiality demanded of a Mayor. It was a genuine and deep-seated desire for peace.

Bute gave to many charities with an open hand, especially educational ones. He became aware, perhaps from simply buying a paper from a ragged urchin at a street corner, of the numerous Glasgow children selling newspapers. As usual he got his secretary, Francis Anderson, to make enquiries on his behalf, in this case from the Provost of the Cathedral, Fr Alexander Munro,[68] who did so much work for the poor of Glasgow. At first, Munro thought there was no especial cause for concern about the newspaper sellers in particular, but Bute funded much of the school soup kitchen, and Munro investigated the case. All the priests struggling to provide for the Catholic poor in Glasgow needed any assistance they could get. As Aspinwall comments: 'Their poverty was horrendous. In 1861, 28,269 families lived in a single room in Glasgow. Twenty years later conditions were even worse, with almost 40,000 living in one room and over 44,600 in two rooms'.[69]

Munro provided a very vivid picture of the lives of these children:

The total number of news boys and girls in town [Glasgow] does not reach 200 . . . Two thirds of all are boys. One lot are over 14 years of age & are on the streets all day selling papers, cleaning boots, selling matches or running a message . . . Less than half are Catholics. They don't go home till night. In the middle of the day they generally go in pairs in threes and fours to an eating house where they get tea & bread & butter for 1½d or a bowl of soup for 1d.

The other class is that of children under 14. These are mostly at school. They go on their beats at 4 o'clock & must be home by 7. The parents are prosecuted if any of these young ones are found selling articles on the streets after that hour. In the central district most of these were daily attenders at the feeding school which I opened for the last three years.[70]

Munro was doubtful if a central shelter would attract the Catholic children, but certain that many of them would avoid the Red Cross shelter, where they must agree to learn Protestant religious views. Much as he wanted help, Munro concluded in exasperation to Anderson: 'The miseries of the news children are just those of our poor school children – neither more nor less.'[71] In response to this Bute urged that Munro might make further application to him for funds, and Munro replied: 'The generosity of the Marquess to me last year was so great that I cannot venture, even at his own request, to ask him so soon for a second donation.'[72]

Bute, dogged once his sympathy had been roused, disagreed, and provided money for the project. By March of the following year, Munro was able to report. He had by now revised his view that the news vendors were no more unfortunate than the schoolchildren. About seventy children were attending his shelter, and he had made no effort to exclude Protestants. The fact was, however, that

> fully four fifths are Catholics! They are a hungry lot & get through any quantity of soup & solids. Some are a sad sight in clothes & person. But on the whole they are not so destitute looking as one would have expected, seeing an occasional specimen of obtrusive nakedness at a street corner. They behave well & of course promise better.[73]

Their takings from paper selling were meagre, at best a shilling a day. Munro found 'more than a half knew their catechism & prayers while some were 'woefully behind',[74] and some of the oldest promised to come to be prepared for Easter confession and communion. With such large numbers, and with the dual aim of physical and spiritual welfare, it would be, as Munro ruefully remarked, 'a big field' for development.

During this year, 1887, one of Bute's main charitable preoccupations continued to be the choir school at Oban. Upon the departure of Rolfe, Bute, determined there should be no further misunderstandings of any kind, drew up a list or rules for those involved with his school:

> The happiness and health of the boys is before all other considerations. Next to this come the church services and their secular education. They will have whole holidays upon Sundays and Days of Obligation and Devotion. It must be seen that they get plenty of exercise, learn to swim, &c. They will have a good long walk in the country with freedom to play, at least twice or three times a week. No one will have the right to inflict corporal punishment upon them. If any of them be in the opinion of both the chaplain and Mr Clements incorrigibly bad, he must be sent home. Great prudence must be used not to overburden them with lessons. Among lessons must be reckoned religious instruction, and in regard to this must be considered that the Church Office contains in itself almost a complete course of Scripture.[75]

Bute was without a priest for the school: he himself had let Bérard go, and before Christmas, the Bishop had had enough of Beurms. Bute reached a degree of desperation over the provision of a choir priest. He sent P. A. Wright,[76] despite knowing he was mentally ill, and liable to accuse others of crimes.[77] Wright and Clements each spent their time attempting to get the other dismissed.

All that summer, Clements bombarded Bute with accounts of the boys, and their (lack of) ability. The other problem was to find a suitable cantor. Mr Kelly demanded payment over the odds, then, with the help of M. Duhamel, thrashed the boys,[78] something Bute had expressly forbidden. It took until October for Clements to finally be satisfied. He could at last report:

> Mr Crowley makes a great difference, and what is more is taking no small interest in his work.
>   I am more pleased to tell your Lordship this, for I have felt telling, that the others we have are practically useless.[79]

Bute decided that the way out of his worst problems at Oban was to place it all in the hands of women, and three sisters of 'the Servants of the Sacred Heart ... came and took charge of the boys'.[80] This finally solved the question of the physical and educational welfare of the boys, but did nothing to ease the constant struggle to find boys with the right musical ability.

Not all of the demands upon Bute were for money. Occasionally, appeals that came to him touched his own life and attitudes deeply. One which brought home to him his own privileged position came early in 1886, and showed him all too bleakly how vulnerable the poor could be in areas where he took freedom for granted. In the Victorian era, telling fortunes for money was a crime. All sensible people knew that it was mere superstition, and that the planets moving above them had no power to predict the future, and anybody telling fortunes was a rogue and a charlatan. A future when newspapers carried columns of such predictions was beyond imagination.

Bute, as so frequently, was less Victorian and more modern, or, if one prefers, more mediaeval. When his first son, John, was born, a Cardiff man, William Jordan, had sent him a chart for the birth: a setting-out of the positions of the stars and planets and an account of what these foreboded for the life of young Dumfries. However, he had the timing of the birth slightly wrong, and Bute wrote back to give the accurate time:

> On this he immediately sent me a new Natus. As I saw that the pages of trigonometry &c must have cost him a great deal of time,

I insisted on giving him a present. He accepted it at last, but with great reluctance.

Later on, I wished to have an ornamental ceiling designed for a room at Mount Stuart of this kind. I am not sufficiently scientific myself to be able to do it. I knew one other person who is a great believer in astronomy [i.e. Condor] but I could not ask him, as he is an eminent Civil Engineer in full employment . . . so accordingly I applied to Jordan . . . I paid him for the design a sum rather under what a professional man would charge for the equivalent amount of time spent in work.

This seemed fair enough to Bute, since Jordan was a professional, a teacher of navigation, once employed by Greenwich Observatory, though now 'a cripple, very old, in weak health and very poor'.[81] Nobody would think of prosecuting a man for accepting a fee from the Marquess of Bute. Of course, Bute was not his only client. Jordan had not been suspicious when two young female servants visited him, asking to have their fortunes told. Jordan had asked their date of birth. After a little banter, he had told one that:

there was a dark brown young man for her . . . Her young man was to be a porter or inspector on the line, and when she was 50 years of age, she would have sufficient money to keep her husband and herself without working. She was likely to be married between 23 and 24 and would be rather fond of the young man.[82]

She and her friend came back for their horoscopes the next day, and Jordan accepted money. It was a fatal mistake. The two girls were police *agents provocateurs*. Jordan was brought before Cardiff Police Court, charged with 'with being a rogue and a vagabond and professing to tell fortunes and rule planets'. According to *The Western Mail*, William Jordan was 'a patriarchal-looking man'.[83] *The Cardiff Times* was rather less in favour of him, and saw

a short, obese man, dressed in a brown suit. His hair and beard are white, and his eyes deep set under bushy eyebrows, and the whole impression of his face one of keenness combined with cunning. He was smiling continually during his trial, and seemed to enjoy the points elicited during the evidence as much as any other person.[84]

It did not even help his case that the girls finally admitted that Jordan 'did not mention any sum or ask for money',[85] for the police considered that 'he has ruined scores of young girls by unfitting their mind for ordinary work, and they have been trying for a long time to catch him'.[86] Nor did it help that the papers very generally disapproved of employing young girls as police agents. Jordan was sentenced to three months hard labour. Bute appealed at once to the most powerful and politically active man he knew personally, Rosebery, who was at this time Foreign Secretary under Gladstone. He drew attention to Jordan's age, and his infirmity, that he was not used to manual labour, and he asked him to approach his colleague, Mr Childers the Home Secretary, to ask for a reprieve.[87]

Bute liked best to spend his money on philanthropy which combined education and Roman Catholicism. He did not just give to institutions, but to individuals as well. His interest in travel and languages meant that he was approached from many countries for the money and other kinds of support which he regularly provided. He sponsored two young men through their education. Both were of Eastern origin, speaking Arabic as a first language. They had converted to Catholicism. Bute soon came to believe that Amîr Nassîf's conversion was a sham, 'a politic stroke aimed at the pockets of Catholics in general, and at mine in particular'.[88] Bute was as usual hypersensitive to being exploited for his wealth. Yet what at the time seemed like a decisive break turned out not to be so. Nassîf returned to Egypt and kept in touch with Bute. When Bute revisited the country with his adolescent daughter, Nassîf was employed to teach her Arabic, and his wife escorted her on many trips throughout the country.[89]

Yousif Hamîs was another matter. Since he appeared perfectly sincere, Bute exerted himself for him. Hamîs wanted to study medicine at Edinburgh University. One problem was the entry qualifications: he did not have nearly enough Latin to pass the qualifying exam. Bute plainly thought it unnecessary a doctor should have excellent Latin, and besieged the University with enquiries, getting conflicting answers. In the end, clarification came from the Principal of the University, Sir Alexander Grant. If Mr Hamîs wanted 'merely to study medicine' he could do so without taking any entry examinations. If he wanted to graduate but not become a British Empire doctor concessions would be made. If he wished to be a registered doctor no concessions were possible.[90] It would seem that Hamîs chose the middle option, as he substituted Arabic for Latin in his entrance examinations.

He entered the University in 1881. His academic career was not covered in glory. In 1885 he wrote to tell Bute of his 'great misery and suffering'[91] at failing his exams, later adding that he had not told Bute at once because of his 'shame for being unsuccessful'.[92] John

Anderson at last had a message to say that Hamîs 'had really passed his examination in the middle of last month. His reason for not writing to Lord Bute was that, looking at the number of times he had failed, he did not think that he had any right to feel proud of having eventually passed.'[93] Bute recorded very little about his charities in his diaries, which are at best laconic, but he did record: 'Heard Yousif Hamîs has passed his medical exams at last.'[94]

Bute was in no danger in forgetting the need to make provision for his own children in the midst of his charities. Before he had completed the purchase of Cumbrae he had decided to leave it in his will to his youngest son, Colum. This sparked a new project, the idea of ensuring each of his children were left an estate of their own, and finally decided him to purchase Falkland Estate. He had first made enquiries about this in the summer of 1885.[95] What he wanted was simply to buy the old Palace, but Mr Bruce would only sell the whole estate, and not the Palace separately:

Lord Bute said that he did not wish to purchase any large extent of land in Fife and that nothing more therefore needed to be done at present but that he wished the matter brought before him again if the Estate was advertised for sale.[96]

In the summer of 1887, Bute's agents were once again negotiating, this time to buy the whole Falkland Estate, including the House of Falkland, where Bute had stayed as a child, the estate running along the foot of the Lomond hills, and the old Palace itself.

Went over with [Lord Bute] and Lady Bute the particulars of Falkland and they both agreed to offer the sum which Mr Hamilton Bruce was willing to accept viz.:– £192,000 and his Lordship authorised this to be done.[97]

On the 3 August, the sale was completed. Bute had a new estate, and two new architectural projects.

13   Mayor

'The gratification with wh. I received such a mark of confidence ...'[1]

On Christmas Eve that year, Margaret celebrated her twelfth birthday. The Christmas celebrations were marked by magical moments, hearing 'people singing the "Adeste"'[2] in the silent Mount Stuart woods, bounded by sea and hills, and also by comic drama:

> to St Margaret's [Orphanage], wh. found just newly being burnt down, Katie Woods having turned the tap of the paraffin cask for fun, & then the maid put a light to it to prove it wasn't water. Scene & screaming.[3]

The lighting of the Christmas Tree there, a week later, must have been something of an anticlimax to both budding pyromaniacs. As usual, the celebrations continued well into January, and the children performed their play (St George and the Dragon, with 'Mgt. very well as the P[rince]ss',[4] as her proud father commented) on 17 January.

At the start of February, Bute, Gwen and the two older children left for Italy. Pope Leo XIII had celebrated his Jubilee as a priest at the end of January, and celebrations were in full swing. The Scottish contingent presented their congratulations on 15 February, and Bute had been chosen to read an address from the laity, 'Latinised by Dowy',[5] and the family spent the first part of Lent in Rome, in miserable weather, then fled to the sun of Naples.

As always, his health and spirits improved in the sun and he enjoyed having a new set of church services to critique. He was trying to collect true ghost stories, but he reported in disappointment that there were very few to be had.[6] In Venice, where they travelled next, ghosts were also 'little heard of', but there was a belief in helpful brownies, though not much in witchcraft, except for spells to create love or impotence.[7]

He also became interested in Giordano Bruno.[8] Bruno was a sixteenth-century radical and philosopher. He was not only scientifically unorthodox (like his contemporary Galileo) but also a sceptic in theology. He died at the stake. Bruno became a hero to those supporting the new movements for free thought in the 1880s and thus a villain to the pro-clerical movement. Neither side had really grappled with the thoughts of the historical man. With all the interest in Bruno, Bute decided to write on the subject.[9]

The first of two essays on the subject is an attempt to present impartially the accounts of his trial before the Venetian Inquisition. Bute had few sympathies with the arch-sceptic,[10] but he put the facts clearly. However, in the second part of this essay, published later the same year, it is not upon Bruno but on the Inquisition that Bute pours his real scorn, because they held the only accounts of Bruno's final trial and refused to release them:

> It is surely impossible that the authorities of the Inquisition can be so entirely blind to the nature of the popular reputation which that Tribunal already enjoys as to suppose that any possible revelation could make it worse than it is.[11]

The Butes returned home just in time for John's seventh birthday, and the following Sunday he was for the first time put into 'boy's clothes'.[12] The Butes were leaving Chiswick House, which they had rented as a London home, and where two of the children had been born. Bute was interested in St John's Lodge, which nestles in the Regent's Park. It was at once more central and more secluded than Chiswick House. He first looked at the outside of it, and then viewed it with Gwen. They set in motion the legal proceedings to lease it.

Then Bute and Gwen left Britain once again and went to Bayreuth, mainly to see *Parsifal*. Bute regarded this opera, with its themes of purity, fall and redemption, as a religious experience, although he cherished no illusions as to the private life of its creator.

> It seems to me that when Wagner wrote the 2nd act of Parsifal, he cannot but have remembered how he had himself yielded utterly to a far worse temptation. Probably there are things in it of wh. Mrs Wagner(?) [*sic*] alone, if anyone, now knows the real sense.[13]

Bute was both shocked and distressed by the audience and after enduring applause in a number of other performances, he wrote to Cosima Wagner, complaining of those

> entirely incapable of appreciating the drama, and so utterly callous to the feelings of others, that they actually attempt to applaud. To clap at the deaths of Tristram and Isolde or of Tanhäuser & Elizabeth, is brutal enough, but to give Parsifal a greeting which might be fit enough for the Grande Duchesse de Gerolstein, is intolerable . . .

He suggested she use the technique used in Glasgow to forbid applause at performances of *The Messiah*, printing comments on tickets, and displaying notices in the corridors, forbidding applause due to 'the sacredness of the subject'.[14]

With all these excitements and travels, it was September of 1888 before Bute went to his new property at Falkland for the first time. He was very pleased by it:

> I am rather surprised by this place – wh. I last saw in 1860, when here with Lady Elizabeth Moore, & where I had often visited with my Mother – does not awake more vivid recollections. Contrary to the usual rule in such cases, it all seems much larger, really fine, and the Palace imposing.[15]

At Falkland, Bute had bought two properties. The first was a handsome early Victorian house by William Burn, in the Jacobean style. It was to prove invaluable to Bute as a base for the east of Scotland especially while he worked on his new enthusiasm, one of his most successful projects, and perhaps the finest of all Victorian recreations of earlier buildings, Falkland Palace.

Falkland is set at the edge of the only hills in Fife, the Lomonds. Even in the mediaeval period it was within reach of Edinburgh, and of course the combination of hills, woodland and open land offered superb hunting. The MacDuff family had had a residence there, which had been famous for its 'great tower' and when it came by marriage into the hands of Robert, Duke of Albany, younger son of Robert II, the castle began to be known as a palace. With reason, for the Duke was the protector of Scotland, and having refused to yield power to his elder brother, he imprisoned that brother's son in Falkland, where he died. James IV had abandoned the old fortification and built a miniature Renaissance palace. His son continued the work. It was there he died tragically early and, it was said, of a broken heart. Even after the Union of the Crowns reigning monarchs had visited, the last being Charles II. Bute spent a fortnight at Falkland, visiting the palace daily. He famously summed up its then state: 'It has suffered much from being restored as a ruin – said to be by Mr Tyndall Bruce under the advice of Sir W. Scott.'[16] The shortness of the visit did not prevent him getting his hands dirty: 'In afternoon to Palace, where cleared chimney at end of Great Hall. Frightful dust of soot & jackdaw nests.'[17]

Not surprisingly, when he addressed the British Archaeological Society as President in August, he found a space to speak of restoration and destruction, pleading for a careful, conservationist approach to the then ongoing recreation of 'the great Dominican church' in Stirling.[18]

After the excitements of Falkland, he returned to London for a brief spell, and shopped for wedding presents, for Gwen's cousin Phillipa, now thirty-six, was marrying a medical doctor, Edward Stewart. Phillipa was ecstatically happy, telling Gwen:

> I assure you I am quite as much in love in my old age as if I was as young as you were & I am very happy. Of course you will think I am engaged to a 'perfect fool' because that is your opinion of doctors but I really must beg leave to differ with you on this occasion.[19]

This was also the year that the 'inflammable' Winefred, Gwen's youngest sister, finally married. Meetings between the other sisters and Winefred, for years, earned Bute's laconic comment 'Usual row'.[20] Winefred had indeed entered a convent, only to leave it again (before taking any binding vows). Then, a year before, she had become engaged to a Mr Henry Cowan. Bute had, once again, been cast in the role of family mediator over this proposed match. He had written to Cowan, sympathising:

> My own belief on the subject of marriage is that its true happiness can only exist by mutual affection, founded upon mutual respect and sanctified by religion. Where such a strong, exclusive and enduring feeling exists, I should regard it as wrong to let almost any obstacle stand in the way.[21]

All the same, Cowan and Winefred hardly knew each other and Bute suspected a 'temporary fancy'. Bute's advice was that the pair should wait, and Mr Cowan should find some 'position' which would allow him to support a wife. He privately confided that he was resigned to supporting Cowan in some post or other himself. The pair did become engaged, only for Winefred to 'shamefully jilt him, at the more shameful instigation of [William] Middleton',[22] whom Winefred married this year. The Butes did not attend the wedding.

Bute, however, had an excellent excuse. He was attending a 'hydropathic' in Strathpeffer. This was in part yet another attempt to get his psoriasis under control. He had made two further attempts at allowing himself to be coated with chrysophanic acid, and each had ended in acute inflammation of his eyes. In the end he decided that the cure was worse than the disease, and returned to the less perfect but less dangerous cure of taking the waters. In addition, he had developed a 'sinus' in his scrotum.

The word sinus comes from the Latin for a bay. The result of an infection, it is an opening in the scrotum which gently weeps. The doctor at Strathpeffer treated it, and at the time it appeared to be cured. Bute complained, as usual, of the effects of 'waters' designed to cure him, here especially 'the numbed, dull sense of incapacity, especially for brain work',[23] but he walked up Ben Wyvis with his doctor, visited the ruined cathedral at Fortrose, and pressed on with his current intellectual project, a translation of 'The White Lady' by Ivan Turgenieff.[24] It is a ghost story, or rather a spirit story, of something like a succubus who, seeking her own birth as a mortal soul, destroys the man whom she enchants, finally dying herself, and bringing upon him decay and mental confusion which are, it is implied, shortly to be followed by his death. Bute was translating the work from French (not the original Russian) into English. It was finally published in the *Scottish* in 1889.[25]

It seems an extraordinarily dark and erotic subject, but Bute very much had his own views on what was indecent. He went in the spring of 1889 to see Shakespeare's *Merry Wives of Windsor* for the first time.

the gross indecency of wh. is beyond anything . . . It is amazing how anybody can talk about the indecency of Emile Zola & swallow the ineffable filth of the play above mentioned. They have not read Zola, or perhaps the other, or only ever heard the expurgated version . . .[26]

This was the year in which Henry Vizetelly, who had published Zola in English, was jailed under the Obscene Publications Act.[27] Turgenieff was a radical, who wrote against the oppression of the peasant by the aristocrat. Zola was not merely a radical but an anticlerical, deemed obscene for the way he wrote of prostitution. One cannot even account for Bute's attitude by explaining that he was attracted to Zola by the stance the author took in defending Dreyfus. Bute, who had a huge respect for the Jewish religion and who routinely visited synagogues on a Saturday, would have been greatly moved by Zola's courage in standing against authority to prevent injustice, but '*J'accuse*' was not published until Bute was dying.

Bute spent most of the spring of 1889 at Falkland. He intended to employ William Frame for both the modern House of Falkland and the ancient Palace. Frame was wildly excited at the prospect of his first major independent work: 'I have received instructions from Lord Bute to visit him at Falkland Palace & I anticipate a lengthened stay there.'[28] He found a prospective assistant, who he hoped would 'help . . . in the measurements & making of drawings'[29] of the Palace. But Bute was not prepared to finance an assistant for drawing, and Frame started single-handed. He was not well, describing a condition where 'pain takes me in the lungs every time I breathe',[30] which sounds very like pleurisy. However, he did indeed begin work on the House of Falkland, making a 'delightful'[31] new dome in the entrance hall. In it he placed, surely acting under Bute's instructions, heraldic glass which commemorates the women associated with the House. Not only had the House been repeatedly inherited through the female line, but Bute was always motivated by a desire to bolster his children, and his eldest child was now growing up fast. Her self-image was being formed and Bute had a high opinion of the worth of women, and not simply as ornaments. Margaret was being particularly well-educated. Now fourteen, she had, among others, a native Greek-speaking governess,[32] Helen Snakos, who arrived not knowing a word of English.[33] The girl's artistic abilities were encouraged as well, and for the important religious and family festival of Easter, she took delight in 'dressing the table' for Easter luncheon 'with Easter eggs and flowers in the Italian manner'. In further celebration, Colum, now three years old, joined the adults for luncheon for the first time.[34]

Bute worked best on projects which fired his imagination. He combined an ability for painstaking research of detail with delight in a good romantic story. He found both at Falkland, and spent April and May beavering away at 'the Exchequer Rolls regarding Falkland'.[35] He had a new helper, who soon blossomed into a new friend, his Falkland factor, Major Woods. But his health was troubling him, and he went back to Dumfries House, in easy reach of Glasgow, for ever more consultation and treatment.

The treatment for the psoriasis was so inhumanly uncomfortable that the wonder is Bute could even try it, let alone persevere on and off for several months. He was condemned to wear an India-rubber shirt next to his skin, which was first painted with chrysophanic acid. Not surprisingly he told his friend Grant:

I am very much pulled down with the remedies for the psoriasis, and am ... very likely to undergo an operation for wht they call a <u>sinus</u>, which ... has recurred. So I am not very cheerful.[36]

The recurrence of the sinus was ominous. The repeated infection suggests that the re-infection was occurring from another source. But as Bute cheerfully reported a little later, the operation itself had not been unduly distressing:

the Professor of Surgery at Glasgow[37] cut the scrotum open at one side. Of course I was under chloroform and have hardly suffered any pain at all, they do these things so well. But of course I am bandaged up and can hardly move about. The wound is not quite closed up yet.[38]

Bute was operated on at the St Enoch's Hotel, Glasgow. It was unthinkable that a man of his class should go to a hospital, and Dumfries House was too far away for the doctors. He spent four days on the sofa there, mainly reading proofs of the *Scottish*, often with his editor, fast becoming his friend, William Metcalfe, before taking the train back to Dumfries House. He then spend a glorious Scottish June convalescing.

The days here have all been the same. Fine & hot, dry, sometimes sunny, sometimes sultry. Nearly always in dressing-gown sitting at top of the steps. Sometimes Shaw, or one of the others, such as F[rederick] A[nderson] to see me. Finished Bikelas VII essays, dictating.[39]

What is noticeable about Bute's illnesses is that while he did to some degree rest physically, he nearly always remained intellectually active. He was translating further essays by Demetrios Bikelas[40] on the origins of Christian Greece including the first days of modern independence. In Britain, the history of this country was little known, so the work was ground breaking. Unfortunately Bikelas was an author who lacked all the flair so evidently possessed by Bute, and although the latter did his best, the essays are anything but a gripping read. As in the case of Turgenieff, Bute was not translating from the original language, but from French.

Bikelas came to stay that summer, and Bute proposed taking him to

Mochrum, Falkland, and Mount Stuart. There is nothing to show him but the country. What is the use of showing (e.g.) the remains of [Linlithgow?], to a man who generally sees the Parthenon out of his bedroom window?[41]

What happened as a result of Bikelas's visit accounts for why Gwen was never again confined to a sofa for nine months.

> I had hoped my wound had healed and I racketed all about the country with the Greek for a fortnight, till I was certainly very tired (he liked Galloway, by the way, best of all, and was extremely interested everywhere in the Scotch dialects) and after he left, I wore my India rubber next-the-skin costume one day. That night, the wound troubled me, next day it was very sore, Saturday last I was in pain and travelled [to Dumfries House] with lint on it. When I undressed at night, I found that the creature had burst, and the lint was saturated with matter. I sent for the doctor on Sunday mng. who said part of the hollow was not filled up, and that an abscess had developed. This was a mental relief to me, as I was fearing that the sinus had re-formed, and that I should have to go though the whole operation &c. again. He comes every morning to stuff in a piece of lint steeped in carbolic, with a probe, and I am bound up. I can toddle about gently, and take a drive with precautions, but I am to avoid travel for some weeks.[42]

The cure sounds exquisitely painful, but what Bute regretted most was that it meant he was unable to travel to the consecration of his friend Colin Grant as Bishop of Aberdeen. The two men had at last steered the committee in charge of the Proprium, of which neither was chairman, through its troubles. They had discussed the historical validity of various hagiographies, Bute reporting that:

> Fr McSuibhne is here, and I am making him read the Lives of St Brigid. As he does so, the word 'impossible' occasionally escapes his lips, & he has not, I believe, yet met with anything he regards as fit to be put forward in the guise of a historical fact.[43]

Bute and Grant had struggled over second Nocturns. Nocturns are readings in the service of Mattins which was at one time a night service. Each reading had a function, and the second Nocturn provided some history of the saint or edifying details of their martyrdom. Bute complimented Grant that 'Your two new 2nd Nocturns are a wonderful improvement upon our first work',[44] later commenting that he thought it was a Frenchman who invented the phrase 'to lie like a 2nd Nocturn'.[45] They shared a sense of humour, and a delight in playing with words. Now, with the Proprium being printed in draft form, for circulation among the clergy for their views, Bute joked that 'The very thought of the subsequent labour of criticising their criticisms almost makes the sweat burst from my pores and a feeling of mental confusion pass over my brain.'[46]

There were so few of the clergy of whose personal qualities and learning Bute wholeheartedly approved. It delighted him that a colleague and a friend who commanded his unqualified respect was being ordained to the episcopate. Grant declared that he was 'touched' but 'conscious of so many wants in myself for the office of Bishop that I cannot think I approach your estimate'. Both the Butes planned very special presents to mark the occasion. Gwen wanted to work a gold thread mitre for the Bishop with her own hands, and

> I myself wish to ask you to let me give you a Pastoral Staff made on one of the old Cellini models, as they have only heads and joints/ embossed rings. I had thought of making these of metal and the wooden parts of the four traditional woods of the cross – palm, cedar, cypress and olive.[47]

He was totally unprepared for the shock of the announcement of Grant's death at the end of September. Grant had kept to himself the symptoms of kidney failure[48] which abruptly ended his life so soon after his consecration:

> Heard with the utmost grief of the death of Bishop Grant of Aberdeen. The loss is very great to me personally. The loss to historical science, especially that concerning Scotland, is so terrible as to cause a sort of despair.[49]

There was nobody to replace Grant as a mentor for church history, but in other areas, Bute's work for the church was looking as though it might be successful at last. Bute had spent a few happy days at the end of 1888 'digging' for ancient ecclesiastical remains at Whithorn, and he had organised, although not attended, a celebration of the Saint's life in that area. Now in 1889 he funded the setting up of a new foundation. The original order of religious at Whithorn had been Premonstratensians, or Norbertine Canons, and apparently

> The Right Rev. Dr. McLachlan, the present Bishop of Galloway, had long cherished the desire to make a link between the present

and the past of his diocese, by inviting the monks of Prémontré to return to the district in which their predecessors once so successfully laboured.[50]

Bute tried very hard to keep his backing secret, but, as the bishop pointed out, it was impossible to deceive the Fathers or others into believing that there was anybody else in that wretchedly poor diocese who had the money to fund such a project.[51] At the time, all looked set fair for a successful 'mission'.

Moreover, it looked for a time, at the end of 1889, as though the problems of Oban choir school were finally resolved. Bute had succeeded in getting a pair of priests to act as chaplains to the choir school at Oban. In the spring he had engaged an Italian priest, Francis Savelli, who had found himself a subordinate, Francis De Carolis, who delighted Clements:

> Holy Week functions went fairly well – Fr De Carolis is an acquisition, he has a fine voice and understands Gregorian music. He is a big man, rather stouter than Fr Simon – with a good appearance.
>
> We begin daily sung mass next Monday.
>
> In June the Bishop intends to hold a Synod. We are to sing a Pontifical Mass.[52]

Savelli was able to tell Bute exactly what he had always wanted to hear about the choir: 'Here is perfect peace within all, and the services are daily performed in good order to the glory of Almighty God.'[53]

It was too good to last. First there were the usual bitter complaints about Clements, who followed Bute's instructions, and refused to listen to counter-orders from the priests, which exasperated them (though not of course Bute). Then, as an Anglican, and not apparently an especially high church one, he did not reverence the Blessed Sacrament, 'and during May devotions to the BVM he didn't go to the service, but was outside the chapel playing with his dog'.[54] There was also the usual lack of help from the Bishop or his subordinates. Savelli had sung Mass daily at 10 a.m. for a year, and complained it had damaged his health. When he had asked the Provost to act as his deacon for a service, he received a letter which put him in 'deepest affliction' and made him feel unable to approach them again, but

> I [did] not write to your Lordship about it, for I believed to give you very trouble and sorrow, seeing the ingratitude of them towards the great and innumerable benefits made by Your Lordship to them ...

But, excuse me, My Lord, I prefer to pass all this in silence and to suffer alone.[55]

After that, the two chaplains started playing off against each other, and trying to drag Gwen in as umpire. Savelli alleged that De Carolis had threatened the Bishop that Bute would destroy the cathedral, and had told him it would be better if he got back to his old church, and generally insulted him in Bute's name. Savelli accused him of wanting to ruin the choir in hopes of becoming Bute's private chaplain.[56] Somehow Savelli overplayed his hand, and Bute became enraged at him and dismissed him.[57] Bute continued to be totally satisfied with De Carolis, and the Bishop continued to be wholly exasperated with the whole scheme.

At this inauspicious point, Bute's friend Grissell made enquiries into de Carolis's background. He was, it seems, prompted by a comment Bute had made, and by an 'ungracious' letter from de Carolis to Bute about Savelli. What Grissell found he 'considered it a duty' to tell Bute, which are always words to chill the heart.

> The real reason for [de Carolis] having to leave S Lorenzo in Damso was that he actually forged the signature of one of the minor Canons to a promissory note for 200 lira. This canon is none other than Don Vincenzo Leusi whom you must have met again and again, for he was Lord Cardinal Howard's chaplain for many years and remained so till the end. The man from whom de Carolis hoped to get the money had the wisdom before paying it to call on Don Vincenzo about it when the clear forgery was discovered, and Don Vincenzo tells me that he himself still has it for he thought it prudent not to destroy it. De Carolis had not only closely copied the signature but had added the word 'accetto'. To hush up so great a scandal for which he is still liable to be prosecuted the chapter thought it better to let him leave.[58]

De Carolis was also in debt to the tune of 2,000 lira. Bute was deeply distressed. He had at last found a man who was very suitable in every other respect to act as chaplain to the choir school, who followed his directions. How extreme his distress is shown by the letter he wrote when Grissell pressed him to reply to him.

> As you urge me to write to you, I will. But I implore you not to make me do more than I can. I cannot do much more. Your action has already has plunged me into a continuous correspondence in

many quarters for now about two months past, day after day, hour after hours . . . all with one unwavering result of harass and distress.

He wished that Grissell had either never heard the story or decided never to repeat it, and said that assuming de Carolis was guilty, which Bute did not believe, the cleric had honestly been trying to turn over a new leaf, and now had no income for himself or with which to support his aged parents. True or false, the stories had set a Mrs Bunman onto Bute, and Bute believed (rightly or wrongly) she was desperate to cause his choir of male voices to be abolished and the Bishop's mixed choir, in which she sang, to be put in its place:

> it is possible that the Pro Cathedral at Oban may be destroyed by your action, and so the Orphanage and all the rest of it. Please spare me writing more . . .
> The whole affaire is causing me pain and vexation beyond expression. For days past I have not been able to put pen to a little historical paper I was working at. Last night the misery the thought caused me was so great that I could not stay in bed.[59]

The Bishop had always wanted the money to go on something else – almost anything else. But the money was not on offer for anything else. It was once again a question of who chose to spend Bute's money: should he simply hand over large sums to others to do as the church hierarchy thought fit, as though it was not really his money, but something owing to them? Did the laity have a role in religious matters, or did ordination and that alone give the right to decide religious policy? Loyal and liturgically-minded McSwiney thought Bute's gift was wholly to the Bishop's advantage.

> I am concerned . . . that the Bishop proves so intractable. The Cathedral establishment and services didn't (does not) cost his Lordship a shiver and from report I know full well that whenever the offices clash with his special arrangements, the hours of the services are changed without a murmur. Hampered as he is by the paucity of his co-operators, it is strange that he should seek to do away with an institution which insures the permanent presence of two priests in Oban, without any pull on his scanty resources.[60]

The Bishop's story is sympathetically told by Roderick Macdonald: 'The bishop became impatient of continuing difficulties, and at last decided that the public daily Office must be abandoned, at least in part.'[61] Bute, anxious and intense, appealed to the Cardinal Prefect of Propaganda, and then asked another person also[62] to bring pressure on the Prefect. That both sides used what power and influence they could muster is perhaps not surprising, given the hierarchical nature of the Catholic Church, and the web of influence which governed it. What is more disturbing is the extent to which Bute was prepared to use the helpless to put pressure on the bishop. If the office was suppressed, it was inevitable that the school, largely an orphanage of twenty-four boys who sang the office, would be disbanded; there was no other reason for their being gathered in Oban. It was hardly necessary for Bute to add threats. He did. He asked his Rothesay parish priest, George Smith, to 'let him [the Bishop] know'[63] that Bute would not only take away the tin cathedral, but also abandon schemes for hospitals at Oban and Benbecula.

The Cardinal Prefect of Propaganda suggested that the bishop was to provide the clergy for the school choir, but at Bute's expense. He also suggested that Mattins, Lauds, Prime, Sext and None would only be said if the bishop so wished, but that Terce would be said daily, Vespers would be said and not sung except on Sundays or feast days, and Compline should always be said. There was to be no full daily office. Bute resigned himself to what was not, in his view, even a compromise, and he did not carry out his threats. If neither quite got what they wanted, it can fairly be said that neither had really deserved to do so.

But Bute was not always purblind to the difficulties of others, or unsympathetic to priests of his church. On occasion he could be warm, sympathetic and gentle: though it must be admitted that he usually only showed these admirable traits when fighting for the underdog. Mr Henry Laverty had been the priest at Hurlford, who had moved to the new St Sophia's at Galston. Bute knew him as a committed and very hard-working priest. He moved on to Cumnock, another demanding charge working with the very poor. While there he suddenly suffered a crisis of faith, for reasons nobody could fully explain, and determined to become an Anglican. He wrote to Bute renouncing his charge, and thanking his patron for his kindness.[64] Bute wrote back a letter full of compassion and good sense. He appreciated that Laverty's sense of honour led him to resign from his one source of income. He suggested that the priest should not speak publicly on his doubts, and

shd. continue to observe carefully those things to wh. you are bound either as a Catholic or as a clerk in Holy Orders. There is a great difference between complying with certain things oneself & telling other people that they are obligatory. I wd. also entreat you to pray to God for light & guidance, & to commend yourself to the intercession of the BV. You know that the temptations against faith, like some of another sort, are better not thought of or reasoned with.[65]

He offered to provide Laverty with the cure which had worked for himself, a trip to the Holy Land, and ended by thanking him for all his kindness towards Bute.

Laverty brought down on himself the wrath of all around him. The organist at Cumnock, John Denham, took the opportunity to claim that Laverty had taken offence at Bute's letter, which made no impact at all on Bute's attempts to help a man with the whole weight of the hierarchy bearing down on him in fury. Charles Eyre, the Archbishop of Glasgow fulminated that

> Your Lordship's view that a pervert can be called 'honest' and bonafide in his secession from the Catholic Church is theologically untenable. It is admitted on all hands that any Catholic who abandons the church is not a mere blunderer but a downright sinner against the fundamental virtue of faith.[66]

Eyre made the further classic mistake of assuming that depression and anxiety could not coexist. The Bishop of Galloway offered retreat and penance.

> Of course the prodigal is welcome – heartily welcome back – & so far as his personal reconciliation with the church is concerned we shall be too glad to afford him every possible facility. The usual process in such cases as his is that he be put on a course of penance in some house of Retreat, & after a sufficient term of satisfaction & preparation, that he be absolved & reconciled in due form.[67]

As if the blood was not chilled enough by this suggested course of action, the Bishop helpfully pointed out that, while Laverty would then in theory be able to function as a priest, there would actually be nowhere he could have a charge or earn a living in Galloway diocese, or 'in the three Kingdoms'.

Bute, knowing the agitation so often part of depression from his own painful experience, argued passionately that Laverty was distressed and depressed, and needed calm and kindness, and offered to fund it. It was not available even for ready money. Bute's diagnosis was almost certainly correct. As Laverty recovered slightly he himself put it down to 'financial worry, melancholy and neuralgia' – he had been 'almost in despair'.[68]

Bute again urged Laverty to go to Jerusalem, a trip which Bute would fund, where he could stay with the Franciscans and get work teaching English:

> I think that what you need is entire change of scene & occupation, the absence of contentious subjects, rest and quiet. I hope that you found you had been misinformed about your dog, & that you have him with you & in good health.[69]

The end of the story is lost. When last heard of, Laverty had despaired of reinstatement by the Catholic Church, and left.

As if this was not enough to tax Bute, the monastery he had founded at Whithorn was already failing, and nobody could see any way of putting things right. The Bishop of Galloway put the matter in a nutshell. The Prior, though humble and holy, was incapable of managing the mission, and was probably becoming senile. Nobody in the order in England could be sent to replace him, as none of them spoke English.[70]

It did not help that Bute was having a miserable year personally in 1890 as well. In February he had had influenza with his temperature rising to 104°f.[71] It left him feeling unwell for weeks afterwards. Bute was also missing his beloved Margaret. She was now fourteen and in May had started at St Leonard's School for Girls, in St Andrews, living in St Regulus' Hotel in the town with her governess, Miss Cuthbert, and attending as a day girl. The Butes had expected their daughter would shine a little more brightly than she did. Margaret enjoyed the social life, which posed its own worries of inappropriate friendships to Gwen. How reassured she was by Margaret's account of her school is not certain:

> I like school very much, it is the form. I have no time for arm in arm or anything of that kind, only lessons, laughing going up and down stairs at school, and biscuits or a bit of cake at a quarter to 11.[72]

At first the school were confident that when Margaret discovered that her inaccuracies cost her marks she would mend her ways. Her end of term report at Christmas 1890 was acid indeed:

10th of 14

Latin. Her work is satisfactory on the whole, but more energy might with advantage be expended on it.

Greek is improving; but she has not as yet much grasp of the more ordinary forms of accidence of the simpler sorts of syntax.

History. Takes a decided interest in her work. She hardly seems to realise this is not enough or that a real effort must be made on her part, if her work is to do her any good.

Head mistress – there is no doubt that if she chose to exert herself she might be one of the first four in this form. I expect that she will make the effort.[73]

She did not return to school after Christmas. Like so much this year, the experiment had not been a success.

Usually, Bute's building projects were his comfort and his delight. But in this Jonah year, even here Bute was doomed to more distress. Twice he went into the public house over the road from the Palace to find his Falkland architect, Frame, drunk and asleep. Bute, always a compassionate man, gave him yet another chance. Frame did not or could not take it. In October, Bute recorded, sadly, 'Frame being drunk again, had to dismiss him.'[74]

Of course, the year was not all gloom. Bute travelled to Oberammergau to see the Passion Play. He successfully hosted a visit by the Duke of Clarence to Cardiff.[75] He continued to show visitors, including Princess Louise,[76] round his excavations and explorations of Falkland Palace. He had begun his work by uncovering the lost original tower of Falkland:

This tower seems to have formed the most prominent feature of the building at the time, and is mentioned as a sort of synonymous term along with 'manor' to designate the whole residence, till a considerably later period ... I was naturally anxious to find any remains of this tower, which has totally disappeared. In excavating the gardens to the north of the standing portions of the Palace, we found the remains of the original enclosing wall, and in the north-east angle a part of a round tower over 50 feet in diameter ... In its centre is the well, sunk in the rock ... This great tower with its high pointed roof must have been the main feature of the early group of buildings, and a prominent feature in the landscape for many miles round. Its great size implies truly noble rooms.[77]

He had written a 'double paper' on the Palace itself and on the death there of David, Duke of Rothesay.[78]

However, his abiding impression of the year was one of unhappiness, coloured as it was by an event which took place at Christmas. Something major crowned the miseries of the year. Bute recorded in his diary:

'25 Dec Sung Mass at midnight. For the only time since 1868 did not communicate',[79] and in his résumé for the year he wrote: 'Not a happy year and a very unhappy Christmas.'[80] Bute plainly wanted to receive. Now, a Catholic feels unable to take communion when he is not, for some reason, in a condition where he may properly and respectfully do so. These would include being unable to forgive somebody, or having quarrelled with somebody, or having a spiritual advisor tell him he should not do so, perhaps because he was unable to admit to his guilt in some matter, or intended to continue in a sinful course of action, and was therefore unable to be forgiven. There is no sign of any disturbance in his relationship with his wife. He records walking with her the following day. The priest in residence was McSwiney, who had the most kindly and helpful of relationships with Bute.

The things which cause Christians most distress are often not the large sins. Usually these can be admitted and forgiven. It is so often small things which assume a disproportionate importance. Whatever his religious difficulty in 1890, it was compelling. The last time he had received communion was 1 November, All Saints Day. There is no record of his taking it at the end of November at the dedication of his chapel in the House of Falkland which was 'solemnly blessed in honour of St Ninian at 10, with the full rite of the ritual, choral'.[81] The year before he had received communion in early December. Bute normally communicated regularly, and invariably on Christmas Day, St Stephen's Day (26 December) and his name feast of St John (28 December) and also on 1 January. This year, he did not communicate on any of these. He wrote to his friend Metcalfe on the last day of the year:

> We have had a very unhappy Xmas. We are to give thanks this evening for the mercies of the past year. It recalled to me the question whether an harvest thanksgiving after a bad harvest is not a mocking of heaven like churching a barren woman. But there are no doubt mercies unacknowledged. Fr. McSuibhne is here, pretty wretched. The constant shadow from the hill renders any gleam of sunlight impossible. I knew before, but I had not realised what it means.[82]

He finally records his confession on 30 January, and his first communion of the year on Candlemas Day (2 February). By then things were taking on an altogether brighter aspect. For a start he had found a new architect to work on Falkland Palace, John Kinross.[83] Kinross was a Scottish-born architect who trained with Glasgow architect John Hutchison.[84] Bute had first met Kinross when he went to the latter's office 'about Queensferry'[85] in the spring of 1890. Bute had recently visited a Carmelite Friary in south Queensferry which was being restored for Episcopalian worship.

> To see Carmelite church. Rather frightened at the restoration. Afraid they are modernising surface of the sedelia & destroying old plaster on walls. Fear they intend turning transept into a porch, by making door where there are remains of flamboyant window.[86]

As Kinross's biographer comments, Bute's 'fears were unfounded',[87] and it seems that the meeting in February established Bute's regard for him. He came in March to visit the Butes, and (in common it must be said with every other visitor) was shown the Palace. But of course at that time, Bute still had Frame working on the designs and drawings. It was only after Frame was dismissed, in November, that Bute records 'in afternoon to Palace, where Mr Kinross. Home with him'.[88] Some agreement was reached, for in December, 'Mr Kinross came for some hours; abt. plan of Palace.'[89] It was a classic case of 'comes the hour, comes the man'. Kinross was as scholarly as Bute himself, with a feel for recreating and invention which went far beyond being merely pedantic. He researched painstakingly:

> The wide range of sources consulted included the master of Works and Lord Treasurer's Accounts, together with the Exchequer Rolls ... the Reverend Robert Scott Milne's The Master Masons of Scotland and their Works ... earlier pictorial representations of the Palace ...[90]

He was as devoted to history as Bute could have wished, and he had what R. R. Anderson and Frame had lacked – a touch of individual flair and a real style of his own. His work on the outside of the Palace was sensitive. The distinctive conical towers on the gatehouse were raised, in accordance with earlier representations (and to something more like that of which Burges would have approved) and a later doorway, which disrupted the regular Renaissance 'bay articulation' of the south 'quarter', was rebuilt as wall.

The temptation to restore the Cross House, thus adding a pleasing Gothic irregularity to this essentially Renaissance building, was too much for both architect and patron. Kinross urged that

> If the south wall were built and the whole roofed the walls would then be perfectly protected and the water kept from percolating through the vault over the guard room in the basement.[91]

The Cross House was investigated, researched and rebuilt in a very convincing manner. Yet delightful as the exterior is, and thorough as the investigation, conservation and restoration, it was with the interiors that Kinross came into his own. The gatehouse exterior had survived, and merely needed its roof restored, and the height of its pitch raised from that of the early Victorian restoration.[92] However, the lower rooms of the south quarter could only be freed up for the extensive interior restoration required if they were not in use – and the Woods family lived there. Major Woods was Bute's factor and assistant in all matters relating to Falkland and its House and Palace.[93] Bute wanted to rescue Woods from the crumbling rooms, probably almost as much as he wanted to rescue the crumbling rooms themselves. Happily the two aims were to be achieved simultaneously. The need for restoration let him keep the fact that the splendid new rooms were to become the new Woods family home a secret. At this point in the proceedings Bute became Mayor of Cardiff. This meant, as Mays points out, that for most of 1891, he was absent from this most exciting restoration.[94]

The surprising news of this had come just before the end of the miserable year 1890, when the council had 'resolved' to elect him, and, presumably knowing something of his temperament, a deputation was sent 'to wait upon Lord Bute and convey to him the purport of this resolution'.[95] It was not usual for an aristocrat to be elected to this kind of office (though they served in the national government through seats in the House of Lords). With his habitual modesty, Bute assumed the role with a good deal of trepidation. He feared that if he made a mess of his term in office, it would lead to other, and perhaps more able, aristocrats being excluded from this kind of public office.[96] Or at least, that was how he rationalised his fear. Perhaps it was a more generalised fear of failing. There is no doubt that he was deeply honoured by the invitation, and it succeeded in healing his fears about his relations with Cardiff. For once Bute had been chosen, not in spite of himself, but for himself. While he held elected office, it was, beyond all doubt, his preferred title: 'Vicar says that he asked the porter this mng. "Is Ld. B. in?" & was answered "His Worship the Mayor had gone to the Town Hall."'[97] Bute was delighted and amused. His actual installation took place on 10 November. However, he could not give his proposed Mayoral dinner that year, due to bronchitis all December, and it was January before he returned to Cardiff to stay and to assume his duties. He was still feverish and ill in January, probably with the epidemic influenza. He continued to see his deputy every day, but in his bedroom or his sitting room at Cardiff Castle. Happily by 4 February, the date set for the postponed mayoral banquet, Bute was up and about again. In one sense the banquet was not an unqualified success:

> Mayoral banquet at Drill Hall, postponed from Nov 9. All very pretty & successful, till just at the vegetable course, when decorations of roof took fire, owing to incandescence & bursting of electric lamp. None injured. Perfect coolness of everyone. John and Ninian with me till after the soup.[98]

In fact there was a major fire, and the guests had to leave the tables as paper decorations burst into flames. When it became clear the situation could not be brought under control, and hot cinders rained on the tables, Bute led the way out. Others, who took it a little less calmly, were amazed at Bute's unruffled behaviour, and thought that 'to this perfect self-possession on the part of the Mayor is to be attributed, in large measure, the calmness of the guests who were bound to emulate his Lordship's demeanour'.[99] It did a good deal to win Bute public approval of the kind he had lacked throughout all his life. The next dilemma was more serious. There was a strike at the docks.

There was a history of trouble over the wages, conditions and employment of seamen, dockers and allied trades all over Britain, and in 1889, Cardinal Manning himself had played a part in sorting out a temporary peace between dockers and employers in London.[100] However, a dispute between the seamen and the ship-owners, which began in 1890, had by February dragged in the Cardiff dock workers.[101] The underlying question was how the unions should operate. The Federation of Dock Workers was favoured by the owners, and offered an 'open shop'. The Union was determined on a closed shop.

> What may prove to be a gigantic drama was opened at the Cardiff Docks yesterday and will be continued at Newport today. The battle between the Unionists and the Federation, if it continues, will be of extraordinary dimensions, without parallel in the history of trade. For whilst the one side has in its ranks an immense number of trained men, the other is infinitely richer in resources. It will be a grand struggle between Labour and Wealth, and so organised is the one and so fleet the other that it is impossible to say which will win.[102]

Bute was in an impossible situation. As Mayor, he was committed to being neutral. As a businessman, he was 'practically owner'[103] of the docks. With great misgivings on the eve of the strike, he attended a dinner.

> Spent all day discussing whether ought to go to Shipowners dinner . . .
> Finally went. Wearisome speeches, except deputy & G.T.C., who
> were very amusing. Left before Federation Toast, wh. hear was
> answered in very bad taste by Laws, notwithstanding their own
> promise to Deputy & W.T.L., & my own strong words.[104]

Laws had made an inflammatory speech. The impossibility of Bute's
position was underlined. Steering clear of trouble in what he himself
did and said would not be enough; others would drag him into it.
Bute took advice and fled: 'From Cardiff to London, to escape the
impossible difficulties of the strike, in wh. I may be called on as Mayor
to intervene in my own affairs.'[105]

His sympathies lay with free trade, but he strongly disliked the
provocative stance and actions of the ship-owners. By nature he
remained a conciliator, and inclined to solve disputes by rational
actions and talk. The debate still rages as to how far trade union action
of this period led to improved wages and conditions, and how far it
decreased the profitability of industry and thus created a 'low wage,
low profitability' culture.[106]

Bute had a good excuse for going to London, to meet Hyacinthe Scott
Kerr, who was engaged to Gwen's widowed brother, Frank. Bute was
still unwell, troubled with a persistent sore throat. He determined on
his usual, and usually successful, measure to get relief from ill-health
and stress. This time he set off for a destination he had not explored
before, both remote and exotic, the Canaries.

He took Margaret with him, and left

> on board the "Ionie" just 8 days late, from Thursday to Saturday,
> because of the strike & then detained at Gravesend by fog. Completely
> manned by blacklegs. Off about 3.30.[107]

and arrived in sight of the peaks of Tenerife on 4 March. His initial
impressions of the island were not favourable: 'One gets very tired of
the unceasing black lava – black roads, black walls, black rocks, black
heaps & ridges of stones, black glens with muddy brown streams
dashing down them.'

There was nothing like a tree except a few small palms:

> Owing to the damp the road-sides are all green, as in England.
> What is really striking is that from the palms to the weeds there
> is hardly a single plant one sees at home. & most of them are
> quite strange . . . The native canaries are green . . . it is difficult to

convey any sense of the ugly black and green landscape, of the most fantastic shapes – black cliffs & hills everywhere, with patches of unwholesome looking green. I am sure the natives are more than half Guanches. [First inhabitants of the islands]. They are yellow, desperately prognathous [having a jutting lower jaw], with small flat noses in the centre of their face.[108]

He was unimpressed by the hotel as well:

> This hotel is quite new. It is just like an immense Scotch hydropathic, and the people & life seem much the same. After dinner they all sit in the common drawing room, where some of them sing & play &c. [109]

And he disliked his fellow guests.[110] In fact the most enthusiastic thing he could find to say in his first days was that 'As I am here & the air is soft & there is no East wind, I shall stay, especially as it is only for a short time & it's a change.'[111]

Suddenly, however, he found he was enjoying himself. The local society amused him:

> I got a letter on wh. my name was appropriately spelled Butte, from the Marchioness of Sauzal, saying she wished to see me. The [school] master said she was one of the leading aristocracy ... I went up to the Villa & called yesterday. Regular Spanish drawing room with Venetians closed, sofa & chairs arranged for precedence, fusty smell, evidently never used. Enter three young ladies. Seated by precedence. Asked in English if I could speak Spanish. Answered, not so well as their English. Slow conversation in English.

The Marchioness was 'a widow of about 50, painted like a wig-block, eyes blackened & all the rest'. They spoke in French, the language they had in common.

> The Marchioness asked whether I wd. like to go into society, wh. I declined on the ground of health. I am told there are about 60 noble families in the island, who live to a great xtent at the Villa, are very xclusive & always marry each other. So you can see what an opening I can give you if you ever come here.[112]

He began to enjoy walking around the island, investigating seaweed on the shore finding some 'like a small semi-transparent bladder, with bright opaline or prismatic colours',[113] and was astonished that 'this afternoon there was tilting at the ring [a form of jousting] (a pastime who I did not know survived anywhere) in the garden. It seemed to be rather a pretty sight and there was a band &c.' [114] What really fascinated him were the surviving fragments of the native language of the islands, which of course gave a clue to the original provenance of the natives, who had been overrun by the Spanish conquest of the islands. His adventures in escaping from the importunate Marchioness (out by a side door and up the nearest cinder hill) amused him very much. In fact, he shortly admitted:

> I am, rather against the grain, obliged to say that this dull, & rather dark & sunless place seems to agree with me. The eczema is going, as far as I can judge, very quickly. [115]

More serious than his skin condition, it now appears for the first time that he was intermittently suffering from albumen in the urine, a sign of kidney failure:

> I went down to Pill box this mng. He xamined the throat, wh. he says is merely congested, nothing serious, and better today. He has been testing the water every two days, and it seems the albumen has been regularly and rapidly diminishing. Today he tried it by 2 tests. The boiling showed no albumen, and the chemical (called, I think, Bryan's) who is the most delicate, only a faint film or trace. He also xamined my eyes, and I understood him that they were all right. I think he rather inclines to the opinion that the skin has had a great deal to do with it, and that this is the real reason why I like hot climates and seek the sunny side of the street. He regrets I cannot stay here longer, and offered me a medical certificate, wh. I declined. I can always come back if needful. I hope with care I may keep right in England, at least in summer. [116]

The question is why Bute's kidneys were beginning to fail. The repeated infection in his scrotum may indicate another underlying cause, probably the infection of his prostate, caused by the dramatic infection of his tooth in 1886. The suggestion is that secondary effects of this infection on Bute's kidneys slowly but surely destroyed them. [117] Bute knew of the danger of damaged kidneys, but he did not yet read his occasional albuminuria as a death sentence. His health was quite restored by his time in Tenerife, he had to get back to his brother-in-law's wedding, and also to his duties in Cardiff, and when he returned in April it was with renewed energy. It was as well. There was increasingly congenial work, but also ordeals to be met: 'In afternoon to Lawn Tennis Tournament with my Lady, Margaret, & Mr Lindsay. Deadly dull: uncivil to ask one to such a thing.'[118] And, for those who do not enjoy watching sport, it is indeed deadly dull.

Meanwhile, Cardiff was getting used to its Mayor, and with some surprise. He did not in the least degree fit the stereotypical picture the town had of an aristocrat, and the local paper commented, tongue securely in cheek:

He has been seen 'prowling around at night on foot' and 'goes about without a foot man in sight' ... the Marquis rarely does anything else but walk. He hates sitting down. He detests a carriage. He loathes a chair ... Health and prudence compel him to spend nearly all his days in walking. He rambles along Cooper's field and round about the Castle. It is simply for his convenience on rainy days that the hideous stretch of blank wall, pierced with red painted peep holes, has made the Castle ugly. It is nothing but a corridor in which he may walk. He even holds his receptions on foot, and the Town Clerk has been compelled to go off to the Garth every weekend in order to get into trim. An audience with the Marquis means two long hours of incessant walking, without a break, and at a rate which would daunt even a hardy rambler. The secret of the activity of the Mayor – apart from his interest in his work – is the necessity which he feels for constant exercise, and the eagerness with which he will make any public engagement an excuse for fresh air. Why then this constant look of bewilderment and awe, when it is whispered that Lord Bute walks.[119]

It was an exaggeration, of course. The castle walkways were there as part of Burges's recreation of mediaeval fortifications. They were merely used by Bute as a walkway as he had a cat-like dislike of getting wet. One is quite sure the Town Clerk did not spend his weekends getting in trim. But Bute exploded the myth of the aristocrat in his carriage with his flunkies and his lack of sympathy for 'the common people', both by his constant walking (so much so that his diary actually records his going anywhere 'in the carriage' as an event) and also by his real interest in the work of Mayor.

His schedule was busy up to July, when he and Gwen went to Bayreuth to hear Wagner: this year *Tannhäuser, Tristan und Isolde,* and *Parsifal.* Then he returned to Cardiff to host, as Mayor, the annual meeting for the British Association for the Advancement of Science. The meeting opened on 18 August, and provided a very mixed programme, with meetings of different 'sections' taking place simultaneously in different venues at the same time. Bute had prepared and read a scholarly paper *On the ancient language of the Natives of Tenerife*. It is an exhaustive and methodical account of the surviving fragments of the original language. He systematically discounted as far as he could the words which betrayed too plain an influence of the Spanish. His tentative conclusion was that the language showed more similarity to Berber than to the native American languages.[120]

As usual, the actual delivery of this paper cost him some trouble, though unlike the lawn tennis, the rest of the week was entertainment very much to Bute's taste; it also brought him and Gwen a pair of new friends. The president of the British Association for that year was Dr William Huggins,[121] the eminent astronomer, and he and his wife and co-worker, Margaret, were received by the Butes. Margaret Huggins was a remarkable woman, a highly motivated researcher and talented artist in her own right.[122] The Huggins were gifted, educated, interesting, passionate and religious, exactly the kind of people who appealed most to the Butes, people remarkable for their interests, and not their birth or wealth.[123] Their faith slightly surprised Bute, for it was becoming less usual to find a scientist who believed in a spiritual world. Dr Huggins at once won Bute's admiration and Gwen developed with Margaret Huggins a close friendship of the kind she rather lacked elsewhere.[124]

As the BAAS meeting drew to a close, Bute was approached by Glasgow City Council and asked if he would accept the freedom of the city. He had given generously to the University, allowing them to build the Bute Halls, and he was the Mayor of Cardiff. Glasgow would be pleased if he would open the new public reading library, the Mitchell Library (built with funds from the eponymous benefactor) and receive the freedom of the City on the same day. Bute was thrown into a panic, in a way which was becoming increasingly rare. He was all too acutely aware of the sectarian hostility pervading the town and University, and he heard that at least one council member, a Mr Chisholm, opposed this new move. Nothing distressed Bute more than this kind of opposition, and he at once begged Metcalfe, his editor and friend, and an unimpeachable Protestant, to discover what he could. The result of the flurry of telegrams between Paisley and Cardiff was an apologetic, and rather surprised, letter of apology from Chisholm to the Provost of Glasgow. Chisholm had plainly underestimated the softness of Bute's skin, and had not realised that his rhetoric could cause Bute to turn down the honour proposed.[125]

The occasion was a great success, and it gave Bute an unparalleled opportunity to put into words just how affected he was by his public office:

> If your Lordship is Provost of the largest town in Scotland, I am Mayor of the largest town in Wales. The choice, to me a most unexpected one – made unanimously by the body wh. is now my council – was not one entirely without precedent, but the precedents were few, and they were mostly remote ... It would be more than idle, it would be unseemly and discourteous as well as untruthful, were I to pretend to conceal the gratification with wh. I received such a mark of the confidence of the citizens of that great commercial centre.

He said that he owed the success of his term of office to 'the excellence of my officials, the kindness of my Council, and the good-behaviour of my townspeople' but that when he reached the end of the year, only the relief he felt in laying down his responsibilities would neutralise his regret.[126] Bute had undoubtedly been daunted by the position to which he was elected. At first, he had accepted only the ceremonial parts of the role that the office brought with it. Elected in November, unwell in December and January and avoiding the dock strike later, it had been 13 April before he presided at a council meeting for the first time. After that, his diary shows, his duties became steadily less of the merely ceremonial and more a matter of real business. He discovered in himself an aptitude, and a liking, for the control and management of committees. He was, it appears, a very quiet chairman, and it could be argued that he was on occasion a manipulative one, but he was also more than merely competent. On the eve of leaving office he offered a shrewd assessment of his colleagues on the council, and the work ahead for the next Mayor:

> Town hall at 11, where Councillor Alderman Rees elected Mayor. Council shows signs of difficulties in the future: Frank Beavan very tiresome, & White very wearisome & talkative.[127]

In complete contrast to 1890, a year which had depressed and diminished Bute, 1891 had been a year of happiness and most unexpected personal growth.

14   St Andrews

'The whole year has been spent in the struggle for the defence of the University'[1]

Being mayor of Cardiff had taken a good deal of Bute's time and energy. He had not had much left to devote to Falkland, his major building project at this time, though Kinross had continued the work. In the bitter cold of January ('22°s of frost',[2] Bute recorded), he went back to Falkland to review the work. He was pleased with the progress, which had included conservation work on the old Palace walls, and re-roofing the standing building, and reforming the conical roofs of the gatehouse.

In addition, the rooms in the gatehouse had been re-lined,[3] and their ceilings had been put in. Bute was surprised how much smaller this made the rooms look. He was taking a child-like pleasure in keeping from the Wood family his intention of moving them into the gatehouse once work was finished.[4] He was delighted with Kinross, who once again came to meet him, dined and spent the night, telling Gwen:

> I went down to the Palace yesterday afternoon with Kinross, and we went over it all again. It seems to me that things have been going very well, and that he is quite to be trusted – And everything is now settled for months of work to come.[5]

Falkland was a convenient place to stay while he worked in Edinburgh on University reform in Scotland, of which he had been one of the Commissioners since 1889.[6] He would not otherwise have left Mount Stuart, for Colum and Ninian both had influenza, and were very feverish. Gwen wrote and telegraphed every day, while Bute worried and tried to comfort himself:

these high temperatures are not so dangerous with children. I know, too, that there is nothing more wh. I can do, as everything will be done wisely & well by you. But I quite agree with you that we shall have to be very careful of them for some time.[7]

Bute had intended to go abroad this spring and now, to give the children a chance to convalesce away from the cold of Britain, Gwen and the boys travelled with Bute as far as Italy. She was joined by her cousin Phillipa, and the latter's husband, Dr Stewart. Bute and Margaret, with Margaret's new governess, Miss Jones, travelled on to Egypt. They also took Rene Condor, the son of Bute's old astrological friend, who was tutoring Margaret in classics.[8] He was not the most useful person as a companion, though he caused father and daughter amusement:

Mr C. is really very silly about a variety of things. He began by saying he would drink no water at all all the time he was in Egypt, as he thought the Nile water might disagree with him, but this has already partly collapsed, as the alternatives were absolute thirst, or getting drunk by the quantity of pure wine. He has an umbrella and has started blue glass spectacles which, (I tried them) prevent one's seeing the beautiful colouring. He also won't eat things served ... He seems likely to be of very little use indeed. He has been out with me twice, but I shan't take him to-day, as he would grumble so.

Margaret was now sixteen and still lame and protected from walking far. She was in excellent health and bouncing good spirits. She had her father's love of languages, and his facility with them, but she only applied herself to systematic learning when she was pressured into it.

Egypt was the home of Amîr Nassîf, who, contrary to Bute's earlier fears, had not been simply manipulating Bute, and Bute and he were back on good terms. He had married, and had a child. He was, as Bute put it 'doing nothing, and expressed a general wish to make himself useful',[9] and at once took Margaret's Arabic lessons over from Bute.

The need to ensure that Margaret's life was not disrupted led to a very regular daily pattern:

I get up sometime after 8, and go into the dining room, where I find Margaret & have my coffee. At 8.30 she goes down to have breakfast with Miss J. and Mr C. About 9 I have my bath. Mgt. begins lessons at 9.30 with Miss J. About that time Pill box comes, and when he is done with me I go to the public bath. (Mgt. does an hour with Mr C. at 11). After my bath I walk alone, and at 12 Mgt. comes to the public garden to meet me. She usually feeds the gazelles. At 12.30 we have collation at a table of our own in the <u>Salle à Manger</u>. Then I write of something, till 3, when Nassîf comes, & I can go out with Mr C. We generally arrange to meet Mgt. & Miss Jones, who go out after tea at 5. And we are in after 6. Dinner at 7. Mgt. goes to bed early, C. later, and I usually leave Miss J. alone at about 10.[10]

Bute and Margaret shared a perfect happy companionship: 'I have just been out with Mgt., strolling about the desert near the town. I enjoy being out with her very much, and so does she, I think, being with me, even if there is nothing to see or do.'[11] This was probably just as well, for Miss Jones could not even manage the limited walking that Margaret could do:

Really the worst thing about Miss J. is her utter physical inability. I think she would be quite incapable of taking a walk with Mgt., unless it were the very faintest potter. She can't bear being in the sunlight, & so on, & so on. But I like her personally, and Mgt. can get enough exercise with me, or Davies. They are going to Sakkara tomorrow, and I shall like to see Miss J. and C. after about 16 miles on donkeys, & going over the place.[12]

Sakkara, or Saqqara, is a vast burial-ground at Memphis with the step pyramid of Djoser, and the tombs of other kings. Miss J. did not attempt the pyramids, up which Margaret scrambled with apparent ease, while her father suddenly became faint halfway up, and had to entrust his daughter to the 'respectable' local men they had with them.[13] Mrs Nassîf accompanied her to the female Turkish bath, and, like her famous ancestress Lady Mary Wortley Montague,[14] she was astonished to find that some of the women were naked except for 'their trinkets, which they kept on'.[15] There were constant small excitements – looking for fossils, seeing a great number of people pass on donkeys and camels, bound for a wedding. There was also a circumcision party:

In it was a very dilapidated cab, containing a matron piled round with her offspring of both sexes and various tender years, with one victim on her lap who was going to be circumcised. Mgt. shows no curiosity on the subject, wh. I was rather afraid she might; she only remarked that the age was different to that of the Jews, and was not the latter 8 days? I replied, yes, as she might remember from New Year's Day [Circumcision of Christ] being the week-day of Xtmas.[16]

If he was shy of some subjects, he was open on others, including Margaret's periods: 'she and I are quite confidential on that subject'.[17] He adored her, and excused all her lapses:

I think, by the way, à propos of what you say of Margaret, that Miss J. sometimes misjudges her. I found e.g. that she had not noticed that she was at all deaf, and had attributed to her hearing, (or seeming to hear) what was said, and her often saying 'What' to intention. Besides which, she sometimes attributes argumentative things Mgt. says to a kind of wish to attack her, or put her in the wrong, wh. I really think is not what Mgt. means, at least consciously.[18]

But Miss Jones's physical weaknesses and the fuss she made over any exertion must have done more than enough to undermine her authority:

Yesterday we went off to the Pyramids again, in order to see the Sphinx &c. We went without Mrs N. Miss Jones, Mgt. and N. in one carriage and Mr C. & me in the other. There was nothing peculiar or interesting xcept the terrible prostration of Miss J., wh., however, they assured me, was almost athletic activity compared to what she had been at Sakkara ... She relapsed into unconsciousness in the train, and from the time she got out of the carriage at the Pyramids till she got into it again, she was literally hardly one minute out of the arms of 2 or 3 men simultaneously. When they had placed her on a very small donkey, wh. tottered slowly forward, they had still to support her from each side, including a sympathetic hand in the small of the back. And when she was off it they tenderly carried her by the arm pits.[19]

Of course, as they were abroad during Lent and Easter, there was a good deal of religious observance.

As far as I can make out, there is a suspension of Lent here as elsewhere [on account of the influenza epidemic], but I shall do it, as I think I am not only able, but shall be all the better. We are to have a maigre [meatless] luncheon every weekday, and abstain on Wednesday & Friday at dinner also. Of course Miss J. and Mr C. said they were much too delicate to fast.[20]

Bute, although he often felt weak from the lack of food, also had the good sense to see he benefited from the regime:

> I am glad to say I am very much thinner. I do not get much to eat, and what there is, is mostly vegetables, as there is always plenty of that (very good 'made dishes' of them) not much meat even on meat days, and very little fish, and often not what I can eat.[21]

The church services did not much impress Bute, being largely in the hands of a red-haired German priest, who ignored the rubrics. The other local priest was a black 'Soudanese', and Bute and Margaret agreed in having reservations about the German and liking the Sudanese. They were distressed at the local attitude to the latter, which became very plain when both were invited to dinner on Easter Monday:

> The Red one (the German) seemed to want to prevent the Black one (who is much the nicest of the two) coming, but I managed to get him told, and he came in late.[22]

Bute was delighted with Margaret's reaction to Egypt, and the east. He responded by buying a property in Jerusalem, to give her an inheritance and a reason to be associated, for all of her life, with an area which meant so much to him.[23]

It was June before he returned to Britain, and to the new house in London, St John's Lodge, which he had leased from the Crown, where he found 'Chapel & extra library very backward'.[24] The work had been in the hands of Trollope & Sons, the building and artistic design firm, but when Bute became dismayed at the work they carried out he turned to a young Scot.[25] The architect was Robert Weir Schultz, the son of a sugar refiner from Greenock, just over the Clyde from the Isle of Bute. He had trained in the office of R. R. Anderson, and after that in the London office of Richard Norman Shaw, five of whose pupils had just founded the Art-Workers' Guild, inspired by William Morris.[26] He first appeared in Bute's life in 1889, showing him drawings of Greek mediaeval churches, from his scholarship-funded travel.[27]

Schultz now undertook the development of St John's Lodge. The property belonged to the Crown and was leased. Bute had already had a lantern created in the entrance hall to take the stained glass from the dome of Chiswick House. The hall had the staircase removed, and access was subsequently from a vestibule by a wooden staircase[28] which had been carved in the Cardiff workshop. It was a gorgeous creation with rich neoclassical swirls of flower and foliage in deep relief in natural wood against a gold background. This was made for the first neoclassical Mount Stuart, and moved sympathetically to St John's Lodge, later but still classical. Perhaps one should rather say it was made for Mount Stuart's owner, Bute. In among the formal, even pretentious swags, nestle little naturalistic carvings which neatly subvert the whole. A beetle feeds on the acanthus leaves. A pair of mice flirt in a swirl of foliage. A squirrel shins up some formalised berries.

Bute commissioned from Lonsdale a re-working of an old theme from Cardiff, Castell Coch and Mount Stuart in a style better suited to the neoclassical villa. On the curved wall behind the dome of the entrance hall he placed re-workings of the three Fates. Giles Worsley suggests they are 'portentously entitled *Birth, Life and Death*',[29] and indeed they do reflect Bute's concern with the cycle of life. The original sketches show these to be closely based on Nicholls's fireplace at Castell Coch, and like Nicholls, Lonsdale uses the Greek form of their names. Clotho is dressed in yellow, mantled in spring green, and spins a golden thread. She is very slim and youthful, backed by apple blossom and misty purple hills. Lachesis is a woman in her middle years, with a full but not heavy figure; her old-gold gown has roses in wreaths and her mantle is rose pink. She holds sceptre and orb and the gold thread crosses her knee. She is crowned, and the apples ripen in the tree behind her, and parrots, doves and finches frolic, and lilies bloom. Atropos is by far the strongest of the figures, and the furthest removed from Nicholls. His Death is merely a stern older woman. Lonsdale's has her face barely visible behind a black veil in black robes. She is almost skeletal, a figure of mystery and terror. Behind her is a broken tree with brown leaves while the hillsides behind her are snow-covered. Above the Fates, Lonsdale threw a re-working of the ceiling of the Great Hall at Mount Stuart, this time painting in ghostly white the figures of the constellations behind their stars, and adding mythological concepts like the moon goddess in her chariot, the beautiful globe balanced in her hand. St John's Lodge inspired changes at Mount Stuart, to which Bute had similar figures added.[30]

Schultz designed a chapel and a theological library contained in an extension. The young John, the Earl of Dumfries, had as his patron John the Baptist. He had been baptised on 22 June, the day before the Eve of St John and it was this John who was the patron saint at St John's Lodge. Schultz was constructing a semi-underground chapel dedicated to him in the garden. Bute, returning from Egypt, plainly did not blame Schultz for the delay in building the chapel, for from now on, meetings, entertainments, and trips with him were a regular part of

Bute's life. As Stamp suggests, Schultz, with his education, charm and energy, provided something which had been missing since the death of the great William Burges.[31]

Towards the end of July the Butes returned to Falkland, and spent a happy and relaxed summer entertaining friends. They lived quietly, and their house parties rarely included the wealthy and landed, or indeed, the politically active. The first visitor in the summer was Fr Hayden, SJ, who had been taking a retreat for nuns[32] in the home of another Scots Catholic family, the Steuarts, at Ballechin House, near Pitlochry, Perthshire, and came to Falkland to act as chaplain for the family for a few days:

> He gives us a long account of the psychical disturbances at Ballechin, noise between his bed & the ceiling like continuous xplosion of petards, so that he cd. not hear himself speak, etc etc.

Their next visitors were the Huggins, and Bute threw them together with Fr Hayden as much as possible, to get a scientific viewpoint on the 'psychical noises'.[33] Mr Huggins very sensibly suggested the use of a phonograph to ascertain the objective reality of the noises. The owner, however, refused to allow this.[34]

Both Bute's architects were regular visitors, and on one occasion Kinross brought Julian Marshall, an expert on the game of real tennis,[35] since there was a remarkable tennis court surviving at Falkland. Marshall fired Bute's imagination to some degree, though as with lawn tennis, one suspects it was a bit of an uphill job.[36]

Angela and her husband also came to spend time, and, rather less pleasantly, the new organist from the church at Cumnock. Replacing both priest and organist had not solved the difficulties there. The constant friction suggests very strongly that the problems were not caused by either, but by the actual situation.

September was spent in Cardiff, where there was another Eisteddfod. Bute delivered, in Welsh, what he later referred to as 'my failure of a speech'.[37] It is the least focused of any extant work by him, and meanders through history and philosophy, without any clear point of departure or arrival. It is so unusual in him to have written a speech which loses its sense of direction that one looks for a cause, which may have been the death of Lady Elizabeth Moore, aged eighty-eight, at the start of the month:

> Afterwards heard that Ly. Eliz. Moore died this day, rather suddenly . . . She has been a great friend of my Mother's, & a second

mother to me, & I am ever grateful to her for her defence of me agst. Gen. Stuart & others in 1860.[38]

General Stuart himself died just two days later. Bute pondered on this:

The coincidence of the death of Gen. Stuart – she died on the Tuesday, he on the Wednesday – was most striking. I hardly see how they can not have anything to do with one another. I get more and more sceptical as to the existence of any such thing as pure accident. I know no theory that would account for it except astrology – which would do so by the theory of certain aspects between points in their nativities and directions (probably of ♄) [Saturn] which has brought them into collision at points during life and produced a coincidence in time of death.[39]

It is not perhaps surprising that for the next two months Bute felt 'a sense of utter uselessness like the influenza'.[40] Despite this he carried on the remorseless round of entertaining his role brought with it, though his patience was not much improved, at any rate in private:

Lord Randolph Churchill, Ld. Wimborne, G. T. Clark, Sir W. T. C. &c. to lunch. Lord R. seemed to me ill-informed, ill-mannered & stupid. I used to know him slightly at Oxford & thought little of him. I wonder whether his wife writes his speeches.[41]

More cheerfully, the excavations at Greyfriars in his great park were having some success:

In the afternoon with Mr Fowler at Blackfriars – (says we did not excavate deep enough – he has found the bones of the Bp. & metal work of his coffin, the only instance of a coffin in the whole place . . .)[42]

His old friend the Bishop of Galloway was dying. Bute went to see him 'in bed, looking very ill . . . he thanked me for what I had done for his diocese, etc, as though considering it likely he might never see me again'.[43] When he wrote up the year in his diary, Bute remembered the 'chief event' as Lady Elizabeth's death. With the benefit of greater hindsight, it was in fact his election as the Rector of St Andrews University.

That Bute allowed himself to be put forward for election at all was a sign of his growing confidence both in public attitudes to Catholicism, and in his own abilities. He had been deeply and personally wounded by the stramash at Glasgow University when he was proposed as rector there in 1883. Attitudes were changing, but when he was again approached by the students of Glasgow University in 1892, he refused to stand. This was in fact to avoid controversy, but he made an excuse of pressure of work. It was only half an excuse.

It was largely by his own desire he was involved in so many projects: literary, architectural, business, and family commitments. Yet he could not just drop them. In every case the lives and livelihoods of others were involved. He had researchers whom he funded working on his intellectual projects. His architectural works employed a team of architects, artists, woodworkers, builders and labourers. In the two years dating from this time, Bute spent over forty thousand pounds on capital building projects.[44] All this money was spent on wages and materials. As his comment on the lavish expenditure of Charles I on his coronation shows, the wealth spread down: 'the general result of expenditure must have been to transfer the wealth of the entertained to the working class by whom the entertainments were prepared'.[45] His academic researches were all published and the *Scottish* rolled off the presses in Paisley each quarter. Bute took his obligations to his printers seriously. In 1898, when *The Art and Book Company* had done a rushed printing job for him, Bute organised a treat for them: a day in the Malverns with transport provided, and a lavish picnic and games.[46] He took time to read to and walk with his children, to teach them to swim, and to serve at Mass, and to share in his pleasures; this was both a moral obligation and a delight to him. The fact he never had to do his own washing, or cooking, did not stop his time being taken up from morning to night. He therefore refused Glasgow, but when St Andrews asked him to be its Rector, he was interested.

Bute had an affection for the little town which went back to his childhood, when he had bathed in the breakers of the West Sands. The University was still faced with possible extinction. There were two interrelated challenges, and it had failed to rise to either of them. The private revenues of the University were derived from its agricultural lands. Financial returns from agriculture slumped in the mid-Victorian period, leaving St Andrews unable to fund bursaries, or found new chairs, or do any work which needed money. The other Scots universities relied on getting undergraduates from the towns which enclosed them, and St Andrews town was tiny. The only nearby urban centre was Dundee. Dundee was an ancient town where new wealth was created due to a sudden surge in demand for the jute spun there. All the worst horrors of the Industrial Revolution were to be found in Dundee: overcrowded housing, poor pay, and mothers leaving their babies in indifferent care to work long hours in the mills, with a correspondingly high level of infant mortality. Yet the Scots working class had always hungered for education, and to 'better themselves'. Dundee was no exception.

Nothing could be achieved without substantial monies. The Baxter family were the heirs of the biggest and wealthiest mill owner of Dundee. At a public meeting in 1872, Dr John Boyd Baxter told a meeting of the Directors of the High School in Dundee that he could place at the head of a subscription list for a college in Dundee the sum of £125,000. This was, in fact, offered by his maiden and elderly sister, Mary Ann Baxter.[47] Dundee College was started, and within a few years had an able Principal in William Peterson.[48] Once the Tay Bridge was built (in the 1870s) St Andrews was an easy commute from Dundee. New Universities were being built in England (London, Durham, Manchester, Birmingham) but with St Andrews so near, the government would not consider upgrading Dundee College. The way forward therefore lay in a relationship with St Andrews. The question was, of what kind. Should Dundee be a subordinate to St Andrews, or should it be equal? Should it only teach subjects not taught in St Andrews or should it, for the sake of convenience, permit duplication, and if so, how much?

The formal connection between Dundee and St Andrews appeared to be finally resolved by the University Commissioners in 1889. It was a solution to the problem which was very definitely favourable to Dundee:

> When the University Commissioners began their work, they remitted the final agreement between the university and the college to University Court and the College Council, and, after labour, these two bodies eventually produced a scheme of 'affiliation'. It was not a very tidy scheme, and its critics were entitled to argue that, under it, Dundee retained substantial independence, while acquiring a formidable interest in the control of the university.[49]

This was how things stood when, in 1892, Bute was elected Rector, fully resolved to do as little as was reasonably proper in the role, and to allow his 'assessor', an official appointed by him, to do most of the donkey-work on his behalf.

> In that position it will be my endeavour to do what I can to serve them, but I am only able to take it on the understanding that the

duties required are very light, as there are so many things I am obliged to do, and I have to make so many journeys (sometimes abroad for health's sake) that I cannot foresee attending as often as I, and I fear, they, would desire.[50]

This was exactly what was expected of a Rector.[51] He appointed Metcalfe as his assessor. He plainly hoped Metcalfe's academic credentials (he was a doctor of divinity) and his Protestantism (he was the Church of Scotland minister of Paisley South) would make good anything he himself lacked.

However, almost at once Bute became alarmed by 'certain proposals wh. seemed to us to saddle St. A. with all the liabilities of Dundee, and enable Dundee to alienate the endowments of St. A.'.[52] He was also worried that Dundee had approximately equal power on the Court (that is the administrative governing body of the University) which he chaired ex officio. St Andrews had always been strongest in the arts subjects, but these were being duplicated in Dundee, while Dundee claimed medical subjects as its own, bitterly opposing any proposal to strengthen St Andrews' provision in this area. Famously, Professor Heddle of St Andrews had announced in 1876 that the choice was 'Dundee or death'.[53] Bute had heard Rosebery speak of the possibility of transferring St Andrews to Dundee, and he saw with alarm that many of the proposals before the Court were tending in that direction. Bute heard very credible, and, to him, disquieting reports that Dundee's Principal, Peterson, had plans for St Andrews which included turning the college of St Mary's into a teacher-training college.[54] Naturally many members of the University were opposed to that, but they lacked organisation. They found a man prepared to take the helm in their Rector. He threw himself into the fight with an energy and a dedication which none could have predicted, and which totally transformed the role expected of him.

The Principal of St Andrews, James Donaldson, suddenly found that instead of having a governing body obedient to him, he had a full-scale mutiny on his hands. He was furious, and made his bitter complaints known. Bute had, he said, 'unfortunately' fallen into the hands of a small clique of churchmen and Tories who had 'poisoned his mind' and Bute 'had not been able to see through them'.[55] In fact a large number of the teaching staff at St Andrews and a majority of the students, as Southgate admits,[56] had been unhappy with the course events were taking. Bute had at first quite liked Donaldson and felt he listened to his (Bute's) schemes with interest.[57]

Members of the United College Dundee opposed Bute, as it was in their interests to make Dundee the only centre for the study of science and medicine. Members of St Andrews teaching staff also had Dundee links. Professor William Knight, the Professor of Moral Philosophy at St Andrews, had been born and lived in Dundee, and it is understandable that his sympathies lay there. The antagonism between Donaldson and Bute takes more explanation. Donaldson had been a member of the council of Dundee College in its early days, and as Hunter Blair comments 'had come to know the businessmen who were its prime movers'.[58] Bute came to believe that Donaldson felt he and his wife would have a wider social and intellectual sphere if the University moved to Dundee.[59] In his turn, Donaldson was utterly thrown that Bute, a Roman Catholic, should speak openly against aspects of his church ('certain prelates' and the Inquisition).[60] He was equally astonished by Bute's habitual refusal to make intellectual differences into personal animosity. On his side, Bute did not understand Donaldson's suave weighing of words, and caution in the public arena.

During this period, Donaldson was confiding his negative impressions of Bute to Bute's supposed friend, the man who had stood him up as best man the night before his wedding, Archibald Primrose, Lord Rosebery, who was on the very eve of taking the premiership from Gladstone (who resigned when his Home Rule Bill for Ireland was defeated in 1894). If there is something more distasteful than both sides of this conflict writing confidentially to the same man, then that something must be the tone of Donaldson's letters. Donaldson had been writing to Rosebery for more than ten years, and their correspondence, though lengthy, had never developed the casual and often intimate tone that Bute's correspondents soon adopted. Instead, Donaldson favoured the downright obsequious. Had Bute been told by anyone, even his wife, that 'your own noble and loveable nature comes out more & more, whenever people have a chance of knowing you'[61] he would at once have remonstrated, or more likely, laughed. Primrose tolerated, even expected it. No wonder that when Bute found out that the students called Donaldson 'Slimy Jemmie', he at once adopted it as his private designation of the Principal, which, if it came to his ears (and Bute was not notably discreet) must have enraged Donaldson.

Bute was installed as Rector in the October of 1893, wearing a gown and hood of his own design, along mediaeval lines. He had some doubts about it himself, 'students assembled to see me pass, cheered, & didn't laugh, so suppose it was impressive, & not grotesque'[62] and Donaldson thought 'he looked very queer with his hood covering his head, as he walked one day through the quadrangle of United College'.[63] He had a photographer come to take his photograph in it on a day when he was feeling very ill with a cold, and suffering his inevitable reaction to having just given a public address. As a positive image of a great and very lively man, the photograph cannot be said to be a success. But his speech had been; even Donaldson had to admit it. It was interesting, light-hearted, learned, had a reasonable number of appropriate jokes, and had been well delivered.

He knew what his opponents were already saying of him, and he used his address to fire a warning shot at them, saying of Peter de Luna, the antipope who had founded the University:

> The more usual charge against him is pig-headed obstinacy. But pig-headed obstinacy is an expression which may be only an abusive term for what others call an unflinching and self-sacrificing devotion to duty.[64]

Those who had called Bute obstinate could reflect he was so only from a sense of duty. He spoke of the gentleness of the Scots Reformers, those ever-powerful and unseen presences in the old grey town, and pointed out that it was commonly the case that countrymen were alike in taste and practice even when they sincerely held different beliefs. He ended by committing himself to a continuing future for the University:

> In the present there are 'fightings within and fears without'. Yet perhaps a voice, however feeble, which speaks here of the past, may aspire to do a little both for the present and for the future, worthy of a noble past.
>
> I pray that some of the words [St Andrew] heard uttered . . . may be realized here . . . 'the rain descended, and the floods came, and the winds blew, and beat upon that house; and it fell not: for it was founded upon a rock.'[65]

Donaldson railed that Bute was in the hands of 'low friends'[66] who were 'reactionary and retrograde'.[67] The facts do not really bear this out. Donaldson has a high reputation: Cant sees him as a humanist, 'shrewd, patient, farsighted'[68] and Southgate as statesmanlike,[69] and this is true of his behaviour, but says little about the aims he worked for. Bute is seen as the villain of the piece, who 'determined that the Rector should once more be the dominant figure in the University'[70] for reasons related to his love of the mediaeval and a liking for personal power. As we have seen, Bute himself when elected was resolved on the exact opposite.

Southgate, in his account of the struggle of Dundee University, which he himself admits is very far from impartial, says that Bute was inspired by contempt for Dundee. This is based largely on the assessment of Bute's motives by those who did not desire to do justice to him, and partly on his use of 'plutocracy' to describe the elite of Dundee, and the word 'abortion'[71] to describe Dundee college. By 'abortion', in this period, Bute meant that that the college was stillborn, or rather, that it was dying before ever being fully formed. This was his response to the presentation of attendance figures by Peterson which were, to say the least, creatively manipulated. Overmuch of the understanding of the fight over St Andrews has been drawn from *The Dundee Advertiser* an invariably partisan and sometimes hysterical[72] witness. The *Advertiser* was owned by John Leng,[73] the Liberal Member of Parliament and one of the governors of United College, Dundee.

Southgate confidently asserts that Bute wished Dundee College 'banished to outer darkness, or failing that a twilight zone'.[74] He brings forward not a shred of evidence to justify this opinion. In fact, Bute was (as we shall see) very happy to have Dundee as part of St Andrews University as long as the tail did not wag the dog. It is as convincing to argue Peterson himself was more responsible for the troubles than Bute and that he had manipulated 'the archaic authorities of the Fifeshire University to sign an agreement all in favour of Dundee'.[75] He fought hard, and by no means cleanly, to keep that advantage, which could only be retained by progressively draining St Andrews of students and prestige. The actual numbers of students at Dundee who intended sitting anything like a full course were very low. It is fair to show, as Southgate does, that the numbers graduating were artificially depressed by the fact that St Andrews did not recognise many of its classes.[76] It is not fair to assume that Bute was insincere in seeking to protect impecunious students at St Andrews. The plight of the middle-class poor – the gifted sons and daughters of clerks, the orphans of solicitors and doctors – was acute, as Bute knew too well. In none of his private and unpublished papers does Bute suggest any dislike to the town of Dundee or its ordinary people. It is true that he came to have a great personal dislike of Peterson and Knight, but then they disliked him equally.

Bute's party was the 'Conservative, Church and St. A. party' whereas Donaldson belonged to the 'Radical, Secularist and D[undee] party'.[77] There, however, the similarities between Donaldson's claims and the facts end. Bute and his party felt that the only way for a Victorian University to grow and to prosper was to have a broad curriculum, including science, and, preferably law. It was also this party who were the staunchest supporters of education for women, not just in the field of the arts, but science and medicine. The battle for the education of women had to some measure been won by this period, and St Andrews had been granting a degree of sorts to them for some time. Bute went further and wanted to see as many women as possible enrolled to study medicine at St Andrews. Not only did students pay fees, they also paid for their degrees. One obvious way to strengthen St Andrews was to get more money by granting more degrees. Bute began exploring the possibility of offering graduation to some of Dr Jex Blake's medical school in Edinburgh, and discussing with her how best to attract female medical undergraduates to St Andrews.

Dr Sophia Jex Blake[78] was the second British woman to become a doctor of medicine, and she only achieved this in the face of overwhelming hostility and obstruction. She had founded her own medical school in Edinburgh, for women only.[79] Her school provided first-rate education, delivered by lecturers who taught at Edinburgh University, but it was not itself a university, and her students needed to graduate. Bute, who as Rector was chairman of the Senate, persuaded St Andrews to recognise the lectures given there, so that her students could graduate through St Andrews University.[80] He went further than this, greatly aided by a bursary granted by Sir William Taylor Thompson. Monies were set aside for both sexes, and specific bursaries aimed to allow women to qualify as doctors.[81] Bute always had supported female education, female employment, and women in the professions. However a pressing need was driving him at this point: to expand St Andrews University to make it viable. He saw that a significant number of women wanted to study medicine in a sympathetic environment, and there was a pool to be tapped in favour of St Andrews. In return he wanted to ensure that women got the education they deserved. St Andrews could never provide the later years of the course, as the town was not big enough to support the general hospital needed for the clinical years of the degree. Dundee was, and this added to claims that it was the best place for the whole medical degree.

Bute was (and still is) attacked as a mediaevaliser who was foolish to want to restore an outdated curriculum in which medicine and law played a part. In fact he was a moderniser. He saw that a modern university could not survive on a curriculum of English, Latin, Greek, modern languages, philosophy and theology. It simply would not attract sufficient numbers. What was needed was to add science, and that meant providing at least the first two years of medicine. Southgate admits that the two years of theoretical background to a medical degree (the *anni medici*) were 'important'[82] to St Andrews. In fact, there was no prospect at all of supporting science in the University without them.[83] It was the numbers of those studying medicine that supported science teaching.

It must at once be said that Bute thought Universities should be 'a place of learning, and not a machine for grinding out graduates and he deplored the tendency to see it merely as a means to the end of a career'.[84] The key word is 'merely'. He understood and sympathised with the desire to earn a living. All those begging letters brought home to him just how essential for happiness and survival this was. The point was that study should be aimed at developing a rounded and developed mind as well. Many of his contemporaries at once recognised him as the modern man he was. A. K. H. Boyd[85] was astonished when he passed a gate and Bute 'in homely tweed' came running two hundred yards down the road to catch up with him: 'I could not but say, gazing on the panting Marquess, and thinking of the unbending, unhurried father, The world is surely coming to an end.' He was only reassured when Bute reappeared for a formal dinner with his order of the Thistle gleaming on his breast, looking as 'the eminent architect and antiquarian . . . ought to do'.[86] Bute took people by surprise.

By March, Bute was disenchanted with the St Andrews University Court, who were 'much worse behaved that the Cardiff Town council';[87] he was beginning to identify in Donaldson a man who was prepared to fight him to the last ditch. At the end of the year, Bute reflected on how much the fighting in St Andrews had cost him.

> The past year has been mainly occupied by slaving for SXA. As Metcalfe says, the people are not worth working for, but the place is. If I had foreseen it, I hardly think that I should have undertaken it, but if I had not, I do not know who else wd. The correspondence alone has been frightful, & men like Thornton & Peterson almost impossible to get on with. Even as it is, things are not so bad as they wd. have been, and I may yet be able to save the House of the Apostle.[88]

The year had not in fact been wholly given over to St Andrews. While working at St Andrews, he made his base in Falkland, and work there was making great progress, benefiting from being under his watchful eye. *The Fife News* gives a rare eyewitness account of Bute at work on architecture:

> Restoration of the Palace. Work in and around this ancient pile is going steadily forward. The Marquis, during his visit, has had placed in a niche over the entrance a shield on which a coat of arms is

represented. Two spaces in the adjoining towers are, we believe, to be likewise filled. Lord Bute, in the quiet way indicative of strength and knowledge, moves about and sees if the whole work has been carried out to his mind.[89]

This year, the focus of attention was the Chapel Royal. This was a genuine work of restoration, at any rate as regards its paintings and furnishings.

In the afternoon to the Palace, whence with Major Wood to the Manse (à propos of Scriptural inscription wh. has been discovered among the nearly obliterated decorations on the N. side of the Chapel Royal.) The minister displayed quite startling ignorance of the history of Protestant versions & then of the ancient languages & the text in them.[90]

Fragments of 'the King's Bench' had been discovered in excavating the cellars, and these had been 'worked into a restored approximation'[91] of the original. It was not a close enough approximation for Bute: 'Vexed to find Royal pew has been beautifully made in oak, as dare not paint this, & had intended deal, coarsely painted like original.'[92] The screen by the entrance only needed restoration, and the ceiling, a beautiful original, was 'rehung on metal beams to ensure its long term stability'.[93] Missing sections were restored and painted so that it was possible to see the difference between new and old, yet the whole, seen from below, made an artistic unity. Excitingly, the original wall-painting survived in enough detail to allow its restoration, which Charlie Campbell was drafted in to do.[94] This wall is in fact a 'blind' wall, facing a corridor, and to give the room symmetry, it had been painted with *trompe l'oeil* windows echoing the real one opposite. In the years since, the actual windows had been changed, but the illusory ones allowed them to be restored to their seventeenth-century forms.

Falkland was not the only Bute building that John Kinross had on hand. As soon as Bute became interested in a place, he bought a historic building there. He had added to his collection 'The Priory' at St Andrews, a Georgian house built on the site of the eponymous Cathedral building, with some of the ruin in its grounds, and built over other parts of it. Bute was ever the archaeologist, and with Kinross having a thoroughly scholarly interest in the same subject, excavations began on the site almost at once, and as Mays indicates, the two men brought infinitely more knowledge, research and expertise to the excavation than had been available to the Cathedral site, in its widest sense, ever before.[95] There were interesting finds of carved heads (a Virgin and an *Ecce Homo* head of Christ) found in the Pends passage. From the Refectory site came rich fragments of carving which showed how beautiful the building must have been. It had been a very considerable building, 'one hundred and eighty feet by twenty eight feet'.[96] Over the next five years, Kinross carried out further excavations and a reconstruction of the crypt under the Refectory, introducing iron supports into existing pillars and building new work in the red sandstone which was easily worked, and avoided misleading as to what was original and what Victorian construction. It was exacting work carried out to Kinross's high standards. Bute let the Georgian villa to a Mr Logan, who took a keen interest in the building.

It seems likely that the gossip was correct, and if things had gone Bute's way, this villa might have become the centre of a reborn Blairs. This idea had undergone considerable change, and he now envisaged the seminary pursuing its usual activities, while its students benefited from appropriate classes at the University. Unfortunately, the Catholic church had just cut the first turf[97] for a new enlarged Blairs. They were reluctant to abandon this expensive project, and Bute was quite clear that Blairs should move bodily, and its students should matriculate as members of the University. The advantage to them would be proper academic study, and to the University a great increase in numbers. There now arose a complicated row over who had said what to whom when, involving Professor Knight, who, it appears, felt that if the college did come, then it should be affiliated exactly as Dundee was: that Blairs should remain where it was, and have its courses (as it would be called today) 'validated' by St Andrews. There would be a financial advantage for the University, almost no change in the education at Blairs, and it would provide another college to vote against St Andrews, which would increasingly be merely one college among many. This was the opposite of what Bute wanted. In addition, the very discussion produced the inevitable visceral sectarian response in many.

Bute's modified idea was not as bizarre as it sounds at first. It would not have raised as many hackles as a plan to 'Catholicise' the University. Given his current relationship with his church it is doubtful if he wanted that any more. It would undoubtedly have killed two birds with one stone, and both the Catholic authorities and those of the University would have benefited: the Catholics by gaining an inexpensive and excellent basic education upon which to build their own theological studies, and the University by a sudden influx of seventy students. What is more, it is likely that a number of upper-class Catholic young men would have joined them, not as ordinands, but as lodgers who would attend their services and some of their subjects. The English hierarchy were still pressing Catholic parents to have those sons who would be sent away to Public School educated at a denominational school and Bute was not moved by the pleas of Br Oswald to send them to Fort Augustus where:

> Our community has greatly increased of late, and I think the teaching staff is on the whole as good as could be desired. And one advantage of a small school like ours is that it is much easier (as we have often found) to consult the special wishes of parents as to special branches of study which they desire to be followed.[98]

All three of the Bute boys were still being taught by tutors. It was late for their eldest, John, known in the family as 'Nohn' and now aged twelve, to be home-tutored, but he struggled with academic work. His tutor described him as 'painfully slow'[99] and reported that he was only just beginning to read for pleasure. His brother Ninian, two years younger, kept up with him with ease. Given the disability of Gwen's brother, this must have given the family anxiety. Bute dearly loved all his children, who continued to play an important part in his life. In April, his youngest reached his landmark seventh birthday, and 'Dear Colum was put into boy's clothes. It is very sad to have no longer a little child.' It was more cheerful to record that 'Nohn served mass (along with me) for the 1st time to-day.'[100] Nohn made his first confession in June, in London, and his first communion on his birthday. After that the family went to Mount Stuart where Bute tried, and failed, to pass on his love of bathing in the icy Scottish sea.[101]

Most of the summer was spent at Mount Stuart. Bute was planning extensive landscaping of the garden. Many years before, Mr Pitman had explained to a bemused landscape gardener that there was very little point in his seeking employment from Lord Bute as 'it was more likely that his Lordship would plan and superintend the laying out of the grounds himself'.[102] He had been doing this with, tradition suggests, the involvement of Margaret. They had picked rhododendrons of such numerous varieties that there would always be one in flower at Mount Stuart (as there is now). He had also laid plans for two lakes, the water from one falling into the other. The ultimate plan was to have an open country walk with the Stations of the Cross on the wayside. The walker would start at the sea and finally reach 'Calvary' by the topmost lake. In Bute's absence, someone had planted 'rows of potatoes and carrots'[103] where he wanted rhododendrons. According to Bute 'next to nothing had been done'[104] (according to Gwen, 'nothing') for the plans for a lake. She was astonished that he took it as 'calmly as he does but he is anything but pleased, only it is a sort of hopeless feeling which comes over one'.[105] She added, feelingly, 'Of course it is very irritating when there are so few things he takes an interest in that when there is something he wants particularly it cannot be done.' This is an odd statement, considering the passion of Bute's commitment to so many projects from building to writing and publishing, and to his children. Jack Stuart, Bute's factor, responded by coming out, and an afternoon was spent in waterproofs in the garden with the gardener. One presumes that the factor was rather better at getting his commands obeyed than Bute himself.[106]

Christmas was spent there, too. It was an exceptionally happy one, though Bute had 'a sort of presentiment that this has been in some sense or other a last Xtmas. – wh God advert in any evil sense'.[107] There was a good sense in which this might be a last Christmas, for, now aged eighteen, Margaret was at last coming out. It is difficult today to imagine the huge contrast that there was for a girl, and indeed her parents, in the Victorian era between being 'in the school room' and 'out'. The Butes were much more liberal parents than many, and Margaret had for a long time enjoyed freedoms and adult privileges not invariably given to others. She had usually dined with her parents for some time, had travelled extensively, and read widely. Now, however, she was free of the controlling hand of a governess, and as soon as the London season arrived in April she went to be presented at a 'Drawing Room'. All the débutantes of the season travelled in court dress, their three 'Prince of Wales' ostrich feathers set in their hair, shivering in their thin white dresses, as their carriages trundled in a queue up to Buckingham Palace. Once inside, each in turn was presented by her mother, or by another senior lady who had herself been presented in her youth, either to the Queen or to her deputy.

It was the high point of the season, and the defining rite of passage for any female of the aristocracy. Therefore when Margaret's turn came on 10 May, there were 'divers people, some of whom to luncheon, to see them off & back at tea'. One of those gathered on this day of heavy showers of rain was Hunter Blair:

> I remember once admiring Lord Bute's state-coach, blazing with innumerable quarterings, standing outside the 'silver door' (so it was commonly called though it was really made of block tin) of his house in Regent's Park. I stood at the entrance with the secretary and comptroller, as my lady drove off in state with her daughter to St James's Palace. As the bedizened coach drove away, a sudden

torrent of summer rain came thrashing down 'there goes a hundred pounds!' groaned Mr A[nderson], as he thought of the drenching and destruction of the gold-laced and embroidered liveries worn by the unsheltered menials.[108]

A photograph also survives. Gwen looks truly lovely in her sculpted court dress, still as slender as a girl, and as graceful. She also looks unbelievably miserable. Margaret, equally resplendent, is bulky and ungainly. She has her father's height, and her father's broad-shouldered, strong physique, and, perhaps due to lack of exercise, is a physical heavyweight, much younger than he was when he became so. It still seemed inevitable that a young woman should be a social animal. Such animals were as prized for their slender beauty as today's 'celebrities' are. Margaret had the attributes to make a splendid career woman, but such a path was unthinkable even for the unconventional Butes. She did not have the physical qualities necessary to excite social admiration. It did not mean, of course, that she would not enjoy herself in other ways.

It was inevitably a season of firsts for her: her first ball, her first opera (by her request *Gli Ugonotti*, as that had been her father's first), and her first fast, before her confirmation, Whitsunday.[109] Bute accompanied his wife and daughter to social occasions, grumbling that it was 'ridiculous' that he was required to wear 'a dress like a General's' to the Court ball because he was Lord Lieutenant of his county.[110] Convention demanded Bute throw a ball, which took place in the grand ballroom at St John's Lodge, where Bute had commissioned stained-glass windows from Nathaniel Westlake depicting Salome's dance for John the Baptist's head. A splendid piece of iconography indeed, combining the themes of dance and St John the Baptist, titular saint of the building, but perhaps slightly ill-omened for the whirling dancers in the room. Outside, Bute arranged for the gardens to be lit by electric light. It is not surprising that the night was 'very successful'.[111]

Although the work for St Andrews had replaced his usual academic study, calmer family pleasures remained. On Sundays they liked to walk to Hyde Park Corner to hear the orators. They often went on to the Zoological Gardens where Bute was a regular visitor. He soon came to know the names of the keepers, and learned and recorded their opinions on many matters from the language of monkeys to the identification of the little rodents he and Margaret had seen in the desert ('Gebelles').[112]

The climax of the worry over St Andrews that year, for him anyhow, was when he spoke on the appeal against the agreement joining the

University and United College Dundee in the House of Lords. He always disliked public speaking, and despite his official support for the Tory party, this was his first ever speech.

> There were only 2 or 3 Peers present, but I was so nervous that I don't know what I said. However, Ld Windsor told me that I was perfectly smooth and lucid, so I suppose that I repeated mechanically the few sentences I had prepared.[113]

Bute and Metcalfe had decided to make this appeal against the agreement claiming it was not legally valid. The speech in the Lords marked the height of the dispute; tempers were rising, and both sides were starting to behave badly. Bute was not an impartial chairman, as he had been an impartial Mayor. He was stage-managing the University Court as much as he could. He provided arguments, wrote letters, and rallied support. Peterson and his supporters came to meetings again and again to find that they were faced, not with open discussion, but formed opinions. They did the same thing, and since they controlled *The Dundee Advertiser* they used that as a wholly one-sided campaigning organ against Bute and his supporters.

Bute still found time to indulge his family. There had been no romance for Margaret during her first season. Her father now hired a steam yacht for her, the *Katomba*, so that she could indulge her passion for sailing. She was captained by Davidson, an experienced man, and Margaret took her throughout the waters of the Clyde, picking up guests, or taking her mother and father for excursions.[114] Bute made no attempt to confine his children to interests he enjoyed, and this summer for the first time Nohn went out shooting with some of Bute's guests.[115] The indoor swimming pool in the basement of the house was in operation, and he gave the boys swimming lessons there. In addition the excavation at the ancient Christian site of St Blane's monastery was well under way, and Bute summoned Mr Schultz to come and take an active part in the work.[116]

The other main summer excitement was experiments in 'crystal vision'. Bute had joined the Society for Psychical Research. During this period, scientific explanation of the world expanded. Many, faced for the first time with the unlikelihood of a historic 'Fall of Man' to explain the cruelty and evil of the world, lost faith not only in a traditional God but in a meaningful and moral world. Others, keeping their faith, sought to establish it more firmly using the investigative methods of science. Others still, beginning to be aware of the limitations of Newtonian science, sought explanations for the anomalies of the older science in the world of spirits. For all these reasons, men of science, and those interested in scientific methodology, began to investigate mental and spiritual phenomena with what they hoped were the methods of science.[117] The SPR was the child of this movement. Many of its members were distinguished scientists. Some of these were decidedly sceptical about the paranormal, for instance Lord Rayleigh[118] and John Joseph Thompson,[119] who were successive Cavendish Professors of Experimental Physics at Cambridge University and both later awarded the Nobel Prize for Physics. Others, like the far more easily convinced Frederick Myers,[120] had no scientific background. Myers was a leading member of the SPR from the beginning. As one of the two joint secretaries, and a leading light of the Society, Myers often visited Falkland, and also Mount Stuart, and became a friend of Bute's.

Myers was an energetic man, well liked, and able in many areas. He had deeply loved his cousin's wife, Annie Marshall, who committed suicide in 1876,[121] and as with so many researchers in this area, he had an intense desire to know that the beloved had survived death and was happy. This drove and distorted his investigations. He was interested in Buddhism, and also in the new field of psychology, though he 'distorted and misinterpreted the latter'.[122] In 1893–4 he submitted an article to the SPR on 'The Mechanism of Hysteria' which was the first publicity in the United Kingdom for the Breuer-Freud studies of hysteria.[123]

One of the leading areas of interest for SPR research was telepathy. Not only did it link into the study of the mind, and how far that could or could not be disassociated from the brain (still an open question in that period) but

> If it were true, after all, that men were capable of communicating in ways far beyond the range of normal sensory powers, then there was surely far more to this world than materialists could fathom, including a possible active role for soul or spirit.[124]

Hence the excitement over telepathy and means of developing it, such as the crystal ball. Bute had his cousin Evelyn Kirwan[125] staying with the family. She was particularly able at using this medium.

> Oct 2. Crystal-vision xperiments in Blue Library before dinner but failure in them after dinner, probably on account of digesting ...

> Oct 3. With E.K. to flower garden for xperiments; says the perfume of flowers is conducive, & suggested incense as possibly useful – she

did not know it is so used in Egypt. Jack Stuart came. With him &
her to the moor, where tried again. He saw a little, but she failed,
probably owing to his presence, talk, xhaustion, or digestion.

Oct 4. . . . went with E.K. to sea-shore for xperiments. She had failed
this morning while dressing (rather sleepy) & after breakfast.

Oct 5. Towards 6 to flower gdn. with E.K. & another crystal-gazing
xperiment. The visions are nearly always black & white, abt. 1 per
minute, last abt. ½ an hour, unaffected by telepathy from me, (unless
in 1 or 2 doubtful cases), or by unseen objects touched.

Oct 7. With my Lady and E.K. to kitchen garden.[126]

His friend Dr Huggins had made him a 'crystal-vision machine'.
Huggins, a fellow SPR member, had (naturally, considering his scientific
training and ability) a caution Bute lacked. When Bute reported to him
that the crystal became hot, he carefully explained that:

Before speculating as to the cause of the crystal being hotter than
the hands in which it had been grasped, I should like to see some
evidence that it is really so. In the case of a true crystal, that is quartz,
the high conducting power for heat which makes a piece of quartz,
which is at the temperature of air, feel colder to a warm hand, than a
piece of glass at the same temperature, might . . . also make a heated
crystal feel hotter to a hand slightly cooler than it really is.[127]

Bute's crystal vision, being an attempt to communicate within this
world, was not forbidden by the Roman Catholic church, which took
a Biblically dim view of séances and attempts to contact the dead.
Telepathy was a matter for which a physical explanation might be
possible. The Society were at that time investigating 'hallucinations',
which they defined as visions of something not there in actuality, but
which appear at first to be real.[128] One of the most widely believed of
all such hallucinations was second sight, as witnessed in the Highlands.
In its classic form, it was the belief that some persons had the capacity
to see visions of others who were carrying symbols of their fate – for
instance a man shortly to drown would be seen covered in fish scales.[129]
More generally the description applied to any kind of foreknowledge
based on a vision.

Peter Dewar, the minister of North Bute, was on terms of some
friendship with Bute. Dewar was a native Gaelic speaker, ministering to

a parish where there were still Gaelic-speaking residents. He met Myers through Bute, and it was agreed that this cultured man, interested in psychical matters, would be the ideal researcher. Bute made a small grant to the SPR and in 1893 Dewar was commissioned to use the monies to send out a questionnaire on the subject throughout the Western Highlands. The results were distinctly disappointing.

> Of 1900 second sight schedules issued, only 54 have as yet been returned, duly filled up. To the question is Second Sight believed in their neighbourhood, 26 return an affirmative and 28 a negative answer. But even those who reply affirmatively have not yet furnished me with any well attested *first hand* case.[130]

A new and revised circular was created with a letter from Lord Bute supporting the appeal for information. It was slightly more successful, and forty-two 'more or less affirmative'[131] replies were received. It may have been this unpromising start which made Bute lose a good deal of confidence in the minister, or simply that he felt he needed more manpower on the enquiry, but that summer he funded enquiries by a woman who had been suggested by Mr Myers in London, who published her accounts of crystal-gazing and telepathy under the irresistible pseudonym of 'Miss X'.[132]

Miss X was Ada Goodrich-Freer, one of the respectable, unmarried, impecunious women who found it so hard to make a living unless they had the money to train as a doctor, the desire to nurse, or the ability to swallow the lot of a governess. Ada Freer was born in 1857.[133] She had the good fortune to be fair and blue-eyed and to look, throughout her adult life, at least ten years younger than she was; and she found it convenient to pretend that she was the age she seemed. She also claimed to come from a 'county' family, which she did not.[134] As regards Lord Bute, the effort to impress was mistaken, for he numbered among his friends those with antecedents every bit as humble as hers, but the mask was, doubtless, more helpful with others. In 1893, at the actual age of thirty-six, but with the assumed character of a very young lady, she obtained a job as an assistant editor to W. T. Stead,[135] whose spiritualist magazine *Borderland* did not attempt the analytical stance of the SPR, which Miss Freer had joined in 1888. It was her desire for respectable anonymity that gave her the delicious soubriquet of 'Miss X', which she was honest enough to admit was a distinct literary advantage to her.

In their furious and vitriolic book *Strange Things*, John Campbell and, especially, Trevor Hall, make a thorough job of demolishing every shred of credibility that Miss Freer possesses. As this present study will show, Hall missed the one final nail in this coffin, through no fault of his own. Yet there is something distasteful about the way in which every possible piece of gossip that could be to her disfavour is piled up. It is quite irrelevant to the case in question that she may have been a lesbian, for which the only evidence is her deep friendship with Miss Constance Moore, with whom she set up house for a number of years, as indeed single ladies in need of financial support and respectability sometimes did, offering mutual chaperonage. The fact that she may, or may not, have been a sado-masochist is equally irrelevant to her honesty and psychical powers.

Of course, driven by financial hardship a lesbian sado-masochist might have become a gentleman's mistress, and might have even have been bisexual and have been in love with the gentleman, as it is alleged Ada Freer was with Frederic Myers. What really beggars belief is that, in the period in question, a gentleman would introduce his mistress to his mother, and that the former should stay at the mother's house in order to write.[136] To suggest such a thing reveals a deep ignorance about the conventions and values of Victorian society. Ada Freer was ambitious and desirous of earning a reasonable living. She worked for Stead, but had reservations about him, as many employees do about their bosses (*pace* Campbell and Hall). She was clever, and universally agreed to be charming.

She approached Bute cautiously and humbly, referring to doubts about her own 'fitness for the task',[137] and asking for a face-to-face meeting. He mentioned meeting her on 30 May, but was much more concerned with taking Metcalfe to the zoo and giving a dinner to the Donaldsons. Neither Miss Freer nor the enquiry into second sight was especially high in the priorities of this busy man. During the summer this changed to some degree. Bute was especially susceptible to certain seductions: laughter, comradeship and frequent and news-filled letters among them. It appears, on any reading of Miss Freer's abilities and motives, that she was singularly well-equipped to supply just these things. John Campbell catalogues with exasperation how Miss Freer succeeded in manoeuvring Peter Dewar out of the enquiry. He was in every point better suited to undertake the work, most especially in that he had the Gaelic. Nonetheless, on Bute's own showing, by the time Miss Freer returned to the Scottish mainland she had started to win his ear.

She visited Bute in London in November and was 'very entertaining abt. her Scotch journey',[138] and gave him in person her impressions of Falkland and St Andrews. A week or so later at Falkland, he had one of his very few personal psychic experiences: 'Heard sharp heavy steps,

which we cannot well xplain, in gallery of Chapel Royal, where Miss
Freer has experienced feeling of horror & dread.'[139] When he wrote to
his wife he had to reassure her that Miss Freer was not becoming one of
his circle of intimates: neither Gwen nor Margaret were ever charmed
by Miss Freer, nor took her claims in the psychic sphere seriously.

> Miss Freer came yesterday p.m. and I took a walk with her in the
> Zool. & the Park. Then I had to write letters hard till dinner. I am
> getting alarmed abt. Miss Swanwick, whose undoubted position in
> the nosegay (a position for wh. Miss Freer is, at the very best, only
> distinctly possible) entitles her, I think, to more attention than I have
> at this time been able to pay her.

'The nosegay' was one of those terms used as shorthand in close
families. Bute liked women, and he had long had what he called a
'nosegay of female friends who charm me'.[140] The nosegay had some
members who were very eminent in their own fields. Anna Swanwick[141]
was eighty-one years old at this time, and Bute regularly visited
her, often taking one or more of his sons. She was a distinguished
translator, a feminist and advocate of women's higher education.
When she was offered an honorary LLD from Aberdeen University,
she told Bute:

> though not personally indifferent to the honour (for as such I regard
> it) bestowed upon me by the Aberdeen University, I prize it chiefly
> as an indication of the higher position now occupied by women, as
> compared with that which they held in my younger days.
>
> I cannot but regard the higher education of women, & the greater
> influence which they exercise in the National life, as one of the most
> important results of the century which is now drawing to a close.[142]

She had assisted in the founding of Girton College and Somerville
Hall, and had published translations of Goethe, Schiller and Æschylus.
She had signed John Stuart Mill's petition for votes for women. To
Bute she was his 'beloved Swanwick'.[143] Mrs Maxwell Scott had
long been a member of the nosegay. Another regular correspondent
and 'distinguished' member was Frances Power Cobbe.[144] She, too,
was a feminist, supporting women's rights, and suffrage. Cobbe was
remarkable in this period on account of her 'female marriage' with
Mary Lloyd, the sculptor. It was only in papers found after her death
that she clearly spoke of the relationship in this way, yet it was apparent
to her contemporaries. Bute had probably become friends with her

through Felicia Skene, another nosegay member, for both women were anti-vivisectionist, as indeed was Bute. A more distant member of the nosegay had been Elizabeth Balch,[145] the American author. A new member was Dr Sophia Jex Blake, also a friend of Frances Power Cobbe, who, like her, found her most intense relationships with other women, latterly her biographer, Margaret Todd. Although Cobbe herself clearly defined her relationship with Lloyd as a marriage, Jex Blake did not attempt to define her sexuality, and in this period there was less concept of what today would be described as lesbian orientations. Nevertheless, it is remarkable how many of Bute's closest women friends had what would today be described in this way.

In other respects too, Bute had unexpected qualities, one being his lack of all anti-semitism. He numbered the wealthy Rothschilds among his friends, and the scholarly A Löwy;[146] in the course of his struggles over St Andrews, he also came to know Dr Adler, the Chief Rabbi of Great Britain.[147] Bute gave land to build a new Synagogue in Cardiff, and was astonished at the outcry against it. With his contacts, he saw how attractive it could be made to Jewish parents of modest means to send their children to St Andrews. Although he sought to keep tests of orthodox belief for those who held theological chairs, at the same time, he campaigned hard to make St Andrews a place which welcomed Jewish students. He was increasingly dreaming of a collegiate St Andrews (on the model of Oxford) where a Jewish college would be added to one for women doctors, one for Catholics, and, yes, even Queen's College Dundee. Bute made it quite plain that he had more hope for the idea of attracting Jewish students than any of the others mentioned. This would, of course, have made Dundee just one college among many, which is, it seems, most emphatically what the supporters of Dundee did not want. Failing a whole college however, he felt that a good deal of growth could be got from simply canvassing the appeal of St Andrews to Jewish students.[148]

It was his opponents, the so-called modernisers and secularists, who put all their considerable energy into ensuring that Jewish students remained unwelcome.

I need not recall to you that the attraction of Jewish students, and, were it possible, of a Jewish Coll., was one of my main designs for the strengthening of SXA – and that this design, just because it wd have such tremendous power for the purpose, has been violently opposed by Chisholm, Donaldson, Knight, Peterson, Burnett &c & Co and was the subject of the unseemly letter by Prof Meiklejohn in wh. he said rather a small group of Jewish students should have 'a comfortable berth in Abraham's bosom' than that they shd. come to SXA.[149]

The best one can say to defend Meiklejohn[150] is that wishing Jewish students dead, rather than at St Andrews, will read in a much more shocking way today than it did then. Bute is probably right that this wish sprang mainly from a desire to see numbers at St Andrews kept down. It should however act as a corrective to the view that the 'Dundee party' were modern and liberal, while Bute was prejudiced and narrow-minded. Bute responded with an outrage that was slow to die.[151]

The next summer he was moved even more deeply to fury. Following his hard work, a Jewish student was applying for admission to St Andrews. The University chose as the day for his examination, the Day of Atonement, and made difficulties about changing this to another day:

> the [Day of Atonement] is, as the Chief Rabbi feelingly wrote to me, the most solemn day in all their year. And the belief that upon that day, God, bound by His Own Word, pardons the sins of the whole year to the fasting penitent ... Anything more defiantly contemptuous of their race & religion than selecting that special one particular day for the xam can hardly be conceived – nor any device better calculated to raise aversion for SXA in the Jewish world. I fear it cannot be inadvertent.[152]

Under pressure from Bute to change the day, Donaldson moved it to the day after the Day of Atonement:

> On Donaldson's plan [the Jewish student] he was to have reached SXA – a place I suppose, strange to him, – at latest abt. noon on Friday, and there pass the D of A alone (or with 1 or 2 others at the outside) presumably in an inn. When night set in on Saturday he wd have been 26 hours without so much as a crumb or a drop of water – unwashed, barefooted, and probably dressed in grave-clothes – the mind being fixed as far as possible upon Sin, Death, and Eternity – and worn out by hours of recitation of the Hebrew prayers. Wd. he be likely in this state to do himself justice in an xam held a few hours later?[153]

Bute became convinced it was a trap to draw him, Bute, into consenting to the idea of an exam on a Sunday, thereby outraging Presbyterian views; possibly so, or just downright disrespect to the Jewish faith.

Either way, it is hardly surprising that the Jewish community did not embrace the idea of a college in a University where they were so plainly not wanted.

Feelings were still running high over the possibility of transferring Blairs to St Andrews as well. The Catholic Church did indeed look into the question in a serious way, and then turned down Bute's offer of money for the new college. There were a multiplicity of reasons for this, one probably being that Angus McDonald, now Archbishop of Edinburgh, was among those advising on the scheme, and another being that the Principal of Blairs had misrepresented Bute's ideas to the utmost extreme:

> the Duke of Norfolk gave on Monday a desperately sectarian dinner in honour of Cardinal Logue. <u>Inter Alia</u> was Stonor, titular Abp of Thessalonica & Canon of SS Saviours (the Cathedral of Rome). I found he had also heard Chisholm's statement that I wished to suppress the Scots colleges of Rome and Valladolid and the St Suplice bursaries, and to have Blairs Col., incorporated into the body of SXA. If you add these together you will observe that the sum wd. be to deprive the Scottish hierarchy of autonomy in – and indeed pretty nearly control of – the training of the clergy wh. wd then have chiefly concerned Knight, & Donaldson & co. And this throws a good deal of light on Ledochowski's saying that Propaganda, in refusing my offer, has wished to preserve the liberty of the Scottish Bps.[154]

The last thing Bute intended was handing over control of clergy training to 'secularists'; he was furious and he gave 'Stonor a piece of my mind'. The real problem, however, was the way in which the Catholic Church viewed the education of its members, lay but especially clergy. There was no concept that a mind exposed to a variety of challenges might become sharper, and a faith which was allowed to be tested might grow. Instead, as McClelland shows,[155] the widespread assumption was that any breadth in education would lead to loss of faith, and most priests and bishops wanted a cloistered training which would keep young men from all possible harm. Faced with such diametrically opposing attitudes to education, it is little surprise that Bute failed not merely to win the day, but to get his viewpoint across.

One of his biggest trials in his work on St Andrews was how often it took him away from Gwen. She had commitments to the boys, who were still educated away from school, and above all she needed to keep chaperoning Margaret. Margaret had to be taken out into society to find her own feet. She had to make female friends of her own age and class, and, hopefully, male acquaintances who might fall in love with her. She could not go anywhere in society alone, and only in society could she do these things. So Gwen was more often separated from Bute, and as the closeness of their marriage had not diminished over time, they both felt it. Here Bute arrives in London for a meeting:

> Everything very nice & ready, including the fire & hot-water in yr. dressing room, & the hot-water bottle in our bed, all of wh., especially the latter when I stretched out in the night, gave me a sense of your being away.[156]

As ever, when they were apart, he tried to ease the separation and cheer her with his most amusing writing:

> Westlake, WTL & Corbett to dinner. Dull. Westlake as usual abt. his health – pill-box fears his nervous temperament & brain activity may induce diabetes – so cdn't dine – but wd. sit at table – where I own his eating & drinking seemed to me indistinguishable from what is generally called dining.[157]

They all gathered at Mount Stuart for a happy Christmas: the usual mix of services, and of fun with the children. It was happy, even idyllic, with a 'vagabond boy'[158] who came and played the bagpipes (reminding Bute of the shepherds in Rome), the children reciting, and the usual round of services. Bute records that 'Mr McDonald came to hear confessions. Iterum me accusavi [Again I accused myself]. Turn with him. He stayed to collation. Fr McSuibhne came. 25 Communicatus sum [I communicated at Mass].'[159]

Once again Bute had a crisis of conscience at Christmas, and it is possible the two were over the same or a similar issue. The difference was that this time the bishop with whom he had had such difficulties succeeded in resolving the issue. It was to be the last unshadowed Christmas Bute was to enjoy.

The year ended in a series of gales, and Bute mourned the 'terrible'[160] destruction of trees. The Christmas holidays continued in January, with a heavy frost, and many happy curling parties, with Bute in-between times 'hard at work for SXA'.[161] The actual work would not have mattered, if Bute had not allowed himself to become so emotionally involved. As it was, he found the letters from St Andrews 'tormenting',[162] and they spoiled his enjoyment of a time with friends and family of which he was very conscious there were a limited number to come.[163] There was just one supernatural experiment during this time, when

Donald and Mrs Dewar (the minister of North Bute Parish and his wife) came to visit, and stay to dinner, and there was 'Thought-reading, apparently muscle-reading & holding the hands.'[164]

Ordinary life resumed, with a move to Dumfries House, meetings with local worthies, and tobogganing in the snow, including the 'xtraordinary descent of Mr Sch[ultz] upon, or rather, with a tea-tray'.[165] Schultz was visiting them at the time when he was working on plans to extend the two wings of Dumfries House, creating a chapel and a room to house tapestries which had come to Bute from the Dumfries wing of the family.[166] These additions were under way in 1897, and were completed after the 3rd Marquess's death. Because the original house is quite compact, these delicious rooms nearly double the footprint of the house.

While Bute was waiting for the outcome of his case in the House of Lords regarding St Andrews University, he got the final verdict rejecting his plans to move Blairs to the University, despite Bute's offer of subsidising the whole college.[167] The Bishop of Galloway was disappointed:

> I heard long ago from some person, I really forget whom, that Rome would object to any condition whatever, but I did not believe it. However it would now appear to be the case ... I am sorry, very sorry, for the adverse decision of the Propaganda. I hope it may all end well but I confess I don't see how we are to manage it.[168]

It was the Monday of Holy Week, 8 April, before news came that the test case in the House of Lords had gone the way Bute and his party desired. His anxiety had been so great that the good news left him feeling 'a little dazed'.[169] It was not the end of St Andrews business, but it would never again be so bitter or all-consuming.

15   Death Sentence

'I am gradually going down'[1]

With the worst and most anxious upheavals concerning St Andrews out of the way, Bute had time for a wider range of interests than he had enjoyed for some time. The family went to St John's Lodge for Margaret to enjoy her second season, and Bute took pleasure in fitting the house up:

> Mr Lonsdale abt. hangings in hall, with Liberty's man (very intelligent as well as obliging) Mrs B giving her advice; then Schultz & Murano glass-man as to electrical fittings, especially garlands in ball-room, & wreaths in dining room. Much advice from all abt. chapel.[2]

The garlands and wreaths must have been very fragile and do not seem to have survived, but some of the other Murano glass fittings still exist. They are electrical chandeliers designed so that the very minimal metal components are not easily seen and decorated with over-sized but naturalistic flowers. Clean, lit, and as part of a decoration of wreaths or garlands, they must have been enchantingly pretty. Bute was also arranging for a statue of St John the Baptist, by the Welsh sculptor William Goscombe John, 'at the end of the garden'.[3]

This summer, Ninian made his first confession, followed by his first communion on his twelfth birthday, and Bute gave him a watch with the family coat of arms on it, with the little crescent (showing he was the second son) picked out in diamonds.[4] Nohn celebrated his fourteenth birthday. He had a reputation in the family for being 'unfortunate', but he was always 'touchingly good'.[5] Life was very busy, happy and varied. On a typical day Bute bought an old Spanish processional cross for the altar at St John's Lodge, dealt with queries about prayer books for a cousin's marriage, had friends to lunch, and took them afterwards across the park to the Zoological Gardens:

> we all had shocks from electric eel. Remarked great intelligence in elephant in picking up & giving keeper last lady's pocket handkerchief, & female (3 years old) chimpanzee in obeying keeper's orders, & apparently counting up to 4.[6]

The Butes were having more of a normal social life than they had had in years, thanks to Margaret's 'season'. Some aspects were, of course, very boring for Bute:

> To Bot[anical] Gdn. to receive Prince & Princess of Wales: deadly dull: her beauty has passed away.[7]
> The Wilfrid Wards to dinner – superficial & pragmatic.[8]

Yet he certainly had huge fun arranging for the lighting of the garden. Frank Anderson, Bute's secretary, kept his colleague, Jack Stuart posted on all the goings on:

> Lady Bute is giving a Garden Party here on Saturday first, they thought of it during the extremely fine weather we have been having, which seems to have broken today and it is dull and very cold, I hope it will take up again by Saturday. If so it will be a very smart party, band of the Coldstreams in attendance.[9]

It remained 'cold and sunless', but the party was 'rather a success altogether'.[10] So was the ball, which followed in June.[11] No wonder. The beautiful house was set in the quiet green space of Regent's Park. Blair reported that 'a priest' could say his daily office in the open air, only occasionally disturbed by sounds from the zoo.[12]

The world was changing. 'Bicals' or 'bikes' were all the rage, and both ladies and gentlemen were riding them. Margaret had one. Typewriters were just beginning to come into more common use, though gentlefolk tended to apologise for using them for personal correspondence. Women were gaining more freedom and being less oppressively chaperoned. Lady Margaret was given a lot of freedom by her parents, taking into consideration her age and 'station in life'. Yachting remained her passion, and once again a yacht was to be hired for her, this time something bigger than the *Katomba* as she was hoping to take her father sailing in the Orkney islands, where he had not been since his boyhood. In the end, the *Christine* was hired, and a suitable skipper found, and not one of the 'Swagger Cowes Johnnies' who would not 'suit Lady Margaret or she them at all'.[13] Whoever was captain had to be able to cope with 'our folk and their extraordinary ways'.[14]

Exasperatingly, there is no further hint of what these ways are, apart from Lord Bute's changing his mind over practicalities very frequently. It is plain they did not include being overly grand, or the 'Swagger Cowes Johnnies' would have suited very well. They may definitely have included the freedom allowed to the nineteen-year-old Margaret, who was taking the train north by herself, though presumably accompanied by her maid, and sailing her own yacht from Stranraer to the Clyde. Anderson took it on himself to order wine and provisions to be sent from Dumfries House to the Isle of Bute: 'of course thinks she will manage everything all right but there are such a lot of things that she has no idea.'[15]

Margaret did indeed take her father on a sailing holiday around Orkney, and he records:

When nearing Stromness yacht struck & stuck on rock, turning somewhat over. In boat to Stromness, where supper at the Mason's Arms. Yacht came abt. 11.30. Slept on board.

> *Media vita in morte sumus*
> *Quem quaerimus adjutorem nisi Te Domine*
> *Qui pro peccatis nostris juste irasceris?*
> *Sancte Deus, Sancte fortis, sancte et misericors Salvator,*
> *Amara morti ne tradas nos!*[16]

Bute's apparent sangfroid was more ruffled than he would have chosen. The rest of the trip was happy and uneventful.

On the way home, the Butes spent a little time in St Andrews, and Bute was delighted with the progress made by Kinross in excavating the Priory, where the 'south foundations of the chapter house' had been uncovered. There was more gossip with supporters, and dinner with the Donaldsons, but the quantity of St Andrews work was less than it had been. Bute was a warm advocate for a new scheme, first proposed now, and eventually put into place. This incorporated Dundee College into St Andrews University and radically reduced the power of Dundee to transfer resources and courses to that college at the cost of St Andrews. He told Metcalfe that the Duke of Argyll

seems rather alarmed at the incorporation scheme – I wish you would write to him to point out its excellences. If it were realised, Dundee would be dead, and no other could ever arise, and we should pocket all it has or is.[17]

It was ungenerous of Bute to wish Dundee 'dead' and exactly what Bute's opponents had always suspected he wanted. Bute had finally come to believe that it was either Dundee or St Andrews, because those promoting Dundee had seen the issues in that way. However, this is the only point[18] where Bute wishes Dundee any ill at all. In the end, the struggle between the two centres of education was only resolved by the link between them being broken, and both survived. Without Bute's intervention, the University of St Andrews would have died before that time.

Bute hit upon a small experiment with the SPR to see if his visionaries and mediums could tell anything verifiable from examining human hair, very much as psychics today purport to tell significant matters about the deceased from holding objects connected to them. Might the spirit guides be able to tell if patients were alive or dead, or diagnose the conditions from which they had suffered? The advantage was that the doctor submitting the hairs, Sir Arthur Mitchell,[19] knew the answers. Some of the hair in question went to each woman: Miss Freer, Mrs Russell Davies and another medium, Katie Wingfield.[20] Miss Wingfield moved in Bute's circles, being the friend of Helen, Countess of Radnor,[21] the sister of Henry Chaplin. Bute was a long-time friend of the Radnors. Miss Wingfield had a 'spirit guide' called Semirus. On this occasion he was stumped. Miss Wingfield admitted that 'the results were not first rate' and that 'Semirus will do nothing at all if he thinks there is the least idea of a test in it.'[22] This was very prudent of Semirus, since according to Sir Arthur:

> Semirus could not easily have been more <u>out</u> than we find him in the cases of A & B . . . I could not have sent your Lordship two more strongly marked cases, & it puzzles me to know why Semirus, if he has more knowledge than the rest of us, is so costive & indecisive.

Sir Arthur knew he was naturally inclined to scepticism, but said he did try to keep an open mind.[23]

Ada Freer was also somewhat dismissive: 'I have not Miss Wingfield's ability to produce impressions at a given moment. Had I been a poet, I could not have been a laureate to write to order!'[24] Her final reading of the hair is not extant and was perhaps communicated to Bute face-to-face. Bute however recorded that 'This xperiment only partially successful with Miss W, Mrs R Davies, & Miss Freer. One thing is

evident: the sensitive cannot perceive if the patient is alive or dead.'[25]
He was not generally uncritical of the claims of mediums:

May 22. At 5, Myers . . . refused to take me to private séance to wh.
he is going, on grounds that nothing would happen if I were there.

May 23. Called on Dr Leaf [then president of the SPR]: trouble
brewing in the SPR if Myers goes on with his spiritualistic (especially
Stainton Moses) rubbish.[26]

Stainton Moses, an SPR member by then dead,[27] was a controversial
Anglican clergyman who was a renowned spiritualist and medium.
In an undated memorandum probably written in 1892 Bute discussed
the possibility that trance mediums were demonically possessed, since
their 'bodies are supposed to be entered and vocal organs used, by
spirits other than their own and of the dead'. It would, he thought,
explain Mrs Leonora Piper, a trance medium renowned for her 'spirit
writing'.[28] Her guide, Dr Phinuit, had been investigated and exposed
as a fraud by the SPR:

I used to look upon Mrs Piper as a mere impostor, but the discovery
of Dr Phinuit's non-existence now inclines me to believe in her
honesty, since, had she been a deliberate impostor, she would almost
certainly have made herself acquainted with the real facts as to some
obscure deceased person, trusting for her confirmation as to the
verification of her statements.[29]

Yet Bute records, without comment, the incredible assertions by Miss
Freer:

To Benediction at Harley House. My Lady & Miss Freer. Walked
back with them. With Miss F in Bot[anical] Gardens. She says Mr
Stainton Moses drank, & agrees with me in believing Mrs Speen
guilty of trickery. Says when ill in England, she, Miss F, used to
xternalise the physical body & go to see friends in New Zealand.
The sight of her physical body inspired her with dislike as the
hindrance to her activity & intelligence.[30]

Her claims linked in with the SPR's interest in establishing that the
mind could be free of the physical brain. In an era which was realising
that it was simply impossible to find a space in the human body in
which to locate the soul, the suggestion that even while living, the

human consciousness could find free itself from the body was of great interest. It is impossible to guess how far, at this date, Bute believed her. Undoubtedly the rest of his family did not. Next year Lady Margaret asked her mother:

> How did dear Ada enjoy her yachting and the Scilly Isles? I hope she won't send her something or other consciousness, or soul, or whatever she sends about, to see us anywhere![31]

Miss Freer had again spent the summer exploring second sight in the Highlands and Islands. As Campbell and Hall suggest, she deliberately sought to discredit Peter Dewar, saying outright that 'the few stories Mr Dewar brought away from Mr MacDonald [*sic*] were not very interesting' and making snide comments at the expense of Presbyterians and their ministers.

However, Dewar was now newly married, and his wife was expecting a child. Moreover some of his parishioners disapproved both of his researches and of the inevitable long absence from the parish that they involved, and it is likely that he did not want to spend another summer travelling round in search of stories. Infinitely less appealing is the way Miss Freer jockeyed the learned and able Catholic folklorist, Rev. Allan McDonald of Eriskay, out of the fame that should rightly have been his.[32]

Some of her letters from this summer have been lost, but the ones that remain are chatty and readable. Particularly gripping is her account of a vision she had at the Priory, St Andrews. She first had glimpses of two possible earlier buildings on the site, and then settled down to wait. It was a wild, wet morning, and she sat there enjoying the storm for a long time. Then came

> sounds as of worship proceeding from the westward & quite near to me. These I am sure had no objective origin because I could always end them immediately by opening my eyes ... I ... [returned] to the same spot by moonlight (what there was of it) this evening after dinner ... I tried to revive the sound but all was silent on that side though I could hear many voices overhead. Suddenly the crypt became light as if a doorway had opened in the N.E. corner behind me. I heard footsteps as if descending the stairs – a black robed figure passed me – later another; I heard two doors close in front of me but could see nothing. Then came the sound of many feet, & a procession passed me walking in single file, I counted 27 tonsured and robed figures ... I heard, after some minutes what

sounded like the distant recital of a prayer & suddenly, in a most distressing manner all was changed & I heard loud coarse voices & the trampling of cattle. After that, only silence & the wailing of the wind, & I came home.[33]

It is a pity that the Augustinian habit is not black, but white. The story is wonderfully and skilfully told. There is enough matter-of-factness in speaking of 'the moonlight – what there was of it', and also her own inability to conjure up the voices again (which so effectively suggests they never were a figment of her imagination) to give the whole thing a feeling of being more than a fairy story. It was quite true that the chapel had been turned into a byre for cattle, and she was not, at that time, supposed to have heard the account of this.[34] Was this fraud, or the kind of imaginative experience which makes it possible for the writers of novels speak of their characters as living people? Bute visited her in October, when he was again staying in London, enjoying walking at night in the closed park, watching the swans sleeping on the water in the misty moonlight.[35]

R. R. Anderson came to stay, bringing news of the researches he had made into Peter de Luna, which were to be embodied in the new marble chapel to be built at Mount Stuart, then Bute moved to Falkland again, to be near St Andrews for the Rectorial election. He had decided, some time earlier, that he would stand again as Rector of St Andrews, come what might. At the time of the first election, he had been morbidly unwilling to stand if there was a contest. This time he decided he would only step down if a Protestant candidate with his own opinions regarding the University could be found:

> To tell you the truth, I am very tired, and I doubt whether I could stand many months more of this kind of thing. My health, wh. is not first class, wd. break down under the continual mental worry, and might break down in serious ways such as albumenuria – from the continual worry & anxiety, with the deprivation of physical xercise & recreation, as well as all mental pursuits congenial to my tastes, as well as the strain of my ordinary business work. Perhaps T., P., C., & K. are calculating deliberately upon this. But I will not resign the Rectorship, nor will I refuse if the students call on me to serve them, nor will I in any case cease to try & serve SXA.[36]

Nobody like this came forward, and he heard with apparent equanimity that Lord Peel was standing against him.[37] The inevitable controversy did not seem to distress him unduly, but he had learned to deal with conflict at some personal cost. There is a close link between anxiety and a rise in blood pressure, and another between high blood pressure and kidney failure. There is no indication in his diary that he was feeling unwell or had summoned his doctor. Indeed, a remark he made to Metcalfe earlier in the month suggests that he was feeling reasonably well. He had worked out a horoscope for the forthcoming Rectorial election and 'The Astrological portents for the election seem to me very bad indeed – and there is a startling element about my own health.'[38] The portents were wrong about the election, but right about his health.

For years, a cryptic cross in Bute's diary, embedded in a banal account of 13 November, remained unremarked. Andrew McLean, intrigued, noted that Bute referred to the day in his yearly summing up: 'To me the main thing in the past year is the announcement made to me by the Dr, on Nov. 13.' The cross marked the day when Bute was told he had Bright's disease, kidney failure. From that day, he knew he was moving steadily to an early death. He did not speak freely of this news, which he had encoded in his diary. It was not until December that he confided in Metcalfe, now one of his closest associates and friends that

> There is no use talking abt. my health recovering. That is not on the cards. It is not a question. The question is what work I may manage to do within the span (wh. may be more or less limited) still left to me.[39]

It was a week after he had been told he had Bright's disease that he had a letter from Miss Freer. He had apparently written to her suggesting he tried to 'appear' to her. She answered that he already had, and she had not mentioned it in her letter 'written just afterwards, because people don't always like to be told these things'.

> I was staring straight out of the window into brilliant sunshine. The dark patch one sees in a bright light took the outline of a figure I have twice seen near you – out of doors, once in your garden at St John's Lodge, once as you passed out of the chapel at Harley House – the figure of a young woman – dead some years I should say – always in the same attitude of bowed head veiled, & outstretched hands parting the heavy black veil. How badly words present a picture – this sounds like a Nun! How can I express the idea? The veil is not tangible, – it is a cloak of mystery – a secret – the action of a revelation. She is not a Nun – she wears a wedding ring. She

has a delicate foreign face – beautiful Italian eyes, Italian in their
depth & softness, sensitive and intellectual. A shadow fell upon the
light, – & for a moment you were there.[40]

Bute instantly identified the figure Miss Freer had seen: 'Letter from
Miss Freer as to the apparitions (apparently) of the late Princess Marie
(Fox) von Liechtenstein.'[41]

The next day he consulted three of his supporters about the St
Andrews Rectorial election, and that night he was too ill and in
too much pain to get to bed. Bute had had a number of distressing
complaints over the years. His psoriasis, the inflammation of his eyes
brought about by the attempt to treat it, and the rubber suit next to
the skin, the abscess in his scrotum; these he bore almost without
complaint. Only the agony of an abscess on his tooth so huge that
the pus dripped down his nose had let him to speak of 'torment'. For
the first time, this November he spoke of 'suffering much' as he spent
his days dictating to his wife a book of Sunday prayers for Catholics
unable to get to Mass, and his nights fitfully dozing in a chair. On
the second day his doctor 'made hypodermic injection'.[42] The next day,
after three days of pain, and nights unable to lie down, he records
receiving a 'letter from Miss Freer abt. another apparition (of M[arie]
F[ox]?) yesterday'.[43] That night he managed to sleep in his bed, and
two days later to take a 'turn' in the garden with his wife.

The following day he heard that he had been re-elected as Rector of
St Andrews, and he went at once to St Andrews. He arrived an invalid
in a closed cab, but the speech he made from a window had all the
old sparkling words:

> I have to thank you for my re-election … I can only say in the
> beautiful language rendered classical by the use of tradesmen that I
> trust by a close and practical attention to business to merit this mark
> of your renewed confidence.
>
> There is a great deal which I should like to say to but you know as
> well as I do that there is a great deal which University commissioners
> must not say out of ground floor windows let alone house tops. I
> have to thank you not only on my own behalf – but as I think – on
> that of the University …
>
> When you did me the honour to bring me into your affairs the
> University was in the midst of the heaviest gale which I believe has
> ever attacked her in the nearly 500 years of her existence …
>
> Well, whatever happens now I hardly think that things can ever
> again be so bad as they have been and if I may venture to look a

little further into the future I cd. even express the hope that the gale is now going down and nearly over ... and that there may be a great calm, a calm full of happiness, and indefinite life in the future generations yet to come for the good of Scotland.[44]

The next day he had a 'wearisome' council meeting, and then returned to Falkland to come to terms with his changed situation.

There was no effective medical treatment. The best that could be done was to place Bute on a low protein diet and forbid him to drink alcohol. His intake of all fluid was restricted. Bute, whose mood had always suffered considerable swings, was very depressed. He was not an alcoholic but like other aristocrats of his period, was accustomed to take a glass of wine with his meals. Now that had gone, and the food he did have caused comment. Faced with his uncompromisingly depressed mood, his wife wrote to Dr Charles Gage Brown,[45] who wrote directly to Bute, urging that his disease was perhaps not as advanced as Bute feared it. Brown had found the albumen 'was not in any great quantity and the casts but few' and he thought Bute 'should rather take heart, and be ready to accept a course likely to do away with any bother'. He thought Bute should look on his new diet as a kind of mix of physical and spiritual discipline. He added:

Her Ladyship tells me you wish to take your meals alone. That will not be to your advantage. Certainly sit in company. It is one aid to digestion.

She also tells me that you certainly seem better in health that seems to correspond with the medical investigating so I hope you are going to take heart, accept a regulated diet and be hopeful. I wish you were in London that I could watch you daily and try and cheer you. That remark about Mackay may deal with a probability. Sir Jas Clarke made a similar and most sad mistake with your own relation Lady Flora Hastings.[46]

Was there a possibility of his condition leading to, or being linked with, cancer? Bute's cup must have seemed very full. Even if his doctors did not take a grim a view of his case (or if they did, hid it from him), Bute felt that all that could possibly be achieved was a delaying tactic; if he took care, he would die over a longer, rather than a shorter time. He was right. The 'casts' in his urine were the symptom of a chronic infection which could have led to amyloid in the kidney – the thickening of the membranes which should filter the blood. This would cause them to leak and destroy his kidney function. The 'casts' may have been due to aggregation of the albumin also occasionally noted in his urine. It seems very likely that all this had originated from an infection in his prostate, undiagnosed and, in this period, untreatable.[47] Bute was dying of the after-effects of a rotten tooth.

Both the Butes knew that the only alleviation for his depression was the intellectual work which would fill his thoughts and keep him from brooding. Two days before the election, Gwen, filled with panic, wrote to Metcalfe, who was perhaps now his closest friend. Her letters had improved over the years and the unpunctuated character of this reflects the stress she was under, with her husband dangerously ill at the age of only forty-eight:

> Lord Bute is better decidedly. We had a specialist here on Saturday & it has come to this that he has to be dieted and he is allowed <u>no wine</u> which he thinks nonsense and does not add to his cheerfulness it is absolutely necessary he shd. have literary work I am writing out at his dictation a little office book we have long projected but cannot you advise him to write on some subject for the Scottish if he will not begin a 'work'; if he cd be made to write with an object it wd be good. Must have his article ready for such a date etc it would be so good for him – he really has nothing much on hand the Pater Nosters but that of course he just takes up and puts down – the doctors are most anxious he should have this work can you help me – the difficulty is for one thing that here are not many subjects of interest ... I am sorry to trouble you, but I know you feel the importance, and <u>I know</u> that it is of vital importance.[48]

The time-scale of the shattering news of Bute's disease, his election as Rector, his plunge into depression, and the communications from Ada Freer is very close. The death sentence, Ada's first communication about the veiled lady and his election all happened in two weeks and a day. Within three weeks, she had said:

> Will you excuse me if I post-pone, say for a fortnight, telling you exactly what I saw? It was an Xtian name, sufficiently common in an approximate form to make it imperative as a test, to get, if possible, the sur-name [*sic*]. This may not be possible, but I should like to try, and telling you part, if correct, might as a matter of association, <u>increase</u> the likelihood of thought trains.[49]

On 9 December, that is less than a month after the diagnosis, she wrote telling him:

Yes, the name was <u>Marie</u>. I am a little perplexed by what you say as to the finding of the surname being no test for you unless it may be that you knew the lady under her married name only ... I had a confused impression the other night that the Marie was followed by a <u>v</u> and (possibly by association <u>with van</u> (from von) I thought of but did not see, 'Holland', but by that time my normal consciousness may have been at work so I do not attach any importance to the impression.[50]

'Another letter from Miss Freer wh. now seems to leave no doubt as to Pss. Marie (Fox) von L.',[51] recorded Bute. Marie was silent and invisible until just before Christmas, when she appeared again to Ada:

I saw the figure again, not very near. She looked at me very earnestly. (This you may be aware is very unusual. Phantasms rarely show consciousness of one's presence) earnestly & so to speak, <u>personally</u>. I felt I was going to be shown something. It struck me that her gestures were intended to imitate <u>you</u>, as one might act a sentence one could not speak. She put her hand to her neck as if in acute pain, – looked again as if to see whether I understood, and made a word with her lips, which I could not distinguish.

A confusion of words came into my head, 'Egypt' was loudest, then 'fox' and '—chester'. I could not catch the first syllable, and 'Go'.

I am ashamed to send what sounds so wretchedly fragmentary. I should not be right if (out of personal vanity shall I say?) I withheld it – but I would it were more.[52]

Fragmentary perhaps but the perfect cliff-hanger. The next instalment came after Christmas, when Miss Freer told Bute that a previous incident had taken a 'new aspect'. She had just heard that a friend of her childhood and youth ('more of a brother to me than my own ever were') had died in California. This suddenly gave importance to an incident in the night between 19 and 20 November, when she had been awakened by 'voices, too distant to recognise' and she got up and wrote 'what came to me, partly what I was induced to write (automatically) partly what I heard'. All of it 'purported to come from my dear old friend Stuart Paulet'. She had put it aside as 'perhaps fanciful'. The knowledge that he had died that night put a different aspect to it, but it had taken until after Christmas for her to write to Bute to enquire if Marie might be 'literally or symbolically' be called 'the Princess'. At the time of the communication, Miss Freer had thought 'the Princess' could be 'some Bourbon he had found in America – he was always getting intrigué with somebody or something mysterious or romantic'.[53] Now, 'the light of your last letter has suggested a clue as to her identity'.

By a further coincidence, and Bute did not believe in coincidences, Miss Freer wrote this letter on the very day that Bute was having Mass offered for the soul of Marie von Liechtenstein.[54] To Bute it was more than a clue, it was a certainty. Paulet's spiritually-communicated letter was low on facts. It spoke of the 'dislocation' of both the Princess and another person, probably Bute, though the letter is a little ambiguous:

She like you had no anchor & less rudder than you ... remember how you used to say I want to be somebody's dog. I've got a home and a big bone, but I want to belong to somebody – it was worse for her you had at least memories.[55]

How deeply Bute had yearned to be 'somebody's dog'. If the words had been his, this must have made him certain the communication was from Marie, and definitely indicates there was more to the broken relationship than questions of her birth. Paulet added the helpful encouragement that 'in Egypt you will learn much, but you must reach – further – get more in touch'.

Bute recorded his feelings four days after receiving this letter, as he summed up the year on its last day:

To me the main thing in the past year is the announcement made to me by the Dr, on Nov. 13. The depression from treatment has been very great. As for the change itself, I now find that my study of things connected with the S.P.R. & cognate thereto, has the effect of very largely robbing it of its terrors – and I cannot help thinking that the action apparently taken by M v L has something to do with it. Still, it is awful, were it only from its greatness, and the unknown conditions of the hereafter, and I must say with Brendan of Clonfert 'Timeo si solus migravero, si tenebraeum fuerit iter; timeo inexpertam regionem, Regis praesentiam, Judicis sententiam' In the meanwhile, there is only to seek to do the will of God. If it may be, I would rather that the separation from my wife should be as short as possible, on account of the grief which I know she will feel, undeserving as I am; and I should be glad if I could be of use to my children, at least till they are settled in life.[56]

Brendan of Clonfert is better known as Brendan the Navigator, and patron saint of Bute the island. Even he, who had faced so many

The solid House of Falkland exterior, designed by architect William Burn, has not changed since Bute visited as a child. (© Falkland Stewardship Trust)

Bute's sense of fun is clearly seen in this 'mural of the winds' over the stair at House of Falkland. Painted in 1898 by Andrew W. Lyons, it is full of caricatures of his friends and family, not yet all identified. (© Falkland Stewardship Trust)

ENEREMVR · CERNVI · ET · ANTIQVVM · DOCVMENTVM · NOVO · CEDAT · RITVI · PRÆSTET · FIDES · SVPPLEMENTVM · SENSVVM · DEFECTVI · GENITORI · GENITOQVE · LAVS · E

The Corpus Christi procession (a procession giving thanks for the sacrament of Holy Communion), another Lonsdale frieze at House of Falkland. (© Falkland Stewardship Trust)

The Chapel Royal at Falkland Palace was largely a restoration. The pieces of the royal pew were found in the cellars, and the pew (on the left side of the chapel) reconstructed. (© K. Bohen)

Falkland Palace, seen against the Lomond Hill, showing a mix of restoration and ruin. (© K. Bohen)

The painted wooden ceiling of the Falkland Palace Chapel Royal is restoration at its finest. The initials and coats of arms are for the visit of Charles I in 1633. (© K. Bohen)

Above. This detail from the Chapel Royal ceiling at Falkland Palace shows the care taken to blend old and new work in a way which, while pleasing to the eye, never deceives the watcher as to what is old and what is new work. (© K. Bohen)

Left. Portraits in oak of Bute's children ornament the door to a cupboard in Falkland Palace. Here are Margaret and 'Nohn'. (© K. Bohen)

Right. A continuing feature of Bute buildings is the detail. Bute had written extensively on the coronations of British Monarchs. This crown on a turret at Falkland Palace appears to be loosely based on, but not identical to, the Scottish crown. (© K. Bohen)

Below. The Crichton Stuart arms ornament a leather chair-back in Falkland Palace. (© K. Bohen)

The Tapestry Gallery down which royalty passed to the chapel of Falkland Palace. (© K. Bohen)

Bute did not share Burges's love of Spartan buildings and minimal plumbing. This wood panelled and marble bathroom ensured the comfort of Bute's Falkland Factor who lived in the Palace. (© K. Bohen)

Sunlight streams into the windows of Falkland Palace, and shows its setting in a little village in magnificent countryside. The Palace provided the Stuart kings with a base for hunting over those wooded hills. (© K. Bohen)

Greyfriars Convent, Elgin, provided architect John Kinross with a large canvas. (© J. Lowndes)

The quadrangle, enclosed on all four sides, is the centre of the monastic buildings at Greyfriars. (© J. Lowndes)

The long wooden barrel vault stretches the length of the chapel at Greyfriars, which is sub-divided to allow the sisters a private worship space, while the congregation of lay people gather in the nave. The two side altars show saints associated with the order. (© J. Lowndes)

Looking down the chapel at Greyfriars from the altar reveals how Kinross shielded the sisters from view, while offering the congregation clear sight lines of the altar. His monumental choir stalls are deliciously simple and graciously imposing. (© J. Lowndes)

Exquisite and economical,
this spiral stair at Greyfriars
ascends to a gallery.
(© J. Lowndes)

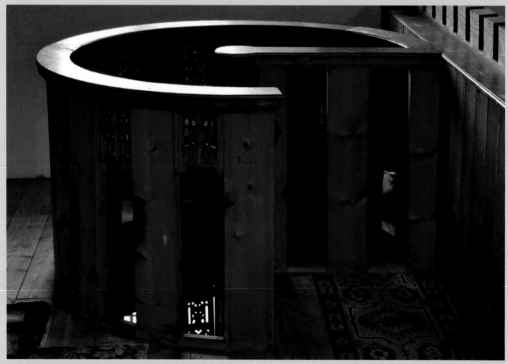

Lady Bute's bedroom at Castell Coch is a creative blend of the work of William Burges and William Frame. If the result in this room is not as rich or unified as Burges, it is lighter and prettier. Over the fire, one can see that Frame did indeed allow Psyche to have a heart-shaped shield. (© Crown Copyright 2011 Visit Wales)

The wash-stand designed by Chapple for Lady Bute's bedroom at Castell Coch. The two towers are to be filled, one with hot, the other with cold water. (© Crown Copyright 2011 Visit Wales)

Thomas Nicholls' Three Fates dominate the Drawing Room at Castell Coch, but the theme is not taken up in the rest of the enchantingly pretty room, sometimes criticised for being more aesthetic greenery-yallery than punchily Gothic. (© Crown Copyright 2011 Visit Wales)

In the ceiling of the Coch Drawing Room, the birds fly home to roost as the stars come out. It is very pretty indeed, although architect William Frame was furious with Charles Campbell over what he saw as the botched painting of the butterflies on the ribs. (© Crown Copyright 2011 Visit Wales)

wonders, feared that last voyage: 'I fear if I go alone, if the journey be dark; I fear the unknown region, the presence of the king, and the sentence of the Judge'.[57] Bute had not quite finished with the princess. He himself had a 'vague' vision of her.[58] At the end of January Miss Freer had a vision of her in Holland Park Gardens, where she walked until she got to the gates of Holland House, 'when she disappeared'.[59] At this point, Lord Bute told Miss Freer that he had identified the Princess with Marie Fox. She arranged an invitation to Holland House, and

> The point most important, I think, is the absolute identification of 'Marie' whose picture hangs by the door of Lady Illchester's sitting room. It was quite unmistakable, only that now her countenance has a gentleness and repose lacking in the portrait . . .[60]

This answers all the points except the ones of most pressing interest, which are whether Miss Freer was a fraud, or self-deluded, or actually saw the Princess. The question cannot, of course, be answered definitively. It is highly suggestive that Ada Freer seems to have begun with details upon which she could backtrack. For instance, had Lord Bute declared at any point that the woman must have been a nun, Miss Freer had laid the basis of a claim that she did not know that the brides of Christ wore wedding rings. It is highly suggestive of fraud that she said the name was a common one, and waited for feedback from Bute before replying that, yes, it was Marie. It was, to put it mildly, also very convenient that she did not mention her 'auditory experience' on a date when she had it, or when she next wrote to Bute.

In Miss Freer's favour it must be admitted that her description of Marie was strikingly accurate from the very beginning. It is only explicable as fraud if Miss Freer had heard the story of Bute and Marie and had got a general description of her from the gossip. The kindly explanation is that Miss Freer was a natural romancer, who was inclined to reinvent the world so that it suited herself, and that she was also inclined to reinvent it for her friends. As her romance of the mysterious figure advanced, she became aware how important it was to Bute, and gently led it to a conclusion which provided a very profound comfort to a dear friend at a crisis in life. There is no doubt this incident was of huge importance to Bute. As he himself records, it formed the basis of his approach to death, and it explains the regard in which he held Ada Freer.

Those intimate enough to learn of his condition were deeply distressed. Huggins told him:

What you say in your letter about yourself has so filled me with grief, greater than I can tell you, my first instinctive feeling was to put it from me, as something too dark to be accepted.

He added kindly but bluntly that it was foolish to argue, as Bute did, that the regime 'cut him off from the small amount of social life he used to have'. He did his friends a great injustice, argued one of the foremost men of science of his age,

> if you do not believe it is your own presence which gives all its charm to your hospitable board, and that any restrictions in food you have to make, can in any sensible degree lessen to your friends the delight of being with you at table.[61]

Bute remained self-conscious about his diet, and at University functions he ate at a separate table, giving rise to comments from those hostile to him[62] that he thought himself above the company.[63] In fairness to him, when he did eat at the same table as guests in Falkland, the sight of him eating a seed mix gruel while others tucked into normal food was considered so extraordinary that it was remembered over a hundred years later.[64]

Bute's health was a good deal better in January, and at the beginning of February he was able to make a 'long speech, proposing a scheme to incorporation of Dundee Coll.'.[65] He was pretty confident in proposing his plans for the expansion of St Andrews, as the University had received the Berry bequest: 'The bequest, of £100,000, was made by David Berry of New South Wales in fulfilment of the intentions of his brother Alexander Berry, a former student of the university.'[66] Bute was buoyantly optimistic about this, commenting to his colleagues:

> Remember that it is possible that we may have Chairs (not Lectureships) not only in English, nor even [only] in History and Botany as well; and money which can be applied to such xpenses as the buildings of the anatomical school.[67]

Of course, it was not all plain sailing. One of Bute's most stalwart supporters had been the distinguished anatomist, Dr Bill Pettigrew.[68] He now refused to teach women medical students, and Bute resigned himself to appointing another lecturer 'in Physiology for the Women, who will herself, I opine, be a woman'.[69] Pettigrew then opposed the appointment of a woman, making difficulties which Bute serenely ignored. Bute resigned himself to bankrolling her salary, and he did the same to enable

Modern Greek to be taught at St Andrews.[70] A site was selected for a new medical school, at the foot of St Mary's Gardens, beside West Burn Lane. There was opposition to funding the building,[71] and once again Bute, acutely aware his time was running out, decided to build it himself.

He was, as Gwen reported, 'wonderfully cheerful considering that he hardly sees a soul'.[72] This was the more remarkable as his health had again deteriorated. He had another abscess in the scrotum, 'neighbouring parts also much inflamed'.[73] He underwent another operation for this. He told Metcalfe:

> I am sorry to say that the change to London has not seemed to benefit me as I expected. I am feeling fit for nothing. Anything tires me. I can do very little. My difficulty in writing is very great. And I am in constant apprehension of becoming useless.[74]

He still had pleasures, and a new building to work upon. He became interested in the old ruins of Greyfriars in Elgin towards the end of 1895, when the nuns had written to him, begging for support. An anonymous nun gave a splendidly naïve account. As she so rightly comments, writing to Bute 'fortunately I mentioned the ruins of the church. That's what decided him.'[75] The property was sold at auction, with the Marquess's agent entering the room and bidding at the last possible moment in the most dramatic way. Bute at once busied himself with getting the right iconography, telling Grissell that the nun's parent 'Order of Our Lady of Ransom or Mercy' was 'nearly extinct, but it exists in Rome'. He asked for copies of their Calendar, missal and Breviary, and actual male and female habits, adding:

> And I want to know how they represent the B.V. de Mercede, and also the Saints of their Order. I have had an idea of a reredos, with the B.V. de Mercede in the middle, between [several saints of the order], and a general mix up of angels clad in the habit of the order.[76]

He handed the commission over to John Kinross, who started work almost at once on restoring the church out of its ruins, while still working on excavation and recreation at the old Priory, St Andrews. Kinross had a remarkably free hand at Greyfriars, but with constant contact with his absent patron. He created a masterpiece. He was working with the 'remains of the fifteenth century buildings'[77] of the original Franciscan friars. He researched other Greyfriars buildings in Aberdeen and Edinburgh, and seeing the similarities with King's College, Aberdeen, allowed that building to influence him.

What he created was a simplicity in keeping, as Mays says, with Franciscan worship, combined with a grandeur of size, space and detail. For years the nuns believed that the choir stalls (inspired by King's College, Aberdeen) must have been designed for monks, for nobody would have made something so impressive for women.[78] By making a stall with a relatively lower back and broader seat, and reducing the (already minimal) fussiness of the outline, Kinross achieved an even more monumental simplicity. The paving stones gave Kinross much trouble to source, as he wanted to use the original quarry, and the lessee appeared 'to have been drunk for the last six months'.[79] It was hard stone, and thus slow to work, and he used it to create a subdued magnificent patterned paving, with slabs interlocking like squared jigsaw puzzles. It is typical of the care taken in the building. At the same time he was pressing forward with the Priory in St Andrews.

The Priory was giving Bute some moments of serious scepticism about the powers of all the sensitives and mediums with whom he was in contact. Mrs Russell Davis's 'Ned' promised to meet Miss Freer, and failed to show up. Miss Freer's 'old friend' Mr Paulet proved equally elusive in the matter of information. This was disappointing in the light of Miss Freer's earlier splendid visions. When required to come up with verifiable facts, all of them failed totally. Bute commented exasperatedly that Paulet:

Can give no information himself, but only verbal xcuses for absence of clairvoyance in Miss F. It seems <u>almost</u> impossible to get anything from the other side wh. is not known to or guessed by somebody on this.[80]

Indeed, but by August Miss Freer had had time to extract an explanation from Mr Paulet (who seemed to differ but little from the guides of the mediums she so despised). Typically, Bute accepted it:

Miss Freer told me in London that Mr Paulet had at last said to her that they can see through earth even less than we can, being further removed from gross matter, & that anything which appears to the contrary sense, is only owing to their power of stimulating clairvoyance in the embodied. We heard before that there was only one person now abt. the Priory, who knew it in old times & still cares for it, & it was he who had caused Miss Freer to see the things wh. she has seen there. This time she saw one (?him) sitting in a stall in the chapter house.[81]

Yet, in other areas, Bute's intellect was as powerful and as independent as ever, and as critical:

> To H of Lords, where interesting conversation with Ld. Halifax – Back by train. Ld. H. has since allowed me to read a lot of private correspondence. The impression of the policy of the Roman Court left on me is most unfavourable, as though the restoration of Temporal Power were an object altogether before the advancement of the Kingdom of Our Lord.[82]

His views may have been somewhat coloured by the fact that some quarters in Rome were still blocking the acceptance of the long-completed Scottish Proprium. Archbishop Eyre opposed the whole project, and he was using what influence he could in Rome, despite the support of the other Bishops for 'honouring our national saints',[83] as Angus Macdonald put it – being, for once, rather on Bute's side. Bute's old friend, Turner, now Bishop of Galloway, was rather franker:

> We quite understand the Glasgow style: everything Scotch is opposed there. In the matter of the new offices, I presume you have heard that one of the Cardinals has blocked their passage with a little of the Roman red tape. I fancy he never heard of the Scottish Reformation, where he wants to prove an uninterrupted cultus among the people in this diocese in reference to St Ninian &c.[84]

At the end of the Season, Bute moved to Cardiff, which did not much please his family or his retainers. He chartered the *Kittiwake* for Margaret this year, and as his secretary told his friend the factor:

> The Charter begins on 15th July and at present it looks as if the yachting this year will be done in the Bristol Channel as My Lord seems bent on spending August & September at Cardiff, which is not a cheerful prospect for any of us.[85]

Despite comment in the papers that Bute disliked London, his secretary knew that he actually enjoyed it, and he had taken a good deal of quiet pleasure in this Season. He moved to Cardiff happily, and in August, he seemed 'particularly well'.[86] Then, he was

> taken ill on the evng. of Aug 22 with violent pain in right side of head, followed by peculiar feeling throughout left half of entire person. Write with greatest difficulty.[87]

He describes the classic symptoms of a haemorrhage in the right side of the brain. Maybe Bute was left-handed. His doctor was puzzled, though he did admit the possibility of cerebral haemorrhage. Summoned to the Castle at 8.45 p.m., he found that Bute had been taken ill while at dinner with an attack of giddiness followed by 'cold clammy sweats' and having difficulty swallowing:

> The pulse was quiet, regular, somewhat fast, but there was no palpitation, breathing quiet, regular, and not at all laboured.
>
> The face, always florid, was not at all changed, the pupils were moderately dilated, but equal and responded well to light, and to accommodation.
>
> There was no headache.

There was nothing the doctor could do except to call back later, and at 11 p.m. he found him walking in the drawing room, 'enjoying a cigarette' and still having trouble swallowing. When he called again on the Sunday Bute was somewhat worse:

> The pupils were somewhat contracted, but equal, and responded to light, and the ophthalmoscope gave negative results. He was sitting in an armchair and complaining that he could only stand by holding on to the table or some other piece of furniture; and on getting him to walk I noticed that he merely shuffled along, and that there was a tendency to fall to the left; but there was no swinging gait and no dragging of either foot.

By evening, it was plain he was even less well, and now 'His Lordship also complained of neuralgic pains over the right brow, the right eye was suffused, and the right upper lid drooped ... There was no occipital headache.' Bute also complained that the 'whole left half of his body had felt colder than the right side'. The doctor still further reduced Bute's diet, and got a second opinion from a London doctor. Gradually, Bute's health improved. Lacking any further means of diagnosis, the doctor could only speculate if Bute had some digestive trouble, or if there had been:

> a sudden organic cerebral lesion such as a light haemorrhage or thrombosis near the internal [corpuscle?] on the right side ... However taking into consideration his Lordship's family history, his own appearance which is that of a prematurely old man for his age, and his enormous size, one must not overlook the suspicion that the

attack <u>may be</u> the precursor of something more serious looming in the future.[88]

The doctor's putative diagnosis was almost certainly right and Bute seems to have suffered a transient ischaemic attack, followed by a stroke. The first cause was the infection destroying his kidneys, and therefore pushing up his blood pressure, making him vulnerable to all forms of vascular disease. Then there was his weight. Bute was by now morbidly obese. In photographs of him in his Rectorial robes, or as Mayor of Cardiff, it is a little hard to tell where the robes end, and Bute begins, but the images suggest a figure of quite amazing bulk. He smoked a great deal. In learning to face stress, and not simply retreat from it, as he had as a younger man, he further pushed up his blood pressure. In fact his medical condition was, almost certainly, caused by a vicious circle of contributory factors triggered by the infection lurking in prostate and kidneys.

Medical matters were not spoken of as freely in Victorian days. Only intimates learned that he was very seriously ill. Thus when the Bishop of Newport forwarded him a letter, he had no idea Bute had had a stroke some eight days before. The letter was from Raphael Merry del Val,[89] chamberlain to the Pope, and his confidential advisor. The 'Merry Devil', who had been born and educated in England, was an uncompromising conservative, both in religion and politics. As we have seen, the Anglo-Catholics in the Church of England could and did claim that not only was their church Catholic, but its ordination was valid, and should be recognised as such by Rome. Viscount Halifax[90] had led a movement by the High Church *English Church Union* which attempted greater dialogue with the Roman Catholic Church. It was counter-productive, for a Roman Commission investigating Anglican orders recommended that they should not be recognised. Merry del Val drafted the Papal Encyclical which declared Anglican orders invalid.[91] It appears both men expected a flood of defections from the Church of England clergy at the shocking news, and they prepared accordingly. They wanted the Anglican clergy to have a soft landing in the Church of Rome, and were prepared to go to some lengths to arrange this.

Therefore Merry del Val wrote to Bute, enclosing a letter from Pope Leo XIII, and actually signed by the Pope himself. In high-flown terms it referred to the plight of Anglican clergymen who converted to Rome, and thereby lost their livings, being 'forced to endure privation and sufferings for which ... their own education ... has [not] prepared them'. Stressing that this was nobody else's idea, but 'Our personal inspiration', Leo XIII reassured Bute that the intention was not to offer the clergy a better income than the one they were relinquishing, but a modest one until they could again support themselves in some way. Of course, he admitted, clergy should not be put off the task of saving their souls by the prospect of poverty, but it would not be surprising if the prospect of poverty hindered the work of grace. Then he offered Bute the chance to become the 'principal collaborator' with the Pope and suggested that Bute should 'co-operate therein with the maximum generosity' which his means allowed. Bute could be 'assured that the All Powerful will give you rich recompense and your name will be ever blessed among English Catholics'. Leo ended:

> We intend to write shortly to the Cardinal Archbishop of Westminster to involve him in our initiative, and instruct him to arrange with you and the Episcopate for the organisation of this work. Meanwhile, we are pleased, as encouragement and as witness of Our fatherly love, to send you and all yours Our Apostolic Blessing.[92]

The timing of this mixture of demand and blackmail could hardly have been worse. Bute had just entered what he knew only too well was a new, and deteriorating, stage of his terminal illness. He was acutely aware of the need to establish all of his children comfortably, and the youngest was only ten years old. He was anxious, and all activities were a burden to him. In such a state of mind, every old fear rose to the top of his mind. He had always suspected that he was simply wanted for his money. Hard on the heels of the rejection of his plans for a genuinely academic education for the Scottish Catholic clergy at St Andrews, and with the Proprium still stalled in Rome, came a demand for Bute to devote a very large proportion of his capital to a project in which he had no interest at all. In fact, as he bitterly complained in a letter to Cardinal Vaughan, who was to have the administration of the proposed fund, 'Rich men are not mere boxes containing money out of which it is to be taken whenever it is wanted and they themselves treated as if they were more insensate than brute beasts.'

Bute attacked, recalling his old pain, when his translation of the Breviary went unacknowledged, remembering the suppression of the Daily Office in Oban, which he blamed on Mrs Bunman's role being reduced by the Cathedral choir and her undue influence on the Bishop, and above all the personal animosity behind the refusal to allow Blairs to move to St Andrews. The grasshopper had picked on an elephant. One may well suspect that in fact the letter originated with Merry del Val, who was passionately committed to encouraging mass conversions from the Church of England, and knew of Bute's

vast wealth. It was certainly he who replied, swiftly and with vitriol.
Blame for the unacknowledged Breviary was laid squarely on Cardinal
Howard, who had presented it, since the Pope was beyond all normal
rules of etiquette such as a simple 'thank you'. It was impossible that
Propaganda or the Pope would take sides in the matter of Blairs.
The suggestion that the office at Oban had been suppressed to please
the Bishop's friend was inevitably beyond all comment. The Holy
Father had signed his letter 'with a hand weakened by 86 years of
a hard life and the infirmities of age' so it was inexcusable that Bute
should not have done the same, even if he was paralysed. In quite
the nastiest letter written to the 3rd Marquess, Merry del Val ends:
'I am returning to Rome early next month and I will use every effort
to diminish the painful impression left upon His Holiness, difficult
as that task may be.'[93]

No Catholic could afford to ignore such a letter, coming as it
did from a source so close to the Pope, and Bute was forced into a
grovelling apology to the Pope. He explained that his failure to reply
arose from his paralysis and his reluctance to allow a secretary to deal
with the matter, and that he had asked to see Merry del Val to whom
he spoke:

I am much grieved to hear from Mgr Merry del Val that Your
Holiness thought that I was wanting in respect in not writing as soon
as the state of my hand permitted me to do so, I beg pardon for my
error, and, as I am now able to write, although with difficulty, I now
do so, humbly to acknowledge the letter signed by Your Holiness
which you were graciously pleased to vouchsafe to send me.[94]

He addressed it to the Pope via Merry del Val, who superciliously
declined to present it, 'the forms of usage at Court and in addressing
a reply to His Holiness requiring much more. I will endeavour to find
an opportunity of mentioning the fact to the Secretary of State or to
the Holy Father without creating any unfavourable impression.'[95]

The affair had a profound effect on Bute. From then on, he assumed
he was *persona non grata* at Rome, or in anything to do with the
larger affairs of the church. He took great precautions to be absolutely
correct in all he did. When he acquired the ruined Abbey of Pluscarden
in the following year, he got the Bishop of Aberdeen to make enquiries
on his behalf as to whether he needed to offer the Abbey back to the
Benedictines who had owned it before the Reformation, or if he could
begin restoration.[96] Bute had restored a lot of religious buildings with
no such queries raised, and his nervousness and his unwillingness to

approach Rome himself or through his own associates is symptomatic of his state of mind.

He was additionally cautious, too, in presenting his interest in ghosts as scientific investigation. He had always been careful that his work with and for the SPR conformed to that allowed by his faith. He had provided the amateur medium Lady Kenmore with a set of guidelines on what was proper for a Catholic back in 1893,[97] that is, matters for proper scientific research. But his sympathies were increasingly drawn toward belief in the 'other world' presented by Katie Wingfield and Ada Freer.

After his first stroke, his life was never the same again. In particular, he missed the free exercise of the ability to write. Gwen, ever devoted, was a very faithful amanuensis. Yet it was hard to have to filter all his words through a third party, even one as uncritical and like-minded as Gwen. Occasionally, as he made a partial recovery, he would take up his pen to write a few words in his own hand. He did this especially when he wanted to speak of his condition. For likeness of mind broke down totally when it came to his illness. Gwen wanted to believe he could get better: perhaps not wholly well again, but certainly much improved, and able, as his doctors suggested, to live for a good long time. Bute could only cope with his condition by removing from the equation the most painful element; false hope. He could manage if he could face the truth squarely, come to terms with it, and move on to considering what he could still reasonably achieve, as a weakened and dying man. Gwen wrote of his improvements, but Bute knew these were only small summits on a downhill road. She could not manage without the illusion that some turn in the road would greatly improve his health. He could not cope with the switch-back of the emotions that inevitably created.

When the students of St Andrews pressed him to agree to another inauguration ceremony as Rector, and to make another triumphant speech, he managed to take up his own pen to write the truth to Metcalfe:

My dear Dr Metcalfe,

There are some other things which I shall be sending you, but I am writing this with a considerable physical effort, in order to spare her Ladyship pain. You must do what you can to prevent the students insisting on another Rectorial address. They cannot know what they are talking about. College Echoes says it ought to be the same session as the election. Anybody who knows what my state was in the winter

1895–6 knows the utter absurdity of this. Since that winter and especially since the brain attack I had in Cardiff

1 – My imagination as well as my spirit are not what they were. I am not capable of the composition.

2 – I cannot follow arguments as I once could, & the necessary train of reasoning wd be beyond my powers.

My memory is the thing in which I feel most difference, & it is xactly on my memory that I shd. have most to depend for matter. I may get better, though I think not. I believe I am gradually going down, & I have engaged a confidential friend to tell me when he sees I must finally stand aside from all public affairs. Meanwhile I really only feel fit intellectually to sit in my sofa or arm chair dictating translation – but I can get though my business in several posts, such as my own, the Comm., the Provostship, and the Rectorship, in a way, though they are all I can do. And I do not xpect to be able to undertake such positions again. And cannot attempt the impossible such as a Rectorial address. If I did, my failure wd. be very painful to myself, and cd. not but be annoying to the students. Please try to make them understand this.

I do not complain. The night cometh when no man can work, sooner or later. It has come to me through over work & anxiety as Rector, and it is perhaps better that way than many others – but I am sure those on whose behalf I have incurred it wd. not try to goad me into a fiasco most distressing to myself & which cd. give no pleasure to them, if they knew what they were doing.[98]

He celebrated his silver wedding that spring with very mixed emotions. His marriage remained, as one of those congratulating him remarked, a matter for real joy and thanksgiving.[99] Yet he celebrated in the knowledge that it was shortly to be ended by death. He presented Gwen with a huge silver Russian icon of the wedding attended by Jesus at Cana in Galilee. He also provided a fund which would give poor girls seeking to marry a small dowry. His proviso was that the same passage of scripture should be read to them, to show 'that the marriage is truly blessed to which Jesus is called by humble prayer, and at which nothing takes place but the natural and harmless gaiety which is consonant with His sacred presence'.[100]

He took what work he felt he could still manage. He became Provost of the little town council of Rothesay, the only burgh on his home island of Bute. It was a small thing after his work as Mayor of Cardiff, but something he could both enjoy and do well. He was also at work on the book his wife had encouraged him to take up, an account of the heraldry of the Royal and Parliamentary burghs of Scotland. He had the collaboration and research of J. R. N. Macphail[101] for this, and the illustrations were provided by the very adaptable and sympathetic Lonsdale. Later he would work on the baronial and police burghs with J. H. Stevenson,[102] and the work would be published posthumously. None of this was exactly gripping to a man who had been used to a much fuller and more demanding life. He now felt he had little to offer the Catholic Church. He could be a dutiful son, and work with individual sympathetic Bishops (and he did indeed start making plans for the provision of the full 'divine office' in Cardiff, where the bishop was an old friend),[103] but he could no longer offer his interest and his energy in the way he once had, for both had been rejected too often and in a way deeply hurtful to him. Instead, he began to pour his energies into funding projects in the world of spiritualism and psychical research.

Before this, most of the studies in which Bute was involved had revolved around collecting word-of-mouth evidence, and personal testimony. This was not merely unsatisfactory in theory, it had turned out to be all but impossible in practice. In December of 1896, Bute and Myers decided that the thing would be for Bute to finance a full-scale investigation of a Scottish house where much ghost activity had been reported: Ballechin House. Bute had first heard of the haunting of Ballechin House from Fr Hayden, the priest who had led a retreat there and had a series of uncomfortable and inexplicable experiences. The house was available for hire, and it was a simple matter to take a holiday let and set up an investigation.

Bute kept Ballechin House supplied with a team of researchers, headed, of course, by Miss Freer. She was universally regarded by visitors, both enthusiastic and hostile, as the most professional of all the investigators who spent time there, which says a good deal more about their lack of impartiality than it does about her possession of it. She was, however, a bright professional journalist, with an assured and charming manner. A sceptic, John Ritchie Findlay, son of the owner of the *Scotsman* (who later became in turn its proprietor), summed up the investigators to Bute, telling him that 'there was hardly a person at Ballechin whose testimony I should set much store [by]'. Miss Freer understood investigation but was not truly impartial. Colonel Taylor was a committed spiritualist. He did not have any 'experiences', but if he had, he would not have considered alternative rational explanations. Mr Powles was exceptionally nervous, telling 'by instinct' if a place was haunted and afterwards having the 'experiences' to justify the claim. 'Mr Shaw the parson' regularly saw 'figures outlined in light against a dark background. These he told me he could see at will.' He too was quite uncritical.

> The following incident illustrates the attitude of mind. Miss Freer came to meet me in a waggonette. The horses startled at the train, & she was thrown out. He saw all that happened, yet he seriously asked her if she thought she had been thrown out by supernatural agencies.

Miss Langton was young, sickly and easily influenced. In fact, the only person upon whose evidence Findlay would have relied at all was Miss Moore, Miss Freer's close friend. Findlay ended bitterly: 'Of course it may be said that it is only persons of this sort are competent to investigate such matters, but if you adopt this position you must abandon all hope of convincing the majority of mankind.'[104]

Miss Langton was not a professional medium, merely it seems a friend of Miss Moore and Miss Freer. Mr Shaw, Mr Powles and Colonel Taylor were all members of the SPR. They were not the only visitors, and, as Miss Freer points out, there were 'eleven ladies, twenty-one gentlemen, and *The Times* correspondent'.[105] No wonder Miss Freer entertained Bute. *The Times* correspondent was thus segregated because after the tenancy of Ballechin had been concluded, a hostile account of the investigation was published in *The Times*, written, it was afterwards revealed, by the leader writer, J. Callendar Ross.[106] This article pulled no punches in denouncing the SPR, and in suggesting that Bute's confidence had been 'grossly abused'. It named the house, which everybody had agreed to keep private, in line with the conventions of the period. It was not a fair article, and even Hall admits that the author either did not know, or ignored, the entirely unbiased testimony of Fr Hayden when suggesting that the house had had no reputation for being haunted before it was let in 1896.[107] It was the first clap of thunder in a storm of protest. Bute unfairly blamed Crichton Browne, and quarrelled with him. The Steuart family, owners of the house, bitterly claimed that they had been deceived by Taylor when he hired the house, and would never have let it had it been known it was for ghost hunting. The good name of their property had been damaged, and they would suffer financial loss.

The alleged hauntings can be condensed into three types of phenomena. The first two were of the kind experienced by Fr Hayden years before, and consisted of the sounds of footsteps and banging on doors, and the sensation of having bedclothes moved or compressed. These were experienced by a number of guests in the 'haunted room', and a number of others experienced nothing, including Sir James Crichton Browne, and Mr Findlay, sceptics, and Colonel Taylor, who was perfectly prepared to believe. In her book, Ada Freer draws particular attention to three classes of sounds. One is of limping steps. These are linked to Major Robert Steuart, a Protestant, who 'died in April 1876'. He had spent much of his life in India, and acquired the belief that the human spirit might, on death, migrate to the body of an animal. He spoke of his intention of returning to earth and inhabiting the body of his favourite spaniel. He may have been taken seriously, because on his death all his dogs were shot. His unmarried housekeeper, Sarah, was hinted to have died of the complications of childbirth at the age of twenty-seven.[108] The sounds of limping in the 'most haunted' room were those of the Major, around the death-bed of his mistress. The other most common noise was the sound of an animal playing, which other dogs in the household noticed, and they are occasionally reported to have encountered apparently canine companions, unseen by the rest of the party.

Several guests (including Fr Hayden, who was not part of this investigation but told Lord Bute of his experiences much earlier) felt as though their bedclothes were being dragged off, and on occasions as though their bed was moved. The other phenomena were visions of a nun and her secular companion in a small glen and occasionally other places in the grounds. These were ascribed to the Major's sister, who had been a nun. Only she belonged to an order which had a very particular kind of habit, and the apparitions wore the standard dress. Then, too, the Major's sister, 'Dear Sister Frances', who had died in 1880, 'was always so fervent and mortified that we could not easily believe she was still in Purgatory'.[109]

In addition there were the typical Victorian parlour séance communications by Ouija board. It was from them that the name 'Ishbel' for the nun was gleaned. Ishbel is the Gaelic form of Isabella, the baptismal name of the nun Sister Frances. Miss Freer made the ingenious suggestion that the visions of the nun might be thought transference from the uneducated Sarah, from beyond the grave, and the incorrect dress due to the limited imagination of Sarah, who neither in this life nor the next moved in circles where she could know the much more refined and elevated nun. Miss Freer offered other explanations, too. The nun might have been a phantasm of some living nun who had once been at Ballechin on a retreat, similar to that given by Fr Hayden. This was supported by a vision of Fr Hayden by Miss Langton. Of course such a theory would be at once acceptable to the SPR which, as seen above, was very interested in the possibility of phantoms of the living, and in thought transference. The most convincing phenomena reported were very like the 'Barisal guns' which are known in United States as 'mistpouffers'. These sound like a distant but very loud explosion, and they are unexplained to this day, though they have been heard by too many (including the present author) to be dismissed as hallucinations. It is tempting to suggest that these may have accounted for most of the noises heard, and for the reputation of haunting.

Bute repeatedly said he was losing his judgement, and the lack of any attempt to get scientific methods of any kind into Ballechin House seems only too clearly to have demonstrated this. Miss Freer said she tried to get a seismograph to record vibrations, but was told a sensitive one would be too hard for an amateur to operate, and one that was easier to operate would be too inaccurate. It is harder to explain the total lack of sound-recording equipment, though a camera was useless as there were few visual phenomena, and what there were appeared in very low light levels. Bute did not suggest it, or even insist upon a better objective basis, and he was funding the investigation. The answer probably is simply that, while not confused or demented, he had indeed lost his critical judgement.

Friends advised Bute not to subject himself to the strain of sleeping in a haunted house, but the temptation was irresistible. He and Gwen spent 26–28 April in the house, sleeping in rooms known not to be affected by the sounds of 'haunting'. He read aloud the Office for the dead, and had:

> A most disagreeable impression, not in the places where he expected it, [which was where the 'nun' had been seen and the rooms where most sounds had been heard] but in No.1 [the room next door to the most haunted one]. The sensation was that of persons being present, and on the second occasion that of violent hatred and hostility.[110]

After this, it was felt that the atmosphere became generally more hostile, and Bute arranged for two priests, the folklorist Alan McDonald and an unnamed bishop, to say Mass in the house. This was done, and each room sprinkled with holy water and prayed in, and the phenomena ceased.

The fact that Bute also believed this investigation could be kept private and not become the subject of gossip in polite society is probably attributable simply to his social naïveté. His was an age which placed a higher importance upon propriety than can be easily imagined in the twenty-first century. Those suggesting that the house was not haunted had as much vested interest in their claims as those who wanted to prove it was. Not only were future lettings put at risk, but there was a suggestion of the disreputable about ghosts and haunting, and the knowledge of a black sheep in the Steuart family did not raise the smile that it might today.

Not only did the Steuarts and Bute quarrel in the aftermath of the affair, Fred Myers had already quarrelled with Miss Freer over his introduction of a Miss Chaston into the house, while Miss Freer was absent. Hall believes this is evidence that Miss Freer was jealous. It is far more likely that she felt that the more or less unchaperoned introduction into the house of a young woman whose career was not what she pretended it had been[111] would jeopardise the whole undertaking. If Bute for one moment had suspected that Myers had introduced his mistress into the house for a convivial week, his fury would have been all-encompassing. Miss Chaston claimed to be a number of things, including a qualified nurse, and she proved to be none of them. Myers now refused to support Miss Freer. He 'wrote to *The Times* at once and said that while he had visited Ballechin representing the Society, he had decided that there was no evidence worth reporting'.[112] This is not at all what he had said earlier. When Bute was privately briefed about this, he sided with Miss Freer. Miss Freer co-wrote with Bute a book called *The Alleged Haunting of B– House*, in which she took her revenge on Myers, and also suggested a variety of sometimes conflicting explanations for the phenomena, from hallucinations to thought transference to unquiet spirits. But then, as their book concludes: 'The editors offer no conclusions. This volume has been put together, as the house at B– was taken, not for the establishment of theories, but for the record of facts.'[113]

Bute increasingly relied on Metcalfe to stand in for him at the St Andrews Court. He did attend a series of meetings in October 1897, when he came to receive the Freedom of St Andrews. He had felt it was approval for his services to the University, which the local newspaper indignantly denied, saying it was for his work on the Priory. Feelings were therefore running high when, on 5 October, Donaldson delivered to the students a speech openly hostile to Bute. Or rather, he delivered part of it, for he was well aware that Bute had the sympathy of the students and was truly their representative. He not only attacked Bute's policies, but launched a personal attack on him as well, suggesting that Bute's mind was dominated by prejudice and emotion. Donaldson always sent his speech in advance to the press, and the Dundee paper was run by those prepared to back him. He did not deliver those parts of his speech which were a personal attack, but instead they were carried in the press. As his biographer comments: 'in including it in a copy sent to the press he would ensure its widespread circulation and avoid any chance of demonstration of dissent in the hall. This is to credit him with a slightly Machiavellian turn of mind ...'[114] Bute, or perhaps the unimpaired Metcalfe, plotted the perfect revenge. Donaldson told Rosebery that at the next meeting of Court, Bute was 'very kind & yielded everything' until the end of the meeting, when he got one of his followers to propose 'that a committee be appointed to consider and report upon the address'. Donaldson told Rosebery that Bute could not have done a more foolish thing.[115] Donaldson's judgement was at fault, not Bute's. The committee decided against Donaldson and he was in effect impeached by the University court.

Bute was increasingly relying upon others to carry forward his work. On the day after he had been told he had Bright's disease in 1895, R. R. Anderson had arrived back from a trip to Saragossa (Zaragoza). He had been researching Peter de Luna, the antipope who had granted St Andrews University its founding charter. Bute's interest had been sparked in typical fashion and his sympathy ignited for the stubborn antihero. Anderson came back in triumph. He had 'been very successful in searching for monuments of Peter de Luna, bringing photographs of 3 splendid reliquaries, a lectern & the lantern (cimboris) all given to him by the Cathedral of Zaragossa'.[116]

There had always been a plan to have two wings to Mount Stuart, reaching out beyond the foot of the old house. The one to the north was to be a chapel, and the one to the south a large conservatory. Plans for the conservatory were scaled down, and in the end it was never built. However, Bute's new enthusiasm for Zaragoza gave an impetus to the chapel. Work was begun on a rosy sandstone ground-level crypt, dedicated to the Virgin. Work was slow and Bute's poor health led him to put more and more of the detail in Gwen's capable hands. She harried Anderson. He replied glumly:

I have thought over and suggested every possible plan for hastening the work, but it is only just to admit that the obstacles the builders have to face are considerable. ... the difficulties of getting hold of men is great. Messrs Devlin say that they are withdrawing men from other works for Mount Stuart, and have also advertised, but with no result, and although willing to offer higher wages in order to secure men, they dare not do so, as they would at once be boycotted by the Master Builder's Association.[117]

Despite the difficulties the crypt was finished, and the simple, arctic, Marble Chapel was finally built. It was faced all in white marble except where the windows showed the glowing sandstone outside. Architecturally it was unremarkable, and it relied for its impact on the dazzling white, only broken by the ruby-red glass in the clerestory, that 'Russian dodge' Bute had longed to try out ten years before. The earliest chapel design is dated 1896 but that scheme was not progressed with. The dates on the plans for the chapel as built are the date the contractors signed the drawings, November 1897 (with Farmer & Brindley, who did the marble work, signing in October 1898).[118] The chapel is as much a reflection of Gwen's taste as of Bute's.

In the autumn of 1897 the decision had been taken to send the two elder boys to Harrow. John was now sixteen, and if he was ever to attend a public school it would need to be now. For years his academic studies had given rise to concern. His brother Ninian, two years younger, kept up with him with ease. In adult life the 4th Marquess was to prove he had an able mind. It seems likely that the problem was, in fact, dyslexia. The boys went to Harrow as day-pupils, boarding in the town with their tutor, René Condor. This would disarm accusations that they were being exposed to harmful Protestant influences. It did almost nothing to reduce their homesickness, and 'Baba', the Earl of Dumfries, seems to have become significantly depressed.

> Baba is getting worse and worse I am sorry to say and Mr Condor says he is going to resign the post of keeping us if Baba stays much longer because he <u>never</u> talks on any occasion whatever therefore the house is as if a continual funeral was going on or something like that, he says today is the very worst day he has had yet, but he said that two or three days ago so I do not know what he means quite.[119]

Inevitably all this tortured Gwen further, especially as she, at least, had huge reservations over sending the boys to school. Although John struggled on at Harrow, his health was 'delicate' for most of the time. Ninian was robust, and while he hated football, he enjoyed squash (as, surprisingly, did John) and alternated between times of hard work when he was near the head of the class, and relapses into idleness. In short, he seems to have enjoyed an utterly normal school life. It seems likely that the desire was to get them away from an atmosphere dominated by their father's slow, brave death. By the next year, twelve-year-old Colum was at prep school, and taking part in a swimming competition.

How far Bute's faculties had been destroyed by illness at this time is shown by the wretched account of his reaction to the stories told to him by James Owens, a Roman Catholic billiard maker in St Andrews with a lively interest in spiritualism. In 1898 Owens had a vision of an unhappy monk, and he contacted Lord Bute, and also the medium Katie Wingfield, about it. The story of the monk, Thomas Platar, was pathetic. His were some of the bones that the excavation of the St Andrews Priory had uncovered. He had been an Augustinian friar, who had stabbed 'his Prior (in 1393) and had in consequence been refused Christian burial, his body having been cast on a dunghill'.[120] Miss Wingfield's control was able to give more details (following a visit from Owens):

> you see he says he was buried or rather his bones were thrown away in the <u>white</u> dress – & his cross taken from him – you see he says he does not want to tell about the buildings but all he wants is to be laid at rest.[121]

What happened next made Bute a laughing stock in St Andrews, and shows how far his mind had declined in 1898. Although it is reported by the hostile Donaldson, the story seems substantially true.

> Lord Bute wrote to the Archbishop and got the required permission. He then sent to London with an order to a tailor to make a dress the same as that which was used by the Augustinian monks. The dress came. The bones which had been taken out of the pit in the garden were wrapped up in this dress and deposited in a crypt which forms part of Lord Bute's restoration. On the morning of July 15 Mr Angus said his mass in the Roman Catholic church and then drove to the Priory with three cabs – for he had to carry an altar, vestments and other apparatus. The altar was set down in the crypt & Lord & Lady Bute, Sir Hunter Blair, a monk of the monastery at Fort William which is to take charge of the Roman Catholic hostel at Oxford, Mr Angus and the billiard maker arrived and again a ceremony was performed, Hunter Blair officiating. After this, the billiard maker took up the bones, & followed by Lord Bute & Hunter Blair marched in procession to the Cathedral grounds, and in a place near to the chapel of St Rule the bones were buried, Hunter Blair & Lord Bute uttering words during the whole procession. The space required was quite small & the grave digger in digging for it came on a stone sarcophagus, on the top of which the bones rest. I asked the priest if Platar's name had been used by him in performing the mass, but he said that he did not, that the words were for person or persons, and it was left to Almighty God to determine who the person was.[122]

It seems incredible that a man who earlier had reported with glee that his friend was snorting 'impossible' over the alleged miracles of St Bridget could possibly be reduced to doing such a thing.

In October he went north with Gwen to participate in the first Mass since the Reformation in the partially restored Greyfriars Convent, where 800 attended, and he and Gwen were the only two at the first Mass for the same length of time at Pluscarden Abbey, celebrated by Hunter Blair. These are the only glimpses we have of Lord Bute in 1898. There are no letters from or to him in the Mount Stuart archive, except a few from Katie Wingfield and none from or to his wife, except those relating to the education of her children.[123] Undoubtedly her family would have written to Gwen to encourage her and help her as she watched the slow decline of the man she loved. The assumption is that afterwards she could not bear to keep these letters.

Bute suffered a debilitating stroke in August 1899,[124] probably at Falkland.[125] He, who had so loved to walk, was moved now in a bath-chair, and Gwen considered having a lift installed for it at Mount Stuart. He made a partial recovery, and the only surviving letters from this period are from Gwen to Metcalfe:

Here we go on slowly – it is a terribly anxious time & the improvement is almost imperceptible. The mind is unharmed but the speech is very indistinct and you may well imagine how sad a time we are passing through. To think that such a mind & body should be so suddenly struck down helpless entirely in the right side & speaking really in such a bad state, the word most wanted not to be got.

Please God things will improve, as I am assured, but at times the outlook is almost unbearably sad.[126]

At the end of the month she added:

We have got Lord Bute downstairs for the first time today – but although it is a good additional step to have made still ... he cannot read anything with comfort nor dictate, nor can any of the old occupations be taken up as wd be the case after any ordinary illness however severe.[127]

He travelled between Mount Stuart, Falkland and Dumfries House. In St Andrews the new medical building was completed, and Gwen told Bute:

'I hear the Medical School at St A is nearly finished' – he said 'I thought it was finished long ago.' I said 'and now they want to put up an inscription saying you gave it and calling it the Bute Medical School' he answered nothing – so I suppose one may take silence for consent. I don't see why it should not be put not that he wd. have put it up himself, it seems to me very proper it should be put up.[128]

In the summer of the next year he was taken on a cruise. Gwen begged Metcalfe:

Please come, I am sure Lord Bute wd. be glad to see you.

As to Lord Bute he is always very much the same, but you will not see him at his best as he is always at his worst when he sees people for the first time, the cruise got rid of certain grooves we had got into, but otherwise he is the same, please do not allude to his being much better.[129]

He became well enough to attend public worship again 'assisting at the Mass' in the charming phrase. Then in his beautiful home in Ayrshire, Dumfries House, on 7 October 1900, he had a further stroke, and lay unconscious until 9 October, when he died in the early hours of the morning. He was fifty-three years old. His wife, Margaret, John and Colum were at his bedside. Ninian was visiting Russia.

For his mother's sake, Ninian tried for a proper sorrow, but his father had been dying for six years, about which Ninian had probably been more realistic than his mother, and Bute's actual death did not mean so much to a young man who felt the whole of his life before him:

It is very sad but 'His will be done on earth as it is in Heaven'. All He does is good. That is why He would not let me be at home. In His wisdom there is all the comfort we need. We must go to him sometime and He knows best when. Think of Him Mother and be as happy as possible. He will help you if you ask Him. 'In prayer is there all comfort'![130]

Obituary

'He set himself above no man'[1]

Bute had made exact arrangements for what was to happen to his body after death. He had the same horror of premature burial that allegedly led some of his contemporaries to arrange to be buried with bells for summoning help should they awake. His doctors were to wait until they saw unmistakable signs that his body was decaying and then remove his heart. Only then was he to be sealed into his coffin. His heart was to be taken back to Jerusalem. It was a beautiful idea, poetic and full of meaning. Full of history, too, for his ancestor Robert the Bruce had also desired his heart to be taken on pilgrimage and left in the Holy Land.

His funeral also was something out of the middle ages. The lead-lined coffin was taken by steamer to the stone pier at Kilchattan Bay, where it was met by a hearse drawn by his own horses. A cross led the procession. Then came the young Lord Bute, Nohn, and after him a double row of clergy, choristers, and incense-bearers. His wife and his daughter were in the single carriage. Everybody else moved on foot, a huge mass of his tenants, his servants, his neighbours. When they reached the gates of Mount Stuart, the day was deepening to dusk. Flaming torches were lit, and the coffin transferred to a hand-bier. Then they moved slowly on to the Shore Chapel, where the simple, impressive service of Vespers for the Dead was started, a public service, relatively accessible to Bute's Protestant neighbours. The emotion of it all was too much for his family, who left before the end. Throughout the night, nuns kept watch by the coffin, praying. The next morning there was a private Requiem Mass for the family and their close friends.[2] Then Bute's lead-lined coffin was placed in a little room at the back of the chapel, avoiding the dark, tide-washed burial ground, and his widow left 'at once' for the Holy Land.

She took his heart in a simple, but exquisite, silver box designed by Lonsdale. She sailed to the Mediterranean, where she picked up Ninian, who had travelled straight there from Russia. Together they went to Jerusalem. Bute's express wishes, made in the year after Colum's birth, were that his heart was

> to be buried on the Mount of Olives, in a place from which the Church of the Holy Sepulchre can be seen, in such a way that it may soonest and most completely mix with the earth.[3]

Gwen found the heart a place beside the Franciscan chapel 'Dominus Flevit'. In later years, she fussed over getting a plaque to mark the spot, and marking the site with flowers. But Bute would not have cared much about these things. His heart had come home to a joy which rose out of sorrow, and his story had drawn to a close.

While Gwen took Bute on his last pilgrimage, the obituaries poured in. Bishop Hedley provided perhaps the most rounded and the most touching:

> Notwithstanding his wealth, his retiring manner, his quiet and scholarly life, in spite of all the barriers that social conditions or personal characteristics placed in the way of free intercourse, it had been felt that he had a human soul, sensitive, unaffected, and kindly nature, and that he set himself above no man . . . Those who had been brought into relation with him in personal, charitable, or municipal matters, or in business, knew well how lowly were his thoughts of himself, and how genuine his concern for all men, high and low.[4]

If Ada Freer had any debts left to pay him, her tribute[5] rendered a full account. Not because it was fulsome, for it was not especially so, but because she left an eyewitness account of his kindness and charming idiosyncrasies. She always had a vivid way with words.

> We once spoke of a lady whose circumstances had become sadly reduced. 'I could not presume to offer her any help,' he said, 'but I did give myself the pleasure of having some pleasant colouring put into her house. I visited at her father's years ago, and everything always looked very cheerful.' He had, in fact, entirely renovated her home from top to bottom.
>
> I remember a somewhat irritated architect complaining that work on a particular part of Falkland Palace was at a standstill because

the swallows were building. Nothing was to be done which might 'interfere with their matrimonial arrangements'. Guests at Dumfries House will recall how the rabbits used to sit up and wash their faces just below the drawing-room window. Woe betide anyone who put down steel traps on any part of the Bute estates: 'There are any number of plants that rabbits don't injure,' Lord Bute would say when a visitor deprecated their appearance in the beautiful gardens. Squirrels and birds were an endless pleasure to him, and he would stand motionless for a long time to watch certain partly albino sparrows that year after year haunted St John's Lodge, while his tall stately figure was well known to every keeper in the Zoological Gardens.

In discussing the unsolved problem of the alleged haunting of B– House, Lord Bute has often said: 'It could be no very evil influence. The place is a perfect aviary.'

Nearly every newspaper in the land carried at least a couple of column inches of obituary. Most were merely formal, mentioning his wealth, his scholarship, his children, his widow. Every mistake that could be made, was made. At least half the obituaries spelt Gwendolen's name wrong, the name of his youngest son proved too much for many to swallow, and was commuted to 'Edmond', Bute was accused of having been an ardent Anglican in his youth, and his publication on the 'altus'[6] was amended to the 'altars'[6] of St Columba.

There were many lives where Bute's passing left a gap. As the newspapers commented, he did not socialise very much with men of his own rank. Bute valued other things in men and women (for many of his friends were women) than their birth. His hospitality was generous, and his company stimulating. Taciturn in general society, he was warm in private. It was said of him that he could fill a dinner table with people who were specialists in a variety of fields, and hold his own in conversation with all of them. He had little interest in small talk, but he was witty and interested in almost every subject of artistic and scientific interest. He was not above gossip of the more general kind, and listened avidly to scandals involving British and foreign royalty. Everybody (except David Hunter Blair, of whom Bute commented, employing the expressive Scotticism 'I feel very sore with him'[7]) agreed that he was an excellent host and that he never behaved as if he had the least consciousness of his rank. In fact, on occasion he would use it to impress those he wanted to win over for one cause or another. He was aware that it mattered to others, but to himself it seemed a trivial thing. He was proud of his lineage, and of his descent from the great saint Queen Margaret, but it was not his ancestor King Robert the Bruce whom he admired, but the squire, later knight, William Wallace. Parentage mattered, family more so, but not rank, and nothing mattered as much as the way the individual worked out their own life. Consequently, he set himself to meet the person before him, and usually bent all his considerable powers on them; this might be a keeper at London Zoo, or a Cardinal of the Church, a Church of Scotland minister, or one of his own children.

Then, slowly, the lives of most of those who had known him returned to normal, except perhaps for his widow's life. Gwen and Margaret went to live for a while in the rural retreat of Castell Coch, and then on the Isle of Millport. Gwen never remarried, and died in 1932.

John, now the 4th Marquess of Bute, did go to Oxford. As an adult he proved to have an acute mind. He had his father's passion for architectural conservation, and worked hard for the preservation of Edinburgh's New Town. He was a committed ornithologist, although unlike his father, he enjoyed shooting. At the age of twenty-four he married Augusta Bellingham, and with her had seven children. He died in 1947. The present Marquess is descended from him in the direct line.

Ninian was twenty-three when he married, and became the father of four children, the eldest of whom, a son called after him, died when only three. Ninian had an early career in the army before entering politics. In 1912 he rejoined the army, and was a Lieutenant-Colonel when he was killed in 1915, leaving his infant son to inherit Falkland. His family are Hereditary Keepers of the Palace to this day.

Colum became a Conservative Member of Parliament. He married Elizabeth Hope, widow of the Marquess of Landsdowne in 1940, and died childless.

Margaret married Colin MacRae in 1909, when she was thirty-four. She had three children. Her only son John was killed in action in Egypt in 1942, leaving her heartbroken.

The question arises of what Bute's achievements were, and what was his lasting legacy. Bute was in the forefront of many movements. He was a committed anti-vivisectionist, and campaigned against cruelty to animals. He was in favour of an increasing public sphere and voice for women, and funded professional education for women out of his own purse. He was one of the first to be interested in the reform of liturgy by looking at, and returning to, older standards, which in time led to the tsunami of liturgical reform in our era. He was an architectural conservationist at a time when the wrecking of buildings in the name of conformity to a gothic ideal was at its peak. He supported the conservation of natural environments all his life. He believed passionately in independence for Scotland, at the vanguard of a movement which has still perhaps not reached its peak. He worked unceasingly at his studies in the history of Scotland at a time when few took such interests seriously. Yet in all these things, although he was active, and lent his energy and his money to the causes he supported, he was only one among many. There is no single cause which would have failed had it not been for his support. He did what others did, albeit in many cases did it somewhat better. In these fields he did not have the creativity to be the one who marked out the path ahead, and instead he was the able supporter, with his shoulder to the wheel.

In one area alone did he change the course of history, and that was in his work for, and salvation of, St Andrews University; and, because of the propaganda of the Dundee faction, this work has not been fairly or properly appreciated in the histories of the two universities. Owing to Bute, St Andrews remained a university in the old town, until the changing tides of education brought it more students and an assured future. Dundee College followed its own path, and it, too, became a full university. By his intervention Bute had done nothing but good.

In his personal life, he showed a courage and a compassion which few people achieve. His utter unpretentiousness in the face of endless sycophancy is remarkable, and his relations with the women around him wholly admirable. He tackled his bouts of depression with remarkable insight and good sense, walking and working himself to health again. Above all, his enormous courage in the face of his oncoming death, and the consistent way he put his wife's emotional needs at this time ahead of his own, inasmuch as he could, is perhaps his finest personal achievement. Yet it is only through his letters and diaries that we have a record of these things, and they have made no impact on the larger world.

Bute also left his buildings. By the time he died, fashions were changing, and within a few years, Bute's buildings were eclipsed. The 4th Marquess advertised Mount Stuart for sale, to be dismantled and re-erected as a hotel. The Victorian Gothic was laughed at, rather than laughed with. It seemed as though the buildings had been expensive monstrosities. Then, really quite suddenly, things changed. By the time all Bute's children had died, the architectural pendulum was starting to swing back. It is perhaps only today that we can appreciate the full range of his architectural imagination from the detailed Gothic humour of Cardiff Castle, to the astonishing stillness of St Sophia's Galston, and from the Renaissance recreation of Falkland Palace, through to the Arts and Crafts detail and finesse of his work at Dumfries House and House of Falkland. Today, the beautiful buildings Bute created are once again appreciated for the extraordinary works of art they are. Bute's final obituary is the awe on the faces of those who encounter them for the first time.

Titles

'Drop the Lord'

Bute's name was of course John Patrick Crichton Stuart, but like many other aristocrats, he rarely used it, and instead used his title as though it was a combination of both surname and first name. One of Bute's requests to his correspondents was 'drop the Lord'. To many, perhaps even to himself, he was simply 'Bute'.

There are instances where surnames and titles are the same (Hastings being one), but most families who have titles have a distinct surname. There was a strong social convention that these surnames should be linked with the titles, and when titles moved sideways, as they sometimes did (there being no heir in the direct line) it was usual for the inheritor to adopt the surname traditionally associated with the title. Thus Patrick McDouall or McDowell (the name is commonly spelt both ways), who became 6th Earl of Dumfries, took the name McDouall-Crichton and his grandson who inherited the title of Dumfries became Crichton Stuart. Lady Edith Hastings married Charles Clifton, and he later assumed her surname, actually before the death of her brother, the 4th Marquess of Hastings, his children thus becoming Hastings, not Clifton. There was, too, a general feeling that it was invidious for the husband and father not to have a title when his wife and son did, especially if he had money of his own.

Many who do not have titles, and all who do, have coats-of-arms: an image unique to that family shown on a shield. How that symbol is shown usually makes it possible to track down the exact person intended. Each married person has their spouse's symbol shown next to theirs, either side-by-side with a divide between the two, or with the shield split into quarters, with the man's arms in the top left (as one looks at it) and bottom right quarters, and his wife's in the others. The eldest son, until he inherits, has his father's arms with a 'label': a straight line with three (occasionally more) lines dropping from it, like an E but with the long line to the top of the shield. The second son has a crescent, resting on its curve, and the third a star. An unmarried woman or widow has her arms shown not on a shield but on a lozenge, a diamond shape. Bute's fondness for coats of arms arose partly from how they enable one to pin-point a person in a symbol. The symbol on the shield arises, of course, from the need to distinguish one knight from another in battle or in a tournament.

Knighthoods cannot be inherited, but baronetcies can. Both give the bearer and his wife a title ('Sir Joseph and Lady Bloggs'). The next title up the ladder of the nobility is Viscount. In Scotland, most viscounts are Viscounts of Somewhere (not so in England). Earls are most usually Earls of Somewhere. Thus the Crichtons were Earls of Dumfries. Earls are referred to as Lord Somewhere and their Countesses as Lady Somewhere, and addressed as 'my Lord/Lady'. If an occasion arises where it is desirable to use Lady Somewhere's first name, she is Josephine, Lady Somewhere, not Lady Josephine Somewhere. Their children are known as Lord Joseph and Lady Josephine, except for their eldest son who is usually given as a courtesy a title already in the family, such as Viscount.

The next step up is to be Marquess of Somewhere, and Marquesses and their Marchionesses are addressed in the same way as Earls and Countesses. Usually their eldest son, before he inherits, is given an honorary title, and this is normally an earldom. Thus young John, or Nohn, Crichton Stuart was the Earl of Dumfries. Becoming Duke and Duchess gives a much grander title. A Duke is his Grace of Somewhere, and his Duchess her Grace, and one addresses them as 'your Grace'.

There are Scottish titles, and British ones. Most Scottish titles can be inherited by women in the direct line, and that includes the earldoms of Bute and Dumfries. That is to say, if an earl has only daughters, then his daughter can inherit the title, which does not pass to his brother's son, as it does in the English and British systems. Thus Lady Edith became Countess of Loudoun but not Marchioness of Hastings. An added complication for inheritance is that very often estates were left 'in the tail male', or entailed. They could only pass to a male heir and that male heir could not dispose of them as he saw fit, but had to pass them to his male heirs intact. Thus Lady Margaret, should she have become Countess of Bute in her own right, could not have inherited the Welsh estates, which would have passed to her cousins. An entail could sometimes be broken but it was difficult and expensive, and also felt to be an incorrect thing to do.

This leaves the question of why titles are created in the first place. Generally, they were seen as a reward for service to the country or monarch, or as a recognition of existing esteem. Thus the 4th Earl of Bute (1744–1814) was promoted to 1st Marquess of Bute in recognition of his father having been Prime Minister, his own service as ambassador for his country, and of his having inherited the bulk of his mother's considerable fortune (she was the only daughter of the famous Lady Mary Wortley Montague). The Bute family also nicely illustrate how, up to the Georgian period, there was a general pressure for an increase in rank. The first recorded Stuart of Bute was Sir John Stuart, born 1360, an illegitimate son of Robert II of Scotland. (His title was a knighthood, not a heritable baronetcy.) His descendant in the direct line, James Stuart, who died in 1662, was the first baronet, and his grandson and namesake was made an earl for services to his monarch over the Union of the Parliaments. He died in 1710.

One suspects that Bute was the first of his line who would be more moved by an elected title, Mayor, than by a hereditary one, both a tribute to the man, and a record of the beginning of a different and more individualistic way of looking at honour.

Notes

Preface

1. BU/89/1/8 Gwen to Angela, 17 July 1872. Gwen was describing how Bute was urging her to wear her most beautiful and formal gown to a Cardiff ball.
2. The Right Rev. Sir David Hunter Blair Bt., OSB, *John Patrick Third Marquess of Bute K.T. (1847–1900) A Memoir* (John Murray: London, 1921), henceforth HB, p. 51n.
3. HB, p. 115.
4. *Ibid.*, p. 104.

Chapter 1: Infancy

1. HB, p. 59.
2. Charles Edward Rawdon-Hastings, 11th Earl of Loudoun 1855–1920.
3. John Crichton Stuart 1793–1848.
4. Maria North 1792–1841, grand-daughter of the Prime Minister.
5. John Davies gives a fascinating account of how the 2nd Marquess of Bute created a thriving industrial complex out of his Glamorgan agricultural land. JD.
6. CCL, B, Bute to Roy 26 Dec. 1844, quoted in JD p. 67.
7. Sophia Frederica Christina Rawdon-Hastings was born in 1809, *SP* vol. II.
8. Flora Mure Campbell 1780–1840, *SP* vol. V.
9. Francis Rawdon-Hastings, 1st Marquess of Hastings KG PC (1754–1828). He had a distinguished military career, a diplomatic career and was Governor-General of India.
10. Patrick James Herbert Crichton Stuart (1794–1859).
11. Patrick McDouall-Crichton, 6th Earl of Dumfries (1726–1803).
12. BU/21/160/20 Bute to Gwen, undated.
13. Lady Flora Elizabeth Rawdon-Hastings 1806–1839, *SP* vol. V.
14. Sir John Conroy, 1st Baronet, 1786–1854. Together with Victoria's mother (the Duchess of Kent) he was responsible for the oppressive system of education she endured and he had put great pressure on her to appoint him her secretary and treasurer, which she resisted.
15. Lady Flora Elizabeth Rawdon Hastings, *Poems by the Lady Flora Hastings, Ed. by Her Sister* (William Blackwood: Edinburgh, 1842).
16. George Augustus Francis Rawdon-Hastings, 2nd Marquess of Hastings, 1808–1844.

17. Barbara, Baroness Grey de Ruthyn, m. George 1831, m. 1844 Admiral Sir Hastings Yelverton d. 1858. Known as 'the jolly fast Marchioness', she was a great follower of hounds, a gambler and a serious palaeontologist.

18. The spelling of the name changed through time from Ruthyn to Ruthven.

19. Mount Stuart mss. Note in Lady Bute's hand.

20. NLS Ms. 3445 f. 322 Bute to Principal Lee, 13 Sept. 1847.

21. NLS Ms. 3445 f. 325 Bute to Principal Lee, 15 Sept. 1847.

22. NLS Ms. 3445 ff. 356–9 Lady Bute to Principal Lee, 11 Dec. 1847.

23. JD, pp. 116–25.

24. *Cf.* NAS GD 152/196/16/2 McNabb to Bruce, May 1848.

25. NAS GD 152/196/8–14 Lady Bute to Tyndall Bruce, letters in the April and May of 1848.

26. The lease to the Dowlais Iron Company had been granted in the eighteenth century upon terms most disadvantageous to the Bute Estate, and the Dowlais Company had also been guilty of a variety of malpractices (JD, p. 39). It was the subject of renegotiation at this date.

27. Mount Stuart mss. Note in regard to the domicile of the Marquess of Bute, prepared for the Court of Session 1860.

28. Mount Stuart mss. Note in regard to the domicile of the Marquess of Bute, undated, in the papers prepared for the Court of Session 1860.

29. NAS GD 152/196/8/6 Lady Bute to Bruce, 21 Apr. 1848.

30. Onesiphorus Tyndall later assumed the name of Bruce, ?–1855. M. F. Connolly, *Biographical Dictionary of Eminent Men of Fife* (Orr: Cupar, 1866). He was a contemporary of the 2nd Marquess of Bute at school.

31. NAS GD 152/196/8/1 Lady Bute to Bruce, 16 Apr. 1848.

32. JD, p. 69.

33. The Dowager Duchess of Northumberland had a jointure of the same sum, but actually received £12,500. The proposed jointure for the Marchioness of Guilford was £2,500. F. M. L. Thompson, *English Landed Society in the Nineteenth Century* (Routledge & Kegan Paul: London, 1963), pp. 102–3.

34. NAS GD 152/196/16/6/9 McNabb to Bruce, 17 May 1848.

35. NAS GD 152/196/8/14 Lady Bute to Bruce, 15 May 1848.

36. *Ibid.*

37. The Tutor-at-Law is always the 'agnate', the closest relative to the father. John Erskine, *Principles of the Law of Scotland* (19th edn, ed. John Rankine: Sweet & Maxwell: Edinburgh, 1895) p. 73.

38. NAS GD 152/196/8–16 Lady Bute to Bruce, 23 May 1848.

39. *Ibid.*

40. Dudley Ryder 2nd Earl of Harrowby, 1798–1882. Lady Harrowby was the daughter of his second marriage to Frances Coutts, *SP* vol. II.

41. Harrowby Papers vol. LXII f. 72, 21 Sept. 1854.

42. Pat Jalland, *Death in the Victorian Family* (Oxford University Press: Oxford, 1996) p. 237.

43. Harrowby Papers vol. LXII ff. 85–6 Lady Bute to Lord Harrowby, 23 July 1855.

44. Harrowby Papers vol. LXII f. 72 Lady Bute to Lord Harrowby, 21 Sept. 1854.

45. NAS GD 152/196/8/14 Lady Bute to Bruce, 15 May 1848.

46. NAS GD 152/196/16/2 McNabb to Bruce, 10 May 1848.

47. NAS GD 152/196/8/16x Lady Bute to Bruce, 23 May 1848.

48. NAS GD 152/196/8/7 Lady Bute to Bruce, date obscure.

49. NAS GD 152/196/8/4 Lady Bute to Bruce, 20 Apr. 1848.

50. NAS GD 152/197/2/14–15 Lord James to Bruce, 6 Mar. 1849.

51. e.g. NAS GD 152/198/2/32 Lord James to Bruce, 5 Oct. 1850.

52. e.g. NAS GD 152/197/2/33 Lord James to Bruce, 4 Jul. 1849.

53. JD, p. 69.

54. NAS GD 152/198/1 Sophia to Bruce, 14 Feb. 1850.

55. NLS 3447 f148 Lady Bute to Dr Hood, 26 Aug. 1853.

56. Harrowby Papers vol. LXII ff. 257–62 Wortley to Harrowby, date illegible. James Stuart Wortley articulated the views of everyone concerned: 'I told him frankly that if I had been in his place, I should have thought it right to have given the mother one of the places outlined to bring up her child at, and I believe this to have been … the opinion that has been expressed by every friend at all he has consulted, but of course it is no small sacrifice of face to change his course now.'

57. Selina Constance Rawdon Hastings, 1810–1867, *SP* vol. V.

58. Adelaide Augusta Lavinia Rawdon Hastings, 1812–1860, *ibid*.

59. Paulyn Reginald Sero Rawdon Hastings, 3rd Marquess of Hastings, 1832–1851, *ibid*.

60. *The Leicestershire Chronicle,* 14 Nov. 1868.

61. Henry Weysford Charles Plantagenet Hastings, 1842–1868, *SP* vol. V.

62. Edith Maud, 1833–1874, *ibid*.

63. Barbara, Baroness Grey de Ruthyn, m. George 1831, m. 1844 Admiral Sir Hastings Yelverton, d. 1858, *ibid*. Known as 'the jolly fast Marchioness', she was a great follower of hounds, a gambler and a serious palaeontologist.

64. Harrowby Papers vol. LXII ff. 64–8 Lady Bute to Lord Harrowby, 1 Aug. 1850.

65. Elizabeth Anne Moore was one of six children of Stephen Moore, 2nd Earl Mountcashell. Her date of birth is not recorded, but she was eighty-eight when she died in 1892.

66. Mount Stuart mss. Lady Bute to Mrs D. Boswell, 10 Feb. 1851.

67. Mount Stuart mss. Bute to Mrs D. Boswell, 22 Jul. 1852.

68. Agnes Strickland, 1796–1874, historian, authoress of *The Lives of the Queens of England,* 12 vols (1840–8) and editor of *The Letters of Mary Queen of Scots,* 5 vols (1864). See *DNB*.

69. Mount Stuart mss. Agnes Strickland to Bute, date unclear.

70. Mount Stuart mss. Yarbrough to Bute, undated.

71. Mount Stuart mss. Flora Yarbrough to Bute, 16 Dec. 1853.

72. Susan Lady North, 1797–1884, *CP* vol. IX.

73. Mount Stuart mss. Aunt North to Bute, 7 Feb. 1857.

74. Mount Stuart mss., 12 Feb. 1857.

75. Sir Francis Hastings Gilbert, 2nd Baronet, 1816–1863. Vice-consul and Consul at Scutari 1853–1863. See Frederic Boase, *Modern English Biography* (Netherton & Worth: Truro, 1892–1921), vol. V, cols. 405–6.

76. Mount Stuart mss. Hastings Gilbert to Lord Bute, 21 May 1850.

77. NLS Ms. 3447 f. 195 Lady Bute to Principal Lee, 26 Aug. 1853.

78. Discovered by Giambattista Donati at Florence on 2 Jun. 1858, it remained visible to the naked eye for over three months and was judged to be among the most beautiful comets ever observed. Patrick Moore, *The Comets* (Keith Reid Ltd: Shaldon, 1973) pp. 59–60.

79. HB, p. 13.

80. Mount Stuart mss. Aunt North to Lord Bute, 5 Mar. 1853.

81. Mount Stuart mss. Henry A. Hunter Blair to Lord Bute, 2 Nov. 1857.

82. Mount Stuart mss. Mrs Tyndall Bruce to Lord Bute, 4 Jan. (no year).

83. Eleanora Boyle, 1816–1891, *SP* vol. II.

84. See *DNB*.

85. John Boyle, 1819–?, *ibid.*

86. NLS Ms. 2851 f. 145 Lady Bute to General Sir George Brown, 26 Nov. 1852.

87. Lord James's daughter, Lady Mary Anne Frances Crichton Stuart, d. 1886, *SP* vol. II.

88. Mount Stuart mss. Nora [Boyle] to Lord Bute, 1 Mar. (no year).

89. *Cf.* Mount Stuart mss. A. Boyle to Lord Bute, 12 Mar. 1861.

90. Hamilla Augusta Boyle, 1813–1875, *SP* vol. II.

91. Mount Stuart mss. Charles Stuart to Lady Elizabeth Moore, 14 Feb. 1860.

92. Mount Stuart mss. Cousin Edith to Lord Bute, 11 Jun. 1858.

93. Harrowby Papers vol. LXII ff. 69–70, 30 Jun. 1854.

94. Mount Stuart mss. Bute's Journal, begun 29 Aug. 1855.

95. Mount Stuart mss. Journal, 1855.

96. *Ibid.*

97. Rev. Samuel Hood, 1782–1872, ordained 1826, Rector of St Paul's Rothesay 1838–72, Dean of Argyll and the Isles by 1854, DD 1870; *St. Paul's Scottish Episcopal Church, Rothesay, Isle of Bute: A Short History*, Ivor Dowse (Rothesay, undated), pp. 6–7.

98. Mount Stuart mss. Journal, 1855.

99. *Ibid.*

100. *Ibid.*

101. *Ibid.*

102. *Ibid.*

103. *Ibid.*

104. Mount Stuart mss. Journal, 1855.

105. *Ibid.*

106. *Ibid.*

107. Charles Edward Hastings, 1855–1920, *SP* vol. II.

108. Flora, 1854–1887, *ibid.* Other children were born from 1865, see the Hastings family tree. The youngest, Egidia, suffered from a disability (a frequent side effect of kidney failure in the mother).

109. BU/21/10/7 Lady Selina, undated.

110. Mount Stuart mss. ? to Bute, 12 Aug. 1857.

111. Harrowby Papers vol. LXII f. 79 Lady Bute to Lord Harrowby, 3 Jun. 1855.

112. Mount Stuart mss. Lady Bute to Mrs Boswell, 22 Jul. 1858.

113. BU/31/2 Bute's diary, 12 Aug. 1866.

114. Mount Stuart mss. *Weekly Journal*, 22 Jan. 1859.

115. Mount Stuart mss. *Weekly Journal*, 17 Dec. 1858.

116. Archibald Boyle, 1822–1874, *SP* vol. II.

117. Mount Stuart mss. *Weekly Journal*, 24 Dec. 1858.

118. Mount Stuart mss. *Weekly Journal*, 8 Jan. 1859.

119. Catherine Sinclair, *Beatrice or The Unknown Relatives* (Simpkin, Marshall, and Co.: London, 1855). Catherine Sinclair was sister to Lady Glasgow, whose property, Kelburn, faces Bute across the Clyde. Donald M. Lewis,

ed., *The Blackwell Dictionary of Evangelical Biography, 1730–1860*, vol. II
(Blackwell: Oxford, 1995).

120. Mount Stuart mss. *Weekly Journal*, 5 Feb. 1859.
121. Mount Stuart mss. *Weekly Journal*, 12 Feb. 1859.
122. Mount Stuart mss. *Trial of the dog.*
123. *Ibid.*
124. *Ibid.*
125. Mount Stuart mss. *Weekly Journal*, 19 Feb. 1859.
126. James Frederick Crichton Stuart, 1824–1891, Lt. Col. in Grenadier Guards,
     SP vol. II.
127. Charles Stuart, 1810–1892, *SP* vol. II.
128. John Boyle 1819–?, *SP* vol. II.
129. JD, p. 70.
130. His identity has not been traced.
131. Stuart's diary, 4 Sept. 1859.
132. Mount Stuart mss. *Weekly Journal*, 20 Aug. 1859.
133. Mount Stuart mss. *Weekly Journal*, 26 Nov. 1859.
134. David Hamilton, pers. com.
135. Mount Stuart mss. *Weekly Journal*, 17 Sept. 1859.
136. Mount Stuart mss. *Weekly Journal*, 13 Aug. 1859.
137. Mount Stuart mss. uncatalogued Bute to Charley, 22 Dec. 1859.

Chapter 2: Custody

1. Also to help nurse her (though much of the work probably fell on her maid
   Locke). Jalland, *Death*, p. 100.
2. Though Sophia never conquered her 'ill opinion and dislike' of Sir William
   Murray. Mount Stuart mss. Stuart's diary, 30 Dec. 1859.
3. Norman Macleod, 1812–1872. See *DNB*. Dr Macleod was the editor of *Good
   Words*, a magazine so strict that three years later, Macleod rejected Anthony
   Trollope's *Miss Mackenzie*. Anthony Trollope, *An Autobiography* (first pub.
   1883: Penguin Books: London, 1993), p. 173.
4. Stuart's diary, 30 Dec. 1859.
5. Stuart's diary, 27 Dec. 1860.
6. Stuart's diary, 6 Mar. 1860.
7. Lady Bute was to rest in the family vault, so required a lead-lined coffin.
   Julian Litten, *The English Way of Death* (Robert Hale: London, 1991), p. 114.
   These coffins were so effectively sealed that the body was frequently preserved
   floating in liquor – probably not embalming fluid, p. 52.
8. Stuart's diary, 6 Mar. 1860.
9. Stuart's diary, 28 Dec. 1859.
10. Stuart's diary, 30 Dec. 1860.
11. BU/21/1/7/3 Lady Elizabeth Moore to Bute, 1 Jan. 1861.
12. *The Buteman*, 6 Jan. 1860.
13. HB, p. 8, footnote.
14. Stuart's diary, 5 Jan. 1860.
15. *The Buteman*, 6 Jan. 1860. Henry John Villiers Stuart, 1837–1914, *BP*. The
    Villiers Stuarts were also Bute's distant cousins, being descended from Lord
    Henry Stuart, son of the 1st Marquess by his first marriage (Henry Villiers

Stuart, Lord Stuart de Decies 1803–1874). Lady Stuart may not have been legally married to Henry Villiers Stuart, both on the grounds that she may have been married to the Austrian Leopold Gersch by whom she had two children, and who was alive at the time of her union with Henry, and on the grounds she had been married by a Roman Catholic clergyman. Their eldest son was Henry Windsor Villiers Stuart, 1827–1895.

16. Stuart's diary, 5 Jan. 1860.

17. Despite the general perception that Victorian women did not attend funerals, the way the close relatives and servants made their way separately to the grave-site was typical for the burial of a woman of Sophia's class at this period. Diane Walker, pers. com.

18. Stuart's diary, 5 Jan. 1860.

19. Stuart's diary, 6 Jan. 1860.

20. BU/21/48/10 Lady Elizabeth Moore to Bute, Nov. 1866.

21. Stuart's diary, 6 Jan. 1860.

22. Rev. John Robertson, *Sermon Preached on the Occasion of the Death of the Marchioness of Bute* (Richard Griffin & Co.: London and Glasgow, 1860).

23. Cpt. Frederick Marryat's *Peter Simple, or the Adventures of a Midshipman* (Saunders and Otley, London, 1834) is an exciting account of the life of a young man at sea, reflecting the personal knowledge of Marryat, who himself became a midshipman aged fourteen.

24. Stuart's diary, 8 Jan. 1860.

25. The originals do not survive but, due to the legal battle that followed, there are numerous official copies.

26. BU/21/1/15 Stuart to Lady Elizabeth Moore, 1 Feb. 1860.

27. JD, p. 50. Richards wholly identified himself with the 2nd Marquess's interests, and was his most trusted ally in south Wales.

28. Francis Edmond Stacey was admitted to King's from Eton in 1850, became a Fellow in 1853 and was called to the bar in 1857. He died in 1885. *AC*, Part II, vol. IV.

29. BU/21/1/15 Lady Elizabeth Moore to Stuart, 2 Feb. 1860.

30. BU/21/1/15 Stuart to Lady Elizabeth Moore, 8 Feb. 1860.

31. Alexander Bruce was a solicitor to the Supreme Court of Scotland.

32. BU/21/1/14 Stuart to Lady Elizabeth Moore, 4 Feb. 1860.

33. BU/21/1/14 Stuart to Lady Elizabeth Moore, 14 Feb. 1860.

34. BU/21/1/14 Stuart to Lady Elizabeth Moore, 8 Feb. 1860.

35. BU/21/1/14 Stuart to Bute, 4 Feb. 1860.

36. Tom Brown, that exemplary hero, threw off for himself all traces of female rule: 'none of the women now, not even his mother's maid, dared offer to help him in washing or dressing . . . he would have gone without nether integuments altogether, sooner than have recourse to female valeting.' Thomas Hughes, *Tom Brown's Schooldays* (first pub. 1857: Parragon: Bath 1999), p. 37. Stuart was simply reflecting the standards of his day in seeking to impress Bute with his superiority to everything female. Yet the intensity with which he did it suggests much about his state of mind.

37. BU/21/1/15 Stuart to Lady Elizabeth Moore, 1 Feb. 1860.

38. BU/21/48/10 Lady Elizabeth Moore to Bute, Nov. 1866.

39. Stuart's diary, 1 Mar. 1860.

40. BU/21/1/123 Counsel for Stuart describing Bute at the Court of Session.

41. BU/21/1/15 Stuart to Lady Elizabeth Moore, 14 Feb. 1860.
42. BU/21/48/6 Mrs Stuart to Bute, Nov. 1866.
43. BU/21/1/24 Transcripts of the Court of Session hearing, 18–20 July 1860.
44. Stuart's diary, 10 Feb. 1860.
45. Stuart's diary, 29 Feb. 1860.
46. Stuart's diary, 5 Mar. 1860.
47. Stuart's diary, 17 Jan. 1860.
48. Stuart's diary, 3 Mar. 1860.
49. Stuart's diary, 5 Mar. 1860.
50. BU/21/33/3 Mrs Lamb to Bute, 8 May 1865.
51. Stuart's diary, 11 Mar. 1860.
52. Stuart's diary, 15 Feb. 1860.
53. Mount Stuart mss. Memorandum for Lady Elizabeth, undated.
54. BU/21/1/22 Georgina Stuart to Bute, 18 Mar. 1860.
55. HB, p. 6, quoting a letter from Bute to Charles MacLean.
56. BU/21/48/11 Lord Harrowby to Bute, 19 Nov. 1866.
57. Mount Stuart mss. uncatalogued. Lady Selina to 'my dear cousin', 5 Jan. 1861.
58. BU/21/1/22 Stuart to Lady Elizabeth Moore, 3 Apr. 1860.
59. BU/21/1/67 Memorandum from Stuart, June 1860. The original suggestion seems to have been made in May but is preserved in a later document prepared for the Court of Session.
60. Stuart's diary, 18 May 1860.
61. Stuart's diary, 9 Jul. 1860.
62. Stuart's diary, 15 May 1860.
63. Theodosia Tyndall was the daughter of Charles Tyndall of Bristol.
64. BU/21/2/56 Mrs Stuart to Bute, 3 Jul. 1860.
65. BU/21/2/57 Bute to Mrs Stuart, 4 Jul. 1860.
66. BU/21/2/60 Mrs Stuart to Bute, 5 Jul. 1860.
67. Stuart's diary, 9 Jul. 1860.
68. Stuart's diary, 10 Jul. 1860.
69. BU/21/2/177 Powell to Maclachlan, 5 Jul. 1860.
70. BU/21/2/37 Lady Elizabeth Moore to Maclachlan, 16 Jun. 1860.
71. In Scotland, a fourteen-year-old boy could legally marry without parental consent, whilst in England, consent was needed up to the age of twenty-one.
72. HB, p. 7.
73. Stuart's diary, 19 Jul. 1860.
74. BU/21/1/124 Transcripts of the Court of Session hearing, 18–20 Jul. 1860.
75. Stuart's diary, 19 Jul. 1860.
76. BU/21/1/124 Transcripts of the Court of Session hearing, 18–20 Jul. 1860.
77. The Scots are notorious for their keeping track of all cousins, no matter how distant, hence this proverbial expression for one held in esteem and acknowledged despite a distant relationship. As Mr Gordon hastened to point out, Lady Elizabeth and Lord Bute had great-grandparents in common. Lady Elizabeth was a great-granddaughter of John Rawdon, 1st Earl of Moria, who was Sophia's grandfather.
78. BU/21/1/124 Transcripts of the Court of Session hearing, 18–20 Jul. 1860.
79. Stuart's diary, 19 Jul. 1860.
80. BU/21/1/124 Transcripts of the Court of Session hearing, 18–20 Jul. 1860.
81. Stuart's diary, 19 Jul. 1860.

Chapter 3: Education

1. For instance simplifying 'John signed. John was a King. It was a document called Magna Charta that he signed. John was afraid of his barons, he did not care about liberty. He signed it at Runnymede. Runnymede is on the Thames. It is not far from Windsor.' He turned this into: 'At Runnymede upon Thames near Windsor King John signed Magna Charta, from fear of his barons, not from love of liberty.' Mount Stuart mss. uncatalogued.

2. BU/21/2/102 Lady Elizabeth Moore to her brother Richard Moore, 22 Oct. 1860.

3. BU/21/2/102 Lady Elizabeth Moore to Richard Moore, 22 Oct. 1860. He might have been forgiven if he had succeeded in taking Bute with him, but Bute retained his dislike of the hunting, fishing and shooting so ubiquitously enjoyed by the nobility, gentry and, increasingly, the middle class. Thompson, *Landed Society*, pp. 136–40.

4. Most of the official letters of this difficult period are now catalogued as BU21/1/ff. and most of the unofficial ones as BU21/2/ff.

5. BU/21/1/149, undated.

6. BU21/2/102 Lady Elizabeth Moore to Richard Moore, 22 Oct. 1860.

7. BU/21/2/149 Bute to George Maclachlan, undated.

8. BU/21/8/221 Charles Stuart to Anderson, 27 Jul. 1861. This of course broke the rules of both honesty and obedience so important in the pantheon of Victorian childhood virtues. F. M. L. Thompson, *The Rise of Respectable Society* (Fontana: London, 1988), p. 126.

9. BU/21/1/149 Lady Elizabeth Moore to Maclachlan, 4 Nov. 1860.

10. The 'drink problem' of the lower classes was far from imaginary. Official sales figures for spirits in 1875 were 1.30 gallons per head, and in 1876, 34.4 gallons of beer. 'Nothing more disheartened the Victorian worker's friend than the calculation of how much money went on beer and spirits that might have been put to "better" uses.' Geoffrey Best, *Mid-Victorian Britain 1851–75* (Fontana: London, 1979), p. 240.

11. BU/21/2/102 Lady Elizabeth Moore to Richard Moore, 22 Oct. 1860.

12. BU/21/2/149 Bute to George Maclachlan, undated.

13. BU/21/2/102 Lady Elizabeth Moore to Richard Moore, 22 Oct. 1860.

14. Mount Stuart uncatalogued. Memorial prepared for Lady Elizabeth by Maclachlan.

15. Stacey married Theodosia Tyndall in 1862, *AC*. Their relationship had been established at Falkland that summer.

16. BU/21/2/152 Lady Elizabeth Moore to Maclachlan, undated. The crisis over, Stacey became a sober lawyer, a partner with his 'rich uncle', married his fiancée, and seems to have led a blameless life.

17. BU/21/1/137 Maclachlan to Lady Elizabeth Moore, 2 Nov. 1860.

18. BU/21/1/149 Note for Lady Elizabeth Moore, 7 Nov. 1860.

19. BU/21/1/137 Col. Crichton Stuart to the Marquess of Bute, 3 Nov. 1860.

20. Randolph Stewart, 1800–1873, 9th Earl of Galloway, *BP*. The family home was at Cumloden in Kirkcudbrightshire. *SP* vol. IV.

21. BU/21/6/1 Maclachlan to Bute, 3 Dec. 1860.

22. Stuart's diary, 28 Aug. 1860.

23. *Glasgow Daily Herald*, 28 May 1861.

24. Harriet Somerset 1811–1885; seventh daughter of the 6th Duke of Beaufort, *BP*.

25. Walter John Stewart, fourth son of the Earl, 1849–1908. *SP* vol. IV.

26. HB, p. 11. These are probably the memories of Lady Henrietta Stewart, who was three years younger than Bute, and later married Mr Algernon Turnor (Disraeli's private secretary); the latter supplied stories of Lord Bute at Oxford to Blair.

27. BU/21/2/156 Lady Elizabeth Moore to Bute, 4 Dec. 1860.

28. Mungo's portrait survives: he is the little dog at Bute's feet in the portrait of him with his mother.

29. BU/21/8/1 Lady Elizabeth Moore to ?(probably Maclachlan), undated.

30. BU/23/4 Bute to Lady Selina, 25 Dec. 1860.

31. Lady Jane Stewart, 1844–1897.

32. BU/21/7/31 Bute, 3 Mar. 1861.

33. We do not know which one.

34. BU/21/7/14 Lady Selina to Bute, 8 Mar. 1861.

35. Eleanora Boyle to Bute, 23 Mar. 1861.

36. BU/21/8/197 Lady Elizabeth Moore to Maclachlan, undated.

37. Harrowby Papers vol. LXII f. 204 Stuart to Lord Harrowby, 23 Oct. 1861.

38. *The Times*, 7 May 1861.

39. *The Scotsman*, 23 May 1861.

40. Mount Stuart mss. Bute to Lady Selina, 30 Jun. 1861.

41. BU/21/13/4 Essex to Galloway, 12 Jul. 1861.

42. BU/21/13/5 Essex to Galloway, undated.

43. BU/21/8/208 Stuart to Anderson, 22 Jul. 1861.

44. *Ibid.*, *cf.* BU/21/13/3 James Frederick Crichton Stuart to Lord Galloway, undated.

45. BU/21/13/2 Essex to Galloway, undated.

46. BU/21/13/3 John Frederick Crichton Stuart to Lord Galloway, undated.

47. BU/57 Bute's diary, 1861.

48. BU/21/48/6 Georgina Stuart to Bute, undated.

49. BU/23/13 Bute to Lady Selina, 20 Jan. 1862.

50. Bute's diary, 4 Sept. 1861.

51. It was very much part of the ethos of the Christian gentleman to be a sportsman and to 'glory in physical toughness': Mark Girouard, *The Return to Camelot* (Yale University Press: New Haven, 1981), p. 136. Bute never enjoyed shooting, and walking and swimming were as near as he got to 'physical toughness'.

52. BU/21/2/239 Stuart to Anderson, undated.

53. Harrowby Papers vol. LXII f. 198 Lord Galloway to Lord Harrowby, 21 Dec. 1862.

54. Harrowby Papers vol. LXII f. 204 Stuart to Lord Harrowby, 23 Oct. [probably 1863].

55. It was not the slight disparity in title that mattered; any marriage between the aristocracy and the gentry was perfectly respectable. It was Bute's money, and the Galloways' lack of it that would have made the match unequal. Thompson, *Respectable Society*, pp. 103–7.

56. BU/21/16/2 Lady Galloway to Bute, 3 Jan. 1862.

57. Brooke Foss Westcott 1825–1901. He co-edited the famous Greek New

Testament which bears his name, and became Bishop of Durham. Reviewing the earliest Greek manuscripts, they carefully considered the evidence for the various readings, and *Westcott and Hort* was for years the basis for scholarly translation, and remains to this day a classic. See *DNB*; Arthur Westcott, *Life and Letters of Brooke Foss Westcott* (Macmillan & Co: London, 1903).

58. Harrrowby Papers vol. LXII f. 237 Westcott to Gen Stuart, 3 Nov. 1864.

59. The by then late Lady Harrowby, daughter of the 1st Marquess's second marriage to Frances Coutts.

60. BU/21/16/5 A. Howe to Bute, undated.

61. BU/63/2 H. Montagu Butler to Bute, 17 Jun. 1863.

62. Harrowby Papers vol. LXII ff. 212–3 Lord Galloway to Lord Harrowby, 2 Dec. 1863.

63. Harrowby Papers vol. LXII f. 215 Lady Galloway to Lord Harrowby, 5 Mar. 1864.

64. HB, p. 33: Erastius was a sixteenth-century. Swiss theologian whose name, unfairly and misleadingly, has been attached to views he did not hold, namely that the state should control the Church, and use it as a prop for its own position.

65. BU/23/13 Bute to Lady Selina, 20 Jan. 1862.

66. *The Sporting Gazette*, 14 Nov. 1868.

67. Henry Blyth, *The Pocket Venus* (Weidenfeld and Nicolson: London, 1966).

68. BU/23/13/19 Bute to Lady Selina, 9 Aug. 1864.

69. Blyth, *Pocket Venus*, p. 116.

70. BU/23/13/19 Bute to Lady Selina, 9 Aug. 1864.

71. He was not alone in this; when Tennyson spoke of the power of the love of one woman to 'keep down the base in man' (Ann Thwaite, *Emily Tennyson: The Poet's Wife* (Faber and Faber: London 1996), p. 165), he was articulating the ideal of a cultural group of religious and idealistic men.

72. BU/23/13/19 Bute to Lady Selina, 9 Aug. 1864.

73. Harrowby Papers vol. LXII f. 221 Smith to Gen. Stuart, 18 Sept. 1864.

74. *Essays and Reviews*, London: Longman, Green, Longman & Roberts, 1861.

75. Harrowby Papers vol. LXII f. 237 Westcott to Gen. Stuart, 3 Nov. 1864.

76. Harrowby Papers vol. LXII f. 284 Bute to Lord Harrowby, 21 Nov. 1866.

77. BU/21/48/11 Lord Harrowby to Bute, 19 Nov. 1866.

78. Harrowby Papers vol. LXII f. 260 Westcott to Lord Harrowby, undated (probably 1865).

79. Harrowby Papers vol. LXII f. 255 Archbishop of Canterbury, 8 Feb. 1865.

80. Of the WHO ICD-10 markers for depression, Bute exhibits four, strongly suggesting he was experiencing a severe depressive episode.

81. BU/21/33/6 Cousin Edith to Bute, 8 May 1865.

82. Harrowby Papers vol. LXII f. 267 Gen. Stuart to Lord Harrowby, 14 Aug. 1865.

Chapter 4: Travel

1. BU/31/1 Bute's diary, 27 Jul. 1866.

2. BU/21/33/2 Georgina Stuart to Bute, 16 May 1865.

3. Sneyd papers/2 Bute to Sneyd, 3 May 1865.

4. BU/21/33/1 Lady Galloway to Bute, 30 Apr. 1865.

5. BU/21/33/1 Georgina Stuart to Bute, 16 May 1865.

6. Sneyd papers/3 Bute to Sneyd, 22 May 1865.

7. Sneyd papers/2 Bute to Sneyd, 3 May 1865.

8. It has not been possible to identify him further.

9. BU/21/33/ A. Stafford to Bute, Dec. 1865.

10. Sneyd papers/3 Bute to Sneyd, 22 May 1865. Public School was designed to 'harden' the boys attending it. Philip Mason, *The English Gentleman* (André Deutsch: 1982), p. 170. Sensitive boys suffered disproportionately.

11. Bute to Mrs Stuart, 29 Jun. 1865.

12. HB, p. 27.

13. Bute to Mrs Stuart, 29 Jun. 1865.

14. Archibald Philip Primrose, 5th Earl of Rosebery, 1847–1929, *SP* vol. VII.

15. Robert Rhodes James, *Rosebery* (Weidenfeld and Nicolson: London, 1963), p. 46.

16. HB, p. 34.

17. Edward Bouverie Pusey, 1800–1882, Regius Professor of Hebrew, Christ Church, Oxford, a leader of the Oxford Movement, *DNB*; H. P. Liddon, *Life of Edward Bouverie Pusey*, ed. J. O. Johnston and R. J. Wilson, 4 vols, 1894–7.

18. Henry Parry Liddon, 1829–1890, later Canon of St Paul's London. J. H. Johnston, *Life and Letters of Henry Parry Liddon* (Longman & Co.: London, 1904).

19. Johnston, *Liddon*, p. 127.

20. William Plomer, ed., *Kilvert's Diary 14 May 1874–13 March 1879* (first pub. 1938–40: Jonathan Cape: London, 1969), p. 320. Kilvert was not particularly hostile to Roman Catholicism; he had an endearing habit of slipping into Roman Catholic churches to pray. *Ibid.*, p. 356.

21. Henry Longueville Mansel, 1820–1871. See *DNB*. Mansel, disturbed by the new and sceptical writings coming from Germany, argued that, whilst belief in God was reasonable, we could know little of him except what he chose to reveal. Mansel's metaphysics have been much criticised. See W. R. Matthews, *The Religious Philosophy of Dean Mansel*, Friends of Dr Williams Library, Tenth Lecture (Oxford University Press: London, 1956).

22. HB, p. 32 quoting Bute to Miss Skene, Christmas Day 1865.

23. At Balliol, G. M. Hopkins was struggling to get by on £75 annually, though his father paid his college expenses and occasionally gave him extra money: Robert Bernard Martin, *Gerard Manley Hopkins, A Very Private Life* (G. P. Putnam's Sons: New York, 1991), p. 28. But the point of attending University was still to 'make a select acquaintance, as much in your own rank as possible' (Lord Monson, quoted in Thompson, *Landed Society*, p. 86), and Bute's own rank was that of the very rich and free-spending aristocracy.

24. Bute had not been there; his flow of words must have confused Liddon.

25. Pusey House, Liddon's diary, 17 May 1866.

26. Augustus J. C. Hare, *The Story of My Life* vol. IV (George Allen: London, 1900), p. 270.

27. George Williams, 1814–1878, was born in Eton, the son of a bookseller and graduated from Cambridge in 1837. He was for a time in charge of Cumbrae College within the Episcopal Church of Scotland on the Isle of Millport, Bute's sister isle in the Clyde. See *DNB*.

28. BU/31/1 Bute's diary, 23 Jun. 1866.

29. Harman Grisewood, 1844–1909, was educated at Harrow, and matriculated at Christ Church, Oxford, aged 18 in 1863. He was for a time a deacon in Anglican Orders, and did not become a Roman Catholic until 1871. W. Gordon Gorman, *Converts to Rome* (Sands & Co.: London, 1910), p. 125.

30. BU/21/42 Sneyd to Bute, 29 Aug. 1866.

31. BU/31/1 Bute's diary, 23 Jun. 1866.

32. Harrowby Papers vol. LXII f. 299 Lady Galloway to Lord Harrowby, 4 Dec. 1866.

33. BU/31/1 Bute's diary, 5 Jul. 1866.

34. BU/31/1 Bute's diary, 6 Jul. 1866.

35. BU/31/1 Bute's diary, 8 Jul. 1866.

36. BU/31/1 Bute's diary, 9 Jul. 1866.

37. BU/31/1 Bute's diary, 13 Jul. 1866.

38. Why Bute felt like this is an interesting question. This is something Williams should have been able to explain. Williams was a friend of J. M. Neale, the Anglo-Catholic who had done more than any other to promote an understanding of the Orthodox Church in England. Neale wrote much about Orthodoxy, but tended to play down the place and importance of the icon in Orthodox worship. It has been suggested that this was in order not to alienate his readers, and so that they did not make the same kind of mistake as Bute. Neale had not travelled widely, ill-health and relative poverty preventing him. Is it possible that he did not properly understand the role of the icon? Or did Bute simply fail to take on board Williams' explanation?

39. BU/31/1 Bute's diary, 15 Jul. 1866.

40. BU/31/1 Bute's diary, 17 Jul. 1866. The Metropolitan was Gregorios, and the correct title of his work *Yearnings after Unity in the East*.

41. BU/31/1 Bute's diary, 18 Jul. 1866.

42. BU/31/1 Bute's diary, 21 Jul. 1866.

43. BU/31/1 Bute's diary, 25 Jul. 1866.

44. BU/31/1 Bute's diary, 21 Jul. 1866.

45. BU/31/1 Bute's diary, 6 Jul. 1866.

46. BU/31/1 Bute's diary, 27 Jul. 1866.

47. BU/31/1 Bute's diary, 31 Jul. 1866.

48. BU/31/1 Bute's diary, 28 Jul. 1866.

49. BU/31/1 Bute's diary, 25 Jul. 1866.

50. The Maronites are an ancient Christian church in full communion with the Roman Catholics. They worship in Syriac (Aramaic) and have their own liturgies.

51. BU/31/2 Bute's diary, 11 Aug. 1866.

52. BU/31/2 Bute's diary, 13 Aug. 1866.

53. BU/31/2 Bute's diary, 11 Aug. 1866. The earlier letters may possibly stand for some such phrase as '*beata dei genatrix qua mater sancta*'.

54. Bute gives a sketch of an oval with one straight end.

55. BU/31/2 Bute's diary, 11 Aug. 1866.

56. BU/31/2 Bute's diary, 16 Aug. 1866.

57. Harrowby Papers vol. LXII f. 267 Stuart to Lord Harrowby, 14 Aug. 1865.

58. BU/21/42 Sneyd to Bute, 29 Aug. 1866.

59. Harrowby Papers vol. LXII f. 267 Stuart to Lord Harrowby, 14 Aug. 1865.

60. Harrowby Papers vol. LXII ff278–87 Charles Stuart to Harrowby, 10 Nov. 1866.

61. BU/21/48/3 Stuart to Bute, 10 Nov. 1866.
62. BU/21/48/4 Bute to Stuart, 13 Nov. 1866.
63. BU/21/48/8 Georgina Stuart to Bute, 15 Nov. 1866.
64. BU/21/61/1 Elizabeth Knox to Bute, 18 Mar. [1867].
65. Harrowby Papers vol. LXII f. 284ff. Bute to Harrowby, 15 Nov. 1866.
66. BU/21/48/11 Harrowby to Bute, 19 Nov. 1866.
67. Harrowby Papers vol. LXII f. 288ff. Stuart to Harrowby, 15 Nov. 1866.
68. Harrowby Papers vol. LXII f. 284 Bute to Harrowby, 21 Nov. 1866.
69. All these letters have been carefully catalogued in Bute's own hand, showing how much this row affected him, and how difficult it was to simply forget it.
70. Sir James Fergusson of Kilkerran, 1832–1907. He was at the time MP for Ayrshire, and his later distinguished career included his serving as Postmaster General and Governor of New Zealand.
71. Harrowby Papers vol. 1077 ff. 127–8 Bute to Henry Ryder, 14 Sept. 1892.

Chapter 5: Oxford

1. Pusey House, Oxford. Liddon diary, 17 Oct. 1866.
2. HB, p. 43.
3. Harrowby Papers vol. LXII f. 291 Mansel to Harrowby, 24 Nov. 1866.
4. Geoffrey Best, 'Popular Protestantism in Victorian Britain', in Robert Robson, ed., *Ideas and Institutions of Victorian Britain* (G. Bell and Sons: London, 1967), pp. 122–4.
5. Mark Girouard identifies a category of 'earnest Victorians' into which Bute's sense of duty and responsibility fits him. 'The Prince Consort set the supreme example of domesticity, purity, religious seriousness and devotion to duty.' Mark Girouard, 'Victorian Values and the Upper Classes', in T. C. Smout, ed., *Victorian Values, a Joint Symposium of the Royal Society of Edinburgh and the British Academy December 1990* (Oxford University Press: Oxford, 1992), p. 52. Yet even Prince Albert was a keen sportsman, and, though fascinated by art and architecture, it is hard to imagine him sitting for hours watching the ladies embroider vestments whilst talking of religion as Bute enjoyed doing. HB, p. 61.
6. Harrowby Papers vol. LXII f. 291 Mansel to Harrowby, 24 Nov. 1866.
7. Liddon diary, 10 Apr. 1867.
8. Harrowby Papers vol. LXII f. 309 James Fergusson to Lord Harrowby, 13 April 1867.
9. Felicia Skene, 1821–1899. See *DNB*; Edith C. Rickards, *Felicia Skene of Oxford: A Memoir ... with Numerous Portraits and Other Illustrations* (John Murray: London, 1902).
10. HB, p. 46, quoting Bute to Miss Skene, Maundy Thursday 1867.
11. Rickards, *Skene*, p. 133.
12. 'Merlin', *The Sporting Gazette*, 18 May 1867.
13. BU/21/51/34. Note of a meeting of 3 Jul. 1867 between Bute and legal representatives to explain the purchase of the Loudoun Estate.
14. HB, p. 48.
15. Mount Stuart mss. uncatalogued, *Journal of a Voyage on the* Lady Bird. This ms. does not have any attribution. However, by comparing it with Bute's diary in the NLS it is possible to deduce that it was written by Dasent.

16. John Roche Dasent, 1847–1914, was later assistant secretary to the Board of Education. NLS Acc 9553.

17. George Webbe Dasent, 1817–1896, Boase vol. V.

18. Frederic Vyner was taken captive by bandits and murdered in 1870 when he was 23. Christ the Consoler, Skelton, was commissioned from William Burges with the money raised for his ransom.

19. Fiona MacCarthy, *William Morris: A Life for Our Time* (Faber and Faber: London, 1995), p. 287.

20. NLS Acc9553 Bute's diary, 31 Jul. 1867.

21. NLS Acc9553 Bute's diary, 11 Aug. 1867. So famous is this that it gave its name to other waterspouts which 'go off' at intervals, though the modern spelling of the generic type is slightly different.

22. NLS Acc9553 Bute's diary, 13 Aug. 1867.

23. NLS Acc9553 Bute's diary, 12 Aug. 1867.

24. Dasent, diary, 21 Aug. 1867.

25. NLS Acc9553 Bute's diary, 21 Aug. 1867.

26. NLS Acc9553 Bute's diary, 22 Aug. 1867.

27. NLS Acc9553 Bute's diary, 23 Aug. 1867.

28. NLS Acc9553 Bute's diary, 29 Aug. 1867.

29. NLS Acc9553 Bute's diary, 30 Aug. 1867.

30. HB, p. 61. Charles Robert Scott Murray, 1818–1882, MP for Buckinghamshire. Gorman, *Converts*, p. 246.

31. Monsignor Thomas John Capel, 1835–1911. See Charles Fitzgerald-Lombard, *English and Welsh Priests 1801–1914* (Downside Abbey, Bath, 1993), p. 3.

32. Liddon diary, 20 Oct. 1867.

33. Johnston, *Liddon*, p. 97.

34. BU/21/33/24 Capel to Bute, 10 Sept. 1868. This letter has formerly been wrongly ascribed the date of 1865, due to the peculiarity of Capel's writing of the numeral 8.

35. BU/21/62/17 Capel to Bute, 30 Mar. 1868.

36. HB, p. 54.

37. *Cf.* BU/21/62/51 Mabel Henry to Bute, 29 May 1868.

38. BU/21/42/4 Elizabeth Knox to Bute, 6 Aug. 1866.

39. His own close friend Addle Hay Gordon was a High Church Scottish Episcopalian, which was of all religious positions the one against which Bute showed most fervour. Yet Addle was one of his most beloved friends.

40. BU/21/65/3 Ethel Wilton to Bute, undated, with envelope postmarked March 1868.

41. BU/21/65/5 Ethel Wilton to Bute, undated.

42. BU/21/65/10 Ethel Wilton to Bute, undated.

43. Not merely black clothes, but cut more modestly than usual and trimmed with crepe. Jalland, *Death*, pp. 301–6.

44. BU/21/65/8 Ethel Wilton to Bute, undated.

45. BU/21/65/9 Ethel Wilton to Bute, undated.

46. BU/21/65/7 Ethel Wilton to Bute, undated.

47. BU/21/65/14 Ethel Wilton to Bute, undated.

48. BU/21/62/52 Lady Elizabeth Moore to Bute, 30 May 68.

49. BU/21/62/118 Capel to Bute, undated.

50. Lady Albertha Hamilton, 1847–1932, *BP*.
51. HB, p. 58.
52. George W. E. Russell, *Portraits of the Seventies* (T. Fisher Unwin, Ltd.: London, 1916), p. 260.
53. John Cumming, 1807–1881, was licensed by Aberdeen Presbytery, and called to Crown Court in 1832. See *DNB*.
54. The degree to which this kind of millennialism stifled charitable action, an aspect of the faith of which Bute would certainly have disapproved, is discussed by D. N. Hempton in 'Evangelicalism and Eschatology', *Journal of Ecclesiaistical History*, 1980, pp. 179–94.
55. BU/21/62/17 Capel to Bute, 30 Mar. 1868.
56. BU/21/62/51 Mabel Henry to Bute, 29 May 1868.
57. *The Tomahawk*, May 1868.
58. BU/21/62/52 Lady Elizabeth Moore to Bute, 30 May 1868.
59. BU/21/62/86 Lady Edith to Bute, 25 Jun. 1868.
60. BU/21/62/30 Emily Freemantle to Bute, 22 Apr. (1868?).
61. BU/21/62/40 Mabel Henry to Bute, undated but almost certainly 1868.
62. BU/21/62/88 Edith Fergusson to Bute, 25 Jun. 1868.
63. BU/21/69/7 Capel to Bute, Holy Thursday Charles Fitzgerald-Lombard, *English and Welsh Priests 1801–1914* (Downside Abbey, Bath, 1993) 1868.
64. HB, p. 66.
65. HB, p. 67.
66. Charles Thomas Biscoe, 1847–1884. *AO*.
67. BU/21/62/79 Colt Williams to Bute, 18 Jun. 1868.
68. BU/21/62/96 Biscoe to Bute, 5 Sept. 1868.
69. *AO*.
70. BU/21/64/3 Invitation, 18 Jun. 1868.
71. HB, p. 30–1. He says that Bute planned to repeat the ball the following year but was forbidden by the authorities, which is clearly incorrect.
72. To fail to take one's degree was not unusual then in the way it is now, because the main purpose of University for upper-class men was social. Because Bute was especially gifted, he was expected to sit his exams and to do well.
73. *The Sporting Gazette,* 14 Nov. 1868.
74. Sir Herbert Maxwell, *Evening Memories* (Alexander Maclehose & Co.: London, 1932), p. 126.
75. BU/21/62/ James Murray to Bute, 2 Apr. 1868.
76. *The Buteman*, 26 Sept. 1868.
77. BU/21/62/118 Capel to Bute, undated.
78. BU/21/33/24 Capel to Bute, 10 Sept. 1865.
79. *The Scotsman*, 14 Sept. 1868.
80. *The Scotsman*, 17 Sept. 1868.
81. *The Times*, 19 Sept. 1868.
82. HB, pp. 69–70, quoting Bute to Miss Skene, 5 Oct. 1868.
83. HB, p. 58.
84. BU/21/62/119 Capel to Bute, undated.
85. Kensal Green had been assured of its success after it was chosen as a final resting-place by Augustus Frederick, Duke of Sussex, in 1843, and later by Princess Sophia: Litten, *Way of Death*, p. 134. Such cemeteries were, and remain, not to everyone's taste. John Morley, *Death, Heaven and the*

Victorians (University of Pittsburgh Press: 1971), p. 44, accuses them of 'snobbery, triviality and lack of taste'.

86. *The Morning Post*, 16 Nov. 1868.

87. Hunter Blair, following a public letter of Capel, gives the place of Bute's reception as the convent of *Marie Reparatrice* at Harley House, home to the Sisters of Notre Dame. There is no mention of the place in the Bute papers, and there was no convent of the Sisters of Notre Dame in Hammersmith. Capel repeatedly exhorted Bute to come to Hammersmith, where there was a convent of the Sisters of the Good Shepherd, and it was a convent of their order that Bute later founded in gratitude at Cardiff. One of two things occurred: either Bute went to Notre Dame and was received there by Capel, who had somehow learned of his whereabouts, or else Bute went to Hammersmith and Capel subsequently lied about the location. It is difficult to see how he could have made a mistake. In May 1868 he promised the Sisters at Hammersmith that Bute would found a convent of the Good Shepherd at Cardiff. (Anon., *A Daughter of the Venerable Mother Pelletier: Sister Mary of the Sacred Heart Ryder* (Convent of the Good Shepherd: London, 1902), p. 202]. This was about the time of Capel's visit to Oxford, and it is just possible that Bute had made such a promise. It is also possible, given Capel's lack of probity with money (to be discussed below) that he had made the promise, trusting to influence Bute afterwards. The promise was not fulfilled until nearly three years later.

Chapter 6: Lothair?

1. HB, p. 73.
2. HB, p. 75.
3. HB, p. 77.
4. *The Glasgow Herald*, 5 Jan. 1869.
5. *The Glasgow Herald*, 7 Jan. 1869.
6. George Earle Buckle, *The Life of Benjamin Disraeli, Earl of Beaconsfield* (John Murray: London, 1916), vol. IV, p. 558.
7. Benjamin Disraeli, *Lothair*, ed. Vernon Bogdanor (Oxford University Press: Oxford, 1975), intro., p. viii.
8. Disraeli was out of office and had 'some real leisure for the first time in many years'. He kept his work on *Lothair* entirely private, and his private secretary, Montague Corry, only knew of it when he 'read the advertisement in the journals'. Robert Blake, *Disraeli* (Eyre & Spottiswoode: London, 1966), pp. 148–9.
9. Russell, *Portraits of the Seventies*.
10. The Right Hon. Benjamin Disraeli, *Lothair* (first pub. 1870: Longmans, Green and Co.: London, 1881 edition), p. 4.
11. JD, p. 26.
12. Disraeli, *Lothair*, p. 26.
13. The description of her table silver which finally rises to a figure of Britannia herself and 'illustrated with many lights a glowing inscription which described the fervent feelings of a grateful client' (p. 29) is not as Braun, *Disraeli* p. 137 suggests, a reflection of Disraeli's love of grandiose table decorations. It is a satire of Mrs Giles's pretensions and lack of taste.

14. Disraeli, *Lothair*, p. 34.
15. Benjamin Disraeli, *Lothair*, ed. Vernon Bogdanor, explanatory notes, p. 377.
16. Disraeli, *Lothair*, p. 62.
17. Disraeli, *Lothair*, p. 173.
18. Disraeli, *Lothair*, p. 112.
19. For example, Thom Braun, *Disraeli the Novelist* (George Allen & Unwin: London, 1981), p. 132.
20. BU/21/93/1 Bute to Gwendolen, later dated 4 Feb. 1872.
21. Disraeli, *Lothair*, p. 42.
22. Critical reaction to *Lothair* was mixed. *Blackwoods Magazine*, vol. 107, pp. 773–96, June 1870, carried a review of such staggering anti-semitism that even sections of the Victorian press protested. *The Quarterly Review*, vol. 129, pp. 63–87, July 1870, was sardonic, remarking 'When Theodora was dead, and Clare Arundel had taken the veil, what was left for Lothair but to return to his old love, Lady Corisande.' Henry James, writing in *Atlantic Monthly*, vol. 26, pp. 249–51, August 1870, was kind. Disraeli might 'not have strictly reproduced a perfect society of "swells", but he has very fairly reflected one.' Further contemporary reaction can be found in R. W. Stewart, ed., *Disraeli's Novels Reviewed* (The Scarecrow Press, Inc: Metuchen, N.J., 1975), pp. 246ff.
23. Bogdanor, *Lothair*, intro., p. ix.
24. JD, *passim*.
25. William Burges, 1821–1881. A full account of his life and work is given by J. Mordaunt Crook, *William Burges and the High Victorian Dream* (John Murray: London, 1981).
26. WB/2 Report on Cardiff Castle, 26 Feb. 1866.
27. Matthew Williams, 'Gorgeously Arrayed in Blue and Gold', *Country Life*, 5 Mar. 1998, pp. 56–9.
28. William Frame, 1846–1905. Crook, *Burges*, p. 83.
29. John Starling Chapple, 1840–1922.
30. Horatio Walter Lonsdale, 1844–1919.
31. Frederick Weeks, 1833–? The dates given in Crook *Burges*, p. 85, are not correct, for in 1920 Weeks was still active.
32. Thomas Nicholls, 1825–1896.
33. BU/89/2/2 Gwen to Angela, undated.
34. Matthew Williams, Keeper of the Collections at Cardiff Castle, pers. com.
35. Mordaunt Crook, *Burges*, p. 264, suggests that 'those astrological complexities were surely of [Bute's] own devising' but it was another ten years before Bute became interested in astrology.
36. Christopher McIntosh, *The Rosy Cross Unveiled* (The Aquarian Press: Wellingborough, 1980), p. 45.
37. Matthew Williams, 'William Burges' Furniture for Cardiff Castle', *Decorative Arts Society Journal*, No. 16 (1991), pp. 14–19.
38. M. Williams, pers. com.
39. Capel had links with the order, which had Houses at both Hammersmith and St Leonard's on Sea, where his home was. The order had been established in England in the middle years of the nineteenth century. It was principally concerned with reclaiming fallen women. John Nicholas Murphy, *Terra Incognita or The Convents of the United Kingdom* (Longmans, Green and Co.: London, 1873), p. 195.

40. Anon., prob. Fr Cronin, 'The Story of the Foundation of the Convent of the Good Shepherd, Pen-y-lan, Cardiff' *Catholic Parish Magazine of St Peter's Cardiff*, November 1922, p. ii.

41. Protestants, as well as Catholics, had institutions for fallen women. Laundries were the usual way of providing the women with work and allowing them to support themselves. It was harder to get admission to the Protestant institutions. 'No girls were ever intentionally admitted who were diseased, otherwise disabled or pregnant.' Olive Checkland, *Philanthropy in Victorian Scotland* (John Donald: Edinburgh, 1980), p. 238.

42. Anon., 'Pen-y-lan', *Parish Magazine of St Peter's Cardiff*.

43. Julia Cartwright, ed., *The Journals of Lady Knightley of Fawsley* (John Murray: London, 1915), p. 233.

44. Giles Stephen Holland Strangways, Earl of Ilchester, *Chronicles of Holland House* (John Murray: London, 1937), p. 434. No letter from or to Marie survives.

45. BL add. ms 52159 f. 245 Charles Douglas to Lady Holland, 14 Mar. 1872.

46. Ilchester, *Holland House*, p. 434.

47. BL add. ms 52159 ff. 224–5 Bute to Lady Holland, 20 Jun. 1871.

48. BL add. ms 52159 f. 242 Charles Douglas to Lady Holland, 14 Mar. 1872.

49. BL add. ms 52159 ff. 226–7 Bute to Lady Holland, 22 June 1871.

50. Mary Catherine Beauchamp, 1844–1876, had married in 1868. *BP* vol. II.

51. BL add. ms 52159 ff. 228–9 Mary Beauchamp to Lady Holland, 10 Jul. 1871.

52. HB, p. 105, quoting Bute to Miss Skene, 29 Jul. 1871.

53. BL add. ms 52159 f. 244 Charles Douglas to Lady Holland, 14 Mar. 1872.

54. *Holland House*, p. 436.

55. *Holland House*, p. 437.

56. BL add. ms 52160 f. 107 Lady Holland to the Rev. C. Comberbach, [6 Mar.?] 1873.

57. BL add. ms 52160 ff. 224–6 Carrie Clark to Miss Probyn, 8 Dec. 1874.

58. BL add. ms 52161 ff. 119–22 J. Browne to Lady Holland, 6 May 1876.

59. BL ad mss 52161 f. 56 Therese von Bülow, 23 Sept. 1875.

60. BU/21/175/120 Bute to Gwen, 11 Jun. 1882.

61. BL ad mss 52159 f. 243 Charles Douglas to Lady Holland, 14 Mar. 1872.

62. BU/21/148/6 Bute to Gwen, undated.

63. BL ad ms 52161 ff. 246–7 C. Comberbach to Lady Holland, 27 Dec. 1878.

64. Fr James McSwiney, SJ, 1827–1905 (ordained 1857). Fitzgerald-Lombard, p. 217. He was the son of a Spittlefields weaver.

65. BU/21/95/1 Capel to Gwen, 23 Feb. 1872.

66. BU/21/93/4 Bute to Gwen, 26 Feb. 1872.

67. BU/21/93/1 Bute to Gwen, 4 Feb. 1872.

68. BU/21/93/5 Bute to Gwen, 28 Feb. 1872.

69. BU/21/93/3 Bute to Gwen, 24 Feb. 1872.

70. It is not possible to give her exact height, but her father called her 'the dearest little darling in the world'.

71. BU/21/93/1 Bute to Gwen, 4 Feb. 1872.

72. BU/21/93/8 Bute to Gwen, 7 Mar. 1872.

73. BU/21/93/7 Bute to Gwen, 7 Mar. 1872.

74. Anon., 'Pen-y-lan', *Parish Magazine of St Peter's Cardiff*.

75. BU/21/93/10 Bute to Gwen, undated.
76. BU/21/93/11 Bute to Gwen, undated.
77. BU/21/93/10 Bute to Gwen, undated.
78. BU/21/93/11 Bute to Gwen, undated.
79. BU/21/93/18 Bute to Gwen, undated.
80. The Marriage Act of 1837 put paid to Fleet marriages, and allowed Nonconformists and Roman Catholics to enter binding marriages in their own churches. Prior to that, all legal marriages needed to be by a Church of England priest, thereby setting up the tradition of Catholics marrying in Church of England buildings.
81. BU/21/93/7 Bute to Gwen, 7 Mar. 1872.
82. That is to say, not the Bute arms alone, but the Bute arms quartered with the Fitzalan-Howard coat of arms.
83. BU/21/93/5 Bute to Gwen, 28 Feb. 1872.
84. BU/21/93/12 Bute to Gwen, 26 Mar. 1872.
85. BU/21/93/12 Bute to Gwen, undated.
86. BU/21/93/14 Bute to Gwen, undated 1872.
87. BL ad. mss. 52159 f. 242 C. Douglas to Lady Holland, 14 Mar. 1872.
88. BU/21/93/13 Bute to Gwen, 1 Apr. 1872.
89. BU/21/94/1 Gwen to Bute, undated.
90. BU/21/93/19 Bute to Gwen, 14 Apr. 1872.
91. BU/21/94/1 Gwen to Bute, undated.
92. BU/21/93/16 Bute to Gwen, undated.
93. *The Morning Post*, 17 Apr. 1872.
94. Phillipa Fitzalan Howard, 1852–1946, *BP*.
95. *The Morning Post*, 17 Apr. 1872.
96. *The Glasgow Herald*, 17 April 1872.
97. BU/96/20/25 Lord Colum to Gwen, 17 Sept. 1920. Bute's youngest son asked his mother if it was true that 'Father never read *Lothair*?' Alas, the answer is not preserved.

Chapter 7: Marriage

1. BU/89/1 Gwen to Angela, 19 Apr. 1872.
2. BU/89/1/19 Gwen to Angela, undated.
3. BU/89/1/2 Gwen to Angela, undated.
4. BU/89/1/3 Gwen to Angela, 25 Apr. 1872.
5. BU/89/1/4 Gwen to Angela, undated.
6. BU/21/95/3 Coutts Bank to Gwen, 11 May 1872.
7. BU/21/185/39 Bute to Gwen, 24 Oct. 1883.
8. BU/91/1/2 Howard of Glossop to Gwen, 24 May 1872.
9. BU/89/1/6 Gwen to Angela, 12 Jun. 1872.
10. BU/89/1/8 Gwen to Angela, 17 Jul. 1872.
11. BU/89/1/7 Gwen to Angela, 25 Jun. 1872.
12. HB, p. 110.
13. BU/89/1/12 Gwen to Angela, 21 Oct. 1872.
14. Girouard, 'Victorian Values', p. 51.
15. BU/89/1/6 Gwen to Angela, 6 Jun. 1872.
16. BU21/94/1 Bute to Gwen, 14 Jun. 1872.

17. Not only was there a high death rate from the illness; it also gave rise to serious after-effects, one of which was already known to be Bright's disease. David Hamilton, pers. com.

18. BU/21/94/2 Telegram from Queen Victoria to Bute, 2 Aug. 1872.

19. BU/21/171/20 Condor to Bute, 7 Apr. 1881.

20. BU/89/1/11 Gwen to Angela, 3 Oct. 1872.

21. BU/89/1/12 Gwen to Angela, 6 Oct. 1872.

22. BU/21/94/1 Gwen to Bute, undated.

23. BU/21/101/3 Bute to Gwen, 27 Jan. 1873.

24. BU/89/1/16 Gwen to Angela, 3 Dec. 1872.

25. BU/89/1/9 Gwen to Angela, 22 Sept. 1872. They were descended from the youngest son of the 1st Marquess of Bute by the latter's first marriage.

26. BU/89/3/2 Gwen to Angela, 1 Feb. 1874.

27. William Burges small notebooks, RIBA library no. 35, pp. 26, 35, 36.

28. *The Buteman*, 28 Dec. 1875.

29. Martin Biddle, *The Tomb of Christ* (Sutton Publishing: Stroud, 1999).

30. Kenneth John Conant and Glanville Downey, 'The Original Buildings at the Holy Sepulchre in Jerusalem', *Speculum* vol. XXXI Jan 1956, p. 8.

31. Conant and Downey 'The Original Buildings' p. 8. *cf.* John Lowden, *Early Christian and Byzantine Art* (Phaidon: 1997).

32. BU/21/101/5 Bute to Gwen, 14 Mar. 1872.

33. BU/21/117/9 Bute to Gwen, Mar. 1875.

34. BU/91/1/2 Lady Howard of Glossop to Gwen, 13 Dec. 1872.

35. BU/21/101/3 Bute to Gwen, 27 Jan. 1873.

36. BU/91/1/7 Howard of Glossop to Gwen, later dated Jan. 1873.

37. BU/21/101/4 Bute to Gwen, 29 Jan. 1873.

38 BU/89/7 Gwen to Angela, 7 Jan. 1878.

39. BU/91/2/2 Lord Howard of Glossop to Gwen, 30 Jan. 1873.

40. BU/21/107/2 Bute to Gwen, 12 Jul. 1874.

41. BU/21/101/2 Bute to Gwen, 25 Jan. 1873.

42. BU/21/101/3 Bute to Gwen, 27 Jan. 1873.

43. BU/21/101/5 Bute to Gwen, 14 Mar. 1872.

44. BU/89/1/16 Gwen to Angela, 3 Dec. 1872.

45. BU/91/8 Lord Howard to Gwen, 20 Jan. 1873.

46. BU/91/4 Lord Howard to Gwen, 16 Jan. 1973.

47. BU/91/12 Lord Howard to Gwen, 7 Feb. 1873.

48. BU/89/2/3 Gwen to Angela, Sept. 1873.

49. David Semple F.S.A., *Second Supplement to St Mirin* (J. & J. Cook: Paisley, 1874), p. 24.

50. Sam McKinstry, *Rowand Anderson: the Premier Architect of Scotland* (Edinburgh University Press, 1991).

51. *The Edinburgh Courant*, 13 Jun. 1873.

52. *Paisley & Renfrewshire Gazette*, 14 Feb. 1874.

53. *Paisley & Renfrewshire Gazette*, 11 Apr. 1874.

54. Semple, *St Mirin*, p. 37.

55. *Paisley & Renfrewshire Gazette*, 14 Feb. 1874. Letter from John Crawford.

56. BU/21/185/17 Bute to Gwen, 11 Jul. 1883.

57. In 1895, Bute himself was to commission the architect Robert Weir Schultz (1860–1951) to survey Wester Kames with a view to restoration. Gavin Stamp,

Robert Weir Schultz, Architect, and His Work for the Marquesses of Bute (Mount Stuart, 1981), p. 43.

58. 'Kilmory Castle', at the farm of Meikle Kilmory.
59. BU/21/175/18 Bute to Gwen, 28 Mar. 1882.
60. BU/85/2 Bateman Invoice, 1874.
61. BU/85/2 Nicholls Invoice, 1874. Thomas Nicholls d. 1895. He was one of the few craftsmen who were given a relatively free hand by Burges. William Goscombe John worked in his studio 1881–6. It is at least arguable that Nicholls was the more creative sculptor.
62. BU/85/2 Campbell Invoice, 1876.
63. BU/85/13 Nicholls Invoice, 1874.
64. Thompson, *Respectable Society*, p. 155. Expressed as a figure based on the Retail Price Index, today that would be worth £28,500,000. Expressed as a figure based on average earnings, today that would be worth £236,000,000. The difference between these two figures very nicely expresses the difficulty in calculating what a pound was worth in the Victorian era.
65. HB, p. 241.
66. Mount Stuart mss. Frame letter book, p. 273.
67. Mount Stuart mss. Frame letter book, p. 51.
68. BU/21/107/2 Bute to Gwen, 12 Jul. 1874.
69. J. S. Black, 'A Short Account of How the Marquis of Bute's Beavers Have Succeeded in the Isle of Bute', *Journal of Forestry and Estates Management*, vol. 3 (1880), pp. 695–8. J. A. Gibson, 'The Bute Beavers', *Transactions of the Buteshire Natural History Society*, vol. 21 (1980), pp. 27–33.
70. BU/21/107/3 Bute to Gwen, undated.
71. BU/89/2/1 Gwen to Angela, 13 Feb. 1873.
72. *The Churchwoman*, 'A personal reminiscence by one who knew him', 9 Nov. 1900.
73. BU/89/2/3 Gwen to Angela, Sept. 1873.
74. *Ibid.* He was called ugly Burges to distinguish him from the painter, J. P. 'pretty' Burgess (Nigel R. Jones, *Architecture of England, Scotland and Wales* (Greenwood Press: 2005), p. 53). It must be doubtful that this is what Gwen had in mind here.
75. BU/89/3/2 Gwen to Angela, 1 Feb. 1874.
76. BU/89/4/1 Gwen to Angela, 23 Feb. 1875.
77. HB, p. 115.
78. *The Buteman*, 23 May 1874.
79. BU/21/108/6 Hay Gordon to Bute, 10 Jun. 1874.
80. BU/21/108/7 Lord Howard to Bute, 4 Sept. 1874.
81. JD, p. 73.
82. JD, p. 273.
83. BU/89/5/74 Gwen to Angela, 23 Aug. 1874.
84. BU/21/117/1 Bute to Gwen, 1 Feb. 1875.
85. JD, p. 143.
86. BU/21/117/2 Bute to Gwen, 2 Feb. 1875.
87. BU/21/117/4 Bute to Gwen, undated, but in series after 117/3, dated 1 March.
88. BU/21/117/5 Bute to Gwen, 3 Mar. 1875.
89. L. V. Shirley was solicitor to the Bute Estate in Cardiff, JD, p. 71.
90. BU/21/117/6 Bute to Gwen, 5 Mar. 1875.

91. JD, p. 73.

92. BU/21/117/8 Bute to Gwen, 6 Mar. 1875.

93. BU/21/117/11 Bute to Gwen, 11 Mar. 1875.

94. BU/21/117/9 Bute to Gwen, undated.

95. Mordaunt Crook, *Burges*, p. 268.

96. BU/21/117/11 Bute to Gwen, 11 Mar. 1875.

97. BU/21/117/3 Bute to Gwen, 1 Mar. 1875.

98. Very approximately, this sum marked the boundary between gentry and aristocracy. Thompson, *Landed Society*, p. 26.

99. BU/21/117/12 Bute to Gwen, 13 Mar. 1875.

100. Later to be Lord Herries of Terregles, 1837–1908. Mark Bence-Jones, *The Catholic Families* (Constable: London, 1992), pp. 215–8. He was one of a large and impeccable Catholic family, and a great sportsman.

101. *The Buteman*, 12 Jun. 1874.

102. BU/21/93/7 Bute to Gwen, undated.

103. *Cf.* BU/21/10/7 Lady Selina Henry, undated.

104. HB, p. 122. quoting a letter of Bute 'to an intimate friend', 10 Jan. 1876.

105. A charitable regular order founded in 1828. Members were always allowed personal possessions.

106. BU/21/93/1 Bute to Gwen, 4 Feb. 1872.

107. BU/21/108/4 Birchall to Bute, undated.

108. Charles Petrie Eyre, 1817–1902; Ushaw College, Durham 1826, deacon 1838, priest 1842, first Archbishop of Glasgow in restored Catholic hierarchy 1878–1902. See *DNB*.

109. BU21/119/1 Eyre to Bute, 5 Jan. 1875.

110. Much philanthropy in Victorian Scotland involved Protestant religious instruction, so the Catholic poor, especially the children, were effectively excluded. Checkland, *Philanthropy*, p. 248. The monetary and emotional support the Catholic poor received from Bute is still remembered in industrial areas of Ayrshire to this day.

111. BU/21/183/4 Richardson to Bute, 22 Jun. 1882.

112. BU/21/149/2 Bute to Henry Lachlan, 22 Jan. 1878.

113. BU/21/117/14 Bute to Gwen, 30 Aug. 1875.

114. BU/21/117/17 Bute to Gwen, 2 Sept. 1875.

115. BU/21/117/16 Bute to Gwen, 1 Sept. 1875.

116. BU/21/132 Papers on Blind Harry.

117. John, 3rd Marquess of Bute, *The Early Days of Sir William Wallace (A Lecture delivered at Paisley, Nov. 16 1875)*, New Edition (Alexander Gardener: Paisley, 1912), p. 7.

118. *Ibid.*, p. 5.

119. *Ibid.*, pp. 37–8.

120. *Ibid.*, p. 39.

121. *Ibid.*, p. 43.

122. *Ibid.*, pp. 56–7.

123. Richard Placid Burchall OSB, 1812–1885.

124. BU/21/119/9 Copy letter Bute to Burchall, 7 Nov. 1875.

125. BU/21/119/10 Burchall to Bute, 24 Nov. 1875.

126. BU/21/119/11 Bute to Burchall, 27 Nov. 1875.

127. BU/21/160/5 Bute to Gwen, 12 Sept. 1879.

128. BU/89/5/4 Gwen to Angela, 21 Dec. 1876.
129. *The Buteman*, 28 Dec. 1875.
130. BU/21/175/137 Bute to Gwen, 20 Jun. 1882.
131. William Gladstone was present for the birth of his children. By contrast the 2nd Marquess had only been allowed to see his wife and baby for a few moments by the second day. NLS Ms. 3445 f. 325 Bute to Principal Lee, 15 Sept. 1847. Alfred, Lord Tennyson fared slightly better, plainly being allowed to spend quite some time with his wife after the birth of their eldest living child. Thwaite, *Poet's Wife*, p. 249.
132. HB, p. 7. footnote.
133. BU/21/119/21 Capel to Bute, 24 Dec. 1875.
134. The full text of this letter is given in the Appendix, p. 239.
135. BU/21/1491/1. Bute to Franchi, not sent.
136. Robert Gray, *Cardinal Manning: a Biography* (Weidenfeld and Nicolson: London, 1985), p. 257.
137. Vincent Alan McClelland, *Cardinal Manning: His Public Life and Influence 1865–1892* (Oxford University Press: London, 1962), p. 119.
138. BU/21/162/6 Bute to Capel, 25 Jun. 1879.
139. BU/89/6/4/ Gwen to Angela, undated.

Chapter 8: Purgatory

1. BU/21/160/7 Bute to Gwen, undated.
2. Prince Leopold, 1853–1884, *BP*.
3. BU/85/20 Pitman to Sneyd, 4 Dec. 1877.
4. BU/85/10 Campbell Invoice, Oct. 1876.
5. BU/89/5/2 Gwen to Angela, 25 Nov. 1876.
6. BU/21/139/3 Bute to Gwen, undated.
7. BU/21/139/4 Bute to Gwen, 24 Feb. 1877.
8. BU/21/139/5 Bute to Gwen, 3 Mar. 1877.
9. BU/89/6/7 Gwen to Angela, undated.
10. BU/89/6/11 Gwen to Angela, undated.
11. BU/89/6/11 Gwen to Angela, 24 Apr. 1877.
12. The Victoria is a coachman-driven open carriage. Both passengers face forward though there is often a small seat facing backwards. There is a hood which can be raised for light rain. It was one of the most popular carriages for summer use, and remains in service, being today the most usual horse-drawn carriage used for weddings.
13. BU/89/6/20 Gwen to Angela, 6 Aug. 1877.
14. BU/89/3/3 Gwen to Angela, 5 Jun. 1877.
15. BU/21/128/2 Bute to Gwen, 9 May 1876.
16. John Martin Robinson, *The Dukes of Norfolk* (Oxford University Press: Oxford, 1982), p. 220.
17. BU/89/6/23 Gwen to Angela, undated.
18. BU/89/6/24 Gwen to Angela, undated.
19. Robinson, *Norfolk*, p. 221.
20. *The Buteman*, 8 Dec. 1877.
21. BU/85/20 Pitman to Sneyd, 4 Dec. 1877.
22. BU/89/6/28 Gwen to Angela, 22 Dec. 1877.

23. BU/21/101/6 Bute to Gwen, undated.

24. BU/89/7/6 Gwen to Angela, Good Friday 1879.

25. Bernard Aspinwall, 'The Making of the Modern Diocese of Galloway', in Raymond McCluskey, ed., *The See of Ninian* (Diocese of Galloway: Galloway: 1997), pp. 126–35.

26. John McLachlan was born in 1826, and ordained as a priest in 1850, appointed Bishop of Galloway at the restoration of the hierarchy in 1878 and died in office in 1893.

27. John Patrick Crichton Stuart, *The Burning of the Barns of Ayr* (Alex. Gardener: Paisley, 1878), p. 3.

28. *Ibid.*, p. 5.

29. *Ibid.*, p. 16.

30. *Ibid.*, p. 11.

31. *Ibid.*, p. 32.

32. BU/35/1 Mabel Henry to Bute, 10 Jan. 1878.

33. BU/35/5/2ff. Papers and copy letters relating to Lady Flora Hastings.

34. BU/35/5/4 The Curse of the Hastings.

35. BU/89/7/6 Gwen to Angela, Good Friday 1879.

36. BU/89/7/12 Gwen to Angela, 28 Aug. 1878.

37. *Cf.* BU/85/1/20 Taylor to Bateman, 10 Sept 1878.

38. HB, p. 218.

39. Matthew Williams, *Lord Bute's Bedroom* (Cardiff Castle Room Notes, unpublished).

40. Matthew Williams, pers. com.

41. James Matthews Duncan, 1826–1890. He was one of the three doctors present at James Young Simpson's discovery of the anaesthetic properties of chloroform. In 1877 he moved south to teach obstetrics and gynaecology at Barts.

42. BU/89/8/2 Gwen to Angela, 11 Feb. 1879.

43. BU/89/8/1 Gwen to Angela, 5 Feb. 1879.

44. BU/21/162/2 Howard of Glossop to Bute, Feb. 1879.

45. BU/89/8/3 Gwen to Angela, 25 Feb. 1879.

46. BU/89/8/4 Gwen to Angela, 24 March 1879.

47. BU/21/160/1 Bute to Gwen, undated.

48. BU/21/185/28 Bute to Gwen, undated.

49. BU/21/176/18 Gwen to Bute, 4 Nov. 1882.

50. BU/21/160/2 Bute to Gwen, undated.

51. BU/21/160/7 Bute to Gwen, undated.

52. BU/21/160/11 Bute to Gwen, undated.

53. Alfred Joseph Stourton, Baron Stourton, 1829–1893, had just succeeded in getting the barony of Mowbray, to which he was co-heir, called out of abeyance in his favour. He was the premier baron of England. Bence-Jones, *Catholic Families*, p. 266.

54. BU/21/160/7 Bute to Gwen, undated. Catholics were encouraged to make lavatorial jokes, 'due to the belief that lavatorial or "dirty" jokes were a preventative against *risqué* or "improper" jokes, which were taboo on moral grounds.' Bence-Jones, *Catholic Families*, p. 227. Bute was not at all shy about sex and very shy about other bodily functions, and regularly transgressed this rule.

55. A common Victorian euphemism for a loo, and the body parts which are employed in it.

56. BU/21/160/4 Bute to Gwen, undated.
57. BU/21/160/22 Bute to Gwen, undated.
58. BU/21/160/7 Bute to Gwen, undated.
59. BU/21/160/5 Bute to Gwen, 12 Sept. 1879.
60. BU/21/160/6 Bute to Gwen, undated.
61. BU/21/160/10 Bute to Gwen, undated.
62. BU/21/160/20 Bute to Gwen, undated.
63. BU/21/160/7 Bute to Gwen, undated.
64. BU/21/160/22 Bute to Gwen, undated.
65. BU/21/175/39 Bute to Gwen, 20 April 1882.
66. BU/21/160/19 Bute to Gwen, undated.
67. BU/21/169/8 Book of press cuttings concerning the Breviary.
68. Book of press cuttings concerning the Breviary, marginal notes. Charles Wordsworth, 1806–1892, Bishop of St Andrews, Dunkeld and Dunblane 1853–92, nephew of the Poet Laureate.
69. A full account of his life can be found in Sheridan Gilley, *Newman and his Age* (Darton, Longman and Todd: London, 1990).
70. BU/21/162/18 Newman to Bute, 3 Dec. 1879.
71. HB, p. 116.
72. JD, p. 73.
73. BU/21/167/2/2 Memorandum of a meeting between Wyndham Lewis and Shirley for the Trust and J. Riches and A. Hood for the Chamber of Commerce of Cardiff and Rees Jones (Mayor), Alderman Alexander, Alderman Jones & the Town Clerk for the Corporation of Cardiff, 29 Dec. 1880.
74. JD, p. 256.
75. BU/21/169/5 Bute to Sneyd, 18 Dec. 1881.
76. BU/21/162/5 Bute to Gwen, later dated 22 Oct. 1880.
77. BU/21/171/20 Condor to Bute, 7 Apr. 1881.
78. BU/21/194/26 Bute to Gwen, 7 Aug. 1884.
79. BU/36/1/12 Bute to Grant, 25 Sept. 1880.
80. BU/36/2/1 Bute to Grant, undated.
81. Colin Grant, 1832–1889. He was born in Glen Gairn, 5 miles from Balmoral Castle.
82. The recognised abbreviation for the Septuagint, the ancient Greek version of the Hebrew Scriptures.
83. BU/36/1/1 Bute to Grant, undated.
84. *Cf.* BU/36/1/4 Grant to Bute, 24 Feb. 1880.
85. BU/36/1/5 Bute to Grant, 2 Aug. 1880.
86. BU/36/1/9 Bute to Grant, 1 Sept. 1880.
87. Crook, *Burges*, p. 328.
88. BU/89/9/3 Gwen to Angela, 22 Apr. 1881.
89. Burges Estimate book, 26 Jul. 1880.
90. Nathaniel H. J. Westlake, 1833–1921. Margaret Westlake, 'N. H. J. Westlake FSA', *British Society of Master Glass Painters Journal* 1929, pp. 58–65.
91. BU/21/168/2 Bute to Gwen, 1 Jun. 1881.
92. BU/21/168/1 Bute to Gwen, undated.
93. BU/21/175/84 Bute to Gwen, 20 May 1882.
94. BU/21/175/137 Bute to Gwen, 20 Jun. 1882.

Chapter 9: Family

1. BU/89/9/7 Gwen to Angela, 23 Jul. 1881.
2. BU/36/2/4 Bute to Grant, 28 Jul. 1881.
3. A thrombosis, encouraged by the practice of lying in bed for two weeks after the birth then enforced on women.
4. BU/36/2/11 Bute to Grant, 10 Aug. 1881.
5. John, Marquess of Bute, *The Altus of St Columba* (Wm. Blackwood & Sons, Edinburgh and London 1882).
6. DA/65/2/8 Bute to Bishop of Argyll, 7 Sept. 1881.
7. BU/36/21 Gwen to Grant, 12 Dec. 1881.
8. BU/36/2/23 Bute to Grant, 29 Dec. 1881.
9. BU/21/175/52 Bute to Gwen, 2 May 1882.
10. BU/89/10/1 Gwen to Angela, 24 Jan. 1882.
11. BU/89/10/2 Gwen to Angela, 26 Jan. 1882.
12. BU/36/2/4 Bute to Grant, 11 Feb. 1882.
13. BU/21/177/1 McSwiney to Bute, 23 Feb. 1882.
14. BU/89/10/4 Gwen to Angela, 9 Mar. 1882.
15. BU/21/175/84 Bute to Gwen, 20 May 1882.
16. BU/21/175/1 Bute to Gwen, 6 Mar. 1882.
17. BU/21/175/5 Bute to Gwen, 13 Mar. 1882.
18. BU/21/175/13 Bute to Gwen, 24 Mar. 1882.
19. BU/21/175/14 Bute to Gwen, 25 Mar. 1882.
20. BU/21/175/20 Bute to Gwen, 29 Mar. 1882.
21. BU/21/175/18 Bute to Gwen, 28 Mar. 1882.
22. BU/21/176/1 Gwen to Bute, undated.
23. BU/21/175/24 Bute to Gwen, 29 Mar. 1882.
24. BU/21/176/5 Gwen to Bute, 25 May 1882.
25. BU/21/176/13 Gwen to Bute, 6 Jul. 1882.
26. BU/21/176/7 Gwen to Bute, 1 Jun. 1882.
27. BU/21/175/13 Bute to Gwen, 6 Jul. 1882.
28. BU/21/175/31 Bute to Gwen, undated.
29. BU/21/175/54 Bute to Gwen, undated.
30. BU/21/175/57 Bute to Gwen, 5 May 1882.
31. BU/89/7/12 Gwen to Angela, undated, 1878.
32. BU/21/175/121 Bute to Gwen, Trinity Sunday 1882.
33. BU/21/175/84 Bute to Gwen, 20 May 1882.
34. Richard Shannon, *Gladstone: Heroic Minister, 1865–1898* (Allen Lane: The Penguin Press: 1999).
35. BU/21/175/122 Bute to Gwen, 14 Jun. 1882.
36. BU/21/185/39 Bute to Gwen, 24 Oct. 1883.
37. BU/21/175/122 Bute to Gwen, 14 Jun. 1882.
38. Aspinwall, *Catholic Experience*, p. 19.
39. BU/175/20 Bute to Gwen, 29 Mar. 1882.
40. R. P. Pullan, Burges's brother-in-law. There is no suggestion elsewhere that he was rather a brute.
41. BU/21/175/10 Bute to Gwen, 2 Mar. 1882.
42. BU/21/175/107 Bute to Gwen, 2 Jun. 1882.

43. Patrick McLaughlin, St Margaret's Ayr 1871–90. C. Johnson, *Scottish Catholic Secular Clergy 1879–1989* (Edinburgh, 1991), p. 198.
44. BU/21/175/133 Bute to Gwen, 18 Jun. 1882.
45. BU/21/175/98 Bute to Gwen, 27 May 1882.
46. BU/21/175/96 Bute to Gwen, 26 May 1882.
47. BU/21/175/122 Bute to Gwen, 14 Jun. 1882.
48. BU/21/175/132 Bute to Gwen, 18 Jun. 1882.
49. BU/21/175/136 Bute to Gwen, 19 Jun. 1882.
50. BU/21/175/144 Bute to Gwen, undated.
51. BU/21/175/137 Bute to Gwen, 21 Jun. 1882.
52. BU/21/175/153 Bute to Gwen, undated 1882.
53. BU/21/175/146 Bute to Gwen, 26 Jun. 1882.
54. BU/21/175/148 Bute to Gwen, 1 Jul. 1882.
55. BU/21/175/162 Bute to Gwen, undated.
56. BU/21/176/12 Gwen to Bute, undated.
57. *Cf.* BU/21/184/2 Gwen to Bute, 21 Oct. 1883.
58. BU/36/18 Bute to Grant, 6 Sept. 1882.
59. BU/36/3/14 Bute to Grant, 25 Aug. 1882.
60. BU/36/2/15 Grant to Bute, 27 Aug. 1882.
61. BU/36/2/18 Bute to Grant, 6 Sept. 1882.
62. Reprinted in John Patrick Crichton Stuart, *Essays on Home Subjects* (Alex Gardener, Paisley, 1904), p. 10.
63. BU/21/177/25 27 Oct. 1882. It was in the style adopted both for village halls and schools in this period, a long broad hall with a few narrow Gothic windows at one end. No evidence has been found as to why Bute's plans were dropped in favour of this one, but one may suppose that impatience to have the school and chapel in operation was the prime cause.
64. BU/89/10/12 Gwen to Angela, 16 Nov. 1882.
65. BU/89/11/4 Gwen to Angela, undated.
66. BU/10/13 Gwen to Angela, 19 Nov. 1882.
67. He knew Hebrew, Aramaic and Arabic.
68. BU/21/185/1 Bute to Gwen, undated.
69. BU/21/185/38 Bute to Gwen, 23 Oct. 1883. and *cf.* BL ad. mss. f. 242 C. Douglas to Lady Holland, 14 Mar. 1872.
70. BU/21/177/29 Bute to Lord Howard, 20 Sept. 1882.
71. BU/89/11/2 Gwen to Angela, 27 Feb. 1883.
72. BU/89/11/4 Gwen to Angela, 1 Mar. 1883.
73. BU/21/185/50 McSwiney to Bute, 11 Mar. 1883.
74. BU/89/11/4 Gwen to Angela, 1 Mar. 1883.
75. BU/21/185/1 Bute to Gwen, undated.
76. BU/21/185/16 Bute to Gwen, 29 Jun. 1883.
77. BU/21/185/1 Bute to Gwen, undated.
78. BU/21/185/5 Bute to Gwen, 25 Apr. 1883.
79. BU/21/185/5 Bute to Gwen, 25 Apr. 1883.
80. BU/21/185/1 Bute to Gwen, undated.
81. BU/21/185/7 Bute to Gwen, undated.
82. BU/21/187/1 McSwiney to Bute, 1 May 1883
83. For generations, the name of the second son of the Bute family had been James, but Bute was not calling the child after his wicked uncle.

84. BU/21/177/21 Colin Grant to Bute, 12 Aug. 1882. In Gaelic speech it is almost impossible to distinguish the letters M and V.

85. BU/21/188/7 Bishop of Galloway to Bute, 2 May 1883. Historically speaking, Bute was quite correct. In the early church baptism and confirmation had been conferred at the same time.

86. BU/36/4/1 Bute to Grant, 9 May 1983.

87. BU/36/4/2 Bute to Grant, 19 May 1983.

88. John Patrick Crichton Stuart, 'Ancient Celtic Latin Hymns', *Essays on Home Subjects*, p. 10.

89. BU/21/185/14 Bute to Gwen, 27 Jun. 1883.

90. BU/21/185/18 Bute to Gwen, 2 Jul. 1883.

91. John Henry Stuart was the son of Bute's factor Henry Stuart, cousin to Bute, being the grandson of the 3rd Earl (see family tree) and brother of Octavia, who married George Sneyd. He would in turn become Bute's factor.

92. BU/21/185/22 Bute to Gwen, 8 Jul. 1883.

93. BU/21/185/22 Bute to Gwen, 8 Jul.

94. BU/21/185/16 Bute to Gwen, 29 June 1883.

95. BU/21/185/17 Bute to Gwen, 1 Jul. 1883.

96. BU/21/185/21 Bute to Gwen, 7 Jul. 1883.

97. BU/21/184 Gwen to Bute, undated.

98. BU/21/185/29 Bute to Gwen, undated.

99. BU/21/185/38 Bute to Gwen, 23 Oct. 1883.

100. BU/21/185/42 Bute to Gwen, undated.

101. BU/21/185/48 Bute to Gwen, 1 Nov. 1883.

102. *The Glasgow Herald*, 10 Nov. 1883. In fact it had been £2,000.

103. *The Glasgow Herald*, 13 Nov. 1883.

104. BU/21/188/18 Guy to Bute, 16 Nov 1883.

105. BU/21/185/36 Bute to Gwen, 21 Oct. 1883.

106. BU/21/185/41 Bute to Margaret, 26 Oct. 1883.

107. BU/21/190/11 Norfolk to Bute, undated.

108. BU/36/5/1 Bute to Grant, 12 Jan. 1884.

109. Uncatalogued Mount Stuart, Gwendolen Hamilton to Miss Arnet, 10 Aug. 1971.

110. Uncatalogued Mount Stuart, Gwen to Bute, 8 Jul. 1884.

111. BU/21/199/30 ? to Bute.

112. Uncatalogued Mount Stuart, Gwen to Bute, 8 Jul. 1884.

113. Uncatalogued Mount Stuart, Gwen to Bute 13 Jul. 1884.

114. There is no trace of Jones' other names, and it has been impossible to find further details of her.

115. BU/21/194/14 Bute to Gwen, 23 Jul. 1884.

116. BU/21/194/32 Bute to Gwen, 14 Aug. 1884.

117. Uncatalogued Mount Stuart, Gwen to Bute, 11 Aug. 1884.

118. BU/21/194/1 Bute to Gwen, 3 Jul. 1884.

119. BU/21/194/6 Bute to Gwen, 16 Jul. 1884.

120. BU/21/194/12 Bute to Gwen, 20 Jul. 1884.

121. BU/21/194/13 Bute to Gwen, 21 Jul. 1884.

122. BU/21/194/34 Bute to Gwen, 15 Aug. 1884.

123. *Ibid.*, p. 135.

124. Hartwell de la Garde Grissell, 1839–1907. An older contemporary of Bute's

at Harrow and Oxford, a Catholic convert, he became an honorary lay chamberlain to Pius IX and left his considerable collection of relics to the diocese of Birmingham and his collection of Papal coins to the Ashmolean.

125. *Cf.* BU/21/194/43 Bute to Gwen, 27 Aug. 1884.
126. BU/21/194/48 Bute to Gwen, 29 Aug. 1884.
127. SCSC Daniel Collins was at St John's Cumnock from 1885–1889.
128. BU/21/176/4 Gwen to Bute, 1882.
129. C. Johnson, *Scottish Catholic Secular Clergy.*
130. BU/21/194/34 Bute to Gwen, 15 Aug. 1884.
131. BU/21/194/26 Bute to Gwen, 7 Aug. 1884.
132. BU/21/194/47 Bute to Gwen, 26 Aug. 1884.
133. BU/21/194/50 Bute to Gwen, 4 Sept. 1884.
134. BU/21/194/51 Bute to Gwen, 6 Oct. 1884.
135. BU/21/194/50 Bute to Gwen, 4 Sept. 1884.
136. BU/21/194/54 Bute to Gwen, 11 Sept. 1884.
137. Uncatalogued Mount Stuart, Gwen to Bute, 22 Sept. 1884.
138. BU/21/194/67 Bute to Gwen, 16 Oct. 1884.

Chapter 10: Mount Stuart

1. Frame Letter Book, to Campbell, 12 Feb 1884.
2. Ian Gow, 'The First Mount Stuart' in Andrew McLean, ed., *Mount Stuart, Isle of Bute* (The Mount Stuart Trust, Isle of Bute, 2001), p. 6.
3. Gow, *Mount Stuart*, pp. 10–11.
4. McKinstry, *Rowand Anderson*, p. 78.
5. McKinstry, *Rowand Anderson,* p. 79.
6. Gow, *Mount Stuart*, p. 10.
7. Mordaunt Crook, *Burges*, p. 34.
8. If one counts the flagpole tower.
9. BU/43/6 Bute's diary, 15 Dec. 1891.
10. BU/21/187/15 Vickers to Bute, 18 Oct. 1883.
11. Mount Stuart uncatalogued, Gwen to Bute, 22 Sept. 1884.
12. Mount Stuart uncatalogued, Gwen to Bute, ?29 Sept. 1884.
13. Mount Stuart uncatalogued, W. Massey to Bute, 11 Oct. 1883.
14. Mount Stuart uncatalogued, W. Massey to Bute, 22 Dec. 1884.
15. BU/21/214/2 Rosebery to Bute, 6 Jan. 1885.
16. Mount Stuart uncatalogued, W. Massey to ?Anderson, 17 Sept. 1885.
17. BU/43/9 Bute's diary 12 Sept. 1894.
18. CCL IX 31, marked Bute general 7, 13 Apr. 1887.
19. BU/21/216/1 Panagiotes Kalogeropoulos to Bute 25 June/7 July 1885.
20. Stamp, *Schultz*, p. 38.
21. BU/13/4 R. R. Anderson to Windsor Stuart, 11 Nov. 1882.
22. Blair, *Bute*, p. 241
23. *Fife News*, 29 April 1893.
24. HB, p. 242.
25. Sneyd Papers, Bute to Sneyd 3 Jun. 1885. Quoted in slightly different words by Gavin Stamp, 'The new Mount Stuart', *Mount Stuart, Isle of Bute* (Mount Stuart Trust, 2001).
26. Frame was at Mount Stuart at that time to discuss Oban Cathedral, but it is

likely that his taking over the new role at Mount Stuart was discussed – in December of that year he was discussing the Family Bedroom with Bute and by May of the following year he was discussing a model of the Horoscope Ceiling there, upon which work had plainly started much earlier.

27. Frame Letter Book, to Campbell, 12 Feb. 1884.
28. Frame Letter Book, to Campbell, 16 Aug. 1886.
29. Frame Letter Book, to Campbell, 3 Jan. 1886.
30. Frame Letter Book, 20 Aug. 1888.
31. Frame Letter Book, 9 Aug. 1888.
32. Frame Letter Book, to Antill, 25 Nov. 1886.
33. Frame Letter Book, to Antill, 23 Dec. 1886.
34. Frame Letter Book, to Antill, 12 Feb. 1887.
35. Frame Letter Book, to Antill, 6 Nov. 1887.
36. Frame Letter Book, 21 Dec. 1889.
37. Frame Letter Book, to Earl, 27 Sept. 1887.
38. Frame Letter Book, to Earl, 28 Sept. 1887.
39. Frame Letter Book, to Nicholls, 18 Jul. 1887.
40. Frame Letter Book, to Nicholls, 5 Nov. 1887.
41. Frame Letter Book, to Nicholls, 21 Sept. 1888.
42. Frame Letter Book, to Nicholls, 28 Feb. 1887.
43. Matthew Williams, 'Lady Bute's Bedroom, Castell Coch: A Rediscovered Architectural Model' *Architectural History*, vol. 46, 2003, p. 271.
44. *Ibid.*, p. 257.
45. *Ibid.*, p. 271.
46. Frame Letter Book, to Campbell, 13 Sept. 1887.
47. Bute's diary, 8 Dec. 1886.
48. Frame Letter Book, to D. Macfarlane, 14 Feb. 1887.
49. Frame Letter Book, to Campbell, 5 May 1887.
50. BU/21/214/44 G. Smith to Bute, 18 June 1885.
51. Frame Letter Book, to Campbell, 17 Dec. 1887.
52. Frame Letter Book, to Campbell, 14 Jan. 1887.
53. They are still extant at Mount Stuart.
54. Frame Letter Book, to Finlayson, 15 Mar. 1888.
55. Frame Letter Book, to Campbell, 13 Sept. 1887.
56. Frame Letter Book, to Mr Worrall, 31 Jul. 1889.
57. Frame Letter Book, to Lonsdale, 13 Dec. 1889.
58. Frame Letter Book, to Campbell, 6 Aug. 1889.
59. Frame Letter Book, to Earl, 1 Sept. 1887.
60. Frame Letter Book, to Earl, 5 Sept. 1887
61. Frame Letter Book, to Nicholls, 25 Nov. 1887.
62. Andrew McLean, Notes for Mount Stuart Guides.
63. Frame Letter Book, to Pembery, 3 Apr. 1888.
64. Frame Letter Book, to F. Anderson, 19 May 1888.
65. Frame Letter Book, to D. Macfarlane, 22 Oct. 1888.
66. Frame Letter Book, to Worrall, 30 Jan. 1888.
67. Frame Letter Book, to Lonsdale, 3 Apr. 1889.
68. BU/43/5 Bute's diary, 1 Sept. 1890. There are two ways of reading this decision. If one assumes that one is looking at the sunny daytime sky (not perhaps unreasonable when one is talking of sun signs), then putting Cancer

to the south suggests one is looking at the summer sky. On the other hand, if one assumes one is looking at the night-time sky, then the opposite is true. In the night sky Cancer is high at midwinter, when the stars are at their best. But the chart which is set up by astrologers for a human birth does not ask which constellation of the zodiac is high in the night sky when the subject is born – to determine the 'sun sign', popularly known as one's 'sign of the zodiac', it asks where in the ring of constellations the sun is sitting. This is, of course, a 'sign' which cannot at the time be actually seen at all, since the sun blinds one to it. Putting Cancer to the south suggests the zodiac in the great hall is seen in the day when the sun is shining, which would be in midsummer. The same hall, seen at night would suggest the opposite – midwinter. But the windows are very hard to see at night.

69. Crook, *Burges*, p. 85.
70. Timothy Lingard, 'Horatio Walter Lonsdale, Architectural Artist', *The Antique Collector* (Dec. 1987), p. 54–61.
71. Lingard, 'Lonsdale', p. 8.
72. Virginia Green 'C20', in J. Mordaunt Crook, ed., *The Strange Genius of William Burges 'Art-Architect' 1827–1881* (National Museum of Wales, 1981).
73. BU/43/4 Bute's diary, 1889.
74. Mount Stuart collection. Uncatalogued.
75. Martin Harrison, *Victorian Stained Glass* (Barrie and Jenkins: London, 1980), pp. 20–28.
76. Harrison, *Glass*, p. 63.
77. Dr David Lawrence, letter to the author, 6 Nov. 2002. Dr David Lawrence is the foremost authority on Burges glass.
78. Frame Letter Book, to Lonsdale, 23 May 1889.
79. Extract from Worrall Ledger by kind permission of Dr David Lawrence.
80. Harrison, *Glass*, p. 11.
81. Lonsdale to Bute, 7 Mar. 1890.
82. Frame Letter Book, to Nicholls, 23 Nov. 1889.
83. Frame Letter Book, to Nicholls, 31 Nov. 1889.
84. Mount Stuart, uncatalogued.
85. BU/43/10 Bute's diary, 24 Sept. 1895.
86. See ch. 15.
87. By this period Bute was Rector of St Andrews University.

Chapter 11: Hierarchy

1. BU/21/194/34 Bute to Gwen, 15 Aug. 1884.
2. *Cf.* BU21/175/146 Bute to Gwen, 26 Jun. 1882.
3. In the 1990s a refugee from the civil wars in former Yugoslavia returned to war-torn Bosnia, as he found life in Cumnock too rough.
4. BU21/209/5 Bute to the Bishop of Galloway, 5 Jan. 1885.
5. BU/21/214/34 Clements to Bute, 28 Apr. 1885.
6. BU/21/199/46 Clements to Bute, 27 Dec. 1884.
7. BU/21/209/4 Collins to Bute, 5 Jan. 1885.
8. BU/21/199/50 Shaw to Bute, 31 Dec. 1884.
9. BU/21/209/1 Collins to Bute, 1 Jan. 1885.

10. BU/21/209/2 Bute to Collins, 2 Jan. 1885.

11. BU/21/209/3 Clements to Bute, 4 Jan. 1885.

12. BU/21/209/5 Bute to the Bishop of Galloway, 5 Jan. 1885.

13. BU/21/209/10 Collins to Bute, 12 Jan. 1885.

14. *Cf.* CUL add. 8316/1/21 Bute to Westcott, 23 May 1883.

15. BU/21/214/22 Collins to Bute, 23 Mar. 1885.

16. BU/21/214/28 Collins to Bute, 26 Mar. 1885.

17. BU/21/214/29 Bute to Collins, 30 Mar. 1885.

18. BU/21/214/67 the Bishop of Galloway to Bute, 20 Jul. 1885.

19. BU/21/225/25 Clements to Bute, 10 Mar. 1886.

20. A full account of St Sophia's Galston can be found in Rosemary Hannah, 'St Sophia's Galston: "the vast space of the interior"', *Architectural History* vol. 46 (2003), pp. 255–68. The first turf was cut early in 1885, and the church 'opened' and 'blessed' at the Mass on Christmas Eve 1886.

21. Mr Henry Stuart Laverty, b. Salford 1854, Cumnock 1889–90.

22. BU/91/26/17 Laverty to Gwen, 1 Sept. 1884.

23. *Ibid.*

24. Mount Stuart mss., uncatalogued, Gwen to Bute, 24 Sept. 1884.

25. Stamp, *Schultz*, p. 12.

26. The following details are taken from Rev. John Carmont, DD, *The Mitchell Trust–Bequest Litigation* 11 Dec 1882–16 Jan 1885 (The Aberdeen University Press Ltd: 1904) DA/32/6, a printed résumé of the case printed by John Carmont after the conclusion of the case, and its final resolution. The facts are not disputed.

27. BU/21/211/3 Copy papers of this case given to Bute by Carmont. The following account is drawn from Carmont's summary of the case presented to Bute and his agents.

28. Giovanni Simeoni, 1816–1892.

29. William Smith, 1819–1892, was appointed the Archbishop of St Andrews and Edinburgh 1885–1892.

30. BU/21/211 Copy letter W. Smith to Carmont, 9 Mar. 1885.

31. CCL IX 31 Bute general 7, 9 Oct. 1884.

32. BU/21/211/5 Opinion by Bute, July 1885.

33. Carmont, *Mitchell*, p. 87.

34. BU/36/6/6 Grant to Bute, 10 Jun. 1886.

35. Angus Macdonald, 1844–1900.

36. It is widely repeated that Bute gave mitres to all the Scottish sees upon the restoration of the hierarchy. This is not true. He gave only to the two sees in which he had a principal residence.

37. DA/65/1/10 Bute to Bishop of Argyll, 31 Jan. 1879.

38. DA/65/1/2 Bute to Bishop of Argyll, 29 May 1878.

39. DA/65/3/1 Bute to Bishop of Argyll, 31 Jan. 1884.

40. DA/65/3/2 Bute to Bishop of Argyll, 17 Mar. 1884.

41. BU/21/194/34 Bute to Gwen, 15 Aug. 1884.

42. DA/65/3/2 Bute to Bishop of Argyll, 17 Mar. 1885.

43. Hereafter abbreviated to the Scottish, as this is how it was always referred to by Bute, his friends and its publisher.

44. Bute, 'Some Christian Monuments of Athens', *SR* vol. VI July and Oct 1885.

45. Bute, The Scottish Peerage, *SR* vol. VII January and April 1886.

46. Letter of Bute, dated 1 Dec. 1886, quoted by HB, p. 133, but now lost.
47. Bute, The Bayreuth Festival, pp. 287–309 SR vol. VIII, 1886.
48. The Marquis of Bute, *The Prophecies of St Malachi* (reprinted from the *Dublin Review*, October 1885).
49. BU/43/1 Bute's diary, 19 Jan. 1886.
50. BU/43/1 Bute's diary, 3 Apr. 1886.
51. BU/36/5/3 Bute to Grant, 13 April 1886.
52. FA210/135/2 Bute to Blair, 7 Apr. 1886.
53. Bute did. Colum has become a common Scottish given name.
54. BU/36/5/3 Bute to C. Grant, 13 Apr. 1886.
55. BU/43/1 Bute's diary, 2 May 1886.
56. *Ibid.*, 7 May.
57. *Ibid.*, 14 May.
58. FA210/135/10 Bute to Blair, 19 May 1886.
59. Dr Julia Lowe, pers. com.
60. BU/36/5/8 23 Bute to Grant, June 1886.
61. David Hunter Blair, 1853–1939.
62. FA210/134/3 Bute to Blair, 31 Oct. 1879.
63. HB, p. 110.
64. Bute was employing him as chaplain at Oban choir school, where he lasted only a few days due to his having become drunk in public.
65. BU/43/1 Bute's diary, 13 Jun. 1886.
66. BU/21/175/142 Bute to Gwen, 24 June 1882.
67. McClelland, *Manning*, pp. 87–9.
68. BU/21/215/2 McSwiney to Bute, 18 Apr. 1885.
69. John R. Watts, *Scalan: The Forbidden College, 1716–1799* (Tuckwell Press: East Linton, 1999).
70. BU/21/219/8 Bute to Archbishop Smith, 1 Aug. 1886.
71. BU/21/219 Purbeck to Bute, 5 Nov. 1886.
72. John Kerr, *Scottish Education, School and University: From Early Times to 1908* (Cambridge University Press: 1913), p. 339.
73. BU/21/219 Purbeck to Bute, 5 Nov. 1886.
74. BU/21/219/1 George Angus to Bute, 16 Mar. 1886.
75. BU/21/225/24 Bute to Archbishop of Edinburgh, 8 Mar. 1886.
76. DA/65/3/5 Bute to Bishop of Argyll, 28 May 1885.
77. DA/65/3/14 Bute to Bishop of Argyll, 13 Oct. 1885.
78. DA/65/4/16 Bute to Rouse, undated.
79. DA/65/4/7 Bute to Bishop of Argyll, 31 May 1885.
80. DA/65/5/2 Bute to Bishop of Argyll, 26 May 1886.
81. DA/65/5/7 Bute to Bishop of Argyll, 25 Jun. 1886.
82. Donald Weeks, *Corvo* (Michael Joseph Ltd: London, 1971).
83. Miriam J. Benkovitz, *Frederick Rolfe, Baron Corvo* (Hamish Hamilton Ltd: London, 1977), p. 7.
84. *Ibid.*, p. 9.
85. BU/21/226/1 Rolfe to Bute, 25 Jun. 1885.
86. BU/43/1 Bute's diary, 29 Jun. 1886.
87. BU/21/226/2 Rolfe to Bute, 1 Jul. 1886.
88. BU/21/226/16 Rolfe to Bute, 11 Aug. 1886.
89. DA65/5/6 Bute to Bishop of Argyll, 17 Jun. 1886.

90. BU/43/1 Bute's diary, 23 Aug. 1886.

91. BU/21/226/21 Bute to Anderson, 2 Sept. 1886.

92. BU/21/226/25 Bute to Anderson, 6 Sept. 1886.

93. Weeks, *Corvo*, p. 20.

94. BU/21/226/19 Rolfe to Bute, 31 Aug. 1886.

95. Benkovitz, *Rolfe*, p. 249.

96. BU/21/226/36 Rolfe to Bute, 17 Sept. 1886.

97. Weeks, *Corvo*, p. 20.

98. BU/21/226/40 Rolfe to Bute, 27 Sept. 1886.

99. BU/21/226/25 Bute to Anderson, 6 Sept. 1886.

100. Francis Beurms, d. 1895 aged 51. *CDS* 1896.

101. BU/21/226/25 Bute to Anderson, 6 Sept. 1886.

102. BU/21/226/28 Anderson to Bute, 9 Sept. 1886.

103. BU/21/226/26 Rolfe to Bute, 5 Sept. 1886.

104. BU/21/226/30 Bute to Anderson, 10 Sept. 1886.

105. DG 75/8/3 Beurms to Turner, 28 Sept. 1886.

106. DA 62/7/3 Beurms to Turner, 28 Sept. 1886.

107. DG 75/8/2 Bérard to Turner, 18 Sept. 1886.

108. DG 75/8/3 Beurms to Turner, 28 Sept. 1886.

109. DG 65/5/1 Bute to Bishop of Argyll, 14 Sept. 1886.

110. Fr Rolfe, *Hadrian the Seventh* (first published 1904, Chatto and Windus, London 1971), p. 382.

111. BU/48/1/14 Bute to Metcalfe, 2 Oct. 1886.

112. BU/43/1 Bute's diary, 4 Oct. 1886.

113. BU/21/226/38 Rolfe to Bute, 20 Sept. 1886.

114. BU/43/1 Bute's diary, 7 Oct. 1886.

115. BU/21/226/40 Rolfe to Bute, 27 Sept. 1886.

116. Rolfe, *Hadrian*, p. 381–2.

117. Benkovitz, *Rolfe*, p. 37. It must be pointed out that Rolfe lived in desperate poverty, and had nowhere else to go next on these occasions.

118. BU/43/1 Bute's diary, 8–9 Oct. 1886.

119. In the early twentieth century he was the author of a number of books, the most famous of which is *Hadrian the Seventh*. It is a *roman à clef*, and a sustained fantasy of what might have happened if Rolfe had been made the first English Pope since the middle ages. Rolfe was rediscovered in the later twentieth century, following a brilliant book, part biography, part narrative of the process of researching a biography, by A. J. A. Symonds, *The Quest for Corvo* (Cassell: London, 1955). Rolfe's works enjoyed a revival and *Hadrian VII* became a successful stage play.

120. BU/21/242/6 Rolfe to Bute, 10 Jan. 1887.

Chapter 12: Charity

1. BU/43/1 Bute's diary, 14 Oct. 1886.

2. BU/43/1 Bute's diary, 19 Jan. 1886. Chrysophanic acid is known to have an irritant effect upon the eyes.

3. *Ibid.*, 5 Nov. 1886.

4. FA210/319 Blair's diary, 12 Feb. 1887.

5. BU43/2 Bute's diary, 14 Feb. 1887.

6. BU/36/7/9 Bute to Grant, 21 May 1887.
7. BU/43/2 Bute's diary, 14 Feb. 1887. Notes for the past year.
8. FA210/319 Blair's diary, 28 Feb. 1887.
9. BU/21/242/35 Blair to Bute, 24 Feb. 1887.
10. BU/21/242/39 Blair to Bute, 24 Feb. 1887.
11. FA210/136/3 Bute to Blair, 26 Feb. 1887.
12. FA210/319 Blair's diary, 28 Feb. 1887.
13. *Ibid.*, 15 Feb 1887.
14. BU/43/2 Bute's diary, 11 Apr. 1887.
15. BU/21/230/5 Bute to Metcalfe, 20 Apr. 1887.
16. BU/43/2 Bute's diary, 3 Mar. 1887.
17. BU/43/4 Bute's diary, 1889.
18. Quoted by Rev. Charles Rogers in *The Book of Wallace*, vol. I (The Grampian Club), Edinburgh, 1889, p. 294.
19. Andrew McLean, 'The Bright Particular Star of the Scottish Home Rulers. Bute and the Scottish Parliament'. Paper for the Symposium 'Bute', Mount Stuart House, 2000.
20. A small area of land there had been in Bute's hands.
21. In the end, Glasgow's cousin, later the 7th Earl, sold his own lands at Irvine and bought Kelburn.
22. CCL IX 31, Bute general 7, 25 Mar. 1886.
23. *Ibid.*, 1 Jun. 1886.
24. Best, *Britain*, p. 97.
25. Readers should remember that Shaw practised what he preached with regards to the reform of punctuation.
26. G. B. Shaw, *Pygmalion* (1915: Harmondsworth: Penguin Books, 1987), ll. 250–60 *passim*.
27. BU/21/237/1 Thompson to Bute, 5 Feb. 1887.
28. BU/21/237/6 Jenny Wotherspoon to Mortimer Herries, 24 Feb. 1887.
29. BU/210/46 Thompson to Bute, 17 Oct. 1885.
30. BU/21/224/17 John Windsor Stuart to Anderson, 28 Sept. 1886.
31. BU/21/237/1 George Thompson to Bute, 5 Feb. 1887.
32. BU/21/237/4 Jeanie Wotherspoon to Bute, undated.
33. BU/21/237/5 Jeanie Wotherspoon to Bute, 15 Feb. 1887.
34. BU/21/237/8 John Anderson to Frank Anderson, 15 Apr. 1887.
35. BU/21/227/1 McSwiney to Bute, 1 Jul. 1886.
36. BU/21/227/4 McSwiney to Bute, 5 Jul. 1886.
37. Burges Small Notebooks 60, 1880, pp. 43–44.
38. BU/43/9 Bute's diary, 16 Jan 1894.
39. BU/21/177/27 A. Hay Gordon to Bute, 13 Dec. 1882.
40. BU/21/177/28 Bute to A. Hay Gordon, 16 Dec. 1882.
41. BU/241/15 Document entitled 'Adam Hay Gordon's Trust' Oct. 1887.
42. BU/43/9 Bute's diary, 14 Jul. 1894.
43. *Cf.* BU/21/194/26 Bute to Gwen, 7 Aug. 1884.
44. BU/21/235/43 Pitman to Bute, 27 Apr. 1887.
45. CCL Bute box IX/30 20 Feb.–7 Mar. 1882.
46. CCL Bute box IX/31 7 Oct.–3 Nov. 1885 and *passim*.
47. *Ibid.*, 8 Oct. 1885.
48. *Ibid.*, 20 Jan. 1886.

49. Greenalls & Whitley finally closed in 1990.

50. BU/21/242/20 Woodward to Bute, 4 Feb. 1887.

51. CU. Add. 8316/1/20 Bute to Westcott, 24 Jun. 1882.

52. BU/21/215/2 McSwiney to Bute, 25 Apr. 1885.

53. CUL. Add 8316/1/22 Bute to Westcott, 28 May 1883.

54. *The South Wales Echo*, 4 Feb. 1891.

55. Plomer, ed., *Kilvert's Diary*, vol. 1, *cf.* p. 37. 'Next to Mrs Corfield's and she was deeply thankful for a blanket and a pair of sheets, having only one blanket and a house full of children.'

56. *Ibid.*, p. 251.

57. Rt. Hon. William Abraham, b. 1842; s. of a working miner; m. 1860, Sarah Williams (d. 1900); d. 14 May 1922, MP (R) Glamorganshire (Rhondda Valley), 1885–1918, Rhondda, West Division, 1918–20. Known as 'Mabon'; he was the miners' agent from 1873; later President of the South Wales Miners' Federation.

58. BU/21/355/34 Mabon to Bute, 27 Jul. 1895.

59. BU/43/9 Bute's diary, 11 May 1894.

60. *The Western Mail*, 26 Apr. 1886.

61. *The Western Mail*, 4 May 1886.

62. BU/43/2 Bute's diary 1887, year summary.

63. *The Western Mail*, 17 Feb. 1893.

64. BU/21/199/15 Jones to F. Anderson enclosing cartoon 21 Feb. 1893.

65. *The Western Mail*, 1 Jun. 1894.

66. *Ibid.*

67. BU/43/6 Bute's diary, 4 Feb. 1891.

68. Alexander Munro, d. asthma 1820–1892, 71 years old. He was a tireless champion of Catholic education. *CDS* 1894.

69. Bernard Aspinwall, 'Children of the Dead End', *The Innes Review* vol LXIII, no. 2, Spring 1992, p. 126.

70. BU/21/216/11 Munro to F. Anderson, 13 Oct. 1885.

71. BU/21/216/12 Munro to Anderson, 2 Nov. 1885.

72. BU/216/14 Munro to F. Anderson, 26 Nov. 1885.

73. BU/21/228/4 Alex Munro to Bute, 24 Mar. 1886.

74. *Ibid.*

75. BU/21/260/1 Directions for Oban Choir School.

76. Patrick Wright, 1835–1889, *CDS*, 1889.

77. FA210/136/1 Bute to Blair, 15 Jan. 1887.

78. BU/21/245/4 Clements to Bute, 21 Feb. 1887.

79. BU/21/245/29 Clements to Bute, 11 Oct. 1887.

80. Rev. Roderick Macdonald, 'The "Tin" Cathedral at Oban: 1886–1934' *The Innes Review* pp. 47–55.

81. NLS 24/ 10085 f. 160 Bute to Rosebery, 15 Apr. 1886.

82. *The Cardiff Times and South Wales Weekly News*, 27 Mar. 1886.

83. *The Western Mail*, 27 Mar. 1886.

84. *The Cardiff Times and South Wales Weekly News*, 27 Mar. 1886

85. *The Western Mail*, 27 Mar. 1886.

86. *The Cardiff Times and South Wales Weekly News*, 27 Mar. 1886.

87. At the time of writing, it has not been possible to find out if Bute's plea was successful. There was a campaign in *The Western Mail* for his release. Jordan died in 1888.

88. BU/21/169/5 Bute to Sneyd, 18 Dec. 1881.
89. BU/43/5 Bute's diary, *passim*, April and May 1890.
90. BU/21/165/4 Sir Alexander Grant to Bute, 7 Nov. 1880.
91. BU/21/210/49 Hamîs to Bute, 10 Nov. 1885.
92. BU/21/210/59 Hamîs to Bute, 25 Dec. 1885.
93. BU/21/241/17 J. Anderson to F. Anderson, 2 Nov. 1887.
94. BU/43/2 Bute's diary, 21 Oct. 1887.
95. CCL Bute box IX/31, 22 Jun. 1885.
96. *Ibid.*
97. *Ibid.*, 27 Jul. 1887.

Chapter 13: Mayor

1. BU/21/286/31 undated, in Bute's hand.
2. BU/43/2 Bute's diary, 24 Dec. 1887.
3. BU/43/3 Bute's diary, 7 Jan. 1888.
4. BU/43/3 Bute's diary, 17 Jan. 1888.
5. BU/43/3 Bute's diary, 15 Feb. 1888.
6. BU/43/3 Bute's diary, 5 Apr. 1888.
7. BU/43/3 Bute's diary, 9 Jun. 1888.
8. 1548–1600.
9. *SR* vol. XII, July and Oct. 1888, p. 69.
10. He was especially shocked by the *Candelajo* Bruno's vernacular play 'The Candle-bearer' (or The Sodomite, which he refused to translate), perhaps because of its pederastic content. His dislike of Bruno may well have originated with this.
11. *SR* vol XII, p. 247, 'The Ultimate Fate of Giordano Bruno'.
12. BU/43/3 Bute's diary, 24 Jun. 1888.
13. BU/43/3 Bute's diary, 26 Jul. 1991.
14. BU/21/285/31 Bute to Frau Wagner, 2 Aug 1891. It is now the tradition at Bayreuth for the first act of the opera to be received with silence, as it is said 'the Master' Wagner desired.
15. BU/43/3 Bute's diary, 5 Sept. 1888.
16. BU/43/3 Bute's diary, 8 Sept. 1888.
17. BU/43/3 Bute's diary, 11 Sept. 1888.
18. *The Glasgow Herald*, 29 Aug. 1888.
19. BU/91/29/11 Phillipa Howard to Gwen, 2 Jul. 1888.
20. BU/43/2 Bute's diary, 15 Jul. 1887.
21. BU/21/242/189 Bute to Cowan, 1 Nov. 1887.
22. BU/43/2 Bute's diary, 16 Jul. 1887. William Middleton d. 1935.
23. BU/43/3 Bute's diary, 30 Oct. 1888.
24. More commonly seen these days as 'Turgenev'.
25. *SR* vol. XIII, 1889, pp. 69–105.
26. BU/43/4 Bute's diary, 25 Feb. 1889.
27. Donald Thomas, *The Victorian Underworld* (John Murray: 2003), p. 154.
28. Frame Letter Book, 22 Mar. 1889.
29. Frame Letter Book, Frame to W. Wilson, 30 Apr. 1889.
30. Frame Letter Book, 29 Apr. 1889.
31. Stamp, *Schultz*, p. 25.

32. BU/91/29/10, undated.
33. BU/21/235/6 2 Jun. 1887.
34. BU/43/4 Bute's diary, 21 Apr. 1889.
35. BU/43/4 Bute's diary, 26 Apr. 1889.
36. BU/36/8/1 Bute to Grant, 11 Jun. 1889.
37. Sir George McLeod, BU/43/4 Bute's diary, 11 Jun. 1889.
38. BU/36/8/4 Bute to Grant, 5 Jul. 1889.
39. BU/43/4 Bute's diary, 2 Jul. 1889.
40. Demetrios Bikelas or Vikelas, 1835–1908. He was a prolific writer and the first president of the International Olympic Committee, and instrumental in persuading the committee that the first of the revived Olympic Games should be held in Athens.
41. BU/36/8/8 Bute to Grant, 10 Jul. 1889.
42. BU/36/8/19 Bute to Grant, 1 Aug. 1889.
43. BU/36/2/1 Bute to Grant, 3 Jan. 1881.
44. BU/36/2/3 Bute to Grant, 1 Apr. 1881.
45. BU/36/2/16 Bute to Grant, 28 Aug. 1882.
46. BU/36/28/16 Bute to Grant, 26 Jul. 1889.
47. BU/36/8/3 Grant to Bute, 29 Jun. 1889.
48. BU/21/262/5 Bishop of Galloway to Bute, 7 Oct. 1889.
49. BU/43/4 Bute's diary, 27 Sept. 1889.
50. BU/21/261/40 extract from *The Catholic Times*, 30 Aug. 1889.
51. BU/21/262/39 Bishop of Galloway to Bute, 24 Jul. 1889.
52. BU/21/260/6 Clements to Bute, 22 April 1889.
53. BU/21/260/10 Savelli to Bute, 24 May 1889.
54. BU/21/260/13 Francis Savelli to Bute, 31 May 1889.
55. BU/21/260/25 Savelli to Bute, 29 Oct. 1889.
56. BU/21/260/2228 Savelli to Gwen, 23 Nov. 1889.
57. BU/21/280/34 Bute to Grissell, 5 Jul. 1890, *cf.* DA65/8/8 Bute to Bishop of Argyll.
58. BU/21/280/32 Grissell to Bute, 2 Jul. 1890.
59. BU/21/280/34 Bute to Grissell, 5 Jul. 1890.
60. BU/21/267/7 McSwiney to Bute, 30 May 1890.
61. Macdonald 'The "Tin" Cathedral', p. 54.
62. Unnamed in the surviving literature.
63. BU/21/280/24 Bute to Smith, 6 Jun. 1890.
64. BU/21/280/14 Laverty to Bute, 19 May 1890.
65. BU/21/280/14 Bute to Laverty, draft on back of Laverty's letter in Bute's hand.
66. BU/21/274/38 Bishop of Glasgow to Bute, July 1890.
67. BU/21//274/36 Bishop of Galloway to Bute, 24 Jun. 1890.
68. BU/21/280/29 Laverty to Bute, undated.
69. BU/21/280/29 in draft on the back of Laverty's letter in Bute's hand.
70. BU/21/274/62 Bishop of Galloway to Bute, 18 Oct. 1890.
71. BU/43/5 Bute's diary, 4 Feb. 1890.
72. BU/94/2/4 Margaret to Gwen, 10 May 1890.
73. BU/94/2/12.
74. BU/43/5 Bute's diary, 30 Oct. 1890.
75. BU/43/5 Bute's diary, 17 Sept. 1890.
76. BU/43/5 Bute's diary, 18 Oct. 1890.

77. *SR* vol. XIX, pp. 297–326 David, Duke of Rothesay. These were not actually published in the *Scottish* until 1892, presumably due to the pressure of the mayoral year in Cardiff.

78. SR, *David*, p. 322.

79. BU/43/5 Bute's diary, 25 Dec. 1890.

80. BU/43/5 Bute's diary, Résumé for year.

81. BU/43/5 Bute's diary, 29 Nov. 1890.

82. BU/21/270/6 Bute to Metcalfe, 30 Dec. 1890.

83. John Kinross, 1855–1931.

84. Hutchison seems to have delegated much of his design work, and this may have benefited his assistant's experience as it later did Charles Rennie Mackintosh, who later trained with him.

85. BU/43/5 Bute's diary, 3 Feb. 1890.

86. BU/43/5 Bute's diary, 21 Jan. 1890.

87. Deborah Clare Mays, *John Kinross, his Life and Work 1855–1931*: unpublished Thesis (1988) University of St Andrews.

88. BU/46/5 Bute's diary, 22 Nov. 1890.

89. BU/46/5 Bute's diary, 19 Dec. 1890.

90. Mays, *Kinross*, p. 81.

91. Mays, *Kinross*, p. 84

92. Mays, *Kinross*, p. 83.

93. *Cf.* BU/21/304/2 Bute to Gwen, 14 Jan. 1892, BU/43/2 Bute diary, 25 Aug. 1892.

94. Mays, *Kinross*, p. 80.

95. Cardiff City Council Minutes, 8 Sept. 1890.

96. BU/21/286/23 Bute's notes, 12 Sept. 1891.

97. BU/46/6 Bute's diary, 10 Jan. 1891.

98. BU/43/6 Bute's diary, 4 Feb. 1891.

99. *South Wales Echo*, 5 Feb. 1891.

100. H.A.Clegg, Alan Fox, A.F.Thompson, *A History of British Trade Unions since 1889*, 2 vols (Oxford University Press: London 1964), vol. I, p. 71.

101. *Ibid.*, pp. 69–77.

102. *South Wales Echo*, 4 Feb. 1891.

103. BU/46/6 Bute's diary, 7 Feb. 1891.

104. BU/46/6 Bute's diary, 5 Feb, 1891.

105. BU/60 Bute's mayoral year diary.

106. Derek Aldcroft and Michael Oliver, *Trade Unions and the Economy 1870–2000* (Ashgare: Aldershot, 2000).

107. BU/46/6 Bute's diary, 27 Feb. 1891.

108. BU/21/292/2 Bute to Gwen, 5 Mar. 1891.

109. BU/21/292/3 Bute to Gwen, 7 Mar. 1891.

110. BU/21/292/5 Bute to Gwen, 11 Mar. 1891.

111. BU/21/292/3 Bute to Gwen, 7 Mar. 1891.

112. BU/21/292/5 Bute to Gwen, 11 Mar. 1891.

113. BU/21/292/8 Bute to Gwen, 18 Mar. 1891.

114. BU/21/292/6 Bute to Gwen, 13 Mar. 1891.

115. BU/21/292/5 Bute to Gwen, 11 Mar. 1891.

116. BU/21/292/8 Bute to Gwen, 18 Mar. 1891.

117. Dr Julia Lowe, pers. com.

118. BU/43/6 Bute's diary, 22 Jun. 1891.

119. *South Wales Echo*, 23 Jun. 1891.

120. John, Marquess of Bute, *on the Ancient Language of the Natives of Tenerife* (John Masters, London. 1891). This is a conclusion which modern research has affirmed, and it is supported by DNA evidence that the peoples of North Africa made a significant contribution to the gene pool of contemporary inhabitants of the Canaries.

121. Sir William Huggins, 1824–1910, astronomer pioneered spectroscopy. His knighthood was granted in 1897. Margaret Huggins (née Murray), 1848–1915, appeared as co-author of his papers, which she illustrated. *DNB*.

122. *DNB*.

123. BU/43/6 27 Aug. 1891.

124. *Cf.* BU/21/396/6&7 Margaret Huggins to Gwen, 11 & 15 May 1898.

125. BU/21/286/23 Chisholm to Bute, 12 Sept. 1891.

126. BU/21/286/31 undated, in Bute's hand.

127. BU/43/6 Bute's diary, 3 Nov. 1891.

Chapter 14: St Andrews

1. BU/43/9 Bute's diary, 31 Dec. 1894.

2. BU/43/7 Bute's diary, 12 Jan. 1892. That is, -12 c.

3. BU/21/304/2 Bute to Gwen, 14 Jan. 1892.

4. BU/43/7 Bute's diary, 15 May 1891.

5. BU/21/304/3 Bute to Gwen, 15 Jan. 1892.

6. HB, p. 185.

7. BU/21/304/2 Bute to Gwen, 14 Jan. 1892.

8. BU/21/304/32 Bute to Gwen, 25 Mar. 1892.

9. BU/21/304/21 Bute to Gwen, Ash Wednesday 1892.

10. BU/21/304/24 Bute to Gwen, 6 Mar. 1892.

11. BU/21/304/27 Bute to Gwen, 13 Mar. 1892.

12. BU/21/304/30 Bute to Gwen, 20 Mar. 1892.

13. BU/21/304/29 Bute to Gwen, 17 Mar. 1892.

14. Lady Mary's daughter, Mary, 1718–1794, married the 3rd Earl of Bute in 1736.

15. BU/21/304/3337 Bute to Gwen, 8 Apr. 1892.

16. BU/21/304/32 Bute to Gwen, 25 Mar. 1892.

17. BU/21/304/38 Bute to Gwen, 10 Apr. 1892.

18. BU/21/304/31 Bute to Gwen, 22 Mar. 1892.

19. BU/21/304/36 Bute to Gwen, 6 Apr. 1892.

20. BU/21/304/21 Bute to Gwen, Ash Wednesday 1892.

21. BU/21/304/37 Bute to Gwen, 8 Apr. 1892.

22. BU/21/304/42 Bute to Gwen, Easter Monday 1892.

23. BU/43/7 Bute's diary, 31 Dec. 1892.

24. BU/43/7 Bute's diary, 8 Jun. 1892.

25. Stamp, *Schultz*, p. 17–19.

26. Stamp, *Schultz*, p. 4.

27. Stamp, *Schultz*, p. 12.

28. Stamp, *Schultz*, p. 17.

29. Giles Worsley, 'A Phoenix Rises', *Perspectives in Architecture* 29, June/

July 1997, pp. 59–61. It is greatly to be regretted that the present lessee of the Lodge, who funded a most beautiful and painstaking restoration of the building, has not felt able to open it to academic research.

30. BU/43/10 Bute diary, 24 Sept. 1895 and *cf.* the dates on the newly discovered sketches for the ceiling figures.

31. Stamp, *Schultz*, p. 14.

32. BU/43/7 Bute's diary, 13 Aug. 1892.

33. BU/43/7 Bute's diary, 27 Jul. 1892.

34. A Goodrich-Freer and the late John, Marquess of Bute, eds, *The Alleged Haunting of B– [Ballechin] House* (C. Arthur Pearson, Ltd: new edn 1900), p. 8.

35. Mays, *Kinross*, p. 82.

36. BU/43/7 Bute's diary, 29 Aug. 1892.

37. BU/43/7 Bute's diary, 31 Dec. 1892.

38. BU/43/7 Bute's diary, 6 Sept. 1892.

39. Harrowby Papers vol. 1077 ff. 127–8 Bute to Henry Ryder, 14 Sept. 1892.

40. BU/43/7 Bute's diary, 20 Oct. 1892.

41. BU/43/7 Bute's diary, 27 Sept. 1892.

42. BU/43/7 Bute's diary, 16 Sept. 1892.

43. BU/43/7 Bute's diary, 22 Nov. 1892.

44. BU/21/356/33 Memorandum. Excluded from this sum are the amounts he spent acquiring Sanquar.

45. 'Charles I', *SR* vol. X 1887, p. 272.

46. BU/21/394/1–7 Art and Book Company to Bute, March 11–20 Apr. 1898.

47. Donald Southgate, *University Education in Dundee* (Edinburgh University Press: Edinburgh, 1982), p. 22.

48. Sir William Peterson 1856–1921, classical scholar and educationalist. In 1895 appointed Principal of McGill University, Montreal, where he 'found a group of largely autonomous schools and transformed it into a University'. *DNB.*

49. Ronald Cant, *The University of St Andrews, a Short History* (St Andrews University Library: 1992).

50. BU/21/299/11 Bute to Student Representative Council St Andrews, 8 Nov. 1892.

51. Cant, *St Andrews*, p. 148.

52. BU21/319/1 Bute to Gwen, 21 Jan. 1893.

53. A. Scott Lowson, *Principal Sir James Donaldson, Education and Patronage in Victorian Scotland*: unpublished thesis, University of St Andrews (1987), p. 380.

54. BU/51/21/6 Metcalfe to Bute, 19 Feb. 1895.

55. NLS MS10014/159–161 Donaldson to Rosebery, Oct. 23 1893.

56. Southgate, *Dundee*, 92.

57. BU/43/8 Bute's diary, 26 Jan. 1893.

58. Blair, *Medicine*, p. 98.

59. BU/43/10 Bute's diary, 7 Aug. 1895.

60. NLS MS10014/164 Donaldson to Rosebery, 12 Dec. 1893.

61. NLS MS10014/8 Donaldson to Rosebery, 28 May 1883.

62. BU/43/8 Bute's diary, 24 Nov. 1893.

63. NLS MS10014/164 Donaldson to Rosebery, 12 Dec. 1893.

64. Rectorial Address, reproduced in *Essays on Home Subjects*, p. 232.

65. Rectorial Address, reproduced in *Essays on Home Subjects*, p. 263.

66. NLS MS10014/159–161 Donaldson to Rosebery, 23 Oct. 1893.

67. Lowson, *Donaldson*, p. 397.
68. Cant, *St Andrews*, p. 125.
69. Southgate, *Dundee*, p. 66.
70. Cant, *St Andrews*, p. 128.
71. Southgate, *Dundee*, p. 97.
72. John S. G. Blair, *History of Medicine in the University of St Andrews* (Scottish Academic Press: Edinburgh, 1987), p. 84.
73. Sir John Leng, 1828–1906.
74. Southgate, *Dundee*, p. 90.
75. *Glasgow Herald* 1895, quoted in Blair, *Medicine*, p. 149.
76. *Glasgow Herald* 1895, quoted in Blair, *Medicine*, p. 103.
77. BU/21/139/4 Bute to Gwen, 25 Jan. 1893.
78. Sophia Louisa Jex Blake, 1840–1912. Physician and campaigner for women's rights. *DNB*.
79. Enid Moberly Bell, *Storming the Citadel* (1953, Constable: London, reprinted 1994), p. 107.
80. Blair, *Medicine*, p. 141.
81. Blair, *Medicine*, p. 143.
82. Southgate, *Dundee*, p. 65.
83. Southgate, *Dundee*, p. 61, 65 and *passim*.
84. BU/21/286/31 Speech in Bute's hand relating to his acceptance of the Freedom of Glasgow, 1891.
85. A. K. H. Boyd, 1825–1899. Church of Scotland minister who had been Moderator of the General Assembly,
86. A. K. H. Boyd, *St Andrews and Elsewhere* (Longmans, Green & Co.: London, 1894), p. 85.
87. BU/43/8 Bute's diary, 4 Mar. 1893.
88. BU/43/8 Bute's diary, 31 Dec. 1893.
89. *The Fife News*, 29 Apr. 1893.
90. BU/43/8 Bute's diary, 24 Apr. 1893.
91. Mays, *Kinross*, p. 87.
92. BU/43/9 Bute's diary, 16 Apr. 1895.
93. Mays, *Kinross*, p. 88.
94. BU/43/8 Bute's diary, 11 Apr. 1893.
95. Mays, *Kinross*, p. 95.
96. Mays, *Kinross*, p. 93.
97. *The Aberdeen Weekly Journal*, 9 Sept. 1892.
98. BU/21/306/38, Br Oswald to Bute, 6 Sept. 1892.
99. BU/37/4 Digby Koe to Gwen, 5 Dec. 1893.
100. BU/43/8 Bute's diary, 2 Apr. 1893.
101. BU/43/8 Bute's diary, 18 Aug. 1893.
102. CCL IX 31 26 Oct. 1884.
103. BU/21/316/60 Gwen to Stuart, 3 Aug. 1893.
104. BU/43/8 Bute's diary, 2 Aug. 1893.
105. BU/21/316/60 Gwen to Stuart, 3 Aug. 1893.
106. BU/43/8/ Bute's diary, 11 Aug. 1893.
107. BU/43/8 Bute's diary, 25 Dec. 1893.
108. Sir David Oswald Hunter Blair, *A Last Medley of Memories* (Edward Arnold & Co.: London, 1936), p. 229.

109. BU/43/9 Bute's diary, 13 May 1894.

110. BU/43/9 Bute's diary, 18 May 1894.

111. BU/43/9 Bute's diary, 4 Jul. 1894.

112. BU/43/9 Bute's diary, 2 Jul. 1896.

113. BU/21/329/65 Bute to Metcalfe, 4 Jun. 1894.

114. BU/43/9 Bute's diary, 28 Jul. 1894.

115. BU/43/9 Bute's diary, 30 Aug. 1894.

116. BU/43/9 Bute's diary, 15 Sept. 1894.

117. Janet Oppenheim, *The Other World: Spiritualism and Psychical Research in England, 1850–1914* (Cambridge University Press: 1985, reprinted 2002).

118. John William Strutt, 3rd Baron Rayleigh, 1842–1919. *DNB*.

119. Sir Joseph John 'J.J.' Thomson, 1856–1940. *DNB*.

120. Frederic William Henry Myers, 1843–1901, Oppenheim, *Other World*.

121. Oppenheim, *Other World*, p. 153.

122. Oppenheim, *Other World*, p. 154.

123. Oppenheim, *Other World*, p. 245.

124. Oppenheim, *Other World*, p. 111.

125. Mary Evelyn Bertha Kirwan, known as Evelyn, b. 1861, m. Count Louis Pomian Lubienski 27 Nov 1895, and d. 1902. She was the daughter of Victoria Louisa Rawdon Hastings, Harry's sister, and John Forbes Stratford Kirwan.

126. BU/43/9 Bute's diary, 2–7 Oct. 1894 *passim*.

127. Mount Stuart uncatalogued Huggins to Bute, 14 Sept. 1894.

128. Oppenheim, *Other World*, p. 22.

129. Oppenheim, *Other World*, p. 17.

130. John L. Campbell and Trevor Hall, *Strange Things* (first pub. 1968, Routledge and Keegan Paul: Birlinn: Edinburgh, 2006), p. 30. Attributed to 17 Mar. 1893.

131. 25 Apr. 1894.

132. Campbell & Hall, *Strange Things*, p. 129.

133. Campbell & Hall, *Strange Things*, p. 102.

134. Campbell & Hall, *Strange Things*, pp. 95–106.

135. William Thomas Stead, 1849–1912. Editor, campaigner and spiritualist. He died when the *Titanic* sank. It is claimed his writings and 'automatic' pictures show premonitions of the disaster.

136. Campbell & Hall, *Strange Things*, p. 134.

137. BU/42/1 Freer to Bute, 28 May 1894.

138. BU/43/9 Bute's diary, 3 Nov. 1894.

139. BU/43/9 Bute's diary, 11 Nov. 1894.

140. BU/21/194/26 Bute to Gwen, 7 Aug. 1884.

141. Anna Swanwick, 1813–1899. *DNB*.

142. BU/21/408/2 Swanwick to Bute, 12 Mar. 1899.

143. BU/21/335/9 Bute to Gwen, 7 Nov. 1894.

144. Frances Power Cobbe, 1822–1904. *DNB*.

145. Elizabeth Balch, 1843–1890 A note by Henry James indicates that 'The Miss B . . . h and Lady G. Incident' was the inspiration for *Mrs Medwin*.

146. Albert, formerly Abraham, Löwy, 1816–1908. An accurate and eminent Hebrew scholar, and one of the first two ministers of Reformed Jewry in Britain. Founded the Anglo-Jewish Association, whose aims were to champion the cause of persecuted Jews and maintain Jewish schools in the Orient. *DNB*.

147. Dr Adler, Chief Rabbi of Great Britain, 1839–1911. He was a controversial

figure: too inclined to compromise with liberal practices for some, and too anti-socialist and anti-trade unionist for others.

148. BU/21/329/97 Bute to Metcalfe, 14 Nov. 1894.
149. BU/21/346/83 Bute to Metcalfe, 7 Jul. 1895.
150. John Miller Dow Meiklejohn, 1830–1902, Professor of Education at St Andrews, *DNB* and date correction: http://www.ed.uiuc.edu/faculty/westbury/paradigm/vol2/Graves.doc.
151. BU/43/9 Bute's diary, 11 Nov. 1894.
152. BU/21/346/83 Bute to Metcalfe, July 1895.
153. BU/21/346/85 Bute to Metcalfe, 19 Jul. 1895.
154. BU/21/346/82 Bute to Metcalfe, 4 Jul. 1895.
155. McClelland, Catholic Education.
156. BU/21/334/3 Bute to Gwen, 31 Oct. 1894.
157. BU/21/335/11 Bute to Gwen, 8 Nov. 1894.
158. BU/43/9 Bute's diary, 24 Dec. 1894.
159. BU/43/9 Bute's diary, 24–5 Dec. 1894.
160. BU/43/9 Bute's diary, 26 Nov. 1894.
161. BU/43/10 Bute's diary, 7 Jan. 1895.
162. BU/43/10 Bute's diary, 15 Jan. 1895.
163. BU/43/10 Bute's diary, 24 Jan. 1895.
164. BU/43/10 Bute's diary, 21 Jan. 1895.
165. BU/43/10 Bute's diary, 12 Feb. 1895.
166. Stamp, *Schultz*, p. 33.
167. BU/21/346/54 Bute to Metcalfe, 4 Apr. 1895.
168. BU/21/346/55 Turner to Bute, 9 Apr. 1895.
169. BU/43/10 Bute's diary, 8 Apr. 1895.

Chapter 15: Death Sentence

1. BU/21/374/7 Bute to Metcalfe, 19 Jan. 1897.
2. BU/43/10 Bute's diary, 30 Apr. 1895.
3. *Ibid.*, 13 Jul. 1895.
4. *Ibid.*, 15 May 1895.
5. BU/21/351/1 Bute to Gwen, 29 Mar. 1895.
6. BU/43/9 Bute's diary, 7 Jun. 1895.
7. *Ibid.*, 12 Jun. 1895.
8. *Ibid.*, 3 Jul. 1895.
9. BU/21/348 /93 Anderson to John Windsor ('Jack') Stuart, 16 May 1895.
10. BU/43/9 Bute's diary, 18 May 1895.
11. BU/43/9 Bute's diary, 14 Jun. 1895.
12. HB, p. 169.
13. BU/21/348/93 Anderson to Windsor Stewart, 16 May 1895.
14. BU/21/348/121 Anderson to Windsor Stewart, 21 Jun. 1895.
15. BU/21/348/151 Anderson to Windsor Stewart, 15 Jul. 1895.
16. BU/43/9 Bute's diary, 25 July. 'In the midst of life, we are in death, of whom may we seek aid, except you, Lord, who justly grows angry at our sins? Holy God, holy and mighty, Holy and merciful Saviour, Hand us not over to bitter death.'
17. BU/21/361/65 Bute to Metcalfe, 19 Aug. 1896.

18. In about a third of the surviving total volume of Bute's papers, which refer to the University of St Andrews and his Rectorship.

19. Sir Arthur Mitchell, KCB, MD, 1826–1909: an eminent pioneering doctor working in the field of 'lunacy'.

20. Catherine E Wingfield d. 1927. *JSPR*, vol. 24, October 1927.

21. E. F. Benson, *As We Were, a Victorian Peep Show* (first pub. 1930: Hogarth Press: London, 1985), p. 305.

22. BU/41/1/2 Wingfield to Bute, 13 Sept. 1895.

23. BU/21/344/25 Mitchell to Bute, 1 Sept. 1895.

24. BU/42/2/10 Freer to Bute, 2 Sept. 1895.

25. BU/43/10 Bute's diary, in a postscript to the 19 Aug. 1895 entry.

26. BU/43/10 Bute's diary, May 1895.

27. William Stainton Moses, 1839–1892. Oppenheim, *Other World*, p. 79.

28. Oppenheim, *Other World*, pp. 147, 156.

29. BU/21/298 undated memorandum in Bute's hand.

30. BU/43/10 Bute's diary, 13 May 1895.

31. Campbell and Hall, *Strange Things*, p. 156.

32. *Ibid.*, p. 238 and *passim*.

33. BU/42/2/12 Freer to Bute, 9 Oct. 1895.

34. BU/21/358/73 W Hogan to Bute, Oct. 23 1895.

35. BU/43/10 Bute's diary, 28 Oct. 1895.

36. BU/21/346/8 Bute to Scott Lang, 15 Jan. 1895.

37. *Ibid.*, 8 Nov. 1895.

38. BU/21/346/118 Bute to Metcalfe, 13 Nov. 1895.

39. BU/21/346/147 Bute to Metcalfe, 3 Dec. 1895.

40. BU/43/10 Bute's diary, 19 Nov. 1895.

41. BU/43/10 Bute's diary, 20 Nov. 1895.

42. *Ibid.*, 23 Nov.

43. There is an extant letter from Miss Freer posted on the day in question, but although she mentions the earlier apparition, and asks if there is any test she could make of the vision's truthfulness, there is no word of any vision in the surviving letter. Either a letter has gone missing, perhaps because Bute read it over frequently, or he misread the existing letter.

44. BU/21/346/127 Speech to students, 28 Nov. 1895.

45. Sir Charles Gage Brown, 1826–1908. He was a graduate of St Andrews University and medical advisor to the Colonial Office.

46. BU/21/342/38 Charles Gage Brown to Bute, 5 Dec. 1895.

47. Dr Julia Lowe, pers. comm.

48. BU/21/346/125 Gwen to Metcalfe, 26 Nov. 1895.

49. BU/42/2/242 Freer to Bute, 5 Dec. 1895.

50. BU/42/2/26 Freer to Bute, 9 Dec. 1895.

51. BU/43/10 Bute's diary, 11 Dec. 1895.

52. BU/42/2/29 Freer to Bute, 20 Dec. 1895.

53. BU/42/2/30 Freer to Bute, St Stephen's Day Dec. 1895.

54. BU/43/10 Bute's diary, 26 Dec. 1895.

55. BU/42/2/31 automatic writing by Ada Goodrich-Freer.

56. BU/43/10 Bute's diary, 31 Dec. 1895.

57. Butler, *Saints* vol. 5, p. 207.

58. BU/42/3/1 Freer to Bute, 6 Jan. 1896.

59. BU/42/3/4 Freer to Bute, 25 Jan. 1896.
60. BU/42/3/5 Freer to Bute, 13 Feb. 1896.
61. Mount Stuart papers uncatalogued, Huggins to Bute, 7 Mar. 1896.
62. Southgate, *Dundee*, p. 100.
63. Lowson, *Donaldson*, p. 411.
64. Pam Shinkins, pers. comm.
65. BU/43/11 Bute's diary, 1896.
66. Cant, *St Andrews* p. 151.
67. BU/21/361/34 Bute to Scott Lang, 19 May 1896.
68. James Bell Pettigrew, 1834–1908, comparative anatomist. *DNB*.
69. BU/21/361/46 Bute to Metcalfe, 16 Jun. 1896.
70. BU/21/361/58 Bute to Gennaelios, 10 Aug. 1896.
71. BU/21/369/26–7 sundry persons to Bute, August 1866.
72. BU/21/360/16 Gwen to Metcalfe, 3 Mar. 1896.
73. BU/43/11 Bute's diary, 20 Feb. 1896.
74. BU/21/360/35 Bute to Metcalfe, 20 Jun. 1896.
75. Author unknown, *A History of Greyfriars* (held by the community at Greyfriars). It was dictated years later.
76. BU/21/366/5 Bute to Grissell, 17 Jan. 1896.
77. Mays, *Kinross*, p. 99.
78. Sister Rose Mary, pers. comm.
79. Kinross quoted in Mays, *Kinross* p. 102.
80. BU/43/11 Bute's diary, 7 May 1896.
81. *Ibid.*, footnote to 7 May.
82. *Ibid.*, 22 Jun. 1896.
83. BU/21/366 /48 Macdonald to Bute, 10 Jun. 1896.
84. BU/21/366/58 Turner to Bute, 5 Aug. 1896.
85. BU/21/363/150 Anderson to Stuart, 23 Jun. 1896.
86. BU/21/361/67 Gwen to Metcalfe, 23 Aug. 1896.
87. BU/43 Bute's diary, 16 Sept. 1896.
88. BU/21/366/62 Notes by Fred Evans.
89. Rafael Maria José Pedro Francisco Borja Domingo Geraldo de la Santisma Trinidad Merry del Val, 1865–1830. *DNB*.
90. Charles Wood, 2nd Viscount Halifax, 1839–1934. *DNB*.
91. *DNB*.
92. BU/21/326/28 His Holiness to Bute (trans. A. Hannah), enclosed by Bishop of Newport to Bute, 29 Aug. 1896.
93. BU/21/326/35 Merry Del Val to Bute, 19 Oct. 1896.
94. BU/21/326/39 draft letter from Bute to Leo XIII, 25 Oct. 1896.
95. BU/21/326/40 Merry del Val to Bute, 2 Nov. 1896.
96. BU/21/373/2–3 Bishop of Aberdeen to Bute, September & October 1897.
97. BU/21/40/1 Myers to Bute, 6 Jan. 1893.
98. BU/21/374/7 Bute to Metcalfe, 19 Jan. 1897.
99. BU/21/376/19 Mrs Grisewood to Bute, 12 Apr. 1897.
100. HB, p. 212.
101. James Robert Nicolson Macphail, 1853–1933.
102. John Horne Stevenson, dates unknown.
103. BU/83/2/18 cutting, probably *Western Daily Mail*.
104. BU/41/5/29 John Findlay to Bute, 3 Mar. 1897.

105. Goodrich-Freer and Bute, *Ballechin*, p. 80.
106. Campbell and Hall, *Strange Things*, p. 185.
107. Campbell and Hall, *Strange Things*, p. 188.
108. Goodrich-Freer and Bute, *Ballechin*, p. 22 and *passim*.
109. BU/21/376/6 Convent of the Holy Sepulchre, New Hall, Chelmsford, to McSwiney, 2 Mar. 1897, enclosed in letter from McSwiney to Bute, 3 Mar. 1887.
110. Freer and Bute, *Ballechin*, p. 194.
111. BU/79 Crichton Browne to Bute, *passim*.
112. Campbell and Hall, *Strange Things*, p. 191.
113. Goodrich-Freer and Bute, *Ballechin*, p. 228.
114. Lowson, *Donaldson*, p. 406.
115. NLS: Rosebery Papers. Ms 100014/196, letter to Lord Rosebery, 15 Nov. 1897, as cited by Lowson, *Donaldson*.
116. BU/43/9 Bute's diary, 14 Nov. 1895.
117. BU/13/20 Anderson to Gwen.
118. Andrew McLean, pers. comm.
119. Falkland papers, Ninian to Gwen, 14 Nov. 1897.
120. NLS MS10014 f. 1197 Donaldson to Rosebery, 9 Sept. 1898.
121. BU/41/1/9 Katie Wingfield to Bute, undated.
122. NLS MS10014 f. 1197 Donaldson to Rosebery, 9 Sept. 1898.
123. BU/21/414 Various persons to Bute concerning his sons' education, 1899.
124. HB, p. 226.
125. Falkland Papers Wood to Anderson, 24 Nov. 1899.
126. BU/21/411/16 Gwen to Metcalfe 6 Sept. 1899. Metcalfe preserved these letters which were later returned to the family, which explains their survival.
127. BU/21/411/21 Gwen to Metcalfe 27 Sept. 1899.
128. BU/21/412/18 Gwen to Metcalfe, 5 Oct. 1899.
129. BU/21/415/20 Gwen to Metcalfe 11 Aug. 1900.
130. Falkland Papers Ninian to Gwen, 11 Oct. 1900.

Obituary

1. BU/83/2/18, cutting probably *Western Daily Mail*, 'Bishop Hedley's splendid tribute'.
2. *The Lady*, November 1900.
3. BU/21/238/150 Lord Bute's private directions to his executors, 20 Dec. 1887.
4. BU/83/2/18, cutting probably *Western Daily Mail*, 'Bishop Hedley's splendid tribute'.
5. *The Churchwoman*, 9 Nov. 1900, 'A Personal Reminiscence'. Neither the piece in *The Lady* nor that in *The Churchwoman* had a byline identifying the author, but both are unmistakably in her style.
6. *Birmingham Argus*, 10 Oct. 1900.
7. BU/49/3/1 Bute to Metcalfe, 10 Mar. 1889.

Bibliography

Published works by Bute

The Early Days of Sir William Wallace, A Lecture Delivered at Paisley, Nov. 16 1875 (Alex. Gardner: Paisley, 1876).

The Burning of the Barns of Ayr: Being the Substance of a Lecture Given at Ayr, Feb. 7, 1878 (Alex. Gardner: Paisley, 1878).

The Altus of St Columba, Edited with a Prose Paraphrase and Notes by John, Marquess of Bute, KT (William Blackwood & Sons: Edinburgh and London 1882).

The Prophecies of St Malachi (reprinted from the *Dublin Review*, October 1885).

On the Ancient Language of the Natives of Tenerife: A Paper Contributed to the Anthropological Section of the British Association for the Advancement of Science, 1891 (J. Masters & Co.: London, 1891).

National Eisteddfod of Wales (D. Hughes: Llanelwy, 1892).

Brendan's Fabulous Voyage. A Lecture Delivered on 19 Jan. 1893, Before the Scottish Society of Literature and Art (New edn, London, 1911).

'Address delivered on November 20, 1893 at the University of St Andrews' (inaugural address as Lord Rector), 1894

The Arms of the Royal and Parliamentary Burghs of Scotland, with J. R. N. Macphail and H. W. Lonsdale (William Blackwood & Sons: Edinburgh, 1897).

The Alleged Haunting of B– [Ballechin] House, with A. M. G. Goodrich-Freer (C. A. Pearson: London, 1900).

The Arms of the Baronial and Police Burghs of Scotland, with J. H. Stevenson and H. W. Lonsdale] (William Blackwood & Sons: Edinburgh, 1903).

Essays on Foreign Subjects (Alexander Gardner: Paisley, 1904).

Essays on Home Subjects (Alexander Gardner: Paisley, 1904).

Translations

The Roman Breviary, 1879.

The Coptic Morning Service for the Lord's Day (J. Masters & Co.: London, 1882).

The Altus of St. Columba, 1882.

Bikelas, D., *Seven Essays on Christian Greece*, 1890.

Archival sources

Bute Archive, Mount Stuart, near Rothesay, Isle of Bute:

BU/21 – Papers of John Patrick Crichton Stuart, 3rd Marquess of Bute.

BU/23 – Additional papers of 3rd Marquess of Bute.
BU/31 – Bute's travel diary for 1866.
BU/35 – Papers of the Hastings family and descendants.
BU/36 – Correspondence with Colin Grant.
BU/43 – Bute's diary (1886 onwards).
BU/57 – Bute's travel diary 1861.
BU/63 – Additional papers of 3rd Marquess of Bute.
BU/85 – Invoices relating to Mount Stuart House.
BU/89 – Papers of Gwendolen Mary, 3rd Marchioness of Bute.
BU/91 – Further papers of Gwendolen Mary.
BU/96 – Papers of Lord Colum Crichton Stuart.
Charles Stuart's diary.
Frame letter book.
WB – papers of William Burges.
Mount Stuart mss. Uncatalogued papers relating to the childhood of the 3rd
    Marquess of Bute.

British Library:
Holland House Papers, add. mss. 52159–52161.

Cardiff Central Library:
The Bute Collection – B IX.

Scottish Catholic Archives

DA Diocese of Argyll and the Isles Archives

DG Diocese Galloway Archives

FA St Benedict's Abbey, Fort Augustus Archives

Harrowby Papers, Sandon Hall, Stafford:
Vols XX and XXI (letters relating to the Bute family).
Vol. LXII (letters relating to the 3rd Marquess's custody).
Vol. 1077 (letters to Henry Ryder).

National Archive of Scotland (NAS):
GD152/196–198 – Bruce family papers.
Minutes of Paisley Abbey Kirk Session.

National Library of Scotland (NLS):
Ms. 1845 – Letters of Russell.
Ms. 2851 – Letters to Gen. Sir George Brown.
Mss. 3445–7 – Letters of Principal Lee.
Acc. 9553 – Bute's Iceland diary.

National Museum of Wales:
Report on Castell Coch.

Paisley Central Library Archive:
Town Council Minute Book.

Pusey House, Oxford:
Liddon's diary.

Royal Institute of British Architects (RIBA) Library
Burges's small notebooks.

Sneyd Papers:
Papers of George Sneyd, privately held.

Worrall Ledger
(privately held).

Periodicals and newspapers
Bell's Life
The Buteman
The Cardiff and Merthyr Guardian
Cardiff Times and South Wales Weekly News
The Churchwoman
The Daily News
The Edinburgh Courant
The Fife News
The Glasgow Daily Herald
The Illustrated London News
Journal of the Society for Psychical Research
The Leicester Advertiser
The Leicester Chronicle
The Leicester Journal
The Leicester Mail
The Morning Post
The Paisley and Renfrewshire Gazette
The Pall Mall Gazette
The Scotsman
The Scottish Review 1888–1900 vols I–XXXVI
The South Wales Echo
The Sporting Gazette
The Sporting Life
The Standard
The Tablet
The Telegraph
The Times
The Weekly Register
The Weekly Supplement and Advertiser for Galston, Newmains Darvel and Hurlford
The Western Mail

Books

Derek Aldcroft and Michael Oliver, *Trade Unions and the Economy 1870–2000* (Ashgare: Aldershot, 2000).

Anon., *A Daughter of the Venerable Mother Pelletier: Sister Mary of the Sacred Heart Ryder* (Convent of the Good Shepherd: London, 1902).

Anon., *Mother Mary of St. Euphrasia Pelletier* (Burns and Oates: London, 1888).

Georgina Battiscombe, *English Picnics* (The Harvill Press: London, 1949).

Mark Bence-Jones, *The Catholic Families* (Constable: London, 1992).

Miriam J. Benkovitz, *Frederick Rolfe, Baron Corvo* (Hamish Hamilton Ltd: London, 1977).

E. F. Benson, *As We Were: A Victorian Peep Show* (first pub. 1930: Hogarth Press: London, 1985).

Michael Bentley, *Lord Salisbury's World* (Cambridge University Press: Cambridge, 2001).

Geoffrey Best, *Mid-Victorian Britain 1851–75* (Fontana: London, 1979).

Martin Biddle, *The Tomb of Christ* (Sutton Publishing: Stroud, 1999).

E. G. W. Bill and J. F. A. Manson, *Christ Church and Reform 1850–1867* (Oxford University Press: Oxford, 1970).

John S. G. Blair, *History of Medicine in the University of St Andrews* (Scottish Academic Press: Edinburgh, 1987).

Robert Blake, *Disraeli* (Eyre & Spottiswood: London, 1966).

Henry Blyth, *The Pocket Venus* (Weidenfeld and Nicolson: London, 1966).

Frederic Boase, *Modern English Biography* (Netherton & Worth: Truro, 1892–1921).

A. K. H. Boyd, *St Andrews and Elsewhere* (Longmans, Green & Co: London, 1894).

Thorn Braun, *Disraeli the Novelist* (George Allen & Unwin: London, 1981).

George Earle Buckle, *The Life of Benjamin Disraeli, Earl of Beaconsfield* (John Murray: London, 1916).

Alban Butler, *Lives of the Fathers, Martyrs, and Other Principal Saints; Edited, revised and supplemented by Herbert Thurston and Norah Leeson* (London: Burns, Oates & Washbourne, 1926–1938).

John L. Campbell and Trevor Hall, *Strange Things* (first pub. 1968, Routledge and Keegan Paul: Birlinn: Edinburgh, 2006).

Ronald Cant, *The University of St Andrews: A Short History* (St Andrews University Library, 1992).

Rev. John Carmont, DD, *The Mitchell Trust – Bequest Litigation* 11 Dec 1882–16 Jan 1885 (The Aberdeen University Press Ltd: 1904).

Edward Carpenter, *Cantuar: The Archbishops in Their Office* (Cassell: London, 1971).

Julia Cartwright, ed., *The Journals of Lady Knightley of Fawsley* (John Murray: London, 1915).

The Catholic Directory for the Clergy and Laity in Scotland (J. Chisholm: Aberdeen, 1888).

Olive Checkland, *Philanthropy in Victorian Scotland* (John Donald: Edinburgh, 1980).

H. A. Clegg, Alan Fox, A. F. Thompson, *A History of British Trade Unions Since 1889*, vol. I (Oxford University Press: London, 1964).

Michael Clifton, *A Victorian Convert Quintet* (The Saint Austin Press: London, 1998).

George Edward Cokayne, *The Complete Peerage of England, Scotland, Ireland, Great Britain and the United Kingdom, Extant, Extinct or Dormant*, vols. I–XIII, eds The Hon. Vicary Gibbs, H. A. Doubleday (St Catherine Press: London, 1910–1940).

M. F. Connolly, *Biographical Dictionary of Eminent Men of Fife* (Orr: Cupar, 1866).

A. Cooke, I. Donnachie, A. MacSween and C. A. Whatley, eds, *Modern Scottish History 1707 to the Present*, vol. 5 (Tuckwell Press: East Linton, 1998).

Crockford's Clerical Directory for 1876 (Horace Cox: London, 1876).

J. Mordaunt Crook, *William Burges and the High Victorian Dream* (John Murray: London, 1981).

John Davies, *Cardiff and the Marquesses of Bute* (University of Wales Press: Cardiff, 1981).

Dictionary of National Biography (Oxford University Press: Oxford).

The Right Hon. Benjamin Disraeli, *Lothair* (first pub. 1870; Longmans, Green and Co.: London, 1881). [All quotations in the text are from 1881 edition.]

Benjamin Disraeli, *Lothair*, ed. Vernon Bogdanor (Oxford University Press: Oxford, 1975).

Ivor Dowse, *St. Paul's Scottish Episcopal Church, Rothesay, Isle of Bute: A Short History*, undated [Rothesay: *c.*1985].

John Erskine, *Principles of the Law of Scotland* 19th edn, ed. John Rankine (Sweet & Maxwell: Edinburgh, 1895).

Charles Fitzgerald-Lombard, *English and Welsh Priests 1801–1914* (Downside Abbey: Bath, 1993).

J. Foster, *Alumni Oxonienses* (Parker & Co.: Oxford, 1888).

Sheridan Gilley, *Newman and His Age* (Darton, Longman and Todd: London, 1990).

Mark Girouard, *Life in the English Country House: a Social and Architectural History* (Yale University Press: New Haven, 1978).

Mark Girouard, *The Return to Camelot* (Yale University Press: New Haven, 1981).

W. Gloag & Robert Candlish, *Introduction to the Law of Scotland* (W. Green: Edinburgh, 1927).

A. Goodrich-Freer and the late John, Marquess of Bute, eds, *The Alleged Haunting of B– [Ballechin] House* (C. Arthur Pearson, Ltd: London, new edn 1900).

W. Gordon Gorman, *Converts to Rome* (Sands & Co.: London, 1910).

Robert Gray, *Cardinal Manning: a Biography* (Weidenfeld and Nicolson: London 1985).

Caroline Grosvenor and Charles Beilby, *The First Lady Wharncliffe and her Family*, vol. 2 (William Heinemann: London, 1927).

Lady Charlotte Guest, *The Mabinogion, from the Llyfr Coch of Hergest, and other Ancient Welsh Manuscripts, With an English Translation and Notes* (Longman, Brown, Green & Longmans: London, 1849).

Augustus J. C. Hare, *The Story of My Life*, vol. IV (George Allen: London, 1900).

Martin Harrison, *Victorian Stained Glass* (Barrie and Jenkins: London, 1980).

Leslie Hodgson, *Heraldry of Mount Stuart* (Edinburgh 2000).

Sir David Hunter Blair, *The Rule of Our Most Holy Father St. Benedict, Patriarch of Monks* (Burns & Oates: London, 1872).

D. O. Hunter Blair, *History of the Catholic Church of Scotland from the Introduction of Christianity to the Present Day* (W. Blackwood & Sons: Edinburgh, 1887–90).

The Right Rev. Sir David Hunter Blair Bt, OSB, *A Medley of Memories* (E. Arnold & Co.: London, 1919).

The Right Rev. Sir David Hunter Blair Bt, OSB, *John Patrick, Third Marquess of Bute, K.T. (1847–1900), A Memoir* (John Murray: London, 1921).

The Right Rev. Sir David Hunter Blair Bt, OSB, *A New Medley of Memories* (E. Arnold & Co.: London, 1922).

The Right Rev. Sir David Hunter Blair Bt, OSB, *Flying Leaves* (Heath Cranton: London, 1922).

The Right Rev. Sir David Hunter Blair Bt, OSB, *Memories and Musings* (Burns, Oates & Co.: London, 1929).

The Right Rev. Sir David Hunter Blair Bt, OSB, *A Last Medley of Memories* (E. Arnold & Co.: London, 1936).

The Right Rev. Sir David Hunter Blair Bt, OSB, *In Victorian Days* (Longmans & Co.: London, 1939).

Lady Flora Elizabeth Rawdon Hastings, *Poems by the Lady Flora Hastings, Edited by Her Sister* (William Blackwood: Edinburgh, 1842).

Thomas Hughes, *Tom Brown's Schooldays* (first pub. 1857; Parragon: Bath, 1999).

Pat Jalland, *Death in the Victorian Family* (Oxford University Press: Oxford, 1996).

Robert Rhodes James, *Rosebery* (Weidenfeld and Nicolson: London, 1963).

Philip Jenkins, *A History of Modern Wales 1536–1990* (Longman: London, 1992).

Christine Johnson, *Scottish Catholic Secular Clergy 1879–1989* (John Donald: Edinburgh, 1991).

J. H. Johnston, *Life and Letters of Henry Parry Liddon* (Longmans & Co.: London, 1904).

Nigel R. Jones, *Architecture of England, Scotland and Wales* (Greenwood Press: California, 2005).

Kelly's Handbook to the Titled, Landed and Official Classes 1899 (Kelly's Directories: London, 1899).

John Kerr, *Scottish Education, School and University: From Early Times to 1908* (Cambridge University Press: Cambridge, 1913).

Florence Becker Lennon, *Lewis Carroll* (Cassell & Co.: London, 1947).

Donald M. Lewis, ed., *The Blackwell Dictionary of Evangelical Biography, 1730–1860* (Blackwell: Oxford, 1995).

H. P. Liddon, *Life of Edward Bouverie Pusey*, ed. J. O. Johnston and R. J. Wilson, 4 vols. (Longmans, Green & Co.: London, 1894–7).

Julian Litten, *The English Way of Death* (Robert Hale: London, 1991).

Leon Litvack, *John Mason Neale and the Quest for Sorbornost* (Clarendon Press: Oxford, 1994).

Elizabeth Longford, *Victoria R.I.* (Weidenfeld & Nelson: London, 1964).

John Lowden, *Early Christian and Byzantine Art* (Phaidon Press: London, 1997).

Fiona MacCarthy, *William Morris: A Life for Our Time* (Faber and Faber: London, 1995).

Vincent Alan McClelland, *Cardinal Manning: His Public Life and Influence 1865–1892* (Oxford University Press: London, 1962).

Raymond McCluskey, *The See of Ninian* (Diocese of Galloway: Ayr, 1997).

Christopher McIntosh, *The Rosy Cross Unveiled* (The Aquarian Press: Wellingborough, 1980).

Sam McKinstry, *Rowand Anderson: The Premier Architect of Scotland* (Edinburgh University Press: Edinburgh, 1991).

Frederick Marryat, *Peter Simple, or, the Adventures of a Midshipman* (Saunders and Otley: London, 1834, 3 vols).

Robert Bernard Martin, *Gerard Manley Hopkins, A Very Private Life* (G. P. Putnam's Sons: New York, 1991).

Philip Mason, *The English Gentleman* (Andre Deutsch: London, 1982).

W. R. Matthews, *The Religious Philosophy of Dean Mansel*, Friends of Dr Williams Library, Tenth Lecture (Oxford University Press: London, 1956).

Sir Herbert Maxwell, *Evening Memories* (Alexander Maclehose & Co.: London, 1932).

Patrick Moore, *The Comets* (Keith Reid Ltd: Shaldon, Devon, 1973).

John Morley, *Death, Heaven and the Victorians* (University of Pittsburgh Press: Pittsburgh 1971).

John Nicholas Murphy, *Terra Incognita or The Convents of the United Kingdom* (Longmans, Green, and Co.: London, 1873).

J. M. Neale, *A History of the Holy Eastern Church: The Patriarchate of Alexandria* (2 vols, John Masters, London, 1847).

J. M. Neale, *A History of the Holy Eastern Church: General Introduction* (2 vols, John Masters, London, 1850).

J. M. Neale, A *History of the Holy Eastern Church: The Patriarchate of Antioch*, ed. George Williams (John Masters: London, 1873).

J. H. Newman, *A Letter to the Rev. E. B. Pusey D.D., on his Recent Eirenicon* (Longmans: London, 1866).

Janet Oppenheim, *The Other World: Spiritualism and Psychical Research in England, 1850–1914* (Cambridge University Press: Cambridge, 1985, reprinted 2002).

Sir James Balfour Paul, ed., *The Scots Peerage* (David Douglas: Edinburgh, 1908).

William Plomer, ed., *Kilvert's Diary 1 January 1870–13 March 1879*, 3 vols (first pub. 1938–40; Jonathan Cape: London, 1969).

Edmund Sheridan Purcell, *Life of Cardinal Manning, Archbishop of Westminster*, vol. 2 (Macmillan and Co.: London, 1895).

E. B. Pusey, *Eirenicon* (Parker: Oxford, 1865).

E. C. Rickards, *Felicia Skene of Oxford: A Memoir ... with Numerous Portraits and Other Illustrations* (John Murray: London, 1902).

Rev. John Robertson, *Sermon Preached on the Occasion of the Death of the Marchioness of Bute* (Richard Griffin & Co.: London and Glasgow, 1860).

John Martin Robinson, *The Dukes of Norfolk* (Oxford University Press: Oxford, 1982).

Rev. Charles Rogers, *The Book of Wallace*, vol. I (The Grampian Club), Edinburgh, 1889.

Fr Rolfe, *Hadrian the Seventh* (first pub. 1904; Chatto and Windus: London, 1971).

George W. E. Russell, *Portraits of the Seventies* (T. Fisher Unwin, Ltd: London, 1916).

David Semple FSA, *Second Supplement to St Mirin* (J. & J. Cook: Paisley, 1874).

Richard Shannon, *Gladstone: Heroic Minister, 1865–1898* (Allen Lane: The Penguin Press, 1999).

G. B. Shaw, *Pygmalion* (first pub. 1915; Harmondsworth: Penguin Books, 1987).

Catherine Sinclair, *Beatrice or The Unknown Relatives* (Simpkin, Marshall, and Co.: London, 1855).

Donald Southgate, *University Education in Dundee* (Edinburgh University Press: Edinburgh, 1982).

Gavin Stamp, *Robert Weir Schultz, Architect, and His Work for the Marquesses of Bute* (Mount Stuart, 1981).

R. W. Stewart, *Disraeli's Novels Reviewed* (The Scarecrow Press, Inc.: Metuchen, NJ, 1975).

Giles Stephen Holland Strangways, Earl of Ilchester, *Chronicles of Holland House* (John Murray: London, 1937).

Agnes Strickland, *The Lives of the Queens of England from the Norman Conquest*, 12 vols (first pub. 1840–8; Longmans, Green, and Co.: London, 1860).

Agnes Strickland, ed., *The Letters of Mary Queen of Scots, and Documents Connected with Her Personal History* 5 vols (Henry Colburn: London 1844).

Lieut.-Colonel Charles Stuart, *Journal of a Residence in Northern Persia and the Adjacent Provinces of Turkey* (Richard Bentley: London, 1854).

A. J. A. Symonds, *The Quest for Corvo* (Cassell: London, 1955).

Donald Thomas, *The Victorian Underworld* (John Murray: London, 2003).

F. M. L. Thompson, *English Landed Society in the Nineteenth Century* (Routledge & Kegan Paul: London, 1963).

F. M. L. Thompson, *The Rise of Respectable Society* (Fontana: London, 1988).

Ann Thwaite, *Emily Tennyson: The Poet's Wife* (Faber and Faber: London, 1996).

Peter Townend, ed., *Burke's Genealogical and Heraldic History of the Peerage, Baronetage and Knightage*, 103rd edn (Burke's: London, 1965).

Anthony Trollope, *An Autobiography* (first pub. 1883; Penguin Books: London, 1993).

J. A. Venn, LittD, FSA, *Alumni Cantabrigienses*, Part II vol. VI (Cambridge University Press: Kraus reprint, 1978).

John R. Watts, *Scalan: The Forbidden College, 1716–1799* (Tuckwell Press: East Linton, 1999).

Donald Weeks, *Corvo* (Michael Joseph Ltd: London, 1971).

Arthur Westcott, *Life and Letters of Brooke Foss Westcott* (Macmillan & Co.: London, 1903).

Articles

Anon. (prob. Fr Cronin), 'The Story of the Foundation of the Convent of the Good Shepherd, Pen-y-lan, Cardiff', *Catholic Parish Magazine of St Peter's Cardiff* (Nov. 1922).

Bernard Aspinwall, 'Children of the Dead End', *The Innes Review*, vol. 43, no. 2 (Autumn 1992).

Bernard Aspinwall 'The Making of the Modern Diocese of Galloway', in Raymond McCluskey, ed., *The See of Ninian* (Diocese of Galloway: Galloway: 1997).

Geoffrey Best, 'Popular Protestantism in Victorian Britain', in Robert Robson, ed., *Ideas and Institutions of Victorian Britain* (G. Bell and Sons: London, 1967).

J. S. Black, 'A Short Account of How the Marquis of Bute's Beavers Have Succeeded in the Isle of Bute', *Journal of Forestry and Estates Management*, vol. 3 (1880).

Kenneth John Conant and Glanville Downey, 'The Original Buildings at the Holy Sepulchre in Jerusalem', *Speculum*, vol. 31 (Jan. 1956).

J. A. Gibson, 'The Bute Beavers', *Transactions of the Buteshire Natural History Society*, vol. 21 (1980).

Mark Girouard, 'Victorian Values and the Upper Classes', in T. C. Smout, ed., *Victorian Values, a Joint Symposium of the Royal Society of Edinburgh and the British Academy December 1990* (Oxford University Press: Oxford, 1992).

Ian Gow, 'The First Mount Stuart', in Andrew McLean, ed., *Mount Stuart, Isle of Bute* (The Mount Stuart Trust, Isle of Bute, 2001).

Virginia Green, 'C20', in J. Mordaunt Crook, ed., *The Strange Genius of William Burges, 'Art-Architect', 1827–1881* (National Museum of Wales, 1981).

Rosemary Hannah, 'St Sophia's Galston: "the vast space of the interior"', *Architectural History*, vol. 46 (2003).

D. N. Hempton, 'Evangelicalism and Eschatology', *Journal of Ecclesiastical History*, vol. 31 (1980).

Timothy Lingard, 'Horatio Walter Lonsdale, Architectural Artist', *The Antique Collector* (Dec. 1987).

Timothy Lingard, 'Horatio Walter Lonsdale, 1844–1919, Architectural Artist', *Catalogue, Gallery Lingard Exhibition*, c.1987.

Rev. Roderick Macdonald, 'The "Tin" Cathedral at Oban: 1886–1934', *The Innes Review*, vol. 15 (Spring 1964).

R. J. Macrides, 'The Scottish Connection in Byzantine and Modern Greek Studies', *St John's House Papers, No. 4* (University of St Andrews, 1992).

R. J. Morris, 'Victorian Values in Scotland and England', *Proceedings of the British Academy*, vol. 78 (1992).

Gavin Stamp, 'The New Mount Stuart', *Mount Stuart, Isle of Bute* (Mount Stuart Trust, 2001).

Hugh Trevor-Roper, 'The Church of England and the Greek Church in the time of Charles I', in David Baker, ed., *Religious Motivation: Biographical and Sociological Problems for the Church Historian* (Basil Blackwell: Oxford, 1978).

Margaret Westlake, 'N. H. J. Westlake FSA', *Journal of the British Society of Master Glass-Painters*, vol. 3, no. 2 (1929).

Matthew Williams, 'William Burges' Furniture for Cardiff Castle', *Decorative Arts Society Journal*, no. 16 (1991).

Matthew Williams, 'Gorgeously Arrayed in Blue and Gold', *Country Life*, 5 March 1998.

Matthew Williams, 'Lady Bute's Bedroom, Castell Coch: A Rediscovered Architectural Model', *Architectural History*, vol. 46 (2003).

Giles Worsley, 'A Phoenix Rises', *Perspectives in Architecture*, vol. 29 (June/July 1997).

Unpublished works

A. Scott Lowson, 'Principal Sir James Donaldson, Education and Patronage in Victorian Scotland', thesis, University of St Andrews (1987).

Sam McKinstry, 'S Sophia's Church, Galston: The Design in Context. A Historical Study'.

Andrew McLean, 'Notes for Mount Stuart Guides'.

Andrew McLean, 'The Bright Particular Star of the Scottish Home Rulers. Bute and the Scottish Parliament'. Paper for the Symposium 'Bute', Mount Stuart House, 2000.

Deborah Clare Mays, 'John Kinross, his Life and Work 1855–1931', thesis, University of St Andrews (1988).

Matthew Williams, 'Cardiff Castle Room Notes'.

Index